PELICAN BOOKS
The Arabs

Peter Mansfield was born in 1928 in Ranchi, India, and was educated at Winchester and Cambridge. He has spent the last thirty years writing and broadcasting about the contemporary affairs and history of the Middle East. In 1955 he joined the British Foreign Office and went to Lebanon to study Arabic at the Middle East Centre for Arabic Studies. In November 1956 he resigned from the foreign service over the Suez affair but remained in Beirut working as a political and economic journalist. He edited the *Middle East Forum* and corresponded regularly for the *Financial Times*, *Economist*, *Guardian*, *Indian Express* and other papers. From 1961 to 1967 he was the Middle East Correspondent of the *Sunday Times*, based mainly in Cairo, and since 1967 he has lived in London but makes regular visits to the Middle East and North Africa. In the winter of 1971–2 he was Visiting Lecturer on Middle East Politics at Willamette University, Oregon. His books include *Nasser's Egypt*, *Nasser: A Biography*, *The British in Egypt*, *The Ottoman Empire and its Successors*, *The New Arabians* and, as editor, *The Middle East: a Political and Economic Survey*. He has also edited a *Who's Who of the Arab World*.

The Arabs

Peter Mansfield

PENGUIN BOOKS

Penguin Books Ltd, Harmondsworth, Middlesex, England
Viking Penguin Inc., 40 West 23rd Street, New York, New York 10010, U.S.A.
Penguin Books Australia Ltd, Ringwood, Victoria, Australia
Penguin Books Canada Ltd, 2801 John Street, Markham, Ontario, Canada L3R 1B4
Penguin Books (N.Z.) Ltd, 182–190 Wairau Road, Auckland 10, New Zealand

First published in Great Britain by Allen Lane 1976
First published in the United States of America by Thomas Y. Crowell
under the title *The Arab World: A Comprehensive History* 1977
Published in Pelican Books in the United States of America by arrangement
with Thomas Y. Crowell
Revised edition published in Pelican Books 1978
Reprinted 1979
Reprinted with Postscript 1980
Reprinted 1981, 1982, 1983
Second edition 1985
Reprinted 1986, 1987

Set by Rowland Phototypesetting Ltd,
Bury St Edmunds, Suffolk
Printed and bound in Great Britain by
Cox & Wyman Ltd, Reading

Contents

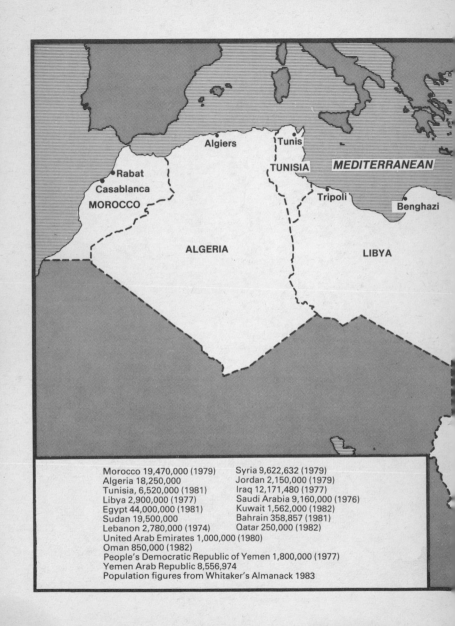

Algiers   Tunis

TUNISIA   **MEDITERRANEAN**

Rabat

Casablanca

MOROCCO

Tripoli

Benghazi

ALGERIA

LIBYA

Morocco 19,470,000 (1979)
Algeria 18,250,000
Tunisia, 6,520,000 (1981)
Libya 2,900,000 (1977)
Egypt 44,000,000 (1981)
Sudan 19,500,000
Lebanon 2,780,000 (1974)
United Arab Emirates 1,000,000 (1980)
Oman 850,000 (1982)
People's Democratic Republic of Yemen 1,800,000 (1977)
Yemen Arab Republic 8,556,974
Population figures from Whitaker's Almanack 1983

Syria 9,622,632 (1979)
Jordan 2,150,000 (1979)
Iraq 12,171,480 (1977)
Saudi Arabia 9,160,000 (1976)
Kuwait 1,562,000 (1982)
Bahrain 358,857 (1981)
Qatar 250,000 (1982)

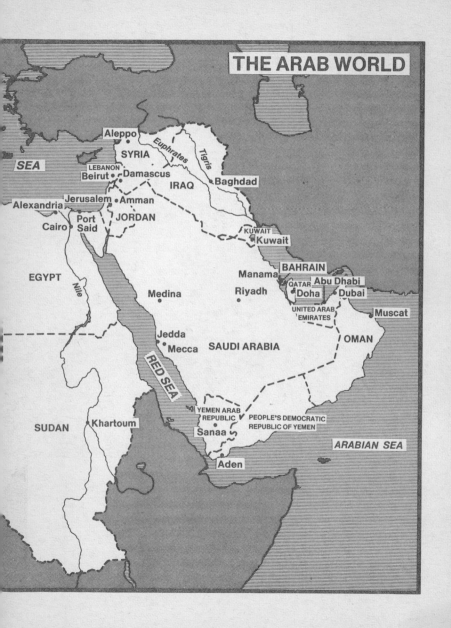

THE ARAB WORLD

Part One
The Arab Past

1. Who are the Arabs?

Before answering this question we have to try to answer another: Who are Arabs? The difficulty is that for many centuries the word 'Arab' had two different meanings. It still has today, although the wider of the two definitions is tending to predominate. But in the past Arab historians and writers, such as the great Ibn Khaldoun of Tunis in the fourteenth century, used the word in either of its senses without explaining which use was intended.

The older of the two definitions referred to some of the Semitic people of the Arabian peninsula. In prehistoric and pagan times two races inhabited Arabia: one was largely nomadic and wandered with their flocks over the great deserts which lie between the river Euphrates and the centre of the peninsula. The others were the inhabitants of the rain-fed uplands in the south – the Yemen. It was the former who were the 'Arabs'. The earliest surviving account of the people of Arabia comes in the tenth chapter of Genesis, which names the descendants of Noah. Noah's eldest son, Shem, is regarded as the ancestor of the Hebrews, Arabs and Aramaeans – the speakers of 'Semitic' languages, the term invented by the German historian A. L. Schlözer in 1781. But the term 'Arab' is not mentioned in Genesis.[1] So far as is known the word first appears in an inscription of the Assyrian King Shalmaneser III announcing his victory over a group of rebellious chieftains, one of whom is referred to as 'Gindibu the Aribi'. From then on Assyrian and Babylonian inscriptions refer frequently to Aribi or Arabu. They are a nomadic people living in the north Arabian desert, and their tribute to their Assyrian overlords was usually in the form of camels, first domesticated in Arabia between about 1500 and 1200 B.C. In the Bible the name Arab is the first word used in the second book of Chronicles (xvii, 11) to refer to nomads from the east bank of the river Jordan in the time of King Jehosophat (c. 900–800 B.C.) ('. . . and the Arabians brought him flocks, seven thousand and seven hundred rams, and seven

---

1. However it has been suggested that the 'mixed multitude' (Hebrew *erev*) mentioned in Exodus xii, 38 as having accompanied the Israelites into the wilderness from Egypt could be a mistake for Arabs (Hebrew *arav*). Hebrew, like Arabic, has no written vowels. (See N. Barbour, *Nisi Dominus*, London, 1946, p. 73.)

thousand and seven hundred he-goats'). But the term most frequently used for Arabs in the Bible is Ishmaelites. This is because after the rise of Islam, Jewish tradition regarded the Arabs as fellow-descendants of the patriarch Abraham, the father of monotheism. The Jews acknowledge that it was only because of the miraculous birth of Isaac to Abraham's elderly wife Sarah that Ishmael, the son of Abraham by his concubine Hagar, was superseded as the patriarch's natural heir whose descendants would inherit the Promised Land. Even then the inheritance would have passed to Isaac's elder son Esau (ancestor of the Transjordanian Edomites, and therefore of King Herod the Great), if his younger son Jacob had not secured it by a trick. From early Christian times the Ishmaelites appear in Jewish tradition as enemies, together with Romans, and as rivals for possession of the Land of Israel.

An Arab was therefore a nomad inhabitant of the central and northern Arabian peninsula. The word itself is probably derived from a semitic root related to nomadism. There are several possibilities, including the word *abhar* which means 'to move' or 'to pass' and from which the word Hebrew is probably derived. In the Arabic language, which developed later than Hebrew, the word *arab* (plural) means 'those who speak clearly' as contrasted with *ajam* or 'those who speak indistinctly' – a term which later came to be applied chiefly to Persians. This does not tell us the derivation of the word but only the definition it was given by the Arabic-speaking people themselves. But Herodotus and later Greek and Roman authors began to extend the terms 'Arabia' and 'Arab' to cover the whole peninsula, and its inhabitants, including the Yemenis of the south-west. The Romans referred to Yemen as *Arabia Felix*. Already the term 'Arab' was broadening. Inevitably also some of the Arabian nomads were settling down around the oases, where a sedentary civilization was possible. One of these was Yathrib in western Arabia, which became Medina after the time of the Prophet Muhammad; another was Petra, the valley hidden among the bare mountains of south Jordan which in the second century B.C. became the centre of the powerful kingdom of the Nabataeans. 'Arabic in speech, Aramaic in writing, Semitic in religion, Hellenistic in art and architecture, the Nabataean culture was synthetic, superficially Hellenic but basically Arabian, and so it remained.'[2] Still another was Palmyra in the central Syrian desert, which achieved high prosperity as a trading centre at a junction of caravan routes and ultimately great political power in the third

2. Philip Hitti, *Syria: A Short History*, London, 1959, p. 61.

century A.D. under the astute and beautiful Queen Zenobia. For a time she defied the legions of the Roman Emperor Aurelian, but was ultimately defeated and brought to Rome in golden chains to be displayed in his triumph.

But while some of the peoples of Arabia adopted a sedentary way of life, the nomadic tribes, who held a strong military advantage over the settlements, remained convinced of the superiority of their own style of living. Moreover, most of the settled peoples showed that they accepted this belief by adopting nomadic values; some of them abandoned their settlements for the freedom of the desert. The great horizons of the desert provided a sense of liberty, but the harsh environment made its own iron laws which moulded the structure of tribal life. Survival depended on the solidarity and self-protection of the tribe, and the system whereby the whole family, clan (that is, group of families), or tribe were held responsible for the acts of any one of them ('life for life, eye for eye, tooth for tooth . . . burning for burning, wound for wound') helped to create such security as there was. There was no written code of laws; individual crimes were restrained by the fear of lasting vengeance. No such restraints however applied to communal acts of violence. Inter-tribal disputes might be settled by an arbiter, a wise authority on tribal customs, but meanwhile they were the excuse for a *ghazu*, or raid, aimed chiefly at driving off your opponents' camels, which for many centuries could be regarded as the national sport of the Arabs.

Desert life was exceedingly harsh. The nomads lived as parasites on the camel, drinking its milk and very occasionally eating its meat. The other staple food was dates, 'the mother and the aunt of the Arabs', as it was known. After one of the rare and irregular rainstorms, which cause dangerous flash floods in the *wadis* or valleys, there would be a brief period of relative ease after which life would once again be centred on the water-holes where a few shrubs and bushes survived.

The nomad Arabs in the first centuries after Christ were animists by religion; that is to say they worshipped trees, rocks or water-springs. Over the years this developed into a polytheism – a belief in a variety of spirits who could be of either sex and were often based on a particular rock or tree shrine. The most famous of these was the shrine at the Ka'ba at Mecca, where the great Black Stone (probably a meteorite) was a place of pilgrimage for centuries before it became central to the religion of Islam.[3] Friendly and helpful spirits were the

3. According to popular legend, the Black Stone was given to Adam on his fall from Paradise.

jinn (i.e. genies), while the hostile and malevolent were *afrit* or *ghul*. In the settled trading and farming communities of the oases the situation was different. Through their contacts with the Christian, Byzantine and Abyssinian Empires and the Zoroastrian Persian Empire they had begun to acquire monotheistic ideas. Agriculture in the peninsula was largely developed by Arabs who had adopted Judaism (although some of the farmers may also have been Jewish refugees expelled from Palestine by the Romans). By the fourth century A.D. the people of southern Arabia abandoned polytheism to adopt their own form of monotheism – a belief in a supreme god known as *al-Rahman*, 'the Merciful'.

It was early in the sixth century A.D. that the Arabian peninsula began to emerge from its isolation to play a part in world affairs. In the north-east the Arabian Kingdom of Hira allied itself with the Persian Empire and in the north-west the Kingdom of Ghassan was usually in alliance with the other great power of the period – Byzantium. In south Arabia the able King Abraha built up a strong state independent of Persia and Ethiopia and even sent his armies northwards into central Arabia. But there was no kind of unity of the peninsula. King Abraha died in about A.D. 570 and south Arabia was occupied by the Persians. The buffer states of Ghassan and Hira also declined, and by the beginning of the sixth century A.D. Arabia was a conglomeration of petty autonomous states.

A stable political background is not essential for the arts, and the sixth and seventh centuries were the great period of Arab heroic poetry. As in the Homeric age of ancient Greece, poetry, which was intended always to be recited aloud in public, was the supreme art. The poverty of the desert nomads made them use words as the chief form of artistic expression. The multiple gods or spirits of Arabia had little hold over their hearts and minds; if anything their religious faith was bound to the honour of the tribe. The poet was the spokesman of the tribe who sang the praises of its heroes and leaders and poured scorn on those of its enemies. He sang magnificently. The images he used were familiar, derived from the elements and the desert with its birds and beasts, but the vocabulary was rich and the sense finely-shaded and allusive. As Richard Burton, the great Victorian orientalist and traveller, wrote of this early Arabic poetry:

The language, 'like a faithful wife, following the mind, and giving birth to its offspring', and free from that 'luggage of particles' which dogs our modern tongues, leaves a mysterious vagueness between the relation of word to word, which materially assists the sentiment, not sense, of the poem. When verbs and nouns have – each one – many different significations, only the radical or general idea suggests itself. Rich and varied synonyms, illustrating the finest shades of meaning, are artfully used: now scattered to strike us by distinctness; now to form, as it were, a star, about which dimly seen satellites revolve.

It is hardly surprising that such poetry almost defies translation. Scholars who have tried have not been poets, and in most cases it would have been better if they had not made the attempt. The poems which the Arabs themselves usually regard as the greatest in their heritage from these early times are the Seven Odes (Arabic: *qasidas*) of Imru al-Qays and others known as the *Mu'allaqat* or 'Hanging Ones' because, according to legend, they were hung in the shrine of the Ka'ba. The first translation into English, which is still in some ways the best, was by the great eighteenth-century orientalist, Sir William Jones.[4] Sir William did not attempt to reproduce the rhymes or rhythm of the original but he reflected its spirit. Here are the closing lines of the first *qasida*, 'The Wandering King'.

O friend, seest thou the lightning, whose flashes resemble the quick glance of two hands, amid clouds raised above the clouds?

The fire of it gleams like the lamps of a hermit, when the oil poured on them shares the cord by which they are suspended.

I sit gazing at it, while my companions stand between Daaridge and Odhaib; but far distant is the cloud on which my eyes are fixed.

Its right side seems to pour its rain on the hills of Katan and its left on the mountains of Sitaar and Yadbul.

It continues to discharge its waters over Cotaifa till the rushing torrent lays prostrate the groves of Canahbel trees.

It passes over Mount Kenaan, which deluges in its course, and forces the white goats to descend from every cliff.

On Mount Taima it leaves not one trunk of a palm tree, nor a single edifice, which is not built with well-cemented stone.

Mount Tebeir stands in the heights of the flood, like a venerable chief wrapped in a striped mantle.

The summit of Magaimir, covered with the rubbish which the torrent has rolled down, looks in the morning like the top of a spindle encircled with wool.

The cloud unloads its freight on the desert of Ghabeit, like a merchant of Yemen alighting with his bales of rich apparel.

The small birds of the valley warble at daybreak, as if they had taken their early draught of generous wine mixed with spice.

The beasts of the wood, drowned in the floods of night, float, like the roots of wild onions, at the distant edge of the lake.

---

4. Supporter of the cause of the American colonists and friend of Benjamin Franklin, who invited him to help draft the Constitution of the Republic. He declined with regret.

Poetry in this era was regarded much more highly than prose, and the poet held an honoured place in nomadic society. According to the North African Ibn Rashid, writing in the eleventh century:

Whenever a poet emerged in an Arab tribe, the other tribes would come and congratulate it. Feasts would be prepared, and the women would gather together playing on lutes, as people do at weddings; men and boys alike would exchange the good news. For the poet was a defence to their honour, a protection for their good repute; he immortalized their deeds of glory, and published their eternal fame. On three things they congratulated one another – the birth of a boy, the emergence of a poet in their midst, or the foaling of a mare.

If the most common poetic themes were praise of the tribe or satire of its enemies, erotic love was also often introduced. Professor Arberry's translation of another part of the same ode of the *Mu'allaqat* conveys something of the magic sensuality of the original:

Out I brought her, and as she stepped she trailed behind us to cover our footsteps the skirt of an embroidered gown.
But when we had crossed the tribe's enclosure, and dark about us hung a convenient shallow intricately undulant, I twisted her side tresses to me, and she leaned over me; slender-waisted she was, and tenderly plump her ankles, shapely and taut her belly, white-fleshed, not the least flabby, polished the lie of her breast-bones, smooth as a burnished mirror.
She turns away, to show a soft cheek, and wards me off with the glance of a wild deer of Wajra, a shy gazelle with its fawn;
She shows me a throat like the throat of an antelope; not ungainly.
When she lifts it upwards; neither naked of ornament; she shows me her thick black tresses, a dark embellishment clustering down her back like bunches of a laden date-tree – twisted upwards meanwhile are the locks that ring her brow, the knots cunningly lost in the plaited and loosened strands;
She shows me a waist slender and slight as a camel's nose-rein, and a smooth shank like the reed of a watered, bent papyrus.
In the morning the grains of musk hang over her couch, sleeping the forenoon through, not girded and aproned to labour.
She gives with fingers delicate, not coarse; you might say they are sand-worms of Zaby, or tooth-sticks of ishil-wood.
At eventide she lightens the black shadows, as if she were the lamp kindled in the night of a monk at his devotions.
Upon the like of her the prudent man will gaze with ardour eyeing her slim, upstanding, frocked midway between matron and maiden;
Like the first egg of the ostrich – its whiteness mingled with yellow – nurtured on water pure, unsullied by many paddlers.
Let the follies of other men forswear fond passion, my heart forswears not, nor will forget the love I bear you.

The seven odes of the *Mu'allaqat* are only the most famous of those which have survived from a great mass of poetry composed in the Arabian desert in the sixth and seventh centuries A.D. But despite the wealth of its literature, this society was poor and unsophisticated, barely touched by civilization. Some of the material and intellectual culture of the Persian and Byzantine Empires had reached it through the caravan routes to the oases. Textiles, food, wine and probably the art of writing reached the Arabs in this way. The training which the armies of the satellite states of Ghassan and Hira received taught them some of the principles of war. Their political organization was a rudimentary form of democracy. The head of the tribe was a shaikh or *sayyid* elected by the elders, but he was

rarely more than a first among equals. He followed rather than led tribal opinion. He could neither impose duties nor inflict penalties. Rights and obligations attached to individual families within the tribe but to none outside . . . He was advised by a council of elders called the *Majlis*, consisting of the heads of the families and representatives of clans within the tribe. The Majlis was the mouthpiece of public opinion.[5]

Much depended on the personality of the shaikh, but however strong his character he could not interfere with the entrenched rights and customs of the clans.

Apart from those who were full members of the tribe by descent, there would be others attached to it. Women and children captured in tribal warfare who were not ransomed became tribal slaves and could be bought and sold. But there were also 'clients' of the tribe who had asked for the shaikh's temporary protection while pasturing their flocks on his land.

The position of women in pre-Islamic Arab society is still disputed. Many Muslim writers maintain that they were held in subjection and that the Prophet Muhammad raised their status. On the other hand there is evidence that some tribes in pre-Islamic times practised a form of polyandry in which paternity was ignored and all inheritance passed through the female line. In earlier centuries there were even some ruling Arab queens in Arabia. Yet by the seventh century there can be little doubt that patrilineal descent and a male-dominated society was the more general rule in Arabia. One of the Prophet Muhammad's earliest prohibitions was against the practice of killing infant girls.

Society in the settled communities was only slightly more complex

5. Bernard Lewis, *The Arabs in History*, London, 1958, p. 29.

and sophisticated. The two most important were Yathrib (or Medina as it was renamed in Islamic times) and Mecca in western Arabia. Yathrib was agricultural, growing cereals and dates. The tribes who lived there had small forts to which they could retreat when attacked by their rivals. There was no concentration of houses or anything resembling a city at this time. Mecca was purely a trading community without farming. By the end of the fifth century A.D. it had overtaken all its rivals to become the commercial centre of the peninsula. Part of its prosperity rested on the fact that two rival trade routes between the Mediterranean and India – the Euphrates–Persian Gulf and the Nile–Red Sea routes – were disturbed by constant warfare. Mecca was dominated by the Quraysh tribe. The leading members of its clans formed an assembly known as a *mala*, which did not however have any legislative or executive powers. Order was maintained through the *lex talionis* and the commercial good sense of the trading community.

It was in this semi-nomadic community – wealthy and sophisticated only in comparison to life in the surrounding desert – that Muhammad was born the son of Abdullah of the Hashim clan of the Quraysh tribe. His actual date of birth is uncertain, but A.D. 571 is most generally accepted. To the nine hundred million Muslims in the world today he was the last in the series of Prophets of God (*Allah* in Arabic), who included Abraham, Moses and Jesus. But even to Christians, Jews and others who do not accept this belief, Muhammad was undeniably one of the few men who have permanently changed the world. Muhammad was an Arab and his first message from God was for the Arabs. Through him this small race of lean and hungry camel-riding nomads, who provoked a blend of contempt and fear in the contemporary civilized world, became one of the most potent forces in the history of mankind. This fact is the cause both of pride and ironic sorrow for their descendants of the present day.

Muhammad's career began when he was over forty. His family was poor, but his material position improved as a result of his marriage at the age of about twenty-five to Khadija, a wealthy widow some fifteen years older to whom he was devoted and who became the first convert to Islam. Little is known about Muhammad's early life; his biography is embellished with stories and anecdotes which were either wholly or partially invented at a later date. It is certain that he had a reputation as a sound and honest businessman and a good husband and father to his daughters. But his calm and trustworthy exterior concealed a man of strong spiritual feelings and driving ambition. He thought deeply about religious matters and cared passionately about the moral and material conditions of his people.

On his trading expeditions and in Mecca Muhammad had direct contact with Christians and Jews. Both tended to look down on the Arabs, whom they regarded as infidels. The Arabs did not reject monotheism out of hand, and the hold of their own polytheistic beliefs (which had never been very powerful) was in decline. But it was clear that these proud and self-willed nomads would not accept Allah in the form in which he was passed on by others. Muhammad was concerned with the morality of Meccan society, where the authority of tribal custom and law was inevitably breaking down in the increasingly urbanized environment. Moreover the whole contemporary civilized world, of which Arabia lay on the fringes, was shaken by the struggle between the two great powers – the Persian and Byzantine Empires. The idea was gaining ground that the world was approaching a new Apocalypse.

After the age of forty Muhammad's religious nature had caused him to retreat periodically to a cave in the bare brown hills outside Mecca to meditate and pray. It was there one night that, according to tradition, the word of God was first revealed to him by the archangel Gabriel. It was a terrifying and overwhelming experience. At first he confided only in Khadija, as he went through a period of doubt and self-questioning – wondering whether he was any different from the *kahins* or soothsayers who were common in Arabia and were consulted as oracles, for a fee, on private or public matters. But the visions returned, and in about 613 Muhammad began to preach in short passages of rhythmic prose. These were taken down in his lifetime on a variety of materials, such as pieces of leather, palmleaves or camel-bone, and grouped together into *suras* or chapters. As a whole they form the Koran, Arabic for 'recitation'. It is beyond dispute that this work contains some of the finest prose in any literature, but the suggestion to any Muslim that Muhammad wrote it is blasphemy. He believes that it was dictated to him by God.

Muhammad's first message to his people in Mecca was from an all-powerful Allah ('your Lord' as he describes himself) who created the whole Universe and 'man from a germ-cell' (Koran xcvi, 1–2) and even now, 'each day is employed in some work' (Koran lv, 29). He had shown man the way of righteousness but some had rejected it. He would summon all his creatures into his presence on the day of resurrection.

> When the trumpet shall sound
> That shall be a day of horror
> Beyond bearing for the ungrateful.
>
> (Koran xxiv, 8–10)

Streams of fire and molten brass shall come upon you and you shall have no help . . .

When the sky shall split, and become scarlet like red leather . . .

On that day shall neither man nor demon be asked about his sins . . .

But the sinners shall be known by their marks, they shall be seized by their forelocks and their feet.

> (Koran lv, 35–41)

The sinners would spin between a hell of fire and an abyss of boiling water. Angels would be assigned to torture them and when their skins were burned they would be replaced by new ones. The blessed, on the other hand, would spend eternity in Paradise, where their highest reward would be the sight of the Divine Being and the chance to praise him unceasingly. Paradise is poetically described as a Garden of Delight where there is no grief, toil or fatigue. The Faithful will recline on silken couches by flowing rivers, enjoying heavenly food and drink served to them by eternally youthful boys circulating among them 'like hidden pearls'. For wives they would have dark-eyed maidens (*houris*), modest and pure.

The sensual nature of this vision of Paradise has often been remarked upon by non-Muslims. Muslim scholars point out that the description is plainly intended as a parable (Koran xlvii, 15). The trees of Paradise correspond to man's good deeds and the rivers to faith. Moreover, the Koran also makes it clear that the wives of the Faithful who are good will accompany them to Paradise. The *houris*, therefore, like the gardens, honey and fruits, are physical manifestations of the spiritual blessings which the doers of good will enjoy in the after-life. Similarly, Islam in no way countenances the suggestion that the beautiful boys of Paradise are intended as catamites for the Faithful.

At first Muhammad preached only to a small circle of friends and relatives. His message to the Meccans was of the simplest: that they should abandon all forms of idolatry and surrender themselves wholly to the one all-seeing and almighty but compassionate God. It was this idea of total submission (in Arabic, *Islam*) which later gave his followers the name Muslims. The only formal rite he enjoined upon them at this stage was to pray, like Jews and Eastern Christians, prostrating themselves in the direction of Jerusalem. Despite the modesty of his message, he soon aroused strong opposition. The fierce individualism of Arab tribesmen was offended by his call for selflessness and surrender. The Meccans also saw Muhammad's movement as a threat to the economically profitable cult of the Ka'ba. Mockery and insults turned into persecution and in 615 Muhammad advised some of his followers to take refuge in the Christian country of Abyssinia. In 619, 'the year of mourning', his wife Khadija and his beloved uncle Abu Talib both died; and the addition of personal sorrows to his political difficulties caused Muhammad to look outside Mecca. He thought first of moving to the hill town of Taif, but the people mocked and snubbed him. 'If you were sent by Allah as you claim,' said one, 'then your state is too lofty for me to address you, and if you are taking Allah's name in vain, it is not fit that I should speak to you.' Deeply depressed by this reaction, Muhammad turned his attention to Yathrib, some 300 miles to the north-east of Mecca. Yathrib was not a commercial city, but an agricultural settlement in an oasis inhabited by rival tribes, of whom several were Jewish. Muhammad's reputation as the leader of a movement which aimed to transcend tribal disputes was sufficient for the people of Yathrib to invite him to be their arbiter. After long negotiations he moved there with a few of his followers in the year 622, which is known as the year of migration (*hijra* in Arabic) and is the starting-point of the Muslim calendar. Yathrib had also been known by the Aramaic name *Medinat* or city, and it now became Medinat al-Nabi, City of the Prophet, or Medina for short.[6]

Henceforward Islam began to develop into a politically organized community as well as a religion. Muhammad was the acknowledged head of this community or *umma*. At first his role was the relatively modest one of the arbiter or settler of disputes and vendettas; but step by step he acquired the authority of a political and military leader. He began to exhibit his qualities of political genius, as he adapted all the powerful Arab traditions of personal honour, brotherhood and tribal solidarity to strengthen the community of the Faithful.

The military role was thrust upon him when war broke out between the Meccans and Medinans. The advantage swung between the two sides, but Muhammad showed his ability to learn from his mistakes and, when the initiative passed decisively into his hands, to strengthen his authority through magnanimity and willingness to compromise. Finally in 630 he took over Mecca against little resistance. He ordered the idols to be overthrown and turned the Ka'ba

6. See Maxime Rodinson, *Mohammed*, London, Allen Lane, 1971, p. 139.

into a Muslim sanctuary, but in all other aspects he treated the inhabitants with tolerance and liberality. Nearly all the Meccans embraced Islam.

There was one people whom Muhammad failed to win over: the Jews. This was not for want of trying. In Medina he promised them freedom to practise their rites and even adapted for Islam certain Jewish rites such as Yom Kippur or the Day of Atonement and the practice of turning towards Jerusalem to pray. But the Jews did not respond, and his relations with them deteriorated. Muhammad ordered his followers to pray towards Mecca instead of Jerusalem. The month of Ramadan, during which Muhammad won his first great victory over the Meccans, replaced the Jewish Day of Atonement as a period of fasting. The Muslims even reverted to the pagan style of parting their hair instead of letting it flow loose according to the Jewish custom which they had adopted earlier. He criticized the Jews as having distorted the teachings of Moses and rejected the Prophet Jesus. The doctrine developed of Islam as an older and purer monotheism than Judaism and Christianity (derived from Abraham, the ancestor of the Arabs and Jews), and as one that had superseded their partial revelations of God. Above all this meant that Islam was an Arab religion for the Arabs. Allah had revealed his truths in the Arabic tongue through Muhammad.

In the earlier stages the relationship between Islam and Christianity was easier than with Judaism. The Koran says (v, 85): 'Those who are most disposed to friendship with the faithful are they who call themselves Christians; this is because they have priests and monks, and because they are free from pride.' But there were few Christians in Mecca and Medina, and the early Muslims did not have to worry about them. In later years a clash became inevitable. Muhammad accepted Jesus as a prophet, but the Christians were (he held) wrong in believing he was the son of Allah who, being uncreated, could not create. The doctrine of the Trinity he found offensive, for there was only one God, Allah. Jesus himself was not responsible for these exaggerations, which he had condemned.

Islam was therefore the ultimate and definitive religion, and Muhammad's message completed those of the earlier prophets. Jews and Christians remained the 'people of the book' and the Faithful were enjoined to give them special consideration. Later they were to have their own protected status in Muslim society. But those who remained Jews and Christians had rejected Allah's message, as it had been transmitted through Muhammad. The religion of Islam was therefore directed towards the pagans – those who were not of the book. Thus although it was an Arab religion in which the Arabs and their language would always hold a special position it was also universal – a message for all mankind.

By 630 Muhammad's authority was firmly established and the unification of the Arabian peninsula was progressing steadily. He was now the head of a state; it was a state of a unique kind, governed by the rules and precepts of the holy book. These transcended, but did not destroy, tribal customs and traditions.

The Medinan chapters of the Koran are therefore chiefly concerned with the structure of society, the protection of the safety, lives and property of its members. The ancient tribal custom of the vendetta was restricted in two ways: the avenger was not to inflict a greater injury than the one he had himself suffered; and if a murder had been unintentional it was made obligatory to accept the blood-price or compensation and not insist on 'an eye for an eye'. Arab Muslim society still had no police force at this stage, so the threat of vengeance was still the basis of internal security in the community. The penalty for thieves was to have a hand cut off, but the Koran does not say who is to carry out the sentence. The protection of the community against threats from outside became the responsibility of the whole *umma*.

As we have seen, the killing of infant girls was strictly forbidden. Whatever it had been in the remote past, the status of women in Arab society immediately before Islam had fallen very low. It was now raised, since they were given the right to own and inherit property. The husband's legal obligations were defined and the maximum number of wives was fixed at four. The pagan custom which obliged a man to marry his father's widows except his own mother was forbidden.

Some twentieth-century moralists, Muslim and non-Muslim, have felt it necessary to apologize for the establishment of polygamy in Islam. They have suggested that the limitation to four wives was really intended as a first stage on the road towards monogamy pointing out that the Koran says 'if you fear that you cannot be quite fair [to all your wives] [take] only one'. They argue that since it is humanly impossible to be perfectly just this amounts to an injunction to be monogamous. The trouble is that the words 'take only one' (Koran iv, 3) are followed by 'or that which your right hand possesses', which means the females who were taken prisoners in war and became slaves. This has been assumed by some to mean permission for the taking of concubines. Others maintain that neither in the Prophet's life nor in the Koran is there any sanction for concubinage. Muslims were enjoined to marry slave-girls if they could not afford to marry free believing women. They were to treat them justly even if their status would remain lower than that of free women.

Whether he accepted concubines or not, Allah clearly permitted polygamy; in certain circumstances he actually encouraged it. (Muhammad practised it himself after the death of Khadija, to whom he was unswervingly faithful in her lifetime.) The Koran says: 'And if you fear that you cannot do justice to orphans, marry such women as seem good to you, two, or three, or four.' This chapter was revealed after the battle of Uhud, in which the Muslims were defeated by the Meccans and the Prophet was himself wounded. Some seventy Muslim males out of 700 were killed, and there was every likelihood that more would be slain in the future, leaving orphans in the care of widows who would have difficulty in providing for them. In such circumstances polygamy was essential for survival, and marriage was declared to be a duty of the Faithful. The need to maintain the numerical strength of the *umma* outweighed concern for the shortage of food supplies, even though the community lived on the edge of starvation. In any case, Malthusian forces were soon to be overcome as the Arabs conquered more fertile lands.

Unquestionably Allah's commands in the Koran raised the status of women in seventh-century Arabia. To a society which never recognized any rights for the woman the Koran says (ii, 228) that in marriage and divorce women should enjoy the same rights against their husbands as their husbands have against them. It is true that the same *sura* of the Koran says that 'men are a degree above them', but this merely acknowledges the fact that the man is the head of the household – something that has hardly been disputed in any civilized society until the present day. It was the scholars and casuists of Islam in later centuries who succeeded in interpreting or misinterpreting the Koran in such a way as to place women in subjection. Seclusion and the veil which were intended to give women privacy and protection in a formerly licentious society became a form of imprisonment. Islam has no clergy; every man is priest and patriarch in his own household. Men exploited this power to dismiss wives at a whim. Divorce, which the Koran commands should only be practised in exceptional circumstances, and which according to one of the Prophet's sayings was 'odious in the sight of God', became a powerful instrument of male tyranny.

Apart from the detailed regulations of family life, the Koran con-

tains a large body of ethical teaching and legal injunction. All intoxi-
cants and games of chance are prohibited. (According to a Tradition,
when this verse of the Koran was revealed, a crier proclaimed the
news in the streets of Medina and in response every jar of wine in a
Muslim household was emptied so that wine flowed in the streets.)
Usury was forbidden, and the eating of swine's flesh. Dieting rules in
Islam are a less strict form of those observed by the Jews. They are
similar to those adopted by the early Christians and involve no eating
of pork or blood, animals that had either died a natural death, had
their necks wrung or been sacrificed to others than God. Penalties are
prescribed for crimes such as stealing, murder and some minor
offences. Slavery is permitted as an institution but some strict limitations are placed on the rights of owners who are commanded to
treat their slaves well. Fraud, perjury and slander are repeatedly
and severely condemned and some rules of social behaviour are laid
down. Together these regulations formed the basis of the structure of
the *shari'a*, or Islamic system of law. The Koran's system of practical
precepts could not provide for every contingency so the early Muslims tried to fill the gaps. The second basis for the *shari'a* is the *sunna*
(the Way) of the Prophet as recorded in the Tradition of his words
during his lifetime. In the year after the Prophet's death his sayings
were still fresh in the minds of his family and companions. Collectively they were known as the *hadith* (Arabic, 'saying'). At first they were
transmitted orally; Arabic script was still in a primitive state. But
although no particular care was taken in their transmission these
earliest traditions have the ring of authenticity. For example, Uqba
ibn Amir said 'someone sent the Prophet a silk gown and he wore it
during the prayers, but on withdrawing he pulled it off violently with
a gesture of disgust and said "This is unfitting for God-fearing men." '
Within two or three generations, however, a number of sayings came
to be attributed to the Prophet as a consequence of theological
controversy. 'Legal maxims, Jewish and Christian materials, even
aphorisms from Greek philosophy, were put into the mouth of the
Prophet and there seemed no limit to the process of fabrication.'[7] It
became a matter of urgent necessity for the Muslim community to halt
the debasement of the Tradition, and a science of *hadith* criticism was
built up during the second and third centuries of Islam. This involved
detailed study of the character of the original source of each *hadith* and
the means by which it was transmitted and their classification in three

7. H. A. R. Gibb, *Mohammedanism*, London, 1953, p. 75.

groups: 'sound', 'good' and 'weak'. In the middle of the ninth century
A.D. two famous *hadith* scholars produced what they claimed to be
collections of sound or genuine *hadith*. These were al-Bukhari and
Muslim. Both were enormously influential in the Islamic world,
especially al-Bukhari whose collection contained over seven
thousand sayings of the Prophet.

But all this lay in the future during the Prophet's lifetime. On his
death in 632 the Islamic religion consisted only of the doctrine and
ritual contained in the Koran. Its core is the *shahada*, or profession of
faith: 'There is but one God, and Muhammad is his Apostle.'[8] In
addition the Faithful were called upon to believe in angels who were
God's servants and messengers (and *shaitans* or devils who try to lead
men astray), and in a series of Apostles of whom Muhammad was the
last: the 'Seal of the Prophets'. These Apostles are not all named in the
Koran, but they included Noah, Abraham, Moses and Jesus among
the most important. They had been sent by God to preach his
uniqueness and to warn against the Last Judgement (which is also a
central doctrine of Islam). Their message was contained in their
books: that of Moses in the Torah or Pentateuch, of David in the
Psalms and of Jesus in the Gospel. All of these books are to be believed
because they confirm one another; only the Koran, God's message
through Muhammad, is the final and perfect revelation.

Apart from these fundamental beliefs enjoined upon the Faithful,
certain obligations or behaviour or ritual are required: prayer, fasting,
almsgiving, pilgrimage. Not all the details of prayer ritual are laid
down in the Koran, but they had already become established during
Muhammad's lifetime. They were to be preceded by ceremonial
ablutions five times a day, with a series of prostrations in the direction
of Mecca accompanied by recitation of the phrase *Allahu akbar* (God is
the most great), the *shahada* and other verses of the Koran. Prayers
could be performed anywhere but ideally they were said in a *masjid*
(place of prostration), or mosque, standing in rows behind an *imam*
who led the movements. Additional prayers are also encouraged,
especially at night. Fasting is required during Ramadan, the ninth
month of the lunar year, when a Muslim is supposed to abstain from
all food and drink during the hours of daylight. The Pilgrimage or *hajj*
to the Sacred Mosque at Mecca is an obligation for every Muslim,
although it is explicitly limited to everyone who has the necessary

8. This is not found in its complete form anywhere in the Koran but the two halves are
brought together to form the *shahada*.

means and the physical ability to reach Mecca. The Pilgrimage season is the twelfth month of the lunar year; some elements of the Pilgrimage, such as the circulation of the Ka'ba and the assembly on Mount Arafat, are laid down in the Koran; others, such as the kissing of the Black Stone set in the walls of the Ka'ba and the stoning of the pillars representing the devil, are not mentioned but have been incorporated into the Muslim ritual because Muhammad observed them during his own pilgrimages.

The giving of alms or *zakat* was an obligation on all Muslims. The law-books later fixed their level as one fiftieth of all income in money or kind. Although *zakat* came to be regarded as a form of state income tax in the Koran, it appears as the means by which the wealthy man can show his righteousness which will be tested at the Last Judgement. *Zakat* means 'purification'. It is to be employed for the poor and the needy, and those employed to administer it, and those who are to be conciliated, slaves and captives, debtors and wayfarers (Koran ix, 60).

These four 'acts of devotion' – prayer, the payment of *zakat*, the pilgrimage and fasting during Ramadan, together with *shahada* or profession of faith – form the five Pillars of Islam.

In addition to the five Pillars, Muslims are enjoined to *jihad*, which means 'striving' or 'exerting oneself', in the Way of God. Today *jihad* is usually translated as 'holy war', although there is nothing in the word to indicate that the striving is to be carried out by the sword or the tongue or any other method. What the Koran does say (ii, 190) is: 'And fight in the way of Allah against those who fight against you but be not aggressive. Surely Allah loves not the aggressive.' Fighting is clearly limited to fighting in defence. The only apparent exceptions are in Koran ix, 5, where the context of the command to 'slay the idolators' shows that the reference is to idolatrous tribes of Arabia assembled at the Pilgrimage, who had first made agreements with the Muslims and then violated them and in Koran ix, 29 where the Faithful are enjoined to fight 'those who have received the Book' (i.e. Jews and Christians) but 'believe not in God nor in the Last Day'. Nowhere does the Koran command Muslims to propagate their faith by the sword.

This in bare outline was the new religion of the Arabs. Its principal characteristic was its unornamented simplicity, its absolute and unconditional monotheism. As such it rejected the Christian doctrine of the Incarnation and Trinity, saint-worship and the relics of the old nature cults which survived in the rites and practices of the Christian

Church. It cannot be stressed too often that Muslims regard their religion as completing and perfecting those of the other People of the Book – the Jews and Christians – who they believed to have gone astray or misunderstood God's message as transmitted to them through Moses and Jesus. In their eyes, the Koran is God's true and final revelation.

The other vital characteristic of simplicity in Islam is that it dispenses with a priesthood. As Richard Burton remarks:

> The Moslem family, however humble, was to be the model in miniature of the State, and every father in Al-Islam was made priest and pontiff in his own home, able unaided to marry himself, to circumcise[9] (to baptize as it were) his children, to instruct them in the law and canonically to bury himself.[10]

The *imam* who led congregational prayers was not a priest; the nearest approach to a sacerdotal order were the *ulama* or scholar-legislators, but there was no question of regarding them as God's representatives. Such an idea would be regarded as blasphemy by a Muslim.

The transformation achieved by the Holy Koran is unparalleled in the history of the world. When Muhammad began to recite his message the Arabs were despised and feared by their more civilized neighbours as licentious and violent nomads living on the edge of starvation, who worshipped idols, stones, trees and heaps of sand. They seemed to have nothing to redeem them except their poetry, which was known only to themselves. Yet before the Prophet's death twenty years later these scattered bands of idolatrous tribesmen had been welded into a single dynamic nation worshipping one all-powerful but compassionate deity. At the same time the sensible social laws of the Koran, skilfully adapted to the needs and conditions of Arabia, had raised the ethical standards of Arab society to an infinitely higher plane. It is hardly necessary to say that none of this could have been imposed through tyrannical force, least of all on the fiercely independent people of Arabia.

9. Circumcision has been practised since earliest times by Muslims, although it is not mentioned anywhere in the Koran.
10. Richard Burton, 'Terminal Essay' to his translation of *The Thousand and One Nights*, Benares, n.d., pp. 181–2.

2. The Great Arab Explosion

When Muhammad died at Medina on 8 June 632 after a painful illness, he left no instructions as to who should succeed him. The Muslim community was in a state of confusion and despair. Muhammad had had no sons. Abu Bakr, father of his young wife Aisha, and a son-in-law Ali, husband of his daughter Fatima, were prominent among his companions. But there was no traditional or legal reason why the succession should pass to them. After lengthy argument within the community, Abu Bakr and Omar, another of the Prophet's companions, succeeded in winning general acceptance for Abu Bakr as *Khalifat rasul-Allah* or successor to the Apostle of God. From this came the term 'caliph'. Ali, the Prophet's son-in-law, only reluctantly submitted to Abu Bakr's authority several months later.

Abu Bakr's first task was to restore his authority among those Arabian tribes who had become rebellious and undisciplined. This was easily accomplished by his own chief marshal, Khalid ibn al-Walid, a former pagan military leader who had been converted to Islam and who was to become one of the greatest Arab generals. With the unity of Arabia restored, the young dynamic state began to look outwards. There were two main impulses behind its expansion: the need to find an outlet for the martial energies of the beduin warriors and the search for booty and supplies to sustain the impoverished Muslim community.

There were two great powers in the Middle East at that time, the rival empires of Persia and Byzantium. Both had been seriously weakened by a series of wars between them, but the Sassanid Empire of Persia, seething with discontent against its despotic military rulers and with heretical opposition to the official Zoroastrian religion, was the more feeble of the two. Byzantium still had the internal strength of its Roman order of administration. But the imperial rule of both Persians and Byzantines was exceedingly unpopular in the provinces which lay on the borders of Arabia, and the people of Mesopotamia were in a constant state of rebellion against their Persian overlords. The Byzantines, on the other hand, imposed their dominant Hellenistic culture and religious orthodoxy on the people of their two principal provinces – the Egyptians, who spoke Coptic (a language derived from Ancient Egyptian), and the Syrians, whose tongue was the semitic Aramaic and who professed the Monophysite heresy which the Byzantine emperors ruthlessly persecuted.

The expansion of the infant Arab caliphate began with a series of probing raids into Mesopotamia. Initially the Arab raiders' objective was limited to the securing of ransom and booty; but as resistance was weak, and as they were joined by tribesmen of the border areas, their ambitions grew. They turned against Syria; the Byzantine Emperor Heraclius, astonished at the sudden emergence of this new threatening power from remote Arabia, sent an army to protect Damascus; it was decisively defeated by Khalid's forces in the crucial battle of Ajnadayn in southern Palestine on 30 July 634.

One month later Abu Bakr died. He was succeeded without interruption by the strong-minded and autocratic Omar, who took the title of *amir al-mu'minin* or commander of the faithful. The Arab advance was unaffected; Khalid's forces swept on through Syria. Damascus fell in 636 and Jerusalem surrendered to the Caliph Omar in 638. Only the Greek strongholds of Ascalon and Tripoli held out and these finally capitulated in 644 and 645. In 639 the Arab general Muawiya was appointed governor of all Syria.

While Khalid was engaged in Syria the Arabs suffered some reverses at the hands of the Persians; but in 636 the new caliph was able to turn his attention to the north-east. In the following summer his forces decisively defeated the main Persian army at Kadisiya. The Arabs drove on to capture the Sassanid capital of Ctesiphon on the Tigris near Baghdad and to occupy all Iraq. But their position in Iraq was still threatened by the Persians on their central plateau. Over the next ten years the Arabs gradually reduced what remained of the Sassanid Empire; its last emperor Yazdajird was killed as he fled before them in 651.

However enfeebled the Persian and Byzantine Empires had been by their own wars, the military successes of the Arabs were astonishing. Their forces consisted almost entirely of undisciplined tribesmen mounted on camels or horses. Their tactics were of the simplest: they would charge the enemy and cast a shower of javelins before wheeling back to a prearranged base line. They would repeat this until the enemy showed signs of breaking and then engage him in hand-to-hand combat. Although they were probably less outnumbered and outarmed by the Persian and Byzantine armies than Arab tradition maintains, the superiority of their enemies should still have been overwhelming. In particular the Arabs had no siege equipment, so they had either to storm the enemy's fortresses or reduce them by a prolonged blockade.

Several years before the final destruction of the Sassanid Empire the conquering Arabs also turned their attention westwards. In the winter of 639 the Arab general Amr ibn al-As appeared at al-Arish, which is still Egypt's eastern frontier, with a force of three thousand cavalry. As in Iraq and Syria the mass of the population, who in this case were Egyptian Christian Copts, were thoroughly discontented with their imperial rulers, the Byzantines, and even welcomed the invaders. Amr easily reduced the fortress of Babylon, near the present site of Cairo; only the great city of Alexandria held out for another fourteen months. For centuries the slanderous myth was widely believed in the Christian world that the Caliph Omar ordered the destruction of the great Alexandrian library, which had been founded by Ptolemy I in the third century B.C. and was one of the glories of the Hellenistic world, on the ground that either its books conflicted with the Holy Koran and must be burned, or they conformed with it and were superfluous. In fact the library had been destroyed in the third century A.D. during a civil war in the time of the Emperor Aurelian. The story was invented in the thirteenth century by medieval Christian propagandists. In fact although the Prophet himself was illiterate, such an action would have been contrary to Islamic tradition. Two of the best-known sayings attributed to the Prophet are: 'Seek knowledge, even unto China' and 'The ink of the scholar is more sacred than the blood of the martyr.'

In November 644 the Caliph Omar was assassinated by a Persian slave. He had failed to appoint a successor but he had designated a special council to select one. They chose Othman, who was weak and vacillating, but a member of the powerful Umayyad family of Mecca. This led to the first serious dissension within the *umma* of Islam and ultimately to the great schism between Sunnis and Shias which divides the Islamic world to this day.

Othman was incapable of maintaining the disciplined and centralized state that had been created by his predecessor. Discontented tribesmen rose in revolt and in June 656 the aged Caliph Othman was murdered while at prayer in his house at Medina.

His natural successor seemed to be Ali, first cousin of the Prophet and husband of his daughter Fatima. But he was opposed by the powerful Umayyads, who included Muawiya, governor of Syria and an outstanding leader, Aisha, the Prophet's widow, and several of his companions. In December 656 Ali was victorious at the battle of the Camel, near Basra, so called because Aisha, 'Mother of the Faithful', rode a camel at the heart of the fighting. Ali was now master of Iraq and he moved his capital from Medina to Kufa. Arabia was henceforth of secondary importance in the Arab Empire in comparison with Syria and Iraq.

Ali's triumph was short-lived. Although a brave fighter and a good general, he was a poor statesman. Muawiya, with the support of Amr the conqueror of Egypt, rose in revolt against him, demanding vengeance for the murder of his uncle Othman. Ali went to meet the rebels, and when he seemed about to win the battle of Siffin near the Syrian-Iraqi border he gave away the victory when Amr conceived the ruse of sending his men into battle with copies of the Koran fixed to the points of their spears, as if calling upon Allah to choose the victor. The more pious among his followers persuaded Ali to halt the fighting. The arbitration through representatives which followed went against Ali. He did not accept the decision, but his camp was weakened by dissension. Several thousands of his followers deserted him and set up on their own. They were known as Kharijites (i.e. 'outgoers' or 'secessionists'), and sects claiming affiliation with the original Kharijites were to appear frequently at later stages in Islamic history. Muawiya regained control of Egypt, and Ali lost the Hejaz to local rebels. Finally, in January 661, he was assassinated by a Kharijite. There was now no serious opposition to Muawiya, who had already had himself proclaimed caliph in Jerusalem. Ali's eldest son, Hassan, who had been set up as a rival caliph in Iraq, was soon persuaded to abdicate. However, there were many who continued to believe in Ali and his descendants as the true caliphs and to regard Muawiya and his Umayyad successors as secular usurpers. They became known as the *Shia* or 'partisans' of Ali as opposed to the *Sunnis* or 'people of the *Sunna*' who are the 'orthodox' majority of Muslims. Around Ali's supposed tomb at Kufa they built the town of Najaf. On the death of Muawiya in 680, Ali's second son Hussein embarked on an abortive revolt against the Umayyads. He was defeated and killed at Kerbala in the following year. Najaf and Kerbala became the twin holy cities of the Shia community. This is the great schism within Islam. Of the 500 million Muslims in the world, perhaps one tenth are Shias. They are the majority among the Arabs of Iraq (although the Sunnis have been politically dominant there), and they are numerically important in Yemen, Syria, Lebanon and eastern Arabia. The fact that since the sixteenth century Shiism has been the ruling faith in Iran has had a crucial effect on relations between Iranians and Arabs.

The Umayyad dynasty lasted from 661 until 750 and it was during their rule that the extraordinary Arab/Islamic expansion reached its peak. By 732 it had extended itself to the Pyrenees and eastwards to Samarkand and the Punjab. Despite persistent efforts, the Arabs were unable to conquer Anatolia (Armenia and Byzantium at that time and Turkey today), and they never succeeded in capturing Constantinople. The Arab northern and eastern borders remained at the foothills of the Taurus mountains.

The original motive force behind the Arab outburst from Arabia was less religious zeal than the pressures of hunger and want on the people of that barren land. As such, it was only one in a series of incursions of the people of the peninsula into the Fertile Crescent. But as the tide of conquest flowed on, the nature of the invasion inevitably changed. A great empire was being established.

At first the fighting was done only by the beduin Arab warriors. Lured on by the vast booty of the luxurious empires they were destroying, they did not settle as owners of the lands they had taken, but went on seeking further conquests. At this stage the Arabs formed the ruling class among Muslims; the Islamic state was essentially an Arab confederation. The idea that non-Arabs should become Muslims, although clearly sanctioned by the Koran, was still so unfamiliar that any converts who were not full members by descent of an Arab tribe had to become *mawali*, or clients, of one of them. Persians, Egyptians, Berbers of North Africa and even Arabs by blood and language who had failed to prove their full membership of the dominant caste became *mawali*. In theory they were equal to the 'pure' Arab Muslims but in practice they were treated with contempt by these Arab warriors and for some time denied more than a residual share in the treasure acquired by their conquests. The beduin Arab leadership showed astonishing adaptability. Muawiya in Syria and Abdullah, the first civil governor, built up navies which effectively challenged the experienced sea power of the Byzantine Empire, despite their lack of naval tradition. Arabs had been sailing the Red Sea and Indian Ocean for centuries but these were the sedentary Arabs of south Arabia. The beduin Arabs had only navigated the desert. In fact, although they built navies their strategy continued to be based on the desert where they enjoyed so many advantages over their opponents. They used it as a means of communication and line of retreat to give them greater mobility and resilience. Accordingly they built their garrison towns as desert ports on the model of Damascus. Fustat, east of Cairo, and Kairouan in Tunisia were cities of this kind, which were known as *amsar* ('metropolis'). These rapidly increased in popularity as the *mawali* flocked to them to set up as traders or artisans.

The 'people of the book' – that is the adherents of the two heavenly religions, Judaism and Christianity – were known as *dhimmis*. They enjoyed religious and personal toleration but not equality before the law. 'Their personal safety and their personal property are guaranteed them at the price of permanent inequality.'[1] Since they paid most of the taxes, mass conversions to Islam created a problem in reducing revenues. Some of the caliphs were reduced to discouraging too many conversions.

Although Jews and Christians were reduced to the level of second-class citizens, they generally welcomed the Arab conquests because of the tyrannical rule of their previous masters. 'Therefore the God of vengeance delivered us out of the hands of the Romans by means of the Arabs . . . It profited us not a little to be saved from the cruelty of the Romans and their bitter hatred towards us.'[2]

The Arabs remained a very small minority in the territories they conquered. It is usually estimated that they numbered no more than a few hundred thousand in the early days of the caliphate. At this stage they had neither the time, experience nor application to transform the existing systems of administration in their new empire. Provided the taxes were paid the structures were generally left intact. But despite the thin admixture of Arab blood, the language spread rapidly among the conquered peoples. It radiated outwards from the garrison towns as they became not only the seats of power but the commercial centres for the surrounding areas.

The vast area of the conquests enforced a change of policy. By 700 Arab manpower was no longer sufficient for the armies, and the *mawali*, but no *dhimmis*, were recruited. However, they were confined to the infantry, with lower rates of pay and a smaller share of booty than the Arab cavalry.

The conquest of the once great Sassanid and Byzantine Empires was achieved with amazing speed. The first real setback for the Arabs came in North Africa at the hands of the Berbers, who were no luxury-loving city-dwellers but warlike nomads like themselves. The

1. G. von Grunebaum, *Mediaeval Islam*, Chicago, 1961, pp. 178–81.
2. Quoted in Bernard Lewis, *The Arabs in History*, London, 1958, p. 58.

origins of the Berbers are mysterious; even the source of the name is uncertain. They have Caucasoid features and hair; many of them are tall, slender, blond and blue-eyed. For some one thousand years from about 1200 B.C. the Berbers were ruled by the Phoenicians, who founded the great Carthaginian state based on Carthage near the city of Tunis. They were succeeded by the Romans after their destruction of Carthage in 146 B.C. Roman rule lasted about 650 years and was followed by the Vandals and the Byzantine restoration (A.D. 429–642). Under the Romans the province of Africa reached a high level of prosperity, relics of which can be seen today in the great Roman cities of Leptis and Sabratha. Agriculture and forestry were extended. But although a minority of the people of North Africa became Latin-speaking Christians, like St Augustine, the greater majority failed to assimilate Roman civilization, in contrast to the population of western Europe. The Punic language of the Carthaginians survived, and since it is a semitic tongue, as closely related to Arabic as Spanish is to French, its prevalence helped the process of arabization when it came.

It took a century for the Arabs to subdue the Berbers and make them part of their empire, but the process was ultimately much more thorough than anything the Romans had achieved. This was partly because of the natural affinity of culture and way of life between Arabs and Berbers and partly because of the assimilating and civilizing power of the Islamic religion. As Ibn Khaldoun pointed out in the fourteenth century:

> The Arabs are the least adapted of all people for empire-building. Their wild disposition makes them intolerant of subordination, while their pride, touchiness and intense jealousy of power render it impossible for them to agree. . . . Only when their nature has been permeated by a religious impulse are they transformed, so that the tendency to anarchy is replaced by a spirit of mutual defence. Consider the moment when religion dominated their policy and led them to observe a religious law designed to promote the moral and material interests of civilization. Under a series of successors to the Prophet, how vast their empire became and how strongly it was established![3]

Christianity was replaced by Islam and Latin by Arabic in all the romanized areas of North Africa. The Latin and Greek population of the cities withdrew to Spain and Sicily. The Berber population retained their language after they had embraced Islam, although there

---

3. Ibn Khaldoun, *Muqadimma*, Beirut, 1900, p. 152, quoted in N. Barbour (ed.), *A Survey of North-West Africa*, London, 1959, pp. 15–16.

was much intermingling of Arab and Berber tribes and even in some cases an exchange of language. Except for the Tuaregs, the blue-veiled nomads of the southern Sahara who write love poetry in an ancient Berber alphabet called Tifinaq, Berbers write their language in the Arabic script.

By the beginning of the eighth century a durable political fusion of Arabs and Berbers had been forged and the last Byzantine cities had been subdued. The great Arab/Berber cities of Kairouan (in Tunisia) and Fez (in Morocco) had been founded and the systematic Arab settlement of the countryside had begun. But the lust for plunder which had lured the Berber tribesmen into Islam, because as *mawali* they were entitled to a share of the booty, had not been quenched and this provided the impulse for the invasion and conquest of Spain. Despite the misgivings of the caliph in Damascus at the further expansion of the already vast Arab Empire, Tariq, an emancipated Berber slave of the Arab governor of North Africa Musa ibn Musair, landed at Gibraltar (Jebel Tariq) with 7,000 men and defeated the Visigothic King Roderic. The crumbling and unpopular Visigothic kingdom swiftly collapsed before the onslaught of the Arab/Berber armies. As in the Byzantine Empire, the various elements of the population had been embittered by the economic and religious oppression of their rulers. The Jews especially welcomed the Arabs and Berbers as liberators. Some of the cities held by the Gothic knights, such as Seville or Merida, continued to resist, but by 714 the whole of Spain and Portugal, except for a small independent state in the north-east, were in Arab hands and three years later their armies broke through the Pyrenees into the fertile lands of France. Here their great advance petered out. Although they continued to raid north-wards and to establish temporary colonies, the climate of central and northern Europe never really attracted them.[4]

The direct influence of Arab/Islamic culture on western Europe was therefore confined to Spain and Sicily (which was finally taken from the Byzantines by the Arabs at the end of the ninth century).

Already before the Arabs drove north across the Pyrenees their lines of communication from the Arab capital to the caliph's capital in Damascus were dangerously stretched. Also the inevitable dissension over the sharing of the spoils of conquest had arisen between the

4. Gibbon over-stressed the defeat of the Arabs by Charles Martel at the Battle of Tours in 732, 'in order to tease the theologians of Oxford about their escape from interpreting the Quran' (Norman Daniel, *The Arabs and Mediaeval Europe*, London, 1975, p. 7), but his interpretation has generally been accepted until recent times.

Arab and Berber soldiers. But in Spain the Arabs were able to consolidate their power. In 755 the Umayyad prince Abdul Rahman, escaping from the massacre of his relatives in Damascus, arrived in Spain and, after a fierce and prolonged struggle against dissension, established a strong centralized government based upon an imperial guard of Berbers and European slaves. It was under him and his successors – notably Abdul Rahman II (822–852) and Abdul Rahman III (912–961) – that the culture of Moorish Spain reached its zenith. Many of the people of Spain were converted to Islam and the converts (*muwallads*) formed a rebellious and active element in the population. The unconverted Christians or Mozarabes (Arabic: *mustarib*) enjoyed a high degree of tolerance and, like the Jews, formed prosperous communities in the cities.

From the end of the eighth century until about 1200 Muslim Spain – or *al-Andalus* as it was called – was the most civilized and materially advanced area of western Europe. Cordoba, with its seventy libraries and 900 public baths, was the most splendid city on the continent. Whenever a European Christian prince needed an architect, physician or musical director he applied to Cordoba. Queen Tota of Navarre brought her son Sancho the Fat of Léon, who had been deposed by his subjects on the grounds of his obesity, to Cordoba to be cured by a Jewish doctor. Muslim Spain became less tolerant under the Berber dynasties, the Almoravides and Almohades of the eleventh and twelfth centuries, but this trend served to spread Muslim culture further as the Mozarabes emigrated to the Christian states of northern Spain.

The boundaries of the Arab/Islamic empire soon reached their maximum extent. In Europe its expansion was halted short of the Pyrenees and Constantinople. Eastward it reached Samarkand and the Punjab with astonishing speed. But although the Arab armies conquered Sind in 712, the province was neither rich nor strategically well placed enough to serve as a base for the extension of Arab rule over the Indian sub-continent. It was not until the end of the tenth century, when Islam had been firmly established in what is now Afghanistan, that the Muslim conquest of India was begun. Similarly it was not the Arabs but the Turks, first the Seljuks, from the eleventh century and later the Ottomans from the fourteenth century, who pressed forward through Asia Minor into the Balkans. Islam spread through Turkestan into China and later into the Malay states, but there it was itinerant traders rather than conquering armies who spread the faith. A similar process took place in Africa. From the newly islamized North Africa, the faith pressed southwards along the ancient oasis highways of the Sahara into central Africa. In most cases it was the ruling classes of these black African states who were converted to Islam. By about 1400 the whole of North Africa, as far south as Lake Chad and from Senegal on the Atlantic to Somalia on the Indian Ocean, was covered with a network of Muslim régimes.

The twin processes of arabization and islamization, although closely linked, were therefore not identical. Arabization began some two centuries before the Prophet Muhammad, with the overflow of Arabian tribes into Syria and Iraq, and reached its greatest impulse during the first decades of the Arab Empire. Islamization lasted much longer and still continues today, especially in Africa. The consequence is that although Arabic language and culture retain a special and predominant place in the world of Islam, only about one fifth of the one sixth of mankind who are Muslims are Arabic-speaking.

Inevitably, the process of empire-building and the arabization of the subject people, changed the Arabs themselves. It even changed the meaning of the word Arab with a resulting confusion which sometimes survives to this day. Initially, as we have seen, those of pure descent from one of the tribes of Arabia, formed a military aristocracy and the spearhead of the advancing Arab armies. But the racial purity of the Arab aristocrats did not apply to their wives. From the early days of the conquests they often married non-Arab *mawali*, with the result that within a few generations many of the Arab generals and governors only had a small admixture of pure Arab blood. The family of Abdul Rahman III, for example, notoriously preferred blonde girls and frequently married Christian slaves from northern Spain. According to the calculations of the Spanish orientalist Julian Ribera, only 0·39 per cent of Abdul Rahman III's ancestry was Arab and the remainder Spanish.[5]

As the conquering Arabs intermarried with non-Arab *mawali* and with non-Muslims, they also gradually gave up their nomadic way of life to adopt a sedentary existence. Ibn Khaldoun pointed out the consequences. Emphasizing that the secret of the strength of nomadic societies is their

strong social solidarity arising out of kinship . . . those Arabs who took up a more sedentary life, however, found themselves, in their quest for more fertile lands and rich pastures, crowding in on other peoples – all of which led to a mixture (of blood) and a confusion of genealogies. . . . This does not mean,

5. Julian Ribera, *Disertaciones y Opusculos*, Madrid, 1928, p. 16.

however, that the Arabs were no longer designated by their genealogies; they merely added to their tribal name a place-name which allowed their rulers to distinguish between them more easily. Later on, however, further mixture took place between Arabs and non-Arabs. This led to a complete confusion of genealogies and a consequent weakening of that solidarity which is the fruit of tribal kinship; hence tribal names tended to be cast aside. Finally, the tribes themselves were absorbed and disappeared and with them all traces of tribal solidarity. The nomads, however, continued as they had always been. 'And God shall inherit the earth and all that are upon it.'[6]

This is how the confusion over the term 'Arab' first arose. Members of the imperial ruling class were proud of being Arab, however diluted their Arab ancestry might be. But they were also inclined to refer disparagingly to those tribesmen who retained their nomadic way of life and refused to settle down. (The contemptuous attitude was cordially reciprocated.) In some parts of the Arabic-speaking world, such as Egypt, the wider use of the term Arab, that is someone of Arab culture, was virtually forgotten. In the nineteenth century an Egyptian Arab was a nomad or semi-nomad who inhabited the desert or the fringes of the Nile valley. The wider meaning was only revived in the twentieth century with the renaissance of Arab national-ism, when Egypt took up its natural position as the most powerful of the independent Arab states. However, the suggestion that Egyptians 'are not really Arabs' is still heard, if with diminishing frequency.

Through large-scale conversion and intermarriage in the Arab Empire, new civilizations rapidly evolved whose cultural level de-pended mainly on the contribution made by the indigenous popu-lations. The Arabs brought little in the way of material civilization – nothing, for example, compared to the Romans – but only their language and religion, although these were of transcendant impor-tance. In places where there was already a long-established tradition of civilized living, as in Tunisia or Spain, for example, a highly developed Arab civilization soon came into existence. In Morocco, which was in a state of relative barbarism in the seventh century, a high level of civilization took much longer to appear.

Until 750 the Arab Empire was ruled from Damascus. The Umayyads at first showed considerable ability as rulers. They quelled the opposition of the Shiites in Iraq and the more serious rebellion of the old Medina theocracy who despised them as secular usurpers of

6. Ibn Khaldoun, *Prolegomena* vol. I, p. 237, quoted in Charles Issawl (trans.), *An Arab Philosophy of History*, London, 1950, p. 107.

the caliphate. Realizing that, with their cultural background and lack of experience, this élite would be incapable of establishing their own method of governing their new provinces, they made no attempt to replace the system of administration inherited from the Byzantines. They only ensured that Arabs occupied all the most senior administrative posts. Arabic was introduced as the main language of government and the currency and other matters were arabized only gradually.

This system worked well for a time; but the stability of the young empire was soon threatened by a series of acute crises. The first problem was financial, and arose from the unexpected early success of the Islamic religion. When the Muslim Faithful had been exempted from taxation, no one had expected the mass conversions of the subject peoples to Islam. As the number of taxpayers rapidly diminished, the empire was faced with an acute shortage of revenues while the demands for increased expenditure were rising. At the same time as the subject peoples poured in from the countryside to the *amsar*, the great military encampments which mushroomed on the edge of the desert, the Arab beduin, who were exempt from taxes, began to settle in their place on land which was formerly the principal source of revenues. Gradually this system was reformed so that taxes were levied on the land itself rather than on the landowners. But this meant that the Arab hegemony was eroded and Ibn Khaldoun's 'tribal solidarity', the basis of Arab strength, was lost. At the same time, the reforms did not come fast enough for the *mawali*, who deeply resented the privileges and favours that were still accorded to the Arabs.

The second great problem for the Umayyads was the feuding among the Arab tribes, which constantly wore away the régime's military power. The bitter animosity of the Shiites and the Kharijites against Damascus also continued. All these various elements of discontent and division were ultimately welded into a revolutionary movement based on Khorasan in eastern Persia, where Arab colonists had settled at the end of the seventh century. This movement of the Abbasids, which first raised its black banners of revolt in 720, took its name from one of the Prophet's uncles, al-Abbas, whose descendants successfully won power for themselves with the help of Persian agents. The movement was joined by many Arabs who were not of the Arab military aristocracy. The Caliph Marwan II, the last of the Umayyads, was an able ruler, but he underestimated the Abbasid threat. The revolutionary movement rapidly advanced westwards and finally overthrew Umayyad rule in 750. (One of the Umayyad princes, Abdul Rahman, escaped the destruction of his family and fled to Spain, where he succeeded in establishing three centuries of Umayyad rule over al-Andalus with his capital in Cordoba.)

So began the golden age of the Arab/Islamic Empire – the Abbasid caliphate. The revolutionary movement which overthrew the Umayyads was a coalition of various elements in rebellion against Damascus. Persians were prominent in the movement, but nineteenth-century orientalists were mistaken in describing these events as a victory of Persian Aryans over Arab Semites. There were Arabs in the movement, although not of pure Arab descent. What had happened was that the Arab tribal aristocracy, having performed its function in the days of imperial expansion, had been ousted by the new class of government officials, landowners and merchants, whose activities were more fundamental to the life of the cities and settled communities. They also included the Muslim scholar-legists, those collectively known as the *ulama* – 'who corresponded socially, though not religiously, to the priesthood of Christendom'.[7]

The Abbasid Empire was more cosmopolitan and more sophisticated than that of the Umayyads. (It was also more religious; the Umayyads were regarded as excessively secular.) Also it was Arab only in a very different sense. The Abbasid caliphs may have been proud of their pure Arab descent (although, as we have seen in al-Andalus, this could have been heavily diluted through the female line); but the empire that they ruled was a synthesis of many elements of which Arab was only one and Persian was predominant. The Arabs still had their racial pretensions to natural superiority, which provoked the rise in the late eighth century of the *shu'ubiya* (or nations) movement. This was not so much a political as a literary protest movement, in which the non-Arabs claimed that they had contributed as much to Islam as the Arabs. Not only the Persians, who in any case felt themselves superior to the Arabs, but other non-Arabs in Syria and Egypt joined in the movement, which often took the form of denigrating the Arabs as barbarian upstarts. At the same time, the significant fact is that the Shu'ubites expressed their ideas in Arabic. The power of the Arab tribal aristocracy had gone for ever, but their language was still extending its empire. In order to achieve equality the *mawali* were obliged to accept arabization. In this vitally important sense the Abbasid caliphate was Arab.

7. Joel Carmichael, *The Shaping of the Arabs*, London, 1967, p. 118.

The Abbasid Empire therefore established the principle of racial egalitarianism which has always since been a feature of the Islamic world. (It would be incorrect to say that all Muslims are racially colour-blind; but that they are much more so than most Christians – especially Anglo-Saxon Protestants – there can be no doubt.) However, the Abbasids were also less democratic in the spirit of their government than the Umayyads. The latter still ruled as desert shaikhs, chosen as *primus inter pares* by their fellow-Arabs and easily approachable to all of them. (The kings of Saudi Arabia have governed their land in much the same way in recent years.) The Abbasids, on the other hand, who moved the capital from Damascus to Baghdad, the site of an ancient Persian village on the west bank of the river Tigris near the old Persian imperial capital of Ctesiphon, adopted a form of despotism which was at least partially inherited from the Persian kings. The caliph ceased to be the mere successor of the Prophet to become the Deputy of Allah Himself – the Shadow of God on Earth, surrounded by an awesome display of power.

Baghdad, the Round City or City of Peace as it was officially called, was to become the most splendid metropolis of the contemporary world. It was two miles in diameter, with three concentric walls each pierced by four gates, through which passed highways radiating from the caliph's palace at the centre to the four corners of the empire. A well-regulated system of tribute and taxation, personally inspected by the caliph, a network of waterways and roads and a postal service of mounted couriers enabled the capital to collect the vast wealth of the empire in the treasure-houses of Baghdad. Skilfully sited as a commercial as well as strategic centre, Baghdad became the focus of a vast trading network. Camels carried cargoes overland to Persia. Ships sailed down the Tigris to Arabia, North Africa and Syria.

Baghdad reached the zenith of its glory under the Caliphs Haroun al-Rashid (786–809) and his son al-Mamun (813–833). With its myriads of mosques, palaces and government offices it was a centre of power, wealth and piety. With its gardens, pavilions and patios it was also essentially a city of pleasure – 'a Paris of the ninth century' in Richard Burton's phrase. No one symbolized this better than Abu Nuwas, the boon companion and friend of Haroun al-Rashid, the lover of wine and boys, who is also one of the greatest of Arab poets. Abu Nuwas was in the forefront of the literary revolution which rebelled against the rigid rules of poetic forms and themes inherited from the pre-Islamic days when Arabs were all desert nomads. Some of the Umayyad poets had rebelled but with limited success. In order to make use of their original talents their most common device was to resort to obscenity.

The new poets protested that they could not be expected to write about the flora and fauna of the desert which they had never seen. Abu Nuwas made his protest in the form of a famous parody of a desert ode or *qasida*.

> The lovelorn wretch stopped at a desert camping ground to question it, and I stopped to inquire after the local tavern.
> May Allah not dry the eyes of him that wept over stones, and may he not ease the pain of him that yearns over a tent peg!
> They said: 'Didst thou commemorate the dwelling place of the tribe of Asad? Plague on thee.' Tell me, who are the Banu Asad?

Something of the spirit of the Abbasid Empire is reflected in the glittering tales of *The Thousand and One Nights*, which is by far the best-known work of secular Arabic literature in the West and has added Aladdin, Ali Baba and Sindbad the Sailor to our folklore. Like the empire, the tales are cosmopolitan. They come from India, Persia, Turkey and possibly Greece as well as Iraq and Egypt.

Haroun al-Rashid and Abu Nuwas both frequently appear in the tales, although the main protagonists, such as King Shahryar and his prime minister's daughter, Shahrazad ('Scheherezade'), who tells him the stories, have Persian names. Stories about Abu Nuwas are found anywhere that Arab culture has spread, from Morocco to India, and most of them are scandalous. The anecdotes may be apocryphal but his reputation was undoubtedly based on fact. Much of the Arab's reputation for sensuality may be traced to him.

> A brook, a bottle, a bench, a way of waiting,
> The body sweetens, the ghost stirs,
> Golden four.[8]

According to *The Thousand and One Nights*, even Haroun al-Rashid was sometimes so shocked by his behaviour that he would consider putting him to death. But he found the poet too amusing to carry out his threat.

On one occasion Abu Nuwas had arranged an orgy with three handsome youths in his house when the caliph walked in. Haroun al-Rashid said with bitter sarcasm, 'I have sought direction of Allah Almighty and have appointed thee *Kazi* [i.e. Judge] of pimps and

8. Translated by Herbert Howarth and Ibrahim Shukrullah; J. Kritzeck (ed.), *Anthology of Islamic Literature*, Harmondsworth, Penguin, 1964, p. 92.

panders.' Unabashed Abu Nuwas replied, 'Hast thou any suit to prefer to me?'

The caliph went away in anger, and the next day when Abu Nuwas appeared at the *Diwan* [council of state], Haroun ordered him to be stripped and an ass's pack-saddle to be bound on his back, a halter round his head, and a crupper under his rump, and thus to be led round to all the lodgings of the slave girls, and the chambers of the Harem, that the women might make mock of him; then to have his head cut off and brought to the caliph.

But Abu Nuwas was a funny fellow, so he made all the girls laugh with his buffooneries, and each gave him something whereby he returned not save with a pocketful of money. When he was met by Ja'afar the Barmecide, Ja'afar said, 'What offence hast thou committed to bring this punishment on thee?' To which Abu Nuwas answered: 'None whatsoever except that I made our Lord the caliph a present of the best of my poetry and he presented me, in return, with the best of his raiment.' When the Prince of True Believers heard this, he laughed, from a heart full of wrath, and pardoned Abu Nawas, and also gave him a myriad of money.[9]

Like many Arabs, Abu Nuwas was bisexual. However, unlike most Arabs he seems to have preferred girls who looked as much like boys as possible:

> Like ephebe she has no hips
> And has even cut her hair
> Soft the pressure of her lips,
> Velvet down on face so fair.
>
> This a double charm doth give,
> Satisfying both their tastes,
> He who for boys doth only live
> And he who likes the lassies' waists.[10]

In fact in *The Thousand and One Nights* he is referred to as the king of the Sodomites, who is prepared to defend the superiority of male attributes.

> When his detractors said to me
> Hair on his lips, alack, we see,
> Wrinkling, spoiling beauty.
> I unto them made answer straight
> How can you this a defect rate
> It is an ornament.

9. Translated by Khati Cheghlou, *Histoires Arabes*, Paris, 1927, and quoted in W. H. Ingrams, *Abu Nawas in Life and Legend*, Mauritius, 1933, p. 31.
10. Ibid. p. 36.

The whiteness of his teeth and face
The down relieves and adds a grace
Like dress to glitt'ring pearls.

It is to me a charming sign
Of new and growing force divine
Which he is acquiring.[11]

11. Trans. J. C. Mardous, *Le Livre des Mille Nuits et une Nuit*, vol. IV, Paris, 1899, p. 107.

3. The Long Decline

The Abbasid dynasty lasted some five hundred years – until the Mongol general Hulagu Khan sacked Baghdad in 1258, had the last caliph kicked to death and, according to contemporary chroniclers, piled some 800,000 corpses in the streets. But the empire's decline, like that of the Roman Empire, had begun long before this. After the death of Haroun al-Rashid in 829 it was shaken by a civil war between his two sons Amin and Mamun. Amin's power was based on Iraq and Mamun's on Persia; Mamun's victory meant an increase in Persian influence in the caliphate, although he kept Baghdad as the capital. In many ways, Mamun's reign was as brilliant as that of his father. Education was especially favoured. Large sums of private and public money were allocated to the mosques which, according to the rule of Islam, were expected to contain a school. The teachers came from every corner of the empire and huge libraries attracted the learned of all nations. Poets, philosophers, orators, doctors and scientists were honoured and highly paid. Knowledge was prized; when one of the caliph's ministers was invited to visit Persia he refused on the ground that he would need 400 camels to carry all his books.

The speed with which the language of poetry-loving, but otherwise scarcely civilized, Arabian nomads imposed itself on the most sophisticated cultures of the ancient world, is astonishing. 'By the eleventh century Arabic not only was the principal everyday vernacular all the way from Persia to Spain, it also had completely ousted as a cultural vehicle ancient cultural languages like Coptic, Aramaic, Greek and Latin from areas where they had had undisputed sway for centuries or millennia.'[1] Although the Arabic language might not be thought suitable for this kind of cultural imperialism, in fact it is ideal for this purpose. From relatively few root-formations the language spreads out as a vast structure of subtle and complex variations, which are ideally suited for the expression of abstract and scientific concepts. Arabic absorbed many foreign words, but these were easily 'arabicized' in a way that was not discordant with the character of the language.

1. Joel Carmichael, *The Shaping of the Arabs*, London, 1967, p. 155.

Like all Semitic languages, the basis of Arabic is the triliteral root. With a few exceptions, there are only three consonants in each verb; but by means of prefixes and suffixes the form of the root is varied to express a great range of related concepts.

Thus, the ideas break, shatter, try to break, cause to break, pretend to break, are among many variations of the fundamental verbal theme which can, or could, be expressed by vowel changes and consonantal arguments without the aid of the supplementary verbs and pronouns which we have to employ in English. The noun, too, has an appropriate form for many diverse things, such as the time and place for an action, bodily defects, diseases, instruments, colours, trades and so on.[2]

Arabic covered the ancient cultures with its mantle but did not suffocate or destroy them. The Persian and the Hellenic were the most important: Persian in literature, especially poetry, and statecraft; and Hellenism in philosophy, science and medicine. (On the other hand, the great body of classical Greek literature – the Homeric epics and the tragedies – were ignored by Islamic civilizations.) Persian culture was to reassert its independence as the Persians gradually threw off the political domination of the Arabs, although the revived Persian language was written in the Arabic script and retained a vast Arabic vocabulary. Hellenism, on the other hand, survived through the civilization of Islam and in turn exerted its own profound influence upon it.

From an early period the doctrines of Islam had been permeated by Greek philosophy; or it might be more accurate to say that as the *umma* expanded, Islam was accepted by men whose minds had been formed by Greek thought and who therefore thought about Islam in terms of Greek philosophy.[3]

The Jews had little direct influence on Islam, except through the early biblical influences on the Prophet Muhammad. It was the spread of Islamic civilization which brought the Jews into contact with Hellenism and enabled them to play their vital creative role in the great cities of medieval Islam such as Cordoba and Toledo. When trade between western Christendom and the East was broken off by the Arab conquest, it was the Jews who resumed it by acting as a link between the two hostile worlds. The ninth-century Arab geographer Ibn Khurradadhbeh described how Jewish merchants from the south of France, speaking 'Arabic, Persian, Greek, Frankish, Spanish and

2. T. Arnold and A. Guillaume (eds), *The Legacy of Islam*, London, 1931, p. vi.
3. A. Hourani, *Arabic Thought in the Liberal Age, 1798–1939*, London, 1962, p. 15.

Slavonic', travel from the western Mediterranean to India and China and back either by landing at Antioch and travelling along the Euphrates valley or by sailing through the Red Sea. 'From the west they bring eunuchs, slave girls, boys, brocade, castor-skins, marten and other furs, and swords. . . . From China they bring back musk, aloes, camphor, cinnamon and other products of those parts . . .'

In the first century of the Abbasid caliphate most of the great works of Greek philosophy and science – Plato, Aristotle, Euclid and Hippocrates – were translated into Arabic. There were few original thinkers; one notable exception was al-Kindi, the first outstanding Islamic philosopher, who was called 'the philosopher of the Arabs'. He was highly appreciated by the Caliph Mamun and died about 870. Al-Kindi was of noble Arab descent in the male line; but most of the famous later Islamic philosophers such as Avicenna (980–1037) were Persian.

Understandably, the first Arab conquerors had no architectural skill or taste. As in other fields, they made use of the ideas and technical skills of the peoples they conquered – Byzantines in the eastern empire, Copts in Egypt and Visigoths in Spain. Just as they employed their stone-masons, plasterers and decorators so they unashamedly used their buildings as stone-quarries for the mosques and palaces they erected.

But in spite of the Arabs' probable ignorance of architecture in the early years of conquest, the remarkable and incontrovertible fact about Muslim architecture is that in all countries and in all centuries it retained an unmistakable individuality of its own, although its origins were so diverse. There was something about it that differentiated it from the work of all the local schools of craftsmanship which were technically instrumental in bringing it into being.[4]

Muslim artisans took over and developed all the crafts of working in metal, wood, stone, ivory, glass and above all pottery and rug-making in which they made their greatest contribution. Islam had taken over from the Jews their repugnance for graven images, and when the Arab/Islamic Empire was in a position to cultivate the arts the prohibition of idols was applied to the plastic reproduction of the human figure. (The Umayyad nobility decorated their hunting lodges with lively frescoes of the human form, and the Umayyads were later

4. Arnold and Guillaume, op. cit., p. 157.

accused of being dangerously secular.)[5] The consequence was that Islamic art tended towards the elaborate development of abstract ornament – the delicate geometric patterns which can be seen at their finest in the mosques and palaces of India, Persia, Egypt or Andalusia. The Arabic script itself, usually in the form of Koranic quotations, was incorporated into the designs to achieve at its best an effect of exquisite harmony.

The administration of the realm of the Abbasid caliphs had been brought to a high peak of efficiency under the prudent care of the Barmecides, a noble Persian family of converted Buddhists who were the grand viziers under the first three caliphs. (The expression 'Barmecide feast', meaning an imaginary banquet, comes from 'The Barber's Tale of his Sixth Brother' in *The Thousand and One Nights*, where a Barmecide serves a series of empty dishes to a hungry guest to test his sense of humour.) But in 803 the Barmecides were ousted from office by Haroun al-Rashid, who was probably jealous of their power, and the administration passed into less able hands. As expenditure of the top-heavy and extravagant court and central government increased, revenues were falling as one by one the more distant parts of the empire fell into the hands of independent dynasties – Spain under the Umayyad Abdul Rahman of Cordoba in 750 and then North Africa under the Aghlabids of Kairouan in 800. The Aghlabids paid no more than nominal tribute to the caliph in Baghdad. The Abbasid caliphs resorted to the disastrous expedient of farming out tax-collection to local military commanders in the eastern provinces. These men thereupon acquired more power for themselves and also became increasingly independent of the central authority in Baghdad.

The first Abbasid caliphs had had to face a series of rebellious movements of a religious character among the Persian peasantry. The

5. The Koran itself gives no support for the widely held belief that it was the Islamic religion which made representations of the human figure impossible. It was the *hadith* literature dating from the second half of the ninth century which was outspokenly hostile and called the makers of figured pictures 'the worst of men'. 'Human and animal figures are less severely prohibited when they occur in what are considered to be degrading contexts. They are specifically allowed on carpets and pillows, since stepping, sitting, or leaning on them are deprecatory acts. The only themes more generally permitted are trees and objects in which there is "no living spirit".' (Richard Ettinghausen, *Arab Painting*, Cleveland, Ohio, 1962, p. 13). In the Koran the word for 'to fashion or form' (*sawwara*) is synonymous with the word 'to create' and God Himself is sometimes called a *musawwir*, a common word for 'painter'. The (figurative) artist therefore came to be regarded as competing blasphemously with God.

most serious was that led by Babak (816–837), who preached the break-up and redistribution of the great estates and defeated four of the Caliph Mamun's generals before he was finally crushed. Thirty years later there was another major revolt of a different character – that of the Zanj or Negro slaves. Unlike the Roman Empire, the Islamic Empire did not look on slaves as the main source of manual' labour; this was carried out by peasants and artisans while slaves were employed as domestic servants or soldiers. But there were exceptions, and one of these was the huge enterprise of draining the marshes of southern Iraq to reclaim the land for cultivation and sell the salt commercially. Thousands of slaves were imported from East Africa for this purpose and in 869 they rose in revolt. At first they had remarkable success. Their revolt spread into southern Persia; they captured Basra and threatened Baghdad. The fact that black troops of the imperial armies sent out to crush them went over to their side was an ominous indication of racial conflict within Islam. Finally, after fourteen years of rebellion, the Zanj were defeated and the head of their leader Ali brought back to Baghdad on a pole.

The empire had been badly shaken but it was not yet seriously endangered by such revolts from below. Of more fundamental importance was the great movement of the Ismailis or 'Seveners', a branch of the Shia who took their name from Ismail, the seventh descendant of Ali, the Prophet's son-in-law. This movement began to grow alarmingly in the middle of the ninth century. Ismaili missionaries spread throughout the empire preaching the return of Ismail's son Muhammad as the Mahdi (or Muslim 'Messiah'), and founding the secret cells of their supporters. The Ismailis fashioned their message to appeal to all the oppressed classes of the Abbasid Empire. They preached greater equality and as a consequence were accused of advocating communism and the common ownership of women.

The Ismailis were rapidly successful. In 901 they won over the rulers of Yemen and in 908 they installed their Imam Ubaydallah as the first caliph of a new rival dynasty in Tunisia, known as the Fatimids after the Prophet's daughter Fatima, the wife of Ali. In 969 the Fatimids secured the great prize of Egypt and founded Cairo, which, with its al-Azhar University, became one of the great intellectual and spiritual centres of Islam. Fatimid power in Cairo grew until it outshone that of Baghdad. In the eleventh century the empire, apart from North Africa and Egypt, included Sicily, Syria and western Arabia. In 1056 a Fatimid general even briefly occupied Baghdad.[6]

But apart from the dismemberment of the empire and the emergence of Muslim powers of competing brilliance in the caliphates of Cordoba and Cairo, the golden age of the Abbasids was beginning to dim before the end of the ninth century. In the very early years of the Abbasids a force of men of pure Arab descent who were loyal to the régime was maintained. But they were gradually disbanded, and the role of protecting the central power of the caliph went to his guards from Khorasan. From the middle of the ninth century the caliph's army, which now consisted of paid troops and no longer of mounted tribesmen spurred by the faith of Islam and the lure of booty, was increasingly recruited from Turks. Some of these were free men but others were Turkish and Circassian slaves from the Caucasus and central Asia who were specially trained for the purpose. It was they who became known as Mamlukes (Arabic *mamluk*, 'owned'). At first the caliphs found them invaluable, since, lacking family ties, they were both more mobile and more reliable than the Arabs and Persians. They were taught to be Muslims and trained for total devotion to the caliph. But as they became more indispensable their desire for power increased. Step by step they encroached upon the government until they formed a ruling caste or pretorian guard with king-making powers. In 945 the captain of the Baghdad troop was given the title of *amir al-umara* or 'Commander of the Commanders' to emphasize his unique importance.

The trend had already begun towards the long period in which the great majority of Arabs (in the new sense of Arabic-speaking peoples) would be ruled by others, men for whom Arabic was not their first language.

In 945 a local dynasty from western Persia seized Baghdad and ruled for the next century as secular sultans with the Abbasid caliph as a religious figurehead. In 1055 the Buwayhids were in turn defeated by a new rising power of central Asian nomads – the Seljuks – who had recently turned Muslim. The Seljuks conquered

6. After the death of the great Fatimid Caliph Mustansir in 1094 the Ismaili movement split into an Egyptian wing and a Syrian/Persian wing. The Egyptian Fatimids were ousted by Saladin in 1171. The Persian/Syrian Ismailis survived, although they in turn divided into two rival groups. It is the descendants of the imams of the major of these two lines who are the Aga Khans of the present day, with millions of followers in India, Pakistan, Iran, Syria and East Africa.

Syria and the greater part of Anatolia (which the Arabs themselves had failed to do). The Islamic Empire was once again briefly united as it had been in the early days of the caliphate. But the difference was that the rulers were Turks and not Arabs or arabized Persians. The Turks, newcomers to the world of Islam, had entered in force and were to remain the dominant element for centuries.

Egypt was not conquered by the Seljuks, but here also the Turks became the ruling class. The Fatimid sultans recruited Mamlukes to free themselves of dependence upon North African and Sudanese troops. They deliberately prevented them from becoming a hereditary caste. The children of the Mamlukes adopted Arabic and became absorbed into Egyptian society, but new recruits were imported from the Black Sea coast and central Asia and specially trained to maintain this curious non-hereditary slave aristocracy.

What of the original Arabs, the lords of the desert who had formed the vanguard of the first great Muslim conquests? Those nomadic tribesmen who had refused to settle down and allow themselves to be absorbed into the cosmopolitan empire of the Abbasids had preserved their precious but poverty-stricken independence by remaining in the deserts, an object of fear and hatred for the people of the settled communities. Wherever the central authority of the state was in decline, they took advantage. In the middle of the eleventh century the Egyptian Fatimid caliph decided to teach his rebellious Tunisian subjects a lesson by letting loose upon them the two Arab beduin tribes of Beni Hilal and Beni Sulaim from upper Egypt. His action was quite disastrous for, unlike the first beduin invasion which brought Islam to North Africa, this was purely destructive. 'Like an army of locusts', as Ibn Khaldoun remarked, the beduin raiders swept through Libya to sack the splendid city of Kairouan in 1056. Writing in the fourteenth century Ibn Khaldoun pointed out that the trouble with the Arabs (he uses the term in the original sense of desert nomads) was that

they are not primarily concerned with establishing law and order or with preventing men from committing evil or aggression against each other. For their main object is to extort money by looting or by fines . . . Lastly, every Arab regards himself as worthy to rule, and it is rare to find one of them submitting willingly to another, be it his father or his brother or the head of his clan, but only grudgingly and for fear of public opinion . . . Mark how all the countries of the world which have been conquered and dominated by the Arabs have had their civilization ruined, their population dispersed, and even the soil itself apparently transformed. Thus Yemen is in ruins, except for a few districts; similarly Iraq, which was so flourishing under the Persians, is devastated; so, too, is Syria at the present day. In North Africa and the Maghreb, which were invaded by the Banu Hilal and Banu Sulaim at the beginning of the fifth century of the Muslim era and ravaged by them during three hundred and fifty years, ruin and devastation still prevail. Yet before that time all the country lying between the Sudan [i.e. black Africa] and the Mediterranean was the centre of a flourishing civilization, as witnessed by the remains of buildings and statues and the ruins of towns and villages. And 'God inherits the earth and its inhabitants and He is the best heir of all.'[7]

The more accepted view today is that Ibn Khaldoun exaggerated the overriding importance of the beduin invasion in the long secular decline of North Africa but that his forceful genius succeeded in imposing his view on subsequent generations. In fact the Beni Hilal and Beni Sulaim were only one of a number of destructive elements – part of a chain reaction which upset the balance of civilization in the Maghreb. What we do know is that in the middle of the eleventh century North Africa entered a period of long, if uneven, decline from which it is now struggling hard to emerge.

7. Ibn Khaldoun, *Prolegomena*, vol. 1, p. 270, quoted in Charles Issawi (trans.), *An Arab Philosophy of History*, London, 1950, p. 57.

4. The West Counter-attacks

At the end of the eleventh century the world of Inner Islam[1] was in a state of confusion. The Seljuks were in the ascendant having captured Jerusalem from the mild Fatimid caliphs of Cairo in 1070 and inflicted a devastating defeat on the Byzantine forces in the following year. But the Seljuk Empire was already revealing its weaknesses. It had been unable to prevent the growth in Syria of the new terrorist sect, an offshoot of the Ismailis, known as the Assassins (from the Arabic *hashshash*, or hashish-eaters, from the means by which they were alleged to have induced ecstasy among their followers). The Seljuk sultans, who had no culture of their own, relied on the Persian bureaucracy to administer the empire, but they could not rid themselves of the idea that sovereignty belonged to a family rather than a single man. Even the most powerful sultans felt obliged to hand over provinces to their relatives to rule as private kingdoms.

It was at this point that western Christendom decided to carry its four-centuries-old battle with Islam into the eastern Mediterranean. At first Islam had been almost wholly victorious, but Christendom's counter-offensive had already begun. Toledo had fallen in 1085 in the first stage of the Catholic reconquest of Spain; the Arab base of Mahdia in Tunisia was taken by the Genoese, the Pisans and their allies took the Italian cities in 1087, and the last Muslims were driven from Sicily in 1091. These campaigns were blessed by the pope as a precedent for the future. The papacy was delighted that the bellicose passions of European military feudal society should be diverted from private wars against the infidel. The idea of Christian Holy War, similar to the *jihad* of Islam, was born.

Now a new and much greater opportunity arose for the use of the swords and spears of Christendom. The traffic of Christian pilgrims to the Holy Sepulchre in Jerusalem was interrupted in the second half of the eleventh century first by the Seljuks' seizure of Anatolia from the Byzantines and then by the conflicts within the Seljuk Empire which raged over Syria and Palestine. This provided the motive for

---

1. A term used to describe the middle-eastern or west Asian Islamic states, in contrast to Outer Islam of central, south-eastern and eastern Asia.

the First Crusade to recover the Holy Land in 1096; but the impulse was the release of the expanding energy of western Europe. In the first place the crusades provided an outlet for the frustrated aggressive instincts of the younger sons of the feudal nobility and in the second it offered a new vent for the commercial ambitions of the great Italian port states such as Venice and Genoa. These had already established entrepôt centres on the Syrian coast for trade with the orient, the vanguard of Europe's economic domination of the Middle East which was to last a thousand years.

The dissensions within the Muslim world gave the First Crusaders initial success. On 15 July 1099 they seized Jerusalem, which had been retaken by the Fatimids from the Seljuk Turks the year before, and massacred thousands of Muslims and Jews. The Holy Sepulchre was safely back in Christian hands. The crusaders then set up a series of small feudal states along the Syrian coast and in Palestine which remained in constant contact with western Europe on which they depended for supplies and new recruits.

But the balance of political and military power had not yet swung decisively in favour of the Christian states. Their successes were due much less to the superiority of their armies than to the divisions between the petty Seljuk states with which they were surrounded, and which were quite ready to ally themselves with the crusaders against their rivals. Also the main centres of Islamic power – Fatimid Cairo and Seljuk Baghdad – were prepared for a time to tolerate their presence.

It was neither a clash nor a fusion between two cultures that was taking place. The Latin Kingdom of Jerusalem was hardly representative of the best of medieval Christendom. It was 'a rude military settlement, without the impulse, or at any rate without the time, for the creation of any achievements of civilization'.[2] Similarly the Saracen[3] enemies they were fighting did not represent the finer aspects of Islamic civilization. It was in Spain and Sicily that the two cultures fused to produce a remarkable mixed civilization which for a time survived the Christian reconquest. (The twelfth-century Norman kings of Sicily read and wrote Arabic. The greatest of Arab geographers produced his monumental treatise at the court of Roger

2. T. Arnold and A. Guillaume, *The Legacy of Islam*, London, 1931, p. 54.
3. The word 'Saracens' (Greek *sarakenoi*) was used by late classical authors to refer to an Arab tribe of the Sinai peninsula. The term was gradually extended to all Arabs and then to all Muslims, until in the Middle Ages the crusaders applied it to all their opponents, whether Arab, Turkish or Persian.

II and dedicated it to him. In Spain, the Mosque Library of Toledo became a resort of Christian scholars after the Spanish reconquest, and it was here that Latin Christendom became familiar with Aristotle in Arabic translation and the efforts of the great Arab Jewish philosopher Moses Maimonides to reconcile Aristotle with the Old Testament.)

The presumptive incursion of the semi-barbarian crusaders into the east Mediterranean eventually produced a strong counteraction from the world of Islam, which was still far from moribund. If it was racked with dissension, so were the crusaders. Sixty years after the First Crusaders arrived in Syria a Seljuk prince Nureddin captured Damascus and established a unified Muslim state to confront them. Nureddin's agent in Egypt was Salah al-Din, known in the west as Saladin, who acted as *wazir* (vizier) to the last of the Fatimid caliphs. However in 1171 Saladin announced the end of the Fatimid caliphate and made himself ruler of Egypt. When Nureddin died three years later Saladin also took over Syria. By 1187 he had recaptured Jerusalem and thrown back the crusaders to a small strip of land along the Syrian coast.

The high point of crusader achievement was past. The Third Crusade led by Richard Coeur de Lion of England, Philip II of France and the Holy Roman Emperor Barbarossa recovered some of the Holy Land ports and gained the right of Christian pilgrims to visit Jerusalem. It also gave the truncated rump of the Kingdom of Jerusalem a new lease of life which lasted a century.

The Fifth Crusade came near to conquering Egypt with the object of exchanging Cairo for Jerusalem, but ultimately failed. The Sixth Crusade briefly recovered Jerusalem in 1229 but lost it again in 1244 to a Turkish army in Egyptian pay. The Seventh Crusade under the saintly Louis IX of France also came close to winning Egypt but ultimately failed like the Fifth. The Eighth Crusade ended with Louis' death in Tunisia in 1270. Over the next thirty years the last crusader strongholds in the Levant were reduced. From then on the European Christian powers were too occupied with their own wars, such as the Hundred Years' War between England and France, or those against more immediate infidel threats such as the Ottoman Turks or the Moors in Spain, to have much time for thought about the Holy Sepulchre.

What lasting impression did the crusaders leave on the Islamic world of the eastern Mediterranean apart from a chain of imposing fortress-castles, of which the Krak des Chevaliers (near the present-day Syrian/Lebanese border) is the most magnificent? The answer is very little that was positive.

There was an important economic legacy in the trading colonies in the Levant which flourished under the crusaders and which were encouraged to stay after the crusaders had been defeated. The Muslim authorities believed that this was to their advantage. As Saladin wrote to the caliph of Baghdad in 1183: 'The Venetians, the Genoese and the Pisans bring into Egypt choice products of the West, especially arms and war materials. This constitutes an advantage for Islam and an injury for Christianity.' The Church agreed with Saladin's view and denounced the traffic, threatening the Christian merchants with excommunication. This had no effect at all. In later centuries, when the balance of economic power swung decisively in favour of Christendom, the Muslim authorities came to regard Christian commercial enterprise as a threat. By then they lacked the power to suppress it.

The crusades had a lasting adverse effect on Muslim society. Whereas the Muslims had been fairly tolerant of the Christians and Jews – the *dhimmis* or people of the two other monotheistic religions – the brutal treatment of Muslims by the crusaders during the three centuries of their occupation made the Muslim leaders, especially the Mamluke sultans and later the Ottoman sultans, much harsher in their attitude towards anyone suspected of collaborating with the infidel invaders. At the time of the First Crusade the Islamic world had declined from the peak of its golden age but was still superior to medieval Christendom in tolerance and breadth of intellectual interest. By the time the crusaders abandoned their last Syrian castles this was no longer so.[4]

It would be untrue to say that the crusades were solely responsible for this deterioration. Early in the thirteenth century, when John of Brienne, titular king of Jerusalem, was launching the Fifth Crusade into Egypt in the hope of exchanging Damietta for Jerusalem, a new and even more serious threat to Islam arose in the east. The great Genghis Khan had succeeded in uniting the nomadic tribes of Mongolia and imposing the rule of his nomad élite over a vast

4. For the Arabs, who of all people have perhaps the most lively feeling of their own history, the aggressive invasion of the crusaders is still a vivid popular myth. It is no cause for surprise that they like to compare Zionists of today with the crusaders and to point out that although the latter may have stayed for three centuries they were eventually ejected as an alien body.

empire of sedentary peoples. In 1219–25 he advanced through Turkestan into Iran and Afghanistan and westwards to the Caucasus and south Russia. Genghis Khan died in 1227 and the Mongol advance paused; but thirty years later Prince Hulagu, brother of Mangu Khan and grandson of Genghis advanced through Persia where he wiped out the Assassins, and into Iraq. In 1258 Hulagu captured Baghdad and put Mustasim, the last of the Abbasid caliphs, to death. This execution was historically insignificant because the Abbasid caliphate had been a mere shadow for more than two centuries, but the swarming hordes of Hulagu's armies finally destroyed all the magnificent public works and the wonderful irrigation system of lower Mesopotamia, which had suffered a long period of decline but was still in operation. As in North Africa two centuries earlier, the locust hordes of nomad warriors devastated nearly everything of cultural and economic value. Mesopotamia was incorporated into the Mongol Empire and cut off from the Islamic world of the eastern Mediterranean. Some restoration was attempted under Hulagu and his successors but it had little result. After three centuries of maladministration, interrupted by civil war, Mesopotamia (Iraq) was incorporated into the Turkish Ottoman Empire. This brought stability of a kind but it remained a stagnant and neglected province until the break-up of the empire after the First World War.

But Hulagu was not only destructive. His wife Dokuz Khan was a Christian and she encouraged him to be tolerant of Christianity. The Christian minorities in Syria and Palestine therefore hoped he would advance further westwards to defeat their Muslim masters. (European Christians even dreamed of achieving their frustrated aims by converting the Mongol Khans to Christianity. Pope Innocent IV and St Louis of France both sent missions to the Mongol court for this purpose, but without success.) In 1259 Hulagu's armies marched into Syria, took Damascus and Aleppo, and reached the Mediterranean. It seemed that the Mongol Empire might extend into Egypt and North Africa to become even more extensive than the Arab Empire. After the death of Saladin in 1193, his Syrian-Egyptian sultanate was divided among his heirs. These soon quarrelled with each other and the unity of the empire collapsed. In 1250 Turanshah, the last free sultan, was killed by his own Mamluke guards and although his widow Shagarat al-Durr, one of the most remarkable women in Muslim history, called herself sultana and was recognized in Egypt, the Syrian princes refused to pay her homage. Aybak, the Mamluke commander in Egypt, married Shagarat al-Durr and became the first in a long line of Mamluke sultans which lasted three centuries. Aybak only ruled for seven years. In a fit of jealousy Shagarat al-Durr had him murdered; the slave women of his first wife then beat her to death with their slippers.

Syria and Egypt appeared to lie at the mercy of Hulagu's armies, but Aybak's successor Qutuz rallied his forces in Syria and won a surprise victory over Hulagu's forces at Ain Jalut in Palestine on 3 September 1260. An outstanding Mamluke officer in Qutuz's army named Baybars quarrelled with Qutuz, killed him and took the Egyptian throne.

Like most of the first Mamluke sultans, Baybars was a Turk, a Qipchaq from the northern shores of the Caspian Sea. He was able and enlightened but totally ruthless. Like Saladin, but with more permanent success, he united Egypt and Syria under his rule. He drove back the invading Mongols and destroyed all but the last remnants of the Crusader strongholds.

One of Baybars' shrewdest, if most cynical, acts of statesmanship was to establish a refugee scion of the Baghdad caliphate as a puppet caliph in Cairo, in order to give his secular government an aura of legitimacy. Baybars set the tone for the three centuries of Mamluke rule, which were violent, extravagant, artistically creative and cruel. As we have seen, the dynasty was hereditary only in the sense that each Mamluke ruler imported his Turkish or Circassian slave successor, who was trained in Egypt while his own sons usually became absorbed into the mass of the population. While these were arabized, the ruling class remained Turco-Circassian and frequently could not speak Arabic. The Mamluke aristocracy held land in virtual ownership in return for military service in the cavalry. Consequently they were never rooted in the land. Their feudalism was military rather than agricultural and they usually lived in the capital or the principal town of whatever district their fiefs were located in. In Syria the task of day-to-day administration was carried on by civil servants who were drawn from local Arab families, with their tradition of religious learning.

The Mamlukes were strictly orthodox in religion and Islamic religious culture flourished under their rule. However, the fact that for both political and religious reasons they tended to oppress the religious minorities such as the Druzes, Maronite Christians, Ismailis and the Alawites (an extreme form of Shiism) made them deeply unpopular with these powerful groups and ultimately helped to undermine their rule in Syria.

Mamluke rule in Syria and Egypt lasted until 1516–17, when it was overthrown by the new rising Muslim power from the north – the Ottoman Turks. During these three centuries the Mamlukes were responsible for holding together Muslim society in the Middle East against its Christian crusader and Mongol enemies. Life was violent in their times, but many of the Mamluke sultans possessed a keen artistic sense. This was a period of high creativity in the arts, as the great mosques, schools and tombs in Cairo of men such as Qalawun, Hassan and Qait Bey still bear witness. Politically and economically, however, the Mamluke sultanate declined fairly steadily from its apogee under Baybars. The system of choosing a successor to the sultan by election deteriorated into one in which the head of the strongest of several warring factions, each with its own private army, seized the throne.

The Mamlukes, with their fierce courage, remained a formidable military force although the Muslim world was beginning to fall behind Christendom in the science of warfare. But their most shattering defeat was not at the hands of the crusaders, whom they virtually eliminated, but their other old enemy the Mongols. In 1400 Timur (or Tamerlane, properly Timur Leng – 'the lame Timur'), after successfully invading both Russia and India, turned westwards to Syria. He sacked Aleppo and Damascus, killed tens of thousands and transported the world-famous skilled Syrian artisans to Samarkand in central Asia. Syria, which had enjoyed some prosperity under the early Mamluke sultans, who had encouraged irrigation and other public works while trade was carried on by Venetian merchants on the coast, never really recovered. As the hard-pressed Mamlukes now endeavoured to squeeze as much money as they could from the lucrative transit trade between Europe and the East they caused an inflationary spiral and provoked retaliation. But much worse was to come. At the end of the fifteenth century the adventurous Portuguese opened up the trade route to India via the Cape of Good Hope. In May 1498 Vasco da Gama's ship reached India and returned to Lisbon laden with spices. A century later the Dutch followed the Portuguese to reach Java.

The Mamluke fleets attempted to ward off the Portuguese threat, but in vain. Their ships were outclassed; the Portuguese soon dominated the Indian Ocean and penetrated into the Persian Gulf and the Red Sea. In the Mediterranean the spice trade remained in the hands of the Venetians and Egyptians for another century; but Egypt and Syria were increasingly by-passed by world trade and declined into the economic backwater in which they were to remain until modern times.

Mamluke power was now in irretrievable decline. However, it was not replaced at this stage by the Christians but by a new Muslim Empire based in Asia Minor. The Turks had entered the Islamic world first as slaves and then as mercenary adventurers. In 1258 the Mongol invasion which brought the moribund Abbasid caliphate to an end has also destroyed the Seljuk sultanate in Asia Minor, but before the end of the thirteenth century the foundations of the Ottoman Empire had been laid on its ruins by Othman, a Turkish mercenary recently converted to Islam. He and his successors gradually extended their rule throughout Asia Minor and their influence into the Balkans, until in 1453 Mohammed II, 'the Conqueror', took Constantinople and overthrew the Byzantine Empire. He began to rebuild the impoverished and crumbling city and to repopulate it with Muslims, Christians and Jews from various parts of his realm. Constantinople developed into Istanbul, the focus of a vast new Islamic Empire which for a time would benefit from a much stronger political and administrative framework than the Arabs ever possessed in their golden age.

It was Mohammed II's grandson Selim I (known as the Stern and Inflexible) who carried on the process of empire-building. After a crushing victory over the Shiite Shah Ismail of Persia in 1514, which enabled him to add Upper Mesopotamia and Kurdistan to his empire, he turned against the Mamlukes who had formed what he regarded as a treacherous alliance with Shah Ismail against him. Late in 1516 he advanced into Syria. The Mamluke Sultan Qansaw al-Ghawri came from Cairo to meet him, and in a great battle at Marj Dabiq, north of Aleppo, the Mamluke forces were decisively defeated and the sultan was killed. The following January the Ottoman forces advanced into Egypt and took Cairo. Tuman Bey, the last of the Mamluke sultans, was beheaded by Selim's executioners.

While Selim was in Cairo a deputation from the Arab Sharif of Mecca came to offer him the keys of the Holy City and the title of protector of the holy places. It was left to his successors in the eighteenth century to claim the universal leadership of Islam through the title of caliph.

Selim I's successor Sulaiman I (1520–66), called by his subjects 'the Lawgiver' and by Europeans 'the Magnificent', developed the best fleet in the Mediterranean and extended his rule along North Africa to include Algiers, Tunis, Tripoli and Oran. By the time of his death in

1566, the Ottoman Empire included nearly all the Arabic-speaking world except Morocco in the far west. Virtually all of Sunni Islam of that period (excluding India) was united under Turkish rule against Persia, where the Shiite dynasty of the Safavids had established itself at the beginning of the sixteenth century. For the next century the Turkish and Persian Empires continued to dispute for control of Mesopotamia, until finally it too came under Ottoman rule.

5. Ottoman Subjects

The great majority of the people who spoke Arabic became subjects of the Ottoman Empire in the sixteenth century. In the western half of the Arab world, only Morocco succeeded in maintaining its independence, but at the expense of closing itself almost entirely to the outer world. The result was that its civilization remained in a state of frozen medievalism. The Algerians, Tunisians and Tripolitanians, on the other hand, finding themselves under attack from the Portuguese and the victorious Spaniards (who had completed their reconquest of the Iberian peninsula by recapturing Granada in 1492), called upon their most powerful co-religionists the Ottoman Turks, who had naval forces in the eastern Mediterranean, to help them. When the Turkish admirals had succeeded in driving out the Spanish they established their own régime. Tripoli, Tunis and Algiers became the capitals of the three *ojaks* or Regencies into which Turkish North Africa was divided.

In the eastern half of the Arabic-speaking world, only a few areas maintained, with the help of their geographical remoteness, any real independence. The Mamluke governor of Yemen surrendered to the Turks in 1517. The Ottoman forces succeeded with great difficulty in quelling the fiercely independent Shiite Zayidi mountain tribesmen in order to incorporate them in the empire. But they were expelled in the 1630s and Yemen recovered its independence. As we have seen, the Sharif of Mecca recognized Ottoman suzerainty; but outside the relatively civilized Hejaz, the beduin remained in their deserts beyond the reach of Ottoman control.

However, it would be an error to suppose that incorporation into the Ottoman Empire meant a *loss* of independence for the settled populations of Syria and Egypt. For over two centuries they had been ruled by Mamluke Turks and Circassians, and it was they who had fought against the Ottoman armies and been defeated while their Arabic-speaking subjects looked on with virtual indifference. Egypt and Syria became separate provinces of the empire instead of an independent sultanate; but in many ways the status of the majority of the people improved.

In fact the Arabic-speaking provinces were

regarded by the Ottoman ruling class, at least in the beginning, with a certain deference which they did not accord to the rest of the sultan's dominions – for the very reason that its inhabitants did speak the sacred language, while most of them at the same time professed the dominant religion.[1]

The mainly Christian inhabitants of the sultan's European dominions – which at their greatest extent in the second half of the sixteenth century included the whole of present-day Romania, Yugoslavia, Greece (including Crete), Bulgaria, Albania and Cyprus as well as part of Hungary, Poland and Russia's Crimean coast – were tolerably well treated at this stage. They were organized in *millets* or religious minority communities, each of which had internal autonomy under an ecclesiastical functionary with temporal powers in matters of personal status, and they enjoyed a considerable degree of individual and communal freedom. Yet, like the *dhimmis* of the first Arab Empire, they were undoubtedly second-class citizens in many important respects. They were known as the *rai'yah*[2] which means the 'shepherded people', and they were distinguished from Muslims by their clothing and headwear. Their lives and property were only secure at the will of their Turkish rulers. The Christian and Jewish subjects were not allowed to ride a horse or carry arms. They could not join the Ottoman army or the civil service.

These discriminatory laws did not apply to the Muslim non-Turkish subjects of the empire who were mostly Arabs. (The status of Christian Arabs such as the Maronite Catholics of Mount Lebanon lay somewhere between that of the Muslim Arabs and the Christian non-Arabs in the empire such as Armenians. They were not members of the Islamic *umma* but they spoke Arabic and by the eighteenth century they began to share in the culture of the sacred language.) A new Ottoman ruling class of governors and administrators was imposed on the Arab provinces of the empire, such as Syria, Iraq and Egypt; but unlike the Mamlukes, they did not settle down and adopt them as their homeland. They were frequently posted to other, perhaps non-Arab, parts of the empire and on retirement they usually returned to Turkey. Under these circumstances there was no question at this stage of the Turkification of these Arab societies. Turkish may have become the language of government but Arabic retained its honoured status and in practice a large share of political power passed

1. H. A. R. Gibb and H. Bowen, *Islamic Society and the West*, London, 1950, vol. I, p. 160.

2. The name was originally applied to all the subjects of a Muslim ruler, but was later limited to those non-Muslim subjects who paid the poll-tax.

into the hands of the local élite of shaikhs, *ulama* and landowners. In the second half of the nineteenth century it became customary to talk of the inveterate antagonism between Turks and Arabs. Certainly elements of this developed, both because the quality of Ottoman imperial rule deteriorated and because the haphazard attempts to modernize the empire in the nineteenth century did involve increased attempts at Turkification, such as the move, which was especially resented by the Arabs, to impose Turkish as the language of education for all except religious studies. But Turco-Arab hostility was far from universal or God-ordained. The bitterness engendered during the closing decades of the Ottoman Empire and the Arab struggle for independence could not efface at one blow the close affinity derived from centuries of symbiosis within an Islamic community. Moreover for four centuries the Turks were the protectors of this community against the ever-increasing powers of the Christian West. Ultimately they failed, but for the first two centuries it was Christendom that was on the defensive.

Therefore although the Arabs were Ottoman subjects for four centuries, in no sense were they slaves. The question arises of why this dynamic and creative people should have remained politically quiescent and socially stagnant for so long.

The Arabs of today regard the four centuries of Ottoman rule as a dark period in their history. It seems so in two respects: firstly, although they formed the majority of the Muslim subjects of the empire and the unique connection between Arabness and Islam remained, they were under Turkish domination; secondly, as citizens of the major Muslim world power they shared in the general decline in the material strength of Islam in relation to Christendom (or 'the West' as it came to be known in the nineteenth century). Finally, as the ultimate humiliation, most of the Arabs came under Western and non-Muslim rule as Turkish power declined.

The sense of shame which the Arabs feel about these centuries is the more powerful because of the intensity of their sense of past greatness. This is a characteristic of all Muslims, but especially of the Arabs because of their unique place in Islam.

The Arab sense of bygone splendour is superb. One cannot begin to understand the modern Arab if one lacks a perspective feeling for this. In the gulf between him and, for instance, the modern American, a matter of prime significance has been precisely the deep difference between a society with a memory of past greatness, and one with a sense of present greatness.[3]

3. W. C. Smith, *Islam in Modern History*, Princeton, 1957, p. 95.

All Muslims, whether educated or illiterate, have a strong feeling for history. The story of the triumphant – and inevitable – development of their faith is a vital and intrinsic element in the Islamic religion in a way that it is not for Christianity or Buddhism (although it is not all-important as it is for Marxists, for whom events in this world are of supreme significance because there is no other). In the lowest period of their fortunes therefore Muslims almost came to feel that history had let them down. What had gone wrong? It was a fearful predicament for a faith which first throve on its sense of inevitable success. Yet Islam did not collapse in adversity. On the contrary, it revealed an extraordinary inner strength and cohesion. But, as we shall see, the cost of this withdrawal to almost impregnable positions was to widen further the material and technological gulf between Islam and the West.[4]

If all Muslims feel some bewilderment about the course of history, the Arabs feel it most intensely. As Wilfred Cantwell Smith has pointed out, 'Arab Islam . . . is uninterested in and virtually unaware of Islamic greatness after the Arab downfall. For it, in 1258 (the fall of Baghdad), or for Egypt in 1517 (the Turkish conquest), Islamic history virtually came to an end.'[5] The fact that for at least two centuries Europe trembled with fear before the Muslim Turks, the conquerors of Byzantium, or that the Islamic faith saw one of its greatest periods of expansion during this period, is not a source of pride to the Arabs.

The question is therefore why the Arabs, with this supreme sense of their own historical role as rulers and conquerors, should have apparently submitted to Ottoman rule with such supine acceptance for so long. It is important to remember that modern Arabs are no different from any other peoples in that those who are not trained historians tend to see their past in a schematic idealized form. The Ottoman conquest of the lands inhabited by a majority of Arabic-speaking peoples did not mean a loss of Arab independence (apart from the fact that political independence in its twentieth-century

4. The material success of Christendom has had a rather different effect on Christians. Unlike Islam, Christianity first appealed to the oppressed and throve on persecution and adversity. But as Christians (especially white Anglo-Saxon Protestants) became much richer than everyone else in the eighteenth and nineteenth centuries this came to be regarded as proof of its superiority as a social system. In some Protestant communities the amassing of wealth was even taken as proof of godliness. It is hardly surprising, therefore, that the current economic difficulties of many Western countries are sometimes blamed on the retreat from Christianity, *pace* the correspondence columns of the London *Times*.

5. W. C. Smith, op. cit., pp. 94–5.

sense would have meant nothing in the fifteenth century). As we have already seen, Arabs had been ruled by Turks or Circassians long before Sultan Selim I added Egypt, Syria and Arabia to his dominions in 1516–17. But there was an important change in the fact that they now became subjects of a highly centralized empire, which in the early stages was efficiently administered from Constantinople. The ruling élite which held authority in this empire was of mixed racial origin, including Arab, but its hallmark was that it spoke Ottoman Turkish, the language of government. Members of the former ruling families of different parts of the empire were drawn into this powerful oligarchy.

It is a paradox of Islam that as a social system it is at once the most democratic and the most authoritarian of religions. It is democratic because it has no established church hierarchy to intercede between God and the faithful. It has no bishops or archbishops and certainly no pope. In theory every individual (male) Muslim is his own priest. We have seen how there are two great 'roots of the Faith' in Islam: the Koran and the Tradition, that is the Word of God as recited by his Prophet Muhammad, and the personal example of the Prophet through his acts and sayings as they have been handed down to posterity. But because 'in religious matters the humblest Muslim stands on a level with the caliph or his chief *qadi*'[6] a third root of faith had to be added – the voice of the people or 'consensus' of the faithful (*ijma* in Arabic). This does not mean the democratic counting of votes of the Muslim community to reach decisions on points of law or ethics at any given time but, 'the slowly accumulating pressure of opinion over a long period'.[7]

Nevertheless, *ijma* is a democratic principle in the sense that it means the acceptance of the will of the majority; and as such it was a natural cause of alarm to men of wealth and authority who tried to limit it to the consensus of the learned (just as votes in Western democracies were once limited to educated, male, property-owners). But the attempt was a failure, as H. A. R. Gibb shows in one striking example from the seventeenth century:

When the use of coffee began to spread in the Near East the jurists almost unanimously took the view that coffee-drinking was unlawful and punishable with the same penalties as wine-drinking, and a number of persons were actually executed for indulging in this vicious practice. But the will of the

6. H. A. R. Gibb, *Modern Trends in Islam*, Chicago, 1947, p. 10.
7. ibid., p. 11.

community prevailed, and today coffee is freely consumed even by those puritans who reject *ijma* in principle altogether.[8]

But, like all applications of democracy, *ijma* could be highly illiberal in practice. 'Consensus' means the rule of the majority and leaves no room for minority or eccentric opinion; and when a consensus had been reached on any given point it was irrevocable. The counterpart of *ijma* sounds to the modern ear both democratic *and* liberal. This is *ijtihad* or the 'right of individual interpretation', which was intended to apply to those points of law on which general agreement had not been reached. But although some Islamic modernizers have put forward *ijtihad* as a libertarian, individualist principle which would have met with the approval of John Stuart Mill, it was never intended to mean 'freedom of judgement' but merely a zealous attempt (the word *ijtihad* means literally 'exerting oneself') to discover the proper application of the Koran and tradition to a particular situation. Nevertheless, it was regarded as a sufficiently dangerous and subversive principle by the early orthodox scholars of Islam for them to be trying continually to narrow its field. Finally, the leading Ottoman jurists of the early years of the empire declared in a famous phrase, 'the Gate of Interpretation has been closed'. In more recent times Islamic modernizers attempted to reopen the Gate but their efforts have been in vain and are likely to remain so until they can secure the support of the *ijma* or the consensus of the community.

So it was that within some six centuries of the death of the Prophet Muhammad the majestic body of Islamic Sacred Law – the *shari'a* – had been immutably fixed. However, it would be misleading to suggest that Islam has been monolithic and intolerant of variety to a unique extent among religions. Apart from the remarkable fact that Sunni Islam incorporates four schools of law – the Hanafi, Maliki, Shafei and Hanbali, which are all considered orthodox – it has also succeeded in embracing two entirely different approaches to God within its system without splitting apart. These are the belief in a remote, all-powerful and transcendant deity which was that of nearly all the major scholars of Islam, and the mystical, almost pantheist view of an immanent God which in Islam is known as Sufism (from the Arabic for wool, *suf*, because of the connection with the undyed woollen garments worn by the Muslim ascetics). Sufism dates back to the earliest days of Islam and some see it as a direct inheritance from the life of the Prophet himself. It is true that one of the greatest of early

8. ibid.

Sufis, al-Hallaj, was finally, after many years of travel and teaching, arrested, imprisoned and brutally executed in Baghdad in 922. Shortly before his death he recited:

> Prophecy is the Lamp of the world's light;
> But ecstasy in the same Niche has room.
> The Spirit's is the breath which sighs through me;
> And mine the thought which blows the Trump of Doom.
> Vision said it. In my eye
> Moses stood, on Sinai.

Al-Hallaj suffered martyrdom, but two centuries later al-Ghazali, one of Islam's greatest philosophers who embraced Sufism and wrote his classic *Ihya ulum al-din* ('The Renaissance of Religious Sciences') to put forward his system of harmony between mysticism and theology, is praised and honoured. He became professor of religious sciences at the famous Nizamiyyah College in Baghdad. Gibb describes him as 'a man who stands on a level with Augustine and Luther in religious insight and intellectual vigour'.[9] In fact in the century after al-Ghazali's death Sufism won a mass popular following in the Middle East and North Africa as well as in the newly islamicized lands of Asia and black Africa. For a time the movement helped to reinvigorate the 'orthodox church' of Islam and to give it a more popular character, although when the orthodox *ulama* became alarmed at its success and its more heretical features, they counter-attacked by imposing a strict control over the Muslim educational system, which was consequently confined in a rigid strait-jacket for centuries.

Heretics in Islam have been condemned by the orthodox, but they have rarely been persecuted and still more rarely have they been burned at the stake. Since the great schism between Shia and Sunni there have been no major religious wars within Islam. It has had no reformation; Protestant Christians often comfortably assume that this is what it lacks. But neither has there been an Islamic counter-reformation or inquisition.

But the remarkable tolerance of classical and medieval Islam towards variations in belief and practice did not diminish its tendency towards political absolutism. The Prophet Muhammad successfully laid the foundations of a monarchical state among his Arab tribal followers. Unlike the tribal shaikhs who preceded him, Muhammad combined the executive, judicial and legislative functions. He was the ruler who interpreted and applied the law. After his death, as we

9. H. A. R. Gibb, *Mohammedanism*, London, 1953, p. 139.

have seen, the *ulama* or scholar-legists of Islam gradually took away the legislative function from his successors the caliphs as they built up the body of the Sacred Law (the *shari'a*), and finally closed its gates. But the caliphs retained the executive and judicial functions, and the function of the caliph or imam was to uphold the Sacred Law. It was during this period that the classical doctrine of the caliphate was developed. In retrospect it is easy to see why it took the form of extreme political passivity or acceptance of the *status quo*. The Sunni interpreters of the law had little to go on because the Prophet had made no provision for the choice of his successor, or the powers he should exercise. At the same time these canonists could only accept that the Islamic *umma* was divinely guided; therefore the way in which the caliphate developed must be ordained by God. Moreover, the need for a strong and stable political structure during these early and formative years of Islam was obvious; rebellion against authority would be patently disastrous. The result is the 'political quietism' which must be regarded as a characteristic of Islamic states. In addition to this, the Abbasids increased their political power by adopting the practices and traditions of the old Persian Empire. They became kings 'by divine right', remote, secluded and far above their subjects.

The Islamic jurists held that the caliphate was an essential and divine institution. It is true the caliph was to be elected; however his electors were not the whole community but a small group of specially qualified men. On occasions he could be nominated by his predecessor. Although the caliph could delegate certain functions he remained ultimately responsible for all acts of government. In return, the faithful were commanded to obey him strictly and to refrain from all acts of revolt. It is true that the jurists provided for the deposition (or impeachment) of a caliph guilty of serious heresy or immorality, but since there was no statutory body empowered to decide on impeachment the caliph had little to fear from this quarter. Moreover, the Faithful were forbidden even to rebel against an unjust caliph. One of the sayings of the Prophet recorded in the first century of Islam was:

> Do not abuse those who bear rule. If they act uprightly, they shall have their reward, and your duty is to show gratitude. If they do evil, they shall bear the burden, and your duty is to endure patiently. They are a chastisement which God inflicts upon those whom He will; therefore accept the chastisement of God, not with indignation and wrath, but with humility and meekness.

Some two centuries later the standard version of the Sunni creed by al-Ashari reads:

We uphold the prayer for peace for the imams of the Muslims and sub-mission to their office, and we maintain the error of those who hold it right to rise against them whensoever there may be apparent in them a falling-away from right. We are opposed to armed rebellion against them and civil war.

However, such a doctrine of the caliphate could clearly only remain intact as long as the caliph remained in fact the supreme executive authority. With the decline of the Abbasids and the break-up of the Islamic Empire the new Turkish and Caucasian military class was in the seat of power. The Arab *ulama* might retain their prestige and authority as interpreters of the law, but the caliphs were reduced to a shadow. After the Mongols' destruction of Baghdad in 1258 they were mere puppets at the court of the Mamluke sultans of Egypt.

As the power of the caliphs declined and with it their ability to see that the Sacred Law was upheld another danger arose: from about the tenth century a new invasion of Arabian tribes into Syria and Sinai and across the Nile into North Africa. These beduin had never been fully islamicized or replaced their ancient customary laws with the *shari'a*. Their appearance meant a revival of the tribalism or solidarity (*asabiyya*) of the tribe which the first caliphs had striven so hard to transform into the *asabiyya* of the Islamic community.

For these reasons, medieval Islamic thinkers generally regarded the new era of secular kingship as inevitable. They might differ in their views on the obligations of rulers and on the proper sanctions against misrule but they were agreed on the necessity for strong government. If the caliph could no longer protect the *umma* and oppose the assaults of the Shia Ismailis, Druzes or Mongols, then a sultan or military governor must do it. So these medieval political philosophers de-livered themselves of opinions which are anathema to the modern libertarian. Military expenditure must be as high as the monarch can possibly afford. 'The king's enemy is his treasury and his friend is the army; when one is strong the other is weak.' They agreed that some aspects of monarchical rule might be almost intolerable, but they had to be endured because 'sixty years of tyranny are better than an hour of civil strife'.

These men were under no illusions about the extent of decline from the high ideals of the early caliphate. As usual it was al-Ghazali who faced the matter with the greatest honesty when he wrote:

An evil-doing and barbarous sultan, so long as he is supported by military force, so that he can only with difficulty be deposed and that attempt to depose him would cause unendurable strife, must of necessity be left in possession and obedience must be rendered to him, exactly as obedience must be rendered to emirs. . . . Government in these days is a consequence solely of military power, and whoever he may be to whom the holder of military power gives his allegiance, that person is the caliph.

Al-Ghazali lived in the most turbulent days of the decline of the Abbasid Empire and he knew what he was talking about.

Nearly three centuries later, when Baghdad had fallen and the Mamluke sultans had set up their puppet caliphs, it was the chief Hanafite *qadi* of Egypt who gave his formal judgement on the legitimacy of this secular absolutism. He wrote:

As for the third method [of acquisition of the Imamate], that whereby the contract is made by oath of allegiance exacted by force, this is when a person possessed of military power exercises compulsion. If the office of Imam is vacant at the time, and one who is not fitted for it aspires to it and compels people by his might and his armies [to accept him] without [receiving] an oath of allegiance or without nomination by his predecessor, his office is contractually assumed and obedience is to be rendered to him, in order that the unity of the Muslims may be preserved. That he should be barbarous or evildoing no way invalidates this, in the most authoritative view. When the Imamate is thus contractually assumed by one person by means of force and military superiority, and thereafter there arises another who overcomes the first by his might and his armies, then the first is deposed and the second becomes Imam, for the reasons of the well being and unity of the Muslims which are stated above.[10]

This stark assumption that might alone creates right could not be permanently satisfying for all Muslims. It did not even require the Muslim ruler to uphold the Sacred Law but only to prove himself stronger than his rival or predecessor.

There was a different concept that was developing over the centuries and was to have its major influence in the Persian and Turkish rather than the Arabic-speaking lands of Islam.

From an early period the doctrines of Islam had been permeated by Greek philosophy; or it might be more accurate to say that as the *umma* expanded, Islam was accepted by men whose minds had been formed by Greek thought and who therefore thought about Islam in terms of Greek philosophy.[11]

These men tried to reconcile Platonic and Aristotelian ideas with

10. Ibn Jemaa, Chief Hanafi *qadi* of Egypt 1291–4 and 1309–24. Quoted in Gibb and Bowen, op. cit., vol. I, p. 32.

11. A. Hourani, *Arabic Thought in the Liberal Age 1798–1939*, London, 1962, p. 15.

Islam. The task was not easy because whereas Plato saw the ideal ruler as the philosopher-king, guided only by truth attained by reason, a Muslim must believe that the ruler's virtue lies in his ability to uphold the Sacred Law which is the will of God. However, if the caliph-imam wisely administered the *shari'a* under divine guidance would he not be assuming the role of the philosopher-king? The view was best put by al-Dawwani, a learned Persian jurist whose works were widely read throughout eastern Islam:

> The governor is a person distinguished by divine support, that he may lead individual men to perfection and provide a corrective order for them. The philosophers designate him 'the absolute sovereign', and the moderns [i.e. the Islamic philosophers] call him the imam and his function the imamate. Plato calls him 'the controller of the world' and Aristotle calls him 'the civic man'.

Such a doctrine at least restored the idea that virtue and wisdom as well as power are necessary attributes of a good ruler. However the central idea, that he who had established himself as the ruler should be obeyed and only rebelled against in extreme circumstances, remained. When, like the first Ottoman sultans, he had secured this power over nearly all the people of Islam, this injunction to obedience was still more powerful.

So it was that under the Ottoman Empire, caliphate and sultanate became almost synonymous. Muslims divide the world into the *dar al-Islam* or *dar al-khilafa* (i.e. domain of Islam or domain of the caliphate) and the *dar al-harb* (domain of war), and the Ottoman Empire was most certainly the *dar al-khilafa* in the eyes of its Muslim subjects. This did *not* mean that the sultan was regarded as or claimed to be a direct successor in the line of the first caliphs of Medina, Damascus and Baghdad. He was always referred to as the sultan or by the Persian title of 'Padishah of Islam' and never as caliph. He was not even given the title of 'Commander of the Faithful', which is all the more remarkable because the first Ottoman sultans greatly extended the area of *dar al-Islam*. It is ironic, but not surprising, that it was only when the empire was irretrievably in decline at the end of the eighteenth century that the sultans assumed the title of caliph.

But if Sultan Selim I, who conquered Syria, Egypt and Arabia, or Sulaiman the Magnificent, who extended the empire into the Balkans and Mesopotamia, were not in the line of succession of the Abbasid caliphs, their empire was a new style in the historical development of Islam. The sultan, although later rivalled by the Moghul emperors of India, was the greatest Muslim ruler in the world, the defender of

Sunni Islam against the Shia emperor of Persia and the conqueror of large areas of Christendom. The Islam of the early sultans and their Turkish warriors may have been unorthodox but they fulfilled their obligation to uphold the Sacred Law more conscientiously than any previous Islamic dynasty. Moreover, when the empire absorbed the centres of Islamic orthodoxy in Egypt and Syria, it became more orthodox Sunni in character. This made it much easier for the Arab subjects of the empire to accept the rule of the House of Othman. Once it had been accepted it was a long time before it was questioned, even by those who rebelled against the iniquitous rule of one particular sultan. If he was deposed because he had been declared unfit to rule by the guardians of the law he was replaced by another member of his family.

Throughout the empire, these guardians of the law – the *ulama* – were mainly of Arab origin except for those in the highest positions. But they had no share in the process of government; this they had long since renounced and, as we have seen, rationalized the process through their doctrine of Islamic kingship based on power. From time to time they would act as spokesmen for the people when their grievances became intolerable. But rebellion in the sense of overthrowing the seat of government was not in their minds.

What was the organization of this Turkish Empire which lasted for four centuries before its Arabic-speaking majority finally rose in revolt? If judged only by the quality of its rulers, it is amazing that it survived for so long after reaching its peak in the sixteenth century.

If the first ten sultans of the house of Osman astonish us with the spectacle of a series of able and intelligent men rare if not unique in the annals of dynastic succession, the remainder of the rulers of that line provides an even more astonishing series of incompetents, degenerates and misfits.[12]

This was due to the way in which the succession was decided. Like their Seljuk predecessors, the early Ottomans habitually made their sons and nephews provincial governors and the most successful and ambitious of them became rivals for the throne. Sultan Mohammed II, the Conqueror, issued a *kanun* (law) requiring his descendants to celebrate their succession with the slaughter of their brothers. After Mohammed III had inaugurated his reign in 1595 with the murder of nineteen brothers, the potential heirs to the throne were kept in

12. Bernard Lewis, *The Emergence of Modern Turkey*, second edn, London, 1968, pp. 22–3.

protective isolation in special pavilions in the palace, with the result that they lacked the administrative experience as provincial governors that had been earned by earlier sultans.

Yet despite the fearful deterioration at the head, the imperial system established by the earlier sultans had sufficient inner strength to survive for a long time.

The empire was originally created by free-born Turks and by 'turkized' Muslims mostly of Asian origin, who formed the cavalry and performed the same role as the Arabian warriors of the first Islamic conquests. As the empire expanded, the sultans rewarded this élite cavalry by making them feudal landowners. They were given the right to collect and keep the land-tax from certain districts. But alongside this feudal cavalry, the early sultans also had troops whom they paid regularly from their treasury. Originally these were also free-born Muslims, but in time they included an increasing number of slaves. The *shari'a* laid it down that the only persons eligible for enslavement were non-Muslim inhabitants of the domain of war. As the first Ottoman conquests were within the domain of war there was a plentiful supply of new slaves for the sultan's armies. However, the conquests in the domain of war came to an end and were directed mainly towards Muslim Asia. So just at the time that enthusiasm among Muslims for service in the Ottoman army began to wane, the supply of slave soldiers also began to dry up. (Muslims were not eligible for enslavement and, although there were born slaves within the domain of Islam who could be bought by the sultan, their numbers were always declining because good Muslims were encouraged to manumit their slaves and because in any case slaves borne by slave women to free masters were free.)

The sultans therefore resorted to a strange expedient which was to give the empire its peculiar character. They took to making periodical levies of their Christian subjects (Albanians, Bosnians, Bulgarians and Armenians), taking them from their parents when they were in their teens and training them for the service of the state.

Although these men technically lost their free status to become slaves there was nothing servile about them (any more than there was about the slave dynasties of the Mamlukes). They were the absolute property of the sultan and as long as they were soldiers they were not allowed to marry. But the fact that they were slaves did not imply any social inferiority. Anyone, including the sultans themselves, might have had a slave mother. Moreover, they soon acquired an extraordinary degree of power – 'nearly every post in what has been described as the "Ruling Institution" of the Empire, was filled either by a Christian conscript or by a slave otherwise acquired'.[13]

The disadvantage of this system was that it was against the Sacred Law, because slaves should only be acquired by the capture or purchase of non-Muslims outside the domain of Islam. But the advantages were considerable: first, their property belonged to the sultan and reverted to him on their death; and secondly, because they had been cut off from their own families and background they were likely to concentrate their loyalties on the sultan. The most promising of them were trained in special palace schools and promoted by gradual stages to the highest government posts. Others performed various functions in the Imperial Household, but the great majority were enrolled in the standing infantry – the famous corps of Janissaries (*yeni-cheris* or new troops in Turkish).

This extremely odd system whereby Muslims were virtually excluded from the administration of the Ottoman Empire probably could not have endured. Eventually the Muslims were bound to rebel against it, and in fact by the eighteenth century it had been destroyed. But it meant that the free-born Muslims of the empire (most of whom were Arabic-speaking) lacked experience of government administration and when they did eventually capture all the key posts at Istanbul the results were usually disastrous. Moreover, the tradition of the system was so strong that even these free-born Muslims were regarded as slaves of the sultan, who could put them to death without trial. The Ottoman sultanate was an unfettered despotism even when the throne was occupied, as it often was during the empire's decline, by an incompetent weakling.

The empire was so vast and varied that the sultan's absolute power could not control it all directly. There had to be some devolution. In the days of rapid growth of the empire new provinces were added in a haphazard manner, but after it had reached its peak in the sixteenth century the system had to be reorganized; and when this was done it remained in much the same form until the end of the nineteenth century. The empire was divided into between thirty and forty provinces or *vilayets* ruled by a governor-general or *vali* (Arabic, *wali*). The vilayets were subdivided into *sanjaks* headed by a *mutasarrif*. In the Arabic-speaking parts of the empire the arrangement, with some variations over the years, was that present-day Iraq was divided into four provinces – Basra, Baghdad, Mosul and Shahrizur; Syria into

13. Gibb and Bowen, op. cit., vol. I, p. 43.

four – Aleppo, Damascus, Tripoli and Sidon; western Arabia into two – Hejaz and Yemen (eastern and central Arabia were still under Arab beduin control); and the North African territories into four – Egypt, Tripoli, Tunis and Algiers.

The *wali* was directly responsible to the central government in Istanbul but he enjoyed extensive autonomous executive and judicial powers including the right to grant feudal lands. This was of the greatest importance because a military feudalism was the basis of the Ottoman system. The practice of granting feudal fiefs to warriors instead of paying them was not invented by the Ottomans; it had started during the collapse of the Abbasid Empire. But the Ottomans developed and extended it because it had the advantage of creating a feudal land-owning class which might have been imposed on the rural populations of the conquered territories but now had an attachment to their soil and therefore did not appear simply as military occupiers.

The intention of Sultans Selim and Sulaiman, who acquired the Arab territories for the empire, was to establish a permanent Ottoman supremacy over them but not to change them fundamentally and certainly not to 'turkize' them. 'The modest ambitions which had contented the Conqueror and the Law-giver remained the highest ideals of their weaker successors.'[14] Consequently, the chief characteristic of the Porte[15] was its intense dislike of change and innovation of any kind. Thus although the *walis* and *mutasarrifs* had extensive powers they were not encouraged to show initiative. In fact those which demonstrated ability were regarded with suspicion and often recalled. (In the later Ottoman period they were only appointed for a year at a time to prevent them from putting down roots and identifying with the people of their province.)

The sultan used various means of counterbalancing the *wali*'s powers. First and foremost a body of Janissaries and other troops was established as a permanent resident garrison in the headquarters of every *vilayet*. The *wali* had some authority over them but it was restricted in various ways. The garrisons at Aleppo and Damascus were commanded by officers appointed directly by the Porte. In Egypt there was a further check because Sulaiman the Magnificent deliberately preserved the independence of the Mamluke princes by

14. Gibb and Bowen, op. cit., vol. I, p. 200.

15. A common term for the Ottoman government referring to the High Gate into the government buildings at Istanbul.

allowing them to continue importing white slaves from central Asia to train as cavalrymen. In fact in the eighteenth century a similar Mamluke aristocracy so far recovered its control of Egypt that the Mamluke lords paid only nominal allegiance to the sultan.

In addition to the presence of Ottoman troops only partially under his control the *wali* had a treasurer or *deftedar* and steward or *kethuda* in charge of other branches of the administration, both of whom were appointed directly from Istanbul and not by the *wali* himself. Also the *ulama* (who, it will be recalled, were usually Arabs) enjoyed considerable authority and the right, which they frequently exercised, to send their protests against the *wali*'s actions directly to Istanbul. In Egypt, the chief religious dignitaries and the senior army officers joined with the *wali*'s chief administrators to form a *diwan* or council, under the chairmanship of the steward, which met regularly and decided all administrative matters. The *wali* (or *pasha* as he was known in Egypt) was not permitted to attend.

It would be quite incorrect to suppose that the Ottoman Empire imposed an iron repression on the Arab provinces. The régime was authoritarian and deeply conservative but neither insensitive nor ruthless. Financially it was not extortionate; in many ways it was an improvement on its predecessors.

So far from overburdening their subjects, the sultans had the wisdom to realize that light taxation and simple forms of direct administration were in the interests both of the Treasury and of the population. Before the Ottoman conquest the lands of Western Asia were divided into a number of independent states, and cultivators were rack-rented and merchants fleeced to pay for the upkeep of large and expensive armies and extravagant courts. As provinces of a vast empire with far-flung frontiers, and at peace with one another, their military establishments were reduced to small garrisons, sufficient to maintain internal order and supply a few regiments for the Imperial army when required.[16]

The real extortion came later, when the imperial system began to break down; the empire felt increasingly threatened by the Christian West and therefore compelled to inflate its military expenditure and in some cases, as with the Mamluke *beys* in Egypt, the pre-Ottoman local dynasties recovered their power. Few of the *pashas* or *deftedars* in the early period were guilty of gross financial or economic mismanagement and those who were were speedily called to account.

In many respects the empire was tolerant. This may have been

16. Gibb and Bowen, op. cit., vol. I, pp. 200–201.

more out of necessity than inclination but it was toleration all the same. First there was the natural tolerance enjoined by Islam of the Christians and Jews – the *dhimmis* – who were organized in their own *millets* or religious minority communities with internal autonomy and considerable individual and communal freedom. It is true that the Ottoman state was essentially Sunni Muslim in character and the *dhimmis* were destined to be second-class citizens in many respects. Only a few Christians, mainly Greeks, managed to reach the highest positions in the land. The attitude towards the Shia Muslim subjects of the empire, who existed in large numbers in what are now Iraq, Lebanon and Yemen, was more severe. There was no requirement for Sunni Muslims to treat the Shias kindly and there was a long history of hatred and warfare between them which especially affected the Shias of Iraq, who were so close to the rival and Shia empire of Persia. There were other minorities who were offshoots of Shiism with Christian, pagan and other elements such as the Druzes, Ismailis and Nusairis.[17] But these enjoyed a certain geographical toleration – the toleration of necessity. Most of them lived in remote mountain areas where rigid administrative control would have been difficult if not impossible. Provided they did not cause trouble and paid their taxes they were generally left alone – even when they were as fiercely individualistic as the Druzes are rightly thought to be.

Finally, although the Ottoman sultanate adhered strictly to the doctrines and principles of the *shari'a*, which was what the vast majority of its Sunni Muslim subjects wanted, it also tolerated and patronized the Sufi brotherhoods of mystics who retained a strong popular following. The sultans protected the brotherhoods and gave them financial support although they controlled their activities. The shrine of one of the great Persian Sufi poets, Jelal al-Din al-Rumi, was maintained in Konya as a place of pilgrimage, and a splendid tomb was built for the Spanish-Arabic writer Ibn al-Arabi of Murcia who died in Damascus in 1240.

The Ottoman Empire was therefore 'not so much a single community as a group of communities each of which claimed the immediate loyalty of its members. These communities were regional, religious or functional; or, to some extent, a mixture of all three.'[18]

The functions, rights and duties of these communities – soldiers,

17. Now more commonly called Alawites, they live mainly in the mountains near Latakia. The Syrian President Hafez Assad is an Alawite.
18. Hourani, op. cit., p. 29.

administrators (or 'men of the sword' and 'men of the pen' as they were called), merchants, craftsmen, peasants and slaves – were generally recognized and hallowed by tradition and the sultans respected them. In fact the dyed-in-the-wool conservatism and re-spect for the *status quo* of the Ottoman administration appeared to satisfy the deepest instincts of the people of the empire. There was no rigid caste system; it was perfectly possible for an Ottoman subject to move up or down the social scale or sideways into a different functional group. But this rarely happened; the vast majority of sons followed the trade of their fathers and married into their own group. Similarly, while there was certainly no institutionalized racial dis-crimination of the kind that was practised in later Christian empires,[19] 'there was a certain division of function between languages, and therefore to some extent between linguistic groups. Turkish was the language of government and the army, Arabic of learning and law, Persian a language of polite letters'.[20] On a smaller scale, some trades in the great Syrian and Egyptian cities were virtually the monopolies of certain racial groups: the grocers were Greeks and the jewellers Armenians.

If the vast majority of the people of the empire accepted the role in life into which they were born and expected the same for their sons, they also took it for granted that their rulers, whose function was to maintain the rigid framework of society, were highly privileged. Moreover, they did not expect them to be lenient and mild in the process of government.

The conception of authority implied in the minds of the subjects themselves an assertion of power accompanied by a certain measure of harshness and violence. 'Abd el-Ra'uf Pasha' (says the Christian chronicler Michael of Damascus), was 'mild, just, and peace loving, and because of his exceeding justice the people of Damascus were emboldened against him.'[21]

Similarly, the famous late eighteenth-century Egyptian historian al-Jabarti remarked: 'If the peasants were administered by a compas-sionate *multazim* [tax-collector], they despised him and his agents, delayed payment of his taxes, called him by feminine names . . .'

This attitude of resignation towards authority was strongly rein-forced by the religious authorities who, as we have seen, constantly

19. The distinction between Arab and non-Arab converts to Islam had ceased long since to have any significance.
20. Hourani, op. cit., p. 33.
21. Gibb and Bowen, op. cit., vol. I, p. 205.

warned the faithful against the spirit of rebellion even when their rulers were guilty of gross misgovernment. The combative spirit that existed in Arab society was largely exhausted in feuds between families, clans or tribes. Moreover, mass uprisings or revolutions against the ruling powers in most ages and societies have not occurred when conditions of life were at their worst but when there were signs of an upturn and there were grounds of hope for improvement. No such conditions existed in the Arab provinces of the Ottoman Empire in the seventeenth and eighteenth centuries. Economic conditions were steadily worsening and much of the wealth that was being created was in the hands of foreign Christian merchants.

As we have seen, the cardinal event which turned the eastern Arab provinces of the empire into an economic backwater – the opening of the Cape route to India by the Portuguese – occurred before the advent of Ottoman rule. In fact the process which turned the whole Muslim Near East from a commercial monetary economy to one which was essentially a feudal economy based on subsistence agriculture, was well advanced before Sultan Selim arrived in Cairo. The first Ottoman governments extended the feudal system, especially in Syria, but they also improved and reorganized it and reduced the burden of taxation on the peasantry. Yet this could do nothing to reverse the inexorable trend whereby an economically stagnant Muslim Near East was to fall further and further behind the thrusting and expansionist Christian West. The First Crusaders found much to admire and envy in the living conditions of their Saracen enemies. Eighteenth-century European travellers to the area were unanimous in their descriptions of the human misery that they found. Some of their observations were necessarily superficial; few of them, for example, had much understanding of or sympathy with the Islamic religion. But everything they saw tended to confirm their belief in the superiority of their own system.

Is there an element in the Islamic religion which causes it to be a barrier to economic progress? The answer to this question has been less discussed than taken for granted in the Christian West. A few generalizations about the Muslim spirit of fatalism being a barrier to economic enterprise combined with a vague recollection that the taking of interest on capital is forbidden by the *shari'a* have generally served. More recently it has been assumed that the seclusion of women has been a fatal impediment to the growth in the Muslim states of a modern industrial economy which depends so heavily on their labour.

Yet today is the time for the revision of most of our assumptions about the relation between religion and economic advance. Weber's theory about the unique advantage of Protestantism for capitalist enterprise has to be adjusted in the light of the fact that the Catholic states of southern Europe (and perhaps Latin America?) show signs of overtaking the Protestant states of the north. Now the wheel of fortune has made an unexpected turn as some of the most deprived and poverty-stricken states of the Near East have proved to be the possessors of fantastic wealth which will place them in charge of about half the world's financial reserves within a decade. This will help to show whether the stagnation of the past was the cause of poverty or whether it was the reverse.

Fortunately, this whole question has been examined by a scholar who is equal to the task: Maxime Rodinson, the noted French orientalist and social scientist whose *Islam and Capitalism* was published in English in 1974. Rodinson is a Marxist, if a highly idiosyncratic one, and his conclusions may not be acceptable to everyone; but he has successfully disposed of certain myths. He maintains that there is nothing in Islam – either in the Koran and *sunna* or the Sacred Law that was developed from them – that is especially hostile to capitalist enterprise. (He defines a capitalist enterprise as one in which 'an owner of means of production pays a wage to free workers in order that the latter may, using the aforesaid means of production, produce commodities which the owner will sell for his own profit'.)

The prohibition of *riba* or the taking of interest was subject to many different interpretations, and in any case widely evaded. The proof is that in the Middle Ages

the density of commercial relations within the Muslim world constituted a sort of world market (to use a somewhat anachronistic term) of unprecedented dimensions. The development of exchange had made possible regional specialization in industry as well as in agriculture, bringing about relations of economic interdependence that sometimes extended over great distances. . . . Not only did the Muslim world know a capitalist sector, but this sector was apparently the most extensive and highly developed in history before the establishment of the world market created by the Western European bourgeoisie, and this did not outstrip it in importance until the sixteenth century.[22]

A self-confident and enterprising Islamic bourgeoisie did exist in the Middle Ages but it never succeeded in achieving political power

22. M. Rodinson, *Islam and Capitalism*, London, Allen Lane, 1974, p. 56.

as a class because from around the eleventh century this was in the hands of the Mamlukes and other Turkish and Caucasian military. But this had nothing to do with the Muslim religion; nor did the fact that the private accumulation of capital never attained the European level. We have to look at other factors, such as the destructive invasions of Mongols and others, which made the Turkish military caste necessary for the defence of society, and the fact that high density of population in the Islamic Near East provided an abundant labour-force which made technical innovations unnecessary.

The result of this failure of an Islamic capitalist bourgeoisie to develop and win political power in the eighteenth and nineteenth centuries, as it did in Europe, was that when the European powers invaded and occupied many of the Arab lands in the nineteenth century these were all at a pre-industrial stage. Rodinson rightly criticizes other Marxist writers for claiming that these countries were on the point of arriving at a 'capitalist socio-economic formation at the moment when the impact of Europe was felt', or, in other words, that colonialism actually prevented them from industrializing. He quotes V. B. Lutsky: 'In one way or another the majority of the feudal states of the East were pregnant with capitalism', and comments that

it would be better to say of these societies that they were nubile. And nobody can deduce from the fact that a woman is nubile that she is necessarily pregnant. Some women are barren, and there are others who either refuse or are refused the act that can make them pregnant.[23]

It cannot be proved that Muslim societies would have developed a capitalist formation of the European–American type. It is equally impossible to prove that they were incapable of doing so.

On the contrary, everything seems to point to their possessing the essential structures which, if certain developments had taken place, could, given certain circumstances, have led to something of the kind. The fact is, simply, that these developments, these circumstances, were not there at the time of the European impact. Consequently, the development of capitalism occurred in these countries as something external in origin, an implantation from or an imitation of Europe.[24]

The questions of whether the Arab states – now that they have no need for concern about the accumulation of capital for the industrialization of the whole Arab world if they act collectively – will

23. ibid., p. 135.
24. ibid., p. 136.

succeed in developing forms of economic organization and techniques which are not purely external in origin, whether this could be a more humane form of capitalism (as some Muslim apologists are claiming) or Arab socialism (if such a thing exists) must be left for a later chapter. But one more wise observation of Rodinson must be quoted:

> If the extra-European peoples have not developed a capitalist socio-economic formation, and if the Europeans have achieved such a structure, which is *in a sense* superior, this is not due to the 'shortcomings' of the former or the 'qualities' of the latter. The non-Europeans do not deserve to be punished, nor the Europeans to be rewarded. The former do not need to feel inferior nor the latter to feel proud. Profound social and historical factors, for or against which men could do little, were working in that direction.[25]

We have seen how the agricultural lands of the Arab provinces of the empire were reorganized after the conquest on Ottoman feudal lines. The cultivable land was divided and distributed as feudal fiefs to the mainly Turkish militia. Later these military fiefs were replaced by tax-farms on a commission system. The *multazim*, as the tenant-in-chief of the tax-farm was called, was originally appointed for one year only; but later hereditary rights developed and the *multazim* was able to bequeath the fief to his sons. The mass of cultivators or *fellahin* owned their lands in the sense that they could bequeath them or sell them to other *fellahin*, but each had to pay his annual taxes to the *multazim* who had the right to deprive him of his land if he failed to do this. This meant that although the *fellahin* were independent farmers in the sense that they could alienate their land and decide which crops they would like to cultivate, in practice they were tied to the soil in a form of serfdom. Although taxes were reduced in bad years, in practice the *multazim* usually demanded that the amount should be made up in the next good year. Inevitably, the *fellahin* fell into debt and became the prey of usurers.

Local traditions and customary practices were respected by the Ottoman ruling class and in many respects each individual village enjoyed a certain independence with its shaikh or headman acting as magistrate and arbitrator. But all this was at the very lowest level of existence. Turks and Mamlukes cannot be wholly, or even mainly, blamed for the plight of the *fellah*. In Egypt, for example, he

had pitted his craft against the exploiters and had failed; and failing, the genius of the race, inferior to no other in capacity and depth of feeling, had turned in

25. ibid., p. 134.

upon itself in bitterness and sought revenge, as it were in limiting production to the minimum of its requirements, in a tenacious opposition to all changes, and an almost deliberate harshening of all the conditions of life. The fertility of the soil served only to raise up oppressors on every side, and since, in the *fellah*'s experience, it seemed that only by oppression could anything be gained, he also, by a natural reaction, became an oppressor of his own kind.[26]

Malnutrition and disease meant that the *fellahin* were incapable of physical exertion; and although some of the village shaikhs amassed wealth – as was inevitable in view of the richness of the soil – their deep conservatism prevented them from trying any non-traditional ways of improving cultivation even when they were in a position to do so.

The situation in the Syrian and Mesopotamian countryside was marginally better. The historical reasons for the inertia of the Egyptian *fellahin* did not apply here to the same extent. There was more space and more energy. In Iraq, for example, the tribesmen made an important contribution to the agricultural economy through the growing of rice or the breeding of sheep while retaining their relative independence as semi-nomads or nomads. But in Syria and Egypt the Arab tribesmen were an additional scourge of the settled cultivators. In Egypt they interfered with the vital irrigation canals and in Syria they devastated some of the richest agricultural areas. It is no surprise that the word 'Arab' in its original sense came to have an almost wholly unpleasant connotation.

Thus although Ottoman rule was neither ill-intentioned nor unduly oppressive, the situation of the Arab *fellahin* deteriorated under the empire. The fact that there was no improvement in farming methods and that almost no attention was paid to public works, probably meant that output declined (although few statistics are available). If these were largely negative failings, the situation became much worse in the later stages as the Ottoman government became weaker, the local *pashas* more exorbitant and the Arab beduin tribesmen more predatory. In growing numbers the peasants began to desert the countryside for the towns.

The situation in the cities was very different; in fact they seemed to belong to another civilization. While the villages lived on in their enclosed world, almost untouched by the influence of Islam, the cities were the product of the great medieval Islamic civilization which was essentially urban. The city-dwellers despised the *fellahin* and had

26. Gibb and Bowen, op. cit., vol. I, p. 264.

almost no contact with them except in the purchase of their crops. It is no exaggeration to say that the citizen of Cairo felt more in common with the inhabitants of Damascus or Baghdad than he did with an Egyptian *fellah*. All the Arabic literature of the period belongs to the cities and provides no insight into the life of the countryside.

Because the people of the towns were less down-trodden and poverty-stricken than the peasants, the pashas treated them with greater respect and ensured that the cities were well supplied. Even so there were quite frequent popular uprisings against the more tyrannical governors (sometimes led by the *ulama* despite their injunction against rebellion). Although the police acted with great harshness in suppressing the populace, these uprisings, if sustained, almost invariably ended in the punishment or recall of the offending governor. In this way the Ottoman government in Istanbul, although remote, always appeared as the last court of appeal against injustice.

But if the citizens of the towns could on occasion act in concert in this way, they had no sense of the general welfare of the city and no civic responsibility. As there were no municipal institutions, they had no share in the government of the city. In fact the cities were less of a single organism than a collection of self-contained, and in some ways autonomous, cells. The various quarters of the cities had their own communal buildings – mosques, churches, or synagogues, baths and *souks* – and their own gates. Each had its own shaikh who was responsible for its administration. Some of these quarters were confined to religious minorities – Armenian or Greek Christians, Jews, etc. – and others were occupied by a single family or clan. But more of them were associated with one of the trade corporations and craft guilds, which were the main functional organizations of the Arab cities. There were corporation guilds for nearly everyone – from the crafts such as the jewellers or woodworkers to the professions such as teachers or physicians, manual workers, such as water-carriers and even to beggars, prostitutes and thieves. (Al-Jabarti, the Egyptian historian, reported that in 1718 the beggars' corporation of Cairo gave Ibrahim Bey, the Mamluke governor of Cairo, a horse and saddlery worth 22,000 *paras*.) Each corporation was jealous of its rights and privileges, which had evolved through custom and traditional usage and were laid down in its statutes. These were generally respected by the political governors although they were wary of them because they had a long tradition of association with Islamic heresy and the Sufi mystical brotherhood. Each corporation had a shaikh who was responsible for seeing that its members paid their taxes and acted as an intermediary between the authorities and the citizens.

But they were only remotely similar to the guilds of medieval Europe. They had no real autonomy and the authorities regarded them as convenient instruments of control.

The rigidity of the Islamic guild system is shown by the fact that no master[27] could open a workshop without permission from his guild, which strictly limited the number of workshops and usually decided where a new one should be situated. Even then he never owned the shop but held a lease. He was not allowed to sell his products above the prices which were periodically fixed by the government (with the object of holding prices in the cities down) and he might not make or sell anything that the guild had not sanctioned. No changes of the traditional style or fashion were allowed. Thus in 1807 strict orders were issued to the cobblers of Istanbul (where exactly the same system applied) not to make boots, shoes and slippers with pointed toes which were contrary to ancient tradition.[28]

Industry in the Arab Near East not only failed to progress between the sixteenth and eighteenth centuries; it had deteriorated since the Middle Ages when it was in advance of the rest of the world. Apart from the effect of the switching of most of the Asian trade to the African Cape route and all the wars and natural disasters of the fourteenth and fifteenth centuries, whole industries had been bodily removed by the Mongols to their capital at Samarkand in central Asia.

For all these reasons it is little surprise that the industrial products of the Near East were quite unable to compete with those of Europe, which at this time were growing in number and improving in quality. This was despite the fact that the lack of trade barriers within the Ottoman Empire created a vast 'common market', comparable to that of the medieval Islamic world, which might have provided an opportunity for the growth of industry. Some of the ancient crafts retained their fine quality – wood and metal in Cairo, brocades in Damascus, glass-making in Hebron – but industrial factories hardly existed by the end of the eighteenth century. The only activity which approached the level of an industry was the weaving of textiles – cotton, wool and silk. Spinning was carried out by the women in their homes. Metal and machine industries did not exist. The few pieces of machinery that were used had to be expensively imported and, in

27. There were masters, journeymen and apprentices as in medieval Christian Europe.
28. Quoted in Gibb and Bowen, op. cit., vol. I, p. 283.

view of the cheapness of human and animal labour, it is hardly surprising that this was rarely done.

Superficially, the commercial sector was in better shape than either agriculture or industry. The corporation system was less rigid than for artisans. The merchants of Cairo, Damascus and Aleppo enjoyed high prestige;[29] some were extremely wealthy and lived in great splendour. The Islamic ban on the charging of interest on loans was a handicap but, as we have seen, it was widely evaded. Its chief drawback was that it prevented the growth of a flexible banking system of the kind that was developing in Europe. (Banking in Egypt was mainly in the hands of the Christian Copts and in Baghdad of the Jews.) Although most of the trade to India had been lost the eastern Mediterranean was still an important entrepôt centre. Europe's trade with Persia and the Persian Gulf went through Aleppo and Baghdad, that with western Arabia and the Sudan through Cairo. Above all, the annual traffic of pilgrims to the Holy Cities of Mecca and Medina, which the Ottoman sultans did their best to protect and promote, passed through Cairo and Damascus.

But the splendour of the colourful and bustling markets of Damascus, Aleppo and Cairo (of which traces can still be seen today) gave an illusory impression of general prosperity. In the first place the whole east Mediterranean area was suffering an economic decline which inevitably affected commerce. Egypt, Syria and Iraq might still exchange textiles and foodstuffs. There were even some substantial exports from Egypt to the North African provinces. But the quality and variety of their products were declining. Moreover, the actual business of trading became more difficult as the Ottoman administration weakened, and law and order deteriorated. Egypt and Iraq had virtually no roads; they had water transport but nothing was done to improve this by preventing the silting up of harbours and canals. In Syria and Arabia the camel caravans were increasingly prey to marauding brigands and beduin, and the detachments of road guards showed more enthusiasm for extorting money from the travellers than protecting them.

All this was bad enough; but the most ominous trend, for those few who were aware of it, was that the real wealth that this trade still represented was increasingly passing into foreign hands. In return for imports from Europe of metals and ironmongery, arms, paper,

---

29. The Prophet Muhammad, it will be recalled, married the wealthy widow of a merchant and became a highly successful one himself.

glassware, fabrics and West Indian sugar and coffee the Near Eastern states had little of their own to export. The caravans from the Sudan which brought ivory, hides and slaves took away very little of Egyptian manufacture except a few cotton textiles, but they bought many European goods which the enterprising Cairene merchants imported for re-export. Thus

the external commerce of the Arab countries was of little benefit to them, and in so far as the imports consisted of manufactured articles and luxury goods for the rich, while the exports consisted of raw and unworked materials, it was directly injurious to their industry and to their economic wellbeing.[30]

But this was not all. As we have seen, the early Ottoman sultans gave autonomous rights to their non-Muslim subjects – the Christians and Jews – in full accordance with the law and practice of Islam. But when the Ottoman Sultan Mohammed II conquered Constantinople he found a number of foreign colonies, each with its own well-defined status and privileges which had been granted by the Byzantine emperors.

The presence of these commercially active communities was vitally important to the empire, so Mohammed II gave them certain privileges which came to be known as the Capitulations to persuade them to remain – such as exemption from taxation and the right to be tried in their own consular courts. It would not have occurred to Mohammed the Conqueror that these communities would become economically dominant in his empire, still less that they could be politically powerful. One of his successors, Sulaiman the Magnificent, agreed to grant to the French King Francis I the right to protect European Catholics in Ottoman territory; and France had since then extended this into a general protection including the Ottoman Catholics as well as the European missions working among them.

It was perhaps inevitable that these foreign trading communities should come to monopolize most of the trade with Europe, and by the end of the eighteenth century this was entirely in the hands of Christians and Jews (both European and Levantine). But the Muslim merchants might still have acquired a share in it if they had mixed freely on social and business terms with the foreigners. Ottoman non-Muslims clearly had their place in society even if they were relegated to certain professions and trades, but the foreigners were outside the society altogether. Muslim exclusiveness not only acted as

30. Gibb and Bowen, op. cit., vol. I, p. 307.

a spur to the foreign merchants – since they were shunned by Ottoman society they devoted all their energies to making profit – but further reduced the capacity of the Muslims to compete as their ignorance grew of the Christian business world they despised. Moreover, the foreign merchant communities not only increased steadily in wealth and power but also in size. The Frank (Arabic *franj* – an inheritance from Crusader times) merchants were obliged to make use of as agents and interpreters those of the local population who were prepared to associate with them, and this meant the Syrian and Armenian Christians and the Jews. They made use of another of the privileges granted by the sultans under the terms of the Capitulations which allowed the foreign ambassadors to Constantinople to grant patents of protection, or *berats* as they were called, to a number of persons in their service. The quota was normally fifty, which was renewed for each fresh ambassador. These protégés received all the privileges, including exemption from taxation, accorded to the foreigners whose nationality they would normally acquire. Abuse of the privilege soon became common and *berats* were widely sold at a high price. In 1793 the pasha of Aleppo complained to the Porte that there were now no less that 1,500 *dragomans*[31] in the city enjoying consular protection. A commissioner from Constantinople who investigated declared all but six of the *berats* invalid; but the abuse continued.

In the latter half of the sixteenth century the economic difficulties of the Ottoman Empire were immensely increased by the flood of cheap silver from the Spanish colonies of the New World which caused a violent inflation, and disastrous devaluation of the empire's currency. The crisis was intensified by the government's increasing demands for revenues for the swelling bureaucracy and armed forces. As always, the main burden fell on the peasants.

By the end of the eighteenth century all the Arab provinces of the Ottoman Empire were in a state of economic stagnation or decline. The situation was not uniform; Syria was in a marginally better condition than Iraq or Egypt, but the general picture was the same. Some individual Arabs were prosperous because not all of such wealth as was being created was in the hands of the Turkish aristocracy, and there were some households which maintained themselves in ostentatious luxury. But for the vast mass of the population there seemed little hope of any material progress. A fatalistic resignation was the only attitude that they could adopt.

---

31. Literally 'translators'. The word has a Sumerian root.

Yet an even greater menace to the Arab peoples of the time than the political and economic stagnation was the intellectual sterility of their society. The great Arab/Islamic civilization of the Middle Ages, which had produced such towering creative thinkers as al-Ghazali and Ibn Khaldoun, and scientists and philosophers who could match anyone in the Christian West (despite the internal political struggles and the barbarian invasions to which the world of Islam was subjected) was no longer making any contribution of importance to mankind's knowledge. From being a society which accepted the free flow of ideas across boundaries of religion and race it became enclosed and inward-looking. There were of course some exceptions to the general intellectual mediocrity; the great Islamic tradition of learning could not wholly be destroyed. There were men such as Muradi the Syrian biographer or al-Jabarti the Egyptian historian. But because of their very capacity they showed in their work how much they suffered from being in an intellectual backwater.

How had this come to pass? It should hardly be necessary today to point out that Islam is not fundamentally opposed to learning, but this was one of the beliefs that was bred by the long hostility between Christendom and Islam. Medieval Christian scholars created the myth that it was the Arab Caliph Omar who ordered the destruction of the great library at Alexandria, whereas in fact the library was destroyed two or three centuries earlier through internal Christian dissensions.

In fact the Koran insists on the high value of learning and associates it with wisdom. Men of learning are placed in a position second only to prophets. This attitude was amplified in the Traditions, one of which says: 'Quest for learning is a duty incumbent upon every Muslim, male and female'; and another: 'Wisdom is the goal of the believer and he must seek it irrespective of its source'; or 'Angels spread their wings for the seeker of learning as a mark of God's approval of his purpose'.

Learning was therefore treasured in Islam; but its purpose was also clear: the understanding and propagation by preaching and teaching of God's final revelation to Muhammad. Teachers had to be literate so only literate preachers were sent out to the newly converted communities. The mosques became the first schools in Islam and the Koran the first textbook.

The Koran is magnificent prose-poetry but it is also the least translatable of any great work of literature. In his *Anthology of Islamic*

Literature[32] James Kritzeck quotes the Islamic scholar Marmaduke Pickthall's description of the Koran as, 'That inimitable symphony, the very sounds of which move men to tears and ecstasy' and compares it with Thomas Carlyle's verdict: 'As tedious a piece of reading as I ever undertook, a wearisome, confused jumble, crude, incondite – nothing but a sense of duty could carry any European through the Koran.' Kritzeck observes that the simple explanation for two such differing views is that Pickthall knew Arabic and Carlyle did not. But even to the non-Arab non-Muslim with a deep knowledge of the language, the Koran cannot have the same meaning as to the Arab Muslim for whom every sonorous phrase or inflection has imaginative associations which are part of his culture and civilization.

We have seen how poetry was of supreme importance to the people of Arabia in the Age of Ignorance before Islam. In a sense it was their religion; it was certainly the greatest comfort of their harsh lives. In the Age of Islam the central place of the Koran in the religion and culture of the Arabs ensured that language would continue to be of supreme and unique importance to them. As H. A. R. Gibb remarked in his *Modern Trends in Islam:*

> The spring of mental life among the Arabs, as among other peoples, is furnished by the imagination, expressing itself in artistic creation. One often hears it said that the Arabs have no art. If art is confined to such things as painting and sculpture, the charge may be true. But this would be a despotic and unjustifiable limitation of the term. Art is any production in which aesthetic feeling expresses itself, and it is doubtful whether any people is totally devoid of artistic expression in some form or another, whether it be in music or dancing or ceramics or the visual arts. The medium in which the aesthetic feeling of the Arabs is mainly (though not exclusively) expressed is that of words and language – the most seductive, it may be, and certainly the most unstable and even dangerous of all the arts. We know something of the effect of the spoken and written word upon ourselves. But upon the Arab mind the impact of artistic speech is immediate; the words, passing through no filter of logic or reflection which might weaken or deaden their effect, go straight to the head.[33]

We shall consider in a later chapter the importance of the attitude to language on the psychology of contemporary Arabs and its effect on the modern Arab nationalist movement. At this stage what is important is the way in which the Arab genius developed after classical times. As Professor Gibb pointed out, 'the creative impulses of the

32. Penguin Books, 1964.
33. H. A. R. Gibb, *Modern Trends in Islam*, Chicago, 1947, p. 5.

imaginative life must be furnished with an intelligible object or direction' among all developing peoples and 'this function is assumed by one of two forces, namely religious intuition and rational thought', and he adds that there is no question that it is the former which more immediately attracts and moves the Arab mind.[34] The great appeal of Islam in its early days was that 'the outward simplicity and concreteness of the ideas of the Koran corresponded to the simplicity and concreteness of their imaginative life, and its code of ethics set up a practical ideal, which harmonized with and satisfied their social aspirations'. However, the Koran alone could only provide the foundations for the organization of their society and their laws so religious leaders devoted themselves to building up as soon as possible the superstructure of this kind. In a sense they did this with distaste because such a task necessarily required the use of reason, which inevitably comes into conflict with revelation. This is a problem which confronts all religions; but in the case of Islam there was never much doubt that it was revelation which would win. But reason did not give up without a struggle.

As we have seen, the first peoples to be conquered by Islam were those of the east Mediterranean or Hellenic world, whose minds had been formed by Greek thought. The first Islamic theologians did not reject Greek philosophy out of hand. On the contrary, with the encouragement of the early caliphs (such as the Abbasid Caliph Mamun 813–833), they studied deeply all the sciences of the classical world; and it can be said that the Christian West ultimately recovered much of the knowledge of Greek philosophy that it had lost in the Dark Ages through the Arabs and especially through the great universities of Moorish Spain. The Arabs 'introduced Aristotle to the West centuries before the revival of Greek scholarship which directly preceded the Renaissance and was one of the causes of the Reformation'.[35] The Arabic Aristotle of Spain was one of the principal sources for medieval Christian scholars in the thirteenth century. But the Muslim attempt to adopt the dialectical method of the Greeks, while accepting the insistence of the orthodox theologians that reason and the pursuit of truth must always be subject to revelation, was ultimately doomed to failure. In the tenth century a brave attempt was made to integrate Greek philosophy with Islam by a secret society of philosophers calling themselves the Brethren of Purity, who published a number of tracts in Basra and distributed them throughout

34. ibid., p. 6.
35. T. Arnold and A. Guillaume (eds), *The Legacy of Islam*, London, 1931, p. 29.

the Islamic world. But although these tracts formed an encyclopedia of the entire knowledge of the time, and as such were widely popular, the orthodox theologians were able to suppress their influence through their control of education. Henceforth Arab/Islamic philosophers had either to conform or to express themselves in such obscure terms that only a small minority could understand them.

This rejection of rationalism had a profound influence on the whole history of Arab civilization and thought. As Professor Gibb has observed, it had some advantages for 'the concentration of Arab thought upon the individual events fitted Muslim scholars to develop the experimental method to a degree far beyond their predecessors in Greece and Alexandria' and 'the detailed observations of Muslim investigation materially aided the progress of scientific knowledge and . . . it was from them that the experimental method was introduced or restored to medieval Europe'.[36] But this 'atomism' of the Arab mind, as Gibb has called it in a famous phrase, the tendency to view the universe as a series of separate entities, unlinked by any chain of causality, has many other aspects. The Arab

conceives his society not as an organic whole, compounded of interrelated and interacting parts, but as an association of separate groups – religions, nations, classes – held together only by the ground beneath and the government above. His town is an agglomeration of quarters, guilds, clans, houses, only rarely with any corporate civic identity of its own.[37]

'Atomism' is also a distinguishing feature of Arab culture. Arabic songs and music are a series of repeated and infinitely elaborated themes; there is no climax or finale. Anyone who heard the great Egyptian singer Umm Kalthoum, the most famous of her time in the Arab world, can verify this point. Each of her songs, which might last for two hours or more, had some of the attributes of a great classical symphony and could move her audience to an extraordinary ecstasy, which had little in common with the hysteria of a Western pop idol's fans, and was much more attractive to observe.[38] But unlike a symphony or concerto, her song did not have contrasting movements which together form an organic whole. She achieved her effects through the astonishing and subtle elaboration of individual phrases and sections. The lyrics, which were written by some of the best

36. H. A. R. Gibb, op. cit., p. 8.
37. Bernard Lewis, *The Arabs in History*, London, 1958, p. 141.
38. Although the concentrated devotion she aroused provoked a leading Egyptian intellectual to describe her as 'the opium of the Arabs'.

contemporary Arab poets, were at least as important as the music. No wonder that this use of the language by a great artist had an over-powering effect on her Arab audience.

Arabic art has similar characteristics. It has been limited in any case in the past by the Islamic prohibition on representation of the human figure, but one cannot help feeling that the consequent development of the art of elaborating decorative geometrical patterns was entirely suited to the Arab genius. From the results which have survived, such as the interior walls of the Alhambra of Granada, we know that it achieved magnificent results. But it has meant that contemporary Arab artists who wish to use composition and perspective – and still more to study the harmony of the human figure – must struggle against their own tradition.

All this applies in much the same way to literature – to Arabic history or biography, which are usually presented as a series of events or human characteristics without any attempt by the author to relate them organically; and above all to poetry, the greatest of the Arab arts. An Arabic poem in the classical tradition 'is a set of separate and detachable lines, strung pearls that are perfect in themselves, usually interchangeable'.[39] Exquisite, and at times fantastic, similes and metaphors abound; and in the best poetry they reveal a poetic imagination of the finest quality, although at its worst it could lead to the sterile love of decoration for its own sake. But although in a purely literary sense the poems have structure, the thought behind them does not. Hence epic poetry and poetic drama (or drama of any kind) are virtually unknown in the Arab tradition. Like musicians and artists, contemporary Arab poets, novelists and dramatists who wish to break away from the classical tradition have either to make use of non-Arab (usually foreign) models or start a new tradition of their own.

But all this anticipates the subject of the contemporary Arab world to which we shall return. The important fact at this stage is that the authority of the orthodox theologians was never seriously challenged by those who advocated that Revelation should depend upon Reason. Education was in the hands of the *ulama*.

In the early stages of Islam there was no educational system as such. The great concern was with the teaching of the Koran to the hundreds of thousands of adults who had been newly converted to Islam. The Caliph Omar who established the administrative system of

39. Bernard Lewis, op. cit., p. 142.

the early Islamic state made no provision for the education of children. He is only supposed to have said to the Arabs who had left Arabia: 'Teach your boys swimming,[40] archery, horse-riding and appreciation of poetry.' The question was who was to do the teaching. The *ulama* themselves were busy teaching the newly-converted adults, and the Arab warriors had no time to teach their sons even if education was supposed to be the private concern of parents. So an unorganized system arose whereby private tutors hired themselves out to teach children in the homes. Some of the more enterprising among them would gather a number of pupils from several families into one place which eventually became known as the *kuttab*, the original Islamic elementary school. However, it was a school only in a very limited sense. Some poetry was taught orally and some elementary mathematics, but there were no textbooks other than the Koran.

As the empire expanded, the need arose for administrative officials capable of acting as clerks and accountants. The *kuttabs* were therefore improved and the curriculum extended – especially in mathematics. But there was still no system of higher education. Only the sons of princes and the very wealthy were taught by specially qualified tutors. Scholarship was advanced by the learned men who travelled widely throughout the empire and set up circles of discussion in the mosques. (This process of teaching still survives. In the great university mosques one can see the scholar with his back to a column surrounded by a circle of his disciples.)

Sunni Islam was only stimulated into creating a system of higher education by the heretical Shias. When the Shia Fatimids captured Cairo in 969 and set up their rival caliphate they at once established a comprehensive system of state education to reinforce their challenge to the Sunni caliphate in Baghdad. Their crowning achievement was the founding of al-Azhar Mosque as a centre of higher education. Al-Azhar was restored to Sunni orthodoxy in 1171 when Saladin captured Cairo and destroyed the decrepit Fatimid caliphate. But at the end of the tenth century it belatedly awakened the Baghdad caliphate to the importance of higher education. At both ends of the Islamic world new institutions of learning were created: the *madrassahs*. Because they were essentially instruments in a doctrinal conflict

40. This injunction may seem odd for a desert Arab, but the Arab armies had by this time crossed the great rivers of the Nile and Euphrates and the caliph was notoriously in awe of water. See A. L. Tibawi, *Islamic Education*, London, 1972, p. 25.

these *madrassahs* tended to be dogmatic in their approach to education. At the heart of the curriculum were religious studies: exegesis, theology, jurisprudence and linguistic study of the Koran. Philosophy and logic were frowned upon. The sciences were still studied at this stage, but they suffered increasing disapproval from Islam.

In some respects the *madrassahs* were admirable institutions. The teachers were paid regularly by the state. The students received free tuition and, in the cases of the wealthy institutions such as al-Azhar, free board and lodging. In the great Mustansiriyah University founded in Baghdad in 1234 the facilities for the students included a hospital with an attendant physician to whom they could report when they were sick. But they were certainly not centres of free inquiry and research; the students were not encouraged to think for themselves.

The challenge from the heretical Shias of Cairo was succeeded by the new one from the Sufis that we have described. During the lifetime of the great al-Ghazali there was hope that Sufism, with all the new vigour that it gave to the world of Islam, could be reconciled with orthodoxy. But when Sufism swept through the Islamic world with astonishing popular success it gave rise to religious practices and heterodox concepts which the orthodox *ulama* could not possibly accept. Whereas, for example, the Prophet Muhammad had clearly commanded that it was the duty of all Muslims to marry, the Sufis were influenced by Christian asceticism to the point of recommending that the most admirable Sufi leaders were those who remained celibate. Even worse from the point of view of the orthodox was that the founders of Sufi orders came to be worshipped as saints. Nothing could be more contrary to the original spirit of Islam. (Some of the Sufi orders were highly fanatical and encouraged practices of self-mortification with roots in pagan times, such as glass-eating or fire-walking. Others such as the Bedawiya, which was founded in Egypt in the thirteenth century and became widely popular among the *fellahin* of Lower Egypt, was well known for the orgiastic practices, inherited from the Ancient Egyptians, which were carried on at fairs near the tomb of the founder of the order at Tanta and continued until recent times.)

The orthodox clergy of Islam were therefore obliged to counter-attack. This was no counter-reformation and there was no witch-hunt of heretics. Sufism was both too widespread and popular and too amorphous simply to be suppressed. It continued to survive as an intrinsic part of the body of Islam. What the *ulama* could do was to reinforce their control over the educational system of Islam, to try to ensure not only that no heretical ideas were taught but that the students should never enter any fields which might lead them to them.

Originality and vitality were gradually crushed out of existence; the field of study was restricted, except among a favoured few, by a narrowing circle of traditional subjects taught by rote and endlessly reproduced in lifeless commentaries. The theology of Islam as taught in the *madrassahs* remained in the grip of the dead hand, so going far to give colour to the charge of petrified medievalism which has been laid against the *ulama* almost down to our present day.[41]

The Muslim Arab world continued to produce great minds and creative thinkers, of whom the greatest in the Middle Ages was Ibn Khaldoun. They argue against any stultification of the human intellect. 'Knowledge and teaching are natural to human society,' wrote Ibn Khaldoun.

This is because man, who shares with the other animals such animal traits as sensation, movement and the need for food and shelter, is distinguished from them by his ability to think. This ability guides him in the pursuit of his livelihood; in his association, for economic purposes, with his fellow-beings; it guides him in the society which comes into being because of that association; it also disposes him to accept what the Prophets transmit to him from God and to base his acts on their teachings.[42]

As this last sentence makes clear, Ibn Khaldoun, like al-Ghazali before him, remained firmly within the Islamic tradition and it is part of the greatness of Islam that this should be so. But it meant that even Ibn Khaldoun could not see the dangers of extreme orthodox control. As far as he was concerned, knowledge increases when, and only when, 'society is flourishing and civilized'. He acknowledged that 'learning has almost disappeared in North Africa' but this was due to 'the weakness of the states existing there and the disruption of society, with the ensuing decline or disappearance of the crafts'. On the other hand, learning was flourishing in Cairo in Egypt 'which has had a large population and an advanced civilization for thousands of years, so that the crafts, and among them learning, are securely rooted and highly developed in that city'. He noted that one of the

41. H. A. R. Gibb, *Mohammedanism*, London, 1953, p. 145.
42. Ibn Khaldoun, *Prolegomena*, vol. II, p. 363, quoted in Charles Issawi (trans.), *An Arab Philosophy of History*, London, 1950.

causes of this admirable situation was that the Mamluke chieftains of Egypt, fearing that their sultan might use his powers to oppress their children, had gone out of their way to endow mosque schools, shrines and almshouses and install their children as supervisors, with the result that Cairo had become the great centre of learning of the Islamic world, attracting scholars to it from Morocco and Iraq.

But because Ibn Khaldoun accepted the orthodox view which rejected any rationalistic approach to the search for knowledge and truth, he also was hostile to the sciences and philosophy. He argued against the study of natural science unless the student had first been steeped in the religious sciences, and he was violently opposed to the study of alchemy (as chemistry was called in the Middle Ages). From the twelfth century onwards (that is after the death of al-Ghazali in 1111) all the sciences in which the Arabs had once excelled were at a standstill or in decline – medicine, mineralogy, physics, botany. There was no free spirit of inquiry, and knowledge became something of a fixed quantity within strictly defined boundaries which the universities were intended to provide.

Here and there was some free spirit who was prepared to challenge the prevailing orthodoxy. At the time of the Black Death in four-teenth-century Spain, for example, the great Arab scholar and phys-ician, Ibn al-Khatib of Granada, insisted that the epidemic was a contagion and not merely a divine punishment, as the *ulama* insisted. In his treatise *On Plague* he had the courage to write: 'It must be a principle that a proof taken from the Traditions has to undergo modification when in manifest contradiction with the evidence of the perception of the senses.'

But such spirits were rare and in fact the field of medicine offers the most striking decline in scholarship and research. The most famous of the European travellers to Egypt in the eighteenth century, the Marquis de Volney, wrote that the most one could expect to find in the way of a local doctor was a man who knew how to bleed and cauterize a wound, and that even the valets of European visitors were consulted for their medical knowledge 'as if they were Aesculapius'. In the prevailing intellectual atmosphere the pseudo-sciences flourished. Not only were the occult practices of the Sufi leaders popular among the public, as would be expected, but even some of the orthodox shaikhs became skilled in the use of amulets and charms, while the science of astronomy in the Islamic Near East was little more than astrology.

The stagnation at home was compounded by the almost total lack of contact with the outside world. In medieval times the lack of curiosity was due to a sense of superiority – which on the whole was justified. Professor Bernard Lewis quotes the tenth-century geographer Masudi as writing:

> The peoples of the north are those for whom the sun is distant; their bodies are large, their natures gross, their manners harsh, their understanding dull and their tongues heavy . . . their religious beliefs lack solidity . . . those of them who are farthest to the north are the most subject to stupidity, grossness and brutishness.

Even Ibn Khaldoun was only mildly interested four centuries later:

> We learn by report that in the lands of the Franks on the north shores of the sea, philosophical sciences are much in demand, their principles are being revived, the circles for teaching them are numerous, and the number of students seeking to learn them is increasing.

But he saw this as no cause for alarm and certainly not for trying to emulate the Franks by reviving the teaching of philosophy. 'God knows best what goes on in those parts,' was his comment.

The invasions of the world of Islam by crusaders, Mongols, the Catholic kings of Spain and others destroyed many of the great Muslim seats of learning and contributed to the hardening of attitudes. From its triumphant early days, when Islam was ready to study and absorb what it needed of the civilizations it had conquered, it became exclusive and defensive, intent on the preservation of the Islamic *umma*. The temporary revival of Muslim military power in the Ottoman Empire caused no liberalization of attitudes. On the contrary, infidel ideas and influences were both shunned and despised. Although it was the Arabs who introduced paper into Europe in the eighth century (after learning how to manufacture it from the Chinese when they captured Samarkand in 704) they rejected mechanical book-printing for centuries because it was an infidel invention unsanctioned by God.

So it was that when at the end of the eighteenth century the West began its invasion of the very heartland of Islam – the Arab provinces of the Ottoman Empire – its peoples were in no position to meet the onslaught. In knowledge, technology and material strength the West was infinitely superior and the Arabs had very little idea why.

6. The West Invades

For some two centuries after Sultan Mohammed II conquered Constantinople from the Byzantines in 1453, the Ottoman Empire was the scourge and envy of western Europe. By the end of the sixteenth century the European dominions of Turkey reached their greatest extent when the island of Crete surrendered to the Turkish forces. These then included all of present-day Romania, Bulgaria, Greece, Cyprus, Albania, Yugoslavia and parts of Hungary, Poland and Russia's Crimean coast. This was the peak; and although the Ottomans twice reached the gates of Vienna, they never succeeded in taking it.

Although the Ottoman frontiers in Europe remained roughly unchanged until the end of the seventeenth century, the empire's power in relation to the West was already in decline. In fact it might be said that a new phase in the apparently endless conflict between Islam and Christendom had begun. The first thousand years which had started with the Arab conquests were generally in Islam's favour, despite the loss of Sicily and Spain. But the tide was clearly seen to have turned with the crushing defeat of the Turkish forces by King John Sobieski of Poland in 1683.

The European Christian powers went decisively over to the offensive. During the eighteenth century the Ottomans suffered defeat three times at the hands of the Russians and in 1774 a turning-point was reached when the sultan was obliged to grant political independence to the Tartars and hand over substantial territories to the Empress Catherine the Great. The most important clause from Turkey's point of view was the one which ultimately allowed Russia to claim the right to protect all the Orthodox subjects of Turkey. Originally the treaty only accorded Russia the right to build a church in Constantinople and to make representations for the protection of officials of the church, while Turkey undertook to protect the Christians. But this clause was later interpreted by the Russians as giving it the right to protect all Orthodox Christians in the Ottoman Empire. The sultan's European dominions began to crumble at the edges as the province of Bukovina was taken by the Austrians in the following year.

So far Ottoman losses had only affected the Christian and not the Arab provinces of the empire. The Christian powers could claim that their aim was to lift the Turkish yoke from their European co-religionists. But at the turn of the century something very different occurred, although it was no part of the Muslim–Christian struggle but of the rivalries between the European powers themselves.

In 1798 the young Napoleon Bonaparte, popular and triumphant after his crushing defeat of the Austrian armies which had brought temporary peace to Europe, proposed to the Directory which was ruling France that he should strike at the source of the arch-enemy Britain's wealth and power by occupying Egypt and threatening the route to India. But he was not only concerned with the military aspect of the expedition. He later remarked to a friend: 'In any undertaking I would have combined the experiences of the two worlds, exploiting for my own profit the theatre of all history, attacking the power of England and, by means of that conquest, renewing contact with the old Europe.'[1] In other words, France was to lead the way in a European penetration of the ancient and mysterious East. Bonaparte's head may have been full of fantasies ('I saw myself founding a religion,' he told the same friend, 'marching into Asia, riding an elephant, a turban on my head and in my hand the new Koran that I would have composed to suit my needs.') But he took some severely practical steps towards their fulfilment. The botanists, astronomers, cartographers, artists and archaeologists he took with his soldiers aroused through their incomparable *Description d'Egypte* the interest of the whole of Europe in this ancient land – the link between the Mediterranean world and the African and Asian continents. In the secret decree of 12 April 1798 one of the aims of the Egyptian expedition was given as arranging to have the isthmus of Suez cut through to ensure 'the free and exclusive possession of the Red Sea for the French republic'. Napoleon visited Suez but, owing to his engineers' mistaken calculation that the scheme was technically impossible, he abandoned the idea.

Thus although the Egyptian expedition may be counted a military failure,[2] and although Napoleon's attempts to appeal to the Egyptians by appearing dressed as a Muslim were quite unconvincing, the whole episode was of cardinal importance. It was

1. Comtesse de Rémusat, *Mémoires*, Paris, 1893, vol. I, p. 274.
2. Britain was concerned, but the threat to India never developed. Napoleon himself abandoned his troops in 1800 and the remainder of his depleted force evacuated Egypt under the eyes of British troops a year later.

significant in two ways. Britain had for some years been concerned with European threats to its Indian possessions. But it was Russian expansion that was seen as the danger; and when the Prime Minister William Pitt in 1791 first laid the foundation of Britain's Near Eastern policy that was to last for more than a century, it was that the Ottoman Empire should not be allowed to disintegrate in case its ports should fall into Russian hands.

From the time of Napoleon's expedition it was France that was seen as the principal menace and it began the long Anglo-French rivalry for political control over the Arab lands. It was as an immediate reaction to Napoleon's landing in Egypt that Britain signed its first 'treaty of protection' with an Arab ruler – the sultan of Muscat – giving it exclusive rights on his territory. As always, it was the security of the route to India, whose possession made Britain a world power, which mattered to the British government. But Britain had still not fully realized that Egypt ('the most important country' as Napoleon is said to have called it on reflection in his exile at St Helena) was the key.

The other significance of Bonaparte's expedition was its impact on the Egyptians and through them on all the Arab peoples of the Ottoman Empire. Such a short period of French rule could not of course transform deeply entrenched institutions and habits of Egyptian society. But it planted a seed that would grow. It was not only the military, technical and scientific superiority of the French that struck the more open-minded members of the Egyptian élite, but the independent spirit of the individual French soldier. The egalitarian ideas of the French Revolution made their first penetration of the closed society of the Near East.

The Ottoman authorities were naturally appalled and outraged that French Revolutionary ideas with their overtones of atheism should have penetrated the empire, although they were unable to immunize it from their influence. On the other hand their sense of superiority towards the infidel was not so great that they were unaware that they were falling behind the West in important respects. Since the empire was based on military power they were most ready to borrow or imitate Western military techniques, and from the early eighteenth century reforms in military and naval training had been introduced. Also, the doubts of the *ulama* were overridden and book-printing introduced, although it remained under the strictest government control.

The empire could still produce formidable fighting troops, and the largely Albanian force that the sultan sent to Egypt in 1799 was no exception. But the consequences of this expedition were nearly fatal to the empire. Among the officers of the Albanian contingent was a young man with exceptional qualities of leadership – Muhammad Ali. The situation that he found in Egypt was that the Mamluke beys, having recovered most of their former power from the weakening Ottoman authorities during the eighteenth century, had acquired the position of domestic tyrants who were allowed to do virtually as they pleased as long as they paid the annual tribute, which of course they extorted from the *fellahin*, to Constantinople. However Napoleon's troops, by defeating and humiliating the Mamluke beys, destroyed their authority – which they were unable to recover after the departure of the French. Muhammad Ali seized his opportunity and ultimately achieved a situation in which the *ulama*, acting as spokesman for the Egyptian people, asked him to take control. In 1805 the Ottoman sultan recognized him as viceroy of Egypt. Muhammad Ali ruthlessly suppressed the Mamluke beys and easily defeated a British expeditionary force which had unwisely been dispatched to restore their power.

The attitude towards Muhammad Ali of most modern Egyptians is ambiguous. He had no love or sympathy for the Egyptians as such and would never have regarded himself as one of them. His driving force was personal ambition. Yet the modern national movement of Egypt dates from his time. He was a political and military leader of genius, who within a generation turned Egypt into a major Mediterranean power which was only prevented from overthrowing the Ottoman Empire itself by the intervention of the great powers of Europe led by Britain.

Muhammad Ali was ruthless in his methods and his overriding objective was to strengthen his armed forces. The industries he built were intended to feed his military power; and in order to increase his revenues he turned the whole country into what amounted to one vast state farm. Most of his factories were uneconomically run and few of them survived his death, but outside forces, as we shall see, were partly to blame for this, and it remains undeniable that he tried to set Egypt on the road to industrialization. Today there are few who would deny that Egypt must have industries if it is ever to solve its economic problems.

Since the Mamluke fief-holders had latterly so exploited the countryside, Muhammad Ali's destruction of them benefited the *fellahin*. During the forty-four years of his rule as pasha of Egypt (1805–49), one million new acres of land were brought under the plough, new irrigation works were completed – including the great Nile Barrage at the apex of the Delta north of Cairo – and the basis of modern departmental government established. One of Muhammad Ali's most remarkable achievements was in education. Overriding or ignoring the opposition of the *ulama* – the men who had helped him to power – he opened new secondary schools where mathematics, technical subjects and Italian, because it was the language of international commerce, were taught by foreign instructors. He founded colleges of medicine and engineering, also with foreign teachers, and sent selected students to Europe for further training. As with his industries, there was much to be criticized in his methods and aims. His purpose was to create an educated corps of army officers and not to establish a public education system for the whole population. Nevertheless, he proved that innovation was possible for a determined ruler of Egypt and his educational reforms went far beyond the cautious changes that were being introduced by his nominal masters in Istanbul.

For all his innovations and reforms in industry, irrigation and education Muhammad Ali imported foreign experts and instructors. The connection with France established by Bonaparte's expedition was maintained, and most of those who held the key positions – such as Mugel in irrigation or Clot Bey, the head of the public health service – were French. It was a vital part of his achievement that he never allowed foreign influence to become excessive. Unlike his successors, he never became subject to European political control or indebted to European bankers.

If Muhammad Ali's reputation as a statesman ultimately rests on the changes he wrought inside Egypt, his most astonishing achievement was to turn this impoverished and enfeebled province of the Ottoman Empire into a Mediterranean power. He and his eldest son, Ibrahim Pasha (who had many of his father's qualities and was a military genius), created a formidable army of a quarter of a million men which won repeated victories throughout the Near East. On the face of it, there could hardly be less promising material for a conquering army than the Egyptian *fellahin*. Bullied and downtrodden by centuries of alien rule, they showed no martial qualities or appetite for military life and had to be recruited by savage and brutal means. But Ibrahim Pasha proved that, if properly trained and led by their Turkish and Albanian officers, they fought with discipline and courage. They lacked the panache in attack of the black Sudanese troops but they were especially good in holding defensive positions, and their health stood up much better than the Sudanese in colder Western climates.

In 1811 Muhammad Ali's suzerain asked him to send an expeditionary force to Arabia to quell the fanatically puritanical Islamic revival movement of the Wahhabis who were contesting the sultan-caliph's authority over the Holy Places. This was the first test of the pasha's armies; the task took seven years but they succeeded. Then in 1820 Muhammad Ali turned south and invaded central and western Sudan. After bloodily suppressing the resistance of the Sudanese tribes, he established the seat of government of an Egyptian dependency under the nominal suzerainty of the Ottoman sultan at the village of Khartoum, near the junction of the Blue and White Niles. In 1840 Egyptian rule was extended to include the future Kassala province of eastern Sudan.

After Muhammad Ali's Sudanese successes, the Ottoman sultan unwisely invited him to help suppress his rebellious Greek subjects. He was initially successful, but the British and Russian fleets intervened on behalf of the Greeks to defeat the combined Egyptian and Turkish navies at Navarino in 1827. Five years later the Greeks secured their independence. This did nothing to restrain the ambitions of Muhammad Ali and his son. When the sultan refused Ibrahim Pasha the governorship of Syria as a reward for his assistance, he proceeded to seize it and was formally recognized by the sultan in 1833. At one time Ibrahim Pasha's armies were threatening Istanbul and at this point the sultan, faced with Britain's refusal to help, was forced to ask the Russians to save him. He was obliged to sign the humiliating Treaty of Hunkiar Iskelessi (1833), which not only gave Russia the right to intervene in Turkish affairs, but included a secret clause permitting Russia to insist on the closing of the Dardanelles in time of war.

By now Britain was thoroughly concerned. Palmerston, the Prime Minister, was uneasily aware that through his conquests Muhammad Ali now controlled the two main routes to India – the Red Sea and the Euphrates valley. Moreover, Palmerston's primary interest was that Ottoman Turkey should remain a bulwark against Russian expansion southward and eastward into the Levant; and now here was Russia stepping in as the saviour of the Ottoman Empire. His hopes that France might act as a brake to Muhammad Ali's ambitions by the pasha's close friendship with the French government were deceived. Palmerston launched a major diplomatic offensive to bring the powers of Europe together in cutting Muhammad Ali back to size.

He was ultimately successful; the treaty of London concluded in 1841 by Austria, England, Russia and Prussia declared the 'Egyptian Question' to have been resolved. Muhammad Ali was forced to return Syria to the sultan and to accept a limitation of 18,000 men to his army. But Palmerston did not care if Muhammad Ali remained ruler of Egypt provided he no longer threatened the Ottoman Empire. Accordingly, Muhammad Ali was able to preserve the hereditary rights of his dynasty which he had extracted from the sultan and his semi-independent power as viceroy. (Farouk, the last king of Egypt, who abdicated in 1952, was his great-great-grandson.) It would be a grave error to regard Muhammad Ali's challenge to the Ottoman sultan as an Arab movement against Turks. Arab nationalism was an almost inconceivable idea at the time. Apart from the fact that he himself was a member of the Ottoman élite who never learned Arabic, his officers were Turks or Circassians; and although they came to identify themselves with Muhammad Ali's Egypt and were quite prepared to fight for it against Ottoman troops of similar racial origin, they would never have thought of themselves as being involved in an *Arab* movement. Ibrahim Pasha, who had close contact with Europe and European officers, was strongly influenced by nineteenth-century European nationalist ideas. He did learn Arabic and toyed with the idea of re-creating an Arab kingdom of the Arabic-speaking parts of the Ottoman Empire – a concept which was supported by some romantically minded deputies of the French parliament. But in reality Ibrahim Pasha identified himself with the Arabs no more than his father, and the revived Arab kingdom remained a romantic ideal.

Muhammad Ali remained the undisputed ruler of Egypt; but he was a broken man as his foreign ambitions had collapsed. Yet another less-publicized agreement forced upon him by Europe was even more ominous for Egypt's future. An Anglo-Turkish commercial convention of 1838, which Britain had the power to enforce, meant that British manufactures, which were cheaper and of better quality than anything his factories could produce, were able to enter Egypt with an eight per cent *ad valorem* duty only. This meant the inevitable collapse of Egyptian industry.

This whole episode demonstrated two things with abundant clarity. One was that the Christian powers of western Europe were prepared to intervene in the Islamic Near East whenever they felt their interests were threatened. The other was that the only effective protection left to the Ottoman Empire was that these interests should conflict. Henceforth, not only the sultan's European possessions were lost one by one; but the powers began to seize the Arab provinces. The first to do so was not Britain but France.

France Takes the First Share

As we have seen in Chapter 3, the formerly prosperous North African coast suffered a long period of disastrous decline. The smiling countryside of the North African Berbers which had flourished under the Romans and the first three centuries of Arab rule enjoyed only intermittent recovery after the beduin invasions, and had now disappeared for ever. The complex irrigation system collapsed and has not even been restored to this day. Whole villages disappeared as the Berbers took to the hills and remained there.

Since that time, the Maghreb has been the land of paradox which it still remains: a land of poor, overpopulated mountains, inhabited by stolid farmers still speaking the Berber tongue; while the potentially rich coastal plains are underpopulated and given up, like the High Plains of the interior, to the sheep of nomadic herdsmen, most of them Arabs or at any rate arabized.[3]

It was only in eastern Algeria and especially Tunisia, helped by the influx of Andalusian Muslims expelled from Spain, that the ancient and prosperous Mediterranean-style agriculture survived.

The consequences for the Mediterranean world of the Catholic reconquest of Spain and Portugal and the expulsion of the Moors[4] were to last for two centuries or more. Fearing a counter-attack by the Moors, Spain and Portugal carried the war into Africa with raids and the seizure of ports such as Tangier, Melilla, Algiers, Tunis and Tripoli. But in the sixteenth and seventeenth centuries Spain and Portugal were much more concerned with their empires in the New World and Asia so the Moroccan dynasties were able to recover these possessions. Only the Spanish enclaves of Ceuta and Melilla remain on the North African coast today.

The answer of the North African Arabs to the raids by Spain and Portugal was not to launch a counter-invasion – of which they were not capable – but to wage a prolonged war against the shipping of any Christian state in the Mediterranean. The men who did this were the

3. Samir Amin, *The Maghreb in the Modern World*, Harmondsworth, Penguin Books, 1970, p. 16.

4. After the fall of Granada in 1492 the remaining two or three million Muslims were given the choice of emigration or conversion to Christianity. Those who chose to remain were only nominally converted and in 1610 the remainder of the Moriscos, as they were called, were forcibly expelled.

corsairs, and their ships were privateers, which meant that they were owned and manned by individuals but permitted, and indeed encouraged, to attack the shipping of any state with which their government happened to be at war. This proviso was often loosely interpreted and the corsairs were essentially pirates. It was their activities which gave the North African Barbary[5] states such a fearsome reputation in Europe. But the famous seamen of the Christian states were hardly any different. Thus when Sir Francis Drake, the greatest of heroes to British schoolboys, set out on one of his famous voyages to the New World in a ship which was fully equipped for war, he had no commission from Queen Elizabeth's government because England and Spain, although not on friendly terms, were not at war. He merely felt, as he put it, 'the general Licence of the Times would be his justification'. Christian captives of the Barbary corsairs were sometimes treated appallingly and sold as slaves.[6] Less is heard of the sufferings of Muslim captives of the Christians, who also could be sold in the great slave markets of Pisa or Genoa.

As we have seen, while Morocco preserved its independence, the Algerians, Tunisians and Tripolitanians called in the newly rising Muslim power of Muslim Turkey to their aid and eventually came under Turkish domination or control. In the early sixteenth century the Turks divided the area into three *ojaks* or regencies with their capitals at Algiers, Tunis and Tripoli respectively. Their frontiers correspond roughly to those between the Maghreb states today. But these frontiers had no natural or historical justification and the authority of the Turkish governors hardly ran into the interior. Similarly, the sultan of Morocco's effective rule did not extend beyond the Atlantic plains or *bled el-maghzen* – government country – while the Berber tribesmen remained masters of the mountains of the interior: *bled el-siba* or 'land of dissidence'.

The three regencies of Algiers, Tunis and Tripoli were essentially maritime city states. Their prosperity depended on trade (and successful piracy), although there were some agricultural exports such as wheat, fruit and tobacco from the surrounding areas. There was a small upper class, many of whom were of European origin, and like their counterparts in Syria and Egypt they imported the luxuries of Europe for their own use. Although many of the descriptions of them

---

5. The word is derived from 'Berber'. The brothers Barbarossa, corsairs who founded the Algerian state in the early sixteenth century, were probably of Albanian origin, like Muhammad Ali of Egypt.

6. The most famous of these was Cervantes, author of *Don Quixote*.

by contemporary Christian writers were highly unfavourable and some were prejudiced (Spanish monks, for example, who wished to raise money to ransom Christian captives), other European travellers between the sixteenth and eighteenth centuries told of Algiers and Tunis as fine cities with some splendid houses and gardens and overflowing markets. But the underlying reality was the same as in the eastern provinces of the Ottoman Empire. The real wealth and military power of the North African Muslim states was steadily dwindling in relation to Europe.

For about a century after their incorporation into the Ottoman Empire the three regencies were ruled directly from Istanbul through a governor. But in view of their distance from the capital, it was probably inevitable that they should acquire a large measure of autonomous power which was shared between the local Ottoman élite. In Tunis a hereditary dynasty was founded in 1705 by Hussein Bey, a Turkish general of the Janissaries of Cretan origin, and lasted until Tunisian independence and the declaration of the republic under President Bourguiba in 1957. In Tripoli at about the same time a similar dynasty was founded by Ahmad Caramanli, who anticipated Muhammad Ali by inviting his main Turkish and Circassian rivals to a banquet and massacring them. The situation in Algiers, the most powerful of the three regency states, was somewhat different. After a series of Turkish governors, most of whom were assassinated, Algiers became an oligarchic republic with a president known as the dey, who, like the doge of Venice, was appointed for life. The dey's task was not easy. He had to cope not only with the local corps of Turkish Janissaries but also the Corporation of Corsairs, whose privateering provided most of his income. Fourteen of the total of twenty-eight deys were assassinated. The interior of the country was divided into three provinces, each of them under a bey who was responsible for collecting taxes from the people. But since these supplied only a small proportion of the revenues of Algiers, the dey's government took little interest in the interior. Such law and order as was maintained was achieved by playing off the tribes against each other. Thus although the deys were despots they had no tight control over the mass of the population.

The wealth of the three regencies was derived mainly from the corsairs and therefore declined as the European states learned how to deal with them. In the early period, the corsairs went as far afield as northern Europe and even reached Iceland; but by the end of the seventeenth century they had ceased to threaten the coasts of Europe.

Henceforth, the corsairs were responding to European attacks on their own territory, as well as their shipping. The European states endeavoured to negotiate treaties with the regencies to secure their shipping from the privateers, but these treaties were constantly breaking down and the European fleets would launch punitive raids against the corsair ports such as Algiers. But the fault was certainly not always on the side of the Barbary states. According to de Grammont, the French historian of Turkish rule in Algiers:

Careful examination of the facts produces overwhelming evidence that in the majority of occasions the first wrongs were committed by the westerners, though it can certainly be granted that the dey's government was always quick to profit from circumstances where he had any excuse, however small, to break the peace and begin hostilities which were certain to be profitable to him.[7]

The European navies became increasingly effective and the Barbary states declined. Whereas there were 35,000 Christian captives in the prisons of Algiers in the seventeenth century there were only 1,200 when the British admiral Lord Exmouth bombarded the city in 1816. The population of the city fell from 100,000 at its height in the seventeenth century to about 40,000 at the time of the French occupation in 1830. At the same time, the number of Muslim captives in Christian hands increased. Two thousand Muslim slaves were released by Napoleon as a gesture to the dey of Algiers when he captured Malta in 1798. By the beginning of the nineteenth century the corsairs were no more than a minor irritation for Europe.

The last Western power to be seriously incommoded by the corsairs was not European but the newly independent United States of America. Having no navy, it could not protect its shipping, which had been guarded by Britain when it was a colony. It therefore negotiated treaties with the Barbary states, under which its shipping would have protection in return for payments of money and goods. But these agreements were always breaking down as the United States failed to pay at the agreed time or the Barbary states raised their demands for 'protection money'. It was an action of this kind by the Caramanli ruler of Tripoli which provoked the extraordinary war between Tripoli and the United States which lasted from 1801 to 1805. The most notorious action of the war was the march from Alexandria by the US consul in Tripoli, William Eaton, with a motley force including

7. H. D. de Grammont, *Histoire du massacre des turcs à Marseille en 1620*, Paris, 1879, p. 6.

some US marines ('From the halls of Montezuma to the shores of Tripoli'), with the aim of deposing Yusuf Caramanli and replacing him with a rival named Hamed. The expedition was a failure, but General Eaton, the rank to which he was promoted by Hamed, went into history as the colourful symbol of the first United States military intervention in the Middle East. General Eaton was hawkish in outlook. 'Shall America,' he asked, 'who, when in an infant state, destitute of all apparatus of war, without discipline and without funds, dared to resist the whole force of the lion's den of Great Britain to establish her freedom, now that she has acquired manhood, resources and experience, bring her humiliation to the basest dog kennel of Barbary?'[8]

General Eaton had his way, and in 1815 a newly-formed American navy was able to send a squadron to Algiers under Commodore Decatur, which secured a more satisfactory treaty from the Algerians.

The British bombarded Algiers in the following year and also imposed a new treaty, under which they paid no more than £600 a year for consular privileges. Henceforth the republic's income from privateering was virtually nil. This did not mean, however, that the European powers ceased to be interested in the North African coast. France had built up a highly profitable commerce based on a trading post near Bône in eastern Algeria, which it had fortified. In 1830 Hussein, the last dey of Algiers, decided that this French privilege should cease.

It was this decision which gave rise to what is one of the most celebrated incidents in the history of European imperialism. The dey gave an audience to the French consul to discuss the much-delayed payment of a debt to two Algerian Jews for the delivery of wheat to France. The dey informed the consul that he would not allow a single French cannon to remain on Algerian soil and that French merchants would in future only enjoy the same rights as other merchants. The audience became heated and, according to the report of the British consul of the time, the French consul said things 'of a very gross and irritating nature'. The dey himself reported to the Ottoman sultan that the consul insulted the Muslim religion and 'the honour of Your

8. But General Eaton also professed his belief that there was an affinity between Islam and American religion. He once told some Arab shaikhs that God had promised a separate heaven to Americans but in this they would be free, if they wished, to make up parties to visit the paradise of Muhammad or the heaven of the papists. The shaikhs were hugely amused but said they doubted whether he would be able to visit the paradise of Muhammad unless he had become a sincere Muslim during his lifetime.

Majesty, the protector of the world'. Feeling intolerably provoked, the dey struck the consul 'two or three light blows with the fly-whisk which I was holding in my humble hand'.

This outrageous insult was the pretext for the French invasion and occupation of Algeria which lasted 132 years. France claimed that its motive was the final suppression of Algerian piracy, but this had long ceased to be a serious menace. The real reason was to preserve France's privileged trading position on the North African coast and this developed into an operation of outright colonial acquisition. The shaky régime of the French King Charles X was shortly to be swept away in the revolution of 1830. The invasion of Algiers was a last gesture to restore the régime's prestige by redeeming the failure of Bonaparte's expedition to Egypt.

There are signs that the French government's original intention was merely to depose the dey and set up an Arab ruler and administration in his place. One of the propaganda leaflets issued before the invasion said:

We French, your friends, are leaving for Algiers. We are going to drive out your tyrants, the Turks who persecute you, who steal your goods, and never cease menacing your lives . . . our presence on your territory is not to make war on you but only on the person of your pasha. Abandon your pasha; follow our advice; it is good advice and can only make you happy.[9]

The French force of 37,000 landed on 14 June 1830 at Sidi Farrouj, west of Algiers. Resistance was brave but hopeless and on 5 July the dey signed an act of capitulation, which included in Article 5 'The exercise of the Muslim religion will remain free; neither the liberty of any class of the inhabitants nor their religion, nor their property, nor their commerce and industry will be impaired in any way. The commander-in-chief gives this undertaking on his honour.' The French general also promised that 'the religion and the customs of the Algerians will be respected. No soldier of the army will be permitted to enter a mosque.'

These undertakings were not fulfilled because France's policy turned into one of full-blooded colonization. Mosques were turned into churches. Muslim holidays were no longer officially observed and tribal lands were confiscated. Ultimately Algeria was even to be declared an indivisible part of France – something which only a generation ago most Frenchmen would have taken for granted. Yet

9. Cf. British propaganda to the Egyptians at the time of the Suez invasion of 1956, which was aimed to encourage them to rise against President Nasser for their own good.

such a policy was doomed to failure in the end. However great the French achievement might be, the Muslim Arabs, who would always form the vast majority of the population, could not be turned into Frenchmen, even if an Algerian élite could be formed by French culture. This would have required the transformation of France into something quite different.

Once the French had decided to occupy and annexe the whole country, they soon discovered that the task was far from easy. In fact it was to take at least forty years for the whole country to be 'pacified'. As the peasants saw their tribal lands being taken away from them they resisted violently. In the west the focus of resistance was the great Arab Amir Abdelkader, who fought the French for fifteen years. He received support from all over the country including the Berbers of the Kabyle country (who were to give the French so much trouble a century later). Writing when the French occupation had finally succeeded, the historian Gafferel said that Abdelkader 'knew how to concentrate around himself the scattered forces of Arab nationality . . . it was against an entire nation, inspired by the double fanaticism of patriotism and religion, that the war had to be waged'.

France's difficulties provoked a ruthless and savage repression. The notorious General Bugeaud who was in charge of pacification said to his troops in 1841: 'Soldiers, you have often beaten the Arabs. You will beat them again, but to rout them is a small thing; they must be subdued.' And he said to the French civilians in Algiers: 'The Arabs must be reduced to submission so that only the French flag stands up on this African soil.' Wherever there was resistance, punitive expeditions were organized. As one French historian wrote in 1853:

> Our soldiers returning from the expedition were themselves ashamed . . . about 18,000 trees had been cut down; houses had been burnt; women, children, and old men had been killed. The unfortunate women particularly excited cupidity by the habit of wearing silver ear-rings, leg-rings and arm-rings. These rings have no catches like French bracelets. Fastened in youth to the limbs of girls they cannot be removed when they are grown up. To get them off our soldiers used to cut off their limbs and leave them alive in this mutilated condition.[10]

On his return from a similar expedition in 1846 General Bugeaud declared: 'We have burnt a great deal and destroyed a great deal. It may be that I shall be called a barbarian, but as I have the conviction

10. M. Baudicourt, *La Guerre et le gouvernement de l'Algerie*, Paris, 1853, p. 160.

that I have done something useful for my country, I consider myself as above the reproaches of the press.'

Inevitably such repression increased the bitterness of the resistance. But ultimately the 'pacification' was successful in that the national spirit of the Algerians was subdued for more than a generation. Abdelkader made his submission to France in 1847 and although there were some subsequent fierce uprisings over the next three decades (the rebellion of 1871 pinned down 80,000 French soldiers for a whole year) the country could be declared at peace and safe for European tourists by 1880.

We have dwelt on the French occupation of Algeria at some length because it must be regarded as the most extreme case of Christian European colonization of an Arab/Muslim country. The French set out deliberately to gallicize the country and to destroy all the symbols of Algerian nationality. French was made the language of government and higher education – the only means of advancement in any profession. Superficially it was successful in that even some of the French-educated Algerian élite came to believe there was no such thing as an Algerian Arab nation in any sense. This is why the reappearance of the Algerian spirit, which had spent several decades underground, was greeted in so many quarters with such disbelief.

Most other parts of the Arab world were to come under European occupation, but in no case (except possibly the Italian colonization of Libya) was such a total form of domination attempted. This was partly because of rivalries between the European powers; each of them watched the others to see that they did not annexe territories too close to their own vital interests. It was also because the spirit of imperialism itself had changed and become more sophisticated. Instead of direct colonial government, advantages were seen in indirect rule which left most of the indigenous institutions intact but merely ensured the physical domination of the territory. This gave rise to the quasi-imperialism which was to be such a feature of relations between Europe and the Arabs.

The next European encroachment on the Arab world was at the opposite end: the toe of the Arabian peninsula. Britain, concerned as always with the protection of the sea-route to India, decided to establish its own staging-post at Aden. This had a flourishing trade and splendid fortifications in Roman times but was in considerable decay when Europe, in the form of the Portuguese fleet, first attacked it in the sixteenth century. When the British took it with a force dispatched from the Bombay presidency in 1839 it was no more than a fishing village of 500 inhabitants. The pretext was provided by a local petty ruler, the sultan of Lahej, who had committed some acts of piracy against shipping in the area.

Nominally southern Arabia was part of the Ottoman Empire but the sultan was in no position to forestall the British action even if he had thought it sufficiently important. The Aden settlement, as it was called, was simply attached to the Bombay presidency. But it formed a base from which Britain steadily extended its influence into the tribal hinterland and northwards into the Persian Gulf. It was able to ensure that no other European power gained a foothold on the coasts of Arabia.

Syria was the next part of the Arab world to provide a pretext for European intervention. The ten years of Egyptian rule under Ibrahim Pasha (1831–40) had brought disturbing changes to this conservative region. He had centralized and improved the administration, introduced conscription, and established a public state education system while allowing the Catholic and Protestant mission schools, which were already active, to continue to operate. He even tried to establish the principle of equality between Christians and Muslims. But the increased taxation that these reforms required, conscription and the attempt to take arms away from civilians were unpopular, and when Ibrahim Pasha was forced out of Syria in 1840 the people rose to help the Ottoman forces against him. The manner in which Ottoman rule was reimposed was disastrous. Even when the empire had been at its height and its administration effective, the mountains of Lebanon had been left largely to themselves under their local ruling dynasties. The system was based on an entente between the Druzes, who were mainly landlords, and the equally independent-minded Maronite Catholic peasants.[11] This system the Ottoman government now set out to destroy in order to be able to impose direct rule on Mount Lebanon. Its task was made easier because the Druze landlords were already alarmed by the growth in number and strength of the Maronites who, through the mission schools and their contacts with Europe, were undergoing a cultural revival. The attempt by the Druze landlords to impose their authority led to the civil war of 1860 in

11. Druzes are an occult sect, an offshoot of the Ismailis, from whom they parted company in the early eleventh century, when they accepted the Fatimid Caliph Hakim as the final incarnation of the Deity. The Maronites are a Uniate Church which reaccepted the authority of Rome in the early eighteenth century in return for the right to retain its oriental rites and customs.

which many Christians were massacred.[12] When these events had repercussions in further massacres in Damascus[13] the powers of Europe intervened. The Emperor Napoleon III sent an army which landed at Beirut and stationed troops in the main square (still known to some as the Place des Canons). A conference of five powers – Britain, Russia, France, Austria and Prussia – was held and agreed on a new arrangement, which the Porte had no choice but to accept, whereby Mount Lebanon became a specially privileged district or sanjak detached from the vilayet of Damascus, with a clear Maronite majority, a Christian governor and chief of police. Ties between Europe and this small but crucial portion of the Ottoman Empire were naturally strengthened by these events.

The Suez Canal

Until the middle of the nineteenth century, a direct confrontation between British and French interests in the Near East had been avoided. France had sympathized with Muhammad Ali but had withdrawn from backing him against Palmerston's decision to put a stop to his ambitions. On the other hand, Britain recognized and accepted both France's special role as protector of the Christians of the Levant and its conquest of Algeria. Both Britain and France supported the general policy of maintaining the existence of the Ottoman Empire as a brake to the ambitions of Russia, and had even joined as allies with the Ottoman sultan in the Crimean War of 1852–4.

However, the danger of a direct clash between Britain and France now arose over Napoleon's 'most important country' Egypt, which acquired an immensely increased significance for all the powers through the opening of the Suez Canal in 1869.

As we have seen, Napoleon was keenly interested in the building of a Suez Canal but rejected it as unfeasible. For similar reasons the British government, although its own engineers' report in 1830 said that it *was* technically possible, was strongly opposed to the idea, foreseeing correctly that it would ultimately force Britain to occupy

12. It is still widely believed in Lebanon, although without any hard historical evidence, that the Maronites were encouraged and supported by the French and the Druzes by the British.

13. The Algerian hero Abdelkader, by now in exile in Damascus, used his authority to protect the lives of several thousands of Christians. The French presented him with a medal inscribed with the words: 'Amir of North Africa, Defender of Arab nationality, Protector of oppressed Christians.'

Egypt in order to protect its precious imperial route to India. As Lord Palmerston remarked:

> We do not want Egypt or wish it for ourselves, any more than any rational man with an estate in the north of England and a residence in the south would have wished to possess the inns on the north road. All he could want would have been that the inns should be well-kept, always accessible, and furnishing him, when he came, with mutton-chops and post-horses.[14]

French interest was maintained, and in the early 1830s their vice-consul in Egypt, a young genius named Ferdinand de Lesseps, became concerned with a Canal scheme which had the support of Muhammad Ali Pasha. However, de Lesseps had to wait until 1854, when Said, one of Muhammad Ali's sons who had been his boyhood friend, became pasha of Egypt, before he could sign an agreement under which the Canal company which he had formed could build and operate the Canal.

Britain still kept up the struggle and used all possible pressure on the Ottoman sultan, who still had to give his consent, to prevent the work from starting. But de Lesseps had the steadfast support of the Emperor Napoleon III, and the cutting of the Canal finally began in 1859.

Said Pasha died in 1863 and was succeeded by his nephew Ismail, a man of intelligence, vision and energy, but of disastrous misjudgement in financial matters. His extravagance earned him the title of Ismail the Magnificent, but destroyed Egypt's independence.

Ismail was quite capable of seeing the immense significance of the Canal for Egypt and the rest of the world. Work on the Canal was pushed ahead until it was opened in great pomp and splendour by the French Empress Eugénie in 1869. Britain had by now fully accepted the inevitable, and the Prince and Princess of Wales were among those who attended the opening. However, Britain's continued pressure on the sultan to withhold his final approval for the Canal had eventually forced Ismail to accept the decision of a commission of arbitration headed by Napoleon III which intended to settle the status of the Suez Canal Company in Egypt once and for all. The emperor's decision meant that in return for the Company's relinquishment of its right to use free forced labour and of various lands and navigation rights on the Suez Isthmus, Ismail (and therefore Egypt) had to pay a crippling sum of compensation. Moreover, the

---

14. A. E. M. Ashley, *Life and Correspondence of Palmerston*, London, 1879, p. 338.

Company's concession ran for ninety-nine years from the date of opening (1869); its status in Egypt was now secure and internationally guaranteed. It had all the means of developing into an autonomous state within Egypt.

This was a problem for the future. The immediate effect of Napoleon III's award was to sink Ismail and Egypt more deeply into debt to European bond-dealers. Moreover, by means of heavy bribes to the Ottoman sultan, Ismail about this time secured his ambition of making himself a virtually independent sovereign with the title of khedive or viceroy, and the right to raise loans and grant concessions in Egypt's name without reference to the Porte. This not only increased the debts further but made them the liability of the Egyptian state. Instead of extending Egypt's independence, Ismail was ensuring its destruction.

The irony was that the positive social and economic achievements of Ismail's reign were considerable. Ports were extended, railways laid, new canals dug and over a million acres reclaimed from the desert. More money was spent on education and the first government girls' school in the Ottoman Empire was founded. Perhaps of greatest importance was that the judicial system was radically changed by the introduction of Mixed Courts which ended the immunity of Europeans to a major part of civil law. European observers were astonished to find Egypt acquiring many of the aspects of an advanced nineteenth-century state. In January 1876 the Alexandria correspondent of *The Times* could write: 'Egypt is a marvellous instance of progress. She has advanced as much in seventy years as many other countries have done in five hundred.' Ismail could claim: 'My country is no longer in Africa; we are now part of Europe.'

It was Ismail's financial folly, which his creditors were ready to exploit to the full, that made Egypt a European protectorate. As Palmerston had foreseen, Britain now had a powerful direct interest in Egypt – the roadside inn on the route to India. The interest acquired a solid financial basis in 1875 when the British Prime Minister Disraeli, with the help of a loan arranged by the London Rothschilds, bought the desperate Ismail's 44 per cent share in the Suez Canal Company. This daring coup delighted most Europeans except the French, who were now the principal rivals of the British in Africa. Henceforth, Britain and France would be scrutinizing every move of the other in Egypt. When Ismail asked for a British financial adviser, France sent one also. Seeing no alternative, the two men cooperated in presenting proposals for reform which amounted to the imposition of an Anglo-French control of Egypt's finances. This Dual Control, as it was called, endeavoured to retrieve the situation but it was now hopeless. While the bond-holders would not accept any reduction in their rate of interest, which was the only way of reducing the intolerable burden of Egypt's national debt, no more revenues could be squeezed in taxes out of the poor *fellahin*. Britain and France then decided that since the source of the trouble was Ismail's unlimited power and the way in which he treated Egypt as his personal property, the solution was to make him delegate some of his power to responsible ministers and hand over his vast personal estates (20 per cent of Egypt's cultivated land) in return for a fixed royal salary or civil list. Unwisely, Britain and France insisted that an Englishman and a Frenchman should be included among the responsible ministers. It was therefore easy for Ismail to turn the tables by blaming Egypt's financial difficulties on the ministers who had been forced upon him. When Egyptian army officers who had not been paid for months became mutinous, Ismail dismissed the government with its European ministers and appointed his own.

Britain and France still shrank from direct intervention in Egypt, if only because it would have required a degree of cooperation between them for which they were not prepared. But their hand was forced when the Austrian and German[15] governments intervened to protest at Ismail's new government's proposal to reduce temporarily the rate of interest payments on the national debt to 5 per cent. Britain and France put pressure on the Ottoman sultan to order Ismail to abdicate in favour of his son Tewfik. The Ottoman government was also in appalling financial straits and the sultan was in no position to refuse. On 30 June 1879 Ismail, after collecting his crown jewels and some £3 million in cash, sailed from Alexandria on his yacht the *Mahrousa*. Eighty-three years later his grandson Farouk, the last king of Egypt, was to leave in much the same way.

Ismail had gone but Egypt's problems remained and the weak and colourless Tewfik was no man to cope with them. His position was now much more difficult because the arbitrary oppression of his father's régime had finally provoked the formation of a national movement among the long-suffering Egyptians. It was probably inevitable that the vanguard of this movement should be formed by

15. Headed by Bismarck and the new major power in Europe.

those officers of the army created by Ibrahim Pasha who were of true Egyptian or *fellahin* origin and resented the domination of the Turco-Circassians who held all the key positions in the country. They found a leader in the massive and dignified figure of Colonel Arabi, the son of a small farmer of Lower Egypt.

As *The Times* pointed out on 12 September 1881: 'The army, we must remember, is the only native institution which Egypt now owns. All else has been invaded and controlled and transformed by the accredited representatives of France and England.' At the beginning the army was only concerned with its own grievances – its missing pay and the unfair promotion of the Turco-Circassians – but when Arabi and his followers successfully combined to force the khedive to dismiss the deeply unpopular and reactionary Circassian minister of war who had tried to arrest them, the army became the focus of a national movement which included all classes of Egyptian society: big and small landowners, traders, craftsmen and *ulama*.

At first the British and French representatives in Egypt, who had almost unanimously detested Ismail, were inclined to sympathize with this new movement. Arabi was behaving with calm and moderation, he had the support of the more conservative elements and although his movement was clearly taking up the slogan of 'Egypt for the Egyptians' this did not seem to threaten European interests at this stage, because it was directed primarily, and not unreasonably, against the Turkish ruling class.

Unfortunately for Arabi, international factors which were quite beyond his control were preventing the cautious, step-by-step advance of his movement which was essential for its success. These factors were the double-dealing of both the Khedive Tewfik and the Ottoman Sultan Abdul Hamid and the attitude of the French government. While Tewfik was giving the impression to Arabi and his allies that he sympathized with their demands and accepted the principle of constitutional government he was telling the sultan that Egypt was in a state of rebellion and, significantly, that Arabi was aiming to form an Arab Empire with himself at its head. Abdul Hamid sent reassurances to both Tewfik and Arabi and waited to see who came out on top. The French government, on the other hand, which had only recently occupied Tunisia,[16] was deeply alarmed that the sultan

16. Under a classical imperialist arrangement, whereby Britain took Cyprus in return for allowing France a free hand in Tunisia. (See below, p. 130.)

might try to raise a pan-Islamic resistance movement against them in North Africa through Egypt. Accordingly, it was strongly opposed to any Turkish intervention in Egypt and therefore to anything, such as the deposition of Tewfik, which might provide an excuse for it. The attitude of the British government of W. E. Gladstone was that anything, including the dispatch of Turkish troops to Egypt, would be preferable to an Anglo-French occupation. On the one hand Britain was committed to an Anglo-French entente, which meant accepting France's position in North Africa, as a barrier to Bismarck's ambitions in Europe. On the other hand, it was a cardinal aim of British policy to prevent France from gaining a predominant position in the eastern Mediterranean. The British government was convinced that if either Britain or France were to intervene militarily in Egypt, war between them was inevitable. It therefore agreed to the dispatch of an Anglo-French Joint Note to the British and French consuls-general in Cairo, which informed Arabi and his colleagues in hectoring tones of the two governments' determination to maintain the khedive on his throne. The effect was to unite the motley coalition of interests around Arabi more than ever before. The Chamber of Notables, which Ismail had established in 1866 as a façade to convince Europe of his liberalism, now came to life and showed its determination to function as a real parliament by voting the budget. When Britain and France objected on the ground that Egypt's debts were such that the Chamber could have no power of decision on the spending of its revenues, a deputation from the Chamber forced the reluctant khedive to appoint a new government in which Arabi was minister of war and the key posts were all held by native Egyptians. A few days later the khedive was obliged to promulgate an Organic Law which gave Egypt proper representative institutions and made him a constitutional monarch.

In this way the Egyptian nationalists threw down the gauntlet to Europe. The trouble was that although Arabi had overwhelming popular support in the country, there were many among the educated élite whose nerve was beginning to fail. There were wealthy landowners in the Chamber of Notables, who felt that it was one thing to install a mildly liberal form of constitutional government which would put political power in their hands, but another to have Egypt under the control of a popular movement led by Colonel Arabi. They also rightly saw that European intervention was now almost inevitable.

However, the National party still appeared to be united; and when in May 1882 the British and French decided to send a joint squadron to Alexandria as a show of force, Arabi's popularity rose to a new height. The danger now was that the popular feeling would produce the kind of incident which would provide the pretext for intervention. This is precisely what happened. Relations between Christians and Muslims deteriorated as every European in Egypt came under the suspicion of wanting an Anglo-French occupation. On 11 June serious rioting broke out in Alexandria in which several hundred people were killed or injured, including at least fifty Europeans. The British consul was seriously wounded.

There is very little doubt that Arabi had no responsibility for instigating these riots; they were the last thing he wanted. They seem to have spread spontaneously after a brawl between a drunken Maltese and an Egyptian donkey-boy. But European officials on the spot reported that it was the military who started the rioting and this version rapidly spread throughout the city. In Britain's Liberal government led by Gladstone there were imperialists and anti-imperialists, of varying depths of conviction. Gladstone had in the past several times expressed his horror at the prospect of occupying Egypt and his support for the idea of 'Egypt for the Egyptians'. The whole cabinet, with the exception of the aged Radical John Bright, now swung in favour of intervention to overthrow Arabi, although they still hoped that it could be done by Ottoman troops on Britain and France's behalf.

Abdul Hamid might have been overawed by the military power of Britain and France but he was not prepared to act as an agent for their interests. He therefore stalled and it soon became apparent that he would do nothing. This left Britain alone, because at this crucial moment the French attitude had changed. At the end of January 1882 the government led by the dynamic imperialist-minded Gambetta fell and was replaced by one led by the milder and more cautious de Freycinet. The new French government believed that Britain was being unnecessarily bellicose, while the British suspected that France was secretly planning to do a deal with Arabi. Accordingly, when Britain issued an ultimatum to Arabi requiring him to dismantle the fortifications he was erecting in Alexandria harbour, de Freycinet refused to be associated with it and ordered the French fleet to sail to Port Said to protect the Suez Canal; British suspicions were therefore confirmed.

When Arabi rejected the ultimatum the British fleet bombarded the forts for ten hours.[17] The Egyptian troops evacuated Alexandria, leaving the city in flames. The Khedive Tewfik, who, while outwardly approving Arabi's actions, had been waiting to see who came out on top, now put himself under Admiral Seymour's protection. Britain's problem had not been solved because the bombardment of Alexandria did not cause Arabi to fall, as the British government hoped, and the Sultan Abdul Hamid, still hedging his debts, refused to declare Arabi a rebel. Some members of the British cabinet still clung to the dwindling hope that a full-scale invasion of Egypt could be avoided, but one by one they went over to the imperialist forward party. Paradoxically, it was France's defection that made this possible. Gladstone himself disliked more than anything the idea of an Anglo-French occupation of Egypt.

With the whole country in a jingo imperialist mood the House of Commons voted overwhelmingly to finance an expeditionary force for Egypt, with Gladstone declaring: 'The insecurity of the Canal is a symptom only and the seat of the disease is in the interior of Egypt, in its disturbed and its anarchical condition.' In fact Egypt was a long way from anarchy. The administration was running quite as well, if not better, than before the National party took power, and after the Alexandria riots law and order were being reasonably maintained.

But the die had been cast. The British force of 30,000 men under Sir Garnet Wolseley sailed up the Suez Canal and took Arabi's force, which totalled 10,000 plus an accompanying rabble of hastily-recruited *fellahin* in the rear. The battle of Tel el-Kebir resulted in 10,000 Egyptian dead; the British lost fifty-seven dead and twenty-two missing. In his official report on the battle Sir Garnet Wolseley wrote: 'I do not believe that at any previous period of our military history has the British infantry distinguished itself more than upon this occasion.'

Wolseley's troops went on to occupy Cairo. Arabi surrendered and was eventually sent into exile in Ceylon, while the khedive was

17. There is strong evidence that the ultimatum was a deliberate provocation. Lord Northbrook, the First Lord of the Admiralty, had earlier reported to Gladstone: 'If we want to bring on a fight we can instruct B. Seymour [the British Admiral] to require the guns to be dismantled. My advisers do not think they will do much harm where they are.' In fact the fortifications were being built in the eastern harbour, out of sight of the British fleet in the western harbour. A British Radical MP later illustrated the situation in the House of Commons: 'I find a man prowling about my house with obvious felonious purposes. I hasten to get locks and bars, and to barricade my windows. He says that is an insult and threat to him, and he batters down my doors, and declares he does so only as an act of strict defence.'

confirmed on his throne as a British puppet. In a famous laconic decree he announced: 'The Egyptian army is dissolved.'

Britain had achieved its immediate objective but had no clear idea what to do next. Annexation of Egypt was out of the question because the other powers, especially France, had too many interests to allow Britain a monopoly in this vital area. The result would almost certainly be a European war. On the other hand, if Britain was to withdraw its troops almost immediately, there was no guarantee that the satisfactory *status quo* would be maintained. The National party had been destroyed but it could well revive.

The solution that was actually adopted was a typical British compromise, in that it evolved out of the circumstances rather than resulted from any planned act of policy. British troops continued in occupation; but Egypt remained nominally an autonomous viceroyalty of the Ottoman Empire under the suzerainty of the sultan. At the same time British control was exercised by its consul-general from behind the khedival throne and a screen of Egyptian ministers in a system which one of the greatest British imperialists, Lord Milner, was to call the Veiled Protectorate. Although the European powers continued jealously to guard what they considered to be their rights in Egypt under the Capitulations and the Commission of the Debt, British authority was absolute in most things that mattered for the next half of the century. One of the reasons for this was that from 1883 to 1907 it was exercised by one of Britain's most remarkable proconsuls – Sir Evelyn Baring (later Lord Cromer), who held the position so long and acquired such prestige that few British ministers dared to thwart him.

The British occupation of Egypt, which ultimately lasted seventy-four years, was to have profound consequences for the West's relations with the Arabs. Once Britain controlled this most important country of the Arab Near East and stood astride the Suez Canal, Egypt became a vital British interest. It was never formally incorporated into the British Empire but it was emphatically part of the imperial system. Thus although British statesmen could see advantages in withdrawing from Egypt in order to avoid the danger of the clash of interests with other European powers, leading to war, there were always weightier reasons for remaining.

The fact that it was Britain and not France or Britain and France together (as it might so easily have been if Gambetta's government had not fallen) which controlled Egypt meant that Britain was the major power in the east Mediterranean until the middle of the twentieth century. It was the sponsor of the Arab Revolt against the Ottoman Turks when it finally took place and was the decisive voice in the settlement after the First World War which gave the independent Arab states the shape they have today. It was also Britain which bore the major share of responsibility for what the Arabs all regard as the greatest catastrophe in their recent history: the loss of Palestine to Zionist Jews.

It was also of major importance that the occupation of Egypt gave Britain control over the Sudan. This had to wait some sixteen years because, just at the time the British forces landed in Egypt, the Egyptians were in the process of losing their vast quasi-empire on the Upper Nile to the national-religious forces of Sudanese tribesmen led by the Mahdi.[18] For some years Britain was too preoccupied with Egypt's problems to consider the reconquest of the Sudan. But Egypt would not be secure until this had been accomplished, and when the time came it was an Anglo-Egyptian force under a British commander, Herbert Kitchener, which advanced by stages up the Nile to reoccupy Khartoum in 1898. The solution for Sudan's status devised by Cromer was another typical pragmatic British compromise. The Sudan was made an Anglo-Egyptian Condominium with the Union Jack and the Egyptian flag flying side by side over the governor-general's palace in Khartoum. But the equality of status of Britain and Egypt was only a fiction. The governor-general and almost all the senior officials were always Englishmen, and policy was made in London, not Cairo.

Sudan, with its vast territory stretching into tropical Africa and the one third of its population who are non-Muslim and non-Arab, is peripheral to the Arab world. Its political and strategic importance for Britain related to the imperialist scramble for the African continent, and it was this aspect of Kitchener's conquest of the Sudan which so nearly led to war between Britain and France in 1898. Just when Kitchener had slaughtered the Mahdist forces at the battle of Omdurman, a French expedition under Captain Marchand struggled through from West Africa to plant the tricolor on the banks of the Upper Nile at Fashoda. Britain and France were on the brink of war for weeks, until France gave way to *force majeure*. But in one respect Britain's acquisition of the Sudan was of major significance for its relations with the Arabs. The question of who controlled the waters of

18. *Mahdi* means literally 'the [divinely] guided one'. There is no mention of one in the Koran or the Hadith, but early in Islamic history the Muslim masses came to believe that one would appear to destroy the injustice and iniquity in the world.

the Upper Nile was a vital concern for all Egyptians. 'Egypt is the gift of the Nile,' said Herodotus. Consequently, the Egyptian people as a whole and not only the nationalist politicians were never resigned to the loss of the Sudan. The blatant hypocrisy of Anglo-Egyptian equality in the Condominium exacerbated their feelings, and the 'Sudan Question' became the major source of disharmony in Anglo-Egyptian relations. As we shall see, more than anything else it prevented Britain from reaching a satisfactory settlement with Egyptian nationalism in the first half of the twentieth century.

France did not abandon its interest in the eastern Mediterranean after the British occupation of Egypt, but its influence in the area was mainly a cultural one. It maintained and strengthened its links with the Christian populations of the Levant through the schools and missions. French also remained the European language most commonly spoken by the Muslim upper classes throughout the area, including Egypt although it was under British political control. But henceforth France's interest in the Arab world was concentrated on the Maghreb – the area that was universally known until the middle of this century as French North-West Africa.

After the conquest of Algeria, French interest turned to Tunisia. The ruling beys of this country accepted the authority of the Ottoman sultan in foreign affairs, but internally they had absolute authority. Life was dominated by the cities, especially the capital, where a small cultured élite maintained something of the intellectual tradition of Ibn Khaldoun.

In the first half of the nineteenth century the beys found that their authority was declining in the face of the growing political and commercial power of Europe and the deteriorating social and economic situation within the country. They made an attempt to confront this situation by building up a modern army and civil service; but these had to be paid for and the only way to do this was to increase prosperity by encouraging European merchants to settle in the country. This improved trade, but also increased the capacity and willingness of the European powers to interfere. In 1857 Muhammad Bey endeavoured to introduce a positive reform plan which stated as a principle that all individuals had the right to liberty and security before the law and that there should be complete equality between Muslims and non-Muslims. In 1860 the Tunisian élite, under the influence of European ideas, even secured the issue of a constitution which provided for a limited form of representative government. Although this experiment collapsed within a few years because the bey was not sincerely willing to give up his authoritarian powers and the country was too subject to the rivalries of the European powers to be able to work out its own, it was the first of its kind in any Arab country. It was not forgotten by the Tunisians and it remained as a symbol of the later struggle for independence through the name *destur* (Arabic for 'constitution') adopted by the nationalist party. Despite the collapse of the constitution, the attempts at financial and administrative reforms continued, especially under the premiership in the 1870s of Khair al-Din, an exceptionally able Circassian who was a representative of the best of the Ottoman élite. He had been brought to Tunis as a young man in the Mamluke style and devoted his career to the service of the Tunisian state. Khair al-Din and other like-minded Tunisian officials and thinkers still retained hopes of progress and development for the country as an autonomous region of the Ottoman Empire; but the opportunity was taken from them by Europe.

France's occupation of Algeria did not mean that Britain was prepared to regard the whole of North-West Africa as a sphere of French influence. There followed a prolonged struggle over Tunisia, which holds a key position between the western and eastern halves of the Mediterranean. The new united kingdom of Italy was also developing its own imperialist ambitions in the area. During the years of the *Risorgimento* Italian nationalist patriots such as Garibaldi had found refuge in North Africa, and colonists from southern Italy and Sicily began to settle there. In Tunisia the Italian colony was especially numerous and active so this country became the prime object of the Italian government's attention when it began to look for a 'fourth shore' for the settlement of its exploding population.

As we have seen, Britain abandoned its interest in Tunisia to France at the Congress of Berlin in 1878 in return for a free hand in Cyprus. Thereafter, a French occupation of Tunisia was only a matter of time. This time a pretext was found in a raid into Algeria from Tunisia of some mountain brigands. Two French expeditionary columns, one from Algeria and the other from the sea, occupied the country without a fight, and the bey signed a treaty authorizing France to occupy the country and take charge of foreign affairs and finance. Two years later a new agreement gave France a protectorate and not a colony like Algeria; in theory the traditional framework of administration remained. In fact the bey and his government, reduced to two ministers – the premier and a 'minister of the pen' – were no more than a façade. Real power was in the hands of the French resident-general and *controleurs civils* and the country was directly administered by France. Nevertheless, in some real respects the nature of the occupation was a great improvement on that in Algeria. There was no systematic attempt to destroy the native culture or declare it nonexistent. Lands were not confiscated and mosques were not turned into churches. The relative mildness of the régime meant that the struggle for independence was less bitter when it came.

The Ottoman government could do nothing to prevent the loss of another of its Arab provinces. Italy bitterly renounced its ambitions and turned its attention further east to the rather less promising territory of Libya, which it occupied thirty years later. Like the French in Algeria, the Italians tried to convince the Arab population of Libya that they had come to liberate them from the Turkish yoke.

By occupying Tunisia, France secured the eastern flank of Algeria. Its attention was then directed towards Morocco on the western flank. But here the situation was greatly complicated by acute competition among the powers of Europe. Britain was especially concerned over the control of the Straits of Gibraltar. As a Mediterranean maritime power Italy was also interested. Morocco's most immediate European neighbour, Spain, although in a weakened state and no longer an imperial power, having recently lost Cuba and the Philippines, still maintained its right to a say in the affairs of Morocco, a country with which it had such close historical affinity and where it had preserved its territorial enclaves of Ceuta and Melilla. But the real problem was Germany. After the Franco-Prussian war of 1870–71, Germany had sympathized for a time with France's expansion in North Africa as likely to take French minds away from thoughts of revenge. This was despite the fact that France looked on its North African possessions as a potential source of manpower to balance Germany's advantage in population. However, by the end of the nineteenth century, imperial Germany had become concerned at being left out in the scramble for Africa and no longer accepted any French monopoly of interest in the Maghreb.

In 1904 France and Britain came to the arrangement known as the Entente Cordiale, which ten years later led to their alliance against Germany in the First World War. Part of this agreement was that, in return for France's abandonment of its remaining rights to interfere in Egypt, which it had jealously preserved for so long, France would have a free hand in Morocco. France and Italy came to a similar arrangement acknowledging Italy's exclusive interest in Libya; and later in the same year (1904) France and Spain concluded a secret agreement which divided Morocco into two spheres of influence – a Spanish one in the north and a much larger French one in the south.

Germany still far from accepted Franco-Spanish control of Morocco as a *fait accompli* and insisted especially that all the powers should have equality in the pursuit of their economic interests in the country. This led to a series of diplomatic crises, culminating in the incident of 1911 when Germany sent a gunboat to Agadir and nearly sparked off a European war. Under the agreement which settled this crisis, Germany accepted France's right to pacify and organize Morocco in return for a guarantee of economic equality for all the powers.

Morocco's fate was sealed. The last independent sultan was forced to sign the treaty of Fez in 1912 which made his country a French protectorate. Later in the same year Spain signed an agreement with France (not with the sultan) defining the limits of its zone.

Throughout all these developments, the Moroccans, though proud of their jealously preserved independence and ancient culture, had been little more than passive and helpless spectators. The last sultan of real ability – Moulay Hassan (1873–94) – had enjoyed some success in playing off the powers against each other, and had even succeeded in reducing their ability to interfere in Morocco's internal affairs. But his efforts to modernize the country by sending students to study abroad and other measures did not even achieve the qualified success of Muhammad Ali's reforms in Egypt. It came too late. Morocco's fossilized medieval society could not be transformed in a generation, and the technical and material strength of Europe was too powerful.

Moulay Hassan's successors were lesser men. Civil war broke out and France sent troops into eastern Morocco. The sultan's army was in no position to prevent the French protectorate when it came. However, if the French occupation of Tunisia was more respectful of the country's personality than that of Algeria, this was even more true of Morocco. This was partly because the personality was so intense. Morocco had never been part of the Ottoman Empire; its ruling dynasty was indigenous and it had no Turco-Circassian aristocracy. It was also because the first French resident-general, Marshal Lyautey, was a colonial statesman of genius, who, although an intensely French patriot, both loved and understood the nature of Morocco.

The fact that Morocco could put up no organized resistance to France and Spain did not mean that their pacification of the country was simple. The Berber chieftains or *Caids* of the Atlas Mountains submitted to France and became the main pillars of French colonial policy in the interior; but in the Rif mountains in the north a national leader of exceptional ability, Abdel Krim, arose and inflicted a series of defeats on the Spanish and French during the 1920s. Abdel Krim was only finally defeated by the dispatch of a large French army under Marshal Pétain, and the country was not entirely pacified until 1934.

By the beginning of the twentieth century the whole of North Africa from the Red Sea to the Atlantic had come under direct or indirect European control. The Ottoman Empire had lost all its western Arab provinces. To the east, Britain was the paramount power on the southern and eastern fringes of the Arabian peninsula through its occupation of Aden and its treaty-relationships with the Arab rulers of the small Persian Gulf states.[19] Ottoman rule remained over Syria, Iraq and the Hejaz and was even extended in Arabia during the nineteenth century through the occupation of al-Hasa in the east of the peninsula in 1871 and of Sanaa, the capital of mountainous Yemen, in the following year. (Ironically, it was the opening of the Suez Canal in 1869 which made these Turkish military expeditions possible.) In large areas of the interior of the peninsula – notably the principalities of Nejd and Shammar ruled by the families of Ibn Saud and Ibn Rashid – the beduin tribes retained much of their independence in the desert which nobody coveted.

The vast majority of the Arab peoples were ruled either by Christian Europeans or Muslim Turks. The nature of this rule was different both in method and objectives, just as it varied between one European power and another. It is therefore no cause for surprise that Arab reactions towards their rulers should have differed from one Arab country to another, and that when the Arab renaissance took place in the twentieth century it was far from being a homogeneous national movement.

19. These treaties were originally imposed on the rulers in the 1820s, with the backing of the Royal Navy, to bind them to refrain from piracy. In 1892, alarmed at the infiltration of Turks, Iranians, French, Russians and others into an area which Britain had come to regard as its own preserve, the British government entered into the so-called Exclusive Agreements with the rulers, under which they agreed never to cede any part of their territory except to the British government nor to enter into agreement with any government other than the British and not to admit foreign representatives without British consent.

7. The Seeds of Arab Nationalism

The Egyptian historian al-Jabarti, who was an eye-witness of Napoleon's invasion of his country, records what happened when the English fleet which was chasing him arrived off Alexandria. A small boat was lowered and ten Englishmen came ashore. They met the notables of the city and told them they were searching for the French fleet. 'You will not,' they said, 'be able to drive them off. We shall stay here with our fleet to defend your port and we want nothing of you except water and food.' But the notables replied: 'This is the sultan's country; neither the French nor any other people have any rights in it. Please go away.'

The notables answered in the spirit of Muslim defiance of the infidel. They did not reply to the Englishmen as Egyptians – still less as Arabs. The Ottoman Empire, for all its weaknesses and failings, which were only apparent to the tiny minority with enough knowledge of Europe for purposes of comparison, was still the protector and preserver of the Islamic *umma*.

The only serious challenge to this view from among the Arab peoples before the nineteenth century came from the central Arabian deserts in the movement led by Muhammad ibn Abd al-Wahhab. He and his followers demanded a return to the pure Islam of its earliest days. They denounced all the later accretions of saint-worship and Sufism as well as the whole structure of Islamic orthodoxy which had been built up over the centuries and which the Ottoman Empire claimed to represent. They equally attacked the revival of pre-Islamic practices and beliefs among the desert tribes of Arabia who had never really accepted Islam. Abd al-Wahhab's special wrath was directed towards the Ottoman sultan and his government 'including its ungodly inclination towards the filthy devices of the Frankish infidels'.

Before his death in 1787 Abd al-Wahhab joined forces with Ibn Saud, head of a small tribal dynasty in central Arabia. In 1806 the Wahhabi forces led by the Amir Muhammad al-Saud occupied Mecca and had the public prayers read in his name instead of that of the Ottoman sultan. This was an Arab movement in that it was inspired by racial pride in the achievements of Muhammad and his followers in the earliest days of Islam and it was anti-Turkish in that the

Wahhabis believed that the Ottoman sultans had forfeited their right to the caliphate. But its appeal was to Islamic rather than Arab solidarity. It was far removed from modern secular Arab nationalism.

As we have seen, the Ottoman sultan's response to the Wahhabi challenge was to ask Muhammad Ali to send forces to repress it. Ibrahim Pasha's army ejected the Wahhabi tribesmen from Mecca and prayers were said again in the name of the sultan. Muhammad Ali and Ibrahim were spurred by ambition and success to turn against the sultan and came near to replacing his empire with their own. But this empire could hardly be Arab. It is true that Ibrahim Pasha was quoted by a French visitor as saying, 'I am not a Turk. I came to Egypt when I was a child, and since that time, the sun of Egypt has changed my blood and made it all Arab.' The same Frenchman went on to give his opinion that Ibrahim's aim was to found an entirely Arab state and 'give back to the Arab race its nationality and political existence'.[1] But it seems likely that Ibrahim was expressing himself in terms which the Frenchman, imbued like most of his fellow-countrymen with romantic nationalist ideas, would understand and appreciate. Certainly there is nothing to show in Ibrahim's actions that he followed up the idea. Under Muhammad Ali's dynasty the domination of the Arab majority by the Turco-Circassian aristocracy in Egypt became stronger.

From the end of the seventeenth century, when Ottoman power was well past its peak, the sultans and their advisers had been conscious of the empire's growing weakness in relation to Europe. In the eighteenth century the first moves were made to modernize the army and its weapons, and these were intensified by the reforming Selim III after he came to the throne in 1798. But although it was possible for the sultan to overrule the conservative *ulama* and allow the printing of books for the first time, it was more difficult to reform the armed forces against the opposition of the powerful Janissaries who were naturally opposed to the development of a new army on modern lines. In 1807 the Janissaries rebelled with the support of the *ulama* and the mass of the people, and deposed Selim III. It was not until 1826 that his successor Mahmud II was able to free his hands by disarming and massacring the Janissaries.

This time no one rose in support of the Janissaries: the absolute necessity of reform of the empire stood out not only to the European

1. G. Douin, *Mission Boislecomte*, Cairo, 1927, pp. 249–50.

powers but to its increasingly rebellious Christian subjects.[2] It had also become apparent to the *ulama* and to a developing class of educated young Turkish administrators and diplomats who came to be known as the Young Ottomans. With their support an era of half a century of reforms, known collectively as the *Tanzimat* or *Tanzimat-i-Khayriyah* ('Beneficent Legislation') was inaugurated. Reform of the army took precedence; French and Prussian instructors were imported to train a new type of Turkish officer and conscription was introduced. Training schools for doctors and civil servants were established and for the first time students were sent to Europe for their further education. Central and local administration were reorganized and, in what was perhaps the most far-reaching change for the world's major Islamic state, a system of secular jurisdiction was introduced throughout the empire. Only the law of Personal Status (divorce, inheritance, etc.) remained under the *shari'a* law. In 1840 a new penal code based on the French penal code was adopted. A commercial code was promulgated in 1850 and in 1861 special Tribunals of Commerce were established to administer it.

Contact with the West increased. On the one hand, the Young Ottomans were educated or served as diplomats in the European capitals; and on the other, after the European revolutions of 1848, many of the ablest political liberals found refuge in Constantinople and joined the Turkish service. European customs found their way into the capital. The sultan set the example by wearing European dress and giving dinners and balls in Western style.

The trouble was that all these changes – even the introduction of secular law – were superficial because they left the authoritarian power structure of the empire untouched. The reforms were little more than window-dressing, aimed to catch the attention of Europe. The European powers were interested in the status and condition of the Christian subjects of the Ottomans. Therefore the reforms were proclaimed as being aimed at the security and happiness of all citizens equally, regardless of religion or race. In theory a totally new Western and secular principle of full equality before the law of all subjects was being introduced into the Ottoman Empire. But for this to become a reality it would have required a revolution of hearts and minds among those who administered the empire. (It is worth recording that full equality for non-Protestants had not even been achieved in Britain at

2. The Greek revolt, which was to lead to Greek independence in 1832, had begun and the sultan's forces were unable to suppress it.

this time.) The principle of equality was being established by imperial fiat, and because it depended upon the will of the sultan who had no intention of giving up any of his authoritarian powers it could not be genuine. It was rather as if the Bourbon kings of France had formally adopted the principles of the French Revolution.

The consequence was that the aspirations for equality and independence among the Christian subjects of the empire were aroused without being satisfied, while the ability of the European powers to interfere in the internal affairs of the empire, on the ground that the Christians were suffering from discrimination, was strengthened. The Balkan provinces where the Christians were a majority revolted one by one and either achieved their independence or were absorbed into one of the European states which was supporting them. On the other hand, the Christian communities in the Anatolian provinces, such as the Armenians and Greeks, could not hope to achieve independence for themselves through rebellion. Ultimately these were to suffer massacre or expulsion.

For those Ottoman subjects who were Muslim but not Turkish (of whom the great majority were Arabs) the crisis of the empire had a wholly different impact and meaning. Since Bonaparte's invasion of Egypt in 1798 first opened a crack through which the ideas of the French enlightenment might enter the closed Islamic society of the Near East, thoughtful Arabs began to consider the reasons for the evident growth in wealth and power of Europe in relation to the Islamic peoples. The outstanding example in the first half of the nineteenth century was the Egyptian scholar and writer Rifa al-Tahtawi (1801–73), who was sent by Muhammad Ali as *imam* of the first student mission to Persia, and wrote with perception and admiration about French society and its achievements. He noted the cleanliness, the energetic industry and intellectual curiosity of the French people and their devotion to the education of their children.

In considering the best means for improving the situation of his own country he saw the solution in a modern system of education. He not only advocated a return to the study of the rational sciences as in the days of Arab greatness (and insisted that the *ulama* should be familiar with modern developments in this field) but also held that all citizens should be given a political education to foster a social conscience and a sense of communal welfare. These were revolutionary ideas in Islamic society at that time. He even suggested that rulers, although they should be strictly obeyed as in all Islamic societies, should do their utmost to please their subjects and take account of public opinion.

But although these were radical ideas, al-Tahtawi was not aware of it. Like all his contemporaries, he was concerned with the reform of Muslim society in Islamic terms. His emphasis was not on the introduction of new principles but on the revival of the virtues of the past. This has been the constant theme of Islamic reformers until the present day.

Tahtawi's writings lack a sense of urgency. 'Tahtawi lived and worked in a happy interlude of history, when the religious tension between Islam and Christendom was being relaxed and had not yet been replaced by the new political tension of east and west.'[3] Even the French invasion of Algiers, which took place while he was living in Paris, did not act as warning of Europe's future domination of the Near East and he wrote about it in a surprisingly detached spirit.

A man who considered many of the same problems as Tahtawi was the great Tunisian statesman Khair al-Din (see above, pp. 129–130). He also studied and admired Europe's political, social and economic institutions and proposed that the Muslim peoples should take over the best of them. But, like Tahtawi, he always said that this would not mean contravening Islamic tradition and law. He only warned

those who are heedless among the generality of Muslims against their closing their eyes to what is praiseworthy and in conformity with their own religious law in the practice of adherents of other religions, simply because they have the idea engraved on their minds that all the acts and institutions of those who are not Muslims should be avoided.[4]

There was certainly no question of abandoning Islam for the sake of progress because, in Khair al-Din's view, the progress of Europe had nothing whatever to do with its being Christian. Christianity aims at happiness in the next world and not in this. 'If it were a cause of worldly progress, the Papal state would be the most advanced, not the most backward state in Europe,'[5] he wrote.

Similarly, Khair al-Din did not even consider the dissolution of the Ottoman Empire. On the contrary, he took it for granted that it was the protector of the Islamic community, and if he advocated the introduction of constitutionalism, representative institutions and

3. A. Hourani, *Arabic Thought in the Liberal Age, 1798–1939*, London, 1962, p. 81.
4. Khair al-Din, *Aqwam*, p. 5, quoted in Hourani, op. cit., p. 88.
5. Quoted in Hourani, op. cit., p. 91.

freedom of the press it was to strengthen the empire by improving relations between the rulers and their subjects.

In the last quarter of the nineteenth century the crisis of Islam became much more acute. It was no longer possible for Arab intellectuals to take a detached attitude towards the West as it became apparent that France's occupation of Algiers was not an isolated incident in a relatively remote regency of the Ottoman Empire but a prelude to the imposition of a Western hegemony along the whole southern coast of the Mediterranean. At the same time, the nature of Arab–Turkish relations and the way in which Arabs looked upon their Turkish rulers underwent a change as the result of the accession to the Ottoman throne of one of the most controversial figures in the modern history of the Middle East – the Sultan Abdul Hamid II.

Abdul Hamid, who for thirty-three years presided over the affairs of the dwindling empire – the 'Sick Man of Europe' as it was known – raised high hopes among his subjects when he ascended the throne with his reputation as a devout but enlightened and liberal prince. He appointed as Grand Vizier Midhat Pasha, a reforming Ottoman statesman of genius who carried the best hope of establishing the principle of equality between the Turkish and non-Turkish subjects of the empire. Under Midhat a new liberal constitution was promulgated, which reduced the sultan's aristocratic powers and provided for the democratic election of a legislative assembly.

But it was not long before Abdul Hamid showed his true opinion of both liberalism and democracy. Within a year he dismissed Midhat.[6] For the sake of appearances he allowed the elections under the new constitution to proceed and the first Ottoman parliament actually met in March 1877 with deputies from all parts of the empire. Although the deputies had no parliamentary experience, and the elections were held under strong pressure from Ottoman officials, the debates were lively and revealing. As the Istanbul correspondent of the *Daily News* wrote:

> It was the first time that representatives from such distant places as Baghdad, Albania, Armenia and Syria met together. Their discussions were singularly full of interest and even surprises. Though most of the members spoke of serious grievances which required redress in their own district, they were surprised to learn that their own constituencies were not alone as spheres of misgovernment.[7]

6. Midhat was recalled to be governor of Syria in 1878 but was arrested two years later and put on trial. He died in exile, almost certainly by violence, in 1883.

7. Sir Edwin Pears, *Life of Abdul Hamid*, London, 1917, p. 49.

Such open manifestations of popular opinion were not at all Abdul Hamid's intention. Within a year he had dissolved the chamber and suspended the constitution. It remained suspended for thirty years. The sultan then set about reversing the whole process of decentralization of power which had taken place gradually over the years in the Arab provinces. Through an elaborate system of spies and agents he endeavoured to gather all the reins of government into his own hands in Istanbul and to end the virtually autonomous authority of the local Ottoman governors. He was greatly helped in this by the invention of the telegraph and the railway. But if Abdul Hamid was ruthless he was also cunning and devious. In his dealings with the Western powers he had to use all his abilities as a born intriguer to play off one against another, as witness his conduct during the negotiations which led to the British occupation of Egypt (see above). With the Arab provinces which were still under his control he was quite prepared to use force if it was necessary to suppress any stirrings of rebellion; but he was ready to try persuasion first. He not only treated Arab leaders with great generosity when they visited Istanbul but he appointed Arabs to some of the highest positions in the state. One of them, Izzet Pasha, although known contemptuously to the Turks as 'Arab Izzet', was his second secretary for thirteen years and rose to be the most powerful man in the empire after his master.

But Abdul Hamid's principal appeal to the loyalty of his Arab subjects was through the Islamic religion. His predecessors in the eighteenth century had revived their claim to the caliphate of Islam which had become a purely ornamental title. Abdul Hamid went much further to pose as the champion of Islam and the protector of all of the Faithful (such as Indian Muslims) living under Christian governments. It seems that he was persuaded by some leading Arab shaikhs that he had been mistaken in cultivating the friendship of those European Christian governments and that his real destiny was to reunite Islam against Christendom. He took good care that his reputation for piety should be sustained; and where most of his predecessors had been dissolute he was strait-laced and strict in his religious observances. He surrounded himself at his court with scholars and divines, subsidized mosques and theological schools and liberally financed Muslim missionary activities in Asia and black Africa. All this was of course especially calculated to appeal to his Arab subjects. Arabic was still unquestionably the language of religion in the empire. The most famous mosques and institutions of learning were in the Arab provinces.

The strength of pan-Islamic feeling was increasing as a reaction to the nineteenth-century invasion of the world of Islam by Christian Europe, and Abdul Hamid sought to exploit it. However, although he had some success with the Arab masses, he was less able to convince the leading thinkers and Islamic reformers. The most influential of these was Jamal al-Din al-Afghani (1838–97), a man of electrifying personality and with the capacity of a true revolutionary to stir men's hearts and minds. Although almost certainly a Persian Shiite by birth he claimed to be an Afghan Sunni (hence his name) and his principal appeal was to the Muslim majority. The burden of his message was that they should unite in a great pan-Islamic movement to face the common danger of European expansionism. But his revolutionary temper and the methods he advocated – which included the assassination of despots – constantly placed him in trouble with governments. From 1871 to 1879 he was in Egypt where, tolerated by Khedive Ismail, he acquired a following of bright young Egyptian intellectuals who included Muhammad Abduh, the most enlightened of Islamic reformers of the nineteenth century, and Saad Zaghloul, the future Egyptian nationalist leader and champion of the independence movement against the British. Expelled from Egypt by the Khedive Tewfik, with British encouragement, he went to India and from there to Paris where he was joined by Muhammad Abduh, who had himself been expelled from Egypt for his part in the Arabi revolt, and together they formed a secret society of Islamic reformers and published an influential Arabic periodical *al-Urwa al-wuthqa* ('The Indissoluble Link'). From Paris he went to Persia where he became adviser to the shah, but was expelled in 1891 when he tried to organize popular agitation against the shah's plan to grant a tobacco concession to a European company. (Persia's debts and submission to European commerce were comparable to those of the Ottoman Empire.)

It was at this point that Abdul Hamid invited al-Afghani to Istanbul with the intention of harnessing his potent influence in support of his claim to pan-Islamic leadership. The consequence was that al-Afghani, while treated with honour, ended his days virtually as the sultan's prisoner (although he was able to arrange the assassination of the Persian shah who deported him).

In fact al-Afghani's concept of pan-Islam was incompatible with that of a despot like Abdul Hamid. He believed that it was up to the mass of Muslim people to take their destiny in their own hands, to unite and to force their rulers to govern in their interests and defend them against acquisitive foreigners. His most bitter attacks were against those rulers who were only concerned with their own power and privilege. He was a revolutionary in that he introduced a wholly new concept into the world of Islam – that of secular politics. He himself was a sceptic – even an agnostic. For him

the centre of attention is no longer Islam as a religion, it is rather Islam as a civilization. The norm of human action is not the service of God; it is the creation of human civilization flourishing in all its parts. The idea of civilization is indeed one of the seminal ideas of nineteenth-century Europe, and it is through al-Afghani above all that it reaches the Islamic world.[8]

Because he understood that the concept of the political solidarity of the Islamic peoples was too remote and abstract for the mass of the people, he also emphasized the need for loyalty towards a smaller unit: patriotism towards the national homeland (Arabic, *watan*). He proclaimed the danger of adopting an alien language or culture for, as he said,

a people without unity and a people without literature is a people without language. A people without history is a people without glory, and a people will lack history if authorities do not rise among them, to protect and revivify the memory of their historical heroes so that they may follow and emulate. All this depends on a national [*watani*] education which begins with 'the homeland' [*watan*], the environment of which is 'the homeland', and the end of which is 'the homeland'![9]

It would be wrong to suggest that al-Afghani was the first apostle of modern Arab nationalism. No such concept had formed in his mind, let alone among his small circle of friends and disciples. But if he did not plant the seeds of nationalism, he prepared the ground for the planting because he

transformed the significance which Islam ought to hold in the life of the Muslim . . . His political activity and teaching combined to spread among the intellectual and official classes of Middle Eastern Islam a secularist, meliorist, and activist attitude towards politics, an attitude the presence of which was essential, before ideologies such as Arab nationalism could be accepted in any degree.[10]

The effects of al-Afghani's secular revolution on the outlook of

8. Hourani, op. cit., p. 114.
9. Muhammad al-Makhzumi, *The Opinions of Jamal al-Din al-Afghani*, (in Arabic), Beirut, 1941, p. 257, quoted in Sylvia Haim (ed.), *Arab Nationalism: An Anthology*, London, 1962, p. 13.
10. Haim, op. cit., p. 15.

nineteenth-century Muslims were naturally not instantaneous. The process of transformation took place over many years. In fact al-Afghani's most famous disciple and colleague, Muhammad Abduh, reacted against his secular and utilitarian view of Islam. After being an active sympathizer with the Arabi revolt in Egypt, for which he was exiled, Abduh went to join al-Afghani in Paris. But he parted company with al-Afghani in 1885 and settled in Beirut. There he lectured on theology and interested himself in the state of education in the Muslim schools of Syria, currently in a deplorable condition. In 1888 he was allowed by the khedive to return to Egypt to resume his career in public life.

But he did not return to active politics. Like al-Afghani he deplored the pervasive influence of European culture and material civilization in the Islamic countries, and like him he thought that much of the fault lay with the despotism of Muslim rulers. But, unlike al-Afghani, he did not advocate revolutionary action to rectify the situation; instead he believed in evolutionary change through education. If he was not reconciled to British control of Egypt, he did not actively oppose it. He was the subject of the warm, if somewhat patronizing, approval of Lord Cromer, who helped him to the office of mufti of Egypt, the highest judicial post in the land, which he held until his death in 1905.

Abduh was made a judge because the khedive feared his influence on the young, but his real interest was in teaching and educational reform. His approach was broad, liberal and humane and his views were always expressed with the gentle benevolence which was characteristic of his nature. His aim was not to reject but to reconcile and to harmonize. He realized that the existing educational system divided between the ultra-conservative religious schools, headed by al-Azhar, and the state schools which were concerned only with turning out civil servants, was disastrous. He advocated a more comprehensive system in which the curriculum of the religious schools would be expanded and modernized while that of the state schools should include some moral and religious education. He also proposed that the foreign mission schools, where he rightly believed much of the teaching was inimical to Islamic culture, should be brought under closer control.

Like all Islamic modernizers who are not secularists, he maintained that there was nothing intrinsic to Islam which is irreconcilable with modern science and philosophy. But like most of those who set out on the hazardous quest for a reconciliation between their faith and reason he was assailed with doubts. Both Lord Cromer and his friend, the British arabist and romantic poet Wilfrid Scawen Blunt, believed that he had lost his faith. Although Cromer described him as 'the chief hope of Liberal Islam in Egypt', he regarded his efforts to reform al-Azhar as hopeless because, in his view, 'Islam cannot be reformed, that is to say, reformed Islam is Islam no longer; it is something else; we cannot as yet tell what it will eventually be.'

Cromer was right in the sense that Abduh's reforming efforts were ultimately a failure. It is also true that Cromer did nothing to help him to succeed. Although the man who effectively controlled Egypt for a quarter of a century indignantly repudiated the charge that the British had done nothing to help education, there can be no doubt that its neglect was the worst feature of British rule in Egypt. Even when Cromer had paid off Egypt's debts and the budget was showing a surplus, education was starved of funds.

But could Abduh have succeeded even with Cromer's moral and material support? The answer is almost certainly that he could not. The truth is that, although he was a man of exceptional qualities and powerful influence which long survived his death, he was unable to achieve his aims alone. The reformation of Islam could not be the work of one man. His opponents not only included the religious conservatives – that was to be expected – but also the rising genera-tion of Egyptian nationalists, who resented his passive acceptance of British political control, which Abduh regarded as irrelevant to his aims.

It follows from this that Abduh can hardly be regarded as a prophet of modern Egyptian nationalism, still less of Arab nationalism. Yet in one important sense he was a forerunner of the modern nationalist movement. In his teaching Abduh constantly harked back to a golden age of Islam when the Muslim community was led by *al-salaf* – 'the great ancestors' – and before it was corrupted by all the innovations of medieval Islam which had since become entrenched tradition. Abduh, like the Wahhabis in Arabia and the Muslim Brothers of more recent times, dated the decline of Islam from the time that the caliphs began to introduce Turkish mercenaries to maintain order. Under the despotism of these barbarians Islamic civilization withered. It is highly significant that in one of his notable memoranda on education to the Ottoman governor of Syria, Abduh strongly recommended against the imposition of Turkish instead of Arabic as a medium of instruction in Syrian schools. As we have seen, the earlier Ottoman sultans had shown their respect for Arabic and its special place in

Islam. But at that time education was almost entirely religious. In their educational reforms of the nineteenth century the Ottomans tried to impose Turkish as the language of instruction for all subjects other than religion. Language became a means of asserting Turkish domination in the empire.

This aspect of Abduh's ideas was developed by one of his outstanding disciples – the Syrian Rashid Rida (1865–1935) who came to Egypt in 1897 and founded the influential review *al-Manar* ('The Lighthouse'), which he edited for the rest of his life. Like al-Afghani and Abduh – and indeed all Arab intellectuals of the time – Rida was passionately concerned with finding the reasons for the weakness and backwardness of the Islamic world in relation to the West. Even more than Abduh, Rida saw the answer in the disunity of Islam under the Turks. Although the Turks had conquered vast new territories and their empire had lasted much longer than that of the Arabs, he did not see this as having been advantageous to the Islamic world. On the contrary; 'It is in the countries which were conquered by the Arabs that Islam spread, became firmly established and prospered. Most of the lands which the Turks conquered were a burden on Islam and the Muslims, and are still a warning of clear catastrophe,' he wrote in *al-Manar*. In another article, entitled 'The Civilization of the Arabs', he wrote:

> To care for the history of the Arabs and to strive to revive their glory is the same as to work for the Muslim union which only obtained in past centuries thanks to the Arabs, and will not return in this century except through them, united and in agreement with all races.

This theme was taken up even more forcefully by another Syrian, Abdul Rahman al-Kawakibi (1849–1902), who came to Egypt from his native Aleppo in the year after Rida and published two books which became the first gospels of Arab nationalism. Like Rida, he asserted that the regeneration of Islam must come through the Arabs and specifically the Arabs of Arabia who, he said, had preserved both their sense of freedom and their solidarity or *asabiyya* and suffered from no racial, religious and sectarian divisions. He went further to say that the caliph should be an Arabian Arab living in Mecca and presiding over a revivified and unified Islam.

It may be seen from this that Rida and Kawakibi's ideas were akin to those of the Wahhabis of Arabia who had rebelled against Ottoman rule in the early nineteenth century. Rida in particular was an Islamic puritan and fundamentalist, who showed active sympathy with the efforts of the Saudi Wahhabis to unite the Arabian peninsula under their rule. At the same time, like the Wahhabis, his primary concern was with the regeneration of Islam. Rida was 'more an Arab *Muslim* than a Muslim *Arab*'.[11] Rida and Kawakibi were pan-Islamists rather than pan-Arabs, although, like al-Afghani, they helped to prepare the ground for Arab nationalism. They believed that the Arabs should regain the leadership of Islam, but meanwhile, for good or ill, the sultan was caliph and the chief protector of the Islamic community. Neither Rida nor Kawakibi were thinking at this stage of the break-up of the Ottoman Empire.

That the attitude towards the Ottoman Empire of men like Rida, Kawakibi and other Arab thinkers of the time should be ambiguous was hardly surprising. As we have seen, their chief concern was with the regeneration of Islam in order to throw off the domination of Europe. But they were both Syrians who had left their homes, where they had lived under oppressive Ottoman rule, for the relative freedom of British-controlled Egypt. (Many other Syrians and Lebanese did likewise; for years the Cairo press and publishing world was largely dominated by Syrian-born Egyptians.) Yet Britain, as the foreign occupying power, was undoubtedly the enemy, and any national movement in Egypt, whether it was primarily Islamic, Arab or native Egyptian, was bound to develop as an anti-British force. Egyptian nationalism, which remained dormant for some years after the suppression of the Arabi revolt, began to revive in the 1890s. It appeared to have found a leader for a time in the young Khedive Abbas II, who succeeded his father Tewfik in 1892 on his premature death at the age of thirty-nine. Abbas tried to assert himself as the head of an independent state and reject British tutelage. But he chose his ground badly, as when he tried to call Lord Kitchener to account for the way he was training the new Egyptian army, and ultimately he was humiliated and reduced to a helpless cypher by the formidable Cromer. Abbas had been encouraged to hope for real support from the sultan and from Britain's imperial rivals among the powers, especially France, but this remained confined to verbal encouragement which was of little use when Cromer held the reins of power in his hands.

For Abbas, like nearly all the family of Muhammad Ali, the love of Egypt took second place to concern for his own autocratic power. Egyptian nationalism had a much more genuine leader in the

11. Sylvia Haim (ed.), op. cit., p. 24.

1890s in a slender and passionate young French-trained lawyer named Mustafa Kamel (1874–1908), who for years before his premature death succeeded in stirring the hearts and minds of his fellow-Egyptians with his speeches and articles denouncing the British occupation. Cromer treated him with contempt, as he did all those he called 'gallicized Egyptians'. By this he meant those young men who had managed to secure a Western university education, which, in Cromer's view, cut them off from the real needs of their fellow-countrymen and fitted them only to make inflammatory and irresponsible speeches. Cromer ignored the fact, which was pointed out by some English liberal critics, that it was his consistent refusal to allow educated young Egyptians any real responsibility that made them irresponsible.

Cromer's disdainful attitude towards Egyptian nationalism (he patronized Abbas in his classic apologia *Modern Egypt* and ignored Mustafa Kamel entirely) helped to foster it. Indeed Cromer denied the very existence of an Egyptian nation. He and most of his British colleagues held the view that since the European communities (Greeks, Italians, Maltese, etc.) controlled the country's economic life and produced most of its wealth (in contrast to the 'gallicized Egyptians') they should be given a preponderant and permanent voice in the country's government. Any 'Egypt for the Egyptians' policy was nonsense, said Cromer. 'The only real Egyptian autonomy . . . is one which will enable the dwellers in cosmopolitan Egypt, be they Muslim or Christian, European, Asiatic, or African, to be fused into one self-governing body.'

Ultimately Cromer was brought face-to-face with the reality of Egyptian nationalism by an incident which was a turning-point in the British occupation of Egypt and a major event in the annals of European imperialism. In June 1906 some British officers were shooting pigeons near the village of Denshawai. They had been warned not to do so because the villagers raised the pigeons for food. A group of *fellahin* attacked them and later one officer who had fled back to his unit was found dead from the combined effect of head-wounds and sunstroke. The British soldiers seized a villager standing beside the body and clubbed him to death.

In the ensuing uproar, with the British press and the panic-stricken foreign communities demanding exemplary punishment to prevent a peasants' revolt, fifty-two villagers were arrested and tried, four were executed and hanged outside the village, three were flogged, and others were sentenced to long terms of hard labour. The bitter resentment among Egyptians at all levels wiped out the memory of the beneficial effects of Cromer's rule. Those leading Egyptians, such as the disciples of Abduh, who had been prepared to tolerate, if not to accept, the continuation of the British occupation were converted overnight and Mustafa Kamel gained a million new followers.

But there was one fundamental inconsistency in Mustafa Kamel's position which he never overcame. The hero of Egyptian nationalism was also an enthusiast for the pan-Islamic movement, which in his case meant supporting the rights of the Ottoman sultan, from whom he expected support. When in 1906 Abdul Hamid was building his Hejaz railway to Medina he landed a force at the head of the gulf of Aqaba and laid claim to the whole of the Sinai peninsula. Kamel led the nationalists in a vigorous campaign in his support and it was left to Cromer to champion the cause of Egypt's territorial integrity with the help of a display of force by the British fleet. Cromer's concern was to keep the Turks away from the Suez Canal but there were many patriotic Egyptians who saw no point in abandoning Sinai, which had widely come to be regarded as Egyptian territory, for the rather nebulous cause of Islamic solidarity. This was one of the first and most striking examples of the clash between local nationalism and pan-Islam. In the twentieth century the same type of conflict would arise with pan-Arabism when Syria, Egyptian or Iraqi interests clashed with the cause of Arab unity.

In Egypt it was the local nationalism which predominated over pan-Islam and, until quite recent times, over pan-Arabism also. It was to the cause of 'Egypt for the Egyptians' that the politically active devoted their energies during the first half of the twentieth century. The pan-Islamic element in Mustafa Kamel's nationalism was more tactical than ideological. He hoped for the support of the Ottoman sultan against the British. At the same time he was aware of the danger that it might alienate Egyptian non-Muslims and he went out of his way to encourage Egyptian Copts to join his movement.

It was not inevitable that Egyptian nationalism or patriotism should triumph over the feeling of Islamic solidarity. As we have seen, the sentiment hardly existed at the beginning of the nineteenth century. The notables of Alexandria told the British sailors who were chasing Napoleon that Egypt was 'the sultan's country'. Muhammad Ali secured for Egypt a large measure of independence, but this was to serve his personal ambitions. He could hardly be an Egyptian patriot when he did not regard himself as an Egyptian. In the second half of the nineteenth century those who had most influence on political thought – al-Afghani, Abduh and their disciples – were intent on reforming Islam rather than securing freedom and independence for the Egyptian nation, even if they were able to understand the powerful influence of national (*watani*) feeling.

Colonel Arabi's revolt originated as an army mutiny but developed into a genuine national movement of 'Egypt for the Egyptians'. However, this only lasted a few months before being destroyed at the battle of Tel el-Kebir. The building of a new national movement with foundations among the Egyptian masses took place over many years under the British occupation.

British rule in Egypt was unique of its kind. As we have seen, Cromer and his colleagues dismissed the idea that there was an Egyptian nation. This may have been unwise; but it meant that the national idea was not regarded as a menace which had to be eliminated. Cromer did devise a potentially disastrous plan to give Egypt a constitution which could have given the foreign communities a permanent veto over all legislation, but neither he nor his successors ever got round to implementing it. Whereas the French in Algeria or the Italians in Libya set out to colonize the country in the style of the Roman imperium, the British never attempted the hopeless task of anglicizing Egyptian society.

Cromer's view, which was shared by most other Englishmen in Egypt, was that Britain's role was restricted to keeping the Egyptian inn on the British imperial highroad to India clean and orderly. It should make a profit, the servants must be well treated and the senior staff should be British; but there was no question of transforming it into an all-British hotel.[12]

Britain's insistence on maintaining what it regarded as its vital interests in Egypt and its predominance in the Sudan meant that the struggle with the Egyptian national independence movement was long and sometimes bitter. Cromer's successor Eldon Gorst attempted to introduce some mildly liberal reforms to give Egyptians a larger share of political and administrative responsibility. But Gorst died prematurely in 1911 and his successor, the imperial-minded Lord Kitchener, reimposed a Cromerian iron hand. When Egyptian nationalism, necessarily quiescent during the First World War when Egypt was under the occupation of a vast Allied army, broke out in violent rebellion in 1919 the British were taken by surprise. Yet for all this the amount of blood the Egyptians had to shed to end foreign rule bears no relation to the sufferings of the Algerians in a similar cause.

12. Peter Mansfield, *The British in Egypt*, London, 1971, p. 323.

Even the horror aroused by the Denshawai incident must be regarded as a tribute to the physical mildness of the British occupation.

So it was that when the time came for the Arab awakening and the split in the Islamic world between Turks and Arabs, Egypt remained outside the Arab movement until much more recent times. This did not mean that it was totally detached and indifferent. Cairo, with its hidebound but still prestigious al-Azhar, remained the greatest centre of Arabic/Islamic culture. Muhammad Abduh's influence was still pervasive, even if he would hardly have recognized some of his results. Just as Syrian Arab intellectuals found refuge from Ottoman oppression in British-controlled Egypt, the plans for the Arab Revolt were hatched in Cairo under British auspices. Nevertheless, the impulse for the Revolt did not come from Egypt but from Syria and the deserts of Arabia.

Some misleading impressions have arisen about the true origins of 'the Arab awakening'. The phrase was given wide currency by the book of the same name which was published in 1938. This is an account of the origin and growth of the Arab national movement by a Palestinian Arab Christian named George Antonius, who himself played a leading role in it before his early death in 1942. The work is a masterpiece and its prose style is among the best of any writer for whom English was not his native language. Because of this the book has become a classic and his analysis has widely become accepted as correct.

Antonius traced the origins of the Arab renaissance, after what he calls the 'False Start' under Muhammad Ali and Ibrahim Pasha, to an infant movement in Beirut in the 1880s. This was a secret society, pledged to the eviction of the Ottoman Turks from Syria, which published some seditious posters and pamphlets. But although this society's activities caused a small stir among the foreign community in Beirut they never led to anything. The reason for this was simple. The society was almost entirely composed of educated Arab Christians, the product of the intellectual revival which had been stimulated in Lebanon in the nineteenth century by Catholic and Protestant mission schools. They wanted to secede from the Ottoman Empire in order to cease being second-class citizens as Christians under a Muslim government. They soon realized that they would achieve nothing without the cooperation of Syrian Muslims; but although they could find some common ground in their demand for Arabic to be recognized as the official language in Syria (and Arab Christians played a special role in the revival of Arabic literature in the nineteenth century) Arab Muslims were not seriously interested in the break-up of the Ottoman Empire at this stage. On the evidence of the last surviving member of the secret society, Faris Nimr Pasha (who later became George Antonius's father-in-law), they soon abandoned their objectives as hopeless. Faris Nimr was one of those Syrians who emigrated to Egypt where he prospered under the British occupation, of which he was a warm, although not uncritical, admirer. With two other Syrian Christians he founded the influential newspaper *al-Muqattam*.

At a later stage Arab Christians (such as George Antonius himself) were to play a vital role in the Arab nationalist movement. But the time was not yet ripe during the reign of Sultan Abdul Hamid. The rumbles of discontent among Arab Muslims were ominous and widespread. Denis de Rivoyre, a Frenchman who in 1884 travelled from one end of the Arab-speaking world to the other, wrote:

> Everywhere I came upon the same abiding and universal sentiment: hatred of the Turks . . . The notion of concerted action to throw off the detested yoke is gradually shaping itself. . . . An Arab movement, newly risen, is looming in the distance; and a race hitherto down-trodden will presently claim its due place in the destinies of Islam.[13]

But even this Frenchman – and, as we have seen from the time of Muhammad Ali, the French could be romantically imaginative about nationalism – agreed that the Arab movement was still 'in the distance'. The vast majority of the Arab Muslims had not yet begun to think in terms of a revolt to break away from the Ottoman Empire. A few intellectuals in Cairo like Kawakibi might be demanding that the leadership of Islam should be restored to the Arabs, but they were thinking more of the reform of the greatest Islamic state in the world and not its partition. What they feared most was that the current of Western ideas which was invading the Arab Near East might be the vanguard of a political and military occupation of the kind that had already taken place in North Africa. What they wanted to do was to reform the empire in order to strengthen its defences. It is significant that the first Arab who publicly advocated the break-up of the Ottoman Empire was a Christian, Negib Azoury, in a book which he published in 1905 in Paris, where he was in exile, entitled *Le reveil de la nation arabe*. In this he proposed the creation of a new Arab kingdom with natural frontiers on the Tigris, Euphrates, Suez Canal,

13. Denis de Rivoyre, *Les vrais Arabes et leur pays*, n.p., n.d., pp. 294–5, quoted in G. Antonius, *The Arab Awakening*, New York, 1965, p. 90.

Mediterranean and Indian Ocean and a member of Muhammad Ali's family on the throne. But Azoury's voice was lonely. He had no followers although his book created a stir, and there are strong suspicions that he was a paid French agent.

Abdul Hamid was quite astute enough to make full use of this sense of defensive solidarity. The crowning achievement of his Islamic policy was the building of the Hejaz railway from Damascus to the Holy City of Medina. The scheme was master-minded by his shrewd and energetic second secretary Izzet Pasha. It took seven years to build (1901–8) at a cost of £3 million, of which more than one third was raised in voluntary donations from all over the Muslim world. The declared aim of the project was to facilitate the transport of Muslim pilgrims to the Holy Cities. This it did, but at the same time it made it easier to move troops into the heart of Arabia and thereby strengthened the Porte's control over the outlying provinces of the empire. As the British ambassador to Constantinople wrote in 1907: 'The effect has been that he has commanded, to an unprecedented degree, the blind obedience of his subjects, and reconciled them to a despotism more absolute than has perhaps ever been known in the whole course of history.'

Abdul Hamid administered his despotism through a vast web of spies and agents. He developed the technique of 'divide and rule' into a fine art by exploiting and encouraging tribal discord or family feuds wherever he could. He was certainly not above arranging the assassination of a local leader who disputed his authority. Sometimes, however, such men were too eminent or popular. In this case he issued them with an invitation, which they could hardly refuse, to come and settle in Constantinople where they would be treated with honour and deference but kept under the close watch of the sultan's spies.

Historically the most important of these compulsory guests of the sultan was Hussein ibn Ali, thirty-seventh in line of descent from the Prophet Muhammad and a member of the Hashemite family of Arabia, which by long tradition had provided the holder of the prestigious office of Grand Sharif of Mecca. In 1893 Hussein, at the age of thirty-nine, arrived in the capital with his wife and four young sons, Ali, Abdullah, Feisal and Zaid, to stay for fifteen years in a villa on the Bosphorus. Dignified and imperious, if sometimes wilful and petulant, Hussein became a familiar figure in Constantinople where he had a large circle of admirers. His sons were educated and grew to manhood during this period.

Despite Abdul Hamid's efforts to strengthen the empire through centralization and to increase its military power with the help of a German military mission, which arrived in Constantinople under Colonel von der Goltz in 1883 to begin a programme of modernizing the Ottoman forces, Turkey was still the Sick Man of Europe, weak and vulnerable in its relations with the European powers. Unable to threaten with gunboats, Abdul Hamid was obliged to use every technique of intrigue and diplomacy in his dealings with Europe. His Islamic policy and his self-promotion as the sultan-caliph were aimed to appeal as much to the Muslim subjects of other empires as to his own: to central Asians ruled by the Russian tsar, to the Arabs and Berbers of French North Africa and to the Muslims of British India. He could also exploit the rivalries between the European powers themselves, and here an encouraging opportunity presented itself in the existence of the ambitious and rising power of Kaiser Wilhelm's Germany. The dazzling success of Prussian arms in the 1870–71 war with France encouraged the Turks to invite the Germans to improve their army. But the Germans were looking for economic as well as military expansion and were deeply resentful that Britain and France were so far ahead in the imperial scramble for Africa.

Germany provided the obvious balance for the overweening influence of the two powers which had already seized large areas of the Ottoman Empire, and Germany was looking eagerly eastwards for political and economic expansion – the policy known as the *Drang nach Osten.* The influx of German capital into Turkey amounted to an invasion. German companies obtained concessions to extend the railway system of Anatolia; and in 1898 Kaiser Wilhelm visited Constantinople to carry the line on from Konya to Baghdad. This was the famous Baghdad railway, which among other things (since the intention was to carry it on to Kuwait) would have created a direct link between the Mediterranean and the Persian Gulf and offered a direct strategic threat to the British position in India.

A Turco-German axis was being formed. Kaiser Wilhelm continued his journey from Constantinople to Jerusalem and Damascus, stressing at all times his sympathies for Islam and the sultan-caliph. In Damascus he said: 'His majesty the sultan and the 300 million Muslims who revere him as the caliph may rest assured that they will always have a friend in the German emperor.' It was not lost on Germany's rivals that most of these 300 million were *their* subjects, and not those of the sultan.

But if the Muslim masses were still loyal to the sultan, a reform movement was growing among the élite. Driven underground by Abdul Hamid in the early years of his reign, the Young Ottoman movement, or Young Turks as they were now called, revived in the last decade of the century. Initially, the movement consisted of exiled groups in Europe or Cairo, who joined to form reform societies and publish newspapers and journals attacking the sultan. But they also had links with a growing underground movement inside Turkey which from 1890 onwards began to gather support, especially among the students of the military colleges. In 1895 a clandestine organization of Young Turks in Constantinople adopted the name of Committee of Union and Progress. An attempted coup in 1896 was crushed and its leaders exiled, but the movement continued to grow. Abdul Hamid tried to win over the exiles with a mixture of threats and promises, but they resisted. In 1899 they were joined by one of his own cousins. In 1906 there was a development which was ultimately fatal to Abdul Hamid: revolutionary cells began to be formed by serving officers in the field. Among them was a young captain, Mustafa Kemal, later known as Atatürk, the father of the Turkish Republic.

In the summer of 1908 matters came to a head as the discontent in the army turned into a full-scale mutiny. The Committee of Union and Progress (CUP) came out into the open and formalized the aims of the mutineers in a demand for the restoration of the Midhat constitution of 1876. Abdul Hamid hesitated and then gave way. On the following day he released all political prisoners, abolished the censorship and disbanded his corps of 30,000 spies.

The news that the 1876 constitution had been restored was greeted with enormous enthusiasm in the Arab provinces. An American eye-witness in Syria wrote:

> The whole empire burst forth in universal rejoicing. The press spoke out. Public meetings were held, cities and towns decorated; Moslems were seen embracing Christians and Jews, and inviting one another to receptions and feasts . . . Syria has never seen such rejoicing. Can it be true? Will it last? were questions in all mouths.[14]

Elections were held under the 1876 constitution and the new parliament met on 17 December 1908.[15] Of the 260 members, 119 were

14. H. A. Jessup, *Fifty-three Years in Syria*, New York, 1910, vol. II, pp. 785–7.

15. In his speech from the throne Abdul Hamid said: 'The intellectual progress of the people having reached the desired standard, we have acquired the conviction that parliament should once more assemble as a guarantee of the present and future prosperity of our country . . .'

Turks and 72 Arabs (the remainder being Kurds, Albanians, Greeks, Armenians and other minorities). When it is considered that out of a total population of the Ottoman Empire (excluding Egypt) of about 22 million some 10·5 million were Arabs and 7·5 million Turks, it is clear that even Midhat's liberal constitution did not provide for racial equality.

In fact although the Arabs reacted enthusiastically to the Young Turks' revolution they took little part in it. They were not an important element in the CUP; 'although a few Arabs, most of them army officers, had joined the party and worked hand-in-glove with its leaders, they had done so as Ottoman citizens rather than as Arab nationalists'.[16] Nevertheless the Arabs were entitled to hope that the revolution would lead to greater equality for them with the Turks, even if it did not for the Christian inhabitants of Turkey's remaining Balkan possessions, who generally had little interest in a more liberal Turkey because they were concentrating on achieving their own independence.

Shortly after the coup a new society called the 'Ottoman Arab Fraternity' (*al-ikha' al-arabi al-uthmani*) was founded with great fanfare at a big meeting of the Arab community in Constantinople attended by the CUP leaders. As a gesture of goodwill the CUP decided to end the fifteen years' exile of Hussein ibn Ali and send him to Arabia to take up the post of Grand Sharif of Mecca which had just fallen vacant. They disregarded the advice of Abdul Hamid, who warned against the move.

'Constitutionalism' was the watchword of the day. Japan's victory over Russia in 1905 had had a tremendous impact throughout the Muslim world not only because it was the first case for several centuries of a supposedly backward Asian state defeating one of the Christian powers of Europe, but also of a constitutional government proving more efficient than an autocracy. The Young Turks sincerely hoped that their constitution would do the same for them, but there was a fatal contradiction in their whole attitude towards the meaning of constitutional government.

Among the leading opponents of the Hamidian despotism there were two contrasting ideologies: Turkish nationalism and Ottoman liberalism. The former, which was naturally adopted only by Turks, stood for the continuation and strengthening of the dominance of the Turkish race, language and culture. The latter, which was held by the

16. G. Antonius, op. cit., p. 101.

non-Turks and some liberal Turks, implied the principle of equality for all the Turkish and non-Turkish, Muslim and non-Muslim elements within the empire. This was represented in the Ottoman parliament by the thirty-five members of the Decentralization party; ominously, nearly all its members were non-Turks.

In the first years after their revolution the Young Turks made a sincere attempt to Ottomanize the whole empire. But although the constitution laid down the principle of equality between Muslims and non-Muslims, they privately acknowledged that this was an 'unrecognizable ideal', as one of their leaders, Talaat Bey, said in a speech to members of the local CUP committee at Salonika in 1910.

Ottoman liberalism had been rejected because the great majority of Christian subjects of the empire rejected the attempts to Ottomanize them, which could only be carried out by force. But the Arab Muslims of the empire were soon made to realize that pan-Islam, if adopted by the CUP for tactical reasons, did not mean equality between Turks and Arabs. In fact the CUP was really concerned with promoting a racial policy of pan-Turkism or unity of all the Turkish-speaking peoples in Asia. The CUP very soon shed its professed liberalism. In April 1909 Abdul Hamid had attempted a counter-revolution by inciting the Constantinople garrison to mutiny against the CUP. After an initial success the revolt was suppressed and Abdul Hamid was deposed. The consequence was to make the CUP increasingly authoritarian in its attitudes. The Arabs soon came to feel that they were in a more weakened position in the empire than they had been under Abdul Hamid. One of the first acts of the CUP was to dismiss the sultan's senior Arab advisers, who included Izzet Pasha himself. They denounced them and Arabs in general as reactionary tools of Abdul Hamid. Under external stress, the force of Turkish nationalism soon dominated the weaker strain of liberalism among the new rulers in Constantinople.

The empire was being threatened on all sides by the Christian powers of Europe. In their first four years of power the Young Turks lost all the remaining provinces of Europe (except for eastern Thrace). Austria-Hungary annexed Bosnia and Herzegovina in 1908, Bulgaria finally seceded to become independent, Italy invaded Libya and the Dodecanese, and Greece took Crete. In reaction to these disasters the Young Turks were strongly influenced by pan-Turanian or Turkish irredentist ideas, that is to say the notion that all the Turkish-speaking Muslim peoples of Anatolia and central Asia formed a single nation. These were the ideas that were later developed by the famous Turkish writer Ziya Gökalp. 'One can rightly say that the seeds of the Arab separatist movement began to sprout from the soil of Turkish nationalism from 1909 onwards.'[17]

For these reasons the Arab–Turkish honeymoon was short-lived. The Ottoman Arab Fraternity was banned as politically subversive, and although the important Arab Literary Club was formed in 1909 in Constantinople it could escape suppression only as long as it remained non-political. In 1912 the Ottoman Decentralization party set up its headquarters in Cairo, where British protection gave it relative freedom of action, and it set about trying to impress the rulers of the empire and Arab public opinion with the need for administrative decentralization.

In addition several Arab secret societies were formed, of which the two most important were *al-Qahtaniya*, led by Major Aziz al-Masri (later Inspector-General of the Egyptian army, and noted Egyptian nationalist) and *al-Fatat* or the young Arab society which was founded in Paris in 1911. Al-Qahtaniya aimed to unite the Ottoman Arab provinces in a single kingdom within the empire, which would then become a Turco-Arab dual monarchy along the lines of the Austro-Hungarian Empire. Al-Fatat, the most important of all these societies, aimed at complete independence for the Arab provinces. It moved its headquarters from Paris to Beirut, and then to Damascus, where its membership rapidly increased.

Early in 1913 a group of prominent Arabs who had formed themselves into a committee of reform in Beirut published concrete proposals for reform which, while accepting the authority of Constantinople (as they had to do if they were to avoid immediate suppression), advocated devolution of regional administration to representative local bodies, the adoption of Arabic as a language on an equal footing with Turkish in the Ottoman parliament, and the ending of the practice of conscripting soldiers for service outside their own provinces. When this move aroused a widespread response throughout Syria and Iraq, the CUP dissolved the committee of reform and closed its headquarters.

On the initiative of al-Fatat the movement then shifted to Paris, where an Arab National Congress was held in June 1913. The meeting was hastily organized, and the overwhelming majority of the delegates came from Syria rather than the other Arab provinces of the

17. Zeine N. Zeine, *Arab–Turkish Relations and the Emergence of Arab Nationalism*, Beirut, 1958, p. 77.

empire. However, it aroused considerable interest and caused the CUP to react. Having failed to persuade the French to ban the congress, the CUP sent their secretary to Paris to enter into negotiations with its leaders. The agreement that they reached appeared to be an important victory for the Arabs. Arabic became the official language in the Arab provinces and the medium of instruction in primary and secondary schools, and the important point about localizing military service was conceded. There were to be five Arab governors-general and a minimum of three Arab ministers in the Ottoman government.

But once again Arab hopes were speedily disappointed, as it soon became clear that the CUP had no intention of fulfilling their promises. The concessions were either whittled down until they had no substance or were indefinitely postponed. By the beginning of 1914 the great majority of leading Arabs had abandoned all hopes of reaching an accommodation with the CUP.

In February 1914 anti-Turkish feeling among the Arabs hardened with the arrest and trial of the founder of al-Qahtaniya, Major Aziz al-Masri. He had replaced al-Qahtaniya with a new society, *al-Ahd* ('the Covenant') which consisted almost entirely of army officers, with a preponderance of Iraqis who were the most numerous Arab element in the Ottoman army. When it became known that al-Masri had been secretly condemned to death on a trumped-up charge of having planned to sell Cyrenaica to the Italians, there was a public outcry, which was reinforced by a strong British protest. Eventually al-Masri was released and allowed to return to Egypt.

Even now there was still no sign of open Arab rebellion against the Turks. Ottoman rule was firm in the Arab provinces despite the occasional strikes and disturbances in favour of reform. The Hejaz railway had helped to consolidate the Turkish hold in western Arabia, although the Sharif Hussein was already beginning to justify Abdul Hamid's warnings by causing trouble with the local Turkish governor in asserting his rights and prerogatives.

In the more remote parts of the Arabian peninsula Ottoman authority had always been light. In the Yemen a compromise had been reached in 1911 with the hereditary ruler Imam Yahya, whereby the latter, in return for the acceptance of Turkish suzerainty, acquired virtual independence in the mountainous interior, while the Turks remained in control of the Red Sea Tihama plain. A similar arrangement was made with Muhammad ibn Ali al-Idrisi, ruler of Asir, the province immediately to the north of the Tihama. A new and potentially threatening rebellious Arab force had appeared in the form of Abdul Aziz ibn Saud, the scion of the Saudi family which had formed the alliance with the Wahhabis and occupied Mecca a century earlier. Abdul Aziz had revived the faded fortunes of his house by recapturing the Saudi capital Riyadh and ousting his rival Shaikh Rashid from the Nejd in 1904. He had gone on to seize the east Arabian province of al-Hasa from the Turks in 1913. But this reverse for the Turks was balanced by the close relationship established with the Rashidi tribes who remained in control of the Shammar region of northern Arabia. British influence in Arabia, which had been spreading throughout the nineteenth century through the special treaty relationships established with the petty ruling Arab shaikhs, remained confined to the southern and eastern periphery of the peninsula.

The bitterness of the fighting when the Arab Revolt against the Turks finally broke out, and the atrocities committed by the Turks in their attempts to hold their Arab provinces, do not deny the close affinity between the two peoples derived from centuries of symbiosis in an Islamic community in which racial 'apartheid' was unknown. In principle the governors, senior administrators and judges in the Ottoman Empire's provinces were sent from Constantinople and appointed for one year only to prevent them from putting down roots and identifying themselves with the local community. In practice – especially in the more outlying parts of the empire – a large share of political power passed into the hands of the local élite of shaikhs, *ulama* and landowners, and this was accepted by the sultan's government in Constantinople. Even Abdul Hamid's attempts to reverse the process by centralizing all power in his hands were only partially successful. The ruling groups in the various provinces as well as Anatolia together constituted a real entity: the Ottoman governing class. This may have varied in composition from one part of the empire to another – Arab-Berber in North Africa, Arab-Turco-Circassian in Egypt, Arab-Kurdish in Iraq – but it had common characteristics. Its members mingled freely and frequently intermarried. In the nineteenth century, when the sultan's Arab provinces were reduced to Syria, Iraq and parts of Arabia, they shared a common education in the secondary schools and colleges which had been created by the Ottoman educational reforms. Only a few of the Arab Ottoman élite were educated at the foreign institutions of learning in Beirut or Cairo.

As we have seen, the initial Arab antagonism towards the Turks was more cultural than social or political. The Arabs deeply resented the 'Turkification' of the educational system and the replacement of Arabic by Turkish for all except religious studies. After the bitterness engendered by the Arab struggle for independence, Arab historians writing with hindsight tended to underestimate the value of the Ottoman educational reforms, which began with the education law of 1869 providing in theory for a minimum compulsory schooling of four years from the age of seven. In 1914 there were some 400 state schools in Syria with about 21,000 pupils at the elementary level and about 900 at the secondary and higher levels. In Iraq there were about 170 schools of all grades with about 7,400 elementary and secondary. These numbers may be pitifully small, but it was to be some years before they were improved upon after the overthrow of Ottoman rule when the Arabs were under European rule. As a noted Arab educationalist has remarked:

While the Turks laid no claim to superiority over the Arabs in civilization, the Europeans did so with undisguised arrogance. For in their different ways the British, the French and even the Italians and Spaniards took it for granted that they had special insight into what was in the best interests of their Arab subjects, and accordingly rejected or side-tracked Arab attempts at improving their educational lot.[18]

When the Arab Revolt came it was not an uprising of the whole Arab people to throw off the Turkish yoke. Only a small minority who had become embittered and intransigent as a result of their treatment at the hands of the Young Turks saw it in those terms. Most of the Arab reformers wanted to change the empire in order to strengthen it, and the great majority of the Arab people remained loyal to the caliphate and sultanate. Iraqi officers may have formed the majority in the subversive al-Ahd secret society; it is also true that most Iraqi army officers fought on the Turkish side in the First World War.

18. A. L. Tibawi, *Islamic Education*, London, 1972, p. 85.

8. The Arab Revolt

By the spring of 1914, the Young Turks were deeply regretting their rejection of Abdul Hamid's advice in having sent Hussein ibn Ali back to Arabia as Grand Sharif of Mecca, but they were forced to admit that there was no easy solution. A mere threat to remove him from office had been enough to provoke a violent reaction in the Hejaz. To have used force would have undermined the basis of the pan-Islamic policy which the CUP still relied upon to maintain the loyalty of the Arab provinces.

But if the moral authority of Hussein's office was powerful, it was all he had. There were only a few hundred beduin warriors to defend him against the Ottoman armies. Accordingly, he turned to Britain as a possible ally and in the spring of 1914 he sent his thirty-year-old second son the Amir Abdullah to Cairo to call upon Lord Kitchener, the famous conqueror of Sudan who was now, as agent and consul-general in Egypt, in charge of British policy in the Near East. The meeting was inconclusive. Abdullah did not wish to commit himself at that stage to Britain, while Kitchener also did not want to be committed to an anti-Turkish policy. Britain was still committed to the preservation of the Ottoman Empire for the old nineteenth-century reasons. A war with Germany seemed inevitable, but although the Young Turks had continued some of Abdul Hamid's pro-German policies it was by no means certain that Turkey would enter the war on the German side. They had become concerned by German imperial expansionism and Anglo-Turkish relations had recently improved. It was of the greatest importance to Britain that war with Turkey should be avoided. India contained 70 million Muslim subjects who still regarded the Ottoman sultan as the caliph, or ruler of the Faithful; and no one could be sure if, in the event of war with Turkey, they would fight against the sultan-caliph on behalf of his Christian majesty King George V.

Nevertheless, this first encounter between Kitchener and the young Hashemite prince was to have momentous consequences. It led to the creation of three Arab monarchies, with British support, and a political association between Britain and the Arabs which, although impermanent and in many ways disastrous, was to dominate the affairs of the Near East for a generation.

The first Kitchener–Abdullah meeting had no practical results, but it established a rapport between the two men. In August 1914 the whole situation changed. British diplomacy had failed and Turkey signed a secret treaty of alliance with Germany. The Ottoman Empire was now effectively ruled by a triumvirate of Young Turks – Enver, Talaat and Jemal. But Enver Pasha was the dominant figure of the three and he was inclined towards Germany. On 5 November Turkey declared war on Britain, France and Russia.

This action automatically transformed the nature of Britain's relations with the Arabs. In Egypt it meant that the nominal Ottoman suzerainty was ended. After thirty years of hidden and indirect British rule, Egypt was formally declared a British protectorate; the pro-Turkish Khedive Abbas II was deposed and replaced by his elderly and amicable uncle Hussein Kamel, who was given the title of sultan.

Britain had two main concerns about Egypt: the security of the Suez Canal and the potential effect on the Egyptians of the inevitable call to *jihad* or Holy War against the infidel that would be issued from Constantinople. There were numerous influential Turks in Egypt, especially in the harems of the aristocracy.

The declaration of the protectorate was tactful in stating that the British government was 'animated by no hostility towards the caliphate. The past history of Egypt shows, indeed, that the loyalty of Egyptian Mohammedans towards the caliphate is independent of any political bonds between Egypt and Constantinople.' This may have been wishful thinking, but it was at least partly true. The pro-Turkish feeling that existed among Egyptian nationalists such as Mustafa Kamel had been largely destroyed by the Young Turks. Even the most virulently anti-British among them had no desire to be ruled by Turks in practice. As Lord Kitchener's oriental secretary Ronald Storrs remarked: 'Pious Muslims shake their heads and say, "We wish the Turks all success – from afar," the last portion of the benison receiving the emphasis.'[1]

Pan-Islamic feeling scarcely affected the Egyptian armed forces as had been feared. It was only some Muslim troops in two Indian battalions of the Suez Canal defence force who deserted to the Turks. Those who were caught were shot, and the trouble was prevented from spreading. A succession of Indian Muslim ruling princes were

1. Sir Ronald Storrs, *Orientations*, London, 1937, p. 154.

brought on visits to the Canal zone to help stiffen the morale of the troops.

But if the Egyptians had accepted their transfer from nominal Muslim to open Christian suzerainty with remarkable calm, there was no guarantee that the Arabs in the empire would remain unresponsive to the call to *jihad*. The potential effect on Muslims in India, French North Africa or the Russian Empire was incalculable.

Here the Grand Sharif was the key, because to be fully effective the call to *jihad* had to be issued from Mecca. The Ottoman government at once began to exhort Hussein to endorse the call.

Hussein was confronted with a difficult choice: either he could side with Turkey and hope that after the war the grateful Turks would satisfy Arab aspirations, or he could throw in his lot with the Allies in the hope that they would help the Arabs to win their independence. The success of either policy depended on numerous unforeseeable factors. Hussein's own family was divided, with Amir Abdullah favouring an alliance with Britain and the third son Feisal at that time inclined towards siding with Turkey.

Hussein's policy was to stall the Turks as long as he could while he tried to extract some form of promise of support from the British. In a stream of messages to the sultan, he assured him that he was praying for success in the war against the infidel ('May God lay them low'), but he was sure his sublime majesty would understand that the time was not propitious, as the British might attack the people of the Hejaz and bombard them into rebellion against the Ottoman Empire. Meanwhile, he was sending a comparable flow of secret messages to Cairo to sound out the British and into Syria and Iraq to test the reaction of the Arab resistance groups.

As soon as war broke out, Lord Kitchener was recalled to London to join the war cabinet. But he had immediately grasped the significance of Amir Abdullah's overtures for Allied war strategy and had cabled him: 'If the Arab nation assists England in this war England will guarantee that no intervention takes place in Arabia and will give Arabs every assistance against external foreign aggression.' But Hussein and the Arab nationalists of Syria and Iraq wanted much more than this in return for their momentous and daring action in splitting the world of Islam and joining the Christian powers of Europe against the sultan-caliph.

The trouble was that of all the Allies Britain had done the least to devise a clear Middle Eastern strategy. It had no doubt that the Ottoman Empire would have to go. The Sick Man of Europe who had been kept alive for so long in Britain's interests must be allowed to die. As *The Times* wrote on 3 November 1914: 'Turkey has betrayed the interests of Islam by making wanton war on the Allies, and has thereby pronounced her own death sentence.' But the cabinet had not decided what should happen to Turkey's Arab provinces. The Foreign Secretary Sir Edward Grey told the French ambassador five months after the war had started that the cabinet had agreed that,

when Turkey disappeared from Constantinople and the Straits, there must, in the interests of Islam, be an independent Moslem political unit somewhere else. Its centre would naturally be the Moslem Holy Places and it would include Arabia. But we must settle what else should be included. We, ourselves, had not yet come to a definite opinion whether Mesopotamia should be included in this independent Moslem state, or whether we should put forward a claim for ourselves in that region.[2]

The British-controlled Indian government, on the other hand, was convinced that the immediate occupation of Mesopotamia was essential for the security of India and the Persian Gulf. A new factor of increasing interest had to be considered – oil. This had first been discovered in large quantities in southern Persia in 1908 and its potential importance was already realized. From 1904 onwards, Britain's First Sea Lord, Admiral Sir John Fisher, had been busy converting the British fleet from the use of coal to oil for power, and on the eve of the war the British government bought a controlling interest in the Anglo-Persian Oil Company for £2·2 million. Persia was not part of the Ottoman Empire, but it was known that neighbouring Mesopotamia was also almost certainly rich in oil, and a rather surprising syndicate of British and German interests had secured a concession to exploit all the oil within the empire's borders. A small Anglo-Indian expeditionary force landed and occupied Basra in southern Iraq in the first month that Turkey entered the war.

It was against this background that Hussein began to bargain with the British. He was strengthened by the receipt of a secret emissary from the Arab nationalist societies in Syria assuring him that the Arabs of Syria would take part in a British-backed revolt against the Turks and accept Hussein as 'spokesman for the Arabs' provided he could extract suitable terms from the British. Hussein also tried to elicit the opinion of the leading Arabs in the Arabian peninsula outside his own Hejaz. Ibn Rashid of the Shammar region and the Imam Yahya of Yemen were pro-Turk, while Ibn Saud, Ibn Rashid's

2. Sir Edward Grey, *Twenty-five Years*, London, 1925, vol. II, p. 236.

rival and enemy and ruler of Nejd, al-Idrisi in Asir and the ruler of Kuwait (which was linked to Britain by the treaty of alliance of 1899) were anti-Turk, although they were unable to offer any positive contribution to an Arab revolt. Ibn Saud had been compelled to accept the overlordship of the sultan in 1914, but he now threw this off and on 15 December signed a treaty with the British government which gave Britain a large measure of control over his foreign policy, but acknowledged the independence and territorial integrity of the Nejd and granted him a small annual subsidy.

The negotiations between Britain and the sharif and the agreement which led to his final decision to raise the flag of revolt are embodied in an exchange of letters between July 1915 and January 1916 known as the Hussein–McMahon correspondence. Sir Henry McMahon, the British high commissioner in Egypt, was delegated to act in this matter on the British government's behalf.

This correspondence is of cardinal importance because it became the subsequent basis of Arab nationalist charges against Britain of betrayal. The debate continues to this day and will never be resolved because of the deliberately imprecise style in which the letters were written. (McMahon's letters resemble a Gilbert and Sullivan parody of *The Arabian Nights*. One began: 'To the excellent and well-born Sayid, the descendant of Sharifs, the Crown of the Proud, Scion of Mohammed's Tree and Branch of the Quraishite trunk, him of the Exalted Presence and of the Lofty Rank . . . the lodestar of the Faithful and cynosure of all devout Believers . . . may his Blessing descend upon the people in their multitudes.')

In his first letter Husein proposed that Britain should support the creation of an area of Arab independence embracing the whole of what is now Syria, Lebanon, Jordan, Iraq and the entire Arabian peninsula with the exception of Aden – a British colony administered by the government of Bombay. In the ensuing correspondence the Sharif made a few reluctant and imprecise concessions: he accepted that Britain's treaties with certain Arabian chiefs should remain and agreed to a temporary British military occupation of Mesopotamia. Sharif Hussein did not comment on the claim in McMahon's second letter 'that it is understood that the Arabs have already decided to seek the counsels and advice of Great Britain exclusively; and that such European advisers and officials as may be needed to establish a sound system of administration shall be British'. The most crucial passage of all was the British assertion that 'portions of Syria lying to the west of the districts of Damascus, Homs, Hama and Aleppo, cannot be said to be purely Arab, and must on that account be excepted from the proposed delimitation [*sc.* of Arab independence.]' Hussein neither accepted nor rejected this claim but postponed his decision. The question therefore remains open whether the land of Palestine (which was not an Ottoman administrative region but a widely accepted geographical entity) was or was not intended to be included in the area of Arab independence. British apologists have had to use dubious logic to claim that Palestine lay to the west of Damascus. They have a stronger case in asserting that the sharif always understood that the Allies never intended Palestine to be an independent Arab state. But whatever the balance of right and wrong there can be no disputing the outraged Arab sense of betrayal over this point.

The truth can scarcely be denied that Britain was double-dealing with the Arabs, because at the same time that it was negotiating with the Sharif Hussein over the future of the Asian provinces of the Ottoman Empire it was discussing the same subject with France and Russia and keeping the two sets of negotiations separate. In extenuation it can only be argued that Britain was engaged in a deadly war with Germany and had to take account of the wishes of its principal allies.

The secret Anglo-French–Russian accord, known as the Sykes–Picot agreement after the principal British and French negotiators, was reached in May 1916. The details are unimportant today because they were later modified in practice, but the agreement was a clear decision in principle to divide the whole of Iraq and Syria into spheres of British and French control or influence, leaving only Jerusalem and part of Palestine (on Russian insistence) to some form of international administration.

The Sykes–Picot agreement is described by Arab writers such as George Antonius as a 'shocking document' and it is easy to see why. In the so-called Arab rectangle formed by Syria, Lebanon, Jordan, Israel and Iraq of today, Britain and France planned to assume direct control over the most populous and advanced areas. The land between – which is roughly the Syrian desert – was to form an autonomous Arab region, but clearly this would be so weak and thinly populated as to be at the mercy of British and French power. Only in the backward and impoverished Arabian peninsula were the Arabs to be given real independence.

In the spring of 1916 the Sharif Hussein had no more than an inkling of the scale of Britain and France's plans. His own negotiations with McMahon had not reached conclusions on several vital points, but he could wait no longer to launch his revolt. It was not only that the British were pressing him harder to begin operations, but his means of warding off Turkish suspicions were becoming exhausted while the situation in Syria was bringing matters to a head. At the outbreak of war Jemal Pasha, one of the three leading members of the CUP, had been appointed governor and commander-in-chief of the Ottoman forces in Syria. He was reported to have told his friends as he stepped on the train in Constantinople, 'I shall not return until I have entered Cairo.'

Jemal Pasha's first policy in Syria was to try to secure the wholehearted support of the Muslim majority of the population for the Turkish war effort. But after the failure of his first attempts to invade Egypt across the Suez Canal (when Egyptian troops, so far from mutinying against the British as he expected, actually helped to defend the Canal) his intelligence services made him aware of the great scale of underground Arab anti-Turkish activities. He then resorted to a policy of repression which earned him the name of al-Jazzar, 'the Butcher'. First he took every opportunity to send Arab units of the Ottoman army out of Syria and replace them with Turks, and then he put on trial before a military court a number of prominent Arab civilians who had been implicated in treasonable activities by documents seized in the French consulates. Eleven were promptly executed in August 1915 and twenty-one more the following January.

Jemal Pasha's iron grip on Syria meant that the Sharif could expect little help from this quarter, but he knew he had to act, especially as a large Turco-German force was about to arrive in the Hejaz on its way to Yemen. His son Feisal was in Damascus, where he had been urgently summoned by Jemal Pasha, whose atrocities had by now swung him round to a strong anti-Turkish view.

Hussein recalled him, and on 10 June 1916 finally raised the flag of the Arab Revolt by symbolically firing a rifle at the Turkish barracks in Mecca. First Mecca and then Jedda on the coast fell to the rebels, but the Turkish garrison continued to hold out against the sharif's ill-trained and ill-equipped troops. Though the Arabs fought boldly against lightly armed garrisons, they often ran away from artillery. After one such retreat, the Arabs explained that they had 'withdrawn to make ourselves some coffee'.

In October 1916 Ronald Storrs arrived in Jedda from Cairo to see what could be done to pull the Arab Revolt together. He was accompanied by a slim, blond and very untidy young temporary captain in the intelligence service named T. E. Lawrence.

Lawrence, who as the legendary 'Lawrence of Arabia' was to symbolize Britain's special, if often strained, relationship with the Arabs, was the illegitimate son of an Anglo-Irish baronet. He had shown unusual promise at school and at Oxford, where he had come under the influence of the tall black-bearded D. G. Hogarth, author, don, archaeologist and influential member of the British establishment. Hogarth was an enthusiastic imperialist, and he saw in Lawrence an extremely able young man who would be capable of disseminating his ideas in a crucial area. With Hogarth's encouragement Lawrence spent the years before 1914 travelling in the Middle East, studying the language, habits and history of the Arabs and occasionally spying on the Turks and Germans. During these years Lawrence gained his detailed knowledge of – although, contrary to the legend, no particular affection for – the Arabs, and an abiding hatred of the Turks and French, Britain's biggest rivals in the Middle East.

When war broke out, Hogarth used his influence to have Lawrence sent to Cairo in military intelligence. In January 1916 the brilliant young Colonel Clayton set up his Arab Bureau of intelligence and diplomatic officers (who included Hogarth) to organize Britain's role in the Arab Revolt. Lawrence managed to get himself attached to the Bureau and then to Storrs' mission to Jedda in October 1916.

Lawrence quickly made up his mind about the Sharif's family. In his account of the Arab Revolt, *Seven Pillars of Wisdom*, he wrote:

> The first, the Sharif of Mecca, we knew to be aged. I found Abdullah the second son too clever, Ali the first son too clean, Zeid the fourth son too cool. Then I rode up-country to Feisal the third son and found in him the leader with the necessary fire.

Feisal by this time had been won over to wholehearted support for a revolt against Turkey because of Jemal Pasha's brutal suppression of the Arabs in Syria. He had a splendid presence and was more sophisticated, in a Western sense, than Abdullah, who remained at heart a beduin chieftain. But Feisal was also more naïve and less intelligent than Abdullah, towards whom Lawrence felt a dislike and a distrust which was cordially returned. There can be little doubt that Feisal was deliberately chosen by Lawrence as the ideal instrument for maintaining British control over the Arab national movement and ultimately for achieving Lawrence's personal objective, shared in some form or another by most of his colleagues, of an Arab 'brown dominion' within the British Empire. In return Feisal trusted Lawrence entirely in the firm belief that he would help the Arabs achieve complete independence under the rule of the Hashemite family.

For a while the relationship between Feisal and Lawrence was an open and honest one. But soon Lawrence learned through the Arab Bureau of the Foreign Office's plans to carve up Syria and Iraq between Britain and France after the war. Hogarth and Lawrence were appalled – but not because they believed in the Arab right to independence: the two imperialists simply wanted the hated French to have no share in the eastern half of the Arab world. Consequently, they set out to undermine the Sykes–Picot agreement. Although ultimately they failed, Lawrence did manage to keep the terms of the agreement from Feisal until he was totally dependent on Britain and unable to withdraw from the British-backed uprising.

Feisal soon became the acknowledged leader of the Arab Revolt. By mastering irregular guerrilla tactics, wearing Arab dress and learning to ride camels superbly, Lawrence turned himself into a beduin warrior. An interesting sidelight on Lawrence's personality is shown in a manual for political officers which he wrote in August 1917. In this he implies that he wore Arab dress not because he loved the Arab way of life, but because it was the best way to 'handle' the Arabs. 'If you can wear Arab kit when with the tribes,' he says 'you will acquire their trust and intimacy to a degree impossible in uniform. It is, however, dangerous and difficult.'[3]

The Arab Revolt was strategically important to Britain. It immobilized some 30,000 Turkish troops along the railway from Amman to Medina and prevented the Turco-German forces in Syria from linking up with the Turkish garrison in Yemen. There could have been the most serious consequences for the Allies if the enemy forces in Arabia had made contact with the Germans in east Africa and succeeded in closing the Red Sea to Allied shipping. Arab forces, who were mainly armed tribesmen with a core of regular troops, carried out valuable guerrilla operations on the right flank of the British Expeditionary

3. However, the question of how good Lawrence's Arabic was remains unresolved and is still periodically disputed in the correspondence columns of *The Times*. According to Antonius, Lawrence 'believed that he was sufficiently fluent in it to pass for an Arab in conversation with Arabs. In that, he showed more self-confidence than powers of observation, as anyone could tell who had heard his pronunciations.' G. Antonius, *The Arab Awakening*, New York, 1965, p. 321.

Force from Egypt as it advanced into Palestine. In a daring stroke Lawrence and Auda, 'the Hawk', a famous tribal leader, captured the important port town of Aqaba in July 1917.

Yet none of these operations would have been possible without the help of British gold and supplies, the support of the British navy on the Hejaz coast and the cooperation of several British officers of whom T. E. Lawrence is only the best known. The Arabs made an important contribution to the defeat of the Turks, but there was little they could do on their own. The myth of Lawrence and the Arab Revolt belongs more to Britain than the Arabs. Although there can be no doubt about the devotion and admiration of his beduin followers for 'al-Orens', as they called him, they were relatively few in number and are now dead. For the Arabs as a whole the myth was soon overwhelmed by the squalid betrayal of the post-war settlement.

For the British, on the other hand, the myth has survived much longer. This is despite the fact that in some ways he has been exposed as a charlatan and a fraud. His own best-selling account of his exploits *Seven Pillars of Wisdom* was romantically incautious in its treatment of facts. The truth is that the British desperately wanted to believe in the Lawrence myth. At a time when the belligerents of the First World War were monotonously slaughtering each other in the mud of Flanders, the romantic individualistic character of Lawrence's desert guerrilla campaign had an irresistible appeal, and the British public, encouraged by able propagandists such as the American journalist Lowell Thomas, were quite ready to believe that he had led the Arabs to victory virtually single-handed.

The real truth was that the central responsibility for defeating the Turks lay with the British general Sir Edmund Allenby, who in the autumn of 1917 launched a successful offensive from Egypt, sweeping up into Palestine to take Jerusalem on 9 December 1917. In Iraq also, after a severe reverse in April 1916 when a mixed Anglo-Indian force advancing up the Tigris to Baghdad was surrounded and forced to surrender to the Turks, British troops had finally succeeded in taking Baghdad a year later. A British military administration was set up with Gertrude Bell, scholar, traveller and one of the most remarkable Englishwomen of the century, as oriental secretary.

In the Arabian peninsula the immediate effect of the Arab Revolt had been considerable. Ibn Rashid and the Imam of Yemen remained pro-Turkish but they were now isolated, and at a meeting in Kuwait in November Ibn Saud, the ruler of Kuwait and a number of minor chieftains, declared their open support for Britain and the Arabs. By the time General Allenby arrived in Jerusalem British paramountcy over Arabia, the Persian Gulf and Iraq as well as Egypt was virtually complete.

However, before the end of 1917 two events had occurred which were to lay the basis for the Arab charge of betrayal against the Allies and to poison their relations with the European powers – especially Britain – for at least two generations. The first of these was the public revelation of the terms of the Sykes–Picot agreement. The Sharif Hussein had already got wind of what was happening. In 1916 he had pressed for a landing of Allied troops at Alexandretta to facilitate a simultaneous uprising against the Turks in Syria, but, although this plan was vigorously supported by the British military commanders in the Near East, it was turned down by the British war cabinet, partly because of French opposition to any landing in Syria with other than French troops. In November 1916 the Sharif Hussein was proclaimed 'king of the Arab countries' by his followers, but this was totally unacceptable to the French, who deeply resented Britain's promotion of Hashemite leadership of the Syrian Arabs. A compromise was reached in January 1917, whereby both Britain and France recognized Hussein as king of the Hejaz.

Early in 1917 King Hussein began to become aware of the real intention of Britain and France towards Syria and Iraq, and Sir Mark Sykes himself was sent to Jedda by the British Foreign Office to allay his fears. But although Sykes and Hussein discussed the question of French aims in Lebanon and Syrian coastal areas, with Hussein maintaining the principle that these were as much Arab in character as the interior, Sykes did not inform him of the details of the broader aspects of the Sykes–Picot agreement. For these he had to wait for the Bolshevik Revolution in Russia in November 1917. One of the first acts of the Bolsheviks was to publish selected documents from the archives of the tsar's foreign ministry which were calculated to show Russia's former imperialist allies in the worst possible light. They informed the Turks of the terms of the Sykes–Picot agreement (to which tsarist Russia had been a party) and the Turks understandably lost no time in passing them on to the Arabs as proof of treachery against the Muslim peoples of the Ottoman Empire on the part of the Christian powers of Europe.

Britain was embarrassed by the revelation. When Hussein asked for an explanation he was told that the Petrograd documents only referred to provisional exchanges between the Allies, and it was suggested to him that the success of the Arab Revolt and the withdrawal of Russia from the war had created an entirely new situation. This was true in a sense but the 'new situation' did not mean that the prospects for Arab independence had improved. Hussein and Feisal still put their faith in Britain; they were so dependent upon British support that they had no alternative. But the basis for their trust had been destroyed.

The other powerful threat to Britain's new relations with the Arabs was less apparently dangerous but was to have a more lasting effect. This was the famous Balfour Declaration of 2 November 1917. It was a statement of British government policy, although it took the form of a letter from the British Foreign Secretary, Arthur James Balfour, to a leading British Jew, Lord Rothschild. Its terms, which are deeply ingrained in the minds of most Arabs, must still be recalled for any understanding of the Arab psyche:

> His Majesty's Government view with favour the establishment in Palestine of a National Home for the Jewish people, and will use their best endeavours to facilitate the achievement of this object, it being clearly understood that nothing shall be done which may prejudice the civil and religious rights of existing non-Jewish communities in Palestine, or the rights and political status enjoyed by Jews in any other country.

The Zionist movement is one of the most remarkable phenomena of the twentieth century but it is not the subject of this book. It is the Arab reaction to it which concerns us here, and for this certain points about this brief paragraph must be noted – as much for what it does not say as for what it says. First of all Palestine or the Holy Land was not at that time a geographical or political entity with defined borders, because it was not an administrative division of the Ottoman Empire. The southern half of the area which became the British mandated territory of Palestine after the First World War until the creation of Israel in 1948, consisted of the sanjak of Jerusalem. The western half formed part of the vilayet of Beirut. The city of Jerusalem and the area surrounding it enjoyed special administrative status under direct rule from Constantinople. But the fact that there was no political entity called Palestine in 1917 did not mean that, like Eldorado, it had only a mythical existence. That the Balfour Declaration referred to it is proof enough of this. For Christians, Muslims and Jews throughout the world it had a very real and special meaning.

Who were the inhabitants of the Holy Land at this time? The Ottoman Empire had no vital statistics for its provinces but it is thought that before the 1914–18 war there were about 600,000 Arabs,

Muslims and Christians, and about 80,000 Jews. The Jewish population fell during the war as some left, as refugees, under American and other auspices, and a British census of 1918 gave an estimate of 700,000 Arabs and 56,000 Jews. It is therefore quite understandable that the Arabs, who formed at least 90 per cent of the population, should have resented the Balfour Declaration's reference to them as 'the existing non-Jewish communities in Palestine'. Although they were the descendants of a people who had lived in Palestine for at least a thousand years,[4] this phrase appeared to classify them as intruders. As elsewhere in Syria, the Palestinians had an educated upper class who enjoyed considerable privileges under the Turks and held high posts under their administration.

Of the 50,000 to 60,000 Jews of Palestine the great majority lived in Jerusalem, with smaller communities in towns such as Tiberias, Safed and Nablus. Some of these were the descendants of the remnants of the Jews of Palestine who had been scattered after their final desperate revolt against the Roman Empire in A.D. 132. Palestine was the least prosperous part of Greater Syria, and these Jews existed in much the same poor conditions as their Arab neighbours, with whom they lived in a fair degree of harmony. Some 12,000 Jews of Palestine were different. These were the early Zionists who lived in forty-three agricultural colonies – *moshavim* (cooperatives) or *kibbutzim* (communes) – and with hard work, idealism and the financial help of wealthy European Jews such as the French Baron Rothschild they were aiming to establish the Hebrew language and Jewish culture as well as a flourishing agriculture in *Eretz Israel*, as they termed Palestine. The ideology of these philanthropic, cultural but essentially non-political Zionists was first formulated in the middle of the nineteenth century by German or Russian Jewish writers, such as Moses Hess and Leon Pinsker, who believed that the Jewish people scattered throughout the world in the Diaspora needed a centre of their own where they could foster the revival of Jewish culture and create a basis for political action. They did not believe that assimilation into Gentile society could solve the Jewish problem. Despite the fact that the status and personal security of the Jews in the West in general had immensely improved since the French Revolution, which in turn owed much to the French Enlightenment and the principles of the American Declaration of Independence, persecution continued,

---

4. Some went back much further than this – to the Canaanites, the inhabitants of Palestine when it was invaded by the Jews led by Joshua, and to the Philistines and other non-Jewish peoples of ancient times.

particularly in Russia and Russian Poland. (It was in flight from Russian pogroms that some 600,000 Jews emigrated to the United States in the last two decades of the nineteenth century, to create the foundations of the rich and powerful community which today forms more than one third of all the Jews in the world.)

Although these early Zionists – the Lovers of Zion, the movement was called in Russia – worked hard for the establishment of the agricultural colonies in Palestine, they did not for the most part believe that Palestine could ever become a Jewish state. This would have to be elsewhere in empty territory – perhaps in South America – which the Jews would buy. One of the most distinguished of the Lovers of Zion, Asher Ginzberg, wrote after visiting Palestine in 1891 and 1893: 'Palestine could not absorb the Jewish masses; it should be a cultural and spiritual centre but not the political or economic basis of the Jewish people.'[5] He also diagnosed the source of a century of trouble:

We are in the habit of thinking that all the Arabs are wild men of the desert and do not see or understand what goes on around them, but that is a great mistake. The Arabs, especially the town dwellers, see and understand what we are doing and what we want in Palestine, but they do not react and pretend not to notice, because at present they do not see in what we are doing any threat to their own future. . . . But if ever we develop in Palestine to such a degree as to encroach on the living space of the native population to any appreciable extent, they will not easily give up their place.[6]

In 1897 the Zionist movement was given a wholly new impetus and character by one man – Theodor Herzl, an Austrian Jewish writer and journalist who possessed unusual prophetic force and energy. Convinced by such incidents as the Dreyfus case in France that if such anti-semitic outbursts could happen even in the Land of the Enlightenment all assimilated Jews might be in danger, he launched Zionism as a political movement with the publication of his pamphlet *Der Judenstaat* ('The Jewish State: an Attempt at a Modern Solution of the Jewish Question'). His reasoning was similar to that of earlier Zionist writers, although he did not acknowledge them, but he went much further to make their vision a reality. In 1897 he organized the first World Zionist Congress at Basle in Switzerland.

In 1903, when settlement by the Jews in Palestine was difficult, the British government offered the Zionist Congress a territory in East

5. Quoted in Walter Laqueur, *A History of Zionism*, London, 1972, p. 80.
6. ibid.

Africa for Jewish settlement, but the offer was rejected because the majority of the Zionists could not consider any other home than the Land of Zion (although Herzl himself was at first prepared to accept it). Unlike Ginzberg, Herzl hardly considered the problem of Palestine's indigenous inhabitants. He referred to Palestine as a 'land without people' and urged that it should be given to the Jews as 'a people without land'. It was only just before his death in 1904 at the early age of forty-four that he acknowledged that *Der Judenstaat* must be realized in harmony with the Palestinian Arab population. It remained true that all the leaders of political Zionism from Herzl onwards either ignored or underestimated the problem presented by the fact that Palestine, although poor and backward in many ways, was certainly not empty. There were some members of the British cabinet who expressed their doubts at the time of the Balfour Declaration. Lord Curzon, who later succeeded Balfour as foreign secretary, wrote in a memorandum:

What is to become of the people of this country [Palestine] assuming the Turk to be expelled, and the inhabitants not to have been exterminated by the war? There are over half a million of these, Syrian Arabs – a mixed community with Arab, Hebrew, Canaanite, Greek, Egyptian and possibly Crusader blood. They and their forefathers have occupied the country for the best part of 1,500 years. They own the soil, which belongs either to individual landowners or to village communities. They profess the Mohammedan faith. They will not be content either to be expropriated for Jewish immigrants, or to act merely as hewers of wood and drawers of water to the latter.[7]

Already before the outbreak of the First World War the Palestinian Arabs had begun to resent the activities of the Zionists and their establishment of exclusive Jewish communities. But they hardly regarded Zionism as a threat, for, despite all Herzl's efforts, the movement was still only weak and embryonic on an international level. There was little fear of Palestine becoming a Jewish state within the Ottoman Empire. Moreover the majority of prominent and influential Jews in Europe were unsympathetic to Zionism. They were more concerned with assimilation and the ending of all forms of discrimination against Jews in Gentile society. This was particularly true in Britain, which had gradually become the principal centre of Zionist activity after the death of Herzl. Indeed the two most representative bodies in British Jewry – the Board of Deputies of British

7. David Lloyd George, *The Truth about the Peace Treaties*, London, 1938, vol. II, pp. 730–31.

Jews and the Anglo-Jewish Association – had actually begun a campaign to persuade the British government to resist the demands of the
Zionists.

All this makes it only more astonishing that the Balfour Declaration
should have been issued in November 1917. At the outbreak of the
war Sir Herbert Samuel, the one Jewish member of the Asquith
government, had put forward Zionist ideas to the cabinet but had
been dismissed by Asquith as a dreamer. But in December 1916 Lloyd
George replaced Asquith, and the only Jew in *his* cabinet, Edwin
Montagu, the secretary of state for India, was strongly opposed to
Zionism.

The motives of Lloyd George's government in supporting Zionism
were a peculiarly British blend of self-interest, self-deception and
idealism. On the practical side there was the hope of securing support
for the Allies from Zionists in Germany, Austria and the United
States, who might otherwise have been attracted by the Central
Powers' promises of support and who were repelled by Russian
anti-semitism. British statesmen tended to hold the exaggerated view
of the economic power and influence of world Jewry which was
common at that time. The imperialists in the Foreign Office also saw
an important advantage in having a friendly community in Palestine,
since the war had exposed the vulnerability of the Suez Canal. Prime
Minister Lloyd George and Foreign Secretary Balfour had good
personal relations with the leading British Zionist Chaim Weizmann
(later the first president of Israel), and in return the Zionists, who
were strongly opposed to the internationalization of Palestine, were
prepared to work for a British protectorate over the Holy Land in
return for British support for Zionism. Sir Mark Sykes, who was
delegated by Lloyd George to negotiate with the Zionists, played a
key role in securing the cabinet's acceptance of the Zionist idea,
although before his death he came to doubt the wisdom of what he
had done. On the idealistic side, several British ministers who, even if
they were agnostic in their views, had all been brought up in the spirit
of nineteenth-century Bible-reading Protestantism, were attracted by
the romantic idea of helping the Jewish people to 'return' to their
promised land after two thousand years.

They did not accept the full Zionist demands or objectives which,
however they might be formulated for practical reasons, were always
that Palestine should become a state with a Zionist character and a
Jewish majority. This is why the Balfour Declaration clearly referred
to a *home* and not a *state* and to *a* national home rather than *the* national

home, which is what the Zionists originally wanted. Nevertheless, there were several members of the cabinet who had much more than an inkling of the Zionists' real intentions and approved of them.[8]

The announcement of the Balfour Declaration reinforced King Hussein's fears which had already been raised by his knowledge of Britain and France's intentions. Hogarth was sent to Jedda to reassure him, but the old king was already showing perceptive fears that the Declaration might foreshadow a Jewish state in Palestine. Hogarth reported: 'The king would not accept an independent Jewish state in Palestine, nor was I instructed to warn him that such a state was contemplated.' The king accepted Hogarth's assurances, such as they were, and ended by showing enthusiasm for the advantages that Jewish immigration would bring to the Arab countries.

The situation was rapidly coming to a head because the Ottoman Empire was on the point of its final collapse. After being held up by the severe winter in Palestine and the stiffening of Turco-German resistance, Allenby resumed his advance in September 1918 to drive the Turks out of Syria. Damascus fell on 1 October. The first Allied troops to reach the city were a body of Australian cavalry, but Lawrence arranged for Feisal's Arab forces to make the triumphal entry and install their own governor.

Beirut fell on 8 October and Aleppo on 26 October. Allenby's advance only halted on 30 October when Turkey capitulated (twelve days before Germany) by signing the Mudros armistice. Four hundred years of Ottoman domination came to an end.

Wild Arab rejoicing greeted the liberation of Syria. The civil population had suffered appallingly from the war, because a plague of locusts, combined with the normal disruption of war and the corruption of Turkish officials and Syrian merchants, had caused widespread famine. Between one third and half a million people died out of a total population of about four million.

Relief at the end of Turkish oppression was combined with high hopes for a new independent future. The Hashemites and other well-informed Arabs had doubts about the Allies' intentions, but Britain and France had taken steps to allay the fears of the general public. In the spring of 1918 a group of seven prominent Arabs living in Cairo presented a memorandum asking for a clear definition of

8. See D. Ingrams (ed.), *Palestine Papers 1917–1922: Seeds of Conflict*, London, 1972, p. 46.

British policy. The British reply, which became known as the Declaration to the Seven, was given the widest publicity. Referring to the Arab territories liberated by the actions of the Arab armies, the British government declared its policy in these to be that 'the future government of those territories should be based upon the principle of the consent of the governed'. With regard to those territories still under Turkish rule (that is most of Syria and northern Iraq) the British government merely asserted its desire 'that the oppressed peoples in these territories should obtain their freedom and independence'.

The phrase referring to the 'consent of the governed' in the third category is particularly significant because it was at least nominally the basis of the post-war settlement. It was given immense moral force by its inclusion in July among the 'Four Ends' of peace of the US President Woodrow Wilson, which were to be embodied in the League of Nations Covenant. It was further reinforced by the Anglo-French Declaration of 7 November 1918 which was issued by the British military commands in Palestine, Syria and Iraq, and given even wider publicity than the Declaration of the Seven. This said that the goal of the British and French governments was the complete and final liberation of peoples oppressed by the Turks, and the setting up of national governments and administrations which should derive their authority from the free exercise of the initiative and choice of the indigenous population. Declarations of this kind by the Powers raised the expectations not only of the Arabs of Syria and Iraq, but of the Egyptians and of all peoples in the world who were living under some form of colonial or imperial rule.

9. The Great Deception: the West Disposes

When the war came to an end the Allies described the whole area of the Arab rectangle as Occupied Enemy Territory, to be administered under military law pending a peace settlement. Already the broad lines of the amended Sykes–Picot agreement were becoming clear. Iraq was maintained as a single unit under an Anglo-Indian administration with a British civil commissioner at its head. Occupied Enemy Territory Administration South (OETA South) covered the approximate area of the future Palestine mandate. OETA West comprised the whole Syrian and Lebanese coastal area from Tyre to Cilicia and was under the French, who hastened to stake their claim by landing troops in Beirut at the end of the war. OETA East covered the Syrian interior. Here the main towns were under Feisal's authority but with a significant attachment of British officers on whom the Arabs, with their limited experience in administration, were heavily dependent.

It was against this background that Feisal with Lawrence as his adviser set out to attend the Paris Peace Conference. The Hashemites' dependence on Britain was already very apparent because only British intervention against strong French opposition secured a place for him at the conference table. Even then it was made clear that he represented only the Hejaz and not the Arabs as a whole.

With dignity and determination Feisal attempted nevertheless to voice, in Paris, the aspirations of the Arabs. It was of little use because all the important decisions had already been taken without his knowledge as the British and French prime ministers, Lloyd George and Clemenceau, had reached an understanding on the revision of the Sykes–Picot agreement. The British government regarded French ambitions in the Levant as excessive. Lawrence and his former colleagues in the Arab Bureau went much further in wanting 'to biff the French out of all hope of Syria', as Lawrence wrote in one of his letters. Militarily, Britain was much stronger than France in the Middle East, but the area had to be seen in a world context in which France was still Britain's principal ally despite growing friction between them. In return for France's abandoning its claims to control Palestine, Britain came round to the view that France would have to have a free hand in Syria and Lebanon and a guaranteed share in

Iraq's oil.[1] But Britain felt obligations towards the Hashemites and Lloyd George used his influence with Feisal to persuade him to come to terms with the French before it was too late.

The unfortunate Feisal attempted to retrieve what he could for Arab aspirations. Taking his stand on the doctrines of self-determination preached by President Wilson and restated in the Anglo-French Declaration, he proposed that a commission of inquiry be sent to Syria and Palestine to examine the wishes of the inhabitants. President Wilson enthusiastically accepted the proposal, and his suggestion that the commission should consist of French, British, Italian and American members was endorsed by the Conference. But in reality the French were strongly hostile to the commission, while the British were lukewarm. Eventually all the parties except the Americans withdrew. The American appointees, Henry King and Charles Crane,[2] decided to go on their own, and their report fully explains British and French hostility towards the commission. After exhaustive consultations with the people of Syria they reported that while the overwhelming majority opposed the mandatory system, there was an acknowledged need for outside assistance, provided it came first from the United States or, as second choice, from Britain. On no account did they want it from France. Realizing that the mandatory system was inevitable, the commission recommended that the United States should have the mandate for Syria, and Britain for Iraq, provided that the mandate was of limited duration and that the mandatory was in no sense a colonizing power. They also recommended that Feisal should become king of Syria and that Iraq should have an Arab monarch.

On the Zionist question they declared themselves to have set out with a strong disposition in favour of Zionism and to have found much to approve of in the Zionists' aspirations and plans, but to have concluded that the 'extreme Zionist programme must be greatly modified if the civil and religious rights of the non-Jewish inhabitants of Palestine are to be protected in accordance with the terms of the Balfour Declaration'.

After discussions with Zionist leaders in Jerusalem they had no

1. Oil had already been discovered in Iraq before the war and when Britain occupied Mosul and Baghdad in 1918 it expropriated the 25 per cent German share in the Turkish Petroleum Company which was planning to develop it.

2. Dr Henry C. King was president of Oberlin College in Ohio. Mr Charles R. Crane, a prominent businessman and oriental traveller, was a political supporter of President Wilson, who appointed him US minister to China in 1920.

doubt 'that the Zionists looked forward to a practically complete dispossession of the present non-Jewish inhabitants of Palestine, by various forms of purchase'.

The King–Crane commission's report was ignored by the Allies. It was clearly repugnant to Britain and France, and the United States, after raising so many expectations, was shortly to retreat into a long period of isolation. For years it gathered dust in some Washington pigeon-hole; but it contained some real wisdom and much trouble would have been avoided if more notice had been taken of it.

The commission's report underlined the fact that it was not only Anglo-French imperialist ambitions but also those of Zionism which were likely to conflict with the hopes and aspirations of the Arabs. Allenby's liberation of Jerusalem, although in one sense it could be looked upon as a triumphant last crusade, was generally welcomed by the city's Muslim and Jewish inhabitants as much as the Christians. The leaders of all the communities showed their willingness to cooperate with each other and with the British military authorities. (Most of the Jerusalem Jews were ultra-orthodox and regarded Zionism and the use of Hebrew for other than religious purposes as sacrilege.) However, in March 1918 a Zionist commission arrived in Jerusalem headed by Chaim Weizmann. Its official mission was to act as a link between the British authorities and the Jewish population, to help with relief work and stimulate Jewish educational and cultural activities. But the Zionists themselves saw it as the first step towards their distant dream of establishing a Jewish state in Palestine. Although Weizmann was prepared to be patient and diplomatic in his approach (while never for a moment losing sight of his real goal) this was not the case with some of his associates – especially those who had escaped from Russian persecution. The harassed and over-worked British officials reacted with increasing irritation towards the pertinacious demands of the Zionists. Some of the British were actively opposed to the Zionists while others were sympathetic. Many more tried genuinely to reconcile the terms of the Balfour Declaration with Britain's obligations under the mandate.

In 1918 this by no means seemed impossible. The reality about Palestine, which the Zionists had to face as much as anyone else, was that the country was overwhelmingly Arab and it was Britain's duty as the mandatory power to bring it to self-government as quickly as possible. There was little likelihood that the Zionists would be able to create a Jewish majority in Palestine before this happened and in this case the Arabs would be in the position to decide just what size and kind of Jewish national home should exist in their country. As Jon Kimche wrote in *Palestine or Israel*[3]:

Thus, when Weizmann departed for home in September 1918 his mission and that of the Zionist commission was in effect at an end. They had come to lay the foundations of a Jewish state and they left with Palestine set to become an Arab state – and it probably would have become one but for the Hitler holocaust and the Second World War.

For their part the Hashemites were prepared to give the Balfour Declaration a try, and even to welcome it as likely to help the progress of the Arabs, provided its terms really meant what they said. Feisal met Weizmann in Palestine in June 1918 and was assured like his father that the Zionists did not aim to establish a Jewish state in Palestine. With the enthusiastic encouragement of Lawrence and the Foreign Office he reached an agreement with Weizmann in London in January 1919 which amounted to acceptance of the official Zionist programme for Palestine. Article IV of the agreement read:

All necessary measures shall be taken to encourage and stimulate immigration of Jews into Palestine on a large scale, and as quickly as possible to settle Jewish immigrants upon the land through closer settlement and intensive cultivation of the soil. In taking such measures the Arab peasants and tenant farmers shall be protected in their rights, and shall be assisted in forwarding their economic development.

The agreement referred throughout to 'the Arab state' and 'Palestine' as two separate entities but did not of course say anything about a Jewish state. Feisal, in his weak and lonely position, was reluctant to commit the Arabs on a matter of such importance on his own. He did not even have time to consult his father. But he was under strong pressure and he decided he must put his trust both in the Zionists and the British government. However, he was able to add a codicil which was signed by both parties as follows:

Provided the Arabs obtain their independence as demanded . . . I shall concur in the above articles. But if the slightest modification or departure were to be made, I shall not then be bound by a single word of the present agreement . . .

This was written in Arabic in Feisal's own hand. Lawrence provided a rough translation into English for Weizmann and there is a strong possibility that it was a deliberately misleading paraphrase

3. Jon Kimche, *Palestine or Israel: the Untold Story of Why We Failed*, London, 1973, p. 258.

intended to lead Weizmann to believe that Feisal's proviso was weaker or less comprehensive than it was.[4]

The terrible Arab–Jewish conflict in Palestine was still only potential, and when it gathered force the leadership of the Palestinian Arabs had long since passed out of the hands of Feisal and his father. In 1919 Feisal was much more concerned with his inevitable clash with French imperialism.

While Feisal was away in Paris the former secret Arab nationalist society al-Fatat formed an Arab independence party which gained Feisal's support on his return. Elections were held wherever possible throughout Syria – although they were blocked by the French in OETA West. A General Syrian Congress, meeting in Damascus, called for recognition of the independence of Syria (including Palestine) and Iraq, and the repudiation of both the Sykes–Picot agreement, the Balfour Declaration and the mandatory system. Feisal alone was aware of the harsh realities of power. Bowing to the strong pressure from Britain which he could not afford to ignore, he returned to Paris in November 1919 to reach a provisional agreement with Clemenceau, pending a final settlement, providing for French occupation of the Syrian coastal areas and a French monopoly of assistance to the Arab state in the interior. Feisal's hot-blooded young followers in Damascus refused to accept any such compromise and in March 1920 the General Syrian Congress passed a resolution proclaiming the independence of Syria (including Palestine and Lebanon but with internal autonomy provided for predominantly Christian Lebanon) under Feisal as king. At the same time a similar meeting of Iraqi leaders declared Iraq's independence with the Amir Abdullah as king.

Britain and France reacted swiftly. Declaring that they did not recognize the Damascus resolutions, they hastily convened a meeting of the Supreme Council of the League of Nations, which announced its decision at San Remo on 5 May 1920. Greater Syria was to be partitioned into the two French mandates of Lebanon and Syria and the British mandate of Palestine, while Iraq was to remain undivided as a British mandate. The British mandate for Palestine carried with it the obligation to carry out the terms of the Balfour Declaration.

Feisal now ruled what was perhaps the shakiest kingdom in history. The French made little secret of their intention of establishing

4. See C. Simpson and P. Knightley, *The Secret Lives of Lawrence of Arabia*, London, 1969, pp. 118–19.

direct control over the whole of the Syrian interior as well as the coast and were only waiting for an excuse to occupy Damascus. Enraged by the San Remo decision, Feisal's young officers were only too ready to provide such an excuse by attacking French positions near the Lebanese border. On 14 July General Gouraud, the French commander in Beirut, sent an ultimatum demanding an unqualified acceptance of the mandate and the French military occupation of Aleppo and the main towns of central Syria. Feisal persuaded the reluctant General Congress to accept the ultimatum but the French had already made up their minds. A French column headed by Senegalese and North African Arab troops advanced and took Damascus on 25 July. Syrian forces, backed by the entire population of Damascus, bravely attempted resistance, but could do little against French tanks and planes. The French then 'invited' Feisal to leave Syria. A sad and pathetic figure, he arrived in London at the end of the year at the invitation of an embarrassed British government. The British understandably had a bad conscience about the fate of Feisal's short-lived Syrian kingdom. Winston Churchill, secretary of state for the colonies, told the Imperial Conference the following year that the spectacle of the French operations against Syria 'conducted very largely by black African troops' had been 'extremely painful to British opinion' but 'we have these strong ties with the French and they have to prevail, and we were not able to do anything to help the Arabs in the matter . . .'

One of France's first acts as the mandatory power was to create *le Grand Liban* by enlarging Lebanon at Syria's expense. Lebanon included the Maronite Catholics and other Christian sects who traditionally looked to France as their protector, whereas Syria was a centre of Arab nationalism. The French scheme was to make an enlarged and strengthened Lebanon the basis for its Near Eastern policy. General Gouraud's decree of 31 August 1920 added to the former autonomous sanjak of Lebanon (that is, Mount Lebanon) the coastal towns of Tripoli to the north, Sidon and Tyre to the south and the Bekaa plain to the east. The population of the *Grand Liban* had a small Christian majority, but with the higher Muslim birth rate they were in constant danger of becoming a minority.

The decisions of the San Remo conference were not carried out without considerable bloodshed. Apart from the fighting in Syria, there was an uprising against the Jews by Muslim and Christian Arabs in Palestine, alarmed by the statements and activities of the Zionists who were already demanding that Palestine should be called *Eretz Israel* with the Jewish flag as its national emblem. The Palestinian Arabs had been unable to play any crucial role in the Arab Revolt but they were now united in their fear and dislike of Zionism. In Iraq also, where Arab hopes had been thwarted by the establishment of an Anglo-Indian administration with virtually no Arab participation, there was a major uprising of the tribes of the central Euphrates in the summer of 1920, which cost the British over 2,000 casualties and £40 million (more than three times the total subsidies for the Arab Revolt) to suppress.

British officials in Iraq were divided between those, like Gertrude Bell, who favoured indirect British control through Arab institutions and an Arab (preferably Hashemite) amir and others, like the redoubtable Colonel A. T. Wilson, an arch-imperialist who believed in direct colonial rule which would make Iraq rival the Indian Empire as the brightest jewel in the British imperial crown.

Wilson's ideas were in line with the imperialists in the British cabinet who had argued during the war that Britain should do everything to obtain 'a continuity of territory or of control both in East Africa and between Egypt and India'. Such men even considered 'Indianizing' Iraq by settling thousands of Indians in the country. Eventually it was Gertrude Bell's views which prevailed, but not before Wilson's repressive measures had provoked the costly uprising.

The need for economy and the generally unsatisfactory situation in Britain's new semi-colonial Arab empire called for action. Lloyd George decided on a fresh approach. In order to put an end to the disastrous rivalry in the Middle East between the Foreign Office and the India Office he put the whole problem into the hands of the young Winston Churchill's Colonial Office. One of the Churchill's first actions was to persuade Lawrence to join his newly created Middle East Department as adviser on Arab affairs. After a series of urgent discussions in London in which the exiled Feisal was involved, Churchill called a conference in Cairo in March 1921, to endorse his decisions. Lawrence said later: 'The decisions of the Cairo conference were prepared by us in London over dinner tables at the Ship Restaurant in Whitehall.'

The conference was attended by all the senior officials in Britain's new Arab 'empire' – Sir Percy Cox, high commissioner for Iraq, Gertrude Bell and the newly appointed high commissioner for Palestine, Sir Herbert Samuel, the man who had first put forward the Zionist idea to the British cabinet.

It had already been arranged between Churchill, Lawrence, Cox and Bell that Feisal should be made king of Iraq. This would at one stroke solve the problem of establishing a system of indirect British rule in this key oil-rich Arab state and of compensating Feisal for his lost Syrian throne. It is described by Antonius as a policy of 'Economy with Honour'. Brushing aside Lloyd George's doubts about the reaction of the anti-Hashemite French towards the sudden promotion of the man they had recently expelled from the throne of Syria, Churchill suggested that Iraqi opinion should be prepared well in advance, to give Feisal a good welcome. Gertrude Bell and Sir Percy Cox gave all their considerable energy to this task. (Some members of the British administration, such as H. St John Philby, famous Arabian explorer and father of Kim Philby, the Soviet agent, doubted the wisdom of imposing Hashemite rule on Iraq and favoured a republic. Philby was overruled and resigned.)

Feisal's triumphal arrival in Iraq was carefully staged. A series of meetings of tribal leaders were held throughout the country. Gertrude Bell was usually present to give support. At one point when a tribal leader remarked with tactless honesty that he was ready to swear allegiance to Feisal because he was acceptable to the British, she saved the day by raising her clasped hands as a symbol of British–Arab friendship in equality.

Feisal's most serious rival in Iraq was Sayid Talib. As he left after taking tea with Gertrude Bell and Lady Cox, Talib was whisked into an armoured car and shipped off for a prolonged stay in Ceylon. Finally, Feisal was declared elected king by a 96·8 per cent majority in a plebiscite. Tribal leaders had recognized that he was Britain's choice and Britain had the power. On 23 April 1921 Feisal was proclaimed king of Iraq and Gertrude could write to her father: 'We have had a terrible week but we've got our king crowned.'

Iraq was not the only problem that Churchill had to settle in the Middle East. In November 1920 the Amir Abdullah, Feisal's elder brother, had arrived in Maan (in what was to become southern Transjordan) at the head of a motley army of tribesmen and retainers and announced his intention – probably spurious and certainly unrealistic, since Abdullah was no military genius – of marching on Damascus to avenge his brother's expulsion.

His presence on the East Bank of the river Jordan was not unjustified. This dry, unpromising territory, inhabited largely by beduin, had, in Ottoman times, been virtually independent under its tribal rulers, and during Feisal's brief reign in Damascus it came nominally under his authority. Moreover, although the French were demanding that Britain expel Abdullah, the British felt some obligation towards King Hussein's second son, who now appeared to have no hope of acquiring an Arab throne.

Churchill, accompanied by Lawrence, went up from Cairo to Jerusalem, where he also had the task of reassuring leaders of the Arab community that Britain had no intention of turning its Palestine mandate into a Jewish state. From there he summoned Abdullah to meet him. Like a good oriental salesman Abdullah began by naming some impossible prices: such as that Transjordan should be joined to Iraq with himself as king. Finally he accepted Churchill's proposal that he should 'temporarily' become ruler of the independent amirate of Transjordan, with an annual British subsidy and British advisers, on the understanding that Britain would try to persuade the French to restore an Arab administration in Damascus with Abdullah at its head. Abdullah knew very well that there was no chance of this, but a reasonably secure amirate was worth several hypothetical kingdoms.

The temporary arrangement, therefore, became permanent and Transjordan was incorporated into the Palestine mandate, under the high commissioner in Jerusalem, with the proviso that the mandatory (i.e. Britain) could exclude it from the area of Jewish settlement. This was done and for nearly thirty years Transjordan remained a poor but relatively peaceful desert Arab state under British guidance and protection.[5]

With Feisal in Baghdad and Abdullah in his new capital of Amman, their aged and now bitterly resentful father still presented a problem. Lawrence was dispatched to Jedda to persuade the old man to accept the accomplished fact that Syria, Lebanon and Palestine were all lost to the rule of his family. Hussein's stubborn refusal to sign the treaty which was offered him drove Lawrence into a fury. He wrote home describing the king of the Hejaz as 'conceited to a degree, greedy and stupid'.

In fact Hussein was unable even to hold on to the modest throne that was left him. As soon as the war ended the great desert fighter Ibn Saud set about extending his rule to the remaining areas of the Arabian peninsula that were not under British protection. In 1919 his Wahhabi warriors defeated King Hussein's army; in 1920 they cap-

5. The curious kink in the frontier that was drafted to divide the new amirate of Transjordan from what was to become Saudi Arabia is known as 'Winston's hiccough', because, according to legend, it was drawn by the secretary of state with pen and ruler after an exceptionally good lunch in Jerusalem.

tured the Asir province between the Hejaz and Yemen and in 1921 they finally defeated the last of the Rashidi amirs, his most powerful rivals in Ottoman times. Britain, which was still paying a subsidy to both Hussein and Ibn Saud, restrained him for a time but in 1924 the Wahhabis invaded the Hejaz and captured Mecca. Hussein abdicated in favour of his eldest son, Ali, and retired, a bitter exile, to Cyprus. But Ali's situation was hopeless. Medina and Jedda surrendered and in January 1926 Ibn Saud was proclaimed king of the Hejaz. The Soviet Union was the first country to recognize him.

Britain also acknowledged his new status in the following year through the treaty of Jedda, in which Ibn Saud recognized in return the Hashemites, Abdullah and Feisal, as rulers of Transjordan and Iraq, and the British-protected status of the Persian Gulf shaikhdoms. In 1932 he assumed the title of king of Saudi Arabia, in control of the whole Arabian peninsula except for the shaikhdoms on its fringes which were under British protection and the mountainous kingdom of Yemen which, after the end in 1918 of the Turkish suzerainty that had never been very effective, reverted to its remote and inaccessible state of independence.

There was irony, which the Arabs of the Fertile Crescent bitterly noted, in the fact that the parts of the Arab world which had achieved independence following the break-up of the Ottoman Empire were the most socially, culturally and economically backward, while the more sophisticated areas were placed under the control of Western Christian nations. As in previous centuries it was the beduin Arabs who were able to resist outside control.

For their part, Britain and France made little attempt to conceal the nature of the imperial role they had conferred upon themselves or their contempt for the idealistic notion that it had been conferred upon them as a temporary trust by the world community. As Lord Curzon, who succeeded Balfour as foreign secretary in 1920, said openly in the House of Lords on 25 June 1920:

It is quite a mistake to suppose . . . that under the Covenant of the League, or any other instrument, the gift of the mandate rests with the League of Nations. It does not do so. It rests with the powers who have conquered the territories, which it then falls to them to distribute, and it was in these circumstances that the mandate for Palestine and Mesopotamia was conferred upon and accepted by us, and that the mandate for Syria was conferred upon and accepted by France.[6]

6. *Parliamentary Debates* (*Hansard*), *House of Lords*, 5th series, XL (1920), col. 877.

Curzon, Balfour and Churchill were all men of a nineteenth-century imperial mould, who certainly would not have disagreed with Lord Cromer's view that the people of the world are naturally divided into 'governing races' and 'subject races', and who took it for granted that the British were among the former and the Arabs among the latter. They could not fail to be aware that there was a conflict between the imperial outlook and the liberal principles of the League of Nations, but they had no doubt that their view was the right one – that it was right for the subject races as well as for Britain. Balfour pointed out the dilemma with startling clarity. In a memorandum he wrote on Syria, Palestine and Iraq in August 1919, while the Paris Peace Conference was still in progress, he pointed out that in Syria the population had no choice other than to accept a French-controlled administration after the war. He added:

The contradiction between the letter of the Covenant and the policy of the Allies is even more flagrant in the case of the independent nation of Palestine than in that of the independent nation of Syria. For in Palestine we do not propose even to go through the form of consulting the wishes of the present inhabitants of the country, though the American commission [i.e. the King–Crane Commission, see above p. 180] has been going through the form of seeing what they are. The four great powers are committed to Zionism and Zionism, be it right or wrong, good or bad, is rooted in age-long tradition, in present needs, in future hopes, of far profounder import than the desires and prejudices of the 700,000 Arabs who now inhabit that ancient land.

In my opinion that is right. What I have never been able to understand is how it can be harmonized with the Anglo-French declaration, the Covenant, or the instructions to the commission of Enquiry . . .

In fact, so far as Palestine is concerned, the powers have made no statement of fact that is not admittedly wrong, and no declaration of policy which, at least in the letter, they have not always intended to violate.[7]

It is scarcely necessary to go any further than this to find justification for the Arabs' sense of betrayal by the West and their special bitterness over Palestine. If the West has a feeling today that the Arabs are taking their revenge it should be easy to understand the reasons.

Balfour admitted frankly that the West had deceived the Arabs but thought that it was in everyone's higher interest that it should do so. T. E. Lawrence, who in 1920 appeared to symbolize the ideal re-

---

7. *Documents on British Foreign Policy*, series I, vol. IV, 1952, p. 345.

lationship between Britain and the Arabs, also had a troubled conscience. As we have seen, he shared the imperialist dreams of his colleagues in the Arab Bureau. He wanted the Arabs of the Middle East to be part of the British imperial system which also meant that they should be kept out of French control. But he wanted them to be self-governing within this system. As he wrote to Lord Curzon: 'My own ambition is that the Arabs should be our first brown dominion, and not our last colony.'

Syria was lost to the French, and there was nothing to be done about this, but Lawrence convinced himself that Britain had done its best for the rest. He gave much of the credit to Churchill, for whom he felt a deep admiration which was warmly reciprocated.

As Lawrence wrote in *The Seven Pillars of Wisdom*:

Mr Winston Churchill was entrusted by our harassed cabinet with the settlement of the Middle East; and in a few weeks, at his conference in Cairo, he made straight all the tangles, finding solutions fulfilling (I think) our promises in letter and spirit (where humanly possible) without sacrificing any interest of our empire or any interest of the people concerned. So we were quit of the war-time eastern adventure, with clean hands, but three years too late to earn the gratitude which peoples, if not states, can pay.

In spite of the significant qualifications ('I think' and 'where humanly possible') Lawrence cannot have written these words without some qualms of conscience. However compelling the reasons, Britain had not fulfilled either the letter or the spirit of the promises which inspired the Arabs to revolt against the Turks.

The anomaly whereby those parts of the Arab world which achieved their independence after the break-up of the Ottoman Empire were the most socially, culturally and economically backward was even more glaring in the case of Egypt. Developments here were unrelated to those in Syria and Iraq, but they ran along parallel lines. The main difference was that Egypt had already been effectively under Western control for some thirty years when the war broke out and the fiction of Ottoman suzerainty was formally ended. Strictly speaking Egypt was a non-belligerent in the war, but, under martial law and occupation of a huge Allied force, it was neutral only in name. Egyptian troops helped to defend the Canal zone against the Turks, and some 150,000 Egyptians served in the Camel Transport Service and the Auxiliary Labour Corps and suffered heavy casualties. The social effects of the war were devastating. While some of the big landowners and a new property-owning middle class grew rich from war profits, the mass of the population suffered severely from inflation, food shortages and the army's commandeering of their camels and donkeys. In 1918 the death rate actually exceeded the birth rate in Egypt.

In 1917 the elderly Sultan Hussein Kamel died and was replaced with British approval by his youngest brother Fuad, the surviving son of the Khedive Ismail. Fuad was unsatisfactory because he had been brought up in Italy and had little understanding or knowledge of Egypt (he could hardly speak Arabic), but there was no obvious alternative. He would have liked to have made himself a fully independent ruler but he lacked any true qualities of statesmanship and was certainly incapable of representing the real feelings and aspirations of the Egyptians.

Egyptian nationalism, which owing to the British occupation was anti-British rather than anti-Turk, remained dormant during the war as martial law and the presence of the Allied forces kept it subdued. But the underlying feelings remained and they found a new voice in a craggy middle-aged lawyer named Saad Zaghloul who, although physically and temperamentally very different from Mustafa Kamel, had the same ability to sway the Egyptian masses with his oratory. Before his retirement in 1907 Lord Cromer approved his appointment as head of a newly created ministry of education, and commended him as an ideal type of moderate nationalist who could be expected to work for Egyptian self-government at some distant date in the future. But by the end of the First World War Zaghloul had become an extreme opponent of the British and spokesman for unfettered Egyptian independence.

Two days after the armistice Zaghloul made a formal request to go to London with a delegation (*Wafd*, as his political party came to be known) to present Egypt's case. Balfour, who was preoccupied with the Paris Peace Conference and who regarded Zaghloul as an irresponsible extremist, curtly refused. In a letter to the British high commissioner in Cairo Balfour said that although the British government favoured as always giving Egyptians an increasing share in the government, 'as you are well aware, the stage has not yet been reached at which self-government is possible'. This was because Britain regarded Egypt as a vital link in imperial communication with India and the Far East which must at all costs be kept under British control. The Egyptians on the other hand considered that their cooperation with the Allies in the war gave them at the very least the right to put forward their case for independence. It seemed ludicrous

to them that the desert tribesmen of Arabia should be represented at
the Paris Peace Conference but not the Egyptians with their long
political experience.

When Zaghloul began to rouse the country in protest, the British
bundled him and some of his followers on a train and exiled him to
Malta. This was the signal for a violent uprising which the Egyptians
call the 1919 Revolution. It began in Cairo with strikes by students and
government officials and spread to the countryside. It was put down
only by swift and firm action by the depleted British forces in Egypt.

A surprised and dismayed British government sent out Allenby,
the hero of the Middle East campaigns, as high commissioner with
special powers to restore order. Despite his authoritarian manner,
Allenby held fairly liberal views which favoured allowing the
Egyptians to manage their own affairs as far as possible. Realizing the
extent of Zaghloul's popularity he ordered his release from exile. But
the problem remained of reconciling Egyptian aspirations with those
British interests which were regarded in London as vital. The British
government therefore sent out a mission headed by the colonial
secretary, Lord Milner, to examine the problem.

Milner was an arch-imperialist who had mellowed with age and he
soon realized that the protectorate over Egypt could not be maintained and that the best hope was to abolish it through an Anglo-
Egyptian treaty guaranteeing British interests. These were principally
the right to maintain troops in Egypt to defend the Suez Canal, the
protection of foreign interests in Egypt (that is the Capitulations) and
the status of the Sudan. This last was nominally an Anglo-Egyptian
Condominium but British officials held all the senior government
posts and decided policy. Egyptian nationalists were now demanding
a reassertion of Egyptian authority in the Sudan, but the British
government, with the full support of Anglo-Sudanese officials, had
no intention of allowing its enlightened, if paternalistic, administration of Sudan to be modified.

The problem was to persuade a representative Egyptian to sign a
treaty of 'limited independence' of this kind for Egypt. If Zaghloul
refused there was no one else who could or would take the responsibility and after some hesitation Zaghloul did refuse. As unrest and
violence continued Allenby, seeing there was no way out of the
deadlock, persuaded a reluctant and divided British cabinet to make a
unilateral declaration of Egyptian independence reserving the un-
solved questions as special points to be settled by agreement at some
future date.

The key problems between Britain and Egypt had been shelved but not solved. Egypt had been granted a form of semi-independence which was not accepted as final by any representative Egyptian. However, the declaration did mean that Egypt at once acquired many of the aspects and institutions of self-government, similar to those in Iraq. Sultan Fuad became King Fuad I; a parliamentary constitution on the Belgian model was introduced which gave the king considerable powers, although not enough for his liking, and the number of British officials in Egypt was steadily reduced. But the British army remained in occupation and British officers retained key posts in the Egyptian army. The British high commissioner, who retained his power to intervene in many of Egypt's internal affairs as well as his title, was still very much *primus inter pares* among the other foreign ambassadors who now came to Cairo. Egypt's struggle for independence, often bitter and violent, was to last at least another three decades.

The western wing of the Arab world, which was under French (and Spanish) rule, was not directly affected by the Arab Revolt in the east or the bitter controversies of the post-war settlement. French fears that the heady concepts of Arab independence would affect their North African empire were unwarranted at this stage. The most delicate situation was in Morocco, where 'pacification' was only half completed when the 1914–18 war broke out. In 1914 the French government ordered the Resident-General Marshal Lyautey to send most of his troops back to France to face the German invasion and to fall back on the Moroccan coast. However Lyautey, a colonial ruler of genius, managed to send the troops for which he had been asked and to hold all occupied Morocco as well. The fact that tens of thousands of North African Arabs served in the French army on the western front tended to justify the deep-seated French feeling that the North African empire was necessary to balance Germany's marked superiority in numbers.

It was only Italy that came near to losing its North African colony in the First World War. When Italy entered the war in 1915 on the side of the Allies, the Sanussi of Cyrenaica,[8] with the support of Turkish and German arms, attacked British outposts in Egypt while the Tripolitanians turned on their Italian conquerors. The Sanussi had little

8. The Sanussi Order, which was founded in 1843, called for a return to the purity and spirituality of Islam at the time of the Prophet Muhammud. It had a wide appeal among the beduin of eastern Libya, who still adhere to it today.

success and signed a truce with Britain in 1916, but the Italians were pushed back to the coastal towns and in 1917 seemed on the verge of losing their new possession entirely. When the war ended the Tripolitanian leaders, advised by Abdul Rahman Azzam Pasha, one of the first Egyptian Arab nationalists who twenty-five years later was to be the secretary-general of the Arab League, felt strong enough to declare a republic. But Italy had been on the winning side in the war and was in no mood to give up its new colony. After two years of negotiations with the nationalists Italy turned to repression which was greatly intensified with the advent of Mussolini's fascism in 1922. Marshal Graziani subdued Tripolitania, Fezzan and finally Cyrenaica until he was able to declare a *Pax Romana* in 1932.

10. Western Tutelage and the Rise of Arab Nationalism

One of the anomalous results of the post-war settlement was that it was the most backward of the Arab states which secured their independence. Another was that the Arabs, the allies of the winning side, came under the direct or indirect control of the Western Christian nations while the defeated Turks rose from the ashes of the Ottoman Empire to create a strong and independent republic. This was due mainly to the genius of one man: Mustafa Kemal. Before the end of the war, when Turkey's defeat seemed inevitable, he had headed a group of army leaders who favoured abandoning what remained of the empire and withdrawing to Anatolia to create a nation in the Turkish homeland. His advice was rejected and after the Mudros armistice he was left to extricate the Turkish Seventh Army from Palestine and bring it back to Anatolia with the remaining eastern armies.

The Young Turks fled the country and the new Sultan Mohammed VI formed a new government of men who were ready to accept the terms of the Allies, who were preparing for the dismemberment of Turkey. Italians and French had their claims but above all it was the Greeks who aimed at the annexation of the whole of western Anatolia in which there were substantial Greek minorities 'and thus bring nearer the "Great Idea" – the restoration of the Greek Christian Empire of Constantinople'.[1]

In 1919 Mustafa Kemal was sent by the sultan to Samsun on the Black Sea coast with orders to disband the Ninth Army and not to resist the Greeks. Instead Kemal began to rally the forces of resistance in eastern Anatolia. A new national assembly meeting in Ankara elected him president and rejected the harsh terms of the treaty of Sèvres of August 1920, which would have left Turkey helpless and deprived of some of its richest provinces. The bitter Greco-Turkish war of 1920–22 ended with the decisive defeat of the Greeks. When Mustafa Kemal's forces advanced towards the Dardanelles to drive the Greeks out of European Turkey, a clash with Britain was only narrowly averted. But Turkey's wartime conquerors were in no

1. Bernard Lewis, *The Emergence of Modern Turkey*, 2nd edn, London, 1968, pp. 236–7.

position for a renewed conflict with a formidable resurgent Turkey. The treaty of Lausanne, 24 July 1923, recognized full Turkish sovereignty in nearly all the territories which are now those of the Turkish Republic. Only the frontiers between Turkey and Iraq, which was by now a British mandate, remained to be settled. In December 1925 the Council of the League of Nations awarded the oil-rich vilayet of Mosul to Iraq and in July 1926 a treaty between Turkey, Britain and Iraq accepted the new frontiers as definitive and inviolable.

Although many Turks wanted to retain a constitutional monarchy, Mustafa Kemal (or Kemal Atatürk as he became when European-style surnames were made compulsory in Turkey in 1935) was determined to get rid of the sultan. In October 1923 Turkey was proclaimed a republic with Kemal as president. As an ardent secular nationalist who believed that all the inheritance of the Ottoman Empire should be destroyed and Turkey thoroughly modernized and europeanized, Atatürk would have liked also to be rid of the Islamic caliphate; but here popular opinion was too strong to be overcome by even his great prestige. Atatürk bided his time; and when in 1924 two prominent Indian Muslims, Amir Ali and the Aga Khan, published a statement calling upon the Turkish people to preserve the caliphate, Mustafa Kemal made use of the unfavourable reaction among Turkish nationalist opinion against this foreign interference to abolish it.

The title of caliph has not since been revived. The assumption of it by King Hussein of the Hejaz was not recognized except in the Hejaz, Transjordan and Iraq, and it lapsed some months later with his abdication. In May 1926 a caliphate congress held in Cairo was attended by delegates from thirteen Muslim countries (not including Turkey) but was inconclusive. Since then the caliphate has hardly been an issue in Islamic politics.

The dissolution of the Ottoman Empire and the rise of the secular Turkish Republic meant that Turkish and Arab peoples, whose lives had been intertwined for so many centuries, were now on separate courses. Atatürk's personality and modernizing reforms attracted widespread interest throughout the Arab world, especially among university students and the professional classes, but the concern was not mutual and there was remarkably little intercourse between the two nations. There was antipathy between Turks and Arabs derived from the former imperial/colonial relationship, and Atatürk's policies were aimed to persuade the Turkish people to forget the past glories of the Ottoman Empire and Islam and to concentrate on developing a strong modern state on European lines.

The consequences of this for the Muslims of the world were most apparent to men of Muslim minorities in other nations. One of these was the Aga Khan, the Indian leader who had intervened without success to try to persuade the Turks not to abolish the caliphate. In his memoirs he described how he headed a deputation of prominent Muslims to the British Prime Minister Lloyd George during the Paris Peace Conference:

The reasons for Muslim concern were profound and historic – Turkey stood almost alone in the world of that time as the sole surviving independent Muslim nation: with all its shortcomings, the imperial régime in Constantinople was a visible and enduring reminder of the temporal greatness of Islam's achievements. In the caliphate there was, too, for all of the Sunni sect or persuasion, a spiritual link of the utmost significance . . .

Muslim opposition to the break-up of the Turkish Empire had a basis – however much misunderstood it may have been – of true statesmanship and of understanding of the absorbing political realities of the Middle East. First, we felt that the separation of the Arabs from the Turks (hailed at the time as emancipation from tyranny, although within a few years all Arab nationalists were singing a very different tune) would not lead to the emergence of a single strong Arab nation extending from Egypt to Persia and from Alexandretta to Aden and the Indian Ocean. We foresaw in large measure what actually happened: the formation of a number of small Arab nations, for many years of little more than colonial status, under British and French overlordship. We predicted that the Arabs would in fact merely be changing masters, and where these masters had been Muslim Turks they would now be Christians, or (as ultimately happened in a large part of Palestine) Jews . . . [2]

Between Two World Wars

Five new states were created from the ruins of the Ottoman Empire – Iraq, Syria, Lebanon, Transjordan and Palestine. Their structure and boundaries were decided by the powers with little regard for Arab wishes. They began their existence without any sense of national cohesion or loyalty and this was to make them virtually ungovernable when they became fully independent. The mandatory powers permitted the establishment of representative institutions within narrowly prescribed limits,[3] but these were quite incapable of reconciling the various conflicting interests within the country or of adapting

2. *The Memoirs of the Aga Khan*, London, 1954, pp. 153–4.
3. Except in Palestine, where even this proved impossible (see below, p. 214).

themselves to rapid social change. In other words they failed in their task of building up a national political community.

Since these new Arab states were Western creations their people tend to regard their frontiers as artificial. It was inevitable, however, that a body of interests should grow up around the governments in Baghdad, Beirut, Damascus or Amman. The emotional aspiration for Arab unity was powerful, but the obstacles to its practical achievement steadily increased.

The Anglo-Arab Monarchies

Feisal's throne in Baghdad seemed only marginally firmer than the one from which he had been removed in Damascus. It was true that he had the support rather than hostility of the mandatory power, but this meant that he held an uneasy position between the British and the nationalists, who wanted full independence as soon as possible. Following the uprising of 1920 the British mandatory authorities, partly through necessity and partly through natural inclination, followed more liberal policies, although pursued by a barrage of criticism from the Anglo-Indian officials who remained a powerful element in the country. A nucleus of parliamentary institutions was created in 1924 with departments of state presided over by Iraqi ministers, and the powers of British officials were gradually reduced. But a clash was inevitable because while Britain was not prepared to give up its special position in Iraq 'public opposition in Iraq to any form of external control was rapidly becoming the most urgent national question of the time'.[4] With some difficulty, Sir Percy Cox persuaded a reluctant Feisal and his government to ratify an Anglo-Iraqi Treaty which in 1922, so far from replacing the mandate as Feisal had hoped, embodied all its terms and provided for Britain's special interests.[5] Even then the government stipulated that the treaty must be approved by the parliament (which had not yet been created), and it was not until 1925 that the assembly was elected and persuaded by all kinds of pressure and threats to approve the treaty by a small majority, in the teeth of fierce nationalist opposition. However from then on Iraq had a substantial measure of indepen-

4. *Special Report on Progress of Iraq*, p. 14, quoted in George W. Stocking, *Middle East Oil*, London, Allen Lane, 1970, p. 50.

5. Such as Article 4 under which the king agreed to be guided by the advice of the high commissioner 'on all matters affecting the international and financial obligations of his Britannic majesty'.

dence. Iraqi ministers became fully responsible to an Iraqi parliament and the British officials became, at least in theory, the servants of the Iraqi government.

Britain's major interest in Iraq was oil. (By 1925 the Anglo-Indian government's ambitions for incorporating Iraq into the British Empire and even of settling it with Indian peasants had been finally thwarted.) It had never made much secret of its intention to take control of the Turkish Petroleum Company, the curious mixture of German, Dutch and British interests which held the concession for Mesopotamian oil from the Ottoman sultan. (As we have seen, France took over the German share as a reward for accepting the revision of the Sykes–Picot agreement.) In March 1925 King Feisal and his cabinet ratified TPC's new concession. (Since this was seven months before parliament ratified the treaty defining Britain and Iraq's relations, it never had a chance to pronounce upon the concession. If it had, it would very probably have rejected it.)

However, this was not done without the strong disapproval of the US State Department, which acted as spokesman for American oil interests. The United States may have withdrawn politically from the Middle East when its twenty-year period of isolationism began after the First World War, but it was not liquidating its financial and commercial interests. In a series of sharp notes Washington pointed out to London that the United States had consistently taken the position in the peace negotiations that any alien territory acquired under the Versailles treaty must be held and governed in such a way as to assure equal treatment 'in law and in fact to the commerce of all nations' and accused Britain of quietly seeking control of all the oil resources of Mesopotamia.[6] Eventually, by reaching a private agreement with the British owners of the Turkish Petroleum Company, two American companies – Standard Oil of New Jersey and Socony Vacuum (later Mobil Oil) jointly obtained an equal share with the two British companies and the French company in the Iraq Petroleum Company, as it had now become. Iraqi ministers had very little to say in any of these proceedings.

Oil was struck in large quantities in 1927; and by the mid 1930s, when the oil pipeline from landlocked Kirkuk had been laid to the Mediterranean, Iraq became the second major Middle East oil producer after Iran.

By 1928 Britain was prepared to end the mandate provided that

6. See George W. Stocking, op. cit., p. 53.

British interests could be maintained. France, which believed that Britain was moving much too quickly, strongly disapproved. A treaty was delayed because of nationalist opposition to continued British tutelage in a concealed form and by disagreements among other League of Nations members. Finally an Anglo-Iraqi treaty was concluded in 1930 and ratified at the end of the year. It provided for an Anglo-Iraqi alliance for twenty-five years during which the two countries undertook to consult each other in order to harmonize their common interests in matters of foreign policy. Britain would have the use of certain air force bases in Iraq and existing means of communication, and in return Britain would provide a military mission to help train the Iraqi army. In accordance with the treaty Iraq became a member of the League of Nations in 1932, although Britain's insistence was needed to overcome the doubts of some League members about Iraq's ability to shoulder all the burdens of independence.

By 1932 Iraq had gone some way, against tremendous odds, towards creating a unified modern state. King Feisal I, despite his heavy dependence on British sponsorship, had established himself as a fairly enlightened and independent national leader. But the problems of Iraq's inherent divisiveness remained acute. The incorporation of the vilayet of Mosul into Iraq meant that one quarter of the population was non-Arab: Kurds, Turcomans or Assyrians. (The combative Christian Assyrians were a constant source of trouble which exacerbated religious differences and culminated in a shocking massacre by Iraqi troops shortly after independence. It was especially the Kurds, who had been cheated of their hopes of an independent state in eastern Anatolia after the First World War and who were ruthlessly suppressed by the Turkish Republic, who were to challenge the unity of the Iraqi state.) Even the Arab population was divided between a Shia majority and the politically dominant Sunni minority. Tribal factionalism among the beduin population of the deserts was also a severe challenge to the authority of the state.

Tired and disillusioned, King Feisal I died suddenly in 1933 and was succeeded by his son Ghazi. Handsome and popular, but shallow and irresponsible, Ghazi was widely regarded as a nationalist, which meant being anti-British. He lacked his father's authority and prestige and, as he pursued his playboy existence, rival political factions encouraged tribalism while a series of incompetent, reactionary and increasingly authoritarian cabinets succeeded each other in office. They were opposed by an alliance of reformist middle-class intellectuals and young nationalist army officers inspired by the example of Atatürk. In 1936 these seized power under the leadership of General Bakr Sidqi. The movement ended, as it had begun, with assassination and another military coup. It was a failure because the reformist elements were soon pushed aside; the army was divided and the mass of the population alienated. But it was an event of great significance because it established a precedent for military coups in the Arab world. Despite the coup's failure, the Iraqi army had gained a new self-assurance and a taste for interference in political life. The army faction which overthrew Bakr Sidqi remained a power behind the scenes, capable of making or unmaking cabinets. However in 1938 this group, known as the Seven, was instrumental in bringing to power a pro-British civilian politician, Nuri Said,[7] who was to dominate the Iraqi state for the next twenty years through his strong personality and political finesse. Iraq's importance gave Nuri a special status in the Arab world, which he exploited to the full.

King Ghazi's death on 4 April 1939 in one of the sports cars he loved to drive recklessly was followed by disturbances as the rumours spread that he had been killed by the British for his nationalist views. Nuri Said and the Seven agreed on the choice of the Amir Abdul Ilah, an able if unappealing man who was nephew of Feisal I and brother of Ghazi's widow, as regent for the infant Crown Prince Feisal.

British support was vital to the fledgling Iraqi kingdom both under the mandate and in the early years of independence. It was this which ensured that the vilayet of Mosul went to Iraq rather than Turkey and that the vital question of navigation rights on the Shatt al-Arab river between Iraq and Iran was decided in Iraq's favour in 1937. (The agreement was denounced as unequal and unfair by Iran some thirty years later.) In another sense, however, the British connection was a weakening and divisive factor. British tutelage was detested by Iraqi nationalists, and the overbearing monopolistic powers of IPC over their major natural resource were deeply resented. Eventually these passions would rise and destroy both the monarchy and Nuri Said, who, for all his inability to change with the times, was the first major statesman the country had produced.

Feisal's elder brother Abdullah ruled over a much poorer and less populous domain. Unlike Iraq, Transjordan was a wholly artificial British creation; but despite this, and although its population was

---

7. Nuri was one of the few Iraqi officers in the Ottoman army who had joined the Arab Revolt in 1916. He became Feisal's chief-of-staff.

composed largely of quarrelsome beduin tribesmen, it was easier to fashion into a semblance of a unified nation with which Britain was able for a time to establish a fairly harmonious relationship. More humorous, intelligent and resilient than his younger brother, Abdullah did not allow his poor-relation status to rankle. In fact he showed some contempt for the pompous paraphernalia of the royal court at Baghdad. At the same time he accepted with benign resignation his almost total dependence on Britain. Two outstanding Anglo-Arab administrators, Sir Henry Cox and Sir Alec Kirkbride, were given the chance, as Abdullah remarked in his own memoirs, 'to do good to the Transjordanians, even against their will'.

The most notable British achievement in Transjordan and the partial fulfilment of Lawrence's dreams was the creation of the Arab Legion. This was the Transjordanian army named by Abdullah after the regulars who fought with Feisal in the Arab Revolt. It was the work first of Colonel F. G. Peake, a former commander of the Egyptian Camel Corps, and later of General J. B. Glubb, or Glubb Pasha, as he was always known – the last and most famous of a generation of Anglo-Arabs and as such as controversial a figure as Lawrence.

Peake concentrated on training the villagers to defend themselves; Glubb was mainly concerned with the beduin, from whom he formed a desert patrol as an arm of the Arab Legion. Between them they fairly easily pacified Transjordan internally, and, with greater difficulty, protected its southern and eastern borders against the forays of the old enemy Ibn Saud's Wahhabi warriors, who, on one occasion, advanced in large numbers in a swirl of dust towards Amman only to be repelled by two aircraft and four armoured cars.

As in Iraq, but at a more leisurely pace, Britain transferred its mandatory powers to Transjordan. The 1928 treaty recognized Transjordan's independence but Britain retained control over finance and foreign affairs. In 1939 Britain agreed to the conversion of the legislative council into a cabinet with ministers responsible to the Amir.

That Abdullah temporarily accepted his lot as a penniless desert ruler did not mean that he lacked ambition. On the contrary, he never abandoned his dream of joining some more important Arab lands to his own. The fact that, in the Arab Legion, he had the strongest Arab army in the 1940s meant that he was able to fulfil part of his dream. But this had fatal consequences for him and the stability of his kingdom.

La Syrie et Le Liban

In acquiring the mandates for Syria and Lebanon, France had achieved a long-standing ambition and in the early years of its rule it behaved more in the manner of a colonial government backed by military power than a guardian entrusted by the League of Nations with the task of bringing the territories with which it had been entrusted to self-government as quickly as possible. The press was controlled and nationalist groups suppressed. The basis of France's policy in both Levant states was to strengthen and promote the traditionally Francophile Christian population at the expense of the Muslim Arab elements. As we have seen, this was the purpose behind France's extension of the borders of predominantly Christian Lebanon at the expense of Syria. In the long run this policy was not a success. It created deep resentment in Syria, and although Lebanon, where the Christian population remained dominant in commercial and political life, always caused France less trouble than Syria, the fact that nearly half its population were Muslim Arabs with no special ties with France meant that *le Grand Liban* was never docile.

The terms of the mandate promised a constitution for both countries within three years, but the Lebanese constitution, which was drafted in Paris with little consultation with the Lebanese, was imposed in 1926. It provided for a bicameral parliament and a president. The principle was established that seats in parliament and the cabinet should be distributed on a basis of religious confession.[8] The president was a Maronite Catholic and the prime minister a Sunni Muslim.

In Syria even a French-imposed constitution was much longer delayed. France had extended the size of Lebanon. In Syria it showed its intention of dividing in order to rule more easily by partitioning the country into four separate administrations, two of which were based on regional minorities.[9] The great majority of Syrians, and especially the educated élite, refused to accept this partition. Many of them went further, demanding an independent Syria which should also include Palestine and Transjordan. In 1925 French rule was shaken to the foundations when the Druzes rose in revolt because of local grievances and formed an alliance with the nationalists in Damascus.

8. Since independence the membership of parliament has always been a multiple of eleven, with six Christians to five non-Christians.

9. For the Druzes in the Jebel Druze in the south and the Alawites – an extreme Shia sect who believe that Ali, the Prophet's son-in-law, was the incarnation of God himself.

The revolt subsided gradually, leaving much bitterness, but it led the French to pursue a more conciliatory policy.

In 1930 the French high commissioner promulgated a new constitution which made Syria, like Lebanon, a parliamentary republic, but with France retaining the control over foreign affairs and security. The new constitution failed to satisfy nationalist opinion even in Lebanon. The Lebanese constitution was suspended from 1932 to 1937 and the Syrian constitution from 1933 to 1936. Various factors contributed to a new French effort at conciliation in 1936. The Anglo-Iraqi treaty had made Iraq independent in 1932. A similar Anglo-Egyptian treaty was concluded in 1936. The expanding power of Fascist Italy and the outbreak of the Spanish Civil War raised tension throughout the Mediterranean, and in France itself a left-wing Popular Front government had come to power. A treaty was signed in September 1936 providing for Syrian independence, Franco-Syrian consultation on foreign policy, French priority in advice and assistance, and the retention by France of two military bases. The Jebel Druze and Latakia districts were to be incorporated into Syria.

A similar treaty was negotiated with Lebanon in November, but, although both treaties were ratified by the Syrian and Lebanese parliaments, they were never ratified by the French chamber and remained inoperative. The Popular Front government fell from power and was replaced by more conservative interests, which favoured retaining French control over the Levant states for strategic and economic reasons. There were prospects of the discovery of oil in north-eastern Syria, and the two countries were a convenient stepping-stone on the route to the Far East. Another important factor was that Syrian and Lebanese independence would profoundly influence the Arabs in North Africa. With the growing threat from Nazi Germany with its population of 80 million compared with France's 40 million, France felt the need more than ever to draw on the manpower of its North African possessions.

The prospect of war with Germany also led France to conciliate Turkey over the question of the region or sanjak of Alexandretta, which, with its mixed Turkish, Arab and Armenian population, had been given a separate administration by France and was now claimed by the Turks. In 1937 the sanjak was given an autonomous status, and after a Franco-Turkish commission had ensured a Turkish majority in parliamentary elections, although Arabs and Armenians outnumbered Turks in the population, France agreed to the absorption of the sanjak of Alexandretta (which was renamed the Hatay by Turkey) in

June 1939. Not surprisingly, this act of naked self-interest by the mandatory power caused bitter anger among the Syrians, who do not accept it to this day. In Syrian schools Alexandretta is still shown as part of the Syrian Arab Republic.

The achievements of the French mandatory in Syria and Lebanon were far from negligible, although the great majority of Syrians and perhaps the Lebanese were never remotely reconciled to its rule. France introduced a relatively modern administrative system, customs organization, land registration and cadastral survey. It built many roads and created a department of antiquities. Its economic efforts were limited by the chronic weakness of the French franc on which the Syrian and Lebanese currencies were based. It gave some encouragement to both agriculture and industry, but it aroused considerable resentment by its policy of granting monopolies to French companies, whose profits were repatriated to France.

In the education field its achievements were more controversial. It protected the foreign mission schools and promoted French language and culture. Arab children were taught a French interpretation of history and even learned to sing *La Marseillaise*.[10] But in Syria at least a system of state schools was established, with its teaching mainly in Arabic. In Lebanon France had no need to impose its language and culture on the Christian population, which had already long accepted it as an instrument of education, although Arabic remained the normal medium of conversation for most of them. For the non-Christian Lebanese and the great majority of Syrians the French *mission civilisatrice* was doomed to failure because of the bitter opposition to its rule. In contrast to North Africa, France did not remain long enough to carry through its purpose in the Levant states. Nevertheless, only the most committed francophobe would deny that something of value remained: a French respect for learning in itself, for clarity of expression and intellectual style.

Arabia and the Persian Gulf

As we have seen, most of the vast and thinly populated Arabian peninsula was united by the political and military genius of the desert

10. The Italian statesman Count Sforza recalled on a visit to Syria in 1935 that he saw a class of dark-skinned and black-haired young Arab boys stammering in chorus: '*Nos ancêtres les Gaulois étaient blonds . . .*' (Our ancestors the Gauls were blond . . .) See A. L. Tibawi, *Islamic Education*, London, 1972, p. 142.

warrior Ibn Saud combined with the religious zeal of his Wahhabi followers. His new kingdom was backward and desperately poor. In the early 1920s his annual revenue from all internal sources was £150,000 with an additional British subsidy of £60,000.[11] Ibn Saud was proud and politically independent, but this meant that he did not even have British help to build the nucleus of a modern army, in contrast to his despised Hashemite neighbours in Iraq and Transjordan. Wahhabi Puritanism frowned on all aspects of twentieth-century technological progress from the telephone to the automobile. (The question of whether the bicycle should be permitted was a subject of earnest discussion among the *ulama*.) Ibn Saud, a man of commanding presence combined with great charm and humour, preserved the beduin Arab tradition of retaining executive authority in his own hands, although advancing age meant that eventually he had to relax his personal control. The lack of trained Saudi Arabians meant that he had to recruit as some of his top officials other Arabs – mainly Egyptians, Syrians and Lebanese.

The king had two ways to increase his meagre revenues: to increase the fees for Muslim pilgrims to Mecca, or open the door to Western capitalist exploitation. The British were opposed to the former, and he and his followers had grave doubts about the latter. In 1933, in even more desperate straits because the world depression caused a decline in pilgrimage receipts,[12] the king overcame his fears and granted an oil concession to Standard Oil of California. After bargaining the cash advance was £50,000 against future royalties. The Iraq Petroleum Company competed for the concession, but, since it already had more oil in Iraq than it could handle it was more interested in keeping potential oil lands out of the hands of a competitor than in developing them, and its negotiator was only authorized to offer £5,000. Texas Oil Company, Standard Oil of New Jersey and Socony Vacuum eventually joined with Standard Oil of California to form the Arabian American Oil Company (Aramco) in 1944.

A major oil field was discovered in 1938 and, although its development was held up by the war, it had already become apparent by the Second World War that one of the poorest Arab states was destined to become one of the richest. It was also an event of the greatest

11. Saudi Arabia's total revenues in 1983 were some $40 billion.
12. 'Oh Philby,' the king exclaimed one day to the Arabian traveller, who was not his close friend, 'if anyone would offer me a million pounds, I would give him all the concessions he wanted.' (H. St J. Philby, *Arabian Jubilee*, London, 1952, p. 176.)

significance because for the first time the United States acquired a major interest in the Middle East.

A parallel development took place in the tiny neighbouring shaikh-dom of Kuwait at the head of the Persian Gulf. Kuwait was under British protection, and, as in Iraq, the United States government intervened to overcome British objections to the ruler of Kuwait granting a concession to a non-British concern. In 1934 a seventy-five-year exclusive concession was granted to the Kuwait Oil Company (KOC) owned jointly by the Anglo-Iranian Oil Company (later British Petroleum) and the American Gulf Oil Corporation. Oil was dis-covered in 1938 but, as in Saudi Arabia, development was delayed until after the Second World War, but when it started Kuwait, with its tiny population and area, rapidly became the prototype of the Arab oil shaikhdom with a vast surplus income.

Standard Oil of California and Texaco also secured an oil conces-sion for Bahrain, where oil was discovered in 1932 and began to be exported in 1934. Although the island's oil production and revenues remained on a much more modest scale than those of Saudi Arabia and Kuwait after the Second World War, Bahrain was able to devote funds to education and social services from the 1930s and secured a lead in a generally backward area.[13]

Rivalry between Ibn Saud and the other independent ruler in Arabia, the *imam* of Yemen, over the possession of the Asir province, which lies between Yemen and the Hejaz, led to a brief Saudi–Yemeni war in 1934. The Yemeni forces were quickly routed by Saudi troops led by the young Prince Feisal and a treaty of peace signed on 20 May 1934. Ibn Saud imposed only a minor frontier adjustment, and the moderation of the terms made the *imam* Yahya his friend for life.

Outside Saudi Arabia and Yemen, the Arabian peninsula and the Persian Gulf were under direct or indirect British control. However, the *imam* Yahya (1903–48) never accepted British rule over the Aden protectorate in Southern Arabia. Although in 1934 he signed a forty-year treaty of peace and friendship with Britain which accepted Yemen's southern frontier as the *status quo* until future negotiations could reach a final settlement, it was only an uneasy truce which followed. The threat from Yemen caused the British to intensify their efforts to pacify the interior, which continued in a state of tribal

13. The ruler of Bahrain was assisted in his enlightened, if paternalistic, administration by a British adviser, Charles Belgrave, another distinguished Anglo-Arab, who differed from the rest in that he obtained his post by answering an advertisement in *The Times*.

anarchy. In 1936 and 1937 Harold Ingrams, one more outstanding Anglo-Arab, persuaded the tribes and rulers of the Hadramaut to sign a truce which became known as Ingrams' Peace; and in 1938 the Aden protectorate, divided administratively into the western protectorate and eastern protectorate (the Hadramaut), was formally established under the British Colonial Office. This provided an effective *cordon sanitaire* protecting Aden Colony. The port of Aden had become one of the world's major bunkering stations and a vital link in the lifeline of the British Empire. The colony, formerly administered by the Bombay government, was transferred to the government of India from 1932 and 1937, and then, when the prospect that India would gain independence became a real one, to the British Colonial Office.

Along the western shores of the Persian Gulf many of the frontiers of most of the small tribal states under British protection remained undefined. This was of small consequence until this desolate region was discovered to contain a large proportion of the world's oil resources and ownership of the subsoil became a question of major importance.

Egypt and the Sudan

The manner in which Britain unilaterally declared Egypt's independence, while reserving its right to control what it regarded as vital imperial interests in the country, was a prescription for political instability in the country. While Britain aimed to secure a treaty with Egypt which would place Anglo-Egyptian relations on a permanent footing that would be satisfactory for Britain, Egyptian leaders struggled to secure their full independence. Those Egyptian politicians who might have been prepared to compromise with Britain were constantly outbid by more extreme nationalists, who rejected any idea that Britain should continue to act as Egypt's guardian.

There were now three major political forces in Egypt: the king, Zaghloul's Wafd party and the British, with the last holding ultimate authority. In the years 1922–36 the same pattern repeated itself several times. The king, who regarded the Wafd as his enemy, would dissolve parliament or suspend the constitution and rule for a time through ministers of his own choice. When popular feeling was so aroused that he could do so no longer, elections would be held in which the Wafd invariably won a sweeping victory. But although the Wafd was unquestionably the popular national party, the 1923 constitution, which gave it power, failed to provide a satisfactory and stable basis for Egypt's political life. The Wafd was a coalition of forces which included a minority with a clear idea of the kind of social and economic reforms that Egypt needed. But the party as a whole was dominated by the wealthy landowners who opposed these reforms, while the leading Wafdist politicians were so heavily engaged in the struggle for power with the king and the British that they had no time or energy to prove that the parliamentary system could satisfy Egypt's needs. Liberal constitutionalism failed to take root in Egypt.

British dominance was reduced by the declaration of independence, but it was still quite enough to arouse the angry resentment of Egyptian nationalists under Saad Zaghloul's fiery leadership. Strikes, bombings and the assassination of European officials were frequent throughout 1922–4. Much of the trouble centred on the Sudan as the king and all Egyptian political elements reasserted Egypt's claims, which Britain strongly resisted. The Sudanese were not immune to the Egyptian nationalist fever, which helped to foment a Sudanese uprising against British rule in 1924. But the new generation of Sudanese nationalists had no desire for a resumption of Egyptian rule; this was a reality which Egyptian politicians took many years to accept.

Anglo-Egyptian relations reached their first major crisis in November 1924 with the murder in Cairo of Sir Lee Stack, the governor-general of the Sudan who by convention was also sirdar (commander-in-chief) of the Egyptian army. The prompt punitive action of Allenby, who detested Zaghloul and held him responsible, virtually eliminated Egypt's minor share in the condominium administration and emphasized that Britain was still very much the master of Egypt. According to the standards of the time, Allenby was a liberal who sincerely believed in Egyptian self-government, and he was strongly criticized by the diehard imperialists in the British cabinet such as Winston Churchill. If Allenby failed to reach agreement with Egyptian nationalism it was because this would have required concessions which no British government would have allowed. He was succeeded by the more imperial-minded Lord Lloyd, a close friend of Churchill, who fought on the whole successfully to preserve what was left of British control through the retention of British officials in key ministries such as finance, war and justice.

Zaghloul, the old nationalist warrior, died in 1927 and was succeeded at the head of the Wafd by Nahas Pasha. He was a lesser man, but the Wafd was still the only popular party with mass support. In 1931 King Fuad succeeded in his aim of ousting the Wafd from power.

Suspending the constitution, he called upon Sidky Pasha, an able right-wing authoritarian and millionaire businessman, who amended the electoral law to ensure the defeat of the Wafd in the elections. After two years Sidky fell ill and was succeeded by other men of lesser ability; popular demand for the restoration of the 1923 constitution increased until the king was forced to agree shortly before his death. He was succeeded by his son Farouk, a handsome and smiling but spoiled sixteen-year-old, who was initially received with wild enthusiasm by the Egyptian masses as a new hope for the future when he returned from school in England.

On several occasions between 1924 and 1936 renewed attempts had been made to agree on an Anglo-Egyptian treaty, but they had all broken down on the question of the reserved points in the 1922 declaration of independence – especially the Sudan. But in 1936 the situation had changed. On the one hand the Wafd party, chastened by another five years in opposition, had softened its attitude towards Britain. It had come to accept that it could no longer remain in office against the opposition of both the British and the palace. Britain, on the other hand, saw the advantage of dealing with politicians who had mass popular support. Both Egypt and Britain were thoroughly alarmed by Mussolini's African ambitions – the Italian–Ethiopian war had just begun – and Anglo-Egyptian cooperation for the defence of Egypt seemed essential.

The result was the Anglo-Egyptian treaty of 1936, which took Egypt much of the way towards full independence. The treaty was to last twenty years; both parties were committed to a further alliance in 1956, but Egypt would then have the right to submit to third-party judgement the question of whether British troops were any longer necessary in Egypt.

The British occupation of Egypt was formally ended, but this did not mean that British troops would leave the country. As Egypt's defence capability improved they would be withdrawn gradually to the Suez Canal zone and Sinai, where their number would be limited to 10,000 land forces and 400 air pilots. The treaty contained another provision which ultimately meant that it did not finally settle the Anglo-Egyptian problem. Britain reserved the right of reoccupation with unrestricted use of Egyptian ports, airports and roads in the event of war.

At the same time Egypt gained control over its own security forces for the first time since 1882. The British high commissioner became an ambassador. The British inspector-general of the Egyptian army was replaced by an Egyptian, and military intelligence was egyptianized. The number of Europeans in the police was to be reduced by 20 per cent a year, although an Englishman, Thomas Russell, scourge of narcotics' pedlars, remained head of the Cairo police until 1946. The Capitulations were finally removed and Egypt obtained full rights of jurisdiction and taxation over all residents.

The Sudanese question was shelved in the treaty – and it was a measure of the Wafd's anxiety to reach agreement that they were prepared to do this – but it seemed for a time that a new and more hopeful period had dawned. The treaty seemed popular. The king, the prime minister, and even the domineering British ambassador Sir Miles Lampson, were cheered in the streets. But there was opposition from several quarters – especially among the students. Secure in the knowledge that it remained the only mass political party, the Wafd was hardly aware of the sinister growth of extra-parliamentary forces. The most formidable of these was the Muslim Brotherhood, which had been founded in the 1920s by an Egyptian schoolteacher of charismatic eloquence as a religious revival movement, but which had become increasingly political in outlook and aims. It demanded that Egypt's entire legal, political and administrative system should be based on the Koran and Islamic tradition. The Brotherhood had established a network of branches which undertook the indoc-trination and education of its new members. It also started para-military training for its youth groups, and in the 1940s turned increasingly to terrorism. Other fascist-type groups appeared on the scene, and in response the Wafd formed its own militant organization.

In this turbulent situation, the students played a leading role. They demonstrated so often that they hardly seemed to have time to study. One of the leading high-school demonstrators demanding an end to British interference and a return to the 1923 constitution was a tall and rather solemn seventeen-year-old named Gamal Abdul Nasser. In 1935, when two students were killed by police bullets, he was slightly injured. He considered joining one of the various parties or groups, but found them all wanting. In 1937, taking advantage of the fact that Britain and the Wafd both wanted to see the Egyptian army improved and expanded, and that the Military Academy had been opened to classes other than the landowning aristocracy, he became an officer cadet. Among his contemporaries was Anwar Sadat, and a score of others who a few years later would join him in the clandestine Free Officers' movement in the army.

Palestine

In Iraq and Egypt Britain had to cope with nationalist movements seeking to throw off British tutelage. In Palestine its role was much more difficult because it was dealing with two such movements which were also in conflict with each other: the Arab and the Zionist. Nevertheless, after the rioting of 1920 and 1921 a period of relative peace ensued. The British went out of their way to still the fears of the Arabs that the intention was to turn Palestine into a Jewish state with a Jewish majority, and Sir Herbert Samuel even incurred the abiding anger of the Zionists, who had naturally welcomed his appointment, by temporarily suspending Jewish immigration in 1921. But fundamentally the Palestinian Arabs never accepted the British mandate at all. Their demand was for immediate Arab rule, and this the British were not prepared to concede. For this reason they consistently rejected Britain's tentative steps towards creating representative institutions as a prelude to self-government at some time in the future. Moreover they did this at a time when the Zionists were also opposed to such moves because the Jews were still only a small minority of the population and would have been consistently outvoted.

The symbol of this totally uncompromising Arab attitude was Hajj Amin al-Husseini, a young member of one of the leading Jerusalem Arab families who had studied at al-Azhar university in Cairo and had acted as recruiting officer for Feisal's army under the British occupation. He headed the anti-Jewish demonstrations in April 1920 and was sentenced by a British military court to fifteen years in prison. He absconded but was pardoned by Sir Herbert Samuel, who decided, as a measure of conciliation of Arab opinion, that he should be offered the post of mufti of Jerusalem when the post fell vacant on the death of his stepbrother. In 1922 he was elected head of the Supreme Muslim Council which had been formed by the British mandatory government. From then onwards he was the effective leader of the Palestinian Arabs. If for a period he was prepared to hold his hand, in effect he never altered his determination to wage all-out war against both the British and the Zionists to make Palestine an independent Arab state.[14]

14. There is much to be said for the view of the Zionist writer Jon Kimche that Hajj Amin not only shaped Palestinian Arab policy throughout the inter-war period, but left a legacy of uncompromising refusal to accept or recognize Zionism in any form, which was an agreed principle of all Arabs for long after his personal influence had declined. (See Jon Kimche, *Palestine or Israel: The Untold Story of Why We Failed*, London, 1973.)

The main reason why Palestine was relatively quiet from 1923 to 1929 was that the Arabs saw no real danger of the Zionists taking over the country. Although substantial numbers of Jews came into the country many were leaving, since economic prospects were limited. In 1927 there was even a net emigration of Jews from the country. By 1931 their numbers had risen from about 60,000 or about 8 per cent of the population to 175,000 or about 17·7 per cent of the total.

In 1929 the peace was broken by a severe riot in Jerusalem, which arose from a dispute over religious practices at the Wailing Wall in Jerusalem. Hajj Amin played a leading role in it. Britain's Labour government acknowledged Arab fears of Zionist domination in a policy statement which seemed to favour the Arabs. At the same time a technical report stated that there was no margin of land available for new immigrants. However, when the policy was reversed in an explanatory letter (later named the Black Letter by the Arabs) from the British Prime Minister, Ramsay MacDonald, to Chaim Weizmann, the president of the Jewish Agency (the organization which succeeded the Zionist Commission and constituted a kind of autonomous Jewish government within Palestine), the Palestinian Arabs became convinced that recommendations in their favour on the spot would always be annulled by Zionist influence at the centre of power.

From then on the situation in Palestine deteriorated as the mutual fear and antagonism of the two communities intensified. In 1929 the Palestinian Zionists made up their long-standing differences with the World Zionist Organization and, with British consent, the two created an enlarged Jewish Agency in which half the members came from outside Palestine. The immense increase in Zionist economic power that this implied was deeply alarming for the Palestinian Arabs. At the same time, Arabs and Muslims outside Palestine were becoming increasingly aroused by the problem. In December 1931 a Muslim congress attended by delegates from twenty-two Muslim countries was called at Jerusalem to warn against the dangers of Zionism, and in 1933 a boycott of Zionist and British goods was proclaimed. Palestine had become a powerful catalyst for the growth of Arab nationalist feeling.

Between 1931 and 1935 there was a great surge of Jewish immigration into Palestine. Initially this was encouraged by Zionist funds and the optimistic economic prospects in Palestine at a time when the rest of the world was suffering from a slump. In 1933 Hitler's advent to power in Germany was an additional stimulus as it spread fear throughout the Jewish communities of Europe.

The British authorities in Palestine still vainly hoped for the creation of an Arab-Jewish state in Palestine leading to self-government. Although they were able to set up some working mixed municipal governments, such as that in Haifa, the aims of the two communities were quite irreconcilable on a national level. In December 1935 the British again offered a form of representative government, through a legislative council on which the Arabs would have fourteen seats and the Jews eight. Some of the Arabs would have accepted the proposal, although they would not have been represented in proportion to their numbers and they would, by implication, have been accepting the Zionist aims of the mandate, while the Jews fiercely rejected it because it would have given the Arabs a permanent constitutional majority.

In April 1936 the various Arab political groups in Palestine united sufficiently to form an Arab Higher Committee under Hajj Amin al-Husseini. In reaction against the continuing fear of the growth of Jewish numbers in Palestine and more immediate alarm at the discovery that the Zionists were smuggling in arms for self defence, the Higher Committee called for a general strike which developed into a general Arab rebellion supported by Syrian and Iraqi volunteers.

In 1937 a new British commission of inquiry under Lord Peel declared the mandate unworkable, and for the first time recommended the creation of an Arab and a Jewish state in Palestine with a third small state under British administration for Jerusalem, Bethlehem, Nazareth and the surrounding areas. This idea was rejected by both Arabs and Jews and in the following year was declared unworkable by the Woodhead technical committee.

Arab bitterness was greatly increased by the knowledge that, while it was events in Europe for which they were in no way responsible that was increasing the pressure of Jewish immigration into their tiny country, the Western nations were doing so little to help. A conference called by President Roosevelt at Evian in France in July 1938 to find a solution for Jews suffering from Hitler's terror was a pathetic failure. The United States, Canada and Australia with their vast empty spaces only offered to take a few thousand Jews. Western European countries emerged slightly better, but it was left to the tiny and impoverished Dominican Republic to offer to take the largest number – 100,000. The Zionists, who had no desire to see the conference succeed because they wanted European Jews to go to Palestine and nowhere else, did nothing to help. Some of them actively worked against the conference. But it was the attitude of the

Western countries which the Arabs saw as monstrously hypocritical, and still do to this day.

In 1938 the Arab rebellion was renewed with increasing violence. It was primarily directed against the British but Jewish settlements were also attacked. The Zionists at first generally adopted a defensive attitude when the Arab rebellion broke out, but increasingly went over to the attack. Their secret army, the *Haganah*, which was no secret to anyone in Palestine, expanded and organized itself during these years while the extremist splinter group the *Irgun Zvai Leumi* (National Military Organization) began to develop its potential as a terrorist force.

Britain's next move was to call a Round Table Conference in London in the spring of 1939. This acknowledged the Arab world's interest in Palestine by inviting the independent states of Egypt, Iraq, Saudi Arabia, Transjordan and Yemen to attend, but it broke down in failure. No conceivable compromise was possible between the Palestinian Arabs' attachment to the soil of Palestine and the Zionist determination to turn it into the Land of Israel. (The fact that in some cases, wealthy Arab landowners had sold land over their tenants' heads to the Zionists, and others had grown rich as middlemen with thriving Zionist enterprise, of course did nothing to reconcile Palestinian farmers to what was happening.) In the first days of the mandate the Palestinian Arabs regarded a Zionist takeover in Palestine as a distant threat; they concentrated mainly on demanding an end to British rule. Now, their rustic villages were overshadowed by modern westernized Jewish towns and settlements, and Jewish numbers had risen to nearly half a million or just under one third of the population. Between 1922 and 1939 Jewish colonies had increased from 47 to 200 and Jewish landholdings from 148,500 to 383,350 acres.

It was at this point that the British government decided on drastic action to try to settle the problem in the face of the inevitable oncoming war. A White Paper issued in May 1939 envisaged the creation of an independent bi-national state of Palestine in ten years and the limitation of Zionist immigration to 75,000 over the next five years. After this further immigration would not be allowed 'unless the Arabs of Palestine are prepared to acquiesce in it'. The Arabs were still about two thirds of the population.

The White Paper was naturally anathema to the Zionists, who saw it quite rightly as an attempt to conciliate the Arabs, as the great majority of the population of the Middle East, during the expected war with Germany. In contrast the Arabs, although they officially rejected it on the advice of Hajj Amin, generally welcomed it and their rebellion died down for the duration of the war.

The White Paper turned the Zionist movement emphatically against Britain for the first time, but the outbreak of war in September placed the Zionists in the paradoxical position of having to support Britain against the common enemy of Nazi Germany. The fate of Palestine clearly depended on the outcome of the war.

The Second World War and its Consequences

Although the Middle East – and especially North Africa – was a major theatre of the Second World War, the Arab peoples were not directly involved. The great powers, who were engaged in a mortal struggle, were not concerned with Arab national aspirations for independence except to the very limited extent that they helped or hindered their war effort. (Turkey, the only Middle Eastern state which was both fully independent and militarily significant, belied the hopes of Britain and France by remaining neutral.)

On the other hand, the effects of the war were of the greatest importance for the Arabs and they profoundly influenced the nature of their relations with the dominant western powers. These effects were not all immediate. The defeat of France in 1940 was a decisive factor in the demise of its Arab empire; but, because France was ultimately on the winning side in the war, North Africa only won its independence a decade later. Similarly, Britain actually emerged from the war as the paramount power in the area, with the appearance of being stronger than ever before. It was only after a few years that it became clear that, with the loss of the Indian empire and the exhaustion of the war, Britain's Middle Eastern role was speedily coming to an end. In some respects the United States was taking its place, but with no clear idea of the part it was to play.

Although the British White Paper on Palestine of May 1939 did much to reduce anti-British hostility among the Arabs, there were some who hoped for an Axis victory. This was much less out of any anti-semitism – and still less from any familiarity with Nazi and Fascist doctrines – than the belief that it would liberate them from Anglo-French tutelage.

In Syria and Lebanon the situation was confused by the collapse of France in 1940. Some Arab leaders in both countries turned towards Germany, but most of them preferred to wait and see the outcome of the war. The submission of all the French forces in the Levant to Vichy caused concern to the British, who declared on 1 July 1940 that they would not tolerate a German occupation of Syria and Lebanon, and imposed a naval blockade which caused severe shortages in both countries. The French high commissioner, General Dentz, tried to conciliate the nationalists, who were demanding the relaxation of French control, but the negotiations broke down.

A crisis was reached in May 1941 as a result of a pro-Axis coup in Iraq (see below, pp. 219–20). The Vichy government allowed Germany the use of Syrian airfields to help the Iraqi nationalist rebels; and as soon as the revolt collapsed Britain, declaring that Marshal Pétain had betrayed his undertaking not to act against his former allies, invaded Syria and Lebanon with a mixed force of British and Free French troops. Fighting from 8 June to 14 July was bitter; Damascus was spared, but Beirut was severely damaged. An armistice was signed on 14 July which gave French troops and civilians the choice of repatriation or joining the Free French.

As the Allied forces entered Syria and Lebanon General de Gaulle's representative, General Catroux, issued a declaration to the Syrians and Lebanese announcing he had come to put an end to the mandate and to proclaim them 'free and independent'. The British government supported this announcement. However, it soon became apparent that de Gaulle had every intention of perpetuating what he himself termed France's dominant and privileged position in the Levant. He instructed Catroux to open negotiations on the basis of the 1936 treaties. But these, which had seemed liberal at the time, were now outmoded, and a critical struggle ensued in both countries. In Lebanon some of the Maronite Christians were prepared to accept a continuation of French rule, but the Muslims and a substantial number of leading Christians (who together formed a clear majority in the country) were now seeking full independence. Britain, seeing the wider advantages of attracting Arab sympathies in the war (which was going badly for the Allies in 1942), gave its support to the majority.

A crisis was reached in October 1943 when the Lebanese Prime Minister, Riyadh Sulh, announced a programme, which became known as the 'Charter of Independence' in which the constitution was amended to annul most of the mandatory's remaining powers. It also provided for especially close cooperation with the other Arab states if they would respect Lebanese sovereignty and independence. This doctrine, which was subscribed to by all Lebanese Muslim and

Christian leaders, was known as the National Pact, and became the cornerstone of Lebanese political life.

France's Committee of Liberation in Algiers rejected the Lebanese demands and, when the Lebanese parliament proceeded all the same to amend the constitution, the French delegate ordered the arrest of President Bishara al-Khoury, Prime Minister Riyadh Sulh and most of the cabinet. This provoked a national uprising. Britain intervened to deliver an ultimatum which said that unless the arrested men were released they would be set free by British troops. The French gave way, the president and cabinet were restored to office, and the constitution remained unamended. During 1944 France reluctantly handed over most of its powers to the Syrian and Lebanese governments. But the crisis was not yet over because the French retained control of the security forces or *Troupes spéciales*, which they hoped to use as a bargaining counter to compel the Syrian and Lebanese governments to sign treaties preserving France's special position in the Levant.

In Syria elections held in July 1943 resulted in an overwhelming victory for the nationalists, who demanded the immediate ending of the mandate and rejected France's proposals for a treaty. The situation remained in deadlock throughout 1944 as Syrian resistance stiffened to French demands. The independence of the two countries was recognized by several powers, including Britain and the Soviet Union; and in October 1944 the signing of the protocol of Alexandria gave birth to the League of Arab States, under British auspices. (See below, p. 228.)

The landing of a new contingent of France's terrifying Senegalese troops in Beirut in May 1945 was taken by the Syrian government as a sign that France intended to repeat the events of 1920: to build up French strength in Lebanon in order to advance on Damascus. Serious disorders broke out in several Syrian cities and spread to Damascus. The French responded by bombarding the Syrian capital for the second and last time during their mandate. But 1920 was not to be repeated because this time Britain was not prepared to wash its hands of Syrian affairs. Once again it intervened with an ultimatum and on this occasion it had strong support from the United States government. The French troops were obliged to cease fire and return to their barracks.

Meanwhile the newly created United Nations provided an ideal platform for the Syrians and Lebanese to present their case. Reluctantly the French gave way under international pressure. In July 1945 it was agreed that Syria and Lebanon should have national armies and the *Troupes spéciales* should be handed over to their control. British and French forces were finally withdrawn from both countries in the summer of 1946.

French stubbornness and lack of realism contributed to France's débâcle in Syria and Lebanon. The attitude of Britain (and the United States) was also a major factor, and this was something which Charles de Gaulle neither forgot nor forgave. But it would in any case have been impossible to restore France's pre-war political position in the Levant. France's cultural influence remained as strong as ever in Lebanon after its departure, but in Syria it was largely submerged by the political antagonism aroused by France's conduct of the mandate.

The Second World War showed just how much British control of Iraq had been retained after the country achieved independence in 1932. Stimulated by Axis propaganda, many nationalist groups were hoping for an Allied defeat in the war. Events in Palestine had further exacerbated anti-British feeling. The White Paper of May 1939 was more favourable to the Arabs in Palestine and the pro-British Nuri Said tried in 1940 to use this as a basis for a settlement of all outstanding problems with Britain. But by this time the pro-Zionist Winston Churchill was in power in Britain, and he was not willing to negotiate on this basis. Moreover, the indefatigable Hajj Amin al-Husseini had arrived in Baghdad in October 1939 as a political refugee, having escaped from Palestine where the British authorities had outlawed his Arab Higher Committee, and he was busy mobilizing anti-Zionist and anti-British feeling.

Nuri Said and the royal family however remained steadfastly pro-British, and in September 1939 Iraq broke off diplomatic relations with Germany. In March 1940 Nuri Said resigned and gave way to an aristocratic Iraqi nationalist, Rashid Ali Gailani – a manoeuvre to make him share responsibility for unpopular pro-British policies.

Supported by four leading army officers, known as the 'Golden Square', Rashid Ali moved Iraq cautiously towards a neutral position in the war. He ordered weapons from Italy and Japan that Britain could not supply. Although the war was going badly for Britain, the Iraqi government still did not dare to denounce the Anglo-Iraqi treaty without guaranteed German support. In November 1940 the British government announced publicly that the prime minister of Iraq no longer enjoyed its confidence and began to exert pressure for his resignation. Iraqi resistance hardened, and in April 1941 the Golden

Square carried out a coup to enforce Rashid Ali's restoration to office. Nuri Said and the Regent[15] escaped to Transjordan.

When the Rashid Ali cabinet refused to allow the landing of British troops in Basra, Britain decided to intervene, on the ground that this contravened the Anglo-Iraqi treaty of 1930. Despite the superficially strong position of the Iraqi army *vis-à-vis* the small British forces in Iraq, Britain succeeded in reversing the situation and overthrowing the Rashid Ali régime with little difficulty. A small force crossed the desert from Transjordan, and another from India was landed at Basra. Iraqi morale was low, opinion was divided, and the promised German aid arrived too late and in too small quantities. Hitler was preoccupied with preparations for invading the Soviet Union.

The Rashid Ali government fled and the Regent and Nuri Said returned. Succeeding Iraqi governments cooperated effectively with the Allies, and Iraq became a base for an invasion of Iran to assure that its neutrality remained favourable to the Allies. In January 1943 Iraq delcared war on the Axis powers. But the feelings which had given rise to the Rashid Ali revolt did not disappear. Many Iraqis of later generations were to regard him and his military colleagues as heroes of Iraq's struggle for independence.

The situation in Egypt during the Second World War was similar in some respects to that of Iraq. As soon as war broke out Britain invoked article VIII of the Anglo-Egyptian treaty of 1936 which, in placing all Egypt's facilities at its disposal, implied the virtual military re-occupation of the whole country. Egypt did not declare war on Germany. A few leading politicians were in favour, but the majority were opposed either because they felt it was not Egypt's war or because they were far from certain the Allies would win. On the other hand, Egypt more than fulfilled its obligations under the treaty. German nationals in Egypt were interned and German property placed under sequestration.

Reasonable harmony in Anglo-Egyptian relations was shattered by Italy's entry into the war in May 1940, which brought the fighting into the Middle East and North Africa. Egyptian neutrality suited Britain because of the advantage of Axis acceptance of Cairo as an open city, but a dispute arose over the reluctance of King Farouk and the Prime Minister, Ali Maher, to take action against Italian firms and nationals

15. He fled with the help of the American ambassador, who drove him hidden under a pile of rugs in the back seat of his car to the British air base at Habbaniyah.

in Egypt. Many of the king's closest circle were Italian (including the notorious Antonio Pulli, who rose from the post of palace electrician to become the king's most intimate companion). Among the Egyptian people as a whole there were many who longed for an Axis victory, not out of sympathy with Fascism but because they believed it would rid the country of the British. (One such Egyptian was the young Captain Anwar Sadat, who was caught by British intelligence and interned for spying for the Axis.) Winston Churchill, who had never shown much sympathy for Egyptian nationalist feelings, declared it was intolerable that Cairo should be a 'nest of Hun spies' and gave orders for the dismissal of the pro-Axis Egyptian chief of staff, General Aziz al-Masri (one of the leading Arab nationalists under the Ottoman Empire, see p. 157) and for the withdrawal of all Egyptian troops from the Western Desert to Cairo.

The moral and physical decline of the golden boy-king into a corrupt, frivolous and premature middle age which made him the subject of ridicule had been astonishingly swift. Some glandular defect was partly the cause, but his upbringing had been exceedingly ill-managed. Although not unintelligent, Farouk was spoiled and wilful. From the beginning of his reign, he crossed swords with the domineering British ambassador Sir Miles Lampson, who treated him with avuncular contempt to which Farouk responded with hatred.

Lampson insisted that he get rid of Ali Maher, and the king gave way with reluctant fury. But the British really wanted to see his old enemy the Wafd party under Nahas Pasha in power for the duration of the war. The Wafd was ready to cooperate with Britain and the British realized that the Wafd, as the popular party, would provide effective support for the Allies. Farouk refused to appoint Nahas.

A crisis was reached in February 1942, when General Rommel was advancing into Egypt from Libya. His name was being chanted in the streets of Cairo. It was even said that a suite had been booked in Rommel's name at Cairo's famous Shepheard's Hotel. Farouk, who was already suspect because of his Italian friends, was thought to be on the point of appointing a new prime minister with anti-British and pro-Axis sympathies. On 2 February 1942, the Abdin Palace was surrounded by British tanks and the towering figure of Sir Miles Lampson forced his way into the king's presence to present him with a choice between abdication and forming a Wafd government under Nahas. To Lampson's dismay, because he had hoped to get rid of Farouk, the king gave way and reluctantly sent for Nahas.[16]

For the rest of the war a Wafdist government ensured that the Egyptian home front was made safe for the Allies. The British had secured their immediate objective but in doing so they had probably destroyed the monarchy, the Wafd party and ultimately their own position in Egypt. For all his loss of popularity, Farouk was still Egypt's head of state and his humiliation was an affront to the whole nation. General Muhammad Neguib, who ten years later was to head the Revolutionary Council which replaced the monarchy, wrote to Farouk requesting permission to resign, with the explanation, 'Since the army was given no opportunity to defend Your Majesty I am ashamed to wear my uniform.' The twenty-four-year-old Lieutenant Abdul Nasser, who was stationed at Alamein, began to lay plans for his budding Free Officers' movement to overthrow the monarchy and Egypt's corrupt parliamentary system as an essential step towards ending the British occupation.

Palestine was relatively quiet during the war, although for anyone who was not preoccupied by the conflict with Germany the coming storm was easy to predict. The Arab rebellion died down and Jewish immigration inevitably slowed to a trickle as Jews were prevented from leaving Nazi-occupied Europe. In the early stages of the war the Zionists in Palestine cooperated with the British, despite the latter's enforcement of the provisions of the White Paper, in the hope of being able to form a Jewish army to fight Nazism. Despite Churchill's sympathy, they failed because of British military opposition, and the Zionists turned increasingly against Britain as the war progressed. A series of attacks by two extremist groups, the Sternists and Irgun, culminated in the assassination of Lord Moyne, the British minister of state in Cairo. Palestinian Jewry greatly strengthened itself militarily during the war. Apart from the 27,000 who received training in the British forces, the Jewish munitions industry developed rapidly and the unofficial Zionist forces ended the war well supplied with light arms.

During the war international Zionism shifted its main effort from Britain to the United States, where it gained the support of both major political parties. This event was of the greatest significance, because

16. Lampson brought with him for the king to sign a declaration of abdication which had been drafted by Walter Monckton, who had also written the instrument of abdication of King Edward VIII six years before, and conveniently had recently arrived at the British Embassy in Cairo.

henceforth United States concern with Palestine was to be the principal factor shaping its Middle East policies. A related and equally important development was the successful challenge to the hitherto unquestioned leadership of World Zionism of the cautious Chaim Weizmann by the younger and brasher David Ben Gurion. Weizmann remained the symbol of the World Zionist movement but Ben Gurion took over the leadership of the Jews in Palestine and the last remote hope of a peaceful outcome in Palestine disappeared.

As we have seen, the Palestine problem had already begun in the 1930s to act as a fermenting agent for the modern Arab nationalist movement. Yet the movement was still very much in its infancy at the end of the Second World War. The foundations for it had been laid before the First World War by writers and thinkers like Rashid Rida and Kawakibi, and more remotely by al-Afghani, who had first promoted the idea of Islam as a revolutionary secular political movement. But the concept of a single *Arab*, as opposed to Islamic, nation or *umma* had made very little headway even by the 1930s. The reasons are not far to seek. The view of Islam as a single non-racial community, embattled against the forces of paganism, idolatry and imperialistic Christendom, went so deep among the Arab peoples that it could not be changed in a generation. If the Ottoman Turks were attacked it was first and foremost on the grounds that they were failing in their duty, as the acknowledged military and political leaders, to protect the body of Islam, and only secondly that they were oppressing or abusing their non-Turkish Muslim subjects. It was on this first basis – that the Young Turks had put Islam in danger – that the Sharif Hussein made his appeal to the Arabs to revolt. His son Feisal did develop a rudimentary theory of Arab nationalism as he struggled to preserve a united and independent Arab Syria. 'We are Arabs before being Muslim, and Muhammad is an Arab before being a prophet,' he would say, and in a speech in Aleppo in June 1919 he declared: 'There is neither minority nor majority among us, nothing to divide us. We are one body, we were Arabs even before the time of Moses, Muhammad, Jesus and Abraham.'[17]

But this vague Hashemite dream of an Arab nation united under their leadership had already been shattered by the decisions of the Western imperial powers. In the inter-war period, Arab political leaders in the newly-created states were too heavily involved in their struggle to throw off foreign control to think of uniting all the Arabs.

17. Quoted in Sylvia G. Haim (ed.), *Arab Nationalism: an Anthology*, London, 1962, p. 35.

They could feel sympathy and interest for the struggles of their fellow Arabs in other states – especially the Palestinians who were fighting two enemies, the British and the Zionists – but there was little they could do to help them in practical terms, still less to join with them in a common political organization. Thus where political parties emerged in the inter-war period, like the Wafd in Egypt or the National Bloc in Syria, they tended to be local coalitions of different social elements seeking independence from the protecting power for their own country rather than for all the Arabs.

The Hashemites did not abandon their dream, because they still regarded themselves as the rightful leaders of the pan-Arab movement. But their claim was weakened by the rivalry between Abdullah of Transjordan, whose aim was a 'Greater Syria' of Syria, Lebanon, Transjordan and Palestine, and his younger brother Feisal of Iraq, who did not abandon his claim to the throne of Syria after his ejection by the French. In one sense Feisal's position was stronger because Iraq carried much more political and economic weight than Transjordan, and because in Nuri Said he had one of the most considerable statesmen in the Arab world during the inter-war years. His claim was maintained by the Regent Abdul Ilah, who always desired to become king of Syria and also had ambitions to recover the Hejaz for the Hashemites. In 1943 Nuri Said drafted a proposal, which he presented to the British minister of state in Cairo, for the United Nations to declare that Syria, Lebanon, Palestine and Transjordan would be reunited and an Arab union formed of Iraq and this Greater Syria, which other Arab states might join at will. But although Britain felt benevolent towards Nuri Said, it was never prepared to exert itself to further his Fertile Crescent policies.

The truth is that the Hashemite dream, in any of its forms, never had much chance of becoming reality. The Hashemite kings could never discard their role as instruments of British policy, however hard they might try (and some of them hardly tried at all). Although it was not apparent at the time, the Iraqi Hashemites were destroyed when they were restored to the throne by British bayonets in 1941. King Abdullah briefly realized part of his dream when he took over what was left of Palestine to the Arabs after the first Arab–Israeli war, but it was this very action which destroyed him.

While there were no practical moves towards uniting the Arabs during the 1930s and 1940s, there were writers and thinkers who began to perform the essential task of developing a theory or ideology of Arab nationalism. That the Arabs formed a nation in the twentieth-century meaning of the word was a novel idea, and it was necessary to show that all the ancestors of the Arabs from pre-Islamic times had contributed to the Arab heritage. As the brilliant Lebanese writer Amin al-Rihani said in a speech in 1938: 'The Arabs existed before Islam and before Christianity. Let the Christians realize this, and let the Muslims realize it. Arabism before and above everything.' An eloquent Syrian lawyer from Aleppo, Edmond Rabbath, put forward similar ideas in his famous study *Unité syrienne et devenir arabe*, published in Paris in 1937. The Arabs, he said, were united by a common origin, among Babylonians, Assyrians, Phoenicians and other semitic races, and by a common history, homeland (the Fertile Crescent), language and culture, which between them had forged a single nation. Rabbath was a Christian and therefore naturally made a distinction between Arabism and Islam, although, like most of the Christian Arab nationalists who followed him, he acknowledged the prime importance of Islam to the Arabs as their national religion. But Muslim Arab nationalists made the same point. Sami Shawkat, a leading Iraqi intellectual who was director-general of education, said in a speech in 1939:

We have up to now neglected a most vital aspect of our glorious history; we have made it start at the prophetic message, and this is a period of less than fourteen centuries. In reality, however, the history of our illustrious Arab nation extends over thousands of years, and goes back to the time when the peoples of Europe lived in forests and over marshes . . .

Another Syrian Christian, a Damascus schoolteacher named Michel Aflaq, began to develop and expand his ideas about the *baath* or renaissance of the Arab nation to a small but expanding group of friends and intellectuals. In 1944, when the departure of the French made it possible, he founded his Baathis party in collaboration with another schoolteacher, Salah Bitar, who was to be prime minister at several key moments in Syrian history. Aflaq, a withdrawn ascetic, has been called, with limited accuracy, the 'Gandhi of Arab nationalism'. His writings, which are romantic and idealistic in tone, are far from lucid. His ideas owed something to Marxism and to romantic German nineteenth-century nationalism, but he gave them a specifically Arab character. His central slogan was: 'One Arab nation with an eternal mission.' He stated the three Arab objectives as 'Freedom, Unity and Socialism', but he explained that freedom meant political, cultural and religious liberty as well as liberation from colonial rule. Unity meant not only the political unification of the Arab peoples but their regeneration through the release of the 'hidden vitality' which is the true source of nationalism. His socialism was less a set of specific socio-economic principles than a rather vague means of national improvement.

There was another inter-Arab political party which preceded the Baath and for a time had more influence although it has not survived as a major political force. This was the Syrian Socialist Nationalist Party, or *Parti populaire syrien* (PPS) as it is more commonly known, founded by Antoun Saadeh, another Syrian Christian. More overtly fascist than the Baath, Saadeh's ideas placed great emphasis on strength, discipline, unity and obedience to a single leader as a means of national revival. He was a secularist who demanded the separation of church and state and denounced sectarian divisions. In this he appealed especially to the minorities in the Arab world – Christians, Druzes, Kurds. What is interesting is that it was not an Arab nation but a Greater Syrian nation which had a distinct identity. The Syrians were not Arabs but the people whose natural home had been Syria since prehistoric times. The Syrian nation is the ethnic fusion of the 'Canaanites, Akkadians, Chaldaeans, Assyrians, Aramaeans, Hittites, and Mitannis'. He said that when the Arabs arrived in the seventh century the Syrian character had already been formed.

Antoun Saadeh was a natural charismatic leader with a strong talent for political organization. But his methods brought him into violent conflict with the established authorities in Syria and Lebanon, and led to his eventual execution by the Lebanese government in 1949. The PPS survived his death and even managed to attempt a coup against the Lebanese government in 1961. But it was over-whelmed by the rising tide of pan-Arab nationalism, which rejected the Syrian separation of the PPS. The party tried to come to terms with this trend but it was too late.

One thing all these pan-Arab writers and ideologists of the 1930s and 1940s had in common was a belief in revival or renaissance – a conviction that the long dark period of national decline and subjection was coming to an end and a new era was dawning. The other feature to be noted is that they all – including the Hashemites and Nuri Said of Iraq – excluded Egypt from the new revival and united nation that they foresaw, although they would sometimes declare rather patron-izingly that Egypt could join later if it wished. However, there was one notable exception, who was ultimately the most influential of them all – the writer and historian Sati al-Husri, who was Syrian by origin and Turkish by education. From the 1930s onwards he began to pour out books and articles expressing his pan-Arab ideas. For al-Husri, it was language that formed the nation: 'The Arab nation consists of all who speak Arabic as their mother-tongue, no more, no less.' Today this view is generally accepted, but it was still revolutionary at the time. It followed from this precept that Egypt was very much part of the Arab nation, and for al-Husri it was the cornerstone or centre of gravity. As early as 1936 he was writing: 'Nature has provided Egypt with the qualities and distinctions which oblige her to take up the task of leadership in the awakening of Arab nationalism.'[18]

The reasons why Sati al-Husri felt the need to make this point, and to return to it repeatedly, are clear. The Egyptians as a whole – with a few notable exceptions such as Abdul Rahman Azzam – were not interested in the Arab nation but in the Egyptian nation. Plans for the Arab Revolt may have been laid in Cairo and the proto-ideologists of Arab nationalism such as Rashid Rida and Kawakibi may have worked in Egypt but they were Syrians who had come there because it was free from Ottoman control.

Mustafa Kamel, the leading Egyptian nationalist under British rule, attacked the idea of an Arab caliphate and the break-up of the Ottoman Empire as a nefarious British plot and the great Zaghloul's reply to Abdul Rahman Azzam, when he was urging the cause of Arab unity, was to ask: 'If you add one zero to another and then to another, what sum will you get?'[19] Later Sati al-Husri himself engaged in a prolonged polemic with leading Egyptian intellectuals such as Ahmad Lutfi al-Sayyid, and Taha Hussein, the outstanding Arab writer of his generation, who still advocated a purely Egyptian nationalism.

But if Egyptian thinkers remained sceptical about Arab nationalism, the politicians and the palace who were interested in power began to follow a different trend during the Second World War. In their different ways both King Farouk and Nahas Pasha, the Wafdist leader, saw the important role that Egypt was bound to play in the Middle East after the war – especially now that any possibility of a Hashemite-dominated Arab union seemed highly remote. Moreover, Britain was encouraging pan-Arabism under its sponsorship and certainly included Egypt in any projected Arab union. Whatever Britain's relations with the Hashemites in Iraq and Jordan, its major

18. A. Hourani, *Arabic Thought in the Liberal Age, 1789–1945*, London, 1962, p. 316.
19. See Sylvia Haim (ed.), op. cit., p. 47.

political and military interests in the Arab world were concentrated in Cairo and the Suez Canal zone. In fact the Anglo-American Middle East Supply Centre made Egypt the focus of the Allied war effort in the Middle East and North Africa.

In February 1942 the British Foreign Secretary Anthony Eden made a declaration in favour of Arab unity, which would include Egypt and North Africa as well as all the eastern Arab countries. With strong British encouragement, a general Arab conference met in Alexandria in September and October 1944, attended by representatives of the governments of Egypt, Iraq, Lebanon, Syria, Transjordan, Saudi Arabia and Yemen, and by an observer on behalf of the Palestinian Arabs. The result was the foundation of the Arab League as a loose confederation of independent states, and the signature on 22 March 1945 of the Pact of the League. The Egyptian Abdul Rahman Azzam became the League's first secretary general and Sati al-Husri the head of its cultural department.

Thus it was only partly due to Egypt's natural dominance as the most populous and advanced of the Arab states that it became the headquarters of the first official pan-Arab organization. It was also partly an accident of war and British sponsorship. Certainly Egyptian leadership was far from being accepted by the governments of the other independent Arab states.

North Africa

It had always been a cardinal element in France's policy towards its North African empire to keep it isolated as far as possible from the nationalist currents in the eastern half of the Arab world. In the 1930s this policy had to all appearances been successful. The revolt in the Rif mountains led by the great Berber warrior Abdul Krim, which began against the Spanish in 1920 but spread to French Morocco, was put down, although with great difficulty. Abdul Krim surrendered in 1926. When the Second World War broke out most people assumed that the European government of North Africa was permanent.

The situation was very different from that in the Arab lands in the east under British control and also from the Levant states. In French North Africa hundreds of thousands of European settlers dominated not only professional and business life but occupied most of the best farming land. The idea that they would one day leave or be ejected seemed inconceivable at the time. (The parallel was with South African whites rather than British tea-planters in India.) Moreover, in all three territories – Morocco, Algeria and Tunisia – a new French-trained generation of Arabs was growing up, who, while demanding greater equality and improved conditions for their people, did so in French political terms and seemed to accept the permanence of French rule. Certainly they accepted the dominance of French culture, which they saw as the key to modernization and progress. They argued on the basis of the principles of the French Revolution. Few people were perceptive enough to realize at this stage that if France was prepared to offer real *égalité* and *fraternité* to her Muslim Arab subjects they would one day inevitably fight for their *liberté*.

The first stirrings of this new type of North African nationalism could be observed soon after the defeat of Abdul Krim, the last representative of the traditional variety. In Morocco a group of young nationalists, many of whom were later to be ministers in the country's first post-independence government, was formed in the early 1930s. The fact that they received the cooperation of the outstandingly able and enlightened Sultan Muhammad V greatly strengthened the Moroccan national movement. In Tunisia a dynamic new nationalist party, the *Néo-Destour*, was formed under the leadership of Habib Bourguiba in 1934 and in Algeria the *Parti populaire algérien* was formed in 1936. In Tunisia the struggle with the French authorities had already begun before the Second World War; Bourguiba was held in French prisons from 1938 until 1942, when he was released by the Germans.

Superficially, the situation returned to normal with the full restoration of French control after the final defeat of the Axis forces in North Africa in 1943. In fact it had fundamentally changed. French prestige never fully recovered from the débâcle of 1940, despite the valiant efforts of Charles de Gaulle and the Free French. The presence of large numbers of Anglo-American troops, the creation of the United Nations and the Arab League, and Syria and Lebanon's winning of their independence with British and US support against French opposition all contributed to a decline in French authority and raised questions about the permanence of French rule. The anti-colonial views expressed by President Roosevelt and some of his colleagues all helped to stimulate the desire for national independence in the three Arab Maghreb states. A meeting with Roosevelt in Casablanca in January 1943 opened the eyes of Muhammad V to the profound changes to be expected in the world after the war and led the Moroccan nationalists into the mistaken belief that they could expect American support in the coming struggle with the French. One of the first open symptoms of the new trend was that the Algerian leader Ferhat Abbas, formerly an advocate of Algeria's assimilation to France, having held the view that no Algerian nation had existed in history, presented to the French and Allied authorities in North Africa a manifesto embodying Algerian claims.

France was prepared to make some concessions, although as always they were never enough to silence the nationalists. In 1944 it extended French citizenship to certain categories of Muslims, and in 1946 a law granted them fifteen deputies in the National Assembly and seven senators in the Council of the Republic. But any manifestations of Algerian nationalism were harshly suppressed. Algerian soldiers had played an important part in the liberation of France; in 1945 a demonstration at Setif, carrying Algerian flags on the occasion of the Allied victory in Europe, was brutally broken up by the police. A rising followed in which about 100 Europeans were killed. In the course of French reprisals about 10,000 Muslim villagers were massacred. Although many worse things were to happen during Algeria's war of independence this event is still commemorated by the Algerian republic. It would not be too much to say that from that day Algeria's independence from France became inevitable.

In Tunisia Bourguiba refused to collaborate with the Germans after they had released him from prison, but when French rule was reimposed after the Allied victory his offers of cooperation were rejected by the French authorities; he escaped to Cairo, which he used as a base to campaign for world support for Tunisian independence.

In Morocco in November 1944 a manifesto signed by members of the National party and independents called upon the sultan to begin negotiations with France for the abrogation of the protectorate treaty and the recognition of Moroccan independence. The arrest of leading nationalists caused serious unrest. In a speech in Tangier in 1947 the sultan made himself the spokesman for Moroccan nationalism by claiming Morocco's affiliation with the Arab world and demanding that its legitimate aspirations be satisfied.

In all three Maghreb states France still seriously underestimated the nationalist challenge. One of the reasons was that in all three countries there were powerful and influential elements among the Muslim population, including intellectuals as well as landowners, who, either out of self-interest or emotional conviction, remained loyal and refused to consider the possibility of political separation from France. Yet it was inevitable that the pressure of nationalist demands would increase. Modern hygiene, introduced by the French, produced a tremendous growth in the population. Industry, apart from mining and building, remained rudimentary – manufactured products were supplied from *la mère patrie* – and the expanding population was heavily underemployed. Vast *bidonvilles*, or shanty-towns, grew on the outskirts of the major cities, and such industry as there was developed on the basis of an abundant supply of cheap but inefficient labour.

In all three Maghreb states the European *colons* enjoyed socially and economically privileged positions. In Algeria the number of French settlers had already reached one million by 1930. They were strongly opposed to equality of opportunity for the Algerian Muslims, and the development of higher education was primarily for the benefit of French or French-speaking students.[20] If the French *colons* thought about the future at all, they saw Algeria, Tunisia and Morocco developing into neo-French states in which French language and culture would remain dominant. For their part the indigenous population was becoming increasingly aware that this would mean a permanently subordinate position for all of them except for a small élite who were willing to adopt French culture as their own and discard their distinctive Muslim Arab personality.

In Libya – the link between the Maghreb and the Arab East – Italian rule between the wars closely resembled that of the French in north-west Africa but with a special fascist character. After Marshal Graziani's difficult and often brutal 'pacification' of the 1920s,[21] substantial colonies of peasant families were settled in Tripolitania and Cyrenaica during the 1930s. By 1938 they had increased to 89,000 or about 10 per cent of the total population.

'Civilization, in fact, is what Italy is creating on the fascist shore of our sea; Western civilization in general and fascist civilization in particular,' said Mussolini in 1934. A few Libyans were enrolled in the Italian army. Arab youths were encouraged to form their own fascist organization, to wear black shirts and give the fascist salute. In 1939 they were given their first chance to apply for special Italian citizenship. But the vast majority of the population were kept in subjection, with their leaders silenced or in exile. Tripoli and Benghazi were Italian cities whose centres were forbidden to Arabs after

20. Some of the *colons* were peculiarly arrogant and insensitive in their attitude towards the Arab population. 'No Arabs, Jews or dogs allowed!' was the sign outside the estate of one notorious millionaire landowner outside Algiers.

21. One of his methods was to have captured nationalist Libyans taken up in planes and thrown out.

dark. On the eve of the Second World War, there were 9,500 Arabs in primary schools out of a population of nearly one million, and 102 Arabs in Italian secondary schools. There were no Arab secondary schools at all.[22]

Libya's fate was different from that of its three western neighbours because the colonizing power was on the losing side in the war. When the Italian forces were finally swept out of the country in 1942 a British military administration was set up; but Libya's political future still had to be settled. In 1945 the four big powers were unable to agree. The United States favoured UN trusteeship, the USSR rather oddly asked for the trusteeship of Tripolitania for itself, while France laid claim to the Fezzan, which it was garrisoning with its troops, and favoured the return of Tripolitania to Italian rule. (France was thinking of the security both of its Arab empire in the Maghreb and its colonies in black west and central Africa.) The British, who wanted the trusteeship of Cyrenaica, opposed its return to Italy because they had promised Sayyid Idris, the head of the Sanussi who had helped Britain during the war, that he would never be handed back to Italian rule. A compromise Anglo-Italian plan which would have given trusteeship for Tripolitania to Italy, for Cyrenaica to Britain and for Fezzan to France and was supported by the US but bitterly opposed by the Arab states, was defeated by one vote at the UN.[23]

In default of any agreement, a majority of the UN eventually voted in favour of an independent and united Libya.

The Slide to Catastrophe

With French authority apparently restored in North West Africa, Britain was in the position of paramount power in the rest of the Arab world. In Iraq, Egypt and also in neighbouring Iran, Britain had taken the initiative in installing régimes sympathetic to the Allies and in forcing the French to abandon their control of Syria and Lebanon. It retained a huge military base in Egypt, and the Middle East Supply Centre in Cairo was in the process of initiating economic planning for the whole Middle East. Finally, Britain was the sponsor of the new League of Arab States.

It was true that the United States had become decisively involved in

22. See Ruth First, *Libya: The Elusive Revolution*, Harmondsworth, Penguin Books, 1974, p. 55, and A. L. Tibawi, *Islamic Education*, London, 1972, p. 150.

23. That of the Haitian delegate, who was persuaded by the Arabs to vote at the last minute. A street in Tripoli is named after him.

Middle Eastern affairs, having briefly entered the scene and with-drawn after the world war. American oil interests in the Middle East, held in check by the war, were on the point of rapid expansion. But despite the United States' growing relationship with Saudi Arabia,[24] the State Department was generally prepared to leave the handling of the West's political interests in the Arab world to Britain. American interest was centred on Iran, where the wartime connection estab-lished by the Persian corridor for the supply of Soviet Russia was continued when the war was over. As a counterweight to Soviet pressure, the Iranian government had recourse to American civilian advisers and a military mission. It was Iran that became the first battleground of the Cold War.

There was one crucial exception to this American detachment from political developments in the Arab world: Palestine. This was the focus of American concern with the Middle East, but it had nothing to do with the impending Cold War and was largely a consequence of domestic political considerations.

Britain's hegemony in the Middle East was short-lived; in many respects its apparent political and military strength was false, since the war had exhausted its resources. Moreover, in July 1945 the government of an imperial-minded Winston Churchill was replaced by a Labour administration which had a more realistic view of Britain's future role in the world and was prepared to give indepen-dence to India. Since the protection of communications with the Indian empire had always been the prime reason for Britain's interest in the Middle East this was certain in the long run to transform its strategic concerns in the Arab world.

The change did not take place overnight because old habits of mind die hard. In Egypt, still the centre of Britain's interest in the Middle East, even the Labour government believed rather vaguely that the 1936 Anglo-Egyptian treaty would hold with a few modifications. Military opinion still regarded a major military base in Egypt as a vital necessity. Moreover, the dominating Labour Foreign Secretary, Ernest Bevin, who was just as much a 'cold warrior' as Winston Churchill, supported the British military in their belief that Egypt should be included in a regional defence pact to combat the Soviet threat.

24. King Ibn Saud, although neutral during the war, received Roosevelt's emissary General Patrick Harley several times, and after the Yalta Conference in 1945 Roosevelt went out of his way to meet him.

Internally, the situation in Egypt was rapidly darkening. King Farouk had seized an opportunity to get rid of the Wafd government in 1944 and replaced it with one led by Ahmed Maher. Unlike his brother Ali, Ahmed had long pressed for Egypt to declare war on the Axis to ensure its place in the United Nations. On 24 February 1945 he announced Egypt's declaration of war to parliament; as he left the National Assembly he was assassinated. This action, almost certainly the work of the Muslim Brotherhood, inaugurated a series of political murders by the Brotherhood to which the state secret police retaliated.

When the war ended, Egyptian politicians of all parties believed that as a reward for Egypt's contribution to the Allied war effort. Britain should evacuate Egypt entirely and accept the unity of Egypt and Sudan. Instead Britain was trying to bring pressure on Egypt to join a Western defence pact, while British troops remained in the major Egyptian cities as a constant provocation to Egyptian nationalist opinion.

Against a background of anti-British rioting and strikes the now elderly Sidky Pasha, who had been recalled to form a government and restore order, reached an agreement with Ernest Bevin which accepted the principle of total British evacuation from Egypt. By this time the Labour government had come round to the view that the military attitude that a Suez base was essential was an imperial hangover. As the Prime Minister Attlee later remarked: 'But India had ceased to be a British imperial place of arms and the Suez Canal had never been a particularly good waterway; and the idea of the Mediterranean as a kind of covered passage for Britain had also been exploded.'[25] Predictably, the agreement was bitterly attacked by the Conservative Opposition with Winston Churchill describing the policy of evacuating Egypt and defending the Suez Canal as 'a complete and total contradiction in terms'.

However, this latest and most promising chance collapsed, and once again it was over the Sudan. Vague diplomatic wording led Sidky Pasha to believe that Britain had accepted Egyptian–Sudanese unity under the Egyptian crown, but the British government had no intention of going as far as this. British military opinion held that, in the event of a withdrawal from Egypt, it was even more essential to retain control of the Sudan. After the failure of the Sidky–Bevin agreement, British troops were still withdrawn from the cities to the

---

25. Francis Williams, *A Prime Minister Remembers*, London, 1961, p. 178.

Canal Zone but they remained seven times as numerous as the 10,000 stipulated in the 1936 treaty.

Britain was equally unsuccessful in placing its relations with Iraq on a new footing. British troops left at the end of the war, followed by most of the rest of the corps of British advisers. Only the more recently recruited technicians and specialists remained. But Britain's influence continued to be strong because it still provided the bulk of technical, economic and military aid, although the United States also undertook an increasing share of this role. The pro-Western stand of the Iraqi government aroused increasing opposition from the rising generation of nationalists – university students, the younger army officers and professional men – who were convinced that the country was still governed from the British embassy. In 1948 they were effective in causing the repudiation of a new Anglo-Iraqi treaty to replace that of 1930, which had been signed at Portsmouth by the Iraqi and British foreign ministers. Despite, or perhaps because of, the greatly improved economic prospects due to increasing oil revenues, Iraq was proving as difficult to govern as ever, since new elements of division based on social and economic interests were appearing in addition to those based on racial and religious sectarianism.

A sign that the Cold War had begun in earnest and that Britain was increasingly transferring responsibility for political and military leadership of the West in the Middle East region was the enunciation of the Truman Doctrine set forth in the US president's address to Congress on 12 March 1947, in which he asked for authority to furnish aid to Greece and Turkey (which Britain was no longer able to give) in order to help them to maintain their integrity and independence against the unnamed, but clearly designated, Soviet threat. In October 1947 the Truman Doctrine was extended to Iran, and two weeks later the Majlis repudiated a Soviet–Iranian oil agreement negotiated after the end of the war while Soviet troops were still in the country.

In the face of extreme Soviet hostility, the American involvement in Iran increased. The United States was still hardly involved politically in the Arab world – except in Palestine. Here its intervention was indirect – but of crucial importance.

11. *Disaster in Palestine*

Although President Roosevelt was generally sympathetic to Zionist aspirations, he also took a special interest in the affairs of the Middle East during the Second World War and was aware of the importance of America's growing oil interests in the area. At his meeting with Ibn Saud in 1945 he was impressed by the king's arguments against Zionism and gave his assurances that the US would take no action hostile to the Arabs. In April 1945 he was succeeded by Harry Truman who had a much more limited interest in, and knowledge of, foreign affairs.

Before the end of the war, the Zionist leaders in London began to urge the cancellation of the British White Paper on Palestine of 1939 and to urge the immediate admission of 100,000 Jews to Palestine. Their hopes were raised when a Labour government took office. At the Labour party conference in 1944 a resolution had been passed saying that since there was no sense in a Jewish national home in Palestine unless the Jews were a majority there should be a transfer of population and 'the Arabs should be encouraged to move out as the Jews moved in'. However, as often happens, the Labour party found in office that it was faced with reality which in this case was that the Arabs of Palestine were still two thirds of the population and were quite unwilling to leave unless they were forced out. Ernest Bevin, who as foreign secretary was responsible for Britain's Palestine policy, put up a stubborn resistance to what he regarded as unreasonable Zionist demands, such as that Palestine should at once be declared a Jewish state.

It was at this point in August 1945 that President Truman endorsed the Zionist demand that 100,000 Jews should be allowed immediately into Palestine. At the same time the US Congress called for unrestricted Jewish immigration to the limit of the country's absorptive capacity. Ernest Bevin, although angered at the US intervention which he considered made a complex problem more difficult (Truman had specifically said he could promise no American help to enforce a step which was bound to be fought bitterly by the Palestinian Arabs), decided to set up an Anglo-American Commission of Inquiry. In its report in April 1946 the commission recommended the continuation of the mandate and the immediate admission of 100,000 Jewish immigrants,[1] but criticized the continued existence of Jewish underground forces, estimated at 65,000. President Truman at once pressed for the immediate admission of the 100,000, but the British government insisted on the prior disbandment of the Jewish irregulars. The mandate government now had to deal with illegal immigration on a massive scale and a widespread campaign of Zionist terrorism, which culminated in the blowing up in July 1946 of the King David Hotel in Jerusalem and the British government and military offices which it housed.

Meanwhile the Arab states were attempting to mobilize their diplomatic and military forces on behalf of the Palestinian Arabs through the newly-founded Arab League. But their political and military weakness as well as their internal divisions and rivalries were apparent.

In 1947 the British government finally despaired of reconciling the conflicting interests. It was under strong economic and political pressure from the United States on behalf of the Zionists, but was unwilling to endanger any further its relations with the Arab states. A UN Special Committee on Palestine (UNSCOP) recommended in a majority report the partition of Palestine into Arab and Jewish states, with Jerusalem and its environs to remain under international control. Partition was adopted by the UN General Assembly on 29 November 1947 by a vote of thirty-three to thirteen, with ten abstentions. The favourable vote was secured by strong US pressure on a number of smaller nations; the Soviet Union also voted in favour of the resolution. All the Islamic Asian countries voted against, and an Arab proposal to ask the International Court of Justice to judge the competence of the General Assembly to partition a country against the wishes of a majority of its inhabitants was only narrowly defeated. (It is hardly necessary to point out that no such resolution could conceivably have been passed today, or even ten years later, because of the large Afro-Asian majority in the UN General Assembly.)

The Arabs totally rejected partition, but the Zionists accepted it; the resolution provided for a Jewish state at a time when Jews formed 30 per cent of the population owning less than 8 per cent of the land

---

1. Critics asked not unreasonably why the United States was doing so little itself to help with the problem. Two years after the war only 5,000 Jewish refugees had been admitted into the United States. (See Christopher Sykes, *Cross Roads to Israel*, London, 1967, p. 341.)

area. UNSCOP had intended that Britain should supervise the implementation of partition, but Britain refused. It had always rejected responsibility for enforcing partition on the Arabs. Instead it announced that it would be relinquishing its mandate for Palestine on 15 May 1948.

The UN partition resolution touched off violent Arab protests, which soon developed into communal fighting. Armed volunteers arrived from Syria to help the Arabs, but in general they were no match for the more cohesive, better trained and armed Zionists. Arab villagers, terrified by reports of events such as the massacre of the inhabitants of the village of Deir Yasin by Irgunists, left their homes *en masse*. Haifa fell to the Zionists on 22 April and Jaffa on 13 May – that is, before the British mandate officially ended.

On 14 May 1948 the last British troops left with the high commissioner, and on the same day the Zionists proclaimed the state of Israel, which was promptly recognized by the United States (in accordance with a prior undertaking with President Truman) and by the Soviet Union. Early on 15 May units of the regular armies of Syria, Transjordan, Iraq and Egypt entered Palestine in support of the Palestinian Arabs. They scored some initial successes, and the Egyptians linked up with the Arab Legion near Bethlehem, but the Israelis, fighting desperately in the knowledge that their survival depended on the outcome, launched a violent counter-offensive which ended with an Arab collapse. The overwhelming Arab superiority in population was not reflected on the battlefield, where the total of Arab regular forces engaged was 21,500, compared with Jewish troops estimated at between 40,000 and 60,000. The Zionists were better equipped and they secured important fresh arms supplies from Czechoslovakia while fighting was in progress.

In spite of the efforts of the United Nations, fighting did not finally stop until January 1949, and the conclusion of armistice agreements between Israel on the one hand, and Egypt, Syria, Transjordan and Lebanon on the other, was not completed until July. Israel now comprised nearly 80 per cent of the area of the Palestine mandate, and the number of Arabs within the area of Israel had decreased from between 700,000 and 750,000 to 165,000. Of the 21 per cent of Palestine which remained in Arab hands, the semi-desert Gaza Strip was placed under Egyptian administration, and the substantial enclave on the West Bank of the Jordan, which included the old city of Jerusalem, was annexed by Transjordan in 1950, against strong opposition from the other Arab states, to form the Hashemite kingdom of Jordan.[2]

The Palestine war and the harsh injustices that it caused the indigenous inhabitants left a legacy of bitterness among all the Arabs against Israel and the two Western powers most responsible for its creation – Britain and the United States. (The Soviet Union's role in supporting Israel's 'war of independence' against what it regarded as Western puppet states was largely forgotten by the Arabs when Soviet policy changed in the early 1950s.) It has been the single most powerful factor behind the radicalization of the Arab world and the growth of anti-Western feeling over the past two decades.

Britain's responsibility has been severely but not unfairly judged by the historian Arnold Toynbee:

> Britain was in control of Palestine for thirty years . . . and during those fateful three decades she never made up her mind, or at any rate never declared, what her policy about the future of Palestine was. All through those thirty years, Britain lived from hand to mouth, admitting into Palestine, year by year, a quota of Jewish immigrants that varied according to the strength of the respective pressures of the Arabs and Jews at the time. These immigrants could not have come in if they had not been shielded by a British *chevaux-de-frise*. If Palestine had remained under Ottoman Turkish rule, or if it had become an independent Arab state in 1918, Jewish immigrants would never have been admitted into Palestine in large enough numbers to enable them to overwhelm the Palestinian Arabs in this Arab people's own country. The reason why the state of Israel exists today and why over 1,500,000 Palestinian Arabs are refugees is that, for thirty years, Jewish immigration was imposed on the Palestinian Arabs by British military power until the immigrants were sufficiently numerous and sufficiently well armed to be able to fend for themselves with tanks and planes of their own . . .[3]

After the creation of Israel, the Arabs continued to recall Britain's responsibility. The anniversary of the Balfour Declaration is still commemorated as a black day in the history of the Arabs. But Britain could not be regarded as Israel's principal friend, ally and supporter. This was the United States, and in the 1950s France also was a considerably more important ally and arms supplier for Israel than Britain.

2. Abdullah had changed his title from amir to king in 1946, when Britain recognized his full independence in a treaty. He proclaimed the Hashemite kingdom of Jordan in 1948, but it was not until after the Arab–Israeli war that this was internationally recognized.

3. From Arnold Toynbee's introduction to Sami Hadawi, *Palestine Diary*, Beirut, 1969, vol. I, pp. xii-xiv.

Since the Second World War United States Middle East policy has had two principal concerns: the welfare and security of Israel and the role of the Middle East region in Soviet–American relations (whether Cold War or détente). Whenever these two interests have conflicted – and in the eyes of the dominant voices in Washington this has rarely happened – the first concern has always prevailed. In consequence United States policy has consistently been the despair of those Arabs (and especially Arab governments) who are favourably disposed towards the West[4] and a ready-made justification for those who are naturally inclined to be hostile.

The reasons for American sympathy and identification with Israel, which apparently precludes any comparable understanding of Arab feelings and aspirations, are undoubtedly varied and complex. Arabs tend to see the matter in simplistic terms: either as the dominance of Zionist influence or, in the case of those on the left, in an American imperialist desire to dominate the Middle East through a powerful client state. Some who have studied the question more deeply have suggested some additional factors, such as the desire to expiate a sense of guilt over the meagre contribution of the United States to forestalling the Nazi holocaust of the Jews or the prevalence in parts of the United States of fundamentalist Christian sects who see in political Zionism a fulfilment of Old Testament prophecy. The British pro-Zionist politician and writer Richard Crossman, who was a member of the Anglo-American Commission of Inquiry, plausibly suggested that while Americans tend to identify themselves more with Jewish settlers than the indigenous Arabs, with Europeans it is the reverse. Whatever the reasons, the vast majority of Arabs have concluded, either with or without regret, that the United States is their enemy and far and away the most important reason for this is the Palestine problem.

The deep Arab sense of grievance about Palestine has been kept alive by the existence of the Palestinian Arab diaspora. Through natural increase these numbered about 2·5 million in 1975 (of whom about one million were living under Israeli occupation in the West Bank and Gaza). Some of the better-educated found work and prospered in the neighbouring Arab states and in a few Western countries, but the great majority – their numbers swollen by the second exodus during the 1967 war – were living in camps as stateless

4. And also of those Americans who for one reason or another have devoted themselves to the Arab world.

refugees. A UN General Assembly resolution of 11 December 1948, affirming their right to a choice of repatriation or compensation, has remained a dead letter, although reaffirmed almost every year, since Israel insists that such measures must be part of a general settlement.

Bitter and humiliated, the Arabs made it clear that they had no intention of accepting Israel. In November 1950 the Arab League decided to continue the war-time blockade of Israel on the ground that an armistice did not constitute a state of peace. One direct consequence of the war was to jeopardize the position of the substantial Jewish communities in several Arab states. As the Zionists urged their emigration to the new state of Israel they became the object of suspicion to Arab governments. Five sixths of Iraq's 150,000 Jews left for Israel over the next few years.

12. The Second Arab Revolt

The Arab East

The social and political repercussions of the Palestine disaster were felt throughout the Arab states. Syria, the nerve-centre of the Arab world, was the first to react. In 1947 public opinion turned against the Communists because of the Soviet bloc's support for the partition of Palestine. Now it was the turn of the corrupt and ineffective politicians who were faced with public anger for the failure of the Arab governments in Palestine. Even before the fighting in the Arab–Israeli war had ceased, Colonel Husni Zaim and his army group carried out a bloodless coup d'état. He made himself prime minister and president, abolished parliament and political parties and announced his intention of carrying out sweeping reforms.

Colonel Zaim lasted only a few months before being replaced by another colonel, and the parliamentary régime was twice restored temporarily in the 1950s and 1960s. Yet he was starting a trend which was to sweep away most of the multi-party 'democratic' systems on European models which the Arab states had inherited. It was in Egypt that his trend had consequences which transformed the Arab world.

The effects of the Palestine war on Egypt were as profound as in Syria but typically they took longer to mature. Egypt's participation in the war was far from being a foregone conclusion. As we have seen, the country's pan-Arabism was still superficial. The prime minister, who knew of the inadequacy of the Egyptian army, had grave doubts. But the Muslim Brotherhood wanted to fight for Palestine and the remorseless Hajj Amin al-Husseini, who was in Egypt, exerted a powerful influence. The day that Britain's Palestine mandate ended the Egyptian army crossed the border. It scored some early successes, but by January 1949 it had been beaten back and shut up in the Gaza Strip on the sea and in two small pockets to the north-east.

The main effect of the war on the Egyptian army was to convince the younger officers of the criminal incompetence of the men who were ruling Egypt. Food and medical supplies were inadequate and irregular while arms were obsolete and in some cases worthless. Senior military officers gave contradictory and meaningless orders while some showed downright cowardice. (A notable exception was Major-General Muhammad Neguib, who was seriously wounded.)

Major Abdul Nasser was wounded and distinguished himself in a defensive engagement at the Irak al-Manshia pocket. But the most vivid memory that he and the other Free Officers who fought in Palestine had of the war was the words of one of their heroes, Colonel Ahmed Abdul Aziz, shortly before he was killed: 'Remember, the real battle is in Egypt.'

Even while the war was in progress Egypt's sham democracy began to disintegrate as the extra-parliamentary forces gathered strength. King Farouk did not improve his image by divorcing his popular Egyptian wife when the war was at its height. The most obvious beneficiary was the Muslim Brotherhood, which had gained prestige as some of the Brothers fought bravely as volunteers in Palestine. The prime minister made use of martial law to try to suppress the Brotherhood and was assassinated in the presence of his own police. Two months later the Supreme Guide of the Muslim Brotherhood, Shaikh Hassan al-Banna, was himself shot down – almost certainly by the counter-terrorist police.

The Brotherhood was temporarily weakened, but the violence continued. After an improbable eleventh-hour reconciliation between Farouk and Nahas Pasha, the Wafd returned to power with its usual sweeping victory, which this time was to be its last. British hopes that this would lead to an improvement in Anglo-Egyptian relations were soon disappointed as the Wafd discovered that its only means of restoring its waning popularity was to rouse national hostility towards the British. Still optimistic, the British government, proposed a plan for a combined Middle East command with the US, Turkey and France, as well as Britain and Egypt, in the same week of October 1951 that the Wafd decided on the desperate course of abrogating the 1936 Anglo-Egyptian treaty. The Egyptian government not only cut off fresh food supplies and withdrew Egyptian labour from the British Suez Canal base, but encouraged the formation of volunteer 'liberation' squads to carry out sabotage and guerrilla attacks. These succeeded in making the base militarily useless, as the 80,000 British troops became wholly absorbed in protecting themselves and their families.

British counteraction against guerrilla attacks led almost inevitably to a major incident. On 25 January 1952 a British force surrounded the Ismailia police headquarters and issued an ultimatum to surrender. The post resisted on the orders of the minister of the interior and some fifty Egyptian police were killed. The following day a frenzied Cairo mob, led by the Muslim Brotherhood and other armed militant groups, burned the centre of Cairo, concentrating their attacks on British property and buildings with foreign associations. The regular army delayed intervening to restore order until the evening.

This incident – 'Black Saturday' as it was called – hastened the end of Egypt's monarchy and parliamentary régime. As one helpless government succeeded another, the Free Officers' organization decided to intervene; and six months later, in an almost bloodless coup, they seized power and sent King Farouk – who they wisely decided should not be tried and executed for his crimes against the Egyptians – into exile in Europe.

The Free Officers genuinely feared that Britain might intervene to preserve the monarchy as it had done seventy years before. Certainly the British government considered the possibility, but since British lives and property were not endangered and Farouk was so unpopular, they wisely decided against intervention. However, four years later they showed that they regretted the decision.

The overthrow of Muhammad Ali's adipose great-great-grandson by a group of young Egyptian officers was a seminal event of the mid twentieth century. It was not only a milestone in the long history of Egypt – 'the most important country' in Napoleon Bonaparte's words – but it profoundly influenced the other Arab states and much of the Afro–Asian world.

In the first place the 1952 revolution meant that Egypt was ruled by two native Egyptians for the first time in 2000 years. (T. E. Lawrence had written in a letter in the 1930s: 'Of course Zaghloul was *echt*-Egyptian: it just shows how the natural leader will be of Nile blood; and not a Turk, or Albanian pasha. First Arabi, then Zaghloul.')

The Free Officers, like Colonel Arabi and his *fellah* colleagues, were unmistakably *echt*-Egyptian. Their nominal head in 1952 was the fifty-year-old General Muhammad Neguib who had distinguished himself in the Palestine war. The Egyptian public was not immediately aware that their true leader and organizer was the tall, impressive but somewhat reserved young Colonel Gamal Abdul Nasser. He was to wield nearly absolute control over Egypt's domestic and foreign policies for most of the two following decades and it was his qualities which ensured that the 1952 revolution was much more than a mere military coup.

Like Arabi, Nasser had roots in the Egyptian countryside. His father, who had been from a poor *fellah* family in Upper Egypt, had earned the primary school certificate which enabled him to enter the lower ranks of the Egyptian white-collar class as a post office official. Nasser was born in Alexandria and passed well through secondary school (despite the time spent in leading anti-British demonstrations) to enter the military academy in 1937, together with most of the other Free Officers, when this was opened to the sons of other than beys and pashas as a result of the Anglo-Egyptian 1936 treaty.

As a student and cadet Nasser was a passionate reader of history and political biography – Western, Arab and Islamic – but like most of his colleagues he had adopted no distinctive political ideology at that stage. A few of the Free Officers leaned towards Marxism or to the Islamic reformism preached by the Muslim Brotherhood, but most of them were concerned only with their immediate triple objective which was to overthrow the monarchy, to secure a final British evacuation from Egypt and to reform the social and political system by eliminating the power of the land-owning classes, which had held up change for so long. They were imbued with a deep Egyptian patriotism and a belief in the innate qualities of the Egyptian people, but their interest in Arab nationalism was still fairly remote. 'The real battle is in Egypt,' as Colonel Abdul Aziz had said.

The body of ideas and practice which became known as Arab socialism developed pragmatically over the years; but one major act of social and political reform was carried out immediately after the 1952 revolution. Less than half of 1 per cent of the landowners between them owned over one third of all cultivable land in Egypt, while 72 per cent of cultivators owned less than one *feddan* (1·038 acre) each, amounting to only 13 per cent of the land. The agrarian reform limited all land-holdings to 200 *feddans* and redistributed the confiscated land to *fellahin* families in lots of two to five *feddans*. (The richness of the Nile valley soil makes this just enough to support a family.) The reform also sharply reduced the rents that it was legal for landowners to charge their tenants. This was reform rather than revolution for the Egyptian countryside. It was certainly incapable in itself of solving Egypt's agrarian problems, although, because it was generally successful in avoiding disastrous falls in output (the Egyptian small landowner, though desperately poor, is an experienced and competent farmer), it served as a model for other developing countries. It did succeed in its prime objective of reducing the overwhelming political powers of the big landowners who had successfully blocked social and political reforms for generations.

The Free Officers formed a revolutionary Command Council with Neguib as its president. They abolished the Ottoman titles of bey and pasha and they banned and dissolved the old political parties. This was about all the Egyptian revolution amounted to in its early years. Nasser was heavily involved simultaneously in negotiations with the British and establishing his authority at home both against the challenge from Neguib and the Muslim Brotherhood.

Neguib had been brought in by Nasser and the Free Officers a few months before the July revolution to act as their leader. Through his age and prestige, he could give their movement weight and significance at home and secure international recognition. At first this worked well, but Neguib was by temperament a conservative regular army officer, with a mild taste for reform, who regarded his young colleagues as far too hasty and radical. The Free Officers' difficulty was that Neguib's smiling, avuncular figure was widely popular with the basically conservative Egyptian masses.[1] Nasser used his skill in political tactics, in which Neguib was no match for him, to manoeuvre Neguib into a position of asking for the restoration of political parties and the reversal of most of the reforms the Free Officers were pledged to carry out. Neguib was reduced to a figurehead and eventually removed from office in October 1954.

A more serious and organized challenge came from the Muslim Brotherhood and, to a much lesser extent, from the Communists. The Communists were fragmented groups of intellectuals with little following among industrial workers; but the Brotherhood with its nationwide militant organization was much more formidable. Having played a leading role in undermining the monarchy, it felt that it was entitled at least to a share of power in the new régime and a say in the reforms. The Brotherhood's tendency to violence was its undoing. An assassination attempt on Nasser at a public meeting by one of the Brothers in October 1954 provided grounds for suppressing their organization throughout the country. Nasser's presence of mind in shouting, as the assassin's bullets missed: 'Let them kill Nasser. He is one among many and whether he lives or dies the revolution will go on,' contributed greatly to the wild popularity he later gained among the Egyptian people.

By the end of 1954 Nasser was in undisputed control of Egypt. He had already shown his awareness of the kind of role that Egypt could play in the world in his little book *The Philosophy of the Revolution*, published in 1954, in which he spoke of its location at the coincidence of three circles – the Arab Circle, the African Circle and the Islamic

---

1. He was also well regarded in the West, where he was referred to in the press as 'Egypt's Cromwell', possibly without regard to the fact that Cromwell was followed by the restoration of the monarchy.

Circle. As the biggest, and in some ways the most developed, Arab state, Egypt's qualifications for Arab leadership were obvious, however detached from the Arab world it had been in the past. (Nasser had certainly read the arguments of Sati al-Husri.) In Africa the struggle of the emergent black nations for independence was only just beginning. Nasser remarked: 'Surely the people of Africa will continue to look to us – we who are the guardians of the continent's north-eastern gate and constitute the link between Africa and the outside world.' Similarly, Cairo with its ancient Islamic university of al-Azhar had never ceased to be a major focal point in the Muslim world. This position was enhanced now that secular republican Turkey had opted out of any claim to Islamic leadership.

But one thing was clear at the time of the 1952 revolution: Egypt would have no chance to play this world role until it had freed its hands by settling its problems with Britain. Here the Free Officers took a momentous decision which showed considerable political maturity. In August 1952 they announced their willingness to separate the question of the Sudan from that of the Suez Canal zone in negotiations with Britain, and at one stroke removed what had been the chief obstacle to an Anglo-Egyptian agreement for half a century.

By February 1953 an Anglo-Egyptian agreement was reached for immediate Sudanese autonomy, to be followed by self-determination after three years. In a sense both parties were bluffing. Neither was able to reject the principle of Sudanization of the administration and self-government when the other proposed it. The Egyptians hoped and expected that an independent Sudan would opt for union with Egypt. The British were counting on Sudanese elections resulting in a pro-British (and anti-Egyptian) régime under the conservative Umma party. The British were shocked when the pro-Egyptian parties won the elections, but the Egyptians were equally dismayed when the new Sudanese government opted for full independence and against union with Egypt. Sudanese independence was declared on 1 January 1956.

Nasser and his colleagues were bitterly disappointed over what had happened, but the way was now open to begin the crucial negotiations with Britain. These were not easy because Britain still tended to regard Egypt as a Western protectorate. Although most Englishmen would not have been as explicit as one right-wing Tory MP, Lord Hinchingbrooke, who said: 'The Suez Canal and the area surrounding it are in some essential sense part of the United Kingdom' they felt in their bones that he was right. But this was an emotional rather than a practical difficulty. India was independent and the empire was dying, even if Britons were not yet aware of their post-imperial status. Moreover, even the military no longer regarded Egypt as the centre of Britain's Middle East strategy. Turkey had joined NATO in the autumn of 1952 and the British joint armed forces HQ was moved from Suez to Cyprus in December. The United States, which was quite favourably disposed to the new Egyptian régime, was also strongly urging Britain towards a settlement.

Nasser stood firm in rejecting a British demand to keep 7,000 servicemen in Suez, but he agreed to the reactivation of the base in the event of an outside attack on any Arab states or Turkey. As the negotiations dragged on, he allowed guerrilla attacks on the base area to be resumed as a means of pressure on Britain. Agreement was finally reached in July 1954 on the basis of a British proposal to evacuate all British troops and maintain the base on a seven-year lease with a cadre of civilians on contract to British firms. On 31 March 1956, the 2nd Battalion of the Grenadier Guards and D Squadron of the Life Guards embarked at Port Said and there were no more British soldiers on Egyptian soil. After seventy-four years the British occupation of Egypt had come to an end.

At the signing of the 1954 agreement, Nasser had remarked:

A new era of friendly relations based on trust, confidence and cooperation exists between Egypt and Britain and the Western countries. . . . We want to get rid of the hatred in our hearts and start building up our relations with Britain on a solid basis of mutual trust and confidence which has been lacking for the past seventy years.

For a variety of reasons this was not to happen. Egypt's relations with all the Western powers, but especially Britain, rapidly deteriorated. The British government's initial reaction to the new revolutionary régime in Egypt had been sceptical but reasonably optimistic. Although the Free Officers rejected its patronizing offer of advice to maintain the institution of monarchy as a stabilizing factor, they swiftly showed that they were much more capable of maintaining order than the previous régime. The Wafdist politicians and the ex-king's cronies aroused little sympathy when they were put on trial.

But British goodwill, which was strictly limited, soon vanished with the bitter rivalry over the Sudan and the frequently acrimonious negotiations over the Suez base. Nasser was the chief suspect, and when he replaced Neguib the situation rapidly worsened. The thirty-six-year-old Egyptian colonel became an object of hatred to a degree almost unparalleled in British political life in time of peace. Prime

Minister Anthony Eden in particular entertained feelings towards Nasser which bordered on hysteria.

This was not because of Nasser's policies inside Egypt alone and his resolute refusal to allow his country to be regarded any more as a Western satellite. The new horizons which Nasser had foreseen in his *The Philosophy of the Revolution* were opening in 1955. In April he attended the Afro-Asian conference at Bandung in Indonesia, where the importance of Egypt and its revolution were acknowledged as he was treated as an equal by Asian statesmen such as Nehru of India, Chou En-lai of China and Sukarno of Indonesia. Already his friendship with Nehru and Tito of Yugoslavia was helping him to form his ideas of the advantages of rejecting alignment with the great power blocs and of creating instead a neutral Arab bloc under Egyptian leadership in alliance with other emerging countries in Asia and Africa.

This at once brought him into conflict with British plans for the Middle East.

The United States secretary of state John Foster Dulles had already had some success, as part of his campaign to create a world-wide system of anti-Soviet alliances, in creating an anti-communist bloc in the 'northern tier' states of the Middle East. Early in 1954 a Turco-Pakistani agreement was concluded and there were good prospects of bringing in Iran. Dulles, realizing that the Arab states were generally much more concerned with Israel than with the Soviet threat, decided that the pact should not include the Arab world for the time being. But Britain thought otherwise. Its principal ally in the Arab world, the dominating and fiercely anti-Communist veteran Iraqi leader Nuri Said, was enthusiastically prepared for Iraq to join. Despite all Nasser's efforts to dissuade him, Iraq sighed an agreement with Turkey in February 1955 which became the nucleus of the notorious Baghdad Pact. Britain, Iran and Pakistan all joined later the same year.

This development was anathema to Nasser. Nuri Said made no secret of the fact that he hoped other countries such as Jordan and Syria would join and for Nasser this meant that the whole Arab world would remain within the Western orbit. Through Turkey the Baghdad Pact was tied to NATO and through Pakistan with the pro-Western SEATO alliance. Syria was a special concern because Nasser had inherited the age-old dispute between the rulers of the Nile and Mesopotamia valleys for the control of the territory which lies between them: that is, Syria. While Syria was under French rule, the struggle was in abeyance, but as soon as it achieved independence after the Second World War the fight for influence in Syria began in earnest. As we have seen, the Iraqi royal family had ambitions for a Syrian–Iraqi Hashemite kingdom; and this Egypt, whether monarchy or republic, was determined to oppose.

Cairo's press and radio launched a virulent campaign against the Baghdad Pact. Ahmad Said, the director of Cairo's *Voice of the Arabs* radio station, developed a style of brilliant invective which aroused a response in every Arab country and made his voice as well known in the Arab world as that of the great singer Umm Kalthoum. Ahmad Said's methods were often highly unscrupulous in detail, but they struck a responsive chord in the deep-seated resentment against the old colonial powers among the Arab masses. Meanwhile, Nasser's interest in the African Circle was already being shown through Egyptian support and encouragement for all anti-colonial movements on the African continent. Special fury was roused in Britain by Swahili language broadcasts on Cairo Radio in support of the Mau Mau rebellion against British rule in Kenya.

The Eden government soon came to the conclusion that every sign of hostility towards Britain in the Arab world, whether it was the young King Hussein of Jordan's summary dismissal of Glubb Pasha, the commander of the Arab Legion, or a stone-throwing demonstration against the Foreign Secretary Selwyn Lloyd in Bahrain, was instigated and arranged by Nasser. The personal quality of Anthony Eden's feelings may be gauged from his reaction to the news of Glubb's dismissal. To his junior minister Anthony Nutting, who suggested a measured response, he shouted: 'But what's all this nonsense about isolating Nasser, of "neutralizing" him, as you call it? I want him destroyed, can't you understand?'[2]

There can be no doubt that the very special nature of British hatred for Abdul Nasser, which went far beyond the feelings towards rebellious anti-colonial leaders in the British Empire, such as Nehru of India, Nkrumah of Nigeria, or Makarios of Cyprus, was due to the ingrained British attitude towards the Egyptian people. Of all Lord Cromer's 'subject races' they were the most despised. The concept of the romantic and noble Arab shaikh beloved of English arabists did not apply to Egypt. 'Those Egyptians are such worms (though they can dig)' was the summary of the young T. E. Lawrence's attitude, after employing some *fellahin* on an archaeological excavation. Now here was a simple Egyptian army officer, with no connection with the

2. Anthony Nutting, *No End of a Lesson*, London, 1967, p. 69.

country's Turco-Egyptian governing class, not only defying the traditional Western image of his fellow countrymen but challenging the whole concept that the Arab world was a subordinate part of the Western system.

The United States, which had no long history of involvement with Egypt, took a more relaxed and dispassionate attitude; but it was to become only marginally less hostile. As we have seen, the initial attitude of the Eisenhower administration to the Free Officers' revolution was favourable. While the United States had none of Britain and France's imperial nostalgia about the Arabs – in fact regarded it as tiresome and irrelevant – it had hopes that the new Egyptian régime would represent a new type of nationalist but anti-Soviet force in the Middle East. Nasser's own views were known to be staunchly anti-Communist (in a preface he wrote in early 1955 for an anti-Communist tract entitled *The Reality of Communism* he used all the liberal arguments against Marxism, which he described as the negation of the individual, of religion, liberty and equality), and he had dealt severely with Egyptian Marxists. In Egypt at that time he was widely regarded as pro-American in his tastes and sympathies. He established close and friendly relations with Kermit Roosevelt, one of the senior Middle East hands of the CIA.

But Nasser's real objection to Communists was that they were unpatriotic Egyptians who were loyal to a foreign ideology. He had no more intention of allowing Egypt to become part of John Foster Dulles' anti-communist crusade than of joining the Warsaw Pact. Ultimately, a clash was inevitable between a Dulles who regarded neutralism as immoral and a Nasser who embraced it wholeheartedly after the Bandung conference. Moreover, the fact that the principal allies of the United States in the anti-Soviet front were the same old colonial powers, against which the Arabs were still struggling for their independence, meant that the force of Nasser's neutralism tended to be directed against the West rather than the Communist bloc.

At the same time the Soviets were busy rethinking their policy in order to take advantage of the way the wind was blowing. Lenin's policy had favoured a plan of supporting 'bourgeois nationalism' in the emerging nations, even if it meant the collapse of local Communist parties, on the ground that this was the best way of ensuring the downfall of both imperialism and capitalism. However, this policy was reversed by Stalin who believed that the local Communist parties should be the spearhead of Soviet policy. This applied to the Middle

East where bourgeois Arab nationalism was condemned. As we have seen, the Soviets supported the Zionist 'war of independence' against the Arab states, which they regarded as reactionary and Wester-controlled.

Initially the Soviet attitude to the Egyptian Free Officers' movement was just as hostile. When the new Egyptian leaders jailed Communists they were described as 'fascist' and 'negative'. But the death of Stalin in 1953 opened the way to a new flexibility in Soviet policy. Seeing the advantages of supporting such patently popular 'bourgeois' nationalist leaders such as Abdul Nasser, Soviet strategists under Nikita Khrushchev's leadership reverted to Lenin's policy. In September 1953 the Soviets appointed Mr Daniel Solod, a brilliant Middle Eastern expert, as ambassador in Cairo. Quietly and patiently he worked to improve Soviet–Egyptian relations. The line he gently pressed on the Revolutionary Command Council was that the Soviet Union was only anxious to see Egypt and the other Arab states become genuinely independent of the Western imperialists. It had no intention of trying to draw them into the Soviet orbit, and the economic aid it was offering, unlike that from the West, was tied to no political conditions. In the phrase that became so hackneyed in the 1950s, it 'had no strings attached'.

Despite his inexperience, Nasser was no innocent and he was fully aware of the purpose behind the Soviet blandishments. With his ingrained anti-Communism, he would have much preferred to receive help from the West if he could have obtained it on the scale that he thought was necessary for Egypt and without damage to its independence. By 1955, the need for help was pressing while the chances of getting it from the Western powers were minimal.

In 1950 the three main Western powers – the United States, Britain and France – had together issued what was called the Tripartite Declaration, in which they pledged themselves to action, within or without the United Nations, to resist any attempt by either Israel or the Arabs to change the 1949 armistice lines by force of arms. Of the three, Britain was now extremely hostile to Egypt, as we have seen. France was an even more deadly enemy because it had become convinced, quite incorrectly, that the Algerian rebellion (see below, pp. 267–9), which broke out on 1 November 1954, could be easily suppressed if it was not helped and promoted by the Nasser régime in Egypt. In fact France had already begun major secret arms supplies to Israel before the outbreak of the Algerian rebellion. Partly as retaliation against its loss of Syria and Lebanon and partly to confront the growing nationalist threat in North Africa, France had formed an alliance with the main enemy of the Arabs.

Nasser had more hope of the United States, although it was clear to everyone that the Truman administration's main motive in subscribing to the Tripartite Declaration was to help Israel. The Eisenhower administration, which was notably more sympathetic to the Arabs and less partial towards Israel, had strongly encouraged Britain to reach the agreement which ended the occupation of Egypt. Following this agreement it had immediately offered to supply $40 million in economic aid. But in 1955 Nasser wanted arms for the alarmingly weak Egyptian armed forces.

When Nasser came to power, both reason and instinct told him to avoid involvement with Israel. He was not only confronted by a morass of domestic and foreign problems requiring solution, but the first Arab–Israeli war had exposed the weakness of the Egyptian army. The Israeli premiership of the moderate Moshe Sharett from December 1953 to February 1955 was a period of relative Egyptian–Israeli détente, but in that month the scandal of the Lavon affair – the failure of a plan by the Israeli secret service to force the British to stay in Egypt by simulating Egyptian outrages against British institutions – brought the militant-activist David Ben Gurion back from his temporary retirement on a kibbutz. One week later Israel resumed its policy of heavy reprisal for incursions by individual armed Palestinians with a massive raid on Gaza, which destroyed the Egyptian headquarters and inflicted heavy casualties.

This event was a turning-point in the modern history of the Middle East. It humiliatingly exposed Egypt's continued military weakness and provoked demands for retaliation from the Egyptians, which Nasser could not ignore. He gave permission for the launching of *fedayeen* (commando) raids into Israeli territory but he knew that these were both provocative and militarily ineffective. His real concern was to find a major source of arms supplies, and because the West was refusing to supply more than small quantities on onerous financial terms[3] he turned to the Soviets, who responded favourably. In September 1955 Nasser shocked the West and delighted the Arab masses by announcing an agreement to purchase large quantities of Soviet arms via Czechoslovakia. In the following May he dealt another

3. Although President Eisenhower described Egypt's request for $20 million's worth of arms as 'peanuts', Washington insisted on payment in hard currency since it was fully aware that Egypt, with total reserves of $20 million, would be unable to agree. See Kenneth Love, *Suez: the Twice-Fought War*, London, 1969, p. 88.

blow to American–Egyptian relations by suddenly and without warning recognizing the Peking régime. His main motive was to evade a possible United Nations embargo on arms supplied to the Middle East. As far as most US congressmen were concerned, he had sold his soul to the devil.

The Western powers had still not altogether abandoned hope of keeping Egypt within their orbit. The new régime had set its heart on the building of a giant dam on the Nile near Aswan, which, by increasing the country's hydro-electric supply, would form the cornerstone of Egypt's development programme. In February 1956 a provisional agreement was reached, whereby the World Bank would loan $200 million on condition that the United States and Britain loaned another $70 million to pay the hard-currency costs. The US and Britain imposed conditions which Nasser found hard to accept, since they involved detailed Western control over the Egyptian economy. When, after much heart-searching, he finally decided to accept, the US and Britain had already decided to withdraw the offer. Whether the US and British governments ever seriously expected the project to be approved by Congress and the British parliament is doubtful, but by the summer of 1956 they had decided to administer a sharp rebuff to Nasser, intending to topple him or render him more pliable. On 19 July John Foster Dulles coldly informed the pro-American Egyptian ambassador in Washington that the US had decided not to give any aid to the dam because the Egyptian economy was too unstable for so large a scheme.

The West did not believe that the Russians would step in; above all they did not expect Nasser to retaliate. But he was already evolving his characteristic political strategy: to return blow for blow with the greatest possible speed. He held his fire for a few days, only declaring in a speech that he would shortly be announcing plans to finance the High Dam without Western aid. Then on 26 July – the fourth anniversary of King Farouk's abdication – he addressed a vast expectant crowd in Alexandria. As Arabs all over the Middle East switched on their radio sets they knew something important would happen, but they did not know what it would be.

Until that day, Nasser's speeches had never caught fire but this time he penetrated to the hearts of the Egyptian people. Breaking from classical Arabic into the Egyptian colloquial he laughed and jeered at the West's pretensions to turn back history to the days of de Lesseps and the khedives. The Suez Canal, he said, was 'our canal'. How could it be otherwise when it was dug at the cost of 120,000

Egyptian lives? Building up to a great climax, he told the crowd, now wildly cheering, that the Suez Canal Company, with its headquarters in Paris, was nationalized and the Canal would in future be managed by an Egyptian Canal Authority. Egypt would build the High Dam with the revenues from the Canal and if the imperialist powers did not like it they could 'choke on their rage'.

Even Nasser's enemies among the Arabs could not help being thrilled by this daring and defiant gesture towards the old colonial powers. If Nasser's version of the Canal's history was highly coloured it was essentially correct. The immense profits on the relatively small original investment in the Canal had gone almost entirely abroad. Less than 5 per cent of the shares were held in Egypt, and although an agreement in 1949 increased Egypt's revenues they were still only 7 per cent of the gross profits. The Canal was a symbol of exploitation by the rich developed world.

If the Arabs were delighted by Nasser's action they knew that it was dangerous. Both the British and French governments soon showed their determination to use force to prevent Egypt from gaining permanent control of the Canal. The fact that the act of nationalization was legal under international law because Nasser offered full compensation to the shareholders was implicitly acknowledged by the British Prime Minister Anthony Eden when he dismissed the question of legality as 'quibbles'.

Eden went through the motions of trying to internationalize the Canal by political means, by inviting the principal Canal users to attend a conference in London, but before the conference he ensured that Egypt would not attend by referring to Nasser in a television broadcast in the most insulting terms – 'A man who cannot be trusted to keep an agreement. We all know this is how fascist governments behave.' Egypt announced its refusal to accept international control and since the great majority of Canal users, while disliking in some cases the way in which Nasser had nationalized the Canal Company, were totally opposed to the use of military force, there was no question of imposing outside control through international action. This majority included the United States, a fact which was ultimately fatal for Eden's plans. (The strong personal antipathy between Dulles and Eden did not help the US and British governments to coordinate their policies but it probably was not a determining factor in the American attitude.) The next British and French step was to withdraw all their pilots from the Suez Canal Company in the certain expectation that this would slow or stop traffic and provide an excuse for intervention. But Nasser had put in charge of the new Suez Canal Authority an exceptionally able and dynamic military engineer – Mahmoud Younis. With the Egyptian pilots working overtime and the hire of some extra pilots from sympathetic nations, he managed to keep the Canal running normally and even to increase traffic.

It was when this move failed that Eden began to think of joining a secret Franco-Israeli plan for Israel to attack Egypt with French logistical support. Israel had its own reasons for wanting to invade. It believed that it could force Egypt to accept its existence and to end the state of semi-war which had existed since Israel's creation and which since the Gaza raid had involved *fedayeen* attacks deep into Israeli territory. It also aimed to break the Egyptian blockade of the mouth of the Gulf of Aqaba. France's government led by the socialist Guy Mollet felt that it had nothing to lose for it was already at war with Nasser's brand of Arab nationalism, and Israel was its ally. Eden, on the other hand, could not fail to be aware of the appalling risks he was taking with Britain's remaining interests in the Arab world, which were still considerable if diminished, by joining the chief enemy of the Arabs in an attack on Egypt. He could only hope that Britain's collusion would not be found out.

The Anglo-French–Israeli plan was sealed at a secret meeting at Sèvres in France on 24 October between the Israeli Prime Minister David Ben Gurion and the foreign ministers of France and Britain. (By the end of 1984 no member of Eden's government had admitted that the meeting took place. But it is known to have occurred, because the French and Israelis felt no reason for such secrecy.)

In accordance with the plan, Israel invaded Sinai on 29 October. The next day Britain and France issued a joint ultimatum calling on Egypt and Israel to cease fighting and to withdraw their forces ten miles from the Canal, failing which Anglo-French forces would 'intervene with whatever strength may be necessary to ensure compliance'. Israel, whose forces were nowhere near the Canal at that time, and whose 'withdrawal' would thus entail a massive advance, accepted the ultimatum; Nasser, who by the terms of the ultimatum would have to voluntarily abandon territory he had not yet lost, rejected it.

On 31 October, when the ultimatum expired, British and French planes began to bomb Egyptian airfields and radio stations. The Voice of the Arabs was knocked off the air and within three days almost the entire Egyptian air force, except for the planes sent to Syria for safety, had been destroyed on the ground. On 5 November the Anglo-

French invasion force which had been assembled in Cyprus landed near Port Said and, after capturing the city (which suffered some heavy damage), advanced southwards along the Canal.

In retaliation the Egyptians had blocked the Canal with scores of ships and the Syrians had blown up the oil pipelines and pumping-stations on their territory, thus threatening Western Europe with the possibility of a serious oil shortage.

The whole Arab world was in an uproar as hostility to Britain and France reached fever pitch. World opinion was also overwhelmingly hostile towards the Anglo-French–Israeli action and after the creation of the UN Emergency Force (UNEF) Britain and France were obliged to withdraw.

The threatened break-up of the British Commonwealth, Soviet warnings, and especially the angry opposition of the United States, which had been deliberately kept in the dark about Britain's intentions and now refused to provide aid to relieve the alarming drain on sterling, all contributed to Britain's decision to halt its Suez action. In addition Britain and France had grossly miscalculated the effect of their action on Egypt. First they had believed that the Egyptians would be incapable of managing the Canal on their own and secondly they were convinced that as soon as hostilities had begun there would be a popular uprising against Nasser. The Near East Broadcasting Station in Cyprus issued propaganda messages urging the Egyptians to rebel. In fact the very opposite happened. Nasser himself admitted later that he had no idea how the people of Cairo would react to bombing, but he was entirely reassured on the second day of the invasion when he went publicly to al-Azhar mosque and was surrounded by great crowds expressing their will to resist. In the rest of the Arab world, nearly every transistor radio was switched on to Ahmad Said's Voice of the Arabs as soon as emergency measures brought him on the air again.

Nasser said later that when he saw the first bombers raiding Cairo he at first refused to believe that Britain could have done anything so stupid. In fact, although the Egyptian army withdrew from Gaza and the whole of Sinai and lost 2,000 to 3,000 men killed or taken prisoner by the Israelis, the net result of the whole episode was an almost complete victory for Egypt. As a natural consequence of Britain and France's act of war, the Suez Canal base, with its huge quantities of stores, was taken over by Egypt, and the terms of the Anglo-Egyptian agreement, which could have involved Egypt in another British military occupation in the event, for example, of a Soviet invasion of

Turkey and were therefore highly unpopular with Egyptian nationalist opinion, were cancelled. All the still considerable British and
French property and interests in Egypt were nationalized; the relics of
the nineteenth-century Anglo-French dual control of Egypt were
eliminated.

The effect of the Suez affair on the Arab world was twofold. It
enormously increased Nasser's personal popularity and prestige and
it intensified the underlying anti-Western radical trend in the Arab
countries. The swell of emotion, which began with Nasser's stunning
Alexandria speech announcing the nationalization of the Suez Canal
Company, rose to a new peak within a few months. He was no longer
only the organizer of the Egyptian revolution but the acknowledged
leader of the Arab world, whose picture was displayed in taxis and
cafés from Aden to Morocco. In the same way, the remains of the
ambivalence in Nasser's own attitude towards Arab nationalism were
dissolved in the emotions of Suez. He accepted the role of champion
of the Arab renaissance.

It may plausibly be argued that in the long run Nasser's heady
triumph in humiliating the old colonial powers was harmful both to
Egypt's interests and ultimately to his own reputation. He had raised
expectations in the Arabs which neither he nor Egypt could possibly
fulfil. He was the new Saladin who would unite all the Arabs and
liberate the land of Palestine from the Zionists. But this near great-
power role was quite beyond Egypt's strength and ability. In later
years Nasser partially acknowledged this reality and on many occasions tried to damp down the more feverish expectations. But he
remained the prisoner of Arab hopes, and in 1967 this led him into
near-fatal disaster.

But in 1956 all this lay in the future. The Nasserist tide was still
rising and it was emphatically flowing against the West. The sympathy felt for the United States by the Arabs for its role in halting the
Anglo-French action and in pressing a reluctant Israel to withdraw
from Sinai and Gaza was only very temporary. The Eisenhower-
Dulles administration was still guided by Cold War principles. It
rapidly mended its bridges with Britain, France and Israel and initi-
ated a campaign to reinforce the remaining conservative pro-Western
elements in the Arab world and contain Nasser's popular movement.
This involved joining the Western blockade of hungry and impoverished Egypt, which made it even more heavily dependent on the
Soviet Union, and promoting what came to be called the Eisenhower
Doctrine. In a message to Congress on 5 January 1957 President

Eisenhower promised military and financial aid to any Middle East countries 'requesting such aid against overt aggression from any nation controlled by international Communism'.

The US government believed there were good prospects for its policy, which meant that for the first time it was becoming heavily involved in the maelstrom of Arab politics. It realized quite correctly that the overwhelming popular appeal of Nasserism among the Arab masses was causing anxiety in some areas of the Arab world. Not only Nuri Said of Iraq, but the established rulers of most of the independent states were still basically pro-Western and conservative. They regarded the rising power of Nasserism, aided by Cairo's immensely powerful radio and press propaganda as well as by ubiquitous Egyptian agents, as a deadly threat. Encouraged by the United States, these anti-Nasser forces began to show their hand in 1957.

Fear of radicalism was enhanced in the Arab oil-producing states by their new wealth, the increase of which was now accelerating as a result of the introduction of the principle of fifty-fifty profit-sharing between the oil companies and the governments of the producing states to replace the old systems of royalty payment per ton. But the increased wealth did not necessarily make the régimes in these countries stronger and more stable; if anything social tensions were increased, and Egyptian propaganda lost no opportunity to point out the glaring inequalities of wealth they were causing.

Superficially, the Iraqi monarchy had little to worry about. With British advice, the new oil wealth was not being squandered. In 1950 a development board had been established and was allocated 70 per cent of the rapidly increasing revenues, although it never received the full amount. As investments were made in the economic infrastructure, in flood control and irrigation, and as Iraq's great economic potential began to be realized, the living standards of the mass of the population started to rise slowly but obviously from their low levels. But the lack of any social policy, and the investment in long-term prospects rather than education and social services (which would have brought speedier and more appreciable benefits to the majority), combined with the fact that many of the big development projects merely increased the wealth of the large landowners, tended to encourage the radical and revolutionary forces in the country. Above all, however, the régime was doomed because the Iraqis regarded it as a humiliation. No Iraqi Arab doubted for a moment that both Nuri Said and the regent, who had been restored to power by British bayonets in 1941, were wholly sympathetic to Britain's aims in the

Suez affair even if they deplored the embarrassing way the Eden government had tried to carry them out. The notoriously complacent British diplomats who assured the home government of the solidarity of the régime and the popularity of the British in Iraq were soon to be proved disastrously wrong.

The Saudi monarchy enjoyed the advantage of being indigenous rather than a foreign creation. But the old King Ibn Saud had died in November 1953 and his son Saud who succeeded him was no more than physically of the same stature. Ibn Saud had been unable to cope with the problems created by the new flood of wealth, but his son went far beyond this with his ludicrous extravagances, which not only made him the laughing-stock of the Arab world but actually succeeded in throwing the Saudi kingdom into debt to Aramco. The third major Arab oil producer – Kuwait – was in a relatively fortunate position, because, although it had its share of spendthrift princes, its relatively tiny population of about 200,000 meant that its revenues were enough for the paternalistic but relatively enlightened régime of its ruler to provide social services and improved living standards for all its people.

Of all the Arab states Jordan was apparently the most vulnerable to the radical Nasserite trend. Over half its population were Palestinians and, although their traditional leaders had accepted the union with Transjordan out of necessity, most of them felt no loyalty or sympathy towards their Hashemite rulers. On 20 July 1951 King Abdullah was assassinated in the Jerusalem al-Aqsa mosque by a young Palestinian and was succeeded by his son Talal, who one year later was declared mentally unstable. The throne inherited by his seventeen-year-old son Hussein when he interrupted his British education to succeed seemed every bit as shaky as that of his great-uncle Feisal in Damascus thirty years earlier. His position was not made any easier by the heavy Israeli reprisal raids on Jordanian frontier villages in response to infiltration attacks by dispossessed Palestinians, and his Western connections were under a constant barrage of criticism from Egypt and Syria. Moreover, at that time he could expect no help or sympathy from his fellow-monarchy in Saudi Arabia as King Saud returned his family's old enmity towards the Hashemites. Hussein earned some respite by his dismissal of Glubb Pasha in March 1956[4]

4. As we have seen, Anthony Eden believed that he dismissed Glubb on Nasser's orders, but, as the king makes clear in his own memoirs, he did it because he deeply resented Glubb's dominating position in Jordan and the taunt that he was merely a British puppet.

but anti-Western feeling in Jordan was inflamed by the Suez affair. (Jordan broke off diplomatic relations with Paris but not with London, thereby merely underlining the continuing importance of the British connection to the régime.) A pro-Nasser nationalist government formed after elections in October 1956 terminated the agreement with Britain, and in January 1957 Egypt, Saudi Arabia and Syria signed the Arab solidarity agreement, by which they undertook to make annual payments to Jordan in place of the British subsidy. All British troops were withdrawn from Jordan by the summer of 1957. Jordan seemed destined to leave the Western orbit and to become a republic.

King Hussein defied the prophets for a number of reasons, including luck, his own courageous determination and the divisions among his opponents. Paradoxically, his good fortune probably included Jordan's poverty; there were no oil revenues to create the social tensions that were rising in Iraq. Also republican forces in the Arab world were restrained to some extent from trying to overthrow him by the belief that Israel would intervene to prevent the creation of a Palestinian state on the East Bank. But essentially King Hussein survived because of the personal loyalty of the beduin element, which is predominant in the army, and the American subsidies which replaced those of Britain. In April 1957 King Hussein, with US encouragement and financial support, carried out a coup against his own pro-Nasser government which aimed to establish diplomatic relations with the Soviet Union.

Syria, the heart and soul of Arab nationalism, was the country which seemed most likely to join the Nasserist camp. Although lacking in oil, it was a country of high economic potential. But its remarkable post-independence boom based on investment in the new cotton industry had slowed down by the mid 1950s and the country was acquiring a world-wide reputation for the chronic instability of its régimes. The fall of Colonel Adib Shishakly, the dictator who ruled Syria fairly effectively from 1950 to 1954, brought a return to constitutional government with a parliament apparently dominated by the traditional political parties. But the really significant trend was the growing power of the Baath party which had gained political weight in 1952 by a union with the Socialist party of Akram Hourani, a politician with an important following in central Syria.

The Baath party's prestige and influence were nothing compared to those of Nasser in the Arab world but it had one important advantage over Nasserism in that it was not attached to any individual leader or Arab state. Significant Baathist movements developed during the

1950s in Lebanon, Jordan and Iraq as well as in Syria. The party's disadvantage was its failure to win mass support, so that when Baathists succeeded in gaining power they were unable to hold it except by extreme dictatorial or fascist-type methods.

Syria was the focus of Middle East tension in 1957 as the governments of the Arab states became increasingly divided along Cold War lines with two mutually hostile camps. The unconcealed efforts of the United States and Britain to set up a pro-Western front against Nasser increased tension and gave added force to Soviet propaganda. A British-sponsored plan to join Syria to Iraq under the Hashemites was in the offing.

Both the Soviet Union and the US were particularly concerned with developments in Syria, which Mr Dulles feared was about to become a Soviet satellite. His fears were exaggerated because, although the anti-Western trend in Syria was very real and the Communist party, although small, was a formidable force under the leadership of Khaled Bakdash, the great majority of Syrians, including the Baath, had no intention of becoming part of the Soviet system. They were equally in no mood to accept the Eisenhower Doctrine; instead the Baathists, who held the key posts in the government, led the country into asking Nasser to form an immediate and comprehensive union between Syria and Egypt. This was proclaimed in February 1958 and called the United Arab Republic. In this way the Baathists hoped to run Syria while the umbrella of Nasser's prestige protected the country from the domination of either of the great powers.

This linking of the two radical Arab nationalist states raised the temperature of the Middle East still higher. The two Hashemite kingdoms of Jordan and Iraq made a riposte by forming a federation of their own but this attempt to tie the two thrones together to prevent them from toppling aroused no popular enthusiasm. In March 1958 King Saud, whom the United States had hoped with some optimism to groom as a conservative rival to Nasser for Arab leadership, was forced by the ruling council of Saudi princes and religious shaikhs to relinquish his powers to his brother Prince Feisal, after the Syrians had accused the king of plotting to assassinate Nasser and so prevent the Syrian-Egyptian union. This seemed like another strategic gain for Nasser, because at the time Feisal was regarded as much more pro-Egyptian and less pro-Western than his brother Saud.

Attention now switched to Lebanon, where the country's delicate Christian/Muslim and Lebanese nationalist/Arab nationalist balance was threatened by the efforts of the able and personally ambitious

President Camille Chamoun and his Foreign Minister, Dr Charles Malik, a philosophy teacher turned politician, to place Lebanon firmly in the pro-Western camp. As Lebanese Muslims poured into Damascus to greet Nasser on his first visit to Syria the tensions that had been exacerbated by the Suez crisis developed into a muted civil war throughout the summer, in which the largely Muslim opposition forces, sustained and encouraged from across the border by what was now the northern region of the UAR, aimed to prevent Chamoun from altering the constitution to allow him a second six-year term of office.

The climax of the turbulent summer of 1958 came on 14 July, when Nuri Said and the Iraqi monarchy were overthrown in a violent revolution. It was Nuri Said's decision to help Chamoun which led to his downfall. Brigadier-General Abdul Karim Kassem and his subordinate officer Colonel Abdul Salam Aref had been ordered in early July to proceed with their troops of Jordan. Almost certainly the plan was to invade Syria and destroy the union with Egypt. Instead Kassem and Aref seized power in Baghdad; Nuri Said, the young king, and his uncle the crown prince, were assassinated and an Iraqi republic declared. At one blow the strongest and most effective pro-Western bastion in the Arab world had fallen. Fearing that what remained of their interests in the area would now be overwhelmed, the US answered President Chamoun's urgent request by landing marines in Lebanon and Britain flew troops into Jordan to help protect King Hussein.[5]

But there could be no question of a Western military counter-offensive against triumphant Nasserism. In Iraq there was no sign of any royalist resistance to the new régime, and Britain recognized the Iraqi republic with almost indecent haste. In Lebanon the civil war was ended with a compromise by the election as president of the moderate General Fuad Chehab, the commander-in-chief of the army (which he had kept out of the dispute), and the formation of a government with leaders from both sides. Lebanon's independence had been preserved, but its foreign policy reverted to being less overtly pro-Western and more acceptable to Arab nationalists.

Nasser and Nasserism were at the height of their success. Not only was Egypt in direct control of the heartland of Arab nationalism in Syria, but its principal rival in the Arab world – Nuri Said's régime in Iraq – had been destroyed. Even the isolationist and ultra-reactionary

5. Egyptian propaganda understandably made much of the fact that, in order to do this, Britain asked for, and received, permission to overfly Israeli territory.

Imam Ahmad of Yemen tried to ensure his own future against the new currents and gain their support for his struggle with the British for the control of South Arabia by applying to join the United Arab Republic. A loose federal structure known as the United Arab States was formed of Yemen and the UAR. In those dramatic days of the summer of 1958 it seemed as if the Arab states might be able to unite politically much sooner than the most fervent Arab nationalists had dared to hope.

The Arab West

After the Second World War the three Maghreb states of the western half of the Arab world were left far behind in their struggle for independence as France reimposed its full authority. The other Western powers made no attempt to intervene as they had done in Syria and Lebanon. But the struggle could not be long delayed as the forces of nationalism only grew under French repression.

In Tunisia Bourguiba's Neo-Destour party and other independent groups demanded autonomy and the formation of a Tunisian parliament. The more liberal approach of the French resident-general failed to satisfy these demands, and in 1950 the French government decided to offer Tunisia internal autonomy to be achieved by negotiated stages. A Tunisian government was formed with the Neo-Destour secretary-general, Salah ben Youssef, as a member. This government negotiated some increase in its powers at the expense of French control and the reform of civil service regulations to give priority to the recruitment of Tunisians. But the powerful French colony in Tunisia of about 180,000 opposed the extension of Tunisian autonomy and succeeded in influencing the Paris government to block further reforms. A new resident-general adopted a hard line; he arrested Bourguiba (who had just returned to Tunisia from Egypt) and other senior members of the Neo-Destour, although Salah ben Youssef escaped to Cairo. Growing agitation led to acts of terrorism against French police and against Tunisians who collaborated with the French. The French resorted to counter-terrorism, to combat the organized bands of fighters or *fellaghas* who appeared in the mountains.

In July 1954 an important conciliatory step was taken by the French government of Pierre Mendès-France: it recognized Tunisia's right to full autonomy, and proposed the immediate opening of negotiations for a convention to confirm the new status and regulate French interests in Tunisia. A Tunisian government was formed with the participation of a large number of Neo-Destour ministers, and lengthy negotiations, which were still obstructed by the opposition of the French colony in Tunisia, ended with the signing of the Franco-Tunisian Conventions in June 1955. Habib Bourguiba was allowed to return from France to receive a massive popular welcome.

Three months later Salah ben Youssef returned from Egypt to lead a violent campaign from the left against Bourguiba and his gradualist approach, and against the limitations on Tunisia's independence in the Franco-Tunisian Conventions. Bourguiba won the struggle because he enjoyed the support of the Neo-Destour; Salah ben Youssef fled the country.

In Morocco the French were faced with a similar type of rebellion, but here the focus of the national movement was the sultan, Muhammad V. French intransigence was represented by General Juin, who came from an Algerian *colon* family and was appointed resident-general in 1947. He failed in his attempt to bring pressure on the sultan to dissociate himself from the Istiqlal (independence) party but without success, although the French were able to draw on their supporters among the *caids* or feudal leaders of the countryside as a counterweight to the more nationalist towns. In the early 1950s the national movement spread and consolidated itself even among the tribes. French policy had been aimed at promoting the differences between Arabs and Berbers, and the French native affairs' experts were amazed and incredulous when the conservative and traditionalist Berber tribesmen joined the rebellion of the cities.

The Moroccan national movement had the support of the Arab League, the Afro-Asian bloc in the UN, and a section of French opinion. However, a majority of the French colony in Morocco was in favour of repression and they enjoyed a powerful influence on the weak and short-lived governments of the French Fourth Republic. In 1953 a group of pro-French *caids* (some of whom had personal grievances against the sultan) demanded the deposition of Muhammad V. After deposing and deporting him to Madagascar, the French authorities replaced him with an elderly cousin, Sidi ben Arafa, who could be relied upon to cause no trouble. As a result, Muhammad V became beyond question the symbol of the national spirit.

A clandestine organization replaced the banned political party and launched a terrorist campaign. After several assassination attempts against him, the frightened puppet sultan ceased to appear in public. The French took severe reprisals and one by one the Moroccan opponents of Muhammad V reversed their opinion and rallied to his cause. By 1955 the French had no alternative but to bring back the deposed sultan, who was received with wild rejoicing and the obeisance of all the former pro-French *caids*. By the declaration of La Celle St Cloud of 6 November 1955, France agreed to terminate the protectorate and recognize the independence of Morocco. In return Morocco recognized French interests and accepted 'independence within interdependence' which was to be defined by freely negotiated agreements. These agreements were completed by 2 March 1956 and a full transfer of power was made. A similar arrangement was concluded with the Spanish government for the incorporation of the Spanish zone with the independent kingdom of Morocco.

The Franco-Tunisian Conventions of the previous year still placed severe limitations on Tunisian sovereignty. It was therefore inevitable that when Morocco gained a promise of full independence, Bourguiba should ask for the same for Tunisia. This was finally granted by the government of the socialist Guy Mollet, and proclaimed in a protocol in March 1956. It was left to later negotiations to establish the basis of Franco-Tunisian interdependence to replace the 1955 Conventions.

Bourguiba formed a new government entirely from Neo-Destour personalities. The bey of Tunis, who had taken no part in the national struggle, had become no more than a figurehead. In July 1957 Bourguiba abolished the monarchy and became president of the Tunisian republic, as well as prime minister.

France's willingness to concede independence to Tunisia and Morocco, despite the fierce opposition of the French colonists, was partly motivated by its determination to retain the third North African territory which it had held so much longer and to which it was most closely attached – Algeria. Various proposals for assimilating Algeria with France, although supported by some leading Algerian personalities such as Ferhat Abbas, failed, because France consistently refused to grant Algerians full French citizenship with political rights unless they renounced their personal status as Muslims, which was something that the great majority refused to do. The law was relaxed in 1944 to extend French citizenship to certain categories of Muslims, but they remained a small minority. The incipient rebellion and savage French reprisals widened the gulf between the two communities in Algeria and finally proved the impossibility of assimilation. In 1947 a different, although related, formula was proposed, which just conceivably would have worked if it had been fully applied. The statute of 1947 created an elected Algerian assembly with substantial autonomous powers. It allowed Algerian Muslims to become full French citizens while keeping their Koranic status, reaffirmed the independence of the Muslim religion, and provided for the teaching of Arabic at all educational levels. But, as with the assimilation policy, the implications of full political integration with France were never faced. French politicians from the Communists to the far right affirmed that Algeria was part of France, but were not prepared to face the logical consequence of having 100 Muslim deputies in the French parliament if Algerians were to become full French citizens. At the same time the French settler community in Algeria, which was politically even more powerful in Paris than those in Morocco and Tunisia, prevented the application of the principles of social and political equality to the Muslim Algerians.

It was despair at the lack of progress which caused the Algerian Muslims to break out in open rebellion in the Aurès mountains on 1 November 1954. The appointment of Jacques Soustelle, who had a liberal progressive reputation, as governor-general in 1955 seemed to offer the chance of a fresh start. But it was too late. As the rebellion spread and French reprisals aimed at 'pacification' became increasingly severe, all plans for political reforms were rendered futile. Soustelle himself moved steadily to the right and, from being an object of suspicion to the French settlers, became their idol. During 1956 nearly all the outstanding Muslim political leaders, who had held back when the rebellion began, joined the rebels' political headquarters in Cairo.

In France the election of January 1956 brought to power a Republican Front, which had fought the campaign on a platform of 'peace in Algeria'. But the Socialist Prime Minister Guy Mollet proved incapable of bringing the war to an end and he returned a chastened man from a visit to Algiers, where enraged settlers peppered him with rotten tomatoes. Mollet's policy of trying to suppress the rebellion before holding elections and negotiating with the representatives of the Algerian people was a failure, as was the desperate attempt in alliance with Britain and Israel in November 1956 to knock out the Nasser régime in Cairo, which the French regarded as the external focus of the revolt.

Pacification, which involved the dispatch of a huge French army to Algeria (half a million by the early 1960s), the use of paratroops and the resettlement of some 1¼ million villagers under the supervision of the army, succeeded in eliminating much of the military strength of the rebellion. In Algiers, General Massu, hero of the French right, managed to restore a fair level of security to the capital. But French severity, which included the use of torture to extract information, only widened the gulf between the two communities, and the revolt continued.

In October 1956 the French scored an apparent success when a plane carrying five Algerian rebel leaders headed by Ahmad Ben Bella from Morocco, where they had been guests of the sultan, to Tunis was forced by French military planes to land in Algiers, where the five men were arrested and imprisoned. But the Algerian revolt was rapidly becoming an international issue. The whole Arab world, which had been further embittered by the French role in the Suez affair, took up the cause of the Algerians with enthusiasm. Despite French objections, the subject was discussed at the UN from 1957 onwards, and liberal-minded Westerners, including the young Senator John Kennedy, increasingly expressed public sympathy with the Algerian cause. Although France could be said to be winning the war militarily, it was losing it politically.

However, it was still true to say that the great majority of Frenchmen regarded the separation of Algeria from France as inconceivable. The discovery of important oilfields in southern Algeria in early 1957 gave an increased incentive to hold on at all costs. The French colonists (or *pieds noirs* as they were usually called) retained their powerful influence in Paris. In May 1958 their suspicions that the government was preparing to negotiate with the rebels caused them to launch a successful combined assault on the Fourth Republic in alliance with the French right and bring Charles de Gaulle back to power. In September 1958 the rebels responded by forming their own government-in-exile headed by Ferhat Abbas.

Although it was not immediately apparent, the high hopes placed in de Gaulle by the French settlers were to be totally deceived. With their exceptional powers under the new constitution, the president and his government were no longer subject to the French settlers' blackmail. Step by step and deliberately obscuring the path he was taking, de Gaulle moved towards acceptance of the principle of Algerian independence. As the French right became aware of what was happening, the settlers, in alliance with some elements in the army, twice came out in revolt – in 1960 and 1961 – but were suppressed. Secret negotiations between the government and the rebels began in 1961 and culminated in the Evian agreements, which laid down the principles of future Franco-Algerian social and economic cooperation, and provided for a referendum to be held throughout Algeria on the choice of independence. The French *colons* and the right had not finally despaired and the extremist O A S (*Organisation de l'armée secrète*) launched a terror campaign against the Evian agreements. Some of the settlers proposed that they should try to hold on to a piece of Algerian territory in which they would form a majority. All such plans failed because the great majority of the *colons*, who until then had regarded a French abandonment of Algeria as unthinkable, changed their views almost overnight. In a remarkable manifestation of mass panic, some 800,000 of the 1,000,000 Europeans left the country. In most cases they abandoned their homes and property intact. In the referendum held on 1 July 1962 the Algerians voted by a huge majority in favour of independence in cooperation with France. One hundred and thirty years of French rule in Algeria came abruptly to an end.

The exiled Algerian leaders returned, and a struggle for power ensued between Ben Khedda (who had succeeded Ferhat Abbas as head of the provisional government in 1961) and Ben Bella, who won with the support of the Algerian people's army under Colonel Houari Boumedienne. The handsome, charismatic and strongly socialist Ben Bella became prime minister in September 1962 and president of the Algerian republic in 1963.

13. *Disunity, Frustration and Defeat*

The structural weakness of the united front of radical Arab nationalist states, which seemed to have been forged under Nasser's leadership in the summer of 1958, was soon revealed. Within a few weeks of the revolution in Baghdad, General Kassem had his second-in-command Colonel Aref, who publicly favoured an immediate Iraqi–Egyptian union, arrested and imprisoned. Kassem blamed an abortive revolt of pro-Nasser Arab unionists in Mosul in February 1959 on Nasser and began favouring Iraqi communists at the expense of Arab nationalists. Nasser regarded this as a threat to the whole Arab nation and on his visits to the Syrian region of the United Arab Republic launched a series of bitter attacks on the Iraqi leader. Kassem survived in power for nearly four years by skilfully playing off communists against Arab nationalists, but he and Nasser were never reconciled. Nasser deeply distrusted him, and Kassem, a vain and unstable man, developed a violent and jealous hatred in return.

Nasser's angry attacks on the Iraqi communists led to a serious breach with the Soviet Union which, since the Suez affair, had become Egypt's main supplier of arms and economic aid. An exchange of highly critical speeches between Khrushchev and Nasser did demonstrate that Nasser was not subservient to the Soviets. It also led to a partial rapprochement with the United States, a resumption of American aid to Egypt and some improvement in relations with anti-Soviet Jordan and Saudi Arabia. But it was the failure of the two leading revolutionary Arab states – Egypt and Iraq – to form an effective alliance which was a bitter blow to those Arabs who had hoped for a speedy achievement of Arab unity.

However, the real testing-ground for an Arab political union was the United Arab Republic. Nasser had a large fund of enthusiasm and goodwill on which to draw, in Syria, but the practical and emotional difficulties were immense and in the end Nasser's magical charisma was not enough.

When the Syrian Baathists first proposed the merger Nasser at first was dubious, suggesting a period of preparation leading to an eventual full union. When the Syrians insisted, Nasser gave way, but on condition that he should have absolute authority in both regions of the United Arab Republic. The Syrian Baathists agreed because they believed that Nasser would have to rule Syria through them. But Nasser had no such intention and since the Baathists still had no mass popular following, it was easy for him to see that they failed when they stood for elections to the National Union, Egypt's single political organization, which was now extended to Syria. In October 1959 Nasser appointed Field Marshal Abdul Hakim Amer, his closest associate, as virtual governor of Syria. The Baathist ministers in the UAR government resigned to go into opposition. Nasser never forgave or trusted them again.

Without Baathist cooperation Nasser continued his policy of applying Egypt's social and economic measures to Syria. When the Free Officers came to power in Egypt they had no ideology except a simple nationalist anti-colonialism. Apart from land reform, which was primarily political in its aims, the Revolutionary Command Council's economic policies were initially cautious and conservative. However, during the 1950s Nasser and his colleagues had become convinced that if they were to achieve the rapid industrialization, high growth rates, the expansion of social services and the building of the High Dam, which alone could satisfy popular expectations raised by the 1952 revolution, they must mobilize all Egypt's human and economic resources. Inevitably, this led to a steady increase in the public sector and a series of socialist decrees in 1960 and 1961 nationalized cotton export firms, banks and insurance companies and 275 major industrial companies, and reduced the maximum land-holding from 200 to 100 *feddans.*

It was the application of these measures to Syria, with little regard for the differences in its social and economic structure, which caused all the secessionist forces in Syria to rally. Syria had proportionately a larger educated middle class than Egypt. Its people were more individualistic, more politically aware and also more factional and divided than in Egypt. All the factions which had cause to resent the union began to coalesce: politicians whose parties had been dissolved, merchants, landowners and businessmen who detested Egypt's socialism, army officers and civil servants who found Egyptians placed over them. In general the Syrians, who regarded themselves as the forerunners of Arab nationalism, felt they were relegated to a subordinate position to Egypt.[1] Those Syrian politicians

1. The Syrians' belief in the superiority of their Arabism had an almost racial quality. 'The first case in history of a black nation colonizing a white nation' was a Turkish journalist's cynical description of the UAR to the author in 1958.

who were prepared to enforce socialist legislation in Syria were out of office and hostile.

On 28 September 1961 a group of army officers struck and soon had the country in their hands. Nasser at first thought of intervening but soon realized that coercion was hopeless.

It was the turn of Nasser's enemies in other Arab régimes to triumph. But few Arabs were unreservedly delighted with what had happened. Even those who had reason to fear Nasserism felt some sense of shame and humiliation that this first real experiment in Arab unity had so spectacularly failed. On the other hand, Nasser's admirers, who were still numbered in millions among the Arab people, feared that Nasser might retire to nurse the fingers he had burned so badly in Damascus. Egypt was only a recent convert to Arab nationalism and could easily revert to its former self-absorption.

To some extent this is what Nasser did. He announced it was not imperative for Syria to remain part of the UAR and he would not oppose its re-entry as a separate nation into the UN and the Arab League. Egypt would remain the United Arab Republic but this could be no more than a salve to wounded pride.

According to Nasser's own testimony, the task of ruling Syria absorbed some three quarters of his time. There was a serious need to attend to Egypt's internal affairs because very little had been done to create a political structure to support his leadership. Under a constitution introduced in 1956 Nasser had become President for a six-year term and the Revolutionary Command Council was abolished. But the National Union he had created as a substitute for the political parties had proved highly unsatisfactory both in Egypt and Syria. Nasser believed that the Syrian right wing had managed to infiltrate the Union to launch its coup and, convinced that the Egyptian bourgeoisie might be planning similar action, he launched a precautionary offensive in which the property of most of Egypt's wealthiest families was sequestered.

In May 1962 Nasser produced his 30,000-word Charter of National Action as a blueprint for Egypt's future political development. This started from the proposition that the parliamentary democracy practised in Egypt after the First World War was 'a shameful farce' and its essence was contained in a passage which declared:

Political democracy cannot be separated from social democracy. No citizen can be regarded as free to vote unless he is given the following three guarantees: (a) he should be free from exploitation in all its forms; (b) he should enjoy an equal opportunity with his fellow citizens to enjoy a fair share of the national wealth; (c) his mind should be free from all anxiety likely to undermine his future security.

In accordance with these principles the Charter said that most of the economy should be publicly owned. All the import trade, three quarters of the export trade and a substantial part of domestic trade must be controlled by the public sector. The key difference from a Marxist system was that there was no nationalization of agricultural land, although ownership was limited to 100 *feddans* per family. Private ownership of buildings was also maintained with constant supervision to prevent exploitation.

This new and unique political organization was to be known as the Arab Socialist Union – a pyramidal organization founded on the 'basic units' in villages, factories and workshops and rising through elected councils at the district and governorate levels to the national executive headed by the president. The legislative branch of the ASU was parliament – the National Assembly. In this, as in all the elected bodies of the ASU, half the seats had to be occupied by workers or *fellahin* (defined as anyone owning less than twenty-five *feddans*). By this means Nasser hoped to ensure greater participation in government by the masses. Other important principles referred to the need for female equality and family planning. This was of some importance as it was the first time that Nasser endorsed the need to limit the population. The Charter specifically recognized the need to raise the social levels of the countryside to those of the towns if Egypt was to make real progress.

In approving the Charter without amendment, the National Congress of Popular Powers he had summoned to discuss it demonstrated both the strength and the weakness of Nasser's rule in Egypt. Undoubtedly his leadership was broadly accepted by the people but there was no popular participation in the process of government. Nasser expressed his wish that participation should be increased through the Arab Socialist Union organization but it was doubtful whether democracy could be imposed from the top in this way.

In spite of Nasser's renewed concentration on Egyptian affairs the powerful influence of Nasserism in the rest of the Arab world remained and in the other Arab states there were numerous elements who were still his loyal supporters. In Syria, Iraq and Jordan there were some prominent Baathists who proved that their attachment to Nasser was greater than to the party by throwing in their lot with Cairo. Another factor was that by the early 1960s Nasser had become without dispute one of the leading figures in the Third World. With

Tito of Yugoslavia and Nehru of India he formed the triangular base of the non-aligned movement. Although in practice Nasser's 'African Circle' had never been as important for Egypt as his Arab Circle, for reasons of language, racial and religious affinity, and strategic interest, Egypt was undeniably one of the major states on the African continent which was destined to play a crucial role in the newly created Organization of African Unity. All Arabs felt at the very least some grudging pride that they had produced in Nasser a world figure.

In 1962 Nasser's continuing role in the Arab world was demonstrated by the fact that the governments of Jordan, Syria, Saudi Arabia and Iraq were all attacking him from their various standpoints. The Saudis and Yemenis concentrated mainly on Egyptian socialism, which they said was alien and atheistic. The series of weak governments which succeeded each other in Syria after the secession rather cautiously reversed some of the UAR socialist legislation and concentrated on accusing Nasser and Egypt of criminally tyrannical behaviour during the union. At a meeting of the Arab League in Lebanon in August the Syrians listed their complaints against Egypt in the most violent terms. Nasser withdrew his delegates (who included some leading Nasserite Syrians) from the meeting and announced that Egypt was leaving the Arab League. In reply to the criticism that he was destroying Arab solidarity Nasser said that he was interested only in 'unity of purpose' and not mere 'unity of ranks'. He said the kind of unity proposed by the Jordanians, Syrians and Saudis served only the interests of imperialism. While all the Arab peoples were working towards a single goal, some Arab rulers were working towards different goals. Thus unity of ranks, based on different purposes, would endanger the entire Arab nation. The clear implication was that of all the Arab governments only the Egyptian was really sincere in its Arab nationalism. This argument had a powerful appeal to the Arab masses. Its disadvantage was that in times of crisis, when the Arabs are facing a common danger, there is no alternative to 'unity of ranks'. Egypt has to deal with whatever kind of régime holds power in the other Arab states if it aims to establish a common Arab front.

In September 1962 a major new development in Arabia sharpened the disarray and divisions of the Arab world but gave Nasser the opportunity to recover the initiative. In Yemen, where the ailing but ruthless old Imam Ahmad had died in September and had been succeeded by his son Badr who lacked his steel nerves, a group of army officers revolted and declared a republic. Although they seized the main towns, Badr escaped and, with help from members of his family and Saudi Arabia, rallied support among the tribes. The Yemeni revolutionaries at once appealed to Nasser for help and Nasser responded by sending an expeditionary force to help defend the Yemeni republic.

Egypt's involvement in Yemen, which was to last five years, was to prove costly and difficult. The troops, which Egypt could ill spare, had to be increased at one time to 50,000; they were untrained for mountain guerrilla warfare and their officers were mostly ignorant of the country and its people. Even more than in Syria, the Egyptians soon discovered that a common language and culture were not enough to ensure cooperation with another people. As the Egyptians became increasingly involved in the administration of the politically fragile republic the cry of 'Egyptian imperialism' was raised by their enemies. Egypt's image was not improved by its attempts at 'pacification' through the bombing of defenceless villages.

Yet at the outset the Yemeni revolt gave back to Nasser the political initiative in the Arab world. In showing that his forces could come at once to the aid of the Yemenis his stock rose among the Arab masses. The establishment of the first republic on the Arabian peninsula placed the Arab monarchies on the defensive. Saudi Arabia publicly announced that slavery was abolished in the kingdom. Both Jordan and Saudi Arabia began to help the Yemeni royalists, but several Jordanian and Saudi air force pilots defected to Cairo.

The establishment of the Yemeni republic also affected the position in South Arabia – the last remaining outpost of British rule in the Arab world. Britain had begun withdrawing from its paramount position in the Persian Gulf when Kuwait became fully independent in 1961 and the Anglo-Kuwaiti treaty of 1899 was revoked. Abdul Karim Kassem then promptly revived an ancient claim that Kuwait was part of Iraq. At the request of the ruler of Kuwait, Britain landed troops to defend Kuwait's independence, but these were shortly afterwards replaced, with Kuwait's agreement, by a joint Arab League force. It was apparent that Kuwait's status as an independent state and its acceptance by the international community depended more on the approval of the majority of Arab states than on British military protection.

Britain still retained a small military and naval base in Bahrain, but the Aden base was of much greater importance because it was regarded as the main defence for Britain's substantial economic interests in the Persian Gulf and a vital strategic link with the Far East.

In 1954 Britain had begun a policy of persuading the tribal shaikhs and sultans in the Aden protectorate to federate.

But powerful forces were working against this plan, and ironically they were much of Britain's own making. Aden Colony, the only part of the Arab world under direct British rule, had schools, trade unions and a civil service and was considerably more advanced than any of the tribal shaikhdoms. A strong Arab nationalist movement was developing, which Britain tried in vain to control by a policy of repression combined with limited moves towards self-government. At that time British politicians and administrators assured the Adenis that independence was inconceivable in view of the importance of British interests involved.

The whole British position was made much more difficult by the revolt in Yemen in September 1962. Instead of the repellent and reactionary Imam Ahmad it was the Egyptian-backed republicans who were attacking Britain's federation plans. As the protectorate shaikhs, with Britain's barely concealed approval, gave their support to the Yemeni royalists fighting the republic, Egyptian forces in Yemen gave active assistance to the anti-British nationalist forces in the area. British pressure succeeded in forcing through a merger between Aden Colony and the Federation of South Arabia against the wishes of the Adeni nationalists, who feared that they would come under the control of the tribal shaikhs whom they considered to be feudal and reactionary. From then on the situation in Aden steadily deteriorated as assassinations and bombings became daily occurrences.

It was the familiar scene of the end of a colonial era. As Britain strengthened its forces in South Arabia to contain the rebellion its measures against the nationalists merely increased anti-British feeling, while the Aden base rapidly became militarily useless as the British troops were forced to devote their energies to protecting themselves and their families.

In 1963 events elsewhere in the Arab world began to move swiftly under pressures from the underlying Arab nationalist forces. In February Abdul Karim Kassem was overthrown and shot in a coup led by the Baathists, and Nasser's friend and ally Abdul Salam Aref was installed as president. The new tide soon overwhelmed the weak Syrian régime, which collapsed under the joint pressure from Baghdad and Cairo. Here also the Baathists took over in alliance with Nasserists and other Arab unionist groups. Both the new Iraqi and Syrian régimes pledged themselves to support the new movement of Arab unity. Iraqi and Syrian ministers arrived in Cairo in scenes of great popular enthusiasm for reconciliation meetings with Nasser.

This seemed to be another moment of great triumph for Nasser, since there were now five of what he termed 'liberated Arab states' sharing similar aims and ideals (UAR, Yemen, Syria, Iraq and Algeria). Yemen was in close alliance with Egypt and Algeria was led by Nasser's friend Ben Bella. The other two – Syria and Iraq – had agreed to start immediate negotiations for the formation of a federal union.

But all the warnings provided by the failure of the previous union with Syria were only momentarily forgotten. The mutual mistrust between Nasser and the Baathists was at once revealed in the trilateral union negotiations. Nasser dominated the proceedings with his personality but the fact that he frequently employed his sharp wit at the expense of the less articulate Syrians and Iraqis (Michel Aflaq was a special victim) did not help to endear him to the Baathists. Although a form of agreement on a tripartite federation was reached on 17 April it was still-born. The Syrian Baathists were purging the army of non-Baathist officials and suppressing Nasserist demonstrations. Following the ruthless suppression of an attempted pro-Nasser uprising in Syria in July, Nasser openly and harshly attacked the Baathists for the first time, referring to the 'fascist' régime in Syria. 'To ensure unity,' he said, 'there must be a single Arab nationalist movement.'

Nasser never satisfactorily explained why he had agreed to attempt a new union with Syria and Iraq in spite of his own feelings towards the Baath and the fact that he had already admitted that the first Syrian–Egyptian union had failed because it was ill-prepared. He did say later that he felt that as long as there was a 1 per cent chance of success a union should be tried, but this is hardly an adequate reason for risking Egypt's entire future on such a dubious venture. The truth was that, having become a kind of symbol of Arab unity, Nasser was simply unable to turn down an offer of union from any other Arab state – least of all from an apparently contrite Syria. He had become a prisoner of his own image which had been created in the 1950s.

Egypt's relations with Iraq and Syria rapidly worsened during the summer of 1963. Nasser had some satisfaction in November when the Iraqi Baathists, who had already made themselves deeply unpopular through the violent methods of their extremists and who had renewed the exhausting war with the Kurdish nationalist minority (which had been a major factor in Kassem's downfall), split between their right and left factions and were ousted by President Aref, whom they had tried to keep as a figurehead, and some senior non-Baathist officers. Aref resumed the pressure for union with Egypt that he had started in 1958, but by now Nasser had learned caution. He agreed to regular consultation through an Iraqi–Egyptian joint political command but he suggested to the Iraqis that they should first ensure their own national unity, which among other things meant finding a solution to the Kurdish problem.

The Arab world was now more divided than ever. The bitter recriminations between the radical and conservative camps in the eastern Arab states – exacerbated by the savage royalist–republican civil war in Yemen – also affected the Maghreb. Hopes that the two halves of the Arab world would come closer together once the Maghreb had gained its independence had been belied. Tunisia joined the Arab League in 1958 but immediately withdrew, protesting that the organization was entirely dominated by Egypt. President Bourguiba thereafter bitterly accused Nasser of trying to interfere and overthrow him. Nasser's relations with independent Morocco were better for a time. Although in many respects a feudal monarch, Muhammad V succeeded in securing the cooperation for a time of the Moroccan trade unions and left-wing politicians. He pursued a radical and neutralist foreign policy which secured him Nasser's friendship, and in 1960 Morocco, Egypt, Mali, Guinea and Ghana combined to form a loose organization of radical African states known as the 'Casablanca' group. But Muhammad V died prematurely in February 1961 and his son Hassan, lacking his father's prestige, took strong constitutional power into his own hands and established an authoritarian form of rule with the support of loyalists and the army but in the face of opposition from the Istiqlal and left-wing politicians. Egypt's sympathies by now lay clearly with the new independent and socialist republic of Algeria under President Ben Bella and, when a frontier dispute led to fighting between Algeria and Morocco in 1963, Egypt supported Algeria. Dividing the Maghreb from Egypt and the eastern Arab world was the vast empty space of the impoverished kingdom of Libya – 'a geographical hyphen' as it was unkindly described. Apparently lacking any natural resources, Libya depended heavily on the income from the US and British military bases and its régime was therefore heavily Western-oriented.

Although any form of Arab political union seemed utterly remote in 1963–4, a situation was arising of the kind which obliged Nasser for a time to abandon his insistence on 'unity of purpose' in preference to 'unity of ranks'. The Israelis had completed the work needed to enable them to divert some of the waters of the river Jordan to the Negev Desert. Because of the immense symbolic importance of the Jordan river, this was something that Arab governments had repeatedly sworn to prevent and the Arab masses expected them to act. In their divided condition there was little chance of their taking effective action, but there was a very real danger that one Arab state – most probably Syria – would act on its own and plunge the others into a war with Israel, for which they were unprepared. This was Nasser's nightmare and at Christmas 1963 he issued an invitation to all Arab kings and presidents, which he knew they would find difficult to refuse, to meet the following month in Cairo to discuss how to meet the situation. He skilfully used the occasion to mend his bridges with Arab states such as Jordan, Tunisia and Morocco from which he was estranged and to emphasize the isolation of Baathist Syria, which was now on bad terms with both the Iraqi–Egyptian and the Jordanian–Saudi camps. The heads of state agreed to set up a unified Arab military command under an Egyptian general and also a Palestine Liberation Organization,[2] with its own army, to represent the Palestinian people. They all agreed, although with little enthusiasm, on the choice of the flamboyant and voluble Palestinian lawyer Ahmad Shukairy, to head the PLO. They also decided on plans to divert the sources of the river Jordan in Arab territory in order to forestall Israel's irrigation schemes.

All this was little more than window-dressing. The pressing problem of how to satisfy Arab aspirations for the liberation of Palestine without provoking a potentially disastrous war with Israel had been postponed rather than solved. The dangers had increased because the decisions of the kings and presidents gave the Arabs a false sense that some positive and united action was at last being undertaken. Lebanon and Syria were reluctant to carry out the diversion work on the Jordan tributaries in their territories without more adequate protection than the Arab states could provide, and the mutual trust that was essential if the united military command was to be effective was lacking.

In fact the differences between the radical and conservative camps deepened during 1965, despite the superficial reconciliation of the

2. This was not a government-in-exile nor, because of Jordanian opposition, could the PLO claim control over the West Bank, the part of Palestine still under Arab control. There was much talk of a Palestinian 'entity', wittily described by one observer as a Hovercraft which was unable to land.

Arab summit meetings. It was a peculiarly difficult time for Nasser. On the world stage his role was undiminished. In May 1964 the Soviet Premier Khrushchev made a much publicized visit to Egypt for the inauguration of the second stage of the building of the High Dam – the gigantic project which not only aimed to change the face of Egypt but was the symbol of Soviet aid to the Third World. At one point during the visit Khrushchev showed his irritation with the overwhelming emphasis on Arab nationalism and unity rather than socialism with which he was confronted, by declaring that the only true union is based on the workers and not on nationalism; the clear implication was that nationalism was an outdated concept. This gave Nasser the opportunity to reaffirm his faith in Arab nationalism in a speech saying that the Arab nation had been united only to be artificially divided and that the Arabs still had 'one conscience and one mind'. There can be little doubt that Nasser welcomed this opportunity to emphasize his non-alignment by publicly disagreeing with the Soviet leader on a fundamental point. Later in 1964 Nasser was host both to the second conference of the Organization of African Unity and to a summit meeting attended by fifty-six heads of non-aligned states or their representatives.

Cairo's status as one of the major capitals of the Third World and Nasser's function as a world statesman could not help to solve his domestic difficulties. Rapid and sometimes ill-planned policies of industrialization and economic expansion combined with a reduction in Western aid and the drain of the Yemeni war had placed Egypt heavily in debt and destroyed its credit. The discovery of a nation-wide conspiracy by a revived Muslim Brotherhood revealed a profound ideological and political dissatisfaction in many levels of society. Finally, his health was seriously deteriorating. Nasser had suffered from diabetes since 1956. Through overwork and worry, especially during the Syrian–Egyptian union, this had developed into 'black diabetes', i.e. the blocking of the arteries. Some delegation of responsibility was essential, but of this Nasser was incapable.

The Yemeni civil war not only drained Egypt's foreign exchange but tied down most of its best troops. In August 1965 Nasser made a sudden visit to Jedda in Saudi Arabia to reach an agreement with King Feisal (who had succeeded his brother Saud in name as well as fact when the latter abdicated in December 1964) on the Yemen, which provided for Yemeni self-determination and the ending of all Saudi and Egyptian intervention. The agreement failed to provide a solution because neither side trusted the other to be wholly sincere. In

December 1965 King Feisal went on a state visit to Iran, and in his address to the Iranian Majlis he suggested the need for Islamic unity against subversive and alien influence from outside. Although he was deliberately unspecific, no one doubted he was referring to Egypt and Arab socialism. All the conservative anti-Nasserist forces in the Middle East rallied to what the press called King Feisal's 'Islamic Front' although he never used the term himself. Feisal was a much more formidable adversary as a statesman than his brother Saud, and rapidly increasing oil revenues gave his country a new power and status.

By now events were moving rapidly towards the new Arab–Israeli war which Nasser had wanted to avoid. In February 1966 the Syrian régime, which had begun a rapprochement with Egypt, was overthrown by the radical wing of the Baath party. The new rulers of Syria had no love for Nasser, but they were more strongly hostile towards the Arab kings and, if possible, even more bellicose than their predecessors towards Israel. A new Palestinian guerrilla organization called al-Fatah had begun sabotage operations against Israel in January 1965, and the Syrian Baathists gave it increasing help and encouragement. The deteriorating situation in the Middle East drew the Egyptians and the Syrians closer together. In November Nasser agreed to conclude a new and highly comprehensive defence agreement with Syria which provided for regular joint staff meetings and a joint command for the two countries' forces in the event of war. The Syrians, still deeply suspicious of Egypt, refused to accept any bases on Syrian soil. The question is why Nasser then accepted such a potentially dangerous arrangement which committed him to Syria's defence, without giving him any real control over its military policies. The answer was much the same as in 1963 and 1958. Nasser had the greatest difficulty in rejecting any offer of closer union with any Arab state but especially with Syria, the former province of the UAR.

A few days after the signing of the fateful Syrian–Egyptian defence pact, three Israeli soldiers were killed by a mine explosion near the Jordanian frontier. Although Syria was clearly the main source of Palestinian sabotage attacks, Israel launched its customary heavy retaliation raid against the West Bank village of Samu. Protesting against their inadequate protection by the Jordanian army, the West Bank rose in revolt and was only quelled with difficulty. The Syrians and the Palestinian Liberation Organization tried to add fuel to the fire. Nasser himself in a public speech avoided inciting the West

Bankers further, but he made it clear where his sympathies lay; and when the Jordanian government had regained control King Hussein bitterly criticized Nasser as well as the Syrians. Calling Nasser a political 'trapeze artist', he accused the socialist Arab states of preparing, in cooperation with the Russians, to liquidate the Palestine problem at Jordan's expense by handing over the West Bank to Israel in return for a settlement. More significantly, he taunted Egypt with hiding behind the protection of the United Nations Emergency Force in Sinai. Friends and critics throughout the Arab world had been asking for some time why, if Egypt had the strongest armed forces in the Arab world, as its leaders often claimed, it had not asked for the UNEF to be withdrawn in order that, in retaliation for Israel's diversion of the river Jordan, the Straits of Tiran might be closed to Israeli shipping, as they were before 1956. This was a challenge that Nasser could not disregard. But the military prospects for the Arabs were rather worse than before. As relations between the 'progressive' and 'conservative' Arab camps deteriorated, Saudi Arabia withdrew all its financial support from the joint Arab schemes agreed upon at the Arab summits and the United Arab Military Command virtually ceased to exist.

In the spring of 1967 tension rose to new heights as Israeli leaders issued increasingly severe warnings to Syria that Israel would retaliate heavily if sabotage by Arab commandos inside Israel continued. Soviet, Syrian and Egyptian intelligence combined to warn Nasser that an Israeli attack on Syria was imminent. Nasser's response on 18 May was to ask the UN secretary-general to withdraw the UNEF from Sinai (where, on Israel's insistence, it was stationed only on Egypt's side of the border).

When U Thant complied the road to war was wide open. Once the UNEF had withdrawn from their positions at Sharm al-Shaikh at the mouth of the Gulf of Aqaba Nasser had no alternative to closing the straits to Israeli shipping. If he had not, his armed forces, which his generals were constantly claiming to be the strongest in the Middle East, would have been the laughing-stock of the Arab world.

King Hussein, realizing that war was now probable and that it would be impossible this time for Jordan to stand aside, made a dramatic flight to Cairo on 30 May to sign a Jordanian–Egyptian defence pact. Damascus Radio failed to mention the event and Syria and Jordan remained unreconciled. At the last minute the semblance of a united Arab military command was re-created and some Iraqi troops moved into Jordan.

In spite of its dangerous disunity, the whole Arab world was now in a state of emotional self-intoxication as a final victory over Israel seemed imminent. Arab newspapers were filled with cartoons showing a puny hook-nosed Israeli being crushed by a gigantic Arab soldier. Even Nasser seemed to have abandoned his usual doubts about Arab military capabilities. This was partly because he had unjustified confidence in the abilities of the commander of the Egyptian armed forces, Abdul Hakim Amer, who had enjoyed a free hand in the military sphere for some years. Nasser may have believed that US restraint on Israel would prevent it from attacking, and that he could score a tactical victory without fighting. He himself had promised the Soviet Union that Egypt would not strike first. However, experience should have told him of the high probability that Israel would attack as soon as it became apparent that the international community, despite some bellicose statements by both British and US governments, was not going to force the Straits of Tiran on Israel's behalf.

In a surprise attack on seventeen Egyptian airfields on the morning of 5 June Israel destroyed most of the Egyptian air force on the ground. With complete command of the air, Israeli forces won an easy victory in Sinai and reached the Suez Canal early on 9 June. After destroying the Egyptian air force, Israel could turn against Jordan, which had entered the war on Egypt's side. By the evening of 7 June, with the Old City of Jerusalem and the West Bank occupied, Jordan accepted the UN Security Council's demand for a ceasefire. Egypt accepted on the following day. Israel was now free to turn against Syria, which had confined itself to probing attacks. Israeli troops stormed up the Golan Heights and occupied the key town of Quneitra on the Syrian plateau. Syria accepted the ceasefire on 10 June. Contingents of Algerian, Sudanese and Kuwaiti troops sent to the Suez Canal front could not arrive in time to affect the fighting.

World opinion was not on Egypt's side, as it had been in 1956. On the third day of the fighting King Hussein and President Nasser agreed on the telephone that there was direct Anglo-American intervention on Israel's side. The original basis of the charge was that the Jordanians had detected enemy planes on their radar screens in far greater numbers than they had thought could be accounted for by the size of the Israeli air force. Cairo Radio began to broadcast the charge that Britain and the US were giving Israel military support. Egypt broke off relations with the US (it had already broken with

Britain in 1965 over the Rhodesia question), and Syria and Algeria followed suit. Lebanon, Sudan, and Kuwait withdrew their ambassadors to Britain and the US, while all the major oil-producing states announced an immediate embargo on oil exports to these two countries. A great wave of anti-Western feeling swept the Arab states, sparing only France, because President de Gaulle, alone among the leaders of major Western countries did not appear committed to a pro-Israeli attitude.

Neither Nasser nor King Hussein were able to sustain the charge of direct Anglo-US military intervention and soon abandoned it. Yet the vaguer, but scarcely less damaging, accusation of collusion remained and was accepted by most of the Arabs. One reason was the simple fact that there had been collusion in 1956, which Britain had still not admitted. Another was the subsequent behaviour of Britain and the US, especially the latter, in the United Nations and elsewhere in the international field. The US government gave the impression of being unwilling to do anything that might offend the Israeli state. If in 1967 the US government had done no more than give the green light to the Israelis to go it alone, with a promise to intervene if things went badly for them, did this not amount to collusion?

A sophisticated but plausible version of what actually happened is provided by the Zionist writer Jon Kimche. Writing of May 1967 he says there were two American policies operating on two distinct levels.

Officially, Americans were correct in every way. They went along with the United Nations, with the British and the French, and endeavoured to find an international solution. But they were convinced that the United Nations would remain ineffective, and that all the British might succeed in doing was to get the Americans involved in a conflict in the Middle East. . . . In secret talks which they had with Yariv and Amit, Israel's military and secret Intelligence chiefs, the Pentagon and the CIA were satisfied that Israel could well take care of the situation as long as the great powers did not intervene. The Israelis were, therefore, informed on two distinct levels of the American position. Johnson and Rusk played their version of the Middle East charade with Eban, but did not realize that Eban was taking it all seriously and was unaware of the other half of the American proposal. Helms [head of the CIA] told his Israeli colleagues that Israel would have to conjure up all her inner strength to withstand pressures from outside. Even the Americans might find it necessary to join in these pressures, for they had to protect themselves at all costs against the suspicion of collusion – and they could do so only by ensuring that there was no collusion. But – and this was conveyed to Yariv rather than spelled out in as many words – if Israel wanted to have tangible results this time, she would have to be solid as a rock and not weaken before, during, or after the actual military encounter.[3]

Apart from the general increase in anti-Western feeling the shattering defeat of the Six Day War had many immediate and long-term effects on the Arab world. The first question that arose in the minds of many was: 'Will this be the end of Nasser?' His share of responsibility was clear and on the afternoon of 9 June his sad and bowed figure accounced on television his intention of resigning and handing over to Vice-President Zakariya Muhieddin. 'Arab unity began before Nasser and will remain after him. I always told you that it is the nation that survives . . . I am not liquidating the revolution. But it is not the property of one generation.'

The extraordinary dominance which he had achieved in Egypt, and his position as the generally well-loved father-figure of a nation accustomed to paternalistic rule, meant that he was not allowed to abandom the presidency at a time of such desperate crisis. As soon as he had finished speaking a great roar was heard as people poured into the streets chanting 'Nasser, Nasser,' and calling for him to stay. Similar scenes occurred in Beirut, Damascus, Baghdad and Benghazi, where several policemen were admitted to hospital suffering from shock on hearing the news. The following day the Egyptian National Assembly met to reject Nasser's resignation and vote him full powers for 'the military and political rebuilding of the country'.

Nasser's image was seriously damaged but not destroyed. His health deteriorated further and there can be no doubt that the disasters of 1967 helped to shorten his life. But in one sense Egypt's difficult situation made his position easier, since those who might have challenged his power were restrained by their lack of any practical alternative to his policies. In August 1967 he was faced with a conspiracy to restore his former right-hand man, Abdul Hakim Amer, as head of the armed forces, and in 1968 and 1969 there were serious outbreaks of unrest among students and industrial workers, but he overcame these with a mixture of firmness and mild concessions. While there was considerable dissatisfaction, especially among the professional classes and the intelligentsia, because the old power structure had not been radically changed, the continuing state of emergency with Israel provided a powerful argument for postponing fundamental reforms.

3. Jon Kimche, *Palestine or Israel: The Untold Story of Why We Failed*, London, 1973, pp. 257–8.

Although King Hussein did not share Nasser's responsibility for the war, his kingdom's losses were proportionately even greater than Egypt's. Some 150,000 new refugees had fled across the river Jordan to the East Bank. The closure of the Suez Canal made Aqaba, the country's only port, virtually useless, and Israel's occupation of East Jerusalem and the West Bank ruined the flourishing tourist trade. Jordan's survival as an independent state seemed more than ever in doubt.

King Hussein therefore took the lead in pressing for the holding of an Arab summit to confront the disastrous situation of the Arab world. The meeting was held in Khartoum at the end of August 1967, and the Sudanese government, led by Muhammad Mahgoub, was the force behind its organization. Mahgoub's critics in the Sudan claimed that he was taking an unprecedented interest in Arab affairs because of unwillingness to tackle Sudan's internal problems, but the fact was that Khartoum was the ideal meeting-place for a reconciliation between Arab conservatives and radicals, which Nasser, having realized the limitations of Soviet support, had decided must be achieved.

The Khartoum summit was in reality a compromise between the two sides. The 'front-line states' – that is Egypt and Syria – said that they would continue the struggle provided all the Arab states contributed all their resources. The reaction of the leading Arab oil-producing states – Libya, Kuwait and Saudi Arabia – was to say that they were prepared to contribute handsomely provided they did not have to take measures which would cause them crippling losses, such as cutting off their oil exports to the West. It was agreed that all the oil sales to Britain, the US and West Germany that had been stopped since the war would be renewed, and at the same time the three oil states, Libya, Kuwait and Saudi Arabia, would contribute annually £30 million, £55 million and £50 million respectively to compensate Jordan and Egypt for the damage of the war and its consequences. (It was decided that Egypt should have £95 million and Jordan £40 million.)

Nasser had played well from what looked like a very weak hand. Syria and Algeria remained intransigently in favour of continued punitive measures against the West, but since neither Syria's Baathist President Atassi nor Algeria's Colonel Boumedienne[4] attended the

4. Boumedienne had ousted Ahmed Ben Bella from power in a bloodless coup in July 1965.

conference, this was not an immediate problem. But while Nasser never seriously expected that the oil states would agree to a total economic boycott he was ready to use the threat of this to persuade them to contribute much more than they ever had in the past. In fact his weak hand held a few strong cards. It was not only that Egypt had suffered, and would continue to suffer, the greatest military and economic losses from the struggle with Israel, but the great anti-Western current in the Arab world threw the oil states on the defensive and prevented them from gaining their full political advantage from Egypt's shattering defeat. Nasser still astonishingly retained much of his popularity with the Arab masses, as anyone who mingled with the Khartoum crowds who greeted him could see. (*'Mais, c'est un vaincu!'* exclaimed an amazed French correspondent as young Sudanese mobbed the car that was bringing Nasser from Khartoum airport.) It was the same anti-Western current which two years later was to sweep away the monarchy in Libya.

The Khartoum agreement would have been impossible without a settlement with Saudi Arabia over the Yemen. This provided for the withdrawal of Egyptian forces and the formation of a transitional régime until a plebiscite could be held. Most people expected the republicans to collapse without Egyptian support but the expected did not happen. As the royalists advanced on Sanaa, expecting an easy victory, the republican premier General Amri, with some Algerian and Syrian assistance, rallied his forces and repelled the attack. Royalist tribesmen could still harry the republicans but by 1968 there were signs that the royalist leadership was deeply divided. The royalist cause was also weakened by events in South Arabia where, as Britain withdrew, the ruling shaikhs and sultans were skittled over one by one by the nationalist forces.

Ultimately it was the National Liberation Front which triumphed in South Arabia over its rival, the Front for the Liberation of South Yemen (FLOSY), which was supported by Egypt and the Yemeni republicans. But the NLF was more radical and more bitterly opposed to tribal rule, and its cause was helped by the same anti-Western feelings which had been roused by the June war. For King Feisal the triumph of the NLF or FLOSY was equally unwelcome – especially in the Hadramaut or East Aden protectorate, where he had been establishing close ties with the hereditary rulers. At midnight on 30 November 1967 a second republic – although shaky and impoverished – was born on the Arabian peninsula. It called itself the republic of South Yemen, to emphasize the artificiality of the division of the region by Britain.

When the British Labour government decided in 1966 to withdraw entirely from South Arabia it had been assumed that it would maintain and reinforce its military presence in Bahrain. However, in January 1968 the government made a sudden *volte face* and announced that it would be withdrawing all its forces by 1971. This decision to end Britain's last quasi-imperial connection with the Arab world, which was confirmed by the Conservative government when it came to power in 1970, alarmed the rulers of the small Gulf shaikhdoms, whose survival in the face of Saudi, Iranian and other ambitions had depended on Britain for so long. Because most of them were far too small to form viable independent states, they discussed the formation of a federation in self-defence, but because of the failure of the rulers to devise a constitution which would resolve their internal rivalries, Qatar and Bahrain declared their full independence in 1971 and the remaining seven shaikhdoms of the Trucial Coast formed a Union of Arab Emirates.

The final communiqué at the Khartoum summit meeting was intransigent in its wording. It ruled out Arab recognition of Israel, a peace treaty or direct negotiations. It made no mention of a possible Arab declaration of non-belligerence in return for an Israeli withdrawal from territory it had occupied in the war, which was the basis of President Tito's friendly suggestions. In fact, as so often happens on such occasions, the public declaration concealed the reality of the participants' intentions. Arab pride prevented Egypt and Jordan from negotiating directly with Israel while it remained in occupation of their territory. It was clear that Israel was in no mood to respond to a simple declaration of non-belligerence by withdrawing. But both Egypt and Jordan had already made up their minds to try to seek a solution by political and diplomatic, rather than military, means.

Three months after the Khartoum summit, President Nasser and King Hussein showed their real intentions by formally accepting the British-sponsored UN Security Council Resolution 242 of 22 November 1967, which called for the withdrawal of Israeli forces 'from territories occupied in the recent conflict' and for respect for the right of all Middle Eastern states 'to live in peace within secure and recognized boundaries'.

The deliberate imprecision of the terms of this resolution, which was the only way in which it could obtain the unanimous support of the members of the Security Council, meant that it was to become the subject of endless controversy. Each party to the Middle East dispute interpreted it differently. Israel placed its emphasis on the 'secure and recognized boundaries' which it said precluded any return to the 1949 armistice lines. The Arab states which accepted it – Egypt, Jordan and Lebanon – emphasized the need for withdrawal and the statement of principle of 'the inadmissibility of the acquisition of territory by military means'. The Arab states which rejected it – notably Syria and Iraq – did so because it implied recognition and acceptance of Israel. It could be argued, therefore, that it was worse than useless because it covered the conflicting issues with a cloak of well-intentioned woolly sentiment. It could equally be argued that no UN resolution on such a controversial issue can do more than this, which is to provide a point of reference from which more practical and specific moves towards a settlement can be made.

Such an argument can hardly be resolved since it involves the question of the proper function of the United Nations, but there is one aspect of Resolution 242 which must be condemned: its failure to. mention the Palestinian Arabs except in a cursory reference to the need for 'a just settlement of the refugee problem' in the Middle East. It was some seven years before this singular omission was internationally recognized.

One reason why the failure to mention the Palestinians seemed less odd at the time was that the striking growth of Palestinian consciousness came after the Six Day War. Between 1948 and 1967 the Palestinians pinned their faith mainly on the Arab states to liberate their lost territory, and most of them had been content to merge their identity into a broad Arab, as opposed to Palestinian, nationalism. Even the use of the name Palestine declined. After the 1967 defeat of the Arab regular armies the Palestinians reached a collective conclusion that the restoration of their country depended on their own efforts. The Palestinian guerrilla organizations, which first appeared on the scene in 1965–6, gained support and prestige. Arab governments and individuals, including the minority of Palestinian Arabs in the diaspora who had succeeded in prospering, helped to provide them with arms and funds. Outside the Arab world the cause of the Palestine liberation movement also gained adherents, especially on the left and among students, as many people became aware for the first time of the injustices the Palestinians had suffered.

The largest Palestinian guerrilla organization was al-Fatah[5] – the

5. *Al-Fatah* means 'victory', but it is also the reversal of the Arab acronym of *Harakat Al-Tahrir Al-Falastini* – Palestine liberation movement.

group which had issued its first military communiqué on 1 January 1965, announcing a sabotage attack on Israeli diversion works on the river Jordan. After the June War the leaders of al-Fatah chose from among themselves the pudgy and elusive figure of Yasir Arafat as their spokesman. Arafat, born in 1929, came from a wealthy and educated Palestinian family. He studied in Egypt and became president of the Palestinian Students' Federation in Cairo, but, like many students in Egypt at the time, he joined the Muslim Brotherhood organization and had to leave Egypt under a cloud when the Brotherhood was suppressed by Nasser in 1954. He was able to return to Cairo in 1955 and spent most of the next few years establishing an embryo Palestinian organization in Lebanon, Iraq, Kuwait and western Europe. In Kuwait, where he formed his own engineering firm, he and his friends founded an al-Fatah cell and created an invaluable logistical base for the movement with the help of wealthy Palestinians in the country. He also established links with the leaders of newly independent revolutionary Algeria, which provided al-Fatah with a recruiting centre and guerrilla training grounds. But Algeria was too remote to provide a military base. The only one of Israel's neighbours which was prepared to do this before the 1967 war was the Baathist régime in Syria. (Egypt still insisted on working only with Ahmad Shukairy's Palestine Liberation Organization and was training a Palestine Liberation Army in Gaza.) Al-Fatah therefore established itself in Syria in 1963 and launched its first raids from there into Israel.

By June 1967 al-Fatah was the largest of the clandestine guerrilla groups, but there were others, some of them only consisting of a handful of men. Shortly after the Six Day War representatives of these splinter groups met secretly in Damascus to discuss joint action. But they failed to agree; al-Fatah resumed operations on its own, while three of the small groups combined into the Popular Front for the Liberation of Palestine under Dr George Habash, a Christian Palestinian from Lydda. Habash had founded his Arab Nationalist Movement among Arab students in 1953, when he was studying for his medical degree at the American University of Beirut. Although he and his colleagues were already developing at that early stage a belief in the need for a total revolution in Arab society to stand up to the modern state of Israel, Nasser's successes in the 1950s caused them for some years to place their faith in his strategy and cooperate fully with Nasserism. But they gradually lost faith in the capacity of the Arab states and their regular armies to liberate Palestine, and they moved leftwards to a belief in Guevara-type revolutionary guerrilla action. They began operations against Israel at about the same time as al-Fatah, although on a smaller scale. They concentrated mainly on political action, i.e. reconaissance work through agents inside Israel.

Habash's scepticism about the capacity of the Arab armies was triumphantly confirmed by the Six Day War. When it was formed, his PFLP took the line that the Palestinian struggle against Israel should be pursued by every possible means including plane hijacking, sabotage and acts of terrorism outside Israeli territory. Anything which harmed Israel's interests was justified and if innocent civilians suffered this was sad but could not be helped. His strategy soon clashed with the more orthodox views of al-Fatah's leadership, and attempts to bring him under some form of central control always failed.

From the moment that they began to come into prominence after the 1967 war, the Palestinian guerrilla organizations suffered from their internal divisions, and the popular enthusiasm they aroused only served to conceal their organizational weakness. Their military operations against Israel and the occupied territories were also faced with the greatest difficulties. The open nature of most of the terrain was unfavourable for guerrilla tactics, and severe Israeli counter-measures and lack of cooperation by the inhabitants of the West Bank prevented them from establishing bases in enemy territory.

Palestinian morale was boosted in March 1968 when for the first time commandos joined forces with the Jordanian army to inflict severe losses on an Israeli retaliatory raiding force at Karameh in the Jordan valley. Al-Fatah's new prestige enabled Yasir Arafat and his colleagues to oust the discredited Ahmad Shukairy[6] from the leadership of the PLO and at a Palestinian congress held in Cairo in 1969 Arafat became chairman of the PLO executive on which various small groups as well as al-Fatah – although not Habash's PFLP – were represented.

In reality 1968 was a false dawn for the *fedayeen*. The relative success of Karameh was not repeated and the commando raids on the occupied territories never posed a serious military threat to Israel, whose casualties were considerably higher on the Suez front with Egypt during 1968–9. Although various attempts were made to weld the various resistance groups into a single organization under al-

---

6. 'Ahmad Shukairy, whose many intemperate and conflicting statements had led many cynics to wonder whether he was not perhaps in the pay of the Israeli secret services because of the harm he had done the Palestinian cause.' (John K. Cooley, *Green March, Black September: The Story of the Palestinian Arabs*, London, 1973, p. 102.)

Fatah's leadership, no common and agreed strategy was ever evolved and no single chain of command was established. The division between al-Fatah and the PFLP was not ideological. While Habash believed that an ideological commitment was essential, al-Fatah's leaders held that this could and should be left until after Palestine had been liberated. In 1969 even the small PFLP suffered a division when a group headed by a Jordanian Nayef Hawatmeh, describing itself as being on the extreme revolutionary left compared with the *petit bourgeois* Habash and his followers, split off to form their own Popular Democratic Front for the Liberation of Palestine (PDFLP). The only thing which fully united all the resistance groups was their rejection of UN Security Council Resolution 242, on the grounds that it involved acceptance of Israel and fell short of the total liberation of Palestine. They agreed instead on a common political objective of a non-sectarian, democratic, Palestinian state in which Muslims, Christians and Jews could live together in equality.[7]

Meanwhile the growth of the commando organizations posed a severe internal threat to the régimes in Jordan and Lebanon, where they formed a type of 'state within a state'. Serious incidents multiplied between the guerrillas and both Lebanese Christian paramilitary groups and the Jordanian army. A compromise agreement arranged in Cairo in November 1969 between the guerrillas and the Lebanese army narrowly prevented the situation from deteriorating into civil war, although Lebanon continued to suffer from Israeli retaliation raids against guerrilla activity from the south of the country. The Lebanese forces were too weak and felt no incentive to repel these attacks. The Israelis carried out with total impunity a helicopter raid on Beirut airport on 28 December 1968 in retaliation for the attack on an El Al aeroplane at Athens airport by two PFLP commandos.

In Jordan, on the other hand, a series of agreements between the Palestine liberation forces and the Jordanian government broke down almost as soon as they were made. In September 1970 a civil war broke out which was largely provoked by the extremists among both the Jordanian army and the guerrillas who refused any compromise. Promised Iraqi support for the Palestinians did not materialize and the Syrian army intervened briefly and ineffectively. Fighting ended

7. This of course implies the destruction of the Israeli state, but the question of whether it also means the expulsion of Jews who have entered Israel since its creation has been the subject of fierce debate within the Palestinian movement. Eventually the majority view prevailed that no one who accepted the non-sectarian state should be expelled, but this has never been written into the Palestinian Covenant.

with a truce agreement sponsored by Arab heads of state which apparently left neither side the victor. But over the following months the Jordanian government gradually asserted its authority over the country and restricted the commandos' base areas. By July 1971 the Palestinian resistance had been virtually liquidated as a guerrilla force in Jordan. In Syria and Egypt it was under the control of the regular army, and it was only in South Lebanon that it retained some power of independent activity. The atrocious events in Jordan aroused a bitter desire for revenge among some of al-Fatah's members. When four young Palestinians assassinated the Jordanian Prime Minister Wasfi Tal in Cairo in November 1971 they said they belonged to a group called Black September, which had sworn to avenge the destruction of the *fedayeen* in Jordan.

The destruction of the Palestinian liberation movement as a military force did not mean that the revived spirit of Palestinian Arab nationalism had died. Although the 700,000 Palestinians on the West Bank were temporarily resigned to Israeli rule they did not accept it, and the 300,000 in Gaza continued to show their rejection of it by violent means. Moreover, the events in Jordan created a stir among the Arab minority in Israel itself, whose numbers had risen to nearly 400,000 through natural increase. Many of them discovered, sometimes with surprise, a renewed sense of identification with their former compatriots. Including the Israeli Arabs, there were now about 1,500,000 Palestinians under Israeli rule and since their birth-rate is much higher than that of the Jews, it was clear that their very existence affected the whole future of the Zionist state. Any proposed Arab–Israeli settlement which tried to ignore their separate identity was wholly unrealistic.

Although it was the tragic drama of the Palestinian guerrillas which attracted the most attention in the Arab world during 1968–9, more serious fighting with higher casualties was taking place along the Suez Canal. In accepting UN Resolution 242 President Nasser had publicly declared his readiness to accept a peaceful solution to the Middle East problem. Egyptian diplomacy had some success in promoting the belief that it was Israeli obstruction which was preventing a settlement and a very substantial majority in the UN was now ranged on the Arab side. At the same time he was under no illusion that anything except the strongest US pressure could persuade Israel to withdraw from occupied territory and although the US voted in favour of Resolution 242 and more than once supported Security Council resolutions condemning Israel's annexation of East

Jerusalem, both the Johnson and Nixon administrations repeatedly denied that they either could or would exert pressure on Israel. The renewal of full-scale war was impossible because Israel retained overwhelming military superiority even if the Arabs were united, which they were not. But Nasser could not remain entirely passive. The Egyptian army had been swiftly re-equipped by the Soviets after the June war and was calling for action. The Israelis could not be allowed to remain without cost on the Suez Canal.

Nasser's response was to launch what he himself called a 'war of attrition' against the Israeli forces occupying Sinai. Like the *fedayeen* raids of 1955–6 this was a dangerous and unsatisfactory tactic, but it allowed the postponement of more drastic alternatives. Egyptian probing raids against the Israeli Suez Canal front brought heavy retaliation. The bombardment of the Suez Canal towns required the evacuation of some one million civilians to the interior and Israeli air raids struck deeper into the country. Israeli–Egyptian engagements in 1968 and 1969 were not all one-sided, and Israel's casualties on the Canal were enough to cause real concern in Israel, but Egyptian forces on the Canal Zone suffered fearful losses from the massive Israeli bombardment. In January 1970 Nasser paid a secret visit to the Soviet Union where he secured a promise of increased aid for Egyptian air and ground defences. The number of Soviet military advisers in Egypt was increased from 3,000 to between 8,000 and 10,000; Egyptian defences improved their performance and succeeded in shooting down at least six Israeli planes in the summer of 1970. By this time both sides were ready for compromise. Nasser had not abandoned all hope that a political solution could be achieved through American pressure on Israel, and when the US Secretary of State William Rogers, who had publicly stated his interpretation of Resolution 242 as meaning an Israeli withdrawal to the pre-1967 lines except for 'insubstantial changes', proposed a plan for a Middle East settlement, based on Resolution 242, which took as its starting-point a ceasefire between Egypt and Israel, he accepted it on 7 August.

The radical anti-Western trend which had been intensified by the Six Day War helped to unseat two of the few remaining pro-Western governments during 1969. In Sudan in May the parliamentary régime dominated by the conservative army officers was overthrown in a coup of radical socialist army officers led by Colonel Jaafar Nimeiry. The new régime suppressed the Umma party and moved the country leftwards towards closer relations with Egypt and the Soviet Union. In September 1969 the aged Libyan monarch King Idris was ousted in a similar coup of young Nasserist officers led by an intense twenty-nine-year-old colonel, Muammar Qaddafy. The new régime speedily reached agreement with Britain and the USA for the withdrawal of the last remaining bases in Arab territory.

The support of the two new revolutionary régimes in neighbouring Arab countries was a vital advantage to Egypt in its difficulties. They offered a new strategic depth for its armed forces and the prospect of increased economic help from a wealthy Libya. On the initiative of Colonel Qaddafy, a passionate Nasserist, the three governments began to discuss the formation of a political federation. But none of this could be of much immediate help to Nasser in his confrontation with Israel. The second post-1967 Arab summit meeting which was held after much delay in Rabat in December 1969 was a failure for Egypt. Nasser appealed to the other Arab states to commit all their resources to the struggle and they failed to respond. He was a tired and disillusioned man when he clutched at the straw offered by the Rogers Plan in August 1970.

Before departing for the Rabat meeting Nasser appointed Anwar Sadat as vice-president. The choice was surprising because although Nasser had kept Sadat close to the centre of power he had never entrusted him with any high executive post. He had made use of his abilities as a diplomatic spokesman, and in recent years Sadat had held the post of president of the National Assembly, which was more honorific than powerful. But of the more obvious successors Abdul Hakim Amer had committed suicide after the 1967 war, Zakariya Muhieddin had withdrawn from politics and Ali Sabry, the favourite of the left and the Soviet Union, was too controversial to unite the country.

Although Nasser knew that he was seriously ill, he probably only saw his appointment of Sadat as a stop-gap arrangement. In effect, however, he was designating as his successor a man who was not regarded in Egypt as carrying any weight but was the common target of characteristically Egyptian jokes that pictured him as Nasser's 'yes-man'.

Egypt and Jordan's acceptance of the Rogers Plan threw an already divided Arab world into greater turmoil. Syria rejected the American proposals outright and the Palestinian resistance organized a series of violent demonstrations in Amman, Beirut and elsewhere in which Nasser was denounced as a traitor. Only a few weeks later the bloody civil war between the Palestinians and the Jordanian army broke out. Despite the exhausted and dangerous state of his health and the suspicion and hostility he now aroused among the Palestinians, Nasser threw himself into the task of stopping the civil war. The fighting was not only a tragedy in itself but there was a clear danger of United States intervention – or even joint US-Israeli action – on behalf of King Hussein against the Palestinians and Syrians.

A hastily summoned Arab summit meeting in Cairo succeeded in obtaining a ceasefire in Jordan and in bringing Yasir Arafat and King Hussein together at the conference table. This did not ultimately prevent the destruction of the Palestinian guerrilla movement in Jordan but at least it stopped the civil war and forestalled US or Israeli intervention. As chairman of the summit Nasser surpassed all his previous performances, showing all his old authority and panache in discussion. But the effort was too much for his tired frame. On his way back from the airport, after saying farewell to the ruler of Kuwait, he suffered a major heart attack and died a few hours later. When he was buried on 1 October tens of thousands of Egyptians surged round his coffin in scenes of unparalleled grief.

Gamal Abdul Nasser was a remarkable man. Future ages will look upon him as one of the two or three key figures of the middle years of the twentieth century. For all the diplomatic and military failures of his later years, which cost some of Egypt's hard-won independence by placing it heavily in debt to the Soviet Union, Nasser's influence on the Middle East and much of the Third World was profound. Radical young army officers as far away as Latin America have been called 'Nasserists' as the best way of describing what they stand for. To some extent he succeeded in casting Egypt for the role that he had foreseen for it in his *The Philosophy of the Revolution*. Egypt remains a relatively poor, weak and underdeveloped country, but with courage, persistence, and diplomatic skill remarkable in one of so little experience, he achieved for Egypt some of the attributes of a great power. This estimate was confirmed by his enemies. At a time when relations between France and Egypt were improving as a result of the end of the Algerian war, a prominent French journalist wrote that the difficulty was that the French people had come to regard Nasser as 'a cross between Hitler and Satan'.

But in retrospect his importance may be seen to lie less in his demonstration that a small power can, through daring and determined leadership, play a disproportionate role in world affairs, than in the body of pragmatic social and economic policies which became known as Arab Socialism. The dismantling of the powers of the old bourgeois and feudal classes, land reform, big strides in industrialization, the building of the High Dam and above all the instilling into the Egyptians of the feeling that development could be a national enterprise, were the real legacies of the Nasserist revolution, and certainly there was no part of the Arab world that was too remote to be influenced by them.

When Nasser died he was still the most considerable Arab political figure and his disappearance altered the balance of forces in the Arab world. In Egypt, where he had dominated the country and taken all the major policy decisions for fifteen years, he left a gaping void. However, the fact that all the reins of power were held by the presidency meant that the transition was smooth. There was a feeling of determination among the Egyptians to show their political maturity. Under the constitution Sadat became acting president and after the unanimous approval of his candidature by the Arab Socialist Union higher executive and the National Assembly his confirmation as president by a massive majority in a national referendum was a foregone conclusion. Although endowed with so much authority, Sadat's inheritance was unenviable. The 'no peace, no war' situation with Israel persisted and it soon became apparent that the United States still had no intention of putting enough pressure on Israel to withdraw its forces on any terms that would not be totally humiliating to the Arabs. The advantages of the ceasefire had mainly gone to Israel, which was content to let the *status quo* continue indefinitely. Meanwhile the army and students were showing increasing impatience with Egypt's inertia, and social discontent was exacerbated by the presence of a million refugees from the Canal zone who had poured into Egypt's already overcrowded cities.

Sadat could not even take his presidential powers for granted but had to prove them. A powerful clique among Nasser's former colleagues headed by Ali Sabry (whom Sadat had appointed vice-president) believed they could continue to control the country with Sadat acting as a figurehead. With the help of his own increasing popularity as Nasser's apparently designated successor and the support of the army, Sadat was able to dismiss all his opponents, whom he accused of plotting against him, and establish his own authority. In direct appeals to the nation he promised to reform Egypt's political system, re-establish the rule of law, and restore public liberties in a number of respects. Although 'de-Nasserization' was still a taboo term, a new era had begun.

Sensing a possible shift to the West in one of their most important Third World allies, the Soviet leaders sent a high-powered delegation led by President Podgorny to Cairo in June. The result was the signing of a fifteen-year Egyptian–Soviet treaty of friendship and cooperation. This formalization of Egypt's relations with the Soviet Union was something which even Nasser had always refrained from doing. It underlined Egypt's continued reliance on Soviet support in the absence of any general Middle East settlement.

Despite this alliance with the Soviets, there was a shift in Egypt's diplomatic strategy in 1971. In some important respects Sadat enjoyed advantages over Nasser. The very fact that he lacked Nasser's authority and prestige meant that other Arab leaders were unafraid of the shadow of his influence. It was of the most vital importance for his new strategy that the reasons for the old mistrust between Saudi Arabia and Egypt had now gone. King Feisal emphasized his new confidence in a long and friendly visit to Egypt, which significantly took place shortly after the signing of the new Soviet–Egyptian alliance, something that the Saudi monarch would undoubtedly have condemned in Nasser's lifetime. Sadat was also fortunate when Syria acquired a more moderate and less isolationist régime in November 1970, when the military wing of the Baath party led by General Hafez Assad established its authority over the civilian wing which was responsible for the débâcle of Syria's intervention in the Jordanian civil war. General Assad had the makings of a popular leader and he lacked the complexes of his predecessors in his attitude towards Egypt.

It was not only with the Arab countries that Sadat was able to lay the ghosts of the past. The Shah of Iran and President Nasser had cordially detested each other; the way was now open for a reconciliation between Tehran and Cairo. Although memories of the Suez affair had long faded the British had never quite overcome their hostility towards Nasser, and a new cordiality was now possible in relations with Britain and other Western countries.

This was all very well, but there was only one Western power which could influence Israel: the United States; and this still showed no real sign of making any genuine change in its policy of wholehearted support for Israel. Mr William Rogers, who was nominally in charge of US foreign policy, gave Egypt grounds for encouragement from time to time. When he visited Cairo in May 1971, just two days after Sadat had sacked Ali Sabry, he acknowledged that Egypt had made the major concession for which the United States had always been asking when President Sadat publicly affirmed for the first time in February his readiness to sign a formal peace treaty with

Israel once it had withdrawn from all Arab territory. But Egypt realized by now that the real conductor of President Nixon's foreign policy was Henry Kissinger. The Middle East was regarded as a sideshow. Most serious of all, from Egypt's point of view, the United States and the Soviet Union were moving towards a policy of mutual détente, which would clearly imply an agreement between the two super powers to allow the Middle East situation to remain frozen. This would be quite satisfactory for the United States and Israel, only mildly unsatisfactory for the Soviet Union (and certainly preferable to a new Middle East war, which it expected the Arabs to lose); but it would be disastrous for Egypt. It was therefore some time towards the end of 1971 or early 1972 when the Rogers initiative had clearly disappeared without trace into the sand that President Sadat decided that the stalemate would have to be broken by force.

14. The Search for Hope: 1973–

In 1972 very few members of the Arab public believed that President Sadat had made up his mind. His repeated promises that the 'no peace, no war' would soon be resolved one way or the other were greeted with scepticism. There was serious unrest in Egypt and President Sadat took action to silence his more influential critics in the press. The Cairene political jokes became more bitterly satirical in their references to Sadat. His action in expelling all the Soviet military advisers from Egypt in July 1972 was widely popular, but enthusiasm soon faded as it yielded no dividends. It was apparent that President Sadat had acted spontaneously in the hope of some positive response from the United States but without securing any prior understanding from Washington. Nothing happened except that Egypt's defences were weakened. After more violent student riots in January 1973, mass arrests and the closure of universities, the question was widely asked whether the Sadat régime would last much longer.

Speaking at a rally in Cairo on 28 September 1973 to mark the third anniversary of the death of Gamal Abdul Nasser, President Sadat bitterly attacked the United States. But although he spoke of various ways of tackling the Middle East problem, his audience noticed one startling omission from his speech: any threat to resume the armed struggle if diplomacy failed.

The reaction of President Sadat's critics at home and abroad, especially the students, was one of angry scorn. 'This man can no longer be taken seriously,' they said. None of them knew that the date on which the Egyptian and Syrian armies would attempt to break the Middle East deadlock had already been fixed for one week ahead – 6 October. This was certainly the best kept secret in the modern history of the Arabs.

It is probable that only the Egyptian and Syrian heads of state and military commanders knew the precise date. Both King Feisal of Saudi Arabia and King Hussein of Jordan knew that the decision had been taken to go to war, but King Hussein, who met Presidents Sadat and Assad in Cairo on 10–12 September, said that his impression was that it would be a matter of months rather than weeks before it happened. At this meeting he repeated the assertion that he had made several times since 1967, that Jordan would not become directly involved in a new war with Israel which could only lead to catastrophe. Unlike Egypt and Syria, Jordan had no Soviet missile umbrella and since all its arms and ammunition came from the West it would receive no replacements for its lost equipment while the war continued. Moreover, as soon as the Israelis counter-attacked across the river Jordan they would be able to advance up the Jordan valley to take the Syrian army in the rear. The Syrians and Egyptians accepted this reality. Jordan could help them more by staying out and pinning down substantial Israeli forces on the West Bank.

Egypt and Syria could not count on the military support of any of their fellow-Arabs, except for the detachment of Moroccan troops on the Syrian front. Iraq's intentions were uncertain. The Algerians had withdrawn their forces from the Suez Canal after the 1970 ceasefire. All the same, Egypt and Syria had a marked superiority in numbers. Against Israel's army of 270,000 when fully mobilized, 1,700 tanks and 400 planes, the combined Egyptian and Syrian forces were 380,000 men already under arms, 3,600 tanks and 900 planes. This said nothing of Israel's qualitative superiority in weapons and tactics, which had been proved so often before on the battlefield. On the other hand, many Israelis, including some of their senior generals, had fallen into the dangerous error of believing that their opponents, especially the Egyptians, were lacking in courage and unwilling to fight. This was a view that was widely endorsed in the rest of the world.

The Arabs had one indisputable advantage: surprise, which had always been regarded as an Israeli monopoly in the Middle East. On this occasion, the Egyptians were helped in achieving it by President Sadat's earlier unfulfilled promises to go to war. Like almost everyone else, the Israelis still believed he was bluffing on 5 October. Partly because of this and partly because 6 October was the day of the Jewish Yom Kippur holiday, the Israelis took seventy-two hours to mobilize.

On the first day of the war the Egyptians made their long-rehearsed crossing of the Suez Canal in three sectors and quickly captured the entire Bar-Lev line. This was only lightly held by the Israelis, but it was thought to be able to hold out long enough for reinforcements to arrive. At the same time a force of 500 Syrian tanks and two infantry divisions advanced deep into Israeli-held Syrian territory to advance almost to Israel proper.

For several reasons it was clear from the beginning that the war of October 1973 would be very different from the Six Day War of 1967.

Apart from the fact that the Arabs had the initiative because they struck first, they largely neutralized Israel's qualitative advantage in air power and armour with the improved Soviet missile defence system and the Sagger anti-tank 'suitcase missile' which can be carried by a single infantryman. Above all, the Arab armies showed that they had learned to improve their strategy through experience. Instead of trying to thrust deep into enemy territory, which would have taken them outside the umbrella of the SAM missile defence system, they aimed to use their superiority in numbers to wear down the enemy in a static war of attrition.

Israel struck back first against the Syrians, who offered the immediate threat to its territory. By 12 October they had forced the Syrians back to their main defensive lines, which at their nearest point were some twenty-four miles from Damascus. The Syrians held firm and the front consolidated but the Israelis were able to turn the main weight of their forces against the Egyptians in Sinai. On the night of 15 October the Israelis succeeded in making a brilliant thrust across the Suez Canal through the gap between the Egyptian Second and Third Armies, and in consolidating a bridgehead on the West Bank.

It is hardly surprising that there are different versions of the responsibility for this disaster. In his account, General Saad Shazly,[1] who was undoubtedly the chief architect of the extraordinary achievement of the Canal crossing, claims that the Israeli incursion could have been dealt with if Sadat had not refused for reasons of political prestige to withdraw enough forces back to the west side of the Canal. In his version,[2] Sadat says that Shazly lost his nerve and collapsed and he therefore dismissed him. It is quite possible that Sadat was misled by his other generals as to the true extent of the threat. Whatever the truth, it is undeniable that Sadat's subsequent refusal to admit that the October War was anything but a great victory that he had achieved for Egypt was to prove a fatal weakness for his diplomacy.

In fact the Israelis succeeded in turning their setbacks of the first week of the war into a stunning military victory. But this time the whole world was involved in the outcome of the war in a way that it had never had time to be in June 1967.

In contrast to the Six Day War, some of the other Arab forces made a

1. Saad Shazly, *The Crossing of Suez*, Third World Centre for Research and Publishing, London, 1980.
2. Anwar Sadat, *In Search of Identity*, London, 1978, pp. 257–63.

real contribution. Iraq, after declaring that its dispute with Iran was suspended, contributed three divisions and three fighter squadrons, which suffered heavy casualties on the Syrian front. Jordan sent two armoured brigades to southern Syria. The 1,800 Moroccan troops were involved in bitter fighting at Mount Hermon on the first day. Saudi Arabia, Kuwait, Tunisia, Sudan and Algeria all contributed on a smaller scale, while the PDRY assisted the Egyptian navy in blockading the Bab al-Mandeb straits at the southern end of the Red Sea. This was a move of some strategic significance because it reduced the importance of the Israeli hold on Sharm al-Shaikh at the entrance to the Gulf of Aqaba, which Israel had maintained since 1967 to be essential for its security.

However, the unsheathing of the Arab oil weapon on behalf of the Egyptians and Syrians was of far greater importance than the direct military contribution of their Arab allies. The Organization of Arab Petroleum Exporting Countries, meeting in Kuwait on 17 October, decided that its members should reduce oil production by 5 per cent a month until Israel withdrew from all occupied Arab territories. The normally cautious and conservative Saudi Arabia led the way by cutting back its production by 10 per cent and adding for good measure a total embargo on all oil for the United States and the Netherlands. All the rich industrialized nations were appalled by this action, which placed their economies in jeopardy. The United States was the least directly affected because it was still only marginally dependent on Arab oil, but it could not stand by and watch the collapse of its allies. Moreover, it was deeply alarmed that Saudi Arabia should have taken the lead in defying the West.

The two superpowers were deeply concerned in the October War from the outset. Both of them began by assuming that Israel would walk over the Arabs as in 1967, especially as they were certain that Egypt had been seriously weakened by its ejection of Soviet military advisers in July 1972. After a day or two they realized that this would not happen. The Soviets called upon the other Arab states to join in and on 10 October began a major airlift, followed by seaborne shipments of arms and equipment to Egypt and Syria, and later to Iraq when it joined in the fighting. But by this time the United States, in response to desperate appeals from Tel Aviv where General Dayan was on the edge of despair, had already begun a much larger airlift of more sophisticated equipment to Israel. It was not only the Israeli breakthrough which changed the course of the war.

The decisive turn in the tide of war in Israel's favour on 15

September immediately affected the attitudes of both superpowers. The Soviets set out to persuade the Egyptians to accept a UN-sponsored ceasefire while they still held substantial gains. The United States on the other hand, while pleased that Israel was out of danger, was also anxious to stop the war before Israeli forces threatened to take Cairo and Damascus and provoked direct Soviet intervention. The United States was anxious to preserve what was left of the détente although it was alarmed at the risks the Soviets were prepared to take on behalf of the Arabs. Dr Kissinger responded to a Soviet invitation to come to Moscow on 20 October, and the following day the two governments agreed to sponsor a joint resolution calling for an immediate ceasefire, the implementation of Resolution 242 of 22 November 1967 and negotiations for a peace settlement 'under appropriate auspices'. After both Egypt and Israel had been persuaded to accept the Soviet–American resolution it was passed unanimously by the Security Council and came into effect on the battlefronts on the evening of 22 October as Resolution 338. However, it broke down almost immediately and Israeli troops on the west bank of the Canal raced for the outskirts of Suez city to cut off the Egyptian Third Army. The Soviets promptly proposed another resolution calling for all forces to return to the positions they occupied on 22 October. After amending the Soviet draft, the United States agreed to co-sponsor it and the joint resolution was accepted by the Security Council on 23 October.

The fighting died down, although Israeli and Egyptian forces never returned to the 22 October lines which were much more favourable for Egypt. It was at this point that the Russians and Americans came as close to a direct confrontation in the Middle East as they ever have before or since. When the Russians, in response to an Egyptian request for both Soviet and American troops to be sent to the Middle East to police the ceasefire, threatened to act unilaterally if the US continued to refuse to send any forces to the area, Washington placed its forces on Defence Condition Three in the early hours of 25 October. Within a few hours the Russians backed down and agreed to accept Resolution 340, which provided for a UN Emergency Force in the Middle East from which the troops of the five permanent members of the Security Council were excluded.

So the seventeen-day fourth[3] Arab–Israeli war came to an end. Militarily, the Israelis won, although they did not achieve a crushing

---

3. Fifth, if the 1968–70 war of attrition on the Suez Canal is included.

victory. Politically, the Arabs were left in a more advantageous position than before the war began.

Casualties and losses of equipment were heavy on both sides. The Israelis lost some 2,800 men dead and 8,000 wounded, 840 tanks and 120 planes. The Egyptians lost 15,000 dead and 45,000 wounded, 650 tanks and 182 planes; the Syrians had some 7,000 killed and 21,000 wounded and lost 600 tanks and 165 planes. Although the Arab losses were so severe the total effect of the war was a strong boost for their morale. It had proved not only that their forces could fight with great courage but that their leaders could show ingenuity, enterprise and powers of improvisation which had normally been regarded as monopolies of the Israelis.

The new confidence of the Arabs was also related to the situation in the wider political sphere. The use of the oil weapon showed that, contrary to all the predictions, the Arab states could act with sufficient unanimity in an emergency. Although their first hopes that they could use the weapon to bring the world to enforce an Israeli withdrawal from all the occupied Arab territories proved to be extravagant, they had succeeded in achieving a shift in the world power balance in their favour. Everywhere the Israelis were losing friends. Before the October War seven African states had broken off diplomatic relations with Israel, sixteen more did so either during or immediately after the war and Israel was left with ties with only five African states, including South Africa. On 6 November 1973 the nine EEC countries issued a declaration which interpreted Resolution 242 of November 1967 in a manner strongly favourable to the Arabs. (Even the Netherlands, which was suffering an Arab oil embargo, was one of the signatories.) A similar statement by Japan followed before the end of the year. Some of these new expressions of sympathy for the Arabs were made out of naked self-interest; others showed recognition of the justice of the Arab cause and a dislike of Israel's insistence on holding on to Arab lands. It did not necessarily mark a change in policy; Britain and France, for example, made similar statements on the Middle East before the October War and the introduction of the oil weapon. On the whole, the Arabs were less interested in the motives of their new friends than the fact they were being treated with an unaccustomed respect.

Arab governments were forced to recognize, however, that although Israel's isolation was an advantage, the only outside power which could directly influence Israel's withdrawal from Arab territories was the United States.

The effect of the October War and the use of the oil weapon on the United States was complex. Responding to overwhelming public demand, Washington had provided Israel with the crucial aid which enabled it to turn a near-defeat into a military victory. Also the United States was still in 1974 much less dependent on Arab oil than other industrialized countries. On the other hand, the Nixon–Kissinger administration saw the results of the October War as providing an opportunity for the US to recover some of the influence it had lost in the Middle East and to mend its many broken bridges with the Arab states.

Since a prime aim of President Sadat in going to war in October 1973 had been to break the frozen impasse in the Middle East and enforce a reappraisal of American policy he can be said to have succeeded. His objectives were strictly limited and he attained them, despite the military disaster of Israel's crossing of the Suez Canal. He was already determined to establish a new relationship with the United States before meeting Henry Kissinger; his task was greatly eased by the personal rapport that was rapidly created between the two men. (One of Kissinger's colleagues is quoted as saying: 'Henry likes very few foreign politicians. In fact there are only three: Anwar Sadat, Golda Meir, and Dobrynin, the Soviet ambassador to the US.')

Dr Kissinger brought about troop disengagement agreements between Egypt and Israel (18 January) and Syria and Israel (5 June). Both agreements provided for the separation of opposing troops with thinned-out forces in the forward zones and a UN Disengagement Force in between. Washington resumed relations with both Cairo and Damascus after a seven-year breach. Egypt could begin work on clearing the Suez Canal and restoring the shattered Canal cities to allow the return of some three quarters of a million refugees. The Canal was reopened in June 1975. The Syrian–Israeli agreement, which took place against a background of a Syrian war of attrition against Israel in the Golan Heights, was achieved with much greater difficulty. Under the agreement, the Israelis withdrew from the Golan Heights capital of Quneitra, but since it had been almost totally destroyed by the Israelis before their departure and remained shorn of the surrounding farmlands from which it derives its life, the Syrians made no move to repopulate it.

America's changed relationship with the Arabs was symbolized by President Nixon's tour of the Middle East in June 1974. No previous US president (with the possible exception of President Eisenhower in 1956) would have been able to visit several Arab capitals. Dr

Kissinger's achievements had been remarkable but they were still very limited in scope. Moreover, the entire approach of the Kissinger 'step-by-step' diplomacy aroused doubts or outright opposition from several quarters. The Soviet Union was angered at being kept out of the negotiating process and showed its disapproval of the Kissinger–Sadat friendship by cutting off arms supplies to Egypt early in 1974. Both Soviet and Syrian suspicions that Dr Kissinger's real intention was to break the Arab front by securing a bilateral peace agreement between Israel and Egypt were greatly increased when he secured a second and more substantial Israeli–Egyptian disengagement agreement in September 1975.

The most doubtful of all were the Palestinian Arabs. Their position after the October War was paradoxical. Because of the shift of world power in favour of the Arabs their cause had gained. On the other hand, the Palestinians had played no part in the decision to go to war and had fought only minor actions on the Lebanese border. World recognition of the justice of their claims depended heavily on Arab diplomacy and the key Arab states, notably Egypt, wanted peace.

This paradox was reflected in the debate within the Palestine Liberation Organization. Some of the Palestinian leaders, including the PLO Chairman Yasir Arafat, reached the conclusion that Palestinian aims should be scaled down to the creation of a small Palestinian Arab state to include the West Bank and Gaza, and that the PLO should seek a settlement in cooperation with Egypt through a UN-sponsored conference at which they would be represented. But these Palestinians were bitterly opposed by others who refused to abandon, even temporarily, the more distant goal of making the whole of Palestine a 'democratic, non-sectarian state'. They opposed any Palestinian participation in a peace conference on the ground that it would lead to Arab recognition of Israel.

Yasir Arafat maintained his leadership and his policy with difficulty. An open split in the movement was only avoided because a decision on Palestinian participation in a peace conference could be postponed indefinitely as long as the US and Israel remained opposed. Despite this fundamental weakness in the PLO's position, 1974 has to be regarded as a milestone in the struggle of the Palestinian Arab people for self-determination. In September the UN General Assembly agreed without a vote to include 'the Palestinian question', for the first time since the creation of Israel, as a separate item on its agenda and then invited the PLO to take part in the debate. On 13 November Yasir Arafat, accorded the honours of a head of state, addressed the UN General Assembly. Speaking in Arabic, with a pistol in his hip pocket, he told the Assembly, 'I have come bearing an olive branch and a freedom fighter's gun. Do not let the olive branch fall from my hand.' He emphasized that the target of the Palestinian revolution was never the Jewish people but Zionist aggression and he looked forward to a time when Jews, Christians and Muslims could live together in Palestine in equality.

The UN's action profoundly influenced the decisions of the meeting of Arab heads of state at Rabat in October 1974. Led by King Feisal of Saudi Arabia, who held that the Arabs could hardly do less than the UN, the Arab leaders persuaded King Hussein of Jordan to accept a resolution affirming the right of the Palestinian people to establish an independent national authority under the direction of the PLO 'in its capacity as the sole legitimate representative of the Palestinian people' in any liberated territory.

Other forms of international recognition were soon forthcoming. The PLO was given quasi-official status by various international organizations. It had become a cliché of international politics that the Palestinians lay at the heart of the Middle East problem.

The fact that these diplomatic triumphs failed to give back to the Palestinians any of their territory explains their increasingly bitter sense of frustration. Dr Kissinger's diplomacy succeeded in achieving a second Egyptian–Israeli disengagement agreement in Sinai in September 1975, providing for the demilitarization of the strategic Mitla and Giddi passes and, in a crucial new development, the establishment of early-warning posts in the area manned by 200 US civilian personnel. To persuade Israel to accept, Washington had to put the strongest pressure on Israel to the extent of suspending the economic aid which it desperately needed. Yet the agreement deeply divided the Arab world, as many Arabs felt that through Egypt they had given away far too much for too little. Egypt had recovered its Sinai oil fields and reopened the Suez Canal but the Egyptian Army, the lynch-pin of any Arab force, had effectively withdrawn from the struggle as the two parties had agreed through the Americans not to resort to force to settle their conflict. The Syrians and the PLO bitterly denounced Sinai 2 and the Arab world was as divided as at any time in the past decade. These inter-Arab differences were reflected in the Lebanese civil war of 1975–6, which not only absorbed the attention, while it lasted, of the PLO and all the front-line Arab states but effectively prevented any move towards the Middle East settlement that they all wanted. During 1976 it became increasingly apparent that neither could the war be ended nor any new peace initiative be taken unless these differences could be settled. This was achieved with the help of vigorous Saudi mediation at the Arab summit meetings of Riyadh and Cairo in October 1976 at which, in return for Syria's swallowing its objections to Sinai 2, Egypt accepted Syria's actions in Lebanon. A largely Syrian Arab Deterrent Force was established in Lebanon to keep the peace. This allowed at least the possibility of a new initiative from American diplomacy which had been effectively frozen throughout 1976. From the beginning of his administration President Carter showed an urgent interest in finding a solution to the Middle East problem. Peace prospects were not improved by a right-wing victory in Israel's May 1977 elections but at least it underlined the need for urgent action if a new Arab–Israeli war, which could only be disastrous for the entire international community, was to be avoided.

At least there was now a US Administration which was publicly dedicated to achieving a comprehensive peace in the Middle East. Moreover, on 17 March President Carter had taken his Middle East policy a step further by declaring the need for a Palestinian homeland – a statement that was welcomed by Yasir Arafat. In May President Carter went to Geneva to confer with President Assad of Syria.

Intensive negotiations throughout the summer of 1977 finally produced results. On 19 September Israel's new Begin government submitted a Draft Treaty for an Israeli–Egyptian peace to the US Secretary of State, Cyrus Vance. It was clearly unacceptable to Egypt but it was important that Israel agreed in principle to a resumption of the Geneva Middle East peace conference. This was something the Israelis had never stated publicly before. Then on 1 October the rest of the world was taken by surprise by a Joint US–USSR Declaration calling for 'negotiation within the framework of the Geneva Peace Conference' as the 'only right and effective way of achieving a fundamental solution to all aspects of the Middle East problem'. The Declaration called for 'the resolution of the Palestinian question, including ensuring the legitimate rights of the Palestinian people'. It also said that 'representatives of all the parties involved in the conflict, including those of the Palestinian people' should be included in the Peace Conference.

The Declaration was notable for omitting any reference to UN resolutions. This was a compromise. The USSR wanted to refer to all UN resolutions on the Middle East which were overwhelmingly anti-Israel while the United States wished to concentrate on Resolution 242. The two superpowers therefore agreed to omit reference to any UN resolution. But it was precisely because the Declaration was so clearly a compromise that it gave so much ground for hope. There were still serious obstacles – notably over Palestinian representation at Geneva. The Israelis were resolutely opposed to any PLO presence until the PLO had publicly declared its willingness to recognize the Zionist state, and the United States, through Dr Kissinger, had promised to support Israel in this matter. The Arab states were all committed to the PLO as the sole legitimate representative of the Palestinian people and the PLO felt unable to declare its recognition of Israel as long as Israel rejected the principle of Palestinian self-determination. (Members of Mr Begin's government had made it clear that in reality they were neither in need of nor interested in the PLO's recognition, but that is a different matter.)

Despite the difficulties, the US–Soviet Declaration appeared as a milestone. If the US Government had maintained its resolution to act in concert with the USSR to enforce what would have amounted to an imposed peace on the Middle East it just might have succeeded. But the possibility was never tested. Israel flatly rejected the Declaration and President Carter, apparently surprised by the fury of American Zionists' reaction, began to weaken. He tried to arrange a secret meeting between the Israeli and Egyptian foreign ministers, Moshe Dayan and Ismail Fahmy. Dayan and Secretary of State Vance agreed publicly on a joint US-Israeli approach to Geneva while Dayan confirmed that Israel would neither negotiate with nor discuss a separate Palestinian state.

At least President Carter still remained publicly committed to the principle of the Geneva Conference. But meanwhile President Sadat had decided on a course of action which was to make the convening of the Conference impossible. In September he had responded to secret approaches from the Israelis by sending, without the knowledge of his Foreign Minister, his personal representative to Rabat to meet Moshe Dayan. The Romanian President Ceausescu also acted as mediator to pass on messages from Mr Begin that he was ready to sign a peace treaty with Egypt. At what point he made up his mind to go to Jerusalem is uncertain. He claimed that the idea came to him suddenly while he was flying through the clouds over Turkey on his way to see the Shah of Iran but this is almost certainly romantic hindsight. Since his closest advisers opposed the plan he not surprisingly kept the decision from them. In a routine speech at the annual opening of the Egyptian parliament on 9 November 1977 he almost casually announced that 'Israel will be astonished when it hears me saying now, before you, that I am ready to go to their own house, to the Knesset itself, to talk to them.' A delighted Mr Begin warmly responded and the visit was fixed for 19 November.

Reactions to Sadat's astonishing political coup ranged from simple admiration and delight in most of the world to anger and dismay among the great majority of Arabs. Even those who were ready to give him the benefit of the doubt when he told a group of US Congressmen that Palestine was still the heart of the problem, and that the only way to lasting peace was 'the establishment of a Palestine state in the West Bank and Gaza with a corridor between them' believed that he was overestimating the strength of his position and that the Israelis would get the better of him. Above all they feared that Israel would end by securing its greatest prize: a separate peace with Egypt.

After President Assad had tried to dissuade Sadat from making the visit, Damascus Radio denounced it vehemently. The PLO called it treachery which would not be forgiven. Saudi Arabia expressed 'surprise' and affirmed its view that any Arab initiative should stem from a united Arab stand. Customary Saudi restraint barely concealed the anger.

Whatever were Arab feelings, the hundreds of millions in the rest of the world who watched the event on their television screens were emotionally thrilled by the spectacle. Sadat's speech to the Knesset was eloquent and dignified, invoking the tolerant spirit of the Caliph Omar and Saladin and the equality of Jews, Muslims and Christians in the sight of God. Only committed Zionists could find unacceptable his insistence on Palestinian rights and his rejection of Israel's right to annex Jerusalem. In his impromptu reply Begin also spoke of peace and negotiations without preconditions, but otherwise presented the hardest and most unapologetic Zionist line. The Jews were back in their God-given Land of Israel by right and there was no question of it being divided. He was not specific either about the territory of the Land of Israel or the future of its Arab inhabitants but he left little doubt that he included Judea and Samaria (the West Bank) in its borders and that he regarded the 'Arabs of the Land of Israel' at best as tolerated guests.

Because Sadat's pilgrimage to Jerusalem led to the precise result that his critics predicted – a separate Egyptian–Israeli peace and disaster for the Palestinian Arabs – they could feel that they had been proved right. At a protest meeting in London the Syrian ambassador compared Sadat with the last Fatimid Caliph in Cairo who committed the ultimate treachery of allying himself with the Frankish Kingdom of Jerusalem and was overthrown by Saladin. But Sadat undoubtedly believed he was serving the cause of all the Arabs, including the Palestinians. He was a man of consuming vanity who revelled in the impression he was making on the world, but this was much more than a theatrical gesture to please his new American friends. He was impelled by a strong awareness that his poverty-stricken people were desperately in need of peace. But at this stage he hoped and believed he could achieve it for all the Arabs as well as the Egyptians. Whether he had truly convinced himself that he went to Jerusalem as the magnanimous victor of the 1973 war we shall never know. This could have merely been part of his strategy although he repeated it so often he probably came to believe it. The trouble was that Mr Begin fully understood his weakness and once Sadat had made his gamble he could not afford to lose. It was impossible to tell his people that they were returning to the *status quo* before he set out on his pilgrimage. He had promised in Jerusalem that there would be no more war between Egypt and Israel and this was a promise which had to be kept.

Negotiations began almost immediately in Cairo. President Carter toured the Middle East in January 1978 in a vain attempt to persuade the Arab states to change their attitude, but in Egypt he delighted Sadat by committing the United States to full partnership in the Middle East peace process. Nevertheless, progress was difficult. While inside Israel there was powerful right-wing opposition to withdrawal from Sinai with its Jewish settlements, Egypt was unable to extract any undertaking from the Israelis that would go any way towards satisfying Palestinian aspirations for a homeland. Libya, Algeria, Syria, the PDRY and Yemen formed a group they called the 'Front of Steadfastness' to oppose Sadat. (Iraq shared their views but failed to join because of its régime's antagonism towards Syria.) The more moderate Arab states such as Saudi Arabia and Jordan preferred to await events, forming what was called a Front of Silence.

Sadat responded in kind to the invective of his Arab critics. He broke off relations with the members of the Front of Steadfastness and Iraq and closed down the PLO offices and radio station in Cairo. Taking their lead from the President, the Egyptian media started accusing the other Arabs of having allowed Egypt to do most of their fighting against Israel for them. Newspaper cartoons showed the PLO as carrying on their revolutionary struggle from the night clubs of Arab capitals. Some leading Egyptian intellectuals, such as the novelist Naguib Mahfouz and the playwright Tawfik Hakim, gave respectability to this renewed spirit of Egyptian nationalism, bordering on chauvinism, by suggesting that Egypt had suffered only disaster from its association with the Arab world and should concentrate on its own affairs. Egypt's isolation from the Arabs was rapidly progressing.

In March 1978 attention was diverted temporarily by Israel's first invasion of Southern Lebanon in response to an indiscriminate Palestinian guerrilla raid in Israel which left thirty-seven dead and eighty-two wounded. The Arabs were enraged but unable to respond because the Arab Deterrent Force in Lebanon was not deployed south of the Litani river. (Only Sadat publicly deplored the raid which gave rise to the invasion.) On this occasion, however, the United States associated itself unambiguously with the UN action to persuade the Israelis to withdraw and to establish a peacekeeping force (UNIFIL) in Southern Lebanon. Because of this the action was effective and the Israelis left with their objective of destroying the Palestinian guerrillas in Lebanon only very partially achieved.

President Sadat repeatedly affirmed that he had no intention of abandoning the Palestinian cause, despite PLO ingratitude. He also threatened to break off all discussions when it seemed that the Israelis would insist on holding part of Sinai. But in August, just when it seemed that the negotiations would go the way of all previous attempts at Arab–Israeli peacemaking, it was announced that President Sadat and Mr Begin had accepted President Carter's invitation to a US–Israel–Egypt summit meeting at Camp David on 5 September. It was there that after twelve days of negotiations the meeting ended with two agreements, 'a framework for peace in the Middle East', which was intended to deal with the Palestinian question and 'a framework for peace between Israel and Egypt'.

The second of these was fairly straightforward – providing for the restoration of Egyptian sovereignty over its territory (except for the partial demilitarization of Sinai) and the normalization of relations between the two countries. The former was inevitably more complex, providing for a transitional period in the West Bank and Gaza of a maximum of five years, during which a local 'self-governing authority' would be established to provide 'full autonomy' for the inhabitants and to replace the Israel military government and its civilian administration. There were several loopholes and unanswered questions. Jordan was mentioned as a partner with Egypt and Israel in establishing the self-governing authority, but Jordan had played no part in the negotiations and was showing no interest in taking over the responsibilities the Arabs had delegated to the PLO. The agreements said nothing about the future of the Jewish settlements in the occupied territories or the length of the period during which Israel had agreed to freeze the settlements. It was most significant that there was no apparent link between the two agreements.

Many interested observers had predicted until the last minute that the negotiations would fail because without such a link – which Israel would certainly refuse – Egypt was inevitably destined for a separate peace with Israel, and this was something that Sadat still maintained he would never accept. With hindsight, many of the same observers realized that the one thing Sadat could not accept was failure. Yet even some of his closest advisers were astonished at the concessions he made at the end. His foreign minister Ibrahim Kamil resigned as the agreements were announced.

Was Sadat deceived or self-deceiving? President Carter later admitted that he had a guilty conscience about the extent to which Sadat was misled about Begin's real intentions. In his heart Sadat must have known that Begin would never relinquish *de facto* sovereignty over 'Jordan and Samaria', even if for tactical and legalistic reasons he would refrain from declaring it *de jure.* Sadat deceived himself because he had no choice.

Having taken this perilous step, President Sadat naturally continued to maintain that the 'Camp David process' was the only path to peace and that the two agreements depended on each other. He refused to entertain any criticism from the other Arabs. They held a summit meeting in Baghdad (which a brief and temporary reconciliation between Iraq and Syria allowed President Assad to attend) at which it was agreed to move the headquarters of the Arab League from Cairo to Tunis. Only Oman backed Egypt although Sudan and Morocco were ambiguous in their attitude. Saudi Arabia and the Arab Gulf states stood out against taking any further immediate action against Egypt but Sadat abruptly refused to meet a delegation from the conference which intended to try to dissuade him from proceeding on the Camp David course. In his speeches he heaped insults upon his fellow-Arabs, describing them as 'dwarves', 'paralytics' and sunk in medieval backwardness. So far from them isolating Egypt, which was still the heart and mind of the Arab world, he was isolating them.

The Camp David process continued on its way. Many sceptics still wondered whether Egypt would set its seal on a separate peace. But this is what was achieved, with the help of vigorous American mediation, in the Treaty of Washington signed on 26 March. The state of war which had existed between Egypt and Israel for thirty-one years was ended. The 'second part' of Camp David dealing with the Palestinian question was relegated to an Exchange of Letters between President Carter, Mr Begin and President Sadat confirming the intention to proceed with the implementation of the terms of the 'Framework for Peace in the Middle East'. This annex to the Treaty of Washington was held to have equal force to the Treaty but this deceived no one. Negotiations between Egypt and Israel on Palestinian autonomy dragged on intermittently for more than a year without any substantive progress until they finally broke down over the issue of Jerusalem. On 30 July the Knesset in effect sealed the fate of the second part of the Camp David agreements by passing a bill which declared all Jerusalem, including its eastern Arab part, to be the united and eternal capital of Israel. Crown Prince Fahd of Saudi Arabia called for a *jihad* (holy war) against Israel's action but this merely underlined Arab impotence since Egypt's defection. On the other hand, the main part of the Egyptian–Israeli treaty was implemented. Ambassadors were exchanged in 1980 and Israel's evacuation of Sinai was completed on schedule in March 1982, despite some fierce rearguard action by some of the extremist Jewish settlers in Egyptian territory.

The question remains whether the Palestinians in the occupied territories might, despite everything, have achieved some of their aspirations through the Camp David agreements. There are many reasons why they did not attempt to do so. Although they were not all equally enthusiastic about the PLO, the overwhelming majority regarded it as their true representative and Israel refused to contemplate dealing with the PLO. Israeli claims that only PLO intimidation prevented them from choosing other more reasonable leaders – that is, those who would collaborate with the occupying authority – were as wide of the mark as similar claims by all colonial powers about nationalist movements among people under their control. Moreover, whenever any prominent Palestinians in the West Bank or Gaza, such as the elected mayors, showed signs of developing as political leaders the Israeli authorities dismissed or deported them. At the same time, while Egypt and Israel were negotiating on the Palestinians' behalf, Mr Begin clarified his understanding of what was meant by Palestinian 'full autonomy'. For example, he saw it as autonomy for the people and not for the land they lived on (which for him was part of Eretz Israel). This meant that Israel would retain the right to appropriate land and water rights whenever it considered it necessary. Understandably no Palestinian would consider such an autonomy worth having.

Yet there must be a small doubt that the Palestinians of the West Bank could have used the tactics made famous by Habib Bourguiba with the French colonialists in Tunisia – that is of taking whatever was offered in the way of delegated powers and then promptly asking for more. It meant advancing by short stages from one position to the next. After the Camp David agreements some influential American commentators such as Joseph Kraft believed that the Palestinians could have used these tactics to achieve their aims. An elected autonomous authority, they argued, could have gradually extended its powers until the Israelis woke up to find they had allowed the creation of an independent Palestinian state.

Ironically, it was the lack of United States will or willingness to place any real weight behind the achievement of Palestinian autonomy which prevented this from happening. President Carter and later President Reagan repeatedly affirmed their rejection of Israel's permanent control of the occupied territories but they never made any effective move to prevent Israel's *de facto* annexation of the land. A resolute action of some kind – such as an insistence that US aid to Israel would be limited if there were further extensions of Jewish settlements in the occupied lands – might just conceivably have persuaded some representative Palestinians that it was worth showing an interest in the Camp David peace process. As it was, they were left without hope.

The United States failed to persuade even such moderate and pro-Western friends as Saudi Arabia and Jordan to accept the reality of the Treaty of Washington. Collectively the Arab states decided – some with enthusiasm and some with reluctance – on a total political and economic boycott of Egypt. Only Oman, Somalia and Sudan retained some diplomatic relations with Cairo. The gulf between the way the Arabs and the rest of the world looked on Sadat was now vast. Although several European governments privately doubted whether the Camp David process could achieve a comprehensive peace in the Middle East, they generally kept these doubts to themselves in the knowledge that they could do little to influence events. To Westerners at large, except for those who sympathized with the plight of the Palestinians, Sadat was a heroic statesman. The degree to which the Egyptian President's appearance on American television improved the unfavourable image of the Arabs in general began seriously to worry American Zionists. Nothing symbolized more strikingly the divergence between Western and Arab views than the joint award in October 1979 of the Nobel Peace Prize to President Sadat and Mr Begin. The coupling of the leader of the major Arab state with a man the Arabs still regarded as their implacable enemy seemed to most of them an act of brutal insensitivity.

The year 1979 saw another event which, although taking place outside the Arab world, was to be just as disturbing as the Egyptian–Israeli peace treaty. The Islamic revolution in Iran has been compared, with only modest hyperbole, to both the French and Russian revolutions. Its effects continue; it inspires both admiration and horror. In the Islamic world its influence has been complex and varied and on many levels.

The immediate political significance of the Iranian revolution for the Arabs was powerful and obvious. A strong pro-Western Middle East régime, buttressed by supposedly loyal and numerous security forces equipped with the most advanced Western weapons, had been swept away. Iran and Israel had come to be regarded as the two principal guarantees of American interests in the region and it was no surprise that there were strong, if unpublicized, links between them. Nationalist feelings among the Arabs were delighted by the Shah's downfall and his replacement by a régime which broke all relations with Israel and declared its total support for the cause of Palestinian liberation. Yasir Arafat visited Tehran to be greeted by a uniquely smiling Khomeini. But already the first anomalies in the Arab reaction to the Iranian revolution were appearing because some Palestinians began to wonder how Arafat could enthuse about the establishment of an Islamic order when the PLO stood for the notion of a 'democratic secular state' and so many of the Palestinian leaders were Christians.

For the Iranian revolution also had a deeper meaning. The Shah had not been overthrown by a military coup but by a widely-based popular Islamic movement. Its leader, the seventy-nine-year-old Ayatollah Khomeini, was a man of exceptional charisma but he could never have succeeded without a deep-seated longing among the mass of Iranians to reassert their identity against the brashly Westernizing and essentially secular policies of the Shah.

Khomeini was not the instigator of the concept of Islamic revival or renewal. The desire to re-create a pure and idealized community of

Muslims – misleadingly but probably unavoidably called Islamic fundamentalism – is almost as old as Islam itself. It found expression in Egypt in the 1930s and 1940s in the Muslim Brotherhood and from there spread to other parts of the Middle East. Although in relative abeyance during the high period of pan-Arab nationalism, it had begun to reappear after the disastrous Arab defeat of 1967. It appealed especially to a youth which felt that the ideals and leadership of its parents' generation had failed. From one end of the Arab world to the other there were signs of renewed Islamic piety among university students. Its symbols were the beards of the young men and the modest *hijab* (headscarf) and enveloping garments of the girls.

Although the signs of Islamic revival had been widely noted before Khomeini's triumphant return to Tehran in the spring of 1979 he gave it a powerful new impetus. For here was an Islamic revolution, dedicated to the establishment of a true Islamic order, which had succeeded. To idealistic Muslim youth Utopia seemed attainable. Yet the very success of the Iranian revolution provoked complex and often contradictory reactions in the Arab states. This was inevitable in view of the multiplicity of sects, interests, and political and social orders which exist in the Arab world.

Although Khomeini held up his revolution as an example to all Muslims it was undeniably Iranian and Shiite Muslim in character. But it did have some universal Muslim appeal. As Khomeini denounced the existing régimes in virtually all the Arab states as corrupt, anti-Islamic and worthless, he found a response among the millions of Arabs dissatisfied with the existing order. The Arab régimes therefore had multiple reasons for disliking and fearing the Khomeini revolution. The Arab Gulf states had a special problem because of its appeal to their own Shiite minorities who had some cause to regard themselves as second-class citizens. In Iraq, where the Sunnis are politically dominant but the Shiites are a majority of the Arab population, this threat was compounded by the revival of ancient Persian–Arab rivalries and the breakdown of the opportunistic but effective agreement that Iraq's Baathist régime had made with the Shah in 1975. As the Khomeini régime stepped up its propaganda campaign, calling upon all righteous Muslims in Iraq to overthrow their 'corrupt and atheistic' régime, President Saddam Hussein concluded that Iran presented a mortal threat. Seeing in Iran's post-revolutionary chaos the chance of a swift and easy victory, he made the disastrous error of launching an invasion of Iran in September

1980. A vast new destabilizing factor had been added to the already turbulent Arab scene.

There was no uniform Arab reaction to the war, just as there had been none to the Khomeini revolution itself. As usual, in the Middle East, there were many anomalies. King Hussein, out of a combination of interest and Arab nationalist ideology, openly allied himself with Iraq. The Arab Gulf states were more cautious, preferring to pour money into Iraq to help its flagging war effort without provoking Iran into military retaliation. Nevertheless, their hostility towards Iran became increasingly clear and it was hardly surprising that Iran rejected their repeated attempts to mediate an end to the war.

Syria, in contrast, supported Iran. This owed much less to any affinity between Iranian Shiites and the sub-Shia minority Alawite sect which has dominated Syria under President Assad's régime, than the detestation of Syrian Baathists for their rivals in Iraq. But the alliance with Iran also served the Syrian President a vital purpose in helping to neutralize Syria's own Islamic zealots who might stand for most of the same objectives as Khomeini but were violently opposed to their Alawite/Baathist rulers. Libya also stood by Iran although Colonel Qaddafy was widely suspected by Arab Shiites of having ordered the assassination of the Lebanese Shiite leader, Imam Moussa Sadr. Ayatollah Khomeini's anti-establishment and anti-Western attitudes inevitably appealed to the Libyan leader. Algeria also showed its sympathies for Iran although with much less stridency. It was alone among the Arab states in being an acceptable mediator for Iran and it was too remote for Iran's fundamentalism to threaten its own moderately secularizing policies.

President Sadat's reaction to the Khomeini revolution was immediately hostile. He considered the Shah a friend who had helped Egypt in the 1973 war and ostentatiously invited him and his family to settle in their exile in Egypt. In the West this was regarded as an act of noble courage but in Egypt it further antagonized the Muslim militants who had turned against him after Camp David. Ironically, Sadat had earlier tolerated and even encouraged these Islamic zealots – provided they were not pro-Libyan or resorted to violence – as a bulwark against the left, which he regarded as his real enemy. But now Sadat was as detested by the Muslim Brotherhood and the more extreme sub-groups of Islamic fundamentalists as Nasser had ever been. It was one of these groups which assassinated him in October 1981.

The fact was that the Egyptian people as a whole were profoundly uneasy with the role that Egypt had come to play since Camp David. Certainly peace had not lost its popularity even if it had not brought many of the social and economic benefits that had been expected. Nor was there any new feeling of comradeship for the Palestinians and Egypt's other fellow-Arabs. But there was a sense that Egypt, in playing the role of US surrogate in the Middle East, had lost some of its hard-won dignity and self respect. Even if it was largely the fault of the other Arabs, Egypt no longer occupied the natural position of leadership to which it was entitled. There was growing awareness that Israel, in paying the price of handing back Sinai in order to neutralize its most powerful enemy, had secured the real prize – a free hand to annex and absorb the West Bank.

Many Egyptians had mixed feelings, uncertain whether they were willing to pay the price that leadership demanded. The country was not on the edge of rebellion although Sadat believed it was when, shortly before his assassination, he arrested 1,500 prominent opponents of the right, left and centre. His death was not followed by any mass uprising of the Egyptian faithful as his assassins had hoped. But the failure of the normally sentimental Egyptians to mourn their lost leader was a certain sign of the decline in his popularity and of all that he symbolized.

With Egypt's elimination from the Arab front the leadership role increasingly devolved on Saudi Arabia. But, lacking population and military power, the Kingdom gave its own definition to the role. Its huge financial resources and dominant position within OPEC gave it international status but were of only limited use in attempting to unite the Arabs in common action. Its natural inclination was more towards discreet mediation and conciliation behind the scenes than the adoption of striking diplomatic initiatives. However, in August 1981 Crown Prince Fahd put forward some modest proposals for a Middle East settlement which included a clear, if implicit, recognition of Israel's existence, coupled with the standard Arab demand for Israeli withdrawal from occupied territories and the establishment of an independent Palestinian state, with East Jerusalem as its capital. The Fahd Plan, as it came to be called, was effectively sabotaged at the Arab summit meeting in Fez in November. Iraq, Algeria and Libya failed to attend but it was essentially Syrian opposition which aborted the Plan. As the major Arab power now confronting Israel, Syria, under President Assad, a shrewd, ruthless and experienced political strategist, was beginning to demonstrate its power of veto over all Middle East peace initiatives to which it was opposed. This expansion of the Syrian role has become a major feature of the Arab political scene in the 1980s. Characteristically, the Saudis did not withdraw their Plan but declared it suspended for further discussion.

Egypt's new President Mubarak maintained the essentials of his predecessor's policies but significantly changed his style in relations with the other Arabs. He halted all abuse and multiplied his conciliatory gestures. Gradually many unofficial links were restored. The most striking rapprochement was with Iraq, anxious for the weight of Egypt's support in its war with Iran. But the Egyptian–Israeli Treaty, which President Mubarak had neither the desire nor ability to repudiate, remained an insurmountable obstacle to the restoration of full relations with the Arabs. Here also the Syrian veto was crucial.

The weakness and disarray of the Arab world was strikingly and humiliatingly displayed during the Israeli invasion of Lebanon in the summer of 1982. It was soon apparent that the Israeli objective, ostensibly to clear Southern Lebanon of Palestinian guerrillas (who in any case had for nine months maintained a US-mediated ceasefire), was in reality the annihilation of the entire Palestinian quasi-state that had been created in Lebanon and the establishment of a docile and friendly neighbour under right-wing Maronite domination. The causes of Arab embarrassment were twofold: many Lebanese Christians greeted the Israeli invaders as friends and deliverers while even Muslims and Druzes showed that they had come to detest the Palestinian presence in their country; secondly, the Arab states felt paralyzed and helpless in their inability to influence events. Syrian forces put up some resistance but after Israel destroyed their missile positions without loss of their planes, Syria agreed to a ceasefire. By the middle of June the Israelis had secured a stranglehold on the PLO headquarters in West Beirut.

Nevertheless, the heavy civilian casualties among Lebanese and Palestinians, the huge destruction of property, the callous saturation bombardment of Beirut and not least the strutting arrogance of the Israeli Defence Minister Ariel Sharon, who was largely responsible for Israel's war strategy, helped to swing world opinion against Israel in what must be described as the sixth Arab–Israeli war. The Palestinian fighters, faced with tremendous odds, put up a moderate resistance which was made less effective through lack of strategy and inadequate command structure but which greatly improved when they were confined to Beirut.[4] In Beirut the Palestinian fighters rallied

4. For a study of the subject see 'Palestinian Military Performance in the 1982 War' by Yezid Sayigh, *Journal of Palestine Studies* vol. XII, no. 4, Summer 1983.

and, supported by some Lebanese allies, they were able to demonstrate that what would have been Israel's first occupation of an Arab capital would be extremely costly.

President Reagan was by now showing some public disapproval of Israel's actions. Alexander Haig, a Secretary of State with extreme pro-Israeli views, resigned on 25 June and was replaced by George Shultz, who was regarded as more of an Arab sympathizer. President Reagan was receiving the most urgent appeals from King Fahd (who succeeded to the Saudi throne on the death of King Khalid on 13 June) that he should restrain Israel. The King is believed to have told President Reagan that unless he acted he would be 'unable to hold his family together'. Some angry telephone calls from the White House to Mr Begin influenced Israel in some points such as restoring water and electricity supplies to the besieged citizens of West Beirut. Israel abandoned any idea of occupying the whole city and an agreement was reached through the American mediator Philip Habib for the evacuation of Yasir Arafat and the 13,000 Palestinian fighters under French, Italian and US military supervision. The evacuation began on 22 August and was speedily completed. Nevertheless, following the assassination on 14 September of Bashir Gemayel, the Lebanese President-elect, Israeli troops did move into West Beirut 'to maintain order'. The United States protested vigorously but in vain. Two days later atrocious massacres of Palestinian civilians by Lebanese right-wing militiamen took place in the Sabra and Shatila refugee camps in areas now under Israeli military control, and without any Israeli attempt to foresee or prevent them. Both the PLO and Syria believed that the United States had broken a solemn promise that Palestinian civilians would be protected after the fighters had been withdrawn.

In spite of this there seemed some hope of a better relationship between the United States and the Arabs. On 1 September 1982 President Reagan had issued comprehensive proposals for a Middle East settlement which, although not presented as an alternative to Camp David, were clearly intended to replace this moribund approach with a new initiative. It was the first time for some years that an American President had placed his prestige behind a plan that showed equal concern for Arab and Israeli interests. Although he ruled out any idea of a Palestinian state President Reagan also rejected permanent Israeli control over the occupied territories and proposed instead the establishment of an autonomous Palestinian entity linked with Jordan. Mr Begin bluntly rejected the Reagan Plan but the Arab response was more nuanced. At their resumed summit meeting in Fez later in

September the Arab states, including Syria, agreed on their own set of proposals which, apart from asking that the UN Security Council should guarantee peace and secure borders among all nations of the region, including an independent Palestinian state, were the same as the 1981 Fahd Plan. In spite of crucial differences – notably over an independent Palestine – the Reagan and Arab proposals were not too far apart for their reconciliation to be inconceivable. Israel, on the other hand, rejected them totally, and US-Israeli relations were distinctly cool. The question as ever was whether the United States would be willing and able to throw its full weight behind a plan which Israel was determined to demolish.

In fact this was only one more false dawn in relations between the Arabs and the United States. First the American proposals were still based on the rejection of the Palestinians' right to self-determination and foresaw Jordan acting on their behalf. Secondly they ignored the role of Syria. It was not only that they made no mention of Syria's Golan Heights as among Israeli-occupied Arab territory but they clearly foresaw no role in a Middle East settlement for Syria's ally and sponsor, the Soviet Union. The Reagan Plan maintained the Kissinger doctrine of keeping the Soviet Union out of Middle East diplomacy.

Yasir Arafat, despite his sense of outrage at what he regarded as American dishonour over the PLO evacuation from Beirut, was still prepared to try to meet the Reagan Plan half way by agreeing with King Hussein on the formation of a joint Palestinian–Jordanian negotiating body. A meeting in Algiers in February 1983 of the Palestinian parliament-in-exile, the Palestine National Council, seemed in spite of the extremist rhetoric and calls for military struggle to give Arafat, who successfully dominated the proceedings, a free hand to pursue his diplomacy. It was summed up by a leading US-Palestinian member of the PNC as Flexible Militancy. In fact a deep crisis was developing which was to shatter the PLO. In April Arafat's plan for joint Jordanian–Palestinian action was rejected by his own Fatah executive. At the same time a serious rebellion broke out within the PLO against Arafat's leadership. The rebels opposed what they saw as the abandonment of the armed struggle for diplomacy and conciliation but there were internal reasons for their action: resentment against Arafat's authoritarianism, the venality and incompetence of some of his senior appointments and a general feeling that the Palestinian liberation movement had gone soft and lost its revolutionary fervour.

Arafat, a skilled politician with much more charisma than is apparent on Western television screens, still held many assets. He enjoyed overwhelming support among the one third of the Palestinian people under Israeli occupation and throughout the world he had become regarded as the symbol of Palestinian nationalism – Mr Palestine. But in 1983 his immediate problem was that Syria, with which his relations had long been uneasy or hostile, was backing the rebels for its own purposes of gaining control over the Palestinian national movement. Expelled from Syria by President Assad, Arafat made his headquarters in Tripoli in North Lebanon where he faced attacks by the rebels backed by Syrian and Libyan troops.

The Reagan Plan had spelled out long-term American objectives for a comprehensive Middle East peace but from the time of its announcement the United States policy was to give priority to securing the evacuation of all foreign troops – Israelis, Syrians and the remaining Palestinians – from Lebanese territory to enable the new Lebanese President Amin Gemayel to establish the authority of his régime throughout the country. To this end US marines returned to Lebanon on 25 September to form part of an international peacekeeping force with similar Italian, French and much smaller British contingents. Vigorous American mediation between Lebanese and Israeli negotiators finally produced, on 17 May 1983, an agreement between Lebanon and Israel which fell short of a peace treaty but was clearly intended to establish normal relations between the two countries in every other respect. This would have effectively divorced Lebanon from the other Arabs as much as the Treaty of Washington had done to Egypt, with the difference that Lebanon would be much too weak to stand up for its own interpretation of the agreement and could expect no support from the United States.

Syria, which was not consulted about the negotiations but merely informed of its results, denounced the agreement on the grounds that it had a vital interest in Lebanon which would now come under Israeli hegemony. Since the provision for Israel's withdrawal from Lebanon depended on prior or simultaneous Syrian withdrawal, Syria was in a position to render the agreement unenforceable. Since the Soviet Union had more than replaced Syrian weapons lost in the 1982 fighting and some 7,000 Soviet advisers were helping to man Syria's defence, President Assad was prepared for a head-on challenge of US policy in the region. Meanwhile, on 4 September 1983, Israel, against US wishes, made a partial unilateral withdrawal of its troops to what it hoped would be more secure positions in Southern Lebanon. The

Lebanese war was proving exceedingly unpopular in Israel and Lebanese/Palestinian guerrilla actions were causing mounting casualties.

The US marines were also a target. In November suicide bombers blew up their headquarters and those of the French contingent, leaving more than three hundred dead. Although the United States attributed the direct responsibility to extremist Shiite militia, it considered that Syria must have approved and assisted the action. The United States identified Syria, with its Soviet backers, as the obstacle not only to a settlement of the Lebanese problem but to peace in the whole area. Its response was to move closer to Israel – with Israel's actions in invading Lebanon forgotten and forgiven – by adopting a common strategy and greatly increasing military and economic aid.

The political panorama of the Arab world in 1984 was a dismal spectacle. The capacity of the Arab states collectively to influence world events had declined from the high point it reached in the previous decade. There were several reasons for this of which Arab disunity was the most obvious. The glut in the world oil market in the early 1980s inevitably reduced the international influence of the Arab oil-producers along with their revenues.[5] The extent of this decline could appear exaggerated. Revenues were still enormous and the huge overseas investment of government and private petro-dollars built up during the boom years left the Arab oil-producers with considerable potency in international trade and finance. Moreover since the Arab oil states are low-cost producers their relative importance in the oil market actually increases when prices are falling.

It was the political disarray of their régimes which was most depressing for the Arab peoples. Certain Arab states were being prevented from realizing their considerable potential by special problems: Iraq was unable to end its hopeless war with Iran, Morocco could not solve its Saharan conflict in a manner that satisfied its national pride and the Sudan faced a renewed rebellion in its south. But there were two principal factors behind the general Arab state of weakness. One was Egypt's isolation and the other, linked to the first, was the inability to adopt a common attitude towards the two superpowers. The significance of the absence of Egypt from the Arab front hardly needs stressing. Every Arab knew the bitter truth that it

5. Those of Saudi Arabia, Kuwait, the UAE, Qatar and Iraq are estimated to have declined from \$155 billion in 1981, to \$108·5 billion in 1982 and \$80 billion in 1983.

was the security of the Sinai front which enabled Israel to invade Lebanon and to pursue virtually unimpeded its principal objective – the absorption of what was left of Arab Palestine. It was small consolation that Israel had been frustrated in achieving some of its aims in Lebanon and was suffering its own internal problems – a divided nation with a catastrophic economy. In its new alliance with the United States, Israel appeared once again as the regional super-power that it had been before 1973.

United States Middle East policy created an insoluble dilemma for the Arabs' political leaders. Most of them agreed, with however much distaste, with President Sadat's famous dictum that 'the United States holds 99 per cent of the cards in the region'. Only the United States had the power to restrain Israel's ambitions to establish its hegemony in the Eastern Mediterranean but time and again the hopes of the moderate and essentially pro-American régimes that this power would be used were frustrated. Expectations that the United States' major Western allies might combine to influence American policy towards the more even balance between Arabs and Israelis in which they professed to believe proved equally fruitless. The American view, powerfully influenced by domestic political considerations, remained essentially unchanged beneath the surface. Yet the nature of the moderate Arab régimes prevented them from following the example of Syria and forming an alliance with the Soviets. The certain knowledge that Saudi Arabia would never announce that it was about to purchase Soviet arms reduced Saudi influence in Washington. The United States valued Saudi Arabia's moderate pro-Western policies but took them for granted.

It was at this dark hour in general Arab fortunes that the plight of the Palestinian Arabs appeared to worsen, something that might have been thought impossible. After a decade in which the Palestinians, despite their failure to recover any of their lost territory, had gained ever-increasing world recognition of their problem and its centrality to the stability of the Middle East region, and in which Yasir Arafat and the PLO had been very widely accepted as their representative, the Palestinians lost in Lebanon their last independent foothold in Arab territory. Moreover, the PLO split and came close to destroying itself. The spectacle of Palestinian fighters killing each other outside Tripoli in November 1983 destroyed much of the sympathy gained for their cause by Israel's invasion in the previous year.

No one could say how the Arab régimes might have developed since the end of the colonial era without the aggravation of the

Palestinian problem, but at least it is probable that some of them would have been less tyrannical and paranoid. Certainly their relations with the West would have been better. But even if the PLO were destroyed the Palestinian problem would not disappear, whatever Israeli hopes for such an outcome. The Arab régimes could not resign themselves to Israel's *fait accompli*, and expect to survive. The best prospect for the Arabs, as always, was in the rather more distant future when their weight of advantage in population and resources is bound to be realized. There is a possibility that if Israel pursues its domineering and expansionist policies it will ultimately destroy itself with an implosive force. The fact that this is now the real fear of many of Israel's warmest friends in the world makes it more plausible. The analogy between Israel and the Crusader Kingdoms, which Arabs are fond of quoting, may yet prove its force as Israel surrounds itself with a vastly more numerous hostile population with at least a million of them within its borders. Yet the Crusader states lasted for three centuries and a modern Saladin has still to appear. Unfortunately the much happier prospect of a reconciliation between Arab and Jew, which would enable Israel to feel secure and the Arabs to regard it as a living organ rather than a cancerous growth in the Middle East, seems equally remote in 1984.

Part Two
The Arab World Today

15. The Gulf: the Eldorado States

The four tiny Arab states of the Persian Gulf[1] are one of the most extraordinary features of the twentieth century. The hazards of history and geography have combined to decide that Kuwait, Bahrain, Qatar and the Union of Arab Emirates (formerly the Trucial Coast) instead of entering the modern world as impoverished outlying provinces of one of the bigger states in the area – Iraq, Saudi Arabia or Iran – have become independent members of the United Nations with living standards which are among the highest in the world. Two of them – Kuwait and the UAE – are major financial powers.

The accident of history which helped to bring about this astonishing result was that the Persian Gulf lay along the trade route of the nineteenth century's greatest maritime power – Britain – and its communications with India, on whose possession much of this power was based. Already from the early eighteenth century East India Company agents had given themselves a quasi-official status and from 1770 onwards the Royal Navy became increasingly active in the protection of shipping against pirates. It was to forestall an attempt by Napoleon to establish himself in the Gulf when he was in occupation of Egypt that Britain concluded a treaty with the ruler of Muscat, at the entrance of the Gulf, in 1798. In 1823 it established a Political Agency in the little shaikhdom of Sharja in the lower Gulf and negotiated a series of treaties with the Arab tribal rulers of the coast binding them to refrain from piracy. During most of the nineteenth century British intervention was confined to keeping the peace in dynastic disputes between the rulers and to the suppression of the slave trade, but by the 1890s Britain realized that it could no longer take its Gulf hegemony for granted. The Ottoman Turks, who had extended their rule to al-Hasa in eastern Arabia, and the Persians were infiltrating into the area. Intensified European imperialist rivalries also affected the Gulf. The French were active, the Russians

---

1. Some, although not all, the Arabs of the area reject the term and insist on Arab or Arabian Gulf. Persian–Arabian Gulf would be a suitable compromise but it is cumbersome and I have retained the common world usage, for which I hope I shall be forgiven by my Arab friends.

were increasing their influence in Persia and attempting to establish a naval supply station at the head of the Gulf, and Kaiser Wilhelm's Germany was planning to extend the Ottoman railway from Turkey to Baghdad and Kuwait as part of its *Drang nach Osten* policy. From 1892 onwards Britain entered into a series of treaties with all the Arab shaikhdoms of the Gulf coast. These Exclusive Agreements, as they were called, all took much the same form although they varied in detail. In return for British protection the rulers agreed never to cede any part of their territory except to the British government, not to enter into agreements with any government other than the British and not to admit foreign representatives without British consent. This was their status for half a century in the penumbra of the British Empire. When in the 1930s the world began to become aware that the Persian Gulf and its surrounding areas lay above a vast lake of oil, United States financial and diplomatic pressures were able to ensure that American oil companies secured a major share in the oil concessions. But Britain, with its headquarters in the Political Residency on the island of Bahrain, maintained political control.

Kuwait: First Oil City-state

Kuwait was the first of these states to acquire vast wealth, and thereby it became the prototype of the tiny multimillionaire oil shaikhdom. From 1896 to 1915 it had a ruler of outstanding character, Shaikh Mubarak the Great, who asserted his independence from the Ottoman Empire and asked a willing Britain for protection. After the First World War Britain was able to establish Kuwait's frontiers with Saudi Arabia and with Iraq, which was under British mandate (although the Iraqis have never wholeheartedly accepted Kuwait's independence). As a trading port Kuwait prospered indirectly from the new oil wealth in Iraq and Iran and its population increased to about 75,000 by 1934. But the real dramatic change came in the 1950s, when the export of the oil which had been discovered in 1938 by the Kuwait Oil Company (half British and half American), got under way and revenues began to soar upwards. The small and somnolent mud-walled trading and fishing port was torn apart to give way to a modern concrete city. Shaikh Abdullah, who succeeded as ruler in 1950, was a social and religious conservative but he favoured the spread of education (for girls as well as boys) and rapid economic development. Under his rule, Kuwait became a comprehensive welfare state not only for the native Kuwaitis but also for the immigrant Arabs, Iranians and

Indians who soon came to exceed them in numbers. A poor Kuwaiti became a contradiction in terms.

As I discovered on my first visits in the early 1960s, even the physical appearance of the new generation of Kuwaitis was being transformed. Political power remained in the hands of the ruling Sabah family, but it was divided both traditionally between the Jabir and Salem branches of the family and on the basis of personality. In June 1961 the ruling family felt confident enough to insist on its independence and the 1899 Anglo-Kuwaiti agreement was terminated by mutual consent. However, General Kassem, the unstable and adventurous ruler of Iraq, at once renewed his country's claims and threatened to occupy Kuwait.

The ruler asked for British troops, who landed immediately but were replaced two months later by a joint Arab League force. The Kuwaitis realized that in the long term their survival as an independent state would depend upon their acceptance by the other Arab states rather than British military protection.

Six months after independence the ruling family took the bold step of forming a Constituent Assembly to draft a permanent constitution and two years later a fifty-member National Assembly was elected by all Kuwaiti (male) adults. This surprising experiment in parliamentary democracy by a conservative shaikhdom gave Kuwait a special character. The parliament was dominated by the leading merchant families but a small group of radical nationalist deputies succeeded in acquiring influence out of all proportion to their numbers. In the prolonged struggle between the Arab radical and conservative camps Kuwait took a neutral stand. This greatly added to its influence as did the establishment in 1961 of the Kuwait Fund for Arab Development, a pioneering body of its kind among the Arab oil states, which provided soft loans for viable development projects such as the expansion of Beirut port, the modernization of Sudan's railways, or Tunisian agriculture. Kuwait was answering the common charge that the Arab oil states would refuse to share their wealth with their fellow-Arabs.

On the death, in November 1965, of the much respected Shaikh Abdullah, the succession passed to Shaikh Sabah Salem, with Shaikh Jabir, the finance minister and inspiration of Kuwait's Arab Development Fund, as Crown Prince and Prime Minister. Shaikh Jabir succeeded as Ruler on the last day of 1977.

The enlightened experiment in parliamentary democracy has brought its difficulties. The executive branch in Kuwait, which has increasingly included university-trained young technocrats from out-side the ruling family, has found it factious and disruptive. The National Assembly has at times prevented the government from taking actions it considered essential; at others its conservative major-ity made decisions it regarded as regressive. In 1975 the cabinet resigned, saying that parliament was making government impos-sible. The Ruler suspended the constitution, dissolved parliament and muzzled the press, which had previously been one of the most free in the Arab world. Some saw the influence of Saudi Arabia which had never approved of Kuwait's democratic experiment, but a more important factor was the deteriorating internal security situation, exacerbated by the Lebanese civil war, which especially influenced Kuwait's large Palestinian minority.

However, the ruling family was determined that the principle of an elected legislature should not be finally abandoned and fresh elec-tions under a revised constitution were held in February 1981. But enormous problems remained. With the defeat of the radical candi-dates ensured, the conservative majority was now supreme in the National Assembly, insisting, against the government's wishes, on such actions as banning alcohol for foreign diplomats and segregating education at the prestigious Kuwait University. Adding to the régime's difficulties, the slump in the oil market halved revenues and caused a genuine crash in the Kuwait stock exchange. The Iranian revolution and the Iraq–Iran war created a looming threat. Many of Kuwait's large Shiite minority found inspiration in the Khomeini régime but fervent Kuwaiti Sunnis were generally hostile to the Iranian revolution, and the National Assembly majority wanted to cut the country's subsidy to Syria as punishment for Syrian support for Iran. Kuwait's appearance of neutrality in the Gulf War was difficult to maintain. Since, in addition, a substantial majority of Kuwait's 1·5 million inhabitants (750,000 in 1975) are non-Kuwaitis (including among others perhaps 250,000 Palestinians as well as dissident Ira-nians and Iraqis), internal security is a matter of the greatest concern.

In spite of these menacing dangers, Kuwait has many positive aspects of which its citizens can be proud. Because it was the first of the Arab oil-rich city states and its revenues were generally wisely used, its citizens have reached an advanced level of education and of expertise and sophistication in financial matters. In 1976 the govern-ment wisely decided to build up a reserve out of budget surpluses and a State Fund for Future Generations was established, receiving 10 per cent of all state revenues which could not be touched for twenty-five years. Government and private investments overseas bring in an income of $9 billion a year. Kuwait or Kuwaitis own property or shares from North and South America to Europe and the Far East; 700,000 Kuwaitis exert an influence on the international financial system far out of proportion to their numbers. In fact the decision they have to face is how far they wish Kuwait to risk developing as an international financial centre in its own right, with the Kuwaiti dinar as a world currency and the Kuwait Stock Exchange extended to handling the shares of non-Kuwaiti companies. Financial prudence is of course required and in 1982 Kuwait's outstandingly able Finance Minister, Abdel Latif al-Hamad, warned that the country faced bankruptcy within four years if the increase in government spending was not checked, but the fact is that since all the country's needs for the economic infrastructure have been met a policy of retrenchment can be sustained. It is a question of reducing exaggerated expectations of expansion.

Although Kuwait's investment income will remain of paramount importance, Kuwaitis have no wish to survive purely as a *rentier* state. The government-assisted Shuaiba Industrial area on the coast twenty-five miles south of Kuwait shows signs of taking off and expanding into the growing markets of the Arab Gulf region.

The extreme delicacy of Kuwait's international position (sandwiched between Iraq and Iran) and its highly sensitive internal security have not prevented Kuwait from following its cherished independent line in foreign affairs or allowing considerable freedom to its people. Of the six members of the Gulf Cooperation Council (see p. 356) it takes the most resolutely non-aligned stand. It has diplomatic relations with the USSR and China (of which Saudi Arabia can make use as a channel to the communist powers if it wishes). With the disruption of Beirut, Kuwait has perhaps the most outspoken and independent press in the Arab World. Of all the many social and economic organizations that have been founded in Kuwait the one which probably expresses best the kind of role Kuwaitis would like to play is the Kuwait Institution for Scientific Research (KISR). Established in 1958 and powerfully encouraged by the ruling family, this now has a budget of $40 million and a staff of more than three hundred, many of them distinguished Arabs with Western nationalities. KISR tackles all the main concerns which are those of the region as well as its own: solar energy, sea water desalination, arid zone agriculture, marine biology and pollution.

The survival of Kuwait and its distinctive personality in such surroundings is inevitably at risk. One dilemma it faces is that to grant Kuwaiti nationality on a large scale to non-Kuwaiti immigrant Arabs, in order to cease being a minority in their own country, would dilute the character they are trying to preserve. However, there is an advantage in that the largest single group – the Palestinians – mostly do not want Kuwaiti nationality if it means abandoning their own national rights while they have a vested interest in Kuwait's prosperity to which they have contributed so much. The strains on Kuwaiti society – religious, political and social – are powerful and evident but it has considerable experience and determination with which to withstand them.

Bahrain: Expanding Crossroads

The shaikhdom of Bahrain consists of a group of small islands lying off the coast of Saudi Arabia. With its water supply from natural springs, Bahrain has had a settled population for some 5,000 years. As the island of Dilmun, it was a natural staging-post and entrepôt trade centre between the flourishing civilizations of Mesopotamia and the Indus valley in the Bronze Age, and in the nineteenth century it was the obvious site for the British political headquarters in the Gulf. Its humid climate and vegetation cause it to stand out from the dry and barren region in which it is situated.

Bahrain is different from its neighbours in other important respects. Its oil was discovered and exported by the American-owned Bahrain Petroleum Company in 1934, several years before any other Arab state. It was therefore the first part of this poor and neglected region to be able to provide adequate schools and welfare services for its people. But the oil wells are small; Bahrain never had any chance to become a major producer, and revenues have never increased beyond a few million pounds a year. This also means that Bahrain has not enjoyed the doubtful benefit of becoming a *rentier* state. Diversification of the economy is not only advisable but essential.

The building of schools in the 1930s and 1940s inevitably produced an educated class which became attracted to the radical nationalist ideas which were spreading in the rest of the Arab world. For a time this was tolerated by the deeply conservative ruling family, on British advice. No organized political opposition was allowed but nationalist clubs and committees were formed. The change came in 1956, the year of Suez and the high flood of Nasserism. (This was the year that the stoning of the British foreign secretary's car by nationalist demonstrators helped to convince Anthony Eden, the prime minister, that Nasser was organizing the entire Arab world in an anti-British conspiracy.) The committees were banned and all political activity ceased. On an island with a British military base there was little that the nationalists could do to organize protest. Faced with a choice between prison and devoting themselves to the trade and business for which Bahrainis have a natural aptitude most of them chose the latter willingly enough.

The ruling family's sense of security was not seriously disrupted until 1968 when, after expecting that the British would transfer some of the Aden military base to Bahrain, the British Labour government suddenly announced that it was withdrawing all its forces from the Gulf by 1971. An additional cause for alarm was that the Iranians had a long-standing claim to Bahrain. They referred to it as Iran's sixteenth province and turned away travellers with a Bahraini visa stamped on their passport. Although Bahrain lies close to the Arab side of the Gulf, a high proportion of its third of a million people are of Iranian origin and a historical case could be made out for the claim, which was strongly supported by Iranian nationalists. However, Anglo-American diplomacy persuaded the Shah of Iran to refer Iran's claim to the UN. The UN under-secretary general Vittorio Guiccardi went to Bahrain in March 1970 and reported what anyone familiar with Bahrain knew very well already: Bahrainis were virtually unanimous in wanting Bahrain to be a fully sovereign state. The great majority added that it should be an Arab state. This verdict was accepted by Iran with a good grace.

Bahrain – and especially its ruling Khalifa family – was still faced by the problem of the loss of British protection. Although Nasserism (and Cairo Radio) was no longer a threat, Baathist and other radical elements were active in parts of the Gulf area and the Marxist opposition elements in Oman were regarded as a danger by all the shaikhly rulers. Between 1968 and 1970 Bahrain, with British encouragement, took part in the negotiations for a federation of all the Arab Gulf states, but in the end opted for independence and joined the United Nations in 1971.

Bahrain's future lies in developing in a modern context as the entrepôt, trading and communications centre that it was 3,000 years ago. Forced to diversify because of its small and declining crude oil production, it has made full use of its natural advantages, aware all the time that it cannot take these for granted because the neighbouring Arab oil states are eager to build their own trading and communications facilities. Its growth for the past decade has been phenomenal. Offshore banking facilities introduced in 1976 have flourished to the extent that Bahrain vies with Hong Kong or Singapore. For many international companies Bahrain has replaced Beirut as a regional headquarters and its airport has become one of the best known in the world.

The island's ancient fishing and pearling links with the sea have been replaced by the giant Arab Shipbuilding and Repair Yard (ASRY), for which Bahrain was chosen as the site by the Organization of Arab Petroleum Exporting Countries (OAPEC). This and Bahrain's aluminium smelter have given rise to a series of secondary light industries.

Government is fairly paternalistic. In 1973 the ruling Emir Shaikh Isa introduced a form of constitutional government with an elected legislature but after only twenty months closed it down because, as in Kuwait, it was making life impossibly difficult for the executive. Unlike the Ruler of Kuwait, however, he has not since revived it and governs by decree. However, the ruling family is popular and fully integrated into the community from which it is not separated by any extravagant display of wealth, for which in any case it does not have the means. Socially, the atmosphere is noticeably relaxed and liberal. Much the most serious threat to stability comes from the Sunni–Shia division. The Shiites, who form about 60 per cent of the Bahraini population, have developed considerably in wealth and influence in recent years but the Sunnis remain dominant. Inevitably, the Iranian revolution attracted some Bahraini Shiites and it looked at one time as if the Khomeini régime would revive the Iranian claim to Bahrain, although this has not been pursued. There were serious Shiite disturbances in 1979 and 1980 and an attempted coup with alleged Iranian support in 1982. However, the excesses of the Iranian revolution reduced Iran's attractions for at least the better established Bahraini Shiites.

The foundation of the Gulf Cooperation Council (GCC) in 1981 will greatly benefit Bahrain if the GCC succeeds with its declared aim of diversifying the roles of its six members and avoiding duplication. Bahrain has been suitably chosen as the site for the projected Gulf University. Integration into the community will be served with the completion, due by the end of 1985, of the giant causeway between the Saudi Arabian mainland and the island. Some expect this to mean the absorption of the Bahraini personality into that of the Saudi Kingdom but this seems extremely unlikely.

Qatar: Modest Achiever

Qatar, the smallest of all the independent Arab states, has more oil than Bahrain but is much less favoured in other respects. When oil exports began in 1950 Qatar was a desolate peninsula with a tiny population reduced to desperate poverty by the decline of the pearling industry. Oil seemed to be the sole excuse for its existence.[2]

Qatar was not a second Kuwait; oil company men described it as 'the smallest of the big producers', but with its population of only about 30,000 the £20 million a year it was receiving in revenues by the late 1950s was more than enough to provide education and welfare for all of them, as well as a cluster of palaces for members of the ruling al-Thani family. The economic boom had attracted immigrants and the population had risen to 100,000.

Like the Saudis, but unlike the Bahrainis or the Abu Dhabians, the Qataris are Wahhabis, and it is more than likely that Qatar would have been absorbed into the Kingdom of Saudi Arabia if it had not been for its ruler's Exclusive Agreement with Britain. Like Bahrain, Qatar considered joining in a federation with the other Gulf rulers after Britain's withdrawal but finally opted for independence in 1971. The size of its population just allows Qatar to attain the normally accepted minimum qualification for membership of the United Nations.

In February 1972 the somewhat listless ruler of Qatar Shaikh Ali al-Thani, who spent much of his time abroad, was ousted in a bloodless coup by his more vigorous cousin Shaikh Khalifa who endeavoured to create a more dynamic and efficient administration.

After ten years of Shaikh Khalifa's rule, Qatar had developed against powerful odds into a flourishing and well-ordered city-state with a distinctive identity and a population of about 200,000 of whom some 75 per cent were immigrants. Perhaps because it has no political ambitions Qatar has influence out of proportion to its size among the Arab states. It has not attempted to compete with Kuwait and Bahrain as a financial centre but it has been able to use its oil revenues – gigantic in relation to population even when they declined from $5 billion in 1980 to $3 billion in 1982 – to develop petrochemical and iron and steel industries. It has huge reserves of natural gas to prolong the life of its revenues. The quality of life in the former desert peninsula

2. Visitors were generally unkind. After an American correspondent had described Qatar as 'sticking like a sore thumb into the Gulf', and a British writer had said simply that it was 'the end', the Qataris understandably became suspicious of foreign journalists.

has greatly improved now that Qatar has its own university, television service, theatre company and newspapers. The Ruler has the seemingly impossible ambition to make his country self-sufficient in food production but if a cheaper way of desalinating seawater is developed Qatar is likely to be the first to make use of it.

The United Arab Emirates: Essential Fusion

The United Arab Emirates (UAE) consists of seven tiny sovereign states – Abu Dhabi, Ajman, Dubai, Fujaira, Ras el-Khaima, Sharja and Umm al-Qaiwain – strung out along what used to be known as the Trucial Coast between Qatar and Oman on the Lower Gulf. Until the middle of the twentieth century the only outsiders to take much interest in this unpromising territory with its scattered palms and crumbling mud forts were a handful of British arabists, who advised the Rulers and tried to maintain tribal peace through the Trucial Oman Scouts, the locally recruited defence force.

Then in 1960 oil was struck offshore from the coast of Abu Dhabi. It was a major strike of Kuwaiti proportions; Abu Dhabi was clearly destined for immense wealth. This created several problems. In the first place the Ruler of Abu Dhabi at the time was the eccentric Shaikh Shakhbut. His incapacity to deal with his sudden wealth was total. For example, he rejected any system of cheques or credit and would wake up the startled young manager of the newly established British Bank of the Middle East after midnight, insisting on seeing all his wealth in cash.

In 1966 Shakhbut was deposed by family agreement (with warm British encouragement) and replaced by his brother Shaikh Zaid, the present ruler, who in contrast is decisive, ambitious and quite capable of coping with the twentieth century. As his revenues soared in geometrical progression he presided over the development in a few years of his mud village capital into a modern city with eight-lane highways, office blocks and a major international airport.

Dubai, the most important of the other UAE members, is ruled by another man of remarkable qualities. Shaikh Rashid is an Arab tribal shaikh who happens to be a business genius and he has been quite content to allow Abu Dhabi to conduct the foreign policy of the UAE, provided he can continue to pursue his own interest of making Dubai a major financial and trading centre. After taking over as regent in 1939, Shaikh Rashid first took most of the trade from his neighbours and rivals in Sharja, who allowed their harbour to silt up, and then went on to make the creek of Dubai a flourishing port. For years Dubai's prosperity was based mainly on smuggling – especially gold, which was shipped eastwards on Arab dhows to dodge Indian and Pakistani customs patrol boats. But the sudden oil boom of the 1960s made it possible for Dubai to diversify its trade. Oil was discovered offshore in Dubai waters in 1966, but the revenues are still not the major source of Dubai's wealth. Some foreign experts doubted Shaikh Rashid's wisdom when he insisted that Dubai should have a major international airport but the traffic soon proved him right. When he went on to build what is in some respects the largest port in the entire Middle East, no one dared to criticize. In fact many a sophisticated foreign businessman has been made to look foolish by the lightning commercial acumen of this seventy-year-old desert shaikh with twinkling eyes, who has abandoned none of the informal traditional ways but is entirely at home in the world of advanced twentieth-century capitalism. ('You say you will need 350,000 concrete blocks for! your bridge? I say you can do it with 250,000!' And he is always right.) It is of little surprise that Dubai was reported to be the second largest importer of Swiss watches in the world, although it would not be easy to discover for whose wrists they are all destined. Britain's responsibility lay in the fact that had it not been for British protection the seven small states would hardly have been able to retain their independence in the modern world.

Each of the rulers had come to regard himself as sovereign and independent, but since no one had ever thought of fixing his boundaries in the empty desert it was quite uncertain what territory he ruled. Understandably, each ruler day-dreamed of Abu Dhabi's good fortune falling on him, and fierce disputes over the ownership of oil wells could be foreseen. A British Foreign Office arabist therefore spent many months over several years demarcating the boundaries of the Trucial States by roaming the interior on a camel to inquire from the sparsely scattered tribesmen which cluster of palm trees or dried-up *wadi* they regarded as their own. Finally a map was produced – the official map of the United Arab Emirates – which outshines that of the petty principalities of pre-1870 Germany in eccentricities. Each of the Emirates has a tiny enclave inside the territory of one of its neighbours.

When Britain unexpectedly announced in 1968 that it would withdraw entirely from the region by 1971, the rulers could not fail to be aware that, however much they valued their independence, they were too small to face the world alone. Rulers of six of the seven

Trucial States agreed to form a federation on Britain's departure. Only Ras al-Khaima remained outside because it was refused veto powers but it changed its mind and accepted in 1972. Shaikh Zaid became the first President and Shaikh Rashid Vice-President. The Federal Constitution provided for a Supreme Council of the seven Rulers, a federal cabinet in which Abu Dhabi and Dubai were predominant and an appointed legislative assembly.

Inevitably there was scepticism from the outset about the new state's chances of survival. Similar federations of small tribal states have so often broken down elsewhere and one cynical British official remarked: 'Here all the shaikhs have in common is that their ancestors signed a treaty with Britain to suppress piracy in 1820.' There were rivalries and traditional hostility between some of the ruling families who remained jealous of their borders, although in some cases these had still not been fully established. Moreover, since the new state had only a tiny educated élite without a single lawyer or judge, the entire federal structure had to be created by outsiders.

Nevertheless, the UAE has survived for more than a decade to defy the pessimists. The greatest problem has been the conflict between federation and 'states' rights', with Abu Dhabi generally pressing for a closer federation, including the abolition of borders and the creation of unified armed forces and federal budget and Dubai standing for the retention of most of the independence of individual member-states.

In a compromise worked out in 1979 Shaikh Zaid and Shaikh Rashid met each other half way in these issues. In general, Shaikh Rashid has been content to concentrate on his phenomenally successful business enterprises and leave the conduct of the UAE's foreign affairs to Shaikh Zaid who has managed to represent a strong collective UAE personality to the outside world. Through the Abu Dhabi Fund for Economic Development established in 1971 and many other contributions to aid programmes, the UAE has become one of the largest aid donors in the world.

Many critical problems remain which in the longer term are more important than the slowdown in development caused by a relative slump in oil revenues. Of the total population of just over 1 million only about one quarter are UAE citizens and over half are non-Arabs from the Indian sub-continent and South and East Asia. The social and political tensions this could create can easily be imagined. Although the problem of succession has been settled in the ruling families – always difficult in a region such as Arabia where primogeniture is not the tradition – the strong personalities of Shaikh Zaid and

Shaikh Rashid will not be easily replaced. At the same time a younger generation of UAE citizens – much better educated than their parents – are asking for more representative forms of government. That they include some members of the ruling families is a healthy sign but the balance between the powers of the federal government and 'states' rights' still has to be resolved. But the centrifugal forces should be overcome by the powerful factors of self-interest which hold the federation together.

16. Oman: the Hermit Disclosed

The sultanate of Oman, which stretches for some 500 miles along the toe of the Arabian peninsula and inland on to the edge of the great Empty Quarter, was until recently the most inaccessible part of the Arab world and is still arguably the most romantic. Much of its rocky and lagoon-filled coastline as well as the mountainous interior is of startling beauty. This part of Arabia receives monsoon rains; there is vegetation and agriculture, irrigation on the coastline (where the incomparable Muscat dates are grown) and pasture and cereals in the highland regions which are still largely unknown to the outside world.

Oman was not always so detached from the rest of mankind. In the eighteenth century it was a major sea power in the Indian Ocean, sending naval expeditions to western India and east Africa to harry the Portuguese, and it reached its greatest extent in the middle of the nineteenth century when its possessions included Zanzibar, Mombasa and parts of southern Persia. In the 1860s Oman's Indian Ocean empire split up with the arrival of the steamship via the Suez Canal. Muscat's[1] commercial and maritime power rapidly declined.

In 1798 Britain signed a treaty of protection with the sultan, as a direct response to Napoleon's occupation of Egypt which threatened Britain's sea-routes to India. From then on Britain exerted substantial control over Oman's affairs, although always stoutly maintaining that the sultanate was a fully independent state. British soldiers commanded the sultan's forces – the Muscat and Oman levies – and British civilians undertook the usually unrewarding task of advising his administration. In the 1950s the sultan's British-led troops assisted both in the ejection of Saudi raiders from the Buraimi Oasis and in putting down the rebellion of the Imam Ghalib, who claimed self-rule for the mountainous interior. The Arab League states denounced

---

1. Muscat is the capital and main port. The power of the sultan often hardly extended into the interior, which was autonomous under its own *imams*, and he was frequently referred to as the 'sultan of Muscat and Oman' or merely 'of Muscat'. Today only the name of Oman is used.

British intervention and supported Ghalib although they had no practical means of helping him.

The man who had been sultan since 1932 was an arch-reactionary of great personal charm. His country was desperately poor; total revenues had hardly risen from the £50,000 from customs receipts in his father's time. But in the 1950s his income began to increase slowly with British aid and payments for oil concessions, and the British persuaded him reluctantly to establish a development department. The trouble was that Said ibn Taimur disliked development of any kind. In an attempt to keep out the twentieth century as long as possible, he personally issued all visas for visitors which were kept severely restricted.[2] Government officials and all women were only allowed to leave the country with special permission, which was rarely given. He forbade the inhabitants of the interior to visit the coastal areas and vice versa. The only surfaced road was the few miles between Muscat and Matrah. Medicines, radios, music, dancing, spectacles, trousers, cigarettes and books were all forbidden. Understandably, the sultan had a special dislike of education. On one occasion he told his British adviser: 'This is why you lost India, because you educated the people.'[3]

In 1958 Said ibn Taimur retired to live permanently in his palace at Salala, the capital of Dhofar province in the far southern corner of his sultanate on the borders of South Yemen. He had married a Dhofari woman by whom he had one son, Qabus, whom he kept for years under a form of house arrest after his return from being educated in England, since Said's suspicious tyranny extended to his own family. In 1962 some dissident Dhofaris, who had made contact with other nationalists when they went to find work in the booming Persian Gulf, joined together to form a Dhofar Liberation Front and began guerrilla warfare against the sultan's forces on a small scale. In 1966 some Dhofari soldiers nearly succeeded in assassinating the sultan at a military parade. But the overthrow of the sultan was virtually impossible as long as his rule was upheld by Britain. However, by the late 1960s Britain was having serious doubts. Oil was discovered in substantial quantities in 1968 and revenues began to mount but the

2. Journalists were specially unwelcome. It is believed that this was because of the book *Sultan in Oman* by James Morris who was *The Times* correspondent in the Middle East at that period. Although remarkably sympathetic towards the sultan in general, James Morris made some mild fun of the way he spoke English and this was not forgiven.

3. H. Boustead, *The Wind of Morning*, London, 1971, p. 223.

sultan still refused to contemplate change. It was not only increasingly scandalous that in a nation of 750,000[4] there were only three small primary schools and one hospital (belonging to an American Protestant mission) to deal with a population ridden with endemic diseases such as malaria, leprosy, tuberculosis and trachoma and an infant mortality rate among the highest in the world, but the sultan's attitude meant that contracting firms were deprived of lucrative commissions.

Finally, in July 1973, Said was overthrown in a palace coup and replaced by his son Qabus. He was flown to London to spend the rest of his days in Claridge's Hotel. Although Whitehall understandably denied connivance, there can be no doubt that the coup had Britain's foreknowledge as well as approval. In fact it would have been impossible to plan the coup without the knowledge of the British officers who held all the key posts in the army.

The accession of the thirty-year-old Qabus was understandably greeted with delight by many of his subjects. Most of his father's ludicrous restrictions were lifted, and a serious development programme was started to provide Oman with the roads, schools, clinics, banks and airports which would help to bring the country from the Middle Ages into at least the early part of the twentieth century. Tens of thousands of Omani emigrants who had had no choice but to find work abroad began to return. The former sultan's 500 black personal slaves were declared free.

Unfortunately for the new sultan, the rebellion in Dhofar did not cease with his accession. The Liberation Front had by this time taken on a strongly left-wing character, becoming more Marxist than pan-Arab nationalist. It received support and Soviet- and Chinese-made arms from the left-wing régime across the border in South Yemen, and in areas which were held by the guerrillas the children were taught Marxist principles.

The rebels were small in numbers but the terrain in Dhofar was ideal for guerrilla warfare and the rebellion was difficult to suppress by conventional means. Defying Arab opinion Sultan Qabus imported some 4,000 of the Shah of Iran's troops to assist him, while a few hundred British soldiers and airmen – some on secondment from the British regular army and some hired direct by the Sultan – perpetuated a curious relic of Britain's former quasi-imperial role in

4. Estimates vary between half a million and 1.5 million, the figure the government uses for planning purposes. No census has ever been taken.

Arabia. By 1976 the rebellion had been reduced to a small handful of guerrillas based in PDRY territory although they continued to create enough incidents to be a threat to security. All attempts to mediate between the PDRY and Oman failed until 1982 when the two centres agreed to end hostility and went on to establish diplomatic relations. Although one threat had been removed Sultan Qabus was rather more concerned by the threat he saw in Soviet expansion in the Indian Ocean and Afghanistan, and the greatly increased insecurity caused by the Iranian revolution and the subsequent Iraq–Iran war. Almost alone among Arab leaders, Sultan Qabus relegated the Palestine question to second place among the problems of the region. He was prepared to isolate Oman in the Arab League by supporting President Sadat's peace with Israel. When the GCC was formed he constantly urged on his fellow-members the need to give priority to external threats to security.

Lower oil prices in the early 1980s meant some revision of Oman's ambitious five-year plan begun in 1981. Nevertheless the transformation of this former Arabian backwater proceeded apace with an imaginative emphasis on the development of agriculture and fisheries. While some of the new building was cause for alarm to conservationists, there was no danger than the unique charm of the Omani personality might disappear. One cause for concern for Oman's future was that the Sultan was childless and when his uncle Tariq died in 1982 there was no obvious successor. However, although an increasingly able cadre of commoners was being built up to manage the affairs of government, it seemed likely that a successor would be found within the royal family and, in view of Sultan Qabus's age, the problem was hardly urgent.

17. Saudi Arabia: Financial Superpower

The effect of great and sudden wealth on the tiny desert states of the Persian Gulf has been remarkable. In the kingdom of Saudi Arabia it has produced one of the most extraordinary phenomena of the twentieth century. It is not only that a state which was one of the poorest on the globe when it was created half a century ago is well on its way to becoming one of the richest by any standards, with control over a major part of the world's financial reserves, but that it should have happened to a beduin tribal monarchy ruled on the most fundamentalist and puritanical principles of Islam. The inescapable problem of how to serve both Allah and Mammon has yet to be resolved.

When the kingdom of Saudi Arabia was created by the great Abdul Aziz Ibn Saud in the 1920s it had a population which was roughly estimated at between one-and-a-half and two million in an area about half the size of India. At best a quarter of these were nomadic and scratched a living by cultivating patches of the barren land over a widely scattered area. The rest of the people lived in the small oases, market towns and the Holy Cities of Mecca and Medina. Mecca, the largest, had a population of about 50,000. Government and organization was tribal. Ibn Saud helped to maintain the unity of his kingdom through a series of brief marriages to the daughters of leading tribal chiefs (On his death he had some 300 sons and an uncounted number of daughters.) The tiny revenues of the state were derived from services to Muslim pilgrims to Mecca and a small subsidy from the British government.

This situation had only begun to change by the time of Ibn Saud's death in 1953. Oil was discovered by the Arabian American Oil Company (Aramco) before the Second World War, but exports and revenues only began to increase significantly after 1947. Even so the impact of the new wealth had already begun to cause a severe strain for the desert kingdom and its puritanical Wahhabi traditions before the death of Ibn Saud. Extravagance and corruption were both possible and humanly inevitable. The old king's authority and prestige were enough to prevent the internal tensions from becoming too great during his lifetime.

Ibn Saud's eldest son Saud lacked his father's advantages. The Saudi capital Riyadh became a centre of ludicrously ostentatious personal wealth and a growing network of governmental graft and corruption. The conservative *ulama* were alienated as much as the young generation of Saudis who were attracted by the radical nationalism and socialism of Nasser's Egypt and listened to the blistering attack of Cairo's Voice of the Arabs on the mindless extravagance of the Saudi princes and shaikhs. But King Saud was not content to enjoy his wealth at home. He used it to intervene in Arab politics and even, with encouragement from some Western governments, dreamed of challenging Nasser's leadership of the Arabs.

It was at this point in 1958 that the only group which represented public opinion in Saudi Arabia – the royal princes, shaikhs and *ulama* – joined together to save the Saudi monarchy and the unity of the kingdom by forcing Saud to hand over all his powers to his younger brother, Crown Prince Feisal.

As they well knew, Feisal was a man of very different talents and characteristics from his brother. His life-style was austere. His father had used him for many missions abroad so he had valuable diplomatic experience and as governor of the Hejaz he had gained the respect of the people of his region. This was of special importance because the Hejazis always had doubts about being ruled by the less sophisticated Wahhabis of Nejd, and under Saud their regionalism had threatened the unity of the kingdom.

Feisal began a period of economy and restraint both at home and abroad to restore Saudi Arabia's chaotic finances. But although the Saudi image abroad improved, austerity was unpopular at home – especially among the tribesmen who had received regular subsidies from Saud. Saudi modernist intellectuals saw their opportunity and formed an undeclared alliance with King Saud on the understanding that if they helped him recover his powers some form of representative government would be introduced. Saud did recover his authority in December 1960 when Feisal resigned as Prime Minister but the bizarre vision of Saud as a democratic constitutional monarch was not realized as the small group of progressives went into jail or exile.

Saud's new period of rule was only brief. The republican coup in Yemen in September 1962 was a direct threat to the Saudi monarchy. Saudi Arabia began helping the Yemeni royalists but the loyalty of its regular armed forces was uncertain and the challenge of the new Yemeni republic which began to preach Nasserist-type Arab socialism was serious enough to require some internal reforms, such as the abolition of slavery. In failing health, Saud was obliged to return power to Feisal who once again became the effective ruler of Saudi Arabia. In November 1964 Saud was formally deposed by a majority of the princes and Feisal became king in name as well as fact.

With his new authority, King Feisal instituted a more dynamic foreign policy than before in an unmistakable challenge to Nasser's leadership of the Arabs. A passionate opponent of communism as well as Zionism, which he tended to see as identical, his objective was to emphasize the traditional and religious element in Arabism. He endeavoured to create a new conservative alliance within the Arab and Muslim worlds (popularly but unofficially called his Islamic Front) against Egypt, which he held responsible for the growth of Soviet power and influence in the region. Although the Islamic Front never cohered into an effective group, Saudi Arabian diplomatic influence steadily increased through the combination of King Feisal's personality and growing financial power. But the country was militarily weak and in 1966 it began a major rearmament programme.

Saudi Arabia's role was enhanced by Egypt's disastrous defeat in 1967. The aftermath of the war brought a settlement over Yemen and an end to the open quarrel with Egypt. But the mistrust was too deep for a real reconciliation with Egypt during Nasser's lifetime.

The main handicap to King Feisal's foreign policy was the difficulty of reconciling militant anti-communism with anti-Zionism for as long as the United States remained the main ally of Israel and the Soviet Union supported the Arabs. This was a notably inhibiting factor in the aftermath of the 1967 war. Rather than assist in creating a new pan-Arab alliance, King Feisal concentrated on the cause of Islamic unity and he scored a diplomatic success in 1969 with the holding of a first meeting of Islamic heads of state in Rabat, following the fire which destroyed one of the most sacred Muslim sites, the al-Aqsa mosque in Israeli-held Jerusalem. But when an Arab summit was finally held in Rabat in the following December, Saudi Arabia made a large contribution to its failure by refusing to increase by the amount they desired its financial support for the Arab nations confronting Israel. The Saudi government and private individuals continued to give considerable help to the Palestine guerrilla organization al-Fatah, which King Feisal pointedly preferred to its Marxist rivals such as the Popular Front for the Liberation of Palestine. But King Feisal ignored demands from the socialist Arab states that he should take the lead in using 'the oil weapon' in the Arab cause. The official view of the Saudi government was that oil and politics should never be mixed.

The common view in the West was that King Feisal would not change this attitude, either because he could not risk alienating the United States or because in practice the oil weapon could never be used effectively. It had been tried in 1967 and notably failed. But several new factors were ignored or discounted. The first was that after the death of President Nasser a new and much friendlier relationship between Egypt and Saudi Arabia had developed. King Feisal showed that he was prepared to forgive Egypt's continuing close relationship with the Soviet Union which he had never fully accepted in Nasser's time. At the same time, Aramco had announced vast expansion plans for the 1970s. In 1971 the US was importing about 30 per cent of its oil from abroad – mainly from Venezuela. By the 1980s this would increase to nearly 60 per cent and most of the difference would be coming from Saudi Arabia. This meant both that the American economy was rapidly becoming dependent on Saudi oil supplies and that the Arab states were increasing their pressure on Saudi Arabia to make use of the oil weapon. All the warning signs were ignored in Washington. When the king and his ministers began to say in public for the first time that Saudi Arabia could not indefinitely ignore United States' wholehearted support for Israel, this was discounted. Aramco officials who had been trying to reinforce the warning in Washington cabled back disconsolately to their president in Saudi Arabia that there was 'a large degree of disbelief' that any drastic action was imminent, adding, 'Some believe that His Majesty is calling wolf where no wolf exists except in his imagination.'[1]

So it was that when in the October 1973 Arab–Israeli war Saudi Arabia not only contributed to the Arab oil strategy but took the lead in forming it, the West was taken by surprise. The full significance of what had happened was not immediately realized; the news was dominated by the fighting and Dr Kissinger's subsequent peace missions. Eventually it was understood that Saudi Arabia, having taken the lead, would never be able to relinquish it however much it might wish to, because its oil resources are so much greater than any other state outside the communist world. Almost overnight Saudi Arabia's Oil Minister Shaikh Yamani became a figure of major

1. Anthony Sampson, 'The Oil War', *Observer*, 17 November 1974.

international importance. Any one of his statements was worthy of a headline.

It should have been apparent even before the 1973 Arab–Israeli war that Saudi Arabia was destined for international stardom as a financial superpower. The quadrupling of oil prices in 1973–4 merely hastened the process. In 1975 Saudi Arabia was not only by far the single biggest oil exporter in the non-communist world, with one third of its proved reserves, but its financial reserves were greater than those of the United States and Japan combined. The awesome responsibilities that this involved for the health of the entire world economy could not easily be absorbed but there was no time to wait.

The tragic assassination of King Feisal on 25 March 1975 at the hand of a deranged nephew was an appalling loss for the Kingdom. The austere grandeur of his personality had eased the tension between his people's inward-looking traditionalism and the needs of the twentieth century. He managed to combine his own deep conservatism with an understanding and acceptance of the revolutionary changes that were required if the Kingdom was to become as technically advanced and productive as the industrialized countries. His pride as an Arab and Muslim meant that he could wish for nothing less. He always insisted that Islam was fully compatible with material progress. As he said on one occasion:

> Our religion requires us to progress and advance and to bear the burden of the highest tradition and best manners. What is called progressiveness in the world today and what reformers are calling for, be it social, human, or economic progress, is all embodied in the Islamic religion and laws.

He and his successors have tried to ensure that all but ultra-reactionary opinion in the Kingdom accepted the changes. Often this meant compromise which more impatient Saudis find hard to accept. Thus King Feisal established the principle, often against fierce opposition, that girls have as much right to education as boys with the result that by the early 1980s girls made up nearly 40 per cent of the Kingdom's 1·5 million students and nearly 30 per cent of the 54,000 receiving higher education. Yet Saudi Arabian women remain highly secluded and segregated outside their immediate family circles – forbidden to drive cars or travel without a male relative and excluded from all types of employment which involve working with men. In this respect Saudi Arabia has changed more slowly than any of the other Arab Gulf states. In a country bent on rapidly developing a self-sustaining economy but with an acute labour shortage the segregation of women would appear self-defeating. It can only be justified as giving absolute priority to the retention of traditional values to avoid any loss of Saudi identity.

On King Feisal's death his brother Crown Prince Khaled succeeded smoothly and a younger brother Prince Fahd became Crown Prince. Although held in much affection, the country-loving King Khaled was in poor health and had little appetite for political action. Prince Fahd held the main responsibility for running the government, as he continued to do when he succeeded on King Khaled's death in June 1982. Another brother, Prince Abdullah, long commander of the National Guard, became Crown Prince. The philoprogenitive Ibn Saud insured that the succession could continue for many more years in his sons' generation. There have been no changes in the broad lines of King Feisal's policies since his death, although King Fahd is less socially conservative and has a more easy-going temperament than his brother.

The Saudi monarchy is not an autocracy because the huge family rules through a consensus of its members which they know must be preserved if the dynasty is to survive. Moreover, although care has been taken to spread the family's power throughout the Kingdom by appointing some of the younger princes to provincial governorships and key posts in the armed forces, an increasing share of executive power has had to be delegated to non-royal technocrat ministers of whom Shaikh Yamani happens to be the best known internationally. On the other hand, the family has long delayed introducing any form of constitutional government or representative institutions. ('The Koran is our constitution. Why do we need anything else?' King Feisal replied when I asked him about this in 1966.) In January 1980 the then Crown Prince Fahd announced that Basic Statistics of Government would be issued and a Majlis al-Shura, or Consultative Council, which is in the best Islamic tradition, would be appointed but four years later these were still being considered.

The Saudi government's huge national and international responsibilities mean that major decisions can never be long delayed. Sometimes these responsibilities conflict in an obvious way. As a major donor of international aid, contributor to the International Monetary Fund and above all as the 'swing producer' within OPEC – that is the one which can affect the entire world fuel situation by the level of its output – Saudi Arabia has a large stake in the health of the world economy. In 1979 the Kingdom was producing 8 million barrels of oil a day, selling off far more of its precious and exhaustible national resource than it needed to. Four years later, when its production was down to 5 million barrels a day, its national development plan required a larger output. In each case the principle was the same – the overriding need for stable oil prices.

The broad lines of Saudi Arabia's development were laid down in the 1960s. These were first to give the country a modern infrastructure and then to make use of the Kingdom's enormous resources of oil and gas as the basis for a variety of other industries. The state had to initiate but the objective remains to hand over an increasing share of the economy to the private sector.

By the mid 1980s, with the help of the colossal increase in revenues in the previous decade, much of the infrastructure was in place. The vast and lightly populated desert Kingdom has been knit together through the building of ports, roads, a telecommunications system and a network of airports (those at Jedda and Riyadh being among the world's largest). The number of passengers carried by Saudia, the national airline, increased more than tenfold between 1971 and 1979 as even elderly Saudis in remote areas became as accustomed to taking planes as Western commuters use buses and trains. At the same time two wholly new industrial cities, Jubail on the Gulf and Yanbu on the Red Sea, which are the core of Saudi Arabia's development and are costing more than the putting of a man on the moon, were already more than half in place. All of Saudi Arabia's exploding cities have to be supplied with water, mainly seawater desalinated at vast cost. The pace of development has inevitably caused some strain and overheating and the government was not entirely displeased that a fall in revenues in 1983 required some lowering of expectations.

Apart from the level of the country's oil output – which is fundamental but, as we have seen, partly decided on outside considerations – Saudi planners and their advisers are faced by a series of complex choices and it is not surprising if there is disagreement. There is the question of how far should the Kingdom continue to depend on the immigrants who now form half the labour force. Projections vary widely as to the future increase in Saudi Arabia's own 6 million people. The delicate question of the employment of Saudi Arabia's women has been mentioned. There is also the problem, which all the wealthier oil states have had to face, of maintaining a work-ethic among Saudi youth after years of easy profits and lavish government subsidies which are taken for granted. The Saudi technocrat ministers constantly preach that the country's resources are not inexhaustible. One major decision on economic strategy that has been made remains both controversial and significant. Enormous subsidies to farmers meant that in 1981 Saudi Arabia produced $1·5 billion worth of food out of the $6·5 billion it consumed and the proportion is growing. Astonishingly, the desert Kingdom was due to produce a surplus of wheat in 1984. The US Secretary of State for Agriculture pointed out in 1983 that Saudi Arabia could import cereals from the Middle West at a quarter of the price. His Saudi counterpart tartly replied by pointing out that it was not only a matter of economics but of national interest. The United States itself is spending billions on developing high-cost fuel alternatives to cheap Saudi oil.

Saudi Arabia's responsibility among the Arab states is one that it cannot shed even if it should wish to. It has been greatly enhanced by the isolation of Egypt. King Fahd no doubt wishes that expectations of his influence were not so high – whether in urging the United States to restrain Israel or Syria to restrain itself. (In dealings with the United States especially, King Fahd's natural affability may be less effective than King Feisal's reserved hauteur.) Saudi Arabia has always seen itself as mediator and conciliator among the Arabs rather than as a didactic leader. This was the thinking behind the Saudi peace plan adopted at Fez in 1982. The Saudi mediating role in Lebanon in 1983 was skilfully and vigorously conducted and effective. But the Arabs will still look longingly to Saudi Arabia for the kind of daring and decisive gesture it made in unsheathing the oil weapon in 1973.

Saudi Arabia's friendship with the United States, which contrives to contribute so much to the country's development and military defences, is a cause of difficulty to the régime, partly, but not exclusively, because of the American alliance with Israel. For those Saudis who detest the country's trend and regard industrialization and the import of Western technology, with all that they bring with them, as anti-Islamic and therefore evil, any identification with the United States symbolizes what is wrong. The young fanatics who so shook the régime by seizing the Great Mosque in Mecca in November 1979 shared most of the views of Ayatollah Khomeini even if he did not directly inspire their uprising. As so often happens in such cases, many Saudis who were horrified by their violence and sacrilege, could understand and even sympathize with their motives.

At the time the incident led to absurdly detailed Western forecasts of the imminent collapse of the House of Saud. It is true that there is no shortage of internal and external threats to its survival. Sudden wealth and the breakneck pace of development have created formidable social tensions. They have spawned some corruption at the highest levels. In contrast with the smaller Arab Gulf states with their tiny populations there are still great disparities of wealth and status among Saudi citizens. Yet when all this is said, the true cause for astonishment is the extent to which the deeply traditional semi-nomadic society of a generation ago has been able to assimilate the changes with so little loss of identity. Saudis who commute between their country and the West might be expected to suffer from schizophrenia but few of them do. My own forecast is that if revolution comes in Saudi Arabia it will be created by Saudi women. But this will not be for tomorrow.

The Gulf Cooperation Council

On 25 May 1981 the heads of state of Saudi Arabia, Kuwait, Bahrain, Qatar, the UAE and Oman met in Abu Dhabi to establish a confederation – the Cooperation Council for the Arab States of the Gulf (GCC).

This could be seen as inaugurating a series of practicable steps towards the kind of unity the Arab states had so often envisaged but failed to achieve. The threat provided by the Iranian revolution (with its notable effect on the Shiite minorities in the six Arab states), the subsequent Iraq–Iran war, the alarming Middle East situation and the threat of Soviet expansionism from Afghanistan all acted as catalysts for the creation of the GCC, but there were strong arguments in its favour apart from security anxieties. Iraq, which was already participating in various bodies for regional cooperation among the Arab Gulf states, at first protested that such a regional grouping threatened the principle of unity of all the Arabs. But Iraq's involvement in the war with Iran and GCC members' contributions to its war effort meant that Iraq was hardly in a position to press its complaints. For their part the GCC members stressed the similarity of their political and social structures which by implication excluded Iraq. (In fact the Iraqis, in their Western suits, had always looked the odd men out at the regional meetings they attended.)

The GCC countries chose as their secretary-general an outstanding and forceful Kuwaiti diplomat, Abdullah Bishara, and made Riyadh their headquarters. At the outset they declared simply their intention to coordinate their economic, political, cultural and security efforts. As the secretary-general pointed out on the GCC's second anniversary, the GCC Charter 'does not clearly define the political theory of the GCC'. But he added that the Secretariat had 'come to the conclusion that the consensus is for a confederal structure . . . based on the fact that each country wants to retain its own characteristics'.

There are many points of method and objectives which resemble those of the European Economic Community, although with the important difference that the six have a common language and culture. The Supreme Council, formed of the heads of state, meets annually and the Ministerial Council of the six Foreign Ministers, on whom much of the political burden for the GCC's functioning rests, at least every six months. The Unified Economic Agreement of June 1981 looks forward to the creation in stages of an Arab Gulf Common Market. This would offer free trade throughout the member states and give GCC nationals the right to move, work and reside anywhere in the region while enjoying equal rights of ownership, inheritance, movement of capital and freedom to exercise their chosen economic activity. The first stage towards this goal was reached on 1 March 1983. Progress has also been made towards coordinating investment and development programmes to avoid duplication and in negotiating collective economic and commercial agreements on behalf of the six. Since between them the six own half the world's known oil reserves which they can produce at the lowest cost, they form a formidable economic power despite their relative lack of development. The decline in oil prices only adds to their incentive for joint action.

Wealth does not provide military security. In this case the contrary is true because the Gulf oil fields are such vulnerable, as well as valuable, targets. The GCC members are conscious of their military weakness despite their heavy arms expenditure, among the highest *per capita* in the world. In a deteriorating situation in the region they held joint manoeuvres which they called 'Shield of the Peninsula' in the UAE's Western Desert. But the members have remained opposed to the granting of any permanent land-base for American troops. After the United States concluded a security agreement with Israel in December 1983 it was inconceivable that they would change their minds.

18. The People's Democratic Republic of Yemen: the First Marxist Arab State?

The National Liberation Front led by Qahtan al-Shaabi which triumphed in 1967 so sensationally both over the shaikhs and sultans in South Arabia and over its rivals of the Front for the Liberation of South Yemen, was faced with a daunting prospect. No newly independent state has started life in less promising circumstances. Before independence the mainstay of the economy had been Aden Port and the income from the British military base of about £11 million a year. Now the base was evacuated and with the closure of the Suez Canal after the June 1967 war the bunkering trade was reduced to a trickle. The merchants, money-changers and bankers – many of them foreigners who had been frightened away by the violence which preceded independence – had closed their shutters for good. The interior was better off only because it had never been anything but desperately poor and backward; only 1 per cent of the land was cultivable and yet 75 per cent of the population lived off agriculture. Little of Aden's wealth had ever percolated into the hinterland and the tiny flow of British aid, much of which was spent on building up the South Arabian forces, had hardly begun to affect the problems of social and economic development of the interior before independence. Britain had promised to increase this aid to £60 million for the first three years after independence but this was when it expected to be dealing with a federation of South Arabian sultans under its patronage. To the nationalist and non-aligned Republic of South Yemen Britain would offer no more than £1·8 million, which amounted to £1·25 million after the deduction of South Yemen's financial obligation to Britain.

Qahtan al-Shaabi's first government consisted of young men with views ranging from Maoism to Nasser-type Arab nationalism. His policies were based on Nasserist socialist ideas: development with a combination of state and private capital under state control, and Egyptian-style agrarian reform which meant the distribution of lands seized from the shaikhs and sultans to individual peasant families. Unfortunately for Qahtan, South Yemen did not have any bargaining power to secure the amount of foreign aid which alone might have made this policy viable. The communist states offered a little help but

Western countries saw no advantage in offering aid to such an aggressively neutralist young government while relations with the conservative Arab oil states, such as Saudi Arabia, were outstandingly bad. In the countryside the peasants had neither the capital nor expertise to farm the newly redistributed lands on their own.

All this tended to the advantage of the pro-Chinese communist elements in the National Liberation Front, who had established their own power base in the eastern region from which to challenge Qahtan's authority. In June 1969 these left-wing elements ousted Qahtan al-Shaabi from power to establish the first régime in the Arab world with an openly communist flavour.

Sweeping nationalization measures brought most of the country under state control and an Agrarian Reform Law was passed. The government used Marxist slogans and displayed posters of communist leaders. A new Family Law did much to emancipate women who began to work beside men in factories and offices and to hold senior posts. Yet the régime was still some way from being fully communist. A constitution published in August 1970 declared the state to be Islamic and the government continued – and still continues – to uphold Arab nationalist causes – especially over Palestine – in a way which is not consistent with communist theory or practice. There was a division between the President Rubayyi Ali, who made several moves to improve relations with the conservative Arab oil states, and Abd Al-Fattah Ismail, the more doctrinaire secretary-general of the National Front. To counterbalance the army, which Ismail regarded as conservative, Ismail formed a Cuban-trained People's Militia and proposed merging all political forces into a single Marxist Vanguard party. Faced with a full Marxist takeover the President tried to rally his supporters. The crisis came to a head in June 1978 following the murder of President Ghashmi of the Yemen Arab Republic. The bomb which killed President Ghashmi was carried by an envoy of President Rubayyi Ali but it may have been planted to discredit him. It provoked a violent struggle in Aden in which Ismail was victorious. President Rubayyi Ali was tried and executed; Ismail became head of state and chairman of the new Yemeni Socialist Party which took a strongly pro-Moscow line.

The importance of Aden to Moscow greatly increased during the 1970s. While the Soviet Union wished to support President Mengistu's Marxist régime in Ethiopia its relations with Ethiopia's neighbours Somalia and Sudan had deteriorated. Under Soviet persuasion, the PDRY not only became the only Arab state to withdraw support from Eritrean nationalists but sent some troops to fight with the Ethiopians and allowed Aden to become an important staging-post for Cuban troops.

However, even after Ismail's seizure of power in 1978, the PDRY was not a fully-fledged communist state controlled by an orthodox Marxist party to be compared with Cuba or Afghanistan, and the Soviet Union did not regard it as such. This was made clear in April 1980 when Ismail was ousted as secretary-general and President and replaced by the much less dogmatically pro-Moscow Prime Minister, Ali Nasser al-Hassani. The Soviet Union did not intervene. Ismail had lost popularity precisely because of his doctrinaire theoretical approach which Arabs generally find unappealing. (It was even said that President Brezhnev regarded him as too extreme.) Soviet aid to the PDRY's economy and military defences had been vital but was still meagre and effectively precluded aid from the Arab oil states. These remained wary of the Aden régime which continued to belong to the far left but the way was open for a real improvement in relations. In 1982 this bore fruit in an agreement to end the virtual state of war with Oman which had existed since independence. Marxist theory and practice have brought the PDRY certain advantages: the partial emancipation of women and the mobilization of the country's meagre resources for essential public works (such as road-building and irrigation) and creditable progress in spreading health and education services into the neglected interior, but with all the concomitant disadvantages of the suppression of individualism and greyness in the quality of life. There was a concerted effort to bring ideology into the lives of the whole population.

There has been constant friction between the two régimes in north and south Yemen. In 1972 and again in 1979 this broke out into open warfare. Fighting ended through Libyan mediation the first time and Kuwaiti the second but on both occasions the truce was accompanied by resounding declarations that the two countries would move towards unity. This apparently unlikely ideal is backed by a real feeling among most Yemenis that their country has been absurdly and artificially divided. Powerful forces oppose unity. Saudi Arabia does not wish to see Aden's Marxism extended to the Kingdom's neighbour, while the Soviet Union has similar but opposite reasons for not wanting to see its closest ally in the Arab World absorbed by another state, although there are signs that it has reduced its opposition to unity. The only certainty is that the objective of unity will continue to be discussed between the two régimes and will not be allowed to die. However, it is unlikely to be achieved unless the character of either or both régimes substantially changes.

19. The Yemen Arab Republic: the Awakened Recluse

Yemen, in the extreme south-western corner of Arabia, rivals Oman as the most secluded and inaccessible part of the Arab world. Also, like Oman, it is one of the few regions of the peninsula to have a regular rainfall and parts are therefore green and fertile.

Yemen was not always so detached from the outside world. Although no real evidence has been found for a Queen of Sheba, a kingdom of Sheba or Saba existed in the first millennium B.C. and prospered on the spice trade to the east. To the Romans, Yemen, with its flourishing agriculture and forests, was *Arabia Felix.* However, some time in the sixth century A.D. the great Marib Dam on which much of its farming was based broke down; the pastures and the forests disappeared and Yemen entered a period of long slow decline.

The ruling dynasty of royal imams, which was to last for 1,100 years, was founded in the ninth century A.D. They were Zaidis, a moderate Shia sect, who in the twentieth century formed about 40 per cent of the population of Yemen and inhabited mainly the mountainous interior. The remaining 60 per cent was mostly Sunni Muslim Arabs of the Shafei school who lived on the coastal plain along the Red Sea. Although a minority, the warlike Zaidi tribesmen dominated the more settled and industrious Shafeis. Although Yemen was conquered by the Turks in 1517 the Zaidi interior never came under stable Ottoman control, and after Turkey's defeat in 1918 the imam soon established his authority over the Shafei areas. Yemen became a unified and independent kingdom under the Imam Yahya who was both temporal and spiritual head of his people.

The imam's system of rule ensured that the country remained in a medieval condition. In his extreme autocracy every item of government business depended on his personal decisions and all outside influences were excluded as far as possible. He managed the tribes through a system of alliances and the hallowed Yemeni tradition of taking hostages, whereby one or more of the relations of the heads of important tribes would be held in a prison school maintained by the imam as a guarantee of the tribe's good behaviour.

Many of the vigorous and enterprising Yemenis refused to accept the stagnation of life at home. They emigrated to establish thriving commercial communities in Aden, Singapore and Indonesia. In 1948 discontent caused a revolt in which the eighty-year-old Yahya was assassinated, but his son Ahmad soon succeeded in recovering the throne. His method of government resembled his father's with an additional dose of sadistic cruelty. He trusted no one among his own people. However, he was wise enough to realize that he could not entirely exclude the influences of the new nationalist current that was sweeping the Arab world.

Accordingly in 1958 he attached Yemen to the new United Arab Republic of Syria and Egypt and he secured Arab League backing for his claims against the British-supported sultans in South Arabia. But the alliance with Nasser's Egypt was too bizarre to last. When the Syrian–Egyptian union broke up the Imam Ahmad showed his delight, Nasser declared the UAR federation with Yemen dissolved and launched a propaganda offensive against him.

Opposition from Yemenis in exile and inside the country was growing. They included both progressive reformers who wanted Yemen to join the twentieth century and conservative traditionalists who resented his family's autocracy. In March 1961 Ahmad narrowly escaped assassination and there was an outbreak of sabotage in the towns. Though ailing and rheumatic, the aged despot with piercing eyes succeeded in holding on to power until his death in September 1961.

His son and successor Imam Badr was less fortunate. A far less formidable and ruthless man than his father, he had tried to introduce a few liberal reforms during the latter's absence from the country for medical treatment, which Ahmad had promptly cancelled on his return. On his accession he announced the release of political prisoners and other conciliatory measures. But this was not enough. A group of army officers led by Brigadier Sallal, determined to get rid of the monarchy which had such an atrocious history of oppression, rose in revolt eight days after Ahmad's death, seized Sanaa and declared a republic. But they suffered a fatal setback when they failed to capture Badr, who escaped to loyal tribes in the north and raised the flag of counter-revolution. As a concerted move to destroy the new republic with the help of Saudi Arabia and Jordan began, Sallal appealed to Nasser for help and a large Egyptian expeditionary force arrived almost immediately.

This was the start of a bitter royalist–republican civil war which ebbed and flowed across the northern and eastern parts of the country for the next seven years. The Egyptians, inexperienced both in mountain guerrilla warfare and in dealing with unfamiliar Yemeni tribesmen, suffered heavy losses. They sent reinforcements so that at times they had nearly 50,000 troops in the country. These were enough to ensure that the principal towns and roads remained in republican hands, but the republic never seemed to be strong enough to enable the Egyptians to withdraw. The task of building up a regular army from the unmartial urban Yemenis was difficult, while generous subsidies to the fighting tribesmen were not enough to ensure their continued loyalty to the republic, especially when they could always be outbid by the superior financial resources of Saudi Arabia. (President Nasser declared once in exasperation that he could not cope with Yemenis 'who are republicans in the morning and royalists in the evening'.) It proved impossible to form a stable republican government because of the difficulty of reconciling the traditional xenophobic independence of the Yemenis with their heavy dependence on Egyptian support.

In December 1962 the US recognized the Yemeni republic (followed by fifty nations but not by Britain) in the hope that it would be secure enough for Egyptian troops to be withdrawn. Various attempts to mediate between the two sides ended in failure.

Finally, as a consequence of the 1967 war, President Nasser decided to come to terms with Saudi Arabia and withdraw his troops from Yemen. The royalists launched an offensive against Sanaa but the republicans somewhat surprisingly rallied and succeeded in lifting the siege. The royalists became divided and disillusioned and the moderate republicans who had replaced Sallal after the Egyptian withdrawal came to terms with King Feisal, who cut off his aid to the royalists. This made it possible to end the civil war in April 1970 with a compromise which retained the republic but brought some of the former royalist leaders (but no members of the royal family) into the government. Saudi Arabia recognized the republic, which was forced to rely heavily upon it for financial aid.

The civil war was doubly tragic because the overthrow of the monarchy provided an opportunity for alleviating the sufferings of the Yemeni people. The tyranny of the Imam Ahmad and his father had kept them ignorant, diseased and undernourished. In 1962 in a population of 5 million there were less than 50,000 boys in schools of any kind and there were no schools for girls at all; only a few of the privileged females learned to read the Koran at home. There was only one hospital and this, according to the harrowing description of a French lady doctor who worked there in the 1950s, was unworthy of the name.[1] The most common diseases were tuberculosis in the mountain areas and malaria and amoebic dysentery in the Red Sea plain; other parasitic diseases and syphilis were also common. Although almost any kind of crop can be grown in Yemen on the different levels between the tropical Red Sea plain and the mountain plateaux, the impoverished condition of the farmers and the total lack of roads to move food around the country meant that virtually the whole population was undernourished. Over the years the most valuable cash crop – the famous Yemeni 'moka' coffee – has been replaced in many areas by the planting of *qat*, a laurel-like shrub whose leaves are chewed as a narcotic by most of the population. It ruins the digestive system but provides temporary relief from the misery and tedium of existence.

After 1962 a start could be made in the republican areas on building roads, schools and clinics with a trickle of aid from Egypt and other Arab states, but little could be done while the war continued. In royalist-held areas the situation was appalling.

In December 1970 a new permanent constitution provided for a Consultative Council, partially elected and partially appointed by the President, to be the country's supreme legislative authority. It was hardly surprising that the new republic proved difficult to govern. There are three main political groups in the country: the tribal chiefs, supported by their tribes, the conservative *ulama*, and the younger generation of the towns who include a variety of nationalist/progressive groups. Of these the tribes generally have the support of Saudi Arabia and deplore any move towards union with southern Yemen while it remains under the left-wing PDRY régime. The younger generation, on the other hand, deplores excessive Saudi influence and looks more to union with the south. The failure of the moderate President Abdul Rahman Iriani to cope with the country's political and economic difficulties led to a military coup in June 1974 headed by Colonel Ibrahim al-Hamdi who suspended the Consultative Council and introduced a new provisional constitution under which he headed a military Command Council. President al-Hamdi had a background as a *qadi*, or religious judge, which gave him an advantage in his dealings with conservative elements. A man of considerable political skill, he had some success in unifying the country despite the opposition of powerful leaders who were jealous of their traditional authority, until he was assassinated in October 1977 when

1. See C. Feyein, *A French Doctor in the Yemen*, London, 1957.

he was about to visit Aden. His assailants were unknown but thought to have feared a move towards unity with the south. He was smoothly succeeded by his Vice-President Colonel Ahmad Ghashmi who again introduced a form of representative government in an elected Constituent People's Assembly. President Ghashmi in turn was assassinated in June 1978 when a bag carried by a special envoy of the PDRY President exploded in his presence but the system he had created survived and the Constituent Assembly elected his former close associate Major Ali Saleh to succeed him.

President Saleh had some advantage as a member of the powerful Hashed tribal confederation and he endeavoured to ease the chronic tension between northern tribesmen and urban political groups by bringing tribal leaders into the Assembly. But he was faced with formidable difficulties, including a full-scale rebellion led by dissident officers in a National Democratic Front which was backed by the PDRY. In February 1979 this erupted into full-scale war in the south which caused Saudi Arabia to place its forces on alert. The settlement reached through Arab League mediation involved a firm undertaking by both sides to negotiate the unity of the two Yemeni republics.

The régime's difficulties were far from ended. The National Democratic Front continued their forays and occupied substantial territory in the south-east. President Saleh endeavoured to pursue a delicate course of maintaining friendship with Saudi Arabia, the chief supplier of aid, while emphasizing the country's independence. In October 1981 he visited Moscow and successfully rescheduled Soviet military loans and in December he became the first North Yemen President to go to Aden. These demonstrations of Yemeni non-alignment were popular with most Yemenis who are conscious of the fact that although Saudi Arabia is immensely richer and more powerful, they have their own proud history and are more numerous.

In contrast to the South, North Yemen has opted since independence for a liberal economic system which was probably the only one possible in view of the country's loose-knit unity. Revenue collection is extremely difficult and the government is chronically short of funds. Economic development has depended on foreign aid and remittances from to 1 to 2 million Yemenis working abroad, mainly in Saudi Arabia. In 1978–9 the enormous trade deficit of $1,402 billion was offset by an equally startling $1,423 billion in workers' remittances and the country had a small balance of payments surplus, although the situation has since deteriorated. The emigration of workers created a shortage of skilled and unskilled labour at home while the huge inflow of funds fuelled inflation. Some real progress has, however, been achieved in overcoming the backlog of neglect although much of this is confined to the southern triangle between Sanaa, Taez and Hodeida, the country's main port on the Red Sea. Unfortunately, while imports have soared with the inflow of emigrants' remittances, production of the main export crops such as coffee and cotton has fallen. Only the cultivation of *qat* has flourished. A road network, the starting point for all development, has been laid and thousands of schools built where before there were none; but the task of educating the population in which 47 per cent is of school age is nonetheless more than formidable.

One of the most constructive developments has been the spread of Local Development Associations (LDAs) which, as their name implies, are independently conceived and organized although they rely on the government and foreign aid as well as the locally raised Islamic *zakat* for much of their financing. By the early 1980s, there were more than two hundred scattered throughout the country engaged in constructing roads, schools and clinics and carrying out water projects. An imaginative new government plan linked to the LDAs' aims to tackle the country's gigantic health problem by providing young villagers who are chosen by their local communities with six months' training as health workers or midwives. They then carry out vaccinations and provide basic advice on matters of health and hygiene to their communities. The alternative would be to swallow up resources in providing advanced health care to the Yemeni minority who live in cities. This scheme has already proved successful enough to serve as a model throughout the Arabian Peninsula.

Yemen's present poverty and backwardness do not entirely conceal the reasons why it was *Arabia Felix* to the Romans. The climate on the high plateaux, where three quarters of the people live, is healthy and benign; the land only needs proper cultivation to produce an abundant variety of fruit and vegetables. Above all, it is a country with a unique personality, whether in its astonishing landscape of mountain-perched villages and skyscraper mud palaces decorated with chalk or in people whose long seclusion from the world has only fostered their independence and alertness of mind. Some of this personality must be destroyed by the impact of the twentieth century, but much will surely remain.

20. Syria: the Heart of Arabism

Few parts of the world have been more disputed than the ancient land of Syria. Egyptians, Babylonians, Hittites, Persians, Greeks, Romans, Arabs and Turks fought across it and in turn made it part of their empires. Throughout history, whenever the régimes in Cairo and Baghdad had enough military power they tried to extend their influence in Syria at the other's expense. In the First World War Britain and France discussed secretly how Syria should be partitioned between them, and after the Second World War the United States and the Soviet Union struggled to prevent it from moving into the other's satellite system. It is no cause for surprise that the people of Syria have developed a high level of political sensitivity.

Today the Syrians see themselves as the vanguard of modern Arab nationalism, the movement which originated in the last years of the Ottoman Empire and gathered strength under Feisal's short-lived kingdom of Syria and the twenty-five years of French rule which followed. But the burning nationalism of the Syrians was not enough to give their republic stability when they finally achieved independence in 1945. Their sense of national unity, which emerged in response to foreign oppression, was only intermittent and superficial. While the majority felt that Syria was a central part of the greater Arab nation from which it had been artificially divided by imperialism, there was also a strong local sense of community, which the French had encouraged, among the minorities in parts of Syria – the 160,000 Druzes centred on the Jebel Druze and the 500,000 Alawites of the Latakia mountains. The people of Aleppo, with their large Christian minority, disputed the primacy of Damascus. Either way, there was little sense of loyalty towards the government of the Syrian republic or the European-style parliamentary system. Barely four years after independence Colonel Husni Zaim's briefly successful *putsch* inaugurated a series of military coups and counter-coups which caused Syria to become a byword for political instability. Syrian régimes were as short lived as the cabinets of the French Fourth Republic. The news agencies hardly bothered to report each time the tanks rolled into Damascus to oust the government from power.

During the 1950s political leadership passed gradually from the hands of the old-style nationalist politicians to more radical, neutralist and anti-western elements represented by the Baathists (see p. 261). In 1958 the Baathists sought protection from the hostile pressures which they saw arrayed against them through a merger with Egypt under the triumphant banner of Nasserism. The union collapsed after three-and-a-half years in bitterness and recrimination but the Syrians were deeply unhappy that they, the torch-bearers of Arab unity, should have ended the first attempt to put it into practice. No Syrian politician accepted the insulting title of 'secessionist' which Egypt hurled against them.

When the Baathists recovered power in 1963 from the weak and shame-faced régime which followed the secession, Syria still did not find stability. Since Arab unity is the essence of the Baathists' creed, they had to declare themselves ready to enter a new union with Egypt and Iraq, where their fellow Baathists had also just taken power. But all the reasons why the first union with Egypt had failed remained and this one died before it was born. A link with Iraq alone might have been possible but there the Baathists were ousted from power before the year was out. The Syrians were left on their own, more sensitive and difficult than ever. Three years later the Syrian Baathists split and a more radical group seized power in a coup which for the first time in Syria's modern history involved serious bloodshed. The original ideological founders and organizers of the Baath party, Michel Aflaq and Salah Bitar went into exile. It was as if a neo-communist state were to have repudiated both Marx and Lenin, and many Arabs felt that only the Syrians could have been so perverse.

A remarkable feature of this new régime was that it was dominated by men of the minorities – Alawites and Druzes – rather than the Sunni Muslim majority who provided Syria's political leadership in the first years of independence. Soon the Druzes were ousted and the Alawites were left in control. It is a strange situation, for the Alawites, an extremist Shia sect who believe that the Prophet's son-in-law Ali was an incarnation of God Himself, in the past formed the poorest and least educated social stratum in Syria. Alawite girls were widely employed as maidservants in middle-class Syrian households. But it was because political leadership and the civilian professions were largely closed to them that many Alawites chose a military career and became a dominant group within the armed forces. Since 1966 their communal solidarity has helped to maintain their dominance. This curious régime had no outstanding figures but consisted of a handful of young civilian and military Baathists – several of them doctors who had turned to politics from medicine. Its aspiring *éminence grise* was Salah Jedid, an ex-colonel who preferred to exercise power with the maximum anonymity. During this period Syria showed symptoms of emotional instability which verged on paranoia. While it was on the worst possible terms with all its potential allies in a new war with Israel – Egypt, Jordan and Iraq – it did everything it could to make such a war inevitable. It openly supported the Palestinian guerrillas in their raids on Israel, and taunted Nasser for his lack of militancy. Finally the Syrians persuaded a hesitant Nasser to join in a fatal military alliance which obliged him to come to their defence but gave him no control over their actions. When the Israelis threatened reprisals the Syrians informed Egypt that they expected a full-scale attack. Because this was confirmed by both Egyptian and Soviet intelligence President Nasser took the actions which led directly to the 1967 war: he moved troops into Sinai and asked for the withdrawal of the UN Emergency Force. When the war came, the Syrians only entered the battle after the Egyptians and Jordanians had been defeated and although their troops fought hard their military command ordered the abandonment of Quneitra, the capital of the Golan Heights, some hours before it was reached by the Israelis.

Despite its patent share of responsibility for the disaster, the régime survived the war intact for a time and pursued its perverse policies. While it rejected out of hand the UN Security Council Resolution 242 or any other proposal for a political solution of the Middle East conflict it took much less energetic military action against Israel than Egypt. There was no 'war of attrition' on the Golan Heights in 1968–9. However, a split began to appear in the ranks of the Baathist-Alawite régime between Salah Jedid and the military wing led by the Defence Minister Hafez Assad. Finally Assad was provoked into action by the débâcle of September 1970 when the civilian leaders sent an armoured column without air cover into Jordan to help the Palestinian guerrillas against the Jordanian army. The intervention failed and the Syrian tanks were badly mauled by the Jordanians. It also nearly provoked US intervention and it is probable that Soviet pressure helped to force the Syrians to withdraw.

In November 1970 General Assad ousted the civilian Baathists who refused his offer to compromise with him, and took over the premiership. In the following spring he became president of the Syrian Arab Republic.

A man of remarkable qualities of leadership, he was a formidable political strategist and a daring negotiator who was also ruthless with his opponents. Although an Alawite, he was fairly successful in his early years in making himself regarded as the representative of all the Syrians rather than of one interest or group. The Syrian people were ready to welcome a more personalized rule after a period of government by faceless men. He broadened his Baathist régime by bringing in some Nasserists, communists and independents. But various centres of opposition remained, notably in Sunni Muslim opinion which is strong in the central Hama region. When in 1973 a new constitution was decreed which for the first time failed to declare that Islam was the religion of the state, there were serious disturbances. The Baathists compromised by agreeing that the head of state must be a Muslim.

Over the years the opposition to President Assad's rule led him to place increasing reliance on those he could trust – that is his fellow-Alawites and among them his own clan or family. His brother Rifaat, at the head of the special Defence Brigade, became a second power in the land. His ubiquitous security services, dominated by Alawites, responded to the campaign of assassination and sabotage carried out by the régime's opponents with equal ferocity. This culminated in the horror of Hama where, in February 1982, 500 fighters of the Muslim Brotherhood, after calling upon the population to rise in rebellion, held the city for four days. Security forces recaptured and destroyed part of the city. Estimates of the dead ranged from 8,000 to 25,000.

It could be said that President Assad's régime survived for two main reasons, apart from his own political skill and iron nerves. One was that the extremism of his main Muslim fundamentalist opponents antagonized not only many of the Christian and Muslim minorities who make up 40 per cent of Syria's population but also some of the Sunni majority. They might detest the Alawite régime but they had good reason to fear one that would be dominated by the Muslim Brotherhood. A united opposition front to President Assad was therefore difficult to form. An additional factor was that President Assad's tactical alliance with the Khomeini régime in Iran, while antagonizing Iraq, neutralized some Muslim fundamentalist opinion in Syria. The other reason for President Assad's survival related to external factions and Syria's focal position in the region. As Egypt withdrew from the Arab front and Jordan remained strictly non-belligerent, Syria was alone in confronting Israel. The other Arab states had little alternative to backing President Assad. They were aware that Syria was also pursuing its own ends in the region, in attempting to dominate and control both Lebanon and the Palestinian liberation movement. Some saw this as an attempt to re-create the Greater Syria of pre-1914, but they had to acknowledge that Syria alone, with its defences strengthened by the Soviet Union, stood against an American-backed Israeli hegemony in the region. It was Saudi Arabian aid which was helping Syria to purchase Soviet arms.

President Assad's exceptional negotiating skill enabled him to play a strong game even with a weak hand. His decision to intervene in force in Lebanon in June 1976 to stop the fighting and prevent Lebanon's partition, involved heavy political and military risks and set Syria against its former allies among the Palestinians. But in October he succeeded in having the other Arab states endorse the presence of 20,000 Syrian troops in Lebanon as the major part of the Arab Deterrent Force to keep the peace. There was no alternative. The strain of maintaining a large proportion of Syria's forces in Lebanon was considerable and in 1982 they received severe punishment from the invading Israeli forces. But President Assad always considered that the risks to Syria of withdrawing from Lebanon were greater than those of remaining. The fact remained that Syria was the only Arab state in the field against Israel. In May 1983 it was successfully able to demonstrate that the United States and Israel could not push through an Israeli-Lebanese peace agreement which it regarded as undermining Syria's vital interests. The risks were enormous but were so for both sides as the United States found itself not only in danger of being embroiled in a new Vietnam in Lebanon but one in which the Soviet Union was directly involved.

At the same time President Assad was demonstrating his determination to dominate the Palestinian movement, first by supporting the rebels against Yasir Arafat's leadership of the PLO, and then by expelling Arafat from Damascus. Syrian forces backed the rebels who expelled Arafat and his 4,000 loyalists from Tripoli, their last redoubt in the region.

Many believed that President Assad had overreached himself but it was only his deteriorating health which caused some hesitation in Syrian policy in the winter of 1983–4. It was also a mark of his dominance in Syria.

The huge strain of military spending, which takes two thirds of the budget and is only partially offset by Arab and Soviet aid, does not conceal the fact that Syria has one of the greatest potentials for development of any part of the Arab world and that some progress has been made towards realizing it. The Syrian nation may have doubled from 5 to 10 million during the two decades that the Baathists have been in power but the country is still far from overpopulated.

The wealth is in agricultural land – the vast curved sweep of territory from the north-east to the south-west of the country, which is the central portion of the Fertile Crescent. The first decade of independence was a period of fast growth in the agricultural sector as private landowners brought new lands under the plough for cotton and grain. But this capital investment fell off during the 1950s with the introduction of land reform and three disastrous years of drought which coincided with the Egyptian–Syrian union of 1958–61. The Syrian economy was in need of massive investment in the still rudimentary infrastructure of roads, railways, bridges, ports and, above all, irrigation dams. Less than 10 per cent of the land was irrigated and because the rainfall is so uncertain Syria's output of cereals can vary between one year and another from half a million tons, which means that it has to import huge quantities of food, to 2 million tons, which leaves a large surplus for export.

The drive for development has therefore concentrated on creating a new infrastructure and increasing the output of the land. The great boom area on which much of this effort is concentrated is the far north-east region of al-Jezirah near the Turkish and Iraqi borders, which the Syrians like to call 'our California'. The potential wealth of this area has long been known but it has long been held back by its isolation. Now a railway has been built to link it to Aleppo and the Mediterranean coast. Here at Tabqa on the river Euphrates a vast dam, said to be the largest earth-fill dam in the world, was completed in 1978.

This will be used to restore the ancient fertility of this part of the Euphrates valley. (At present it is barren of vegetation, but in the ninth century the Caliph Haroun al-Rashid, who liked to spend his summers in nearby Raqqa, could travel all the way back to Baghdad under the shade of trees.) The 250 square mile Lake Assad created by the dam will be used to triple Syria's irrigated area by the end of the century. This helps to give the Syrians a quiet confidence about their future. As the director of the project said to me: 'We Syrians believe that before many years water will be as precious as oil and we plan to make use of every drop we can.' New dams are planned for other Syrian rivers nearer the Mediterranean, such as the Nahr al-Kabir in the Alawite mountains, to make the country self-sufficient in fruit and vegetables. (At present Syria rather surprisingly imports many of these from Lebanon.)

Under President Assad, Syria's policies remain socialist and *dirigiste*; the state retains the main responsibility for development and controls foreign and domestic trade and banking, although some limited measures were taken in the 1970s to relax currency and banking controls in order to encourage the repatriation of Syrian and Arab capital and to stimulate the private sector in various ways. The socialist system has caused the disappearance of the feudal landowning class and transferred considerable benefits to the poorer sections of the community, while promoting much of the development the country needed. At the same time it has been inefficient in many areas and created corruption on a massive scale which has been fuelled by the aid that Syria has received from the Arab states. The government has occasionally promised to tackle corruption but has done little to any effect.

The régime is highly repressive and the security forces are omnipresent. Yet even in the troubled 1980s the country gives a more relaxed and open impression than twenty years earlier when foreign visitors could notoriously expect an unsmiling and hostile reception. In the mid-1970s the Syrians began to stimulate what is potentially their biggest growth industry of all: tourism. Subsequent events have not favoured the trend but it would be hard to exaggerate what Syria has to offer.

A tenth-century traveller remarked: 'Syria is a land of blessing, a country of cheapness, abounding in fruits and peopled by holy men.' The holy men are less numerous today but they and their powerful patrons have left their memorials in every corner of the land: the great Umayyad Mosque of Damascus, Queen Zenobia's Palmyra in the Syrian desert, the Aleppo citadel, Krak des Chevaliers (the crowning achievement of the crusaders), the Roman amphitheatre of Busra. The astonishing ruins near Aleppo surrounding the pillar on which St Simeon lived and preached for thirty years form some of the largest surviving Christian monuments which antedate the medieval cathedrals of the West, and Maloula, the lovely hillside village north of Damascus, is one of the last surviving villages whose inhabitants still speak Aramaic, the language of Jesus Christ. This brief list mentions only part of the country's staggering richness in antiquities. It also leaves out the fact that Syria has some of the most beautiful and unspoiled Mediterranean coastline. This provides part of the clue to the reluctance of the Syrians, which has only just begun to change, to make themselves a tourist target. It is not only the caution and suspicion of their political outlook which has held them back from building the hotels and providing the facilities for the tourist hordes from the West who would come if they could. They have seen the example of other Mediterranean countries which are now mourning the ruin of their countryside and coastlines.

21. Lebanon: Arab Supermarket; Ruin or Reform?

All nations require a certain degree of tolerance and compromise between their different communities; for the Republic of Lebanon it is a matter of survival. When after the First World War, France decided to enlarge the old Sanjak of Lebanon, which had enjoyed special privileges in Ottoman times, to make *le Grand Liban* it was founding a new Mediterranean republic with a very special character. Lebanon remains small – half the size of Wales – but it is not, as it might have been, a tiny inward-looking Christian island in a vast Muslim Arab sea. It is a nation with a double nature: Arab and Lebanese. Some of its people are more drawn to one side or the other but experience has shown that if Lebanon is to continue to exist they cannot afford to be exclusive in their loyalties.

The question of the relative strength of the multitude of different religious communities is so politically sensitive that no national census has been taken since 1932 and none since independence.

The population has at least doubled over the past twenty years and in 1983 was estimated at about 3·4 million. Until recently there were up to 1 million non-Lebanese resident in the country of whom about 400,000 are Palestinians.

In the early years of independence it was assumed that there was a small majority of Christians over Muslims and Druzes and it was on this basis that seats in the National Assembly were always in multiples of eleven with six Christian and five Muslim. The Maronite Catholics are the largest Christian group but there are also substantial communities of Greek Orthodox, Greek Catholics, Armenian Apostolics and Catholics. Among the Muslims it has been assumed until recently that the dominant Sunnis outnumber the Shias, while about 6 per cent of the population are Druzes.

The country's political, social and economic system reflects this kaleidoscope of communities. By strict convention the President is Maronite, the Prime Minister a Sunni Muslim and the speaker of the National Assembly a Shia and there is always at least one Greek Orthodox and one Druze in the cabinet.[1]

---

1. According to a Lebanese economist even agriculture is sectarian: Maronites grow most of the apples, Sunni Muslims the citrus fruit and Greek Orthodox the olives.

The dominance of the Christian communities – especially the Maronites – in both politics and the economy (due to various factors – their schools, their contacts with Europe, the support of the French mandatory authorities) has been increasingly challenged in recent years. Lebanese Muslims have demanded and obtained more of the key posts in the civil service. Commerce is still predominantly Christian but several of the new light industries which have been such a successful feature of the Lebanese economy in recent years are owned by Muslims.

By the 1980s it was generally accepted that, owing to the higher birth rate among Muslims and the stronger Christian tendency to emigrate, there was now a majority of Muslims in the country although this could not be certain in view of the impossibility of taking a census. For similar reasons the Shiites almost certainly outnumbered the Sunnis. Christian fears of being swamped by the surrounding Muslim ocean greatly add to Lebanon's political difficulties. The suggestion of some Maronite leaders that the 1·5 million Lebanese emigrants, some two thirds of whom are Christian, should be included in the Lebanese political system is hardly realistic.

The first serious signs of trouble in the muted civil war of 1958 was not a bid by Lebanese Muslims to oust the Christians from their dominant position, although a minority of them may have seen it in this way, but a response to what they regarded as an attempt to upset the compromise on which Lebanon is based. This was embodied in the National Pact between the two communities at the outset of independence which said in effect that Lebanon was at the same time part of, and independent from, the Arab world. The year 1958 was peculiarly difficult for Lebanon. The Nasserist tide was at its height; the Arabism of Lebanese Muslims and the fears of the Christians were equally aroused. But President Chamoun's attempt to guarantee Lebanon's survival by linking it openly with the West only deepened the crisis. This was overcome by an essentially Lebanese compromise, which reinforced the National Pact. Under the wise presidency of Fuad Shihab it seemed for a time that national unity had been strengthened.

This was doubly valuable when Lebanon faced an even more severe test a decade later. Although Lebanon was not involved in the June 1967 war, anti-Western feeling among Lebanese Muslims was fiercely aroused. The subsequent rise in political and military power of the Palestinian guerrilla organizations offered a direct challenge to the Lebanese state which, unlike Syria, Egypt or Jordan, was in no position to control their activities. While most Lebanese had some sympathy with the Palestinian struggle, opinion ranged from those such as the Maronite political leaders Camille Chamoun and Pierre Gemayel who believed that the Palestinians should not infringe Lebanon's sovereignty and that the guerrillas should be excluded from Lebanese territory, to the Druze Socialist party leader Kamal Jumblatt, who felt that it was Lebanon's duty to lend them all possible assistance. All Lebanese were sharply aware of Lebanon's defencelessness in the face of Israeli reprisals and many believed that the occupation of the Litani river basin in south Lebanon was a major Zionist objective for which Palestinian guerrilla attacks from Lebanon would provide Israel with an excuse.

Clashes between the guerrillas and the Lebanese army and armed civilian groups were only prevented from deteriorating into a general conflict through a series of patched-up compromise agreements which were reached through the help of Arab mediation. The situation was made even more difficult as a result of the Jordanian army's suppression of the Palestinian guerrilla bases in Jordan in 1970–71; Lebanon became the last remaining centre of guerrilla activity and the principal target for Israel's reprisal attacks. The 1973 Arab–Israeli war worsened Lebanon's situation because it raised hopes of a solution without satisfying them. Civil war was sparked off by the murder of the Palestinian occupants of a bus in a Christian quarter of Beirut. An attempt to form a government of army officers failed; Lebanon is probably the only Arab country where such a solution can never succeed.

At first, Lebanese forces were mainly the ones involved, but from June 1975 onwards the right-wing Christian militia increasingly entered the fray against the progressives – a collation of Nasserists, Baathists and others under the leadership of Kamal Jumblatt, the Druze politician. The Palestinian leaders at first tried to keep their forces out of the civil war but were drawn in remorselessly until by January 1976 they were fully engaged on the side of the leftists. There followed a period of successes for the leftist-Palestinian forces, who at one time controlled 80 per cent of the country and reduced the rightists to an enclave around Jounieh which they made their capital. In April 1976 the Syrians began to intervene to prevent the country's partition and this led to an odd alliance between them and the Lebanese Christian right. The tide turned against the leftist-Palestinian forces and in August 1976 the besieged Tel el-Zaatar

Palestinian refugee camp in East Beirut fell to right-wing forces with heavy loss of life.

Syria's intervention helped to secure the election of Nicholas Sarkis as the new president but he was unable to take office until September because the stubborn Sulaiman Franjiyeh refused to withdraw. Syrian forces intervened in strength in June but they did not attempt to enter Beirut until their presence as part of the Arab peacekeeping force had been endorsed by the Arab summit meetings in October. After nineteen months of civil war, a ceasefire became effective in most of the country except the extreme south where fighting continued between the Christian militia and Palestinians.

It was not a straightforward civil war although it developed increasingly along those lines. The conflict was fuelled from outside by the supply of arms and money from various quarters (the Arab countries, Israel and probably the CIA) and the Lebanese showed their usual commercial enterprise in securing their needs. Atrocious acts of kidnapping and torture were committed by both sides; some 50,000 were killed, many more were injured and about 1 million Lebanese were driven from their homes. The more fortunate crowded into the hotels of Arab or European capitals; the poor became destitute refugees.

With their customary vigour the Lebanese set about restoring their shattered economy. While Arab aid for recovery was well below Lebanese expectations, the revival of trade and banking and the continuing strength of the Lebanese pound showed that Beirut would not easily lose its pre-eminence in these areas. But it was soon apparent that 1976 was only a respite and not an end to the civil war. The fears and hatreds intensified by the war had not died down; above all the continuing presence of the Palestinian quasi-state in Lebanese territory meant that Israel always found cause to intervene. Moreover, an alliance which was started early in the civil war was developing between various branches of the Christian militia and Israel. Since the 1950s Israeli leaders such as David Ben Gurion and Moshe Dayan had seen the advantages of promoting Christian separatism in Lebanon and the creation of a Maronite-dominated Christian state which would be in alliance with Israel. In Southern Lebanon the Israelis had an opportunity to make a start by establishing a pro-Israeli enclave under a Lebanese Christian officer, Saad Haddad, who received their full support. During and after the civil war Southern Lebanese crossed the 'open border' into Israel for refuge or medical treatment. The great majority were Shiites and some of them, embittered by their suffering and antagonized by the frequently domineering and insensitive attitude of the PLO fighters towards them, joined Haddad's militia.

The danger of a revival of sectarian violence constantly threatened the régime of Elias Sarkis who proved a singularly undynamic president. The Syrians, so far from being an effective deterrent force, soon became detested by the Christians who had welcomed them in 1976 and now demanded their withdrawal. Syrian domination was opposed by some in the other Lebanese camp. The assassination of the leftist Druze leader, Kamal Jumblatt, in March 1977 was almost certainly by Syrian hands but it was followed by Druze attacks on Christian villages and counter reprisals.

In March 1978 Israel launched its first full-scale invasion of Southern Lebanon with the aim of destroying the Palestinian guerrilla bases. The Palestinians melted away northwards and it was mainly the Lebanese who suffered. On this occasion, firm UN Security Council action backed by the United States secured an Israeli withdrawal by mid-June and the installation of a UN International Force in Lebanon (UNIFIL). But the Israelis continued to give strong support to Saad Haddad's border enclave over which UNIFIL had no control and which he later declared to be an independent state of Free Lebanon.

In the summer of 1978 the Maronite camp was weakened by the deep split, reflecting an ancient rivalry, which took place between the Falangists, mainly of Mount Lebanon, and supporters of ex-President Franjiyeh in the north. On 13 June the ex-President's son Tony and his family were massacred by Falangists and Franjiyeh vowed revenge. The Syrians were close to Franjiyeh and their relations with the Lebanese rightists deteriorated. In the autumn the Syrians heavily bombarded East Beirut.

The years 1979–81 were hardly years of peace for Lebanon. Violence between sects and within sects, followed by inevitable reprisals, Syrian shelling, massive Israeli retaliation for Palestinian guerrilla attacks, caused many thousands of dead and injured. Neither UNIFIL nor the Lebanese armed forces, slowly being restored after their collapse in the civil war, was capable of keeping the peace. US mediation only brought very temporary respite.

Much worse was to come. On 6 June 1982 the Israelis invaded and this time did not stop at the Litani river but went on to besiege West Beirut for two months. Thousands died and tens of thousands were made homeless in the cities and villages of the south and the capital.

The Israeli objective was the final destruction of the Palestinian organization in Lebanon. But the question had also clearly been raised as to whether Lebanon itself could survive. This doubt had been expressed before but each time the Lebanese had edged back from disaster. Now it was uncertain whether they could. The initial reaction of much of the Christian population was to welcome the long-anticipated invasion. The Christian militias, grouped together since 1976 in the Lebanese Forces, were headed by Bashir Gemayel, the youngest son of the Falangist leader, Pierre Gemayel. Bashir was increasingly regarded as the warrior-hero of the majority of Christians who regarded both Palestinians and Syrians with fierce hatred. But although the Lebanese Forces looked on the Israelis as allies they did not join the fighting. Both Maronites and Israelis mistakenly considered they could use each other for their own purposes. The bulk of the Lebanese Muslim and Druze militias, who had turned against the Palestinians' presence in Lebanon, did not fight alongside them in resisting the Israelis, although the Shiite Amal militia fought bravely in the Beirut suburbs.

Under the shadow of Israeli guns, Bashir Gemayel was elected President to succeed Elias Sarkis on 23 August. He had already shown his determination not to be used as an Israeli puppet when he was assassinated before he could take office. His elder brother Amin was then elected. A more intellectual and moderate figure than Bashir, Amin could not be the same idol to the militant Christians as his brother (who now became their 'martyr-hero') but he had a much better chance of representing himself as leader of all the Lebanese rather than only the Christians. He was still faced with a task of almost insuperable difficulty in reuniting the country and establishing government authority throughout Lebanese territory. The international force of US, French, Italian and British troops could only be of limited help in these objectives. In some ways, as was soon proved, they made matters worse.

Some success was achieved, with American assistance, in the important task of restoring the shattered Lebanese security forces. But there were greater obstacles. Syrian and Israeli forces still occupied all Lebanon except for the Greater Beirut area while Lebanese Muslims, notably the Druzes and Shiites, refused to acknowledge the régime's authority unless Lebanon was politically restructured to their advantage. But this the Lebanese forces were determined to prevent and President Gemayel was not strong enough to dispense with them. The traditionally warlike Druzes had not resisted the Israeli invasion but now showed equal determination not to be dominated by the Maronites. The Shiites who, having fled northwards from the troubled south over the previous years, now formed a majority of the population of Greater Beirut, were a major factor in the Lebanese equation that could not be ignored.

Israel's dream of a stable Maronite-dominated Lebanon as an ally was already fading. In the Chouf mountains of south central Lebanon where Maronites and Druzes had lived side by side in peace since the mid-nineteenth-century massacres, the arrival of the Lebanese Forces with Israeli backing provoked a miniature civil war. Under pressure from Israeli Druzes,[2] Israel ended by supporting both sides, and when the Israeli forces withdrew south of the Awali river in September 1983 the Druze militia, backed by Syria, won a decisive victory and most of the Maronite villagers became tragic refugees from the Chouf.

President Gemayel rejected Israel's demand for a full peace treaty on the grounds that it would leave Lebanon impossibly isolated from the Arab world with which it has all its cultural and commercial affinities. Israel settled for something nearly as good which was an agreement for non-belligerency and the normalization of political and economic relations. This was achieved, with energetic US mediation, on 17 May 1983 but since its provision for the withdrawal of Israeli forces from Lebanon was conditional on a similar Syrian withdrawal and Syria rejected the entire Lebanese–Israeli agreement as opposing its vital interests, it was worthless. In fact it was worse because the United States was now committed to regarding it as the only solution to Lebanon's problems and Syria as the only obstacle.

President Gemayel was left with very limited assets and options. While what amounted to fifteen years of continuous civil strife had increased the sense of Lebanese identity through the shared suffering of the Lebanese people, this was offset by myriad currents of rivalry and antagonism. Old hatreds had been revived and new ones created. Saudi mediation and Syrian pressure helped but it was still something of a miracle that, in November 1983 in Geneva, a reconciliation conference could be held under Amin's chairmanship which brought together many ancient enemies – his father Pierre, Chamoun, Franjiyeh and Walid Jumblatt, the son of Kamal, who had taken over the Druze leadership. They might refuse to shake hands but they agreed on a formula which reaffirmed Lebanon's

---

2. In contrast to Israel's Muslim and Christian Arab citizens, the Druzes serve in the Israeli Defence Force.

Arab identity and looked to a revision of the Lebanon–Israeli agreement.

This could only be a beginning of the essential task of creating a new structure for the Lebanese state. The suffering of the Lebanese continued with an oppressive Israeli occupation in the south, fighting in Tripoli in the north and the breakdown of the thousandth ceasefire between warring militias in Greater Beirut.

Various suggestions for the reform of Lebanon's political system have been made. They have to match the need for a strong central government with the desire of the non-Maronite Lebanese to end the Maronite ascendancy. Lebanese Muslims are mostly prepared for the presidency to remain in Maronite hands but believe that the President should be elected by popular vote rather than, as at present, by parliament. Another proposal is that there should be two chambers, one to be elected by proportional representation and the other in which the various sects would be represented equally. No other society of mixed races or religions can provide a model because Lebanon is unique.

The economic system which is suited to the Lebanese genius is a form of *laissez-faire* capitalism which scarcely survives anywhere else in the world. But although this system – or lack of system – gives the Lebanese a high level of personal liberty, whose value can hardly be underestimated, it has its darker side.[3] In recent years a growing number of the Lebanese intelligentsia and educated middle class – both Christian and Muslim – have become impatient with the anomalies which make Lebanon at the same time one of the most old-fashioned as well as the most progressive of all the Arab states. Government planning and social services are rudimentary. Attempts by the state to combat inflation, by controlling the rapacity of individual merchants (and other powerful pressure groups such as taxi-drivers) invariably fail. A national education system of a kind exists and a Lebanese University was founded by the government in 1953 but it is the private schools and colleges, many of them religious foundations, which remain the mainstay of Lebanese education and enjoy the highest prestige. In the American University of Beirut the teaching is in English and in the Jesuit University of St Joseph it is in

3. The Arab-American economic historian, Charles Issawi, has suggested that the reason why Lebanon alone among the Arab states has made a success of capitalism is that, like Japan, it passed through a stage of feudalism (*Arab Resources, The Transformation of a Society*, Ibrahim Ibrahim, ed., London, 1983, p. 298). The difference is that in Lebanon feudalism survives in the form of its political warlords.

French. Thus although the Lebanese are the most literate of the Arabs their education does little to aid the cohesion of Lebanese society or to encourage feelings of national, as opposed to sectarian, loyalty.

Despite the glaring anachronisms and anomalies of its social and political system, which provides no kind of model for any other Arab state, Lebanon plays a crucial role in the Arab world. 'The Arabs *need* Lebanon,' a Muslim editor once remarked to me. By this he meant that the liberal atmosphere of Beirut ('You can *smell* the freedom here,' said a wistful Arab cabinet minister on a private visit) provides the forum for the creative struggle of current ideas in the Arab world. It is no surprise that Lebanon has the most readable newspapers written in Arabic, because they avoid the aching dullness which is the result of government control. Even during and after the civil war more than half of all the books being produced in the Arab world were published in Beirut.

A visitor may be struck by the financial acquisitiveness of the Lebanese and the individualism which sometimes merges into personal aggressiveness, but he may also reflect that Lebanon as a nation has never threatened anyone and has provided a home for a unique combination of Christian, Muslim and Druze Arabs, Armenians and Jews.

In many ways the civil war has proved that Beirut is irreplaceable. Other Middle Eastern capitals have taken over some of its functions but none has been able to provide them all. Unfortunately, Lebanon's uniqueness is no guarantee of its survival. It could remain partitioned between Syria and Israel and some Lebanese are convinced that this would be these two countries' preferred solution. Of the tragedy of Lebanon's dissolution there can be no doubt.

22. Iraq: the Dynamic Outsider

The people of Iraq accept the fact that they do not enjoy a good reputation in the Western world. Some regret it, while others do not care; but they cannot deny that it is so. Iraq has abundant human resources of intelligence and energy, but it is widely associated with violent extremism and stubborn perversity. It is difficult to recall that the Iraq of the 1950s, with its pro-Western and anti-Soviet régime, was the West's favourite Arab state. Forecasts based on its vast oil resources, which at that time were more developed than those of any other Arab producer, and huge untapped agricultural potential gave Iraq a 'Scandinavian' standard of living before the end of the century.

Iraq's internal problems have not changed since it was carved out of the dead body of the Ottoman Empire half a century ago; they are essentially political and are the same, although in a peculiarly acute form, as those of any new nation whose people do not form a natural political community with shared ideals. The powerful centrifugal forces in Iraq constantly threaten to tear the nation apart.

A majority of Iraqi Arabs are Shia Muslims,[1] who live mainly in the centre and the south of the country; but the Sunni minority, who live mostly in the Baghdad area and the northern provinces, have been politically dominant since Ottoman days. There are other important minority groups, such as the Christian Assyrians, but it is the problem of the Kurds which is the key to Iraq's instability.

The Kurds are an ancient mountain people who speak an Indo-European group of dialects related to Persian and inhabit a great arc of territory from western Iran through northern Iraq and Syria to eastern Turkey. After the First World War the treaty of Sèvres recognized an independent Kurdish state of Kurdistan, but this was cancelled by the treaty of Lausanne in 1923. A substantial number of Kurds became Iraqis when the League of Nations awarded the vilayet of Mosul to Iraq, and this was accepted by Turkey. Today they form between 10 and 20 per cent of the population of Iraq, although the division is far from clear. There has been much intermarriage, and many Iraqi Arabs have some Kurdish blood.[2] The dissatisfied national aspirations of the Kurds and the fact that the north-eastern region where they live is the richest oil-producing area in the country have been a constant threat to the unity and stability of the Iraqi state since independence. Since 1958 the Kurdish nationalists have been continuously either at war with the Baghdad régime or at best in an uneasy state of armed truce.

A precarious unity was maintained for a time by the monarchy, although its dependence upon British arms and support was ultimately fatal. The high hopes that were raised by the 14 July 1958 revolution were soon belied; the régime of Abdul Karim Kassem (1958–63) was beset by bloody disturbances which were violently repressed. The Baathist régime which followed Kassem's overthrow fared no better. Unpopular and internally divided, it was ousted by an army coup six months later. Iraq was ruled for the next five years by a series of governments dominated by nationalist army officers but including some civilian 'technocrat' ministers. For a few months in 1965–6 a distinguished academic, Dr Abdul Rahman al-Bazzaz, was installed as premier. He attempted to restore civilian rule and representative government and to make peace with the Kurdish nationalists but he was soon removed from office by a group of disgruntled army officers and retired generals. Finally, in July 1968, the Baathists under General al-Bakr succeeded in restoring a Baathist military régime.

For ten years Iraq had enjoyed neither stable nor competent government. Land reform was introduced in 1958 as a political measure to reduce the power of the big landowners which had been left untouched under the monarchy. The act was hasty and ill-conceived; there were long delays in redistributing the expropriated lands to the peasants, who in many cases lacked the necessary technical and managerial skill. The results were disastrous. Neglected lands were overwhelmed by salination, the constant threat to Iraqi agriculture. From being an important exporter of cereals to a hungry world Iraq was forced to import huge quantities to feed its own people. Nationalization measures in industry had similarly unfortunate results; the Iraqi state lacked the administrative machinery to manage large sections of the economy. While all this was happening, Iraq's oil revenues were falling behind those of its neighbours. In 1961 Abdul

2. Again statistics are very dubious but there are probably about 1·5 million Kurds in Iraq, 4·5 million in Turkey, 2·5 million in Iran and 0·25 million in Syria.

Karim Kassem promulgated his Law 80 which expropriated over 99·5 per cent of the Iraq Petroleum concession without compensation and the company responded by cutting output. Iraq was no longer in the front rank of producers.

For some months the restored Baathist régime gave no indication that it was any improvement on its predecessors. Its repression of opposition was both blunt and brutal. Some prominent figures, including the former premier Dr Bazzaz, were arrested and imprisoned on trumped-up charges of spying for Israel. On 27 January 1969 the régime caused an international uproar and deeply embarrassed other Arab governments by hanging fourteen alleged spies, nine of them Jews,[3] and publicly displaying their bodies.

In its foreign relations Iraq was both perverse and uncompromising. It virulently denounced any move by other Arab states towards a political settlement of the Middle East conflict and declared its all-out support for the Palestinian guerrillas. Yet when the civil war broke out in Jordan in September 1970 the 12,000 Iraqi troops who had been stationed there since the 1967 war failed to move. It was left to the detested rival Baathist régime in Syria to intervene, and Iraq became an object of derision to the other Arab states.

Despite its setbacks and failures, the stability and self-confidence slowly improved. This was largely due to the efforts of the vice-president, Saddam Hussein, who established step-by-step his control over the internal security services and the military wing of the Baath to emerge as the strong man of the régime. Although no less ruthless than his rivals, he proved himself considerably more competent and, having ended the internal anarchy, was able to allow some relaxation of the atmosphere of public life.

Iraq's internal unity had been helped by its quarrel with its larger and more powerful neighbour, Iran, which had kept the two countries close to war for a decade. In April 1969 Iran unilaterally denounced the 1937 treaty governing navigation rights in the Shatt al-Arab, the river which forms the boundary between the two countries for some sixty miles from the head of the Persian Gulf. Claiming that the treaty

3. Before the creation of Israel in 1948 Iraq had a flourishing community of about 130,000 Jews. In 1950–51 some 90 per cent of them left for Israel, both attracted by Israeli publicity and afraid for their future in Iraq. Evidence has since come to light that their flight was at least partly caused by Zionist *agents provocateurs*, who carried out acts of sabotage against Jews in Baghdad. See 'How the Iraqi Jews came to Israel' in *Middle East International*, London, January 1973, and Elie Kedourie, *The Chatham House Version and other Middle-Eastern Studies*, London, 1970, pp. 311–12.

was unjust to Iran because it was concluded when Iraq had British protection, Iran deployed its forces along the river banks. But the dispute goes much deeper than this and related to the Shah of Iran's open claim to establish Iranian hegemony over the entire Gulf region, which was fiercely disputed by Iraq. With more than three times Iraq's population and forces equipped with the most sophisticated American arms, Iran was much the stronger party. Moreover, as long as the Kurdish problem remains unresolved a large part of Iraq's army will always be reserved for the north. The Shah helped to ensure the continuing resistance of Kurdish fighters by providing them with arms and support. Iraq succeeded to some extent in righting the balance by forming an alliance with the Soviet Union, which provided arms and technical assistance on a massive scale. The Soviets were developing a major oil field in southern Iraq and their warships made use of the Iraqi naval port of Umm Qasr on the Gulf. Any Iranian attack on Iraq – an option undoubtedly considered by Iran – faced the prospect of a confrontation with the Soviet Union.

Bitter experience has proved that no régime in Iraq is stable as long as the Kurdish problem remains. In March 1970 an agreement was reached with the veteran Kurdish nationalist leader, Mustafa al-Barzani, on a form of Kurdish autonomy. Barzani had been allowed to return from exile in the Soviet Union with some of his followers after the 1958 revolution; from then on he was almost continually at war with the Baghdad government. Four years after the autonomy agreement, Barzani denounced it as having proved to be hypocritical and inadequate and rose once again in rebellion. The Iraqis threw in a large force and fighting was bitter. As usual, the Iraqi forces controlled the valley and main towns of Kurdistan but the Kurdish guerrillas had the advantage in the hill-fighting. The Iraqis succeeded in forcing Barzani back to a narrow strip of territory along the Iranian border where they received some protection from Iranian artillery.

The basis of the Iraqi–Kurdish problem is the total absence of trust between the two sides. The Iraqis are convinced that the real aim of the Kurds is to set up their own independent state in the oil-rich north-eastern region of the country. The Kurdish nationalists deny that they aim to secede but believe that the Iraqis wish to deprive them of their natural right to a substantial share of the oil revenues. (They claim as proof that during the transitional period the Baghdad government tried to move Arabs and other non-Kurds into the Kirkuk region so that the census would not show it as a Kurdish majority area.) When the Iraqi government finally nationalized the Iraq Petroleum Company in 1972 the Kurdish nationalists regarded the action as a deadly threat because it tightened Baghdad's grip on 'their' oil. Barzani was led to make some provocative remarks to an American correspondent to the effect that if the United States provided 'political, humanitarian or military help, open or secret' to his 'small nation of poor and oppressed people' the Kurds 'could control the Kirkuk field and give it to an American company to operate'. Understandably, this only increased Iraqi suspicions.

In March 1975 an unexpected twist of events occurred when the Shah of Iran and the strong man of the Iraqi régime, Vice-President Saddam Hussein were publicly reconciled at the Algiers meeting of heads of state of the OPEC countries. The two countries agreed to settle their differences and although it was not made public, this included an undertaking by Iran to stop helping the Kurdish nationalists. Thousands of Kurds had taken refuge in Iranian territory but the border was then closed by Iranian troops. Shorn of Iran's crucial support, the Kurdish revolt collapsed and Barzani went into exile.

The Iraqi régime gained immensely from the denouement. It went ahead with its plans for Kurdish autonomy although it was mistaken in assuming that the Kurdish problem was finally solved.

The nationalization of IPC was a risky step for Iraq to take. But times had changed in the twenty years since Iran's Premier Mossadegh had tried to do the same in his country, or in the ten years since Kassem had passed his Law 80 in Iraq. Not only Iraq but the oil companies had been losing heavily by the cut-back in production. After vociferously protesting, IPC conceded the loss of its Kirkuk fields in return for fair compensation.

The breaking of the twelve-year impasse in Iraq's oil industry combined with the astronomical rise in oil prices provoked by the 1973 Arab–Israeli war swiftly doubled Iraq's oil revenues. With its relative internal stability, Iraq had the opportunity, after a long period of stagnation and decline, to realize some of the potential which raised so many optimistic hopes in the 1950s.

By the mid-1970s it was apparent that Iraq was carrying some of the increasing weight within the Arab world which reflected its human and material resources. In its foreign policies the Baathist régime remained something of a maverick – independent and radical to the point of extremism although on occasion pragmatic, as in the agreement with Iran. In the October 1973 war the régime sent some 18,000 troops to fight alongside the Syrians but when they accepted the UN ceasefire it ignored Syrian protests and withdrew them. After that it repeatedly offered to revive the Arab northern front against Israel but only on condition that Syria repudiated all UN resolutions aimed at a political solution with Israel. On this basis, it refused to join with Syria in the Arab Front of Steadfastness opposed to President Sadat's peace initiative. But, while denouncing Egypt's policies Iraq consistently refused to break all relations with the Egyptian people. On the basis of its pan-Arab ideology Iraq invited Egyptians to immigrate where they were given unrestricted residence. Hundreds of thousands of Egyptians of various trades and professions took advantage of the offer and they remained even after Iraq took the lead in imposing an official Arab boycott of Egypt after the signing of the Israeli–Egyptian peace treaty.

Iraq did not preclude an improvement in relations with Kuwait, after the settlement of outstanding territorial differences in 1977, or regular consultations with Saudi Arabia. Relations with the Soviet Union were close while the attitude towards the United States was hostile, but a majority of the foreign companies contracted to take part in Iraq's ambitious development plans were from the non-communist industrialized countries, including the USA. The size of Iraq's oil revenues reinforced the country's independence of action. The view of Saddam Hussein, the régime's political strategist, was that time was on the side of the Arabs provided they made full use of their natural advantages and the fact that new 'centres of power' were emerging (such as China and Japan) in addition to the American and Soviet superpowers. For this reason there could be no compromise on Arab claims to Palestine. In fact Iraq's uncompromising stand on Palestine led in 1978 to an open breach with the PLO which blamed Iraq for sponsoring the extremist Abu Nidal group held responsible for the assassination of several leading PLO moderates.

By 1980 Saddam Hussein, who assumed the presidency in 1979, had some reasons for satisfaction with Iraq's situation. The application of huge oil revenues to the country's natural resources was beginning to show results. In health, education, women's emancipation, the treatment of poverty and the redistribution of wealth, Iraq had much to show the Arab states. Moreover, it was the only one to have given practical expression to its pan-Arab ideology. (Officially, Iraq was always referred to as the 'Iraqi region of the Arab homeland'.) At the same time, President Saddam Hussein could look forward to presiding over a meeting of non-aligned heads of state to be held in Baghdad in 1982.

The régime was entirely ruthless in the elimination of its enemies who included communists, pro-Syrian Baathists, unreconciled Kurds and above all Shiite Iraqis who rejected not only Sunni domination but the secularism of the government. A militant Shiite group called al-Dawa (Islamic call) attempted to defy the régime. But stability was not only based on repression. Saddam Hussein regularly toured the country, mixing with the people even in the Shiite areas of greatest dissidence. Care was taken that much of the benefit of the oil revenues should accrue to the deprived Shiite population.

In September 1980, President Saddam Hussein put everything at risk by going to war with the Islamic Republic of Iran. Only two reasons could explain this disastrous decision: one was Iraq's belief, possibly encouraged by émigré Iranian generals, that it could expect an easy victory in view of the chaotic and demoralized condition of the armed forces in post-revolutionary Iran; the other was a feeling that the Khomeini revolution presented a mortal threat to the survival of the Iraqi Baathist régime.

President Saddam Hussein had been wary of the Khomeini revolution from the beginning because the overthrow of the Shah placed the vital 1975 Algiers agreement at risk although it could not at first be openly hostile to a régime which so enthusiastically embraced the Palestinian cause. However, it was not long before Ayatollah Khomeini showed his own contempt and hatred for Iraq's régime and Tehran Radio was calling upon the Iraqi people to overthrow their godless rulers. The threat of subversion of Iraq's Shiite majority was clear.

On 17 September 1980 Iraq denounced the 1975 agreement over the sharing of the Shatt al-Arab waterway bordering the two countries and invaded. It advanced deep into Iranian territory taking the port of Khorramshahr and surrounding the vital oil complex of Abadan. But Iranian morale was higher than expected and Arabic-speaking Iranians in south-western Iran did not support the invaders. For a year the war developed into a stalemate, with heavy casualties being sustained on both sides, but in September 1981 the Iranians forced Iraq back across the Karun river and went in in the following May to recapture Khorramshahr, taking thousands of prisoners. A new stalemate developed although now Iran was back on Iraq's borders.

Not all the advantages were on Iran's side. While neither of the two superpowers decisively supported Iraq in the war, they both tended to favour Iraq, especially as the Iranian threat to the region appeared to grow. France, on the other hand, openly supported Iraq with arms supplies. The Arab Gulf states, while officially neutral in the war, provided Iraq with some $30 billion in aid. Jordan openly supported Iraq and provided an urgently needed free port at Aqaba. Egypt provided substantial quantities of arms. Iran had much greater difficulty in obtaining arms and spare parts. Iraq had command of the air and superiority in armour and artillery. Without too much difficulty Iraq was able to contain the Iranian offensive in the form of 'human wave' assaults conducted mainly by teenage Islamic volunteers rather than regular troops. Moreover, if the Iranian Arabs did not fight for Iraq, neither did the Iraqi Shiites rise *en masse* against their Baghdad régime.

However, as the war dragged into its fourth year it was clear than Iran had the greater stamina. Its casualties were even higher than Iraq's terrible losses but it had three times the population. Moreover, it was able to restore oil exports to about 2·5 million barrels a day while Iraq, deprived of all exits to the Gulf and with the trans-Syrian pipeline closed by the implacably hostile Damascus government which supported Iran in the war, was reduced to a trickle of 600,000 barrels a day, exported through Turkey. It could hope to increase exports through a Saudi Arabian pipeline to the Red Sea but this would take at least a year. Having maintained a good appearance of normality in the first two years of the war Iraq, with disastrously reduced reserves, was obliged to cancel contracts, postpone payments and scale down all its development plans.

By 1982 President Saddam Hussein had reduced his conditions for an end to the war to a ceasefire and a return to the *status quo* before the fighting started. But Ayatollah Khomeini was implacable in demanding his overthrow and the payment of huge reparations. Repeated mediation efforts by Arab and Islamic states, the UN and others, came to nothing. Iraq could only hope for Ayatollah Khomeini's death although this would by no means ensure an end to the war.

Inevitably doubts were raised about President Saddam Hussein's own chances of survival. In the initial stages of the war he appeared frequently in public and among the troops to rally morale but in time he became increasingly concerned with his own security. Amid reports of unrest and attempted coups he retreated to his headquarters, relying only on a few trusted relatives and supporters. But he still had some room to manoeuvre. In November 1983 he made the gesture of dismissing his much-hated brother Barzan, the head of the secret police, and made moves towards reconciliation with some of his political opponents – the communists and one of the two main Kurdish national groups. The softening of Iraq's attitudes due to its weakness helped to bring about a rapprochement with Egypt and even signs of a friendly relationship with the USA. But as long as the debilitating war lasts there can be no question of Iraq increasing its influence in the region. It is suppliant rather than dominant. The Arab Gulf states might be willing to help Iraq financially but when they formed their confederation of the Gulf Cooperation Council in 1981 they excluded Iraq which might otherwise have been able to insist that it had a natural right to membership.

23. Jordan: the Stubborn Survivor

Many obituaries of the Hashemite kingdom of Jordan have been prepared for instant use. There have been many occasions in the past thirty-five years when the external and internal forces gathered against this last of the Anglo-Arab monarchies were so strong and numerous that its survival seemed impossible. But it still lives and the obituaries gather dust on the files.

The state of Transjordan which was created under British auspices in 1921 on the East Bank of the river Jordan as consolation prize for the Hashemite Amir Abdullah was desperately poor and deeply dependent on British protection and support. Yet it was politically viable; it had a fairly homogeneous semi-nomadic population, who mostly accepted Abdullah's rule with loyalty and enthusiasm. All this was changed by the first Arab–Israeli war of 1948–9 and Abdullah's annexation of the West Bank of Jordan – the 21 per cent of Palestine remaining in Arab hands – to form the Hashemite kingdom of Jordan. The new population was more than twice as numerous as the original Transjordanians and half a million of them were destitute refugees. Although a majority of the West Bankers voted in favour of joining the East Bank they did so mainly because it seemed the only alternative to their absorption by Israel. Few of them felt any loyalty towards the Hashemites and some were irreconcilably opposed to them. All of the Palestinians had doubts about being ruled from Transjordan, whose inhabitants they regarded as less advanced than themselves.

The new frontiers were mere armistice lines which often separated villages from their farmlands or water supplies, divided Jerusalem into two hostile and uncommunicating sectors and cut off Jordan from any access to the Mediterranean. The economic prospects were even more unfavourable than the political outlook. When Abdullah was assassinated by a Palestinian youth in July 1951 and a year later his mentally unbalanced son Talal was obliged to abdicate in favour of his seventeen-year-old British-educated son Hussein, there were few who were prepared to gamble on the survival of the monarchy. Indeed, as the Nasserite republican tide gathered strength in the 1950s it seemed doubtful whether there was a future for any of the Arab kings except those in the remoter parts of Arabia.

King Hussein followed a policy which was in harmony with his courageous but volatile nature, of alternately bowing to the storm and sailing directly against it. In December 1955 he gave up any idea of taking Jordan into the British-sponsored Baghdad Pact after serious rioting throughout the country and the resignation of four West Bank ministers. A few months later he earned wild popularity by dismissing Glubb Pasha, the British commander of his army. Elections in October, overshadowed by the Suez affair which influenced all Arab opinion, brought to power a nationalist government which terminated the Anglo-Jordanian treaty and prepared to announce Jordan's final step from the conservative pro-Western camp into the progressive neutralist camp by establishing relations with the Soviet Union and rejecting American aid. It was in April 1957 that King Hussein decided at last to counter-attack. With the help of loyal beduin regiments he foiled an alleged military coup, imposed martial law and dissolved parliament and the political parties. Jordan did not establish diplomatic relations with Moscow and the United States became the main supplier of the outside aid which was essential for the country's survival.

The Jordanian monarchy remained in great peril. The anti-Western tide in the Arab world was growing stronger and a year later swept away King Hussein's last remaining friends and allies – his Hashemite cousins in Iraq. It seemed doubtful whether the kingdom of Jordan could survive the radical nationalist pressures from the revolutionary régimes in Iraq and the United Arab Republic of Egypt and Syria. But events moved in the king's favour. After three years the Syrian–Egyptian union collapsed and the pressure from Damascus was relaxed. At the same time the Saudi monarchy dropped its old enmity derived from the dynastic antagonisms of the Hashemite and Saudi families and became Jordan's ally and supporter in mutual defence of the conservative, pro-Western interests in the Arab world. Internally, King Hussein was able to rely on the unquestioning loyalty of the beduin elements in the army and the traditional leaders of Transjordan as a basis for his rule. Moreover although radical Arab nationalist feeling – Baathist or Nasserist – was strong among the Palestinians of the West Bank, especially the students and the younger generation, there were older members of the conservative West Bank leadership who were prepared to cooperate with the king and take part in his governments. Palestinian ability and enterprise helped to develop Amman from the dusty village it had been in the 1920s into a modern city. Some light industries were created, cultivation was extended, many new roads were built and a new port developed at Aqaba on the Red Sea. Jordan included most of the major sites of the Holy Land and its tourist industry was booming. Political repression was severe and Jordan bore some aspects of an oppressive military régime but the country was well administered and, in relation to its difficult circumstances, remarkably prosperous.

As always, King Hussein was helped by the divisions among his opponents in the Arab world. Danger again threatened when the Baathists recovered power in Syria and Iraq in 1963 and plans were announced for Syrian–Iraqi–Egyptian union. But the project failed, and King Hussein was able to improve his relations with Egypt for a time in a common enmity towards the Baathists, whom President Nasser was now describing as fascists. Despite occasional internal disturbances, which had to be put down by the army, the Jordanian monarchy seemed reasonably secure against anything except assassination of the monarch himself. He took great personal risks but appeared to enjoy miraculous protection. However, Jordan could never ensure its survival through self-isolation from the rest of the Arab world. Since it has the longest frontier with Israel it is the main 'confrontation' state, whatever its government might wish and since a majority of its people are Palestinian Arabs it is inconceivable that it should merely stand aside in an Arab–Israeli conflict. It had stayed out of the 1956 Egyptian–Israeli war, but on that occasion President Nasser had told both Syria and Jordan not to involve themselves. If Syria had joined in the battle it would have been impossible for Jordan to remain neutral. In 1964 the situation was different. There was a real possibility that Syria would involve all the Arab states in a war with Israel over Israel's diversion of the Jordan waters. King Hussein therefore answered President Nasser's invitation to an Arab summit in Cairo and agreed, however reluctantly, to the setting up of a Palestine Liberation Organization and a Palestine Liberation Army. But he still steadfastly maintained Jordan's right to speak for the Palestinians[1] and he refused to allow the PLA to train on Jordanian territory or the PLO to set up its headquarters in Jordan. In May 1967,

---

1. In February 1950 Jordan offered Jordanian citizenship to any Palestinian who asked for it.

realizing that there was no possibility of Jordan remaining outside the war which seemed imminent and inevitable, King Hussein flew to Cairo to sign a defence pact with Egypt.

The results of the Six Day War were disastrous for Jordan. It ended with the entire West Bank under Israeli occupation and the refugee population of the East Bank increased by about 200,000. The tourist industry was undermined and the closure of the Suez Canal made the country's only port almost useless. The Jordanian economy had virtually ceased to exist. The demise of Jordan seemed this time to be certain.

Throughout 1968 and 1969 there were almost daily artillery duels with Israel across the cease-fire lines in the Jordan valley and on several occasions Israel launched heavy air and rocket attacks on Jordanian territory in reprisal for Palestinian commando raids. To add to Jordan's troubles, the rising power and prestige of the Palestinian guerrilla organizations now threatened to undermine the régime itself. The king's attitude towards the guerrillas characteristically varied. At times when he was optimistic about a US-sponsored political settlement between the Arabs and Israel he tended to listen to the advice of the 'ultras' among his supporters, led by his own uncle Sharif Nasser Ibn Jamil, who wanted a confrontation with the guerrillas to restrict their activities. When his hopes of a settlement faded he warmed towards the guerrillas and ordered the army to cooperate with them. However, as the guerrilla organizations acted increasingly as a law unto themselves without obligations to the Jordanian state, clashes with the Jordanian army became more frequent. The trouble was patched up with agreements which at once broke down. Finally, in September 1970 the extremists among both the Palestinians and Jordanians were successful in provoking a showdown. The civil war aroused bitter criticism from the other Arab states. Kuwait and Libya cut off the subsidies they had been paying since the 1967 war. King Hussein agreed to a ceasefire when the army wanted to continue fighting until the bitter end. The Syrian column which intervened was successfully beaten off and the 12,000 Iraqi troops stationed in Jordan remained inactive although the Iraqi government had sworn to protect the guerrillas. But although the civil war ended with an apparent compromise, the Jordanian army had won the upper hand and in the following summer was able to demolish the last guerrilla bases on Jordanian territory. At the cost of the bitter hatred of the *fedayeen*, which led to the creation of the Black September organization and the revenge killing of the Prime Minister Wasfi Tal, Jordan destroyed the 'state within a state' which the guerrilla organizations had created.

Jordan's situation was still disastrous. New hopes raised by the US peace initiative of the summer of 1970 soon fizzled out, and both the Egyptians and Syrians were talking of the inevitability of a new war with Israel. King Hussein declared that Jordan would not fight again because another conflict would only mean total disaster for the Arabs. But if the United States could not or would not force an Israeli withdrawal from the river Jordan there was no other way in which Jordan could recover its lost territory. There were some of the king's Transjordanian supporters who favoured cutting the country's losses by letting the West Bank go and returning to the pre-1948 borders. But this has never been acceptable to the king himself. He has never abandoned his belief in the heritage of the Hashemites as the leaders of the Arab Revolt. He still regards it as his responsibility to speak for the Palestinians and to regain the Old City of Jerusalem for the Arabs.

When Egypt and Syria launched their assault on Israel in October 1973 to recover their lost territory, Jordan compromised. With no air cover to match Israel's Skyhawks and Phantoms and no Soviet missile system, an all-out confrontation with Israel in the Jordan valley would have meant certain disaster. Yet, as in 1967, it would have been well-nigh impossible for Jordan to remain entirely aloof. Its solution was to send two armoured brigades to fight alongside the Syrians.

In the short term this action was fully justified. While the bulk of the Jordanian army was preserved, Jordan had played its role in the battle. In reality, Jordan's diplomatic position was severely weakened in the aftermath of the war which ended with a military stalemate but a tangible political advantage to the Arabs. When, for the first time since 1957, American pressure was brought on Israel to give up some of its conquests, Jordan was ignored. The Israelis saw no reason to make any concessions to Jordan and summarily rejected King Hussein's suggestion that they should negotiate a disengagement agreement in the Jordan valley along the lines of those that had been reached with Egypt and Syria. Jordan was as isolated in the Arab world as it had ever been in the past. Even its former ally Saudi Arabia, the only one of the three major oil states which had continued to provide a subsidy after the 1970 civil war, had come round to the view that the Palestine Liberation Organization, rather than Jordan, should represent the Palestinian people at the United Nations or any Middle East peace conference. This was the decision that was reached unanimously by all the Arab states at their summit meeting in Rabat in October 1974. Having insisted for so long that Jordan should represent the Palestinians King Hussein sadly gave way to the combined pressure of the Arab kings and presidents.

Yet this was far from being the end of the story. King Hussein made no secret of his belief that the PLO would not be able to recover any lost territory without Jordan's help. Jordan continued to pay the salaries of West Bank government officials and provide funds to educational and religious institutions. West Bank mayors were regularly invited to Amman, including some who were publicly supporting the PLO.

Jordan's initial reaction to President Sadat's peace initiative of 1977–8 was cautious and qualified. Although King Hussein was gratified by Egyptian proposals that the West Bank be returned to Jordanian administration as a step towards a peace settlement, he refused to attend the Israeli–Egyptian–American Camp David summit in September 1978 and expressed disappointment over the results because they provided neither for Israeli withdrawal from the occupied territories nor the restoration of Arab sovereignty over them. When Egypt went on to conclude a treaty with Israel in March 1979, Jordan expressed its outright opposition and refused, despite strong US pressure, to join the abortive Egyptian–Israeli negotiations on Palestinian autonomy in the occupied territories. Instead King Hussein moved towards a reconciliation with the PLO and in September Yasir Arafat made his first visit to Amman since the 1970 civil war.

Jordan's recognition of the PLO as representing the Palestinians, which it continued to uphold, relieved it from certain Arab pressures. But its relations with the other Arab states were as uncertain as ever. For a time Jordan was brought closer to Syria by Egypt's withdrawal from the Arab front, which they both deplored. In 1975 and 1976 a series of agreements were signed for Syrian–Jordanian 'integration and cooperation'. But in September 1980 King Hussein declared vigorous support for Syria's arch-rival Iraq in its war with Iran. His motives for this surprising alliance with a régime which had been responsible for the destruction of his Iraqi Hashemite cousins were partly Arab nationalist – the Arab homeland was at risk – and partly Jordanian self-interest. The friendly relations with Syria were destroyed and a series of bomb outrages in Jordan were attributed to Syrian agents.

The quarrel with Syria was probably inevitable even without the Iraq–Iran war because of King Hussein's opposition to what he saw as

President Assad's 'Greater Syria' ambitions, embracing Jordan as well as the Palestinian liberation movement. Jordan's policy was both flexible and determined. When, in the spring of 1983, negotiations with Yasir Arafat to develop a common Jordanian–Palestinian negotiating position in relation to the Reagan Plan for the Middle East proved abortive because of Palestinian opposition, the PLO went on to split between Arafat loyalists and Syrian-backed rebels. King Hussein continued to declare his recognition of the 'historic' PLO leadership as legitimate. At the same time, he widened his options by proposing to recall the Jordanian parliament, with half its members from the West Bank, which had been dissolved in 1974 when he had formally abandoned political responsibility for the Palestinians. In these various ways he served notice that Jordan would be prepared to represent the Palestinians again if they so wished.

The Hashemite Kingdom of Jordan's situation remains, as always, extremely precarious. Neither Iraq in its weakened state nor a more friendly Egypt can balance Syria's hostility. At the same time, King Hussein is fully aware that there are powerful voices in Israel who advocate a 'Jordanian solution' for the Palestinian problem: that is, one in which Transjordan would become the independent Palestinian state inhabited by the bulk of the 4 million Palestinians. In such a situation there would probably be no place for a Jordanian monarchy.

However, after more than thirty years on the throne King Hussein has become the longest-serving Arab head of state. His natural qualities of courage and dedication are now coupled with experience which has made him a political strategist of great subtlety. Not the least of his assets has been his ability to forgive his enemies. Several leaders of former attempted coups against him are today flourishing in Amman. Jordan's human rights record is not impeccable but it shines in comparison with those of most Arab régimes. His frequently expressed pessimism about the Middle East outlook will continue to be combined with an absolute determination that Jordan will survive.

24. Sudan: the Loose-limbed Giant

The republic of the Sudan is a vast subcontinent which links the Arab world with black Africa and belongs to both. In area the size of Europe without Russia, it has a population of about 20 million, although this is increasing by nearly 3 per cent a year and half the nation is under twenty years of age.

The country is divided into two distinct areas: the north (which includes the centre and west) is largely arabized and Muslim in religion. It has about three quarters of the population and includes the capital Khartoum and its twin city of Omdurman on the confluence of the Blue and White Niles. The south, which was first penetrated by Arab slave-traders and occupied by the Turco-Egyptian government after 1860, is inhabited by a variety of negroid tribes (mostly pagan, although some have been converted to Christianity or Islam), who speak Sudanic languages and who in material culture and social organization are African.

As a political entity, the Sudan of the present day is a creation of the Turco-Egyptian period of 1820–85. The capture of Khartoum by the Mahdi in 1885 led to thirteen years of Sudanese nationalist rule – the Mahdiya – until the reconquest by the Anglo-Egyptian forces of Lord Kitchener and the inauguration of the Anglo-Egyptian Condominium in which the British were decisively the senior partner. In the sixty years that it lasted, the political status of the Sudan was a constant source of friction between Britain and Egypt, until the question was finally settled when both countries resigned themselves to Sudan's full independence on 1 January 1956.

When the Sudan became a sovereign independent state, with fledgeling parliamentary institutions inherited from the British, it faced staggering problems. Except for the arid deserts of the north, Sudan's vast sprawling lands have huge agricultural potential. Whereas about one third of the country's land surface could be used, only about one eighth is productive at present. Since the completion of the Sennar Dam on the Blue Nile, cotton has become the mainstay of the economy and the imaginative Gezira Scheme, which was started by the British, has turned the vast triangle of land between the Blue and White Niles into one of the great cotton-producing areas of the world.[1] But the heavy dependence on cotton is dangerous for Sudan and there is an urgent need for diversification and the opening up of new lands. The trouble is that this will require investments on a scale which the Sudanese economy is quite incapable of generating on its own. Khartoum's only link with the Red Sea is the 500 miles of ancient railway to Port Sudan, which suffers severe strain during the cotton-exporting season and is often closed by floods. Most of the country's roads are tracks which are made impassable by rain.

To make any progress with tackling these problems, Sudan needed stable and vigorous government. But there were deep political divisions between the conservative Umma party, centred around the son and grandsons of the Mahdi, and all those who opposed any attempt to impose a new Mahdist hegemony. These included the rival Khatmiyya order of the Mirghani family. As the political factions jockeyed for position, it was left to a handful of able civil servants to tackle the giant problems of development. After only two years of independence the politicians were replaced by a military régime under the benign avuncular figure of General Abboud; but although this began by attempting a few mild reforms it soon became listless and ineffective. In 1964 it was swept away in the 'October revolution' which was carried out by a coalition of the old-style politicians, students, intellectuals and left-wing trade unionists, united only in their desire to be rid of the stagnant military régime. The coalition soon disintegrated and parliamentary elections were won by the Umma, who soon squeezed the left out of power.

Whoever ruled Sudan during those years faced two main political problems – one of them external and the other internal. The first of these was the country's relationship with Egypt and the Egyptians, who had ruled Sudan for much of the nineteenth century and only in very recent years formally abandoned their ambition to reunite the two countries. The Umma party and the Ansar (or 'Followers'), as the warlike Mahdist supporters were called, were always opposed to political links with Egypt. But even those Sudanese politicians who were regarded as pro-Egyptian and the younger generation of

1. The scheme is worked as a three-cornered partnership between the Sudanese tenant-farmers, the government and the Sudan Gezira Board, an autonomous state organization.

nationalists who were attracted to the banner of Nasserism, were usually hostile to any suggestion of patronage or domination by the more advanced and developed 'Big Brother' Egypt. The relationship between the two nations is close and familial. Common interest in the river Nile makes a minimum of economic interdependence inevitable. There is much intermarriage between Egyptians and Sudanese northerners and tens of thousands of Sudanese study in Egyptian schools and universities. It is because the kinship is close that it is sensitive.

Sudan's ties with its neighbours to the north are part of its wider involvement in the Arab world. Although geographically remote from the Arab heartlands, Sudanese Muslim Arabs are far from indifferent to Arab nationalism. Many of them feel passionately about Palestine and would deeply resent any suggestion that they are not part of the Arab nation. The trouble is that Sudan's involvement with the Arabs is bound to conflict to some extent with the unity of the Sudanese people, some 30 per cent of whom are neither Arabs nor Muslims.

Although the Sudan's 'Southern Problem' was not created by Britain but by Muhammad Ali and his descendants who annexed the tropical southern provinces to the north, Britain bears some responsibility for making it intractable. During most of the period of the Anglo-Egyptian Condominium (1898–1956), the British pursued a deliberate policy of preventing the arabization of the south. The language, religion and trade of the northern Sudanese were all excluded wherever possible. Whereas proselytization was banned in the north, it was permitted in the south and the few schools that existed were in Christian missionary hands and the teaching was in English. But although the policy was to insulate southern Sudan as far as possible from the north, there was no positive plan to cut it off entirely and integrate it with the black African territories of Uganda and Kenya, which were also under British rule. The possibility was often discussed but nothing was done. The élite corps of British administrators who formed the Sudan Political Service regarded Sudanese independence as such a remote contingency that there was no cause for urgency.

After the Second World War there was a rapid change of mood. With the imminent prospect of the ending of the British occupation of Egypt and the general momentum towards independence of colonial territories, a decision on the southern Sudan's future could not be delayed any longer. In 1947 the British reversed their previous policy.

Integration with the north was accepted; Arabic was introduced into southern schools and southerners were encouraged to obtain their higher education in Khartoum. The British civil secretary stated the principle that the southerners must be 'equipped to stand up for themselves in the future as socially and economically the equals of their partners in the north'.

Preparation of the south for its role in a united and independent Sudan had been left disastrously late. Negotiations between Britain and Egypt on the Sudan which followed the 1952 revolution in Egypt (see p. 247) led to the acceptance of Sudanese independence by the two Condominium powers. As the date for full independence, which was fixed for 1 January 1956 approached, Sudanese southerners lost confidence in their future as they saw themselves dominated by the more advanced and educated northerners, while the British, who had for so long protected their interests, withdrew. In August 1955 the garrison in the southern town of Torit mutinied against their northern officers. The mutiny was suppressed and its leaders executed, but the rest of the garrison fled to the bush where they formed the nucleus of a guerrilla force which was to carry on the struggle with the north for sixteen years. This savage and largely unreported war was the dominant factor in Sudanese political life and the main obstacle to the country's progress and development. The governments in Khartoum, whether parliamentary or military régimes, tried policies which were a mixture of conciliation and military repression but all of them failed to end the rebellion. Tens of thousands of southerners and some of their political leaders fled across the border into exile in Uganda, but guerrilla fighters grouped under the name Anya-Nya continued the war in the southern jungle with courage and ferocity. Israel, which had a clear interest in keeping the Khartoum government's attention diverted from the Arab world, played an important role in sustaining the rebels with arms, money and tactical advice.

The parliamentary régime which was restored after the October revolution of 1964 lasted five years. It began with high hopes but deteriorated into political bickering irrelevant to the country's problems. The war in the south continued; the administration was corrupt and idle. In May 1969 a new military takeover was led by a thirty-five-year-old colonel Jaafar Nimeiry. The new régime began by adopting fairly orthodox Nasserist policies of non-alignment (but friendship and arms deals with the Soviet Union), Arab unity (including an agreement in principle to join a federation with Libya and Egypt) and nationalization of foreign interests. But there were significant differences from the situation in Egypt. One was the importance of the Sudanese Communist party, the most powerful and influential in the Arab world, which supported the military coup. Initially, the new government included several ministers who were communists or fellow-travellers. Another difference was the continuing strength of the traditional Mahdist elements who were bitterly opposed to the new régime. When the elderly Mahdist leader, Imam al-Hadi (a grandson of the original Mahdi who captured Khartoum in 1885), took refuge with his Ansari supporters on an island in the White Nile, Nimeiry used troops to suppress them. The imam was shot dead while trying to cross the Ethiopian border.

Nimeiry's next confrontation was with his former communist allies, whose role in the government he had whittled away. On 19 July 1971 some pro-communist officers seized power in Khartoum. But their coup was only briefly successful. Troops led by junior officers released Nimeiry and restored him to power. The Sudanese Communist party was ruthlessly suppressed and its leaders executed. Having destroyed his enemies on both left and right, Nimeiry consolidated power in his own hands. He dissolved the Revolutionary Command Council and set up presidential-style government, with himself as Prime Minister as well as President. But his dictatorship was transcended by a liberal act of policy of decisive importance to the whole future of Sudan. Soon after taking power in 1969 Nimeiry, realizing the overriding importance of ending the civil war, had made a formal offer of autonomy to the south. This had been accepted as a basis for negotiation by some of the exiled southern politicians but rejected by the Anya-Nya guerrillas, who refused to believe any northern promises and rejected anything less than full independence. But Nimeiry did not give up, and during 1970 he gradually disengaged Sudan from its political commitments to the Arab world. By opting out of the federation with Egypt and Libya he incurred the special fury of Libya's Qaddafy, who accused Sudan of betraying the Arab nationalist cause. But Nimeiry had realized that a settlement with Sudan's own non-Arab southerners was incompatible with any union with its Arab neighbours.

After suppressing the pro-communist coup Nimeiry devoted new energy to solving the southern problem. He combined a major military drive against the insurgents, using helicopters for greater mobility, with a vigorous diplomatic campaign to come to terms with the rebel leaders through British and Ethiopian mediation. Finally in

February 1972, after months of painstaking negotiations, the representatives of the South Sudan Liberation Movement, who felt the tide of war was turning against them but had become convinced of the sincerity of the Nimeiry régime, accepted an agreement providing for an immediate ceasefire, autonomy for the three southern provinces within the Sudanese republic, and the reintegration of 6,000 Anya-Nya fighters into the Sudanese army.

This agreement was of immense significance for Sudan's future. It meant that work could at last begin on the reintegration of the refugees and the slow and difficult task of developing the impoverished southern provinces. It was of wider importance that it provided evidence of the possibility of integrating a significant non-Arab and non-Muslim minority into the Arab world. It could finally establish Sudan as the natural bridge between the Arabs and black Africa.

Apart from the southern settlement, these years offered up some hopeful prospects for Sudan. Plans were laid to realize the country's immense potential as a source of food, with huge investment by the Arab oil states in the reclamation of uncultivated lands. Behind the agricultural programme was the belief that if the United States were to respond to any future use of the Arab oil weapon by cutting off food supplies, as some American officials had hinted, Sudan might act as granary for the Arab world. In 1978 oil was discovered in the Upper Nile province of west-central Sudan. Reports of the size of the discovery were often wildly exaggerated but it was enough to make a real difference to Sudan's prospects. Sudan was distancing itself from the Soviet Union and in mid-1977 President Nimeiry asked all the Soviet military experts to leave the country. There was some consequent increase in Western aid.

Internal stability was hard to find with two attempted coups by Mahdists and right-wing extremists in 1975 and 1976. The second caused heavy loss of life in Khartoum. President Nimeiry denounced Libya for supporting the rebels and moved closer to Egypt and Saudi Arabia in a defensive alliance which was clearly directed against Colonel Qaddafy. However, in 1977 President Nimeiry made the wise and effective move of agreeing with his most formidable opponent, the young Umma Party leader Sadiq al-Mahdi, on a general reconciliation to build a 'new Sudan'. Al-Mahdi and most other opposition leaders in exile returned home and were integrated into the one-party system they had formerly opposed. Most notably, Hassan al-Turabi, the head of the Sudanese Muslim Brotherhood, joined the government as attorney-general in charge of the reform of the legal system.

President Nimeiry was fairly skilful in exploiting Sudan's relationship with Egypt without appearing to come under Egyptian domination. He did not condemn President Sadat's peace with Israel and refused to follow the other Arab states in breaking relations with Cairo. Instead he tried, albeit unsuccessfully, to mediate between them and Egypt. But at home he was faced by mounting difficulties. The reconciliation policy never really worked; Sadiq al-Mahdi detached himself from responsibility for the régime's actions. Many of the huge development schemes were either long delayed through administrative failure or proved unsound. As Sudan sank deeper into debt, the drastic economy measures proposed by the IMF and other Western aid sources provoked violent social unrest.

President Nimeiry's response was to become even more arbitrary and autocratic in his rule. A Khartoum saying was that 'our President is surrounded by advisers who are advised not to advise anything'. In January 1982 he suddenly dismissed General Abdul Majid Khalil, first vice-president and commander-in-chief of the army, along with twenty-two senior officers. It was assumed they had become too critical of his authoritarianism. In June 1983 he sacked forty judges after accusing the whole judiciary of being 'corrupt, lazy and drunken'. But his most fateful action was to impose by presidential decision the administrative division of southern Sudan into three separate regions. The rationale behind this move was to end the domination of the whole south by the Dinkas, the largest of many tribal groups in the region, in favour of other smaller tribes, and there were arguments in its favour. But according to the 1972 Addis Ababa agreement such a drastic change had to be approved by a referendum in the south. The reality was that the Addis Ababa agreement had failed to break down the wall of suspicion between north and south. The transfer of southern units in the army to north, officially intended to 'seal the ethnic unity of the country', had caused disruption and protest. The 1972 agreement was breaking down and already by the end of 1982 the first signs of a new southern rebellion – to be known as Anya-Nya II – had appeared. This was potentially even more dangerous than Anya-Nya I as it was based on the Nilotic tribes who form half the population of the south and was being joined by trained and armed southern soldiers. In May 1983 mutinies of the Bor and Pibor garrisons were put down only with heavy force.

In the face of threatening bankruptcy and civil war, President Nimeiry did not attempt to secure new allies among political leaders but made a direct appeal to what he saw as the long-frustrated wishes of the northern Sudanese people by declaring in September 1983 the 'Islamization' of Sudan, replacing all the 'colonial' legal system with the full Islamic *sharia*, including a total ban on alcohol, amputation of the right hand for theft and stoning for adultery. To public applause, the army destroyed great quantities of alcoholic beverages in Khartoum. Convicts were released because they had not been tried by Islamic laws. He himself, formerly by his own admission a heavy drinker, had undergone a kind of conversion; in 1981 he published a book entitled *Nahaj al-Islami, Limaza*, or, *Why the Islamic Way*, in which he described how he had moved from his socialist beliefs when he took power to a conviction that a Muslim ruler's duty was to establish an Islamic order.

Comment in the West concentrated on the negative aspects of President Nimeiry's actions, ignoring their widespread popularity. There was evidence that alcohol had become a real social evil in Sudan among all classes, not least among army officers. The prospect of abolishing laws inherited from the colonial era had good public support. But genuine doubts were expressed – not only by foreigners – as to whether Islamic fundamentalism could suddenly be imposed in this way from above. One sceptic was Sadiq al-Mahdi who found himself in jail with some of his supporters. President Nimeiry's 'Islamic revolution' was in line with the aims of the Muslim Brotherhood but its leader Dr al-Turabi had earlier expressed doubts about the wide gulf between government and people.

The question also at once arose of the impact of Islamization on Sudan's predominantly non-Muslim south. Southerners' fears were freely expressed, increasing the menace of civil war. In 1982 Sudan and Egypt signed a Complementarity Agreement providing for the complete harmonization of the two countries' domestic and foreign policies over the next ten years but President Mubarak, in the process of suppressing Egypt's own militant fundamentalists and with a substantial Christian population, made it clear that he would not follow Sudan's example.

The United States was prepared to help alleviate the huge economic problems of Sudan in its key position between Qaddafy's Libya and

Marxist Ethiopia. But the prospect of acting as a pro-American bastion in Africa could hardly be reconciled with President Nimeiry's affirmation of Sudan's Islamic identity and rejection of westernizing influence.

25. Egypt: the Centre of Gravity

With its 45 million people, Egypt is easily the most populous of the Arab countries. About one quarter of the Arab nation is Egyptian by nationality. Its inhabited areas are the most densely populated in the Arab world, because although Egypt is about the size of France and Spain, the Egyptians live only in the valley and delta of the Nile (with a few thousand in the oases of the western desert), which are no more than 4 per cent of the total or roughly the size of Holland. The consequence is that, although Egypt is in many respects the most advanced of the Arab countries, it is also one of the poorest in terms of income per head as its population presses at the edges of its limited natural resources.

To offset its poverty and overpopulation, Egypt enjoys certain vital political advantages in relation to the other Arab countries. As the most ancient of nation states, it has a natural sense of political community which most of the others, with their 'artificial' frontiers, have lacked and are in the painful process of developing. The Egyptian nation, forced in the narrow crucible of the Nile valley over thousands of years, is relatively homogeneous. (The only important minority are the 10 to 20 per cent who are Christian Copts. As the descendants of those who claim to have been converted to Christianity by St Mark in the first century A.D. but not to Islam after the arrival of the Arabs in the seventh century, they are arguably the most Egyptian of the Egyptians.) Control of the river Nile, the nation's lifeblood, offers easy mastery of Egypt. The natural tendency of the Egyptians to defer to strong paternalistic government has often been abused by Egypt's rulers, whether native or alien. Yet the underlying spirit of Egypt survives and, however gradual the process, it will eventually overwhelm or absorb any tyranny.

Modern Egypt was late in diverting its attention from its own struggle for independence to that of the whole Arab nation. When it did so under a leader of exceptional qualities, Gamal Abdul Nasser, it was inevitable that the size and weight of the Egyptian nation should give it a dominant position in the Arab world. Yet the attitude of non-Egyptian Arabs to Egypt is always ambivalent. They acknowledge, as they must, that Cairo is the greatest of Arab cities and a centre of Arab culture and learning. They agree that the headquarters of the Arab League should hardly be anywhere but the Egyptian capital and the Egyptian army is the most considerable force to stand against Israel. But there are elements of resentment in their attitude. This is partly the natural human dislike of being placed in a subordinate position and may be compared with the attitude of Europeans to Americans after the Second World War. It is noticeable that whereas individual Egyptians, who are usually amiable and humorous,[1] are generally popular in the Arab world, anything that smacks of Egyptian officialdom or 'imperialism' is deeply resented. But there is another element in Arab feelings about the Egyptians, which is a doubt whether they are true converts to Arab nationalism. Nasser's charisma buried these doubts for a time but it never eliminated an important school of thought in Egypt, to which many of its most distinguished writers and political thinkers have belonged, who can be described as 'pharaonists', because they believe that the nation is at its best when it is true to the heritage of Ancient Egypt rather than Arab/Islamic culture. Non-Egyptian Arabs may therefore claim that the Egyptians are not wholehearted in their Arabism. Egyptians may ask in return which of the other Arab states, with the possible exception of Syria, can claim to represent the pure spirit of Arab nationalism. From Sumerian Iraq to the Arab–Berber kingdom of Morocco, they all have a complex inheritance.

In the sixteen years of his mastery of Egypt (1954–70) Nasser attempted nothing less than the transformation of the country's political and economic outlook. Nasser was of course aware that, even if he had not worked himself to death at fifty-two, there was no prospect of any substantial increase in the income of the individual Egyptian during his lifetime. But, with the Nile High Dam as a foundation, he hoped for a 'Great Leap Forward' in both agriculture and industry to change Egypt's colonial cotton-based economy into one that could make and export a variety of products and set itself the not unreasonable ambition of becoming the Japan of Africa. At the same time he hoped, through a massive investment in education, health and other services, to raise the social levels of the Egyptian masses.

Some years after his death it was still too soon to say how far he had succeeded in his aims because it will take more than a generation for

---

1. The Egyptians have a marvellous gift for laughter and are famous for their jokes. If Egypt is the Centre of Gravity it is also the Centre of Levity of the Arab world.

the major innovations of his era to achieve their full effects. Some things may be said with confidence. The period of real economic expansion and progress was between 1956 and 1964. Although *per capita* income is only a rough and notoriously inaccurate estimate of human welfare, this certainly increased during those years; and as a result of land reform, price and rent controls, food subsidies and taxation policy there was some improvement in the gross maldistribution of wealth. The average Egyptian, especially in the towns, was noticeably healthier and better fed in 1964 than in 1954. Educational opportunities were also greatly increased. In the 1950s the régime could claim that it was opening two new schools every three days. Inevitably, the quality of the teaching was often low, and there has recently been criticism that expansion was too hasty. Illiteracy has not fallen nearly as fast as was hoped. (One of the besetting problems is that in the countryside the children are kept away from school by their parents to work in the fields.) Nevertheless, by the 1970s Egypt was turning out tens of thousands of teachers, engineers, doctors, pharmacists and administrators. Many of them left to work abroad in other Arab countries of the West, where they could find more and better paid opportunities. They formed a brain drain, which Egypt could ill afford in human terms, although the money they sent back to Egypt helped the balance of payments. After 1964 there was a marked slowing down, which was mainly due to the drying-up of foreign investment aid. (In the 1956–64 period of expansion Egypt was outstandingly successful in securing help from both East and West, but this could not continue indefinitely.) By 1966 Egypt, having learned from some of its errors, was very possibly prepared for a new period of expansion when the disaster of the 1967 war intervened. Since then the need to replace military losses, the immense devastation of the Suez Canal cities and the continuing 'no peace, no war' situation have undermined all Egypt's development plans. As long as some 20 per cent of Egypt's GNP continues to be devoted to military expenditure, there is no hope of breaking the vicious circle of poverty for most of the population. It is as much as any régime can do to hold inflation in check and prevent the existing low living standards from actually falling.[2]

2. An excellent assessment of the economic achievements and failures of the Nasser period is Robert Mabro's *The Egyptian Economy 1952–1972*, London, 1974. He concludes: 'Economic development is a slow and very long process. Governments, however, are under pressure, from within their countries and without, to achieve rapid economic progress. Attempts to markedly hasten the pace – as in Egypt between 1956 and 1964 –

Critics and admirers of Nasser's rule are agreed on one of its aspects: it was highly personal. For fifteen years all decisions on matters of foreign and domestic policy were taken by one man. He dominated all those around him with his presence, and although some of his colleagues among the Free Officers were men of strong character they either forebore to challenge his authority or were squeezed out of the centre of power. (The only possible exception was Nasser's closest colleague Field-Marshal Abdul Hakim Amer whom he allowed a fairly free hand to control the armed forces.) Although Nasser broadly speaking secured the consent of the Egyptian people to his government he never obtained their participation. His attempts to broaden the basis of popular participation, through parliament or the single political organization the National Union, which was replaced in 1972 by the Arab Socialist Union, were sincerely intended but always conflicted with his natural authoritarianism. Moreover, whereas some Egyptians, such as communists or the Muslim Brothers on the extreme right, disputed his authority the great majority were prepared to leave decision-making in his hands. This remained true to an astonishing degree after the disasters of 1967.

Nasser's successor on his premature death therefore inherited a task of appalling difficulty. He not only had to confront the devastating political and economic problems created by Egypt's 'No war, no peace' situation but to do so through a power system moulded to Nasser's image.

Anwar Sadat had the one advantage that, under this system, as the only vice-president he at once became acting president and his candidature for the presidency was virtually unchallengeable. On the other hand, in appointing him in December 1969 to act as head of state in his absence for the Rabat summit meeting, Nasser almost certainly had not thought of him as his inevitable successor. Nasser had never appointed Sadat to any high executive office. He was regarded as loyal by the Egyptian people but as no more than a political lightweight.

As happens fairly often in such cases, Anwar Sadat's stature grew to fill the high office he had inherited. His first and most urgent task was to establish his own authority.

This was challenged almost immediately by Ali Sabry (whom he

---

may turn out to be short-lived because of gaps in resources, which reflect conflicts of objectives competing for scarce means. Not that all that was done in Egypt at that time is lost – on the contrary; the achievements were in many respects impressive.'

had made one of the two vice-presidents) and other senior Nasserist officials who felt that Sadat should either allow himself to be manipulated as a front man or set aside. Two weeks after he dismissed Ali Sabry, this group attempted a bloodless coup by resigning *en masse*. Sadat, strengthened by a crucial promise of loyalty from the armed forces, met the challenge squarely. He formed a new government and put Ali Sabry, the resigning ministers and their associates on trial for conspiracy against the state. In a series of speeches he promised the Egyptians that he would end all previous abuses of police power, restore the rule of law, reform the political system and generally introduce 'freedom and democracy'. He consistently denied any intention of reversing the positive achievements of the Nasser revolution (which he could hardly do since he had been part of it) but only to rectify its mistakes.

The fact that Ali Sabry had been leader of the pro-Soviet wing of the Nasser régime led most observers to diagnose a sharp swing to the right. Others went further to talk of a wholesale dismantling of the Nasserist structure. The popular anecdote of the kind the Cairenes delight in had Sadat on an outing in the presidential limousine arriving at a crossroads. The chauffeur asks the new president which way he should turn. Sadat asks, 'Which way did President Nasser go?' 'Left, your excellency.' 'Well, signal left and turn right!'

But this anecdote was ahead of reality. The dispute with Ali Sabry was over power rather than ideology. Within the extremely narrow options open to Sadat and with almost no prospect of finding an alternative arms supplier to the Soviet Union, there was no real opportunity for a sharp swing to the right away from non-alignment and towards the West. Even at home it was quite unfeasible, in Egypt's tense situation, to think of dismantling the socialist structure and replacing it with a free economy. In the same way the restoration of public liberties was much more easily promised than carried out. It was not only that, in Egypt's semi-war situation, the régime felt quite unable to subject itself to full freedom of criticism, but also that President Sadat, having established his authority, had to defend it. There are no effective checks and balances to presidential power in Egypt except rivals for the office.

However, although Nasser's Egypt was far from being transformed under Sadat there was a discernible change in the tone of public life. The mere removal of Nasser's dominating presence allowed greater freedom of individual expression. Also the presidential style had changed. Nasser was an ascetic who devoted himself to work, which ultimately killed him; his wife was a shy and retiring woman who rarely appeared in public. Anwar Sadat, on the other hand, who visibly enjoyed the good things of life, emphasized the ceremonial and social aspect of his office. His attractive half-British wife Jihan performed the role of Egypt's first lady with more aplomb than many of the presidential consorts of Western countries. In the Sadat era the sequestration orders against the property of the *ancien régime* where reversed. All this combined to make him popular among Egypt's middle and upper classes. Equally it made him an object of suspicion to the left and those of the old Nasserist cadres who had been replaced.

The years 1971–3 were of mounting difficulty for Sadat's presidency. While the American government showed no sign of following up the Rogers Plan of 1970 by enforcing an Israeli withdrawal in Sinai, the Soviet Union rejected Egypt's repeated appeals to supply the type of arms that made an Egyptian crossing of the Suez Canal a feasible alternative. The two superpowers seemed increasingly interested in their own mutual détente. At home Egyptian people were in an angry mood. Left-wing students, encouraged by Palestinians, were demanding action. The army, sitting paralysed on the banks of the Suez Canal, was restive. A million refugees from the Canal towns were heightening the already desperate social problems of Egypt's cities. The public as a whole wondered why it was being called to make sacrifices for a war to recover lost territory which never came. When President Sadat explained why his promised 'year of decision' in 1971 had ended in total inaction with the apparently lame excuse that the Indo-Pakistani war had diverted the attention of the world, and especially the Soviet Union, from the Middle East, he even became an object of derision. The political jokes which circulated about him were more savage than affectionate.

In the summer of 1972 Sadat made what had every appearance of a desperate throw to restore his popularity when he ordered the withdrawal of all Soviet military advisers from Egypt. It was popular because the Soviet presence was disliked – especially by the army. Few Egyptians were happy with the feeling that their former British occupiers had merely been replaced by Russians. Sadat's gesture was dangerous because he had no real alternative to Soviet military aid.

He took no steps to find out beforehand what the US response would be. All he got was an approving nod from President Nixon. Many Egyptians began to have doubts about the rationality of Sadat's action as soon as it was taken.

In order to dominate his critics, Sadat still lacked the authority and prestige which Nasser enjoyed, even after 1967. But Sadat had an advantage which turned out to be invaluable. Because he did not cast the same shadow as Nasser, other Arab leaders did not fear he was trying to impose an Egyptian hegemony. They were much more ready to cooperate on a basis of equality. Ultimately, Sadat was much more successful than Nasser in forming a united Arab front to which each Arab state contributed the resources with which it was most endowed. His greatest success was with the Arab oil states and notably with the most important of them, which had for so long been Nasser's enemy: Saudi Arabia. The Saudi–Egyptian axis became the basis of an Arab political/military strategy in 1973.

Anwar Sadat emerged from the October 1973 Arab–Israeli war with greatly enhanced prestige and authority. His strategy had been devised with skill and foresight. What was most surprising was that it succeeded in deceiving the Israelis. Despite the severe military set-back of Israel's crossing of the Suez Canal in the last week of the war, Sadat broadly won the limited political objectives he had set himself. Foreign journalists who had earlier described Sadat as a man of straw were thinking of ways to eat their words.

The rapprochement between Egypt and the United States, which had been one of Sadat's principal objectives and was exemplified by the exceptionally warm personal relationship he established with Henry Kissinger, had important consequences inside Egypt. The swing towards the West became more pronounced. As American and other Western businessmen poured into Cairo, a series of new laws designed to encourage and guarantee foreign private investment were promulgated as part of the new policy of *infitah* or 'open door'.

The basis of President Sadat's political strategy was his declared view that the United States of America holds 99 per cent of the cards in the Middle East. Through Dr Kissinger's mediation, Egypt reached military disengagement agreements with Israel in January 1973 and September 1975 which made possible the reopening of the Suez Canal in June 1975, the repopulation of the Canal cities and the recovery of Egypt's Sinai oil fields.

The obverse side to these achievements was that Egypt's new relationship with the other Arab states came increasingly under strain as they became aware that Egypt was in the process of withdrawing from the Arab front with Israel. The rapprochement with the United States also ended the close relationship with the Soviet Union which halted military supplies early in 1973.

At home a number of liberalizing measures were taken to restore the authority and independence of the law courts, to dismantle the police state, and to increase political freedom. In 1976 permission was given for three *nawabir*, or political platforms, to be formed, representing respectively the right, left and centre; and following elections in October in which the government centrists won a huge majority, the President said the *nawabir* could now become fully-fledged political parties. But it was made clear that liberalization would be within strict limits. The presidency retained overwhelming powers under the Constitution and the President continued to use these in various ways to control freedom of expression and paralyse his critics.

The *infitah* policy brought some benefits in stimulating the private sector – especially the small entrepreneurs and artisan class and encouraging Western aid, although foreign private investment remained extremely limited. Egypt's socialist system was ripe for reform. But *infitah* also had serious drawbacks. It had raised public expectations of prosperity too high and disappointment was inevitable. It also caused the emergence of a new high-spending millionaire class. Conspicuous corruption and consumption – together with that of non-Egyptian Arabs flooding into Cairo – was an insult to the poverty-stricken Egyptian urban masses.

When severe rioting broke out in all major Egyptian cities in January 1977 in protest against government economic measures aimed to reduce subsidies for essentials, President Sadat blamed the disturbances exclusively on the left. The rioters had chanted the name of Nasser, and President Sadat declared that Nasser and Nasserism had been dead since 1967. From then on he was openly critical of all aspects of the Nasserist era except for the early years after the 1952 Revolution. He condemned the National Charter as valueless.[3]

There was a conflict at the heart of Sadat's ideology. His pro-Americanism and his desire to place Egypt firmly in the Western camp were matched by a very Egyptian type of conservatism. His detestation of the left led him to tolerate and even encourage Islamic militants who were able to gain control of the student unions in most of Egypt's universities. He raised expectations among Egyptian Muslims that the country was moving towards a true Islamic order with full application of the *shari'a* legal system. This alarmed Egypt's

3. See Anwar el-Sadat, *In Search of Identity*, London, 1978. For a devastating comparison of Sadat's earlier adulation of Nasser with his later deprecation see David Hirst and Irene Beeson, *Sadat*, London, 1981.

Coptic minority. Christian–Muslim relations deteriorated to an extent that had been unknown since the 1952 Revolution.

As Sadat moved towards a separate peace with Israel and he joined the United States in denouncing the Khomeini revolution in Iran, which was an inspiration to most Islamic militants, they turned against him. Eventually an extreme group among them destroyed him.

Sadat's decision to make his pilgrimage to Jerusalem in November 1977 was entirely his own. His Foreign Minister believed that there were still real prospects of forming a common Arab approach to a renewed Middle East peace conference, with both the USA and USSR participating, and that this would be infinitely preferable.[4]

Sadat astonished and delighted the outside world with his mission which he performed with courage and dignity. But because he was unable to secure the support or even the acquiescence of any of the other key Arab states and he could not afford to allow his gesture to fail, he was forced into concluding a separate peace with Israel. His violent response to his Arab critics only increased Egypt's isolation.

The Egyptian people showed they had mixed feelings about what was happening. There was a longing and a desperate need for peace. There was also a feeling that Egypt had suffered too much in the Arab cause and that, in the common phrase, the other Arabs including the Palestinians, were ready to fight 'to the last Egyptian'. Some leading Egyptian intellectuals rationalized these feelings by talking of an Egyptian identity and destiny which were separate from those of the other Arabs. At the same time, Egyptians were delighted with the recovery of their territory and the left made no headway with its claim that the demilitarization of Sinai involved a loss of sovereignty. Yet it was apparent that there was a deep and growing uneasiness in Egypt about the trend of events. It was not only that most Egyptians felt that, in spite of everything, Egypt should play a leading role in the Arab world and Sadat's attitude that the other Arabs must first beg Egypt's forgiveness was making this impossible. There were also growing doubts about Sadat's apparent eagerness to replace the Shah's Iran and Israel as the United States' principal surrogate in the region.

Sadat became increasingly intolerant of criticism. Already in 1978 he had done much to destroy his reputation for liberalism. The old Wafd party had revived and was gathering support while the vocal

4. See Ismail Fahmy, *Negotiating for Peace in the Middle East*, London, 1983.

left-wing party was publishing its own highly successful weekly paper. Sadat responded by holding a referendum to endorse measures to remove from politics and the media all those who entertained 'atheist ideologies' and those who had corrupted political life before 1952. The New Wafd then announced it was disbanding and the left-wing Progressive party that it was suspending its activities. In September 1981, seeing a concerted move to overthrow him, Sadat ordered the arrest of some 1,500 personalities from the full extent of the political spectrum, including Muslim divines and Coptic bishops. All they had in common was that they were critical of some aspect of his policies. Sadat's assassination on 6 October 1981 by Muslim extremists was not followed by any general uprising of Islamic fundamentalists. Most Egyptians were shocked by the violence. But they who are accustomed to venerate their leaders entirely failed to mourn the death of Sadat.

Sadat's successor, Vice-President Husni Mubarak enjoyed the same advantage of a smooth succession under the constitution. But although he had acquired some knowledge of international diplomacy in his six years as vice-president, his purely military career had given him no experience in political manoeuvre. His great assets were his personal modesty, a capacity for hard work and a reputation for incorruptibility which was never seriously challenged.

President Mubarak's succession marked an immediate change in the presidential style. He soon released all Sadat's political prisoners except for Muslim extremists accused of acts of violence. In a much improved political atmosphere he engaged in a dialogue with the opposition. At the same time he moved to check the more obvious abuses of the *infitah* policy while maintaining its essentials. He said he wanted to see an *infitah* for industry rather than for consumption.

In foreign policy he ended all the media hostilities with the Arab states and began slowly and patiently to improve his relations with most of them as far as was compatible with Egypt's treaty with Israel. For the treaty he saw no alternative since a renewed war was out of the question. Relations with Israel were cool and became cooler with Israel's invasion of Lebanon in 1982 which stirred much indignation in Egypt. Progress towards 'normalizing' Israeli–Egyptian relations ceased but there was no break and President Sadat's policy of close friendship with the United States remained, and there were only minor gestures towards a reconciliation with the USSR. On the other hand, President Mubarak effectively abandoned the part of the Camp David agreement dealing with the Palestinian question, declaring that Egypt had no mandate to negotiate Palestinian autonomy on behalf of the Palestinians.

Egypt's new ruler could not fail to be aware that he had a narrow space in which to manoeuvre. The country's gigantic social and economic problems could be alleviated but not solved by Western aid, the remittances of 2 million Egyptian workers abroad, oil exports and Suez Canal revenues. After two years of the new presidency there was an inevitable feeling of anti-climax in the country. While the worst errors of the Sadat era had been remedied there was no breakthrough. While President Mubarak had not built up his own political constituency – there was no identifiable cadre of Mubarakists as there had been, and still were, of Nasserists and Sadatists – the opposition could claim that overwhelming powers were still being employed by the presidency to ensure that the country was still effectively a one-party state.

There were signs, however, that President Mubarak's dogged patience was bearing fruit in some respects. Arab disarray made the boycott of Egypt appear increasingly harmful to Arab interests. Yasir Arafat's reconciliation with President Mubarak after his departure from Lebanon in December 1983 was openly welcomed by all the moderate and pro-Western Arab governments and Egypt could claim, with some justification, that its own attitude towards a settlement of the Arab–Israeli dispute was proving to be right. For Cairo to resume its function as the headquarters of the Arab League was still a distant prospect but there were signs that Egypt was returning to the centre of gravity of the Arab world.

No one could doubt that the spirit of the Egyptian nation which has endured so much and for so long will survive whatever new trials it is called upon to face. Nasser never lost his faith that the descendants of the men who built the Great Pyramids would once again astonish the world. As the French archaeologist remarks of the *fellahin* in *The Rediscovered Soul* by Tewfik al-Hakim, Nasser's favourite Egyptian author:

Europe has failed to understand that these people whom we regard as ignorant know many things. The Great Wisdom flows in his blood but it flows without his knowledge . . . Can you really believe that the thousands of years which made up Egypt's past have vanished like a dream without a trace?

26. Libya: the Inveterate Challenger

When on 1 September 1969 a group of young Libyan army officers carried out a brilliantly successful coup to depose the seventy-nine-year-old King Idris (who was in Turkey for medical treatment) and declared a republic, no one in the Arab world knew much about them. A coup had been expected, and hoped for, by the Arab revolutionary régimes. By 1969 the impoverished desert state of the 1950s had become one of the world's leading oil-producers. In that year its exports surpassed those of Kuwait and Saudi Arabia. But it remained a Western satellite with the only significant British and American military bases left on Arab soil. The Egyptians were especially interested in having a sympathetic régime on their western flank, but they expected the coup to come from the more senior officers with whom they were in contact.

It was not long before Nasser and the rest of the Arab world recognized the unusual qualities of the lean, handsome twenty-seven-year-old army captain with burning eyes, who became chairman of the otherwise anonymous Revolutionary Command Council. Promoted to colonel and commander-in-chief of the Libyan armed forces, Muammar al-Qaddafy became at once a formidable force in Arab politics. He could be attacked, deplored and sometimes derided, but never ignored. Some of his colleagues are able men of strong character but he has always dominated them with his personality.

Muammar al-Qaddafy is unusual but he is not *sui generis*. His passionate feelings and attitudes are the product of his Libyan background and of his experiences as a schoolboy and junior officer in the intoxicating heyday of the Nasser revolution. He was born in a beduin family at Sirte on the desert coast of central Libya. Neither he nor any of his colleagues on the Revolutionary Council came from the traditionally dominant tribes or families of Libya. He grew up with a fierce pride in the heritage of his people and a passionate belief in the regenerative power of Arabism and Islam. Gamal Abdul Nasser was and remains his idol. He is convinced that the Arab nation was never closer to achieving its ideal than when the masses accepted Nasser's leadership. But eventually it became apparent that his ambitions went beyond merely following in Nasser's footsteps. He saw himself not only as a new Arab leader but as the creator of an ideology derived from Arab and Islamic values which would show the way to the rest of the world.

Initially he combined his fierce nationalism with a puritanical fundamentalism. He was both a radical revolutionary who detested the corruption, materialism and subservience to the West of Libya's former rulers, and a dedicated anti-communist and social conservative who favoured the strict application of the *sharia* law and opposed the emancipation of women.

The first steps taken by Qaddafy and his Revolutionary Council were to be expected. They secured the agreement of the US and British governments to close their military bases and withdraw. They offered help to the Palestinian guerrilla organization al-Fatah and established regular contacts with the Egyptian régime. In fact they turned the whole focus of Libya's attention towards the east. Under the monarchy Libya had been regarded as belonging more to the Maghreb, the Western half of the Arab world, than to the Eastern half, the Mashrek, and the government had been involved in discussions of Maghreb unity with Tunisia, Algeria and Morocco.

Several reasons combined to make Colonel Qaddafy turn his country round to face eastwards. Apart from his admiration for President Nasser, he looked upon Egypt as the essential nucleus of a union of Arab states. Moreover, the cause of Palestine liberation was the focus of Arab interest. Despite the undeniable prestige and growing influence of Algeria in the Arab world, the Maghreb was too remote from the Arab heartlands to absorb Qaddafy's attention. Nasser responded to Qaddafy's enthusiastic overtures. After the collapse of the Arab summit meeting in Rabat, he flew to Tripoli to sign with Qaddafy and Colonel Nimeiry, who had recently come to power in Sudan, a tripartite pact known as the Tripoli Charter, uniting the three régimes in an Arab Revolutionary Front. Nasser gave Nimeiry the title of 'Guardian of Arab Nationalism'.

At home Muammar Qaddafy pushed forward with his puritan Islamic revolution. Alcohol was forbidden, bars and nightclubs were closed. New regulations required all street signs and public notices to be written in Arabic only. Italian ex-colonists were banned from owning land and the remains of their expatriate colony left in a flood. The Mediterranean-style café and casino life of Tripoli vanished completely. But although the young revolutionaries set out to destroy the overt signs of Western influence they had no intention that Libya should remain an undeveloped desert state living off its oil revenues. After a short breathing-space in which the economy marked time, they stepped up expenditure on agriculture, industry, public works and all the social services. Helped by successful negotiations with the oil companies to increase revenues, they soon increased development expenditure in nearly every sector to five or six times their levels before the 1969 revolution. Since Libya lacked teachers, doctors, administrators and technicians of all kinds, they imported them from Egypt and to a lesser extent from other Arab countries such as Tunisia or Syria. By 1972 there were some 200,000 Egyptians working in Libya.

Nasser's death in September 1970 was a severe blow to Colonel Qaddafy, but it did not stop him from pursuing the cause of pan-Arabism. On the contrary, he seemed to believe that he had inherited Nasser's mantle. The trouble was that he was soon on bad terms with nearly every Arab régime as he found cause to criticize their behaviour. He denounced them for being reactionary and corrupt, for having too close ties with the Soviet Union or for being insufficiently enthusiastic about Arab unity.

In international affairs, Colonel Qaddafy has shown a unique capacity for the provocative gesture. He claimed to be supporting guerrilla organizations in the United States and to be supplying arms to the Irish Republican Army. He gave heroes' burials to the five Palestinian Arabs who were shot during the Munich Olympics massacre and he sent 400 troops by air to help Idi Amin, the Muslim president of Uganda who was expelling the Israeli advisers from his country. However, the Libyan troops were turned back by the Sudanese. He nationalized British Petroleum in Libya as a political protest against Britain's failure to prevent the Iranians from seizing three small Arab islands in the Persian Gulf. Perhaps his most characteristic gesture was to insist that henceforth the passports of any visitors to Libya would have to be written in Arabic as well as English and French. Most Arabs admitted that the action made little sense; if Arabic was needed, why not Chinese or Russian? Yet once again he had touched a responsive chord in their feelings.

Qaddafy was by no means satisfied with gestures of this kind. Libya must be an example to all the other Arab and Muslim states. After a period of reflection in mid-April 1973 he announced his 'cultural revolution' which aimed to purge the Libyan revolution of all anti-Islamic and anti-Arab elements and principles. His five-point programme said that all existing laws must be replaced by new revolutionary laws, all 'perverts and deviationists' must be weeded out and all forms of bourgeoisie and bureaucracy abolished. 'Popular committees' would be established in every sector of society to enable the people to seize power. At about the same time Qaddafy announced his theory of the Third Way between capitalism and communism, which became the official doctrine of the Libyan government. Declaring the need for a new outlook, since capitalism and communism had both failed, Qaddafy said that his Third Way was based on religion and nationalism which are the motive forces of history.

Qaddafy expounded his Third Way ideology in the three volumes of his Green Book which appeared between 1975 and 1979. The second volume, entitled *The Solution of the Economic Problem – Socialism*, was based on the idea that 'whoever possesses your needs controls or exploits you' and concluded that 'in the final stage profit will automatically disappear and there will be no need for money'. The most severe restrictions were applied to housing. Since only one house per family was to be allowed all privately owned rented properties were taken over by the government. A limit of 10,000 dinars was placed on personal bank deposits. With government encouragement, workers took over the management of some two hundred public and private companies. In 1981 the state took over all import, export and distribution functions and a series of state-run supermarkets replaced private retailers. By 1982 the private sector had virtually been eliminated.

It was already apparent from the first volume of the Green Book that the term 'Islamic fundamentalist' was a misnomer when applied to Qaddafy. He saw himself rather as a new Mahdi or spiritual leader who had reopened the gate of *ijtihad* or the exercise of independent judgement. He rejected all the Prophet's Hadith and Islamic jurisprudence based upon them, accepting only the Koran as a source of guidance. In numerous ways he rejected conventional Islamic thinking – from his attitude to private property to the training of girl soldiers to form his personal bodyguard. Inevitably this brought him into conflict with the *ulama*. He was not attempting to make a secular revolution but he was harnessing Islam to its needs. He argues that 'there is nothing in real life . . . for which principles are not found in Islam'. But also since the essence of religion is the unity of God there can be no distinction between the followers of Muhammad, Jesus and Moses; he considers all monotheists to be Muslims. At the same time, since every nation must have a religion and the religion of the Arabs is

Islam he believes that Christian Arabs have adopted the wrong position and should become Muslims in order to be true Arabs.

Years of power have not made Qaddafy any less unpredictable and adventurous. He has quarrelled with virtually every Arab régime, including the PLO leadership. He has denounced them for treachery and corruption and called for their overthrow; in some cases he has actively worked for it. Where he has established cooperation with Arab states such as Syria or the PDRY this has aroused alarm and hostility among others. Friction with Sadat's Egypt reached the stage of open warfare in 1977. Partly because of his inevitable frustration in achieving the unity of the Arabs he has diverted his attention to sub-Saharan Africa, usually with disastrous results, as in Uganda in 1980 or Chad in 1982–3. In 1982 he spared no effort for the summit meeting of the Organization of African Unity to be held in Tripoli. But he had made so many enemies that nineteen countries boycotted the meeting so that the necessary two-thirds quorum was not attained and no formal sessions could take place. Yet his quixotic character has also enabled him suddenly to change course, appearing without warning in an Arab capital to attempt a reconciliation. Something in the Arab character means that he is rarely rebuffed. In 1983, for example, both King Hassan of Morocco and President Bourguiba of Tunisia, who had good reason to believe he had tried to promote rebellion against them, welcomed his overtures towards Maghreb unity. This does not mean that any Arab state would regard him as a reliable ally. The form of unity Syria entered into with Libya in 1980 has notably failed to develop.

While the relations between Qaddafy's Libya and the Arab world have been stormy and uncertain those with the United States have continuously deteriorated. From 1975 onwards he moved closer to the Soviet Union which became his principal arms supplier, although he never withdrew his opposition to the communist system. To the United States, on the other hand, Libya was an international trouble-maker of major proportions. It was seen as a threat to American interests throughout Africa and the Middle East. Colonel Qaddafy was certainly not dissatisfied with this image.

That a country which was carved out of the desert a generation ago and still has a population of little more than 3 million should achieve such international prominence has been remarkable. It can only partly be explained by Libyan oil wealth and its use to promote anti-government movements in various quarters of the world. In fact the revenues declined together with exports by more than two thirds in the early 1980s but with little discernible curbing of Libyan initiatives. In the more affluent 1970s a major part of the revenues was used to build an economic infrastructure and create social services which underpinned the régime. Some austerity was possible without seriously shaking its popularity. Considering the range of interests that Qaddafy had offended – the *ancien régime*, the new middle class, the *ulama* as well as many of his former revolutionary colleagues – it was surprising that no effective opposition front had been formed.

Many of Colonel Qaddafy's precepts are confused and self-contradictory. Much of his political and military strategy – such as his support for Idi Amin of Uganda and his efforts to obtain atomic weapons – has been wildly irresponsible and futile. But with his resilience and charisma and his insistence that a Third Way can be found between communism and capitalism he continues to arouse interest at the very least among the people of the Third World. When in August 1981 Libya openly challenged the mighty US navy which it said was violating its territorial waters and two of its planes were shot down, the feeling merged into sympathy for the Libyan gadfly's defiance of the superpower.

27. Tunisia: the Dogmatic Moderate

Westerners, whose knowledge of the Arab world is limited to occasional press reports, are apt to think of Tunisia as 'the sensible Arab state'. They contrast its generally balanced and moderate view of world affairs with the emotional rhetoric of other Arab countries.

This is not only because Tunisia is pro-Western, and therefore wise, in occidental eyes. The Tunisian republic under its remarkable leader, Habib Bourguiba, has consistently aimed to take the logical and dispassionate view on all issues and especially those relating to the Middle East. Occasionally this has made for a certain complacency, a quiet satisfaction in the knowledge of superior wisdom, which is understandably irritating to the other Arabs.

President Bourguiba's leadership has scarcely been challenged since Tunisia achieved independence in 1956. His hold on the country has only faltered during his periods of bad health when he was absent from the country for long periods. In the 1950s he was a constant and telling critic of Arab policies – especially President Nasser's – and proposed his own cautious strategy of advancing step-by-step from one prepared position to another, which he called 'Bourguibisme'. Nasser and Bourguiba were temporarily reconciled in 1961 when Bourguiba seemed to abandon his own creed by ordering an armed attack on the Bizerta naval base, which the French had refused to give up. A thousand Tunisian lives were lost but the French withdrew.

Despite their differences, Nasser and Bourguiba had much in common. Both were authoritarian, charismatic leaders, who sought to rid their countries of feudalism and foreign control. They shared many views on social and economic reforms. Nasser was more socialist on economic matters, while Bourguiba was more of a secularist, who was known to order women to remove their veils and advised Tunisian workers not to keep the Muslim fast of Ramadan if it interfered with production.

The differences of temperament and character were too strong for the truce between the two leaders to last. In April 1965 Bourguiba's suggestion during a visit to the eastern Arab states that the Arabs should make peace with Israel as a start towards a solution of the

Palestine problem on the basis of the 1947 Partition Resolution brought angry reactions in many quarters of the Arab world, including Egypt. Bourguiba was acting in the way that Nasser most disliked. He was breaking the façade of Arab unity on Palestine, which had only recently been created with difficulty at the summit meetings, and providing an opening for Western sympathizers with Israel to drive a permanent wedge between the Arab states on this issue. In fact Bourguiba's analysis of the Palestine problem and the reasons for past Arab failures was very similar to Nasser's. It was Bourguiba's manner of appearing to lecture the Arabs from a pinnacle of superior wisdom which infuriated the Egyptian leader. Since Tunisia was not directly involved and had suffered no danger or damage from the creation of Israel, he felt it had no right to set itself up as the spokesman of a moderate and rational Arab view of the Palestine question. Impervious to the flood of criticism, Bourguiba counter-attacked, accusing Egypt of exploiting the Arab League for its own purposes. He disdainfully refused to follow Egypt's lead in breaking off diplomatic relations with West Germany when the Bonn government established diplomatic ties with Israel.

After the Bizerta affair of 1961 and the nationalization of French property in Tunisia in 1964, France placed Tunisia in a political and economic quarantine for a time. But Franco-Tunisian relations gradually recovered. Bourguiba was anxious for reconciliation; with uncharacteristic modesty, he even acknowledged his 'lack of experience' at the time of the nationalization of the French settlers' property. At the same time he moved to place Tunisia firmly in the pro-Western camp. An American company was hired to convert the former Bizerta base into a naval dockyard. In 1966 Bourguiba went so far as to express his approval of US raids on North Vietnam.

Tunisia was briefly reconciled with the other Arab states at the time of the June 1967 war. Some Tunisian troops were sent to the front although they did not arrive in time to fight. Tunisia was not immune to the wave of anti-Western feeling which swept the Arab world, encouraged by the belief that Britain and the US had helped Israel. Rioters sacked the British and US embassies and attacked synagogues. Bourguiba at once clamped down on the unrest; the leaders of the demonstrations, who were university teachers and students, were arrested and given heavy jail sentences. This was only part of a long struggle between Bourguiba and left-wing elements in the universities. In 1968 another mass trial of students and teachers accused of plotting to overthrow the government became a major affair as French teachers working in Tunisia, and the French left, took up the cause of the students.

Tunisia was once again at loggerheads with most of the Arab world. When the Syrians accused Bourguiba of betraying the Arab cause, he broke off diplomatic relations with the Arab League. When the Arab League refused to distribute a Tunisian memorandum accusing Egypt of excessive dependence on the communist countries and of pursuing policies which had led to three successive Arab defeats, he decided once again that Tunisia should boycott the League.

In 1969 Tunisia also took a sharp turn to the right in its internal policies when Bourguiba dismissed Ahmad ben Saleh, the young left-wing minister of economy, planning and education who for some years had been responsible for the country's socialist economic policies. His agrarian reform had introduced a modified form of collectivization in which small peasant holdings were grouped into 500 hectare 'agricultural units' to be administered by a single cooperative. Bourguiba had concluded that this policy was a disastrous failure because it was unsuited to Tunisian realities. Ben Saleh was disgraced and put on trial for high treason and abuse of authority. In 1973 he escaped from prison.

Although Bourguiba's authority can hardly be challenged when he is in the country, his bouts of ill health and absences for medical treatment inevitably raise the question of the succession. (Bourguiba's formidable wife, Wassila, whom he married after divorcing his French wife at the time of independence, plays a political role which is unusually forceful for a woman in a Muslim country.) Bourguiba's preference is to keep the Tunisians guessing, while hinting at his own immortality. At a poetry contest held on the occasion of his seventieth birthday in 1973 he remarked:

I must reveal to you, as well as to the rest of the people, another aspect of the personality of Bourguiba. Not only is he a man of political genius who has triumphed over French colonialism, he is also perhaps a great poet. Therefore, I have decided that these poetry contests will be renewed every ten years; I shall meet you again in 1983 for my eightieth birthday, then for my ninetieth, and then, why not, for my hundredth.

Sometimes he commiserates with the Tunisians because of the impossibility of finding a substitute for Bourguiba. 'Abilities as great as Bourguiba's are not found round every corner. They are a miracle of nature that occur rarely in history.'

It is a measure of Bourguiba's standing in the country that the

Tunisians do not find such vanity astonishing. He has had no difficulty in countering any attempts to reduce his powers. At the eighth congress of the country's single political organization, the Neo-Destour party, a former interior minister, Ahmad Mestiri, led a tentative move to liberalize the party's rigid structure. The liberals succeeded in winning the elections to the party's Central Committee. But it made little difference. Bourguiba gathered ultra-loyalist elements around him and had Mestiri isolated and expelled from the party. At the ninth party congress in 1974 he reversed the decisions of the eighth congress and had himself elected president for life.

However, this has by no means meant that his governments have been able to take stability for granted. In 1976 and 1977 the Prime Minister, Hedi Nouira, was faced with increasingly aggressive opposition from students, trade unionists, intellectuals and organized political parties. Followers of the exiled Ahmed Ben Saleh contributed to the unrest. In January 1978 the resignation of Habib Achour, secretary-general of the single trade union federation, was followed by a general strike, clashes between police and demonstrators leaving more than fifty dead and the arrest of Achour and other union leaders. Ignoring protests from international trade union organizations, the government re-imposed its control on the Tunisian unions and put Achour and his colleagues on trial.

President Bourguiba's failing health recovered sufficiently in 1979 for him to resume control of affairs. He marked his seventy-fifth birthday by pardoning Achour and several hundred other political offenders. He confirmed that Hedi Nouira would be his successor but in the spring of 1980 Nouira suffered a stroke and abandoned political life. President Bourguiba replaced him by Mohammed Mzali and subsequently announced that it was Mzali who would ultimately succeed the 'Combattant Suprème' as Bourguiba is officially known in Tunisia.

Since 1979 a new form of opposition to the régime has become prominent: Islamic militants who have received added inspiration from the Khomeini revolution in Iran and call for a fully Islamic state. As would be expected, they have their greatest following among university students. President Bourguiba tried to deal as firmly with them as with all other forms of opposition, making clear that Tunisia will not be diverted from its mildly secularizing policies. He has employed ridicule as well as the prestige of his office. Islamic fundamentalist students invariably wear beards. 'You think that a beard makes you a good Muslim?' he asked of one at a university prize-giving. 'The Emperor Charlemagne wore a beard – was he one also?' Leading members of the fundamentalist Mouvement de la Tendance Islamique have been tried and imprisoned. At the same time, in preparation for his own departure President Bourguiba has taken steps towards a more liberal and democratic régime. At an extraordinary congress of the ruling Neo-Destour in 1981 he approved the principle of party plurality. The Communist party, outlawed since 1963, was licensed and two other parties followed in 1983.

Liberalization is a recognition of the fact that some decentralization of power is inevitable after nearly thirty years of Bourguiba's authoritarian rule of independent Tunisia. However, the difficulties of moving towards democracy were underlined in January 1984 when economic austerity measures inspired by IMF advice and insensitively handled by the government led to widespread rioting. President Bourguiba was forced to intervene and announce the cancellation of the decision to double the price of bread. The crowds declared their love and respect for Bourguiba but blamed the prime minister Mzali. The President declared his continued confidence in Mzali but it was not a good augury for his succession.

Tunisia today is a small Arab Mediterranean state (population about 7 million) aligned economically and politically to the United States and France and heavily dependent on Western Europe for markets, tourism and the export of immigrant labour. Its tourist industry has been a deserved success and it is probably the Arab country best known to Europeans. Apart from the country's assets of climate, beaches and historic sites the Tunisians have pursued an admirable policy of maintaining indigenous styles in their modern architecture. The beauty of their Mediterranean coastline has been enhanced rather than destroyed. The health of the Tunisian economy depends heavily on climate and the world situation. The fact that 60 per cent of the population is under twenty presents immense problems. But within these constraints Tunisia has in many respects provided a model for balanced development among Third World countries. The surprised international reaction to the January 1984 rioting showed that it was judged by high standards.

The fact that Tunisia has played an international role out of proportion to its size has depended largely upon the personality of Habib Bourguiba and his creative and original mind. Bourguiba's Tunisia has made an incomparable contribution to the political life of the modern Arab world through its constant challenging of received ideas and the application of reason to emotional problems. But because the Bourguiba approach, despite his idiosyncratic egoism, reflects something in the Tunisian character it is likely to survive his death. When the Arab states decided in 1979 that the Arab League headquarters should be moved from Cairo, Tunis seemed the obvious alternative. It was far from being a political backwater but it was outside the maelstrom of inter-Arab disputes.

28. Algeria: Austere Revolutionary

The Algerian republic was born in 1962 with high hopes but poor prospects. The 9 million Muslim Algerians had won their independence after one of the bloodiest colonial wars in history, which had given them high prestige and sympathy from other countries of the Third World but had cost them about 1 million lives, uprooted large masses of the rural population and forced thousands more into emigration. For the immediate future the worst disaster was that four fifths of the European *colons*, or 800,000 persons, had suddenly abandoned their Algerian homes. They included nearly all the country's technicians, teachers and administrators.

The young republic was virtually without doctors or engineers. The major city of Oran had no fire service because all the firemen were Europeans.

Apart from the spirit of its people, the country had a great national asset in the oil and natural gas fields which had been discovered in the Sahara during the independence war. The Evian agreements with France which ended the war gave the oil companies, especially those of French nationality, a privileged position. Algeria was getting substantially less for each ton of oil than the other Arab oil producers. But the Algerians were in no position even to consider running their own oil industry at that stage. They had been left with a colonial type of economy which had to be maintained as well as possible, in order to prevent a disastrous fall in output and exports, until it could be transformed into something more suited to the needs of the inhabitants. The European colonists, who owned most of the best land, treated Algeria as little more than a fruit-farm growing oranges, lemons and vines for France. In 1963 French farms left vacant since 1962, together with some large agricultural estates still under French management, were taken over by workers' management committees. The system of workers' self-management, or *autogestion*, became a special feature of the Algerian revolution. It was idealistic because it was an attempt to avoid creating a Soviet-type centralized state bureaucracy, but it was also realistic because there were no Algerian managers with experience of running large estates. It was often inefficient, but there was no real alternative at that stage.

The president of the Algerian republic in the first three years of the republic was Ahmad Ben Bella, one of the leaders of the FLN (National Liberation Front), who had been kidnapped by the French in 1956 and spent the war in prison. Ben Bella had charm and charisma, and began with a large fund of popularity. At home he introduced wide-ranging socialist measures and in foreign affairs he pursued a determined policy of making Algiers one of the leading capitals of the Third World and a focus for all African liberation movements. But his personal style of government aroused increasing discontent inside Algeria. He attempted to eliminate the military leaders from government in order to gather power into his own hands. There was also a widespread feeling that his ambitions for Third World leadership conflicted with the task of tackling Algeria's gigantic social and economic problems. Matters came to a head in the summer of 1965 when Ben Bella was planning to act as a host for a conference of Afro-Asian heads of state to mark the tenth anniversary of the historic Bandung Conference. On 19 June the army, under the defence minister, Colonel Houari Boumedienne, who had helped to bring Ben Bella to power in the early days of the republic, moved to depose Ben Bella in a swift and bloodless coup. In contrast to Ahmad Ben Bella, Houari Boumedienne was shy and retiring. When he came to power little was known about his political ideas except for a vague belief that he was a hardliner of the left.

In fact he turned out to be a gifted and dedicated statesman with a strongly pragmatic approach who steadily grew in stature during his years in power. He gave the country the stability it urgently needed but was denied while chronically disturbed by power rivalries under Ben Bella. This left the régime free to concentrate on the social and economic transformation of Algeria. With remarkable speed it succeeded in gaining mastery over the control and development of its own resources. This enabled Algeria to acquire a position as a spokesman for the developing countries of the Third World in their relations with the advanced industrial nations of both East and West.

At the time of independence it was widely believed that the FLN, which had been the instrument through which Algerian men and women had taken part in the revolution, would be entrusted with ruling the country and 'mobilizing the masses' in the Marxist sense, but this did not happen. The party survived but as little more than a shell. Such mobilization of the masses as took place was through the military commanders. The use of the army as an instrument of social and economic progress was developed and maintained. There were elected popular assemblies for the communes and for the higher levels of the governorates, or *wilayas*, for which elections were first held in June 1974, but Algeria had no national representative institutions.

The country was governed by a small, industrious élite bureaucracy which concentrated on the nation's two most urgent and manifest needs: industrialization and education. Industrialization was essential in order to provide employment for a population which was grossly unemployed during French rule and which is increasing by more than 3 per cent a year. (From 9 million at independence, it reached 20 million by 1984.) A crash programme of training was needed to run the new industries. Young Algerians were sent to any country which would provide the instruction; initially they went mostly to Eastern Europe. They returned to run the *sociétés nationales*, or autonomous state companies, which control nearly all industry. These include the Société Nationale de Sidérurgie, which has in the steel works at Annaba the nucleus of a major steel industry, but inevitably the most important is the state oil company Sonatrach. Step by step, this has succeeded in winning control over Algeria's oil resources against the stubborn opposition of the oil companies, especially the French companies, whose position was reinforced by the special privileges they gained in the pre-independence Evian agreements. The struggle culminated in February 1971 when the Algerians expropriated all French interests. The risks were great for Algeria as output fell by 25 per cent. But the French companies failed to obtain international backing against the Algerians – mainly because they had often stepped in to replace US or British companies which had been nationalized in other parts of the world – and were obliged to come to terms. Cooperation with France was resumed but on a much more equal basis.

Algeria is not, and is unlikely to become, a producer of crude oil on the scale of Saudi Arabia and Kuwait. The price increases of 1973–4 were a windfall benefit, but Algeria needs every dollar of additional revenue for its own development. On the other hand, Algeria *is* a major producer of natural gas. According to present estimates, Algeria has over 5 per cent of the total world supply and its gas fields are much more accessible than those in Siberia.

Algeria has shown determination in its industrialization plans. It has held back consumption with a tough programme of austerity and maintained a high level of investment. In the 1970–73 four-year plan Algeria was probably unique among developing countries in exceeding the planned level of investment and because of this was able to attract foreign investment in spite of its socialist policies.

However, industrialization and rapid economic development will hardly benefit the country unless they are sustained by an educated population. Here the young republic has been confronted by a problem on a wholly different scale from that of its neighbours Morocco and Tunisia. In these countries the French never set out systematically to destroy the nation's personality. In Algeria they succeeded to a certain extent. Algeria needed to be built up from the foundations as an Arab Muslim state. This presented formidable difficulties. In the first place, while the arabization of the French educational system was generally accepted as essential if Algeria was to recover its identity, there was also a clear need to retain French, at least for some time, as the medium in certain branches of higher education and as a means of access to modern scientific thought. Another problem was the lack of teachers. At the time of independence there were about 19,000 teachers in the country but all but 1,700 of those were French as the result of a secret rule restricting the number of Muslim teachers to 10 per cent of the total. In the early stages teachers had to be hired from Egypt, Syria, Jordan or any Arab country which could provide them. A third problem is that a substantial minority of Algerians, mainly from the Kabyle Mountains, speak Berber as their first language, French as their second and Arabic only as a third. The Algerian authorities deny this is a serious difficulty because Berber is not a written language. As the minister of information and culture, Mr Ahmad Taleb, remarked in 1972: 'It is wrong to say that Algeria is made up of Arabs and Berbers. Algerians are Berbers, more or less arabized. Algerian blood is Arab–Berber with Berber dominant. The Algerian people is an Arab–Berber people whose culture is Arab.'

Nevertheless, the Berber demand for cultural identity had not died and there were serious disturbances among the Berber population over the language issue in 1980 and 1981.

Impressive advances in both the spread of education and arabization have been made in spite of the difficulties. At the time of independence only about three quarters of a million Algerian Muslims went to school out of a potential 2·5 million. By 1974 there were 61,000 teachers for the 2·6 million pupils in school and education absorbed about 11 per cent of the GNP – an enormous proportion for any country. Arabization only gathered momentum in the 1970s. Before independence, teaching at all levels was still mainly in French but today all teaching at primary and secondary levels is in Arabic and the teaching at the universities of Algiers, Oran and Constantine is divided into the *ancien régime*, in which French-educated students can end their studies in French, and the *nouveau régime*, which is taught entirely in Arabic.

President Boumedienne described Algeria's political system as Islamic socialism but this better describes what it is not than what it is. It is not dogmatic or doctrinaire and it is peculiar to Algeria alone. The first obvious danger of placing so much power in the hands of a small élite bureaucracy is that, however devoted and hardworking it may be, it will become self-perpetuating and divorced from the mass of the population. A gulf divides the successful Algerian graduate who takes his holidays in France from the mass of Algerian rural and urban workers or from most of the 1 million Algerians who are still working in France.

Another consequence of the failure of the FLN to develop as a ruling party responsible for 'mobilizing the masses' is that Algerian women have not been emancipated at anything like the pace that was expected during the war of independence. Then they played a crucial role alongside the men as nurses or guerrilla fighters. Many believed that the veil would disappear in the cities, whereas today it is more commonly seen in the streets of Algiers, even on younger women, than in any Arab capital except those of Arabia. It is not surprising therefore that some Marxist critics have concluded that Algeria still has to undergo a true revolution. Writing of the Algerian countryside one of them has said:

The real obstacle is a social one; it can be overcome only through a mass peasant movement determined to break away from tradition, with all that this implies in the political sphere (discarding current forms and modes of property distribution, and current methods of exploitation), the ideological and cultural sphere, and, most important of all perhaps, the religious sphere.[1]

However, the régime has never shown any inclination towards a Maoist-type of peasant-based revolution, insisting on the nation's Arab–Islamic character. It is strengthened by the indisputable pride that most Algerians take in their country's new place in the world. Among the Arabs the Algerians enjoy high prestige because of their courage and endurance during their bitter struggle for independence.

1. Samir Amin, *The Maghreb in the Modern World*, Harmondsworth, Penguin Books, 1970, p. 237.

This has given them a special influence in Arab affairs. They cannot be accused of criticizing the Arab frontline countries without direct experience of war. Although Algeria has always shown scepticism of attempts to achieve a political solution to the Middle East conflict and was a leader of the Arab Front of Steadfastness opposed to the Camp David agreements, it has consistently played a moderate and mediating role, maintaining its links with the conservative and pro-Western Arab states. Its role in helping to secure the release of the US embassy hostages in Tehran in 1980 was hardly given adequate recognition.

Although Algeria is concerned with the Middle East conflict, it is naturally in the western Mediterranean that its main sphere of interest lies. The former foreign minister, Abdul Aziz Bouteflika, who was president of the UN General Assembly in 1974, described Algeria as the central country of the Maghreb, on the borders of the Mediterranean with a double attachment to Algeria and the Arab world and thus ideally placed to be the crossroads of Europe, Africa and Asia. President Boumedienne promoted his idea of the western Mediterranean as a 'lake of peace' from which the fleets of the rival superpowers would be excluded. In accordance with this policy, Algeria has moved to strengthen its ties with the western European nations. A special relationship with France remains and no doubt always will. The cultural links are indestructible and hundreds of thousands of Algerians will continue to find employment in France. Moreover, since the settlement of the oil nationalization crisis French diplomacy has shown a shrewd willingness to develop the relationship on a new and more equal basis. At the same time, however, the Algerians are anxious to reduce the scale of French predominance in their trade and cultural life.

West Germany, Italy, Japan, Britain and even the United States, despite continuing opposition to Washington's policies, have all played an important role in establishing the new industries. More and more Algerian students are learning English, with official encouragement, as an alternative to French.

Whatever the importance to Algeria of its Arab and Mediterranean policies, its special contribution to world affairs is as a spokesman for the developing countries of the Third World in their dialogue with the rich industrialized nations. It clearly established its claim at the fourth summit conference of non-aligned nations which was held in Algiers in September 1973 and attended by fifty-seven heads of state. Pressing the view that the main division in the world was between the industrialized powers and the Third World, President Boumedienne warned the conference that détente between the Soviet Union and the US threatened to become 'a source of tension in the relations between the privileged world and the rest of humanity'. He said it was up to the Third World's peoples and leaders 'to provoke a radical transformation in the present situation by counting above all on their potentialities and by mobilizing all their human and material resources for the benefit of their countries'.

That Boumedienne's 'radical transformation' was not a fantastic dream was soon proved by the drastic change in the world oil market after the October 1973 Arab–Israeli war. But although Algeria benefited from the oil price rises, it remained a developing country with fifteen hungry millions to feed. Much of the increase in oil revenues was counterbalanced by the rise in prices of food and manufactured imports. Algeria had no intention of letting the argument lie and in April 1974 sponsored a special session of the UN General Assembly on the issue, at which President Boumedienne and the Algerian delegation presented their case with a wealth of documentation. Although he had some bitter words about the past exploitation of the poor three quarters of the world by the rich nations he looked forward to a possible era of cooperation and justice provided the developing countries could control their own resources.

The movement begun by Algeria gathered momentum to include countries, mainly in Latin America, which have pro-American régimes and are not included among the non-aligned states. The 'Group of 77' non-aligned countries thus brought 104 developing countries together when they met in Algiers in February 1975 to discuss a common attitude towards the second conference of the UN Organization for Industrial Development at Lima in March. Algeria's role as spokesman for three quarters of mankind on the most pressing issue which confronts them has been clearly acknowledged.

In 1976–7 President Boumedienne's régime took some carefully controlled but genuine steps towards democratization. A National Charter issued in 1976 set off an unprecedented national debate. The Charter's basic assumptions of a socialist industrial and agrarian revolution were not challenged and no one could campaign against the Charter, although they could vote against it, but widespread criticism was expressed of the power of the state institutions and the Charter's general concentration on economic affairs at the expense of foreign affairs and discussion of the type of society Algeria was aiming to build. A new constitution providing for Algeria's first nationally elected parliament was approved by a massive majority in a referendum in November 1976 and a People's Assembly was elected the following February to share the process of legislation with the president.

Houari Boumedienne did not live to oversee the development of this new stage in the development of the Algerian revolution. When he died on 27 December 1978 not only the Algerians but the whole Arab world felt the loss of an outstanding leader. However, President Chadli Benjadid has proved a worthy successor. His calm, moderate and reassuring personality has earned him the nickname of 'Chadli the Wise'.

Without any break with the past or the 1976 Charter and consti-tution, President Chadli (he is almost invariably known by his first name) has guided Algeria into a new era. He relaxed the atmosphere by ordering the release from restriction of former political leaders including Ben Bella. Exit visas, which had long been a source of popular irritation for Algerians, were abolished. A new generation which had not known the years of struggle for independence was now a majority of the population and was looking for some relaxation from austerity. It was also time discreetly to replace some of the *anciens combattants* in their entrenched positions by new cadres formed since independence.

In the Chadli era there has been a subtle but significant reduction in central state authority. The private sector of the economy has been stimulated while the sixty-two state companies have been broken up and decentralized. A new effort is being made to encourage agricul-ture whose relative neglect has turned Algeria into a major importer of food. Another discernible trend has been towards greater concen-tration on Algeria's national interests at the expense of its role as a Third World leader. Completion of the great trans-Saharan highways to black Africa has been postponed in favour of improving the country's own road and rail network while the effort to supply the rural areas of Algeria's vast territory with electricity and gas have been greatly intensified.

In February 1983 Algeria's standing in the Arab world was marked when it acted as host to the Palestine National Council, the Pales-tinian quasi-parliament, for its first meeting following the PLO's expulsion from Lebanon. In November 1983 Chadli was the first Algerian head of state to make an official visit to France. He felt able to say: 'The Algerians have no feeling of bitterness or complex about the past.' Although he added that the word 'reconciliation' is a bit strong 'in relation to Algeria and France' he spoke of 'common action and cooperation' between a 'great industrialized country of the North and a country of the South in the process of development and jealous of its independence'.[2] His quiet self-confidence was manifest.

Algeria still faces massive problems apart from its continuing dependence on oil and gas exports at a time of world recession and the need to prepare for its 'post-hydrocarbon' era. President Chadli has attempted to deal with corruption among the privileged élite of the state sector, which causes so much public resentment. Perhaps inevitably, he has had only limited success. The Berber cultural and linguistic problem continues to smoulder while a new danger emerged in 1981 in a clash between the Berber nationalists and Muslim fundamentalists demanding an acceleration of Arabization. The régime has dealt firmly with the problem of Islamic militancy, which is virtually ubiquitous in the Arab world, while emphasizing Algeria's attachment to Islam.[3] But the phenomenon is unlikely to disappear. Ex-President Ben Bella, as a born-again Muslim, has multiplied from abroad his criticisms of the régime's alleged secularism.

The darkest feature of Algeria's foreign relations is the continuing failure to achieve a harmonious relationship with its most important neighbour, Morocco. Algerian support for self-determination for the inhabitants of the former Spanish Sahara represented by the Polisario Front is the biggest single obstacle, although behind this lies a longstanding Moroccan feeling of resentment that Algeria's borders were artificially enlarged by France at Morocco's expense before independence. The idea of the unity of the Greater Maghreb (Morocco, Algeria, Tunisia and perhaps Libya) often falters but never dies and it was in this spirit that President Chadli agreed to meet King Hassan of Morocco in February 1983 after several years during which there had been virtually no communication between the two régimes. The meeting helped to relax the atmosphere between the two countries but the wider hopes of a genuine reconciliation and a solution to the Sahara problem were not fulfilled.

2. See interview with Paul Balta and Jean de la Guérivière, *Le Monde*, 6–7 November 1983.

3. 'Algeria is a country governed by its laws and a constitution which declares Islam to be the religion of the state. Every citizen must act within the law and this is the law of Islam which rejects force and preaches tolerance and social justice.' President Chadli to *Le Monde*, 6–7 November 1983.

29. Morocco: Kingdom of the Far West

In October 1973 the news that a contingent of Moroccan troops was engaged in the thick of the fighting on Syria's Golan Heights was a cause of general surprise in the West. Even the hundreds of thousands of American and European visitors who have experienced more of Morocco than the raffish pleasures of Tangiers have scarcely thought of it as belonging to the Arab world of which it is the tip of the western wing. 'The Moroccans are Berbers not Arabs' was a frequent comment.

Certainly Morocco spent several centuries in a state of relative isolation from the rest of the Arab world, which was partly self-imposed and partly due to the fact that, unlike the rest of the Maghreb, it was never incorporated into the Ottoman Empire. But this very isolation ensured the preservation of its Arab–Islamic culture, and when Morocco finally came under European rule in the twentieth century the French and Spanish made no attempt to supplant or destroy Morocco's heritage. (Marshal Lyautey, the greatest of French imperialists, held a deep respect for Arab/Islamic tradition.) Morocco's present Alawite dynasty not only traces its ancestry back to the Prophet's son-in-law, from whom it takes its name, but has ruled Morocco for 300 years. In modern times this has given the Moroccan royal house one unmatched advantage over other Arab monarchies, such as the Sanussis of Libya or the Hashemites of Iraq who were British creations, the deys of Tunis who were relics of the Ottoman Empire or King Farouk of Egypt who was the great-great grandson of an adventurous Albanian officer. The other good fortune of the Alawites was in producing in the mid-twentieth century an able and courageous representative in Sultan Muhammad V, who identified himself wholeheartedly with the nationalist struggle and suffered exile for it. (If Farouk had done the same, the modern history of Egypt would have undoubtedly been different.)

After independence in 1956 Muhammad V announced his intention of transforming Morocco into a constitutional monarchy and changed his title from sultan to king to emphasize his purpose. At home he maintained friendly relations with left-wing politicians and abroad he pursued a radical nationalist foreign policy which insured him against criticism from the rising republican forces in the Arab world led by Abdul Nasser. But the move towards constitutional parliamentary government was constantly delayed and the king remained a feudal monarch in many respects. The combination of his prestige and political shrewdness prevented the anomalies of his rule from being exposed before his premature death during a minor operation in February 1961.

His son Hassan II enjoyed fewer advantages. He had the loyalty of the army and the masses of the countryside but he was suspect to the left-wing politicians, who had grouped themselves into a new party under Mehdi Ben Barka called the *Union Nationale des Forces Populaires* (UNFP), the trade unions and the students who soon became hostile. Although King Hassan had no taste for parliamentarianism, elections were held under a new constitution drafted by his advisers. But before the elections were completed some of the UNFP leaders were arrested for alleged complicity in a plot and both the conservative Istiqlal party and the UNFP boycotted the rest of the elections. This marked the end of cooperation between the monarchy and the established political parties. The experiment in parliamentary government lasted barely eighteen months. In 1965 the king dissolved parliament and took over all legislative and executive powers. For two years he was his own prime minister until handing over to a cabinet of loyalists. After five years of direct rule by decree King Hassan decided on the wisdom of returning to a modified form of parliamentary government. Elections were held under a revised constitution which left considerable power in the monarch's hands. Since they were once again boycotted by the political parties the new parliament hardly reflected the political opinion of the nation, especially that part of it comprised by the students and urban workers.

King Hassan retained his throne because of the acute conflicts within the splintered opposition and the continuing royalism of most of his people. He was able to pursue pro-Western policies, including close friendship with the United States, although these were anathema to much of the politically conscious part of the nation.[1] Yet some of the king's most loyal supporters were appalled at the risks he was

1. He moved much more slowly towards nationalizing French property than neighbouring Algeria and Tunisia. However, relations with France underwent an acute crisis in 1965–6 as a result of the kidnapping and disappearance in Paris of the exiled UNFP leader Mehdi Ben Barka. A French court tried and condemned to death *in absentia* King Hassan's right-hand man, the defence minister General Oufkir.

taking. Although quite possibly the most intelligent of all the contemporary Arab heads of state he seemed extraordinarily insensitive to the most obvious dangers to absolute monarchy in the twentieth century. The extravagance and corruption of his court and the widening gap between the privileged few and the mass of the population seemed to court the fate of the Bourbons, Romanovs or the house of Muhammad Ali. His intellect told him what reforms were needed but he lacked the application to carry them out.

Nemesis nearly overtook the king in July 1971 when a group of army generals, using trainee NCOs as their dupes, attempted a coup at a royal birthday party in the seaside palace of Skhirat. Several ministers and generals were killed, but the king survived and loyalist forces under General Oufkir restored order. The organizers of the coup were not radical Free Officers, but the people of the Moroccan cities believed that they were and cheered the first news that the attempt had succeeded.

Four generals and six junior officers were summarily executed and more than a thousand officers and men were put on trial for their complicity in the coup, but the king realized that repression was not enough. He announced reforms and a concerted attack on corruption. A new prime minister was charged by the king with changing a system which 'makes the rich richer and the poor poorer'. In March 1972 the king imposed a new constitution of his own making which increased the powers of the government, while keeping many in his own hands, and provided for a new parliament with two thirds of its members elected. But once again elections were postponed indefinitely on the grounds that 2 million voters were not registered.

One year later the king had an even narrower escape when his aircraft was attacked by Royal Moroccan Air Force fighters and nearly shot down over the Mediterranean as he returned from a private visit to France. The king's pilot managed to land miraculously at Rabat and once again the loyalists succeeded in restoring order. This attempted coup was no more from the left than that of the previous year, but was planned by General Oufkir, the king's closest supporter. Oufkir died at the royal palace on the same night, supposedly by his own hand.[2]

This new writing on the wall spurred the king to fresh action to save his throne. He was still unable to find a basis for cooperation with the

2. In a book published in June 1974, a retired French general, Claude Clement, claimed that Oufkir was killed on the king's orders. He also alleged that Mehdi Ben Barka died of a heart attack under torture by Oufkir.

main political parties, but he launched a programme of agrarian reform and moroccanization of foreign property. This caused a serious crisis with France, but was widely popular in Morocco. The king showed new energy and application in the business of government. He appeared more frequently at public gatherings, where he was generously applauded. However, the left-wing opposition was unreconciled, maintaining that in reality the king only exercised power through royal puppets and the police. Students at Rabat University clashed with the security forces and about half of them went on strike. In March 1973 an attack on a police post in the Atlas Mountains and sabotage in the cities led to mass arrests and several executions.

Despite the reforms, the king's rule still partly depended on severe repression. An appeal to Moroccan nationalist pride was therefore shrewdly calculated to strengthen his position. The despatch of 1,800 Moroccan troops to Syria in May 1973, their reinforcement and brave performance during the October war, won wide popular approval in Morocco, disposing of the popular myth that Morocco is insulated from the emotional feeling of the Arab world. King Hassan was not only host to the Arab summit meeting in Rabat in October 1974 but played a crucial role in the decision to recognize the PLO as the true representative of the Palestinians and in persuading his fellow monarch Hussein of Jordan to accept it. He has continued to sustain Morocco's Arab role. He again played host to the Arab summit conferences in Fez in 1981 and 1982 which eventually produced a common Arab approach to peace in the Middle East in the Fez Plan of September 1982. Morocco's physical remoteness from the central Middle East conflict combined with its ideological commitment, make the Kingdom the most acceptable venue for such inter-Arab meetings. In 1977 and 1978 Moroccan troops earned credit and prestige from their intervention to help the beleaguered government of Zaire.

However, if the Arab/Berber Moroccan nation takes pride in its Arabism and its African contribution, it is the claim to the former Spanish Sahara territory which truly rallies nationalist sentiment. With few exceptions, politicians from the far right to the communists support the King in this cause which he has shrewdly exploited. Combined with the Kingdom's own phosphate deposits the Western Sahara gives Morocco 60 per cent of world reserves.

As Spain hesitated while General Franco was dying in 1976, King Hassan called upon the Moroccan people to stake their claim by marching into the territory. Some 300,000 took part in the Green

March. Spain gave way and agreed that Morocco, with Mauritania as a minor partner, should take over the administration of the territory in the wake of the Spanish withdrawal. However, this was at the cost of a serious dispute with Algeria and Libya which supported the independence claims of the indigenous Polisario Front. Since 1976 Morocco has had to conduct an intense diplomatic struggle within the UN and the Organization for African Unity (OAU) against the recognition of the Polisario's so-called Arab Saharan Democratic Republic (RASD). It has also fought a costly and debilitating war against the Polisario guerrillas.

By grouping its regular forces behind a defensive wall around the 'useful triangle' in the western part of the territory which includes the capital and the main phosphate deposits, Morocco can keep out the Polisario, who lack modern weapons, but it is unable to inflict on them a final defeat.

Hopes for a diplomatic settlement rose in June 1981 when King Hassan agreed to an OAU proposal for a referendum in the Western Sahara, but the solution failed because of the King's insistence that the referendum should be purely consultative and Moroccan sovereignty was not in dispute. Algeria insisted that there should be a prior consultation with the Polisario leaders. A meeting between King Hassan and President Chadli in February 1982, after years of frozen relations between the two countries, also created optimism but came to nothing. Morocco suffered a setback when the OAU admitted the RASD to membership but in 1983 it received a boost when the unpredictable Colonel Qaddafy appeared to withdraw his support from the Polisario. Morocco's expensive struggle to keep the Western Sahara continues but without any sign that popular support is wavering.

Apart from the heavy cost of the war – with military spending nearly 6 per cent of GNP – Morocco faces massive social and economic problems. At $7 billion its international debt in 1984 was one of the highest *per capita* in the world. But the country lacks neither resources nor potential. The world price of phosphates has fallen in recent years but the longer-term prospects in a hungry world are good; the USSR is now a major importer. Morocco's own population has increased from 7 million at independence in 1956 to 22 million in 1984 but it has not made the common error of neglecting agriculture. Without this the effects of the prolonged drought in the early 1980s would have been even more disastrous. Output of citrus fruit has more than tripled in twenty years through irrigation which explains Morocco's alarm at the prospect of Spain and Portugal's entry into the EEC. It might have been wiser to concentrate on the backward and inefficient cereal farming to reduce huge imports of American wheat.

In an interview with a Beirut weekly magazine *al-Hawadeth* in March 1974 King Hassan explained his philosophy of government. Describing his role as 'a constitutional monarchy with presidential powers' he went on to claim that the hereditary element provided a fairer and more impartial system than power attained through election. Whereas he had had a long and tough training from his father in the craft of shouldering responsibility, there was no guarantee that voters elected the best or most suitable candidate through the ballot box. He added: 'I do not think there is any contradiction in the fact that power should belong to the people and the nation, and that it should be ruled by a king with an honourable Alawite lineage. To say that power should belong to the nation does not mean that everyone within this nation should rule.'

This remarkable creed helps to explain the paradox of Morocco's monarchy. As the 'sunset King'[3] adds a new wing to one more of his cluster of vast palaces it would seem that he was offering intolerable provocation to his many impoverished subjects. There have been many warnings: for example, food riots in Casablanca in June 1981 which left more than a hundred dead; these were repeated in several cities in January 1984. Yet the monarchy continues to receive support from the whole political spectrum. Left-wingers certainly demand more equality and less corruption but mostly they want to reform rather than destroy the system. This can only partly be explained by the intense Moroccan patriotism which focuses on the Saharan claim. King Hassan is a man of ability who clearly enjoys political manoeuvre and has gained from experience. Although he has harassed and restricted the opposition – and there are numerous political prisoners – he has never attempted to suppress it entirely. A principal left-wing opposition party exists in the Socialist Union of Popular Forces which significantly is more nationalist than the King on the Saharan issue. An elected Moroccan parliament and municipal councils survive even if elections are frequently postponed, and when they take place are heavily influenced to ensure a massive majority for the pro-royalist parties and independents. The Moroccan press is so sycophantic to authority as to be almost unreadable. Nevertheless, freedom of speech and elements of parliamentary democracy have

3. In Arabic *Maghreb* means sunset as well as Morocco.

survived in independent Morocco to a greater extent than in any Arab state with the exception of pre-civil war Lebanon.

The downfall of Emperor Haile Selassie of Ethiopia in 1974 left Morocco as the only monarchy on the African continent with the exception of Swaziland. King Hassan's relaxed approach gives the impression of confidence in the survival of his throne but it is certain that he takes nothing for granted.

Part Three
The Arabs Today

30. Through Western Eyes

Any writer who embarks on an attempt to describe and interpret the contemporary Arab world to Western readers is confronted by a set of formidable difficulties. At the superficial level he encounters a stereotyped vision of the Arabs, and of the Islamic religion which is closely associated with them in the Western mind. A more complex problem is that the average educated Westerner is unaware that he suffers from prejudice towards the Arabs. The New England or Hampstead liberal would be alarmed to find himself making a derogatory generalization about 'the blacks', 'the Chinese' or, still more, 'the Jews'. He feels no such compunction in this thoughts about 'the Arabs'.

Some years ago I heard through my literary agent that a well-known American publisher was interested in commissioning a book on the Arab world which would try to make intelligible to the general reader 'the Arab reluctance to join in the progress of the twentieth century'. This assumption about the Arab character seemed to bear out the need for a book of this kind because, as I wrote in the foreword to a draft synopsis, to most Westerners the word 'Arab' still seemed to conjure up a picture of a shaikh in flowing robes, brandishing an outdated rifle as he urged his camel across the sand dunes to attack a neighbouring encampment. But the reaction of an equally famous London publisher to the offer of the British rights to such a book was also interesting. He said that I was 'setting up a cockshy' in describing the Western idea of the Arabs. This may have been the Western concept of the Arabs some twenty-five years ago, he wrote, but it certainly isn't nowadays, at least among the intelligent public for whom the book is intended.

This made me wonder whether I had exaggerated Western ignorance about the Arabs. I was reminded of a passage in the memoirs of a former American oil company official:

> During our first week at the Aramco school on Long Island, questions were asked of us to ascertain our general knowledge about the Arab world. The questions 'What is Islam?' and 'Who was the Prophet Mohammed?' brought forth some interesting answers. One of our members thought that Islam was 'a game of chance, similar to bridge'. Another said it was a 'mysterious sect

founded in the south by the Ku Klux Klan.' One gentleman believed it to be 'an organization of American Masons who dress in strange costumes'. The Prophet Mohammed was thought to be the man who 'wrote *The Arabian Nights*'. Another said he was 'an American Negro minister who was in competition with Father Divine in New York City'. One of the more reasonable answers came from one of our men who said, 'Mohammed had something to do with a mountain. He either went to the mountain, or it came to him.'[1]

These responses were facetious but the jokes were clearly intended to conceal total ignorance. The question arises whether Europeans, with their longer associations with the Arab world, would fare better than the Americans. My conclusion after studying the matter at both ends for twenty years, is that the difference is only marginal. The outdated view of the Arabs is still widespread and it is constantly reinforced by countless newspaper cartoons and selective television images which concentrate on the romantic and colourful aspect of the Arabs because it provides the most striking contrast with our own world. As for the Islamic religion, the attitude towards it in the Western world is based on an equal mixture of prejudice and ignorance.

One of the main problems was raised at the beginning of this book (see pp. 13–14): the semantic one of 'who or what is an Arab?' The confusion is the fault of no one but is a result of the historical development of the Arab nation through the 'arabization' of other races. But it is reproduced in the minds of Western schoolchildren in a multitude of history and geography textbooks. A few years ago I was asked to revise the entry for the word 'Arab' in a widely circulated children's encyclopedia. This began fairly well: 'The simple meaning of the name Arab is "inhabitant of Arabia", but the people of Arabia have been very important in the history of the world, and have gone on to live in many other countries, so the name is also used to mean anyone who speaks Arabic and claims that he is descended from Shem, who was one of the sons of Noah.' Although I have yet to meet an Arab who claims to be descended from Shem, at least this attempts to explain that there are two historical meanings for the word Arab. But the entry continued:

The Arabs of Arabia are usually medium-sized with long and sometimes curved noses and oval faces. Their skin is brownish and their hair is dark brown or black. Those who live in towns nowadays often wear clothes like European people [*sic*], but the peasants of the villages and the desert tribes

1. Grant C. Butler, *Kings and Camels*, New York, 1960, pp. 16–17.

wear the Arab dress. Many Arabs are highly educated and trained and work as scientists, engineers, or in other professions. Most Arabs who live in towns can read and write. They work as traders, craftsmen and clerks and they usually have only one wife. However, there are many more peasants, *fellahin*, than townsmen. The *fellahin* still live in tribes under the rule of a sheikh, and have tribal laws which are very strictly kept. A peasant sometimes has as many as four wives if he has money to keep them. The sheikhs own land, and employ peasants to work for them. They use camels to carry burdens but usually ride on donkeys.

By this time the child who was trying to learn something about the Arabs could hardly be more confused. The author (or authors?) of this encyclopedia entry, after correctly making the distinction between the two meanings of the word Arab, has mixed them up again. If he was referring to Arabia, there are very few peasant farmers in the peninsula. If he meant the whole Arab world, the great majority do not 'still live in tribes under the rule of a sheikh' and strict tribal law. In the case of Egypt, which is the country most commonly associated with the term *fellahin*, this has not been true for a very long time.

If the expert confuses the modern and classical meanings of the word Arab it is hardly surprising that even the well-informed Westerner makes the same mistake. But there is a more profound reason for the distortion of the Arab image in the West: the anti-Islamic prejudice which has gone deep into our subconscious where it continues to tinge all our thinking. In his *Islam and the West: The Making of an Image*, Norman Daniel traces one of the main causes of this hostility to the shock that was caused to medieval Christians by the Muslim attitude towards Jesus Christ (p. 24). If Muslims had simply denied that there was any truth in Christianity, instead of regarding it as an incomplete version of their own faith, it might have been easier for Christians to accept Islam's existence.

For Christians the prophetic preparation of the Jews leads to a single event, the incarnation, which is the inauguration of the Messianic Kingdom . . . For Muslims too there is just one Revelation, of the only religion, Islam, or submission to God; but it was made again and again through successive prophets. Muhammad's was the final prophecy, but his was not more 'Muslim' than that of Jesus, or Moses, or Abraham 'who was neither a Jew nor a Christian' (according to the Kor\`an, iii, 60). For the Latin it was an impossible imaginative effort so to suspend belief that the association of sacred names, which includes the most sacred of all, would seem anything but grotesque; yet it would be a mistake to imagine that medieval writers were ill-informed. There is evidence that they believed as much as they were willing to believe, and all who knew the Islamic reassessment of the familiar sequence of God's servants found it intolerable. As a result Islam was often deformed when it was presented by Christians.

The leading Palestinian intellectual Walid Khalidi has noted one of the consequences of

the great battle between Christian Europe and the world of Islam which began in the seventh century and ended only with the stemming of the Ottoman tide in eastern Europe in the eighteenth century. All the fears, animosities and suspicions of these times are reflected, sometimes explicitly and sometimes by implication, in the contemporary Western writings (as indeed they are in the Arabic writings of the time), both prose and verse, lay and ecclesiastical. They therefore form part of the literary heritage of every educated European and are embedded in the subject matter of his general reading. Of course, the modern European and American reader would generally dismiss with a smile as quaint any hostile references to the Moor or the Saracen. But he would be less than human if he does not at the same time admit into his subconscious a smaller or larger number of prejudices. One residue of these prejudices is the facility with which the word 'oriental' is still pre-fixed to such words as 'duplicity', 'cruelty', 'servility', and 'despotism'. Another is possibly the general mis-understanding that exists about Islam . . .[2]

Khalidi observes that there is a group of twentieth-century oriental-ists who have arrived at a critical estimation of Islam 'which is at once profound, authoritative and sympathetic'. But they are scholars whose writings influence only a tiny minority. 'To the average and perhaps more than average educated Westerner, Islam appears as a fanatical, bloodthirsty, reactionary, xenophobic, and largely destruc-tive force. The obvious present-day poverty and material backward-ness of most Islamic countries (due to a variety of causes which I cannot go into now) are all too easily equated with Islam itself.' The contribution of the Arab Islamic world to Western civilization through its preservation of the Graeco-Roman heritage during the Dark Ages is usually underestimated. Kenneth Clark in his famous television series on *Civilization* ignored it entirely. It was left to the author/ scientist Jacob Bronowski to make amends in his own series entitled *The Ascent of Man*.

In the nineteenth century the adjective 'fanatical' was almost automatically prefixed to 'Muslim' (or, more probably, the widely used misnomer 'Mohammedan') by journalists, travel writers, or even reputable historians. The underlying prejudice has scarcely

2. Walid Khalidi, 'Arabs and the West', *Middle East Forum*, xxxii, 10 (December 1957), p. 15.

diminished today. Khalidi quoted from a feature article by the Cairo correspondent of the London *Times* on 29 April 1955:

Beyond the garden of the church *you may meet Islam*. [Emphasis added.] A man has died and his wife is mourning her loss, helped by many female friends and sympathizers. They squat in the dust of the village street, all shrouded in black . . . There they sit in the filth (tin cans, fluttering rubbish and indefinable debris), wailing, screeching and clutching their clothes.

Khalidi comments on this that there is no doubt that the correspondent saw these women. 'He saw a group of very poor women in deep distress who happened to be Muslims in a village with obviously rather inadequate town planning and municipal arrangements, but he did not meet *Islam* in the rubbish.'

To cite an even more recent example, a book which appeared in London and was widely noticed by the critics was a vivid account by a young British medical student of a year he spent in the maternity ward of a provincial Algerian hospital. The author had been shocked and angered in his first contact with oriental society both by the people's passive acceptance of feudal traditions and the gap between the authorities' professed ideals of Islamic socialism and practice. The book was a brilliant piece of reportage, although the author could be said to have made little attempt to understand the real nature of the society he was describing. It was the title of the book that was astonishing: *The Private Life of Islam*.[3] It is doubtful whether a reputable Western publisher would consider bringing out an account of a year's experience in a Sicilian hospital under the title *The Private Life of Roman Christendom*.

The prolonged medieval and Renaissance struggle between Western Christendom and the world of Islam was a conflict between equals. There was mutual hostility and even hatred – but there was mutual respect. This changed in the eighteenth and nineteenth centuries, when the European Christian powers achieved overwhelming technical and material expansion. The hostility and fear in the attitude of these powers towards other creeds were replaced by contempt for their lack of practical achievement. Islam was doubly condemned because after nearly dominating the world it had entered a period of long physical decline. In Western eyes, it was a proven failure. Lord Cromer, who ruled Egypt for the British from 1883 to 1907, was a foremost example of this attitude. He divided the people

3. Ian Young, *The Private Life of Islam*, London, Allen Lane, 1974.

of the world into 'Ruling Races' and 'Subject Races' and regarded this as a permanent feature of the universe. Arthur Balfour held a similar view, although he characteristically wrapped it in a mantle of dubious sophistry. In a debate on the situation in Egypt in June 1910 he was replying, as Leader of the Conservative Opposition, to the accusation of some radical MPs that the Tories adopted a superior attitude towards 'orientals'. He said:

Look at the facts of the case. Western nations as soon as they emerge into history show the beginnings of those capacities for self-government, not always associated, I grant, with all the virtues or all the merits, but still have merits of their own. Nations of the West have shown these virtues from their beginning, from the very tribal origin of which we have first knowledge. You may look through the whole history of the Orientals in what is called, broadly speaking, the East, and you never find traces of self-government . . . Conqueror has succeeded conqueror; one domination has followed another; but never in all the revolutions of fate and fortune have you seen one of those nations of its own motion establish what we, from a Western point of view, call self-government. That is the fact. It is not a question of superiority or inferiority. I suppose that a true Eastern sage would say that the working government which we have taken upon ourselves in Egypt and elsewhere is not a work worthy of a philosopher – that it is the dirty work, the inferior work, of carrying on the necessary labour. Do let us put this question of superiority and inferiority out of our minds.[4]

In 1910, many more Englishmen would have agreed with Balfour than with his radical opponents, even if they failed to appreciate the philosophical trimmings of his argument. A few years later came the Great War, which was followed by the European powers' partition of the Middle East and the prolonged struggle of the Arab states for their full independence. This was a new cause of ill-feeling between the Arabs and the West. The Arabs were accused of treachery and ingratitude and a perverse failure to appreciate the benefits that had been bestowed upon them by the imperial powers. A distinction was often made between the 'good Arab', the tribal shaikh, pasha or amir who was prepared to cooperate with the authorities, and the 'bad Arab', who was the radical nationalist of the towns. In this the attitude of the average Westerner towards the Arabs was no different in kind from that towards other 'subject races' such as Indians, south-east Asians or black Africans. But in the case of the Arabs there was and is a vitally important difference which is due mainly,

4. *Hansard*, series V, vol. xvii, 13 June 1910, cols 1140–46.

although not entirely, to the conflict between Arabs and Jews which has its origins in the Balfour Declaration of 1917. The unique position of the Jews in Western Christian and post-Christian society, their persecution and Western guilt feelings of responsibility have all been reflected in attitudes towards the Arabs. Western liberals, socialists and anti-imperialists of all kinds, have generally excluded the Arabs from the sympathy they have accorded to other races struggling for their independence. With very few exceptions, New York liberal intellectuals, European social democrats, left-wing writers, journalists and university dons have found that their pro-Zionism has made them hostile and unsympathetic towards the Arabs. Perhaps the best exponent of this selective anti-imperialism is the eminent British left-wing weekly the *New Statesman* (ex-*New Statesman and Nation*) which under a series of editors since 1931 has consistently supported Indian, African or Latin American nationalism, while remaining cool or even hostile towards Arab nationalism except in those areas, such as South Arabia or ex-French North Africa, where it was not in conflict with Zionism.[5]

The underlying anti-Arab bias of Western liberals has required some self-justification. One of the most common forms of rationalization is related to the small group of distinguished Western arabists, such as France's Marshal Lyautey or Britain's Glubb Pasha. Although these men had a profound and genuine sympathy for the Arabs they were undeniably of a right-wing imperialist cast of mind. From this it was an easy stage to deduce that all Arab sympathizers were, at best, sentimental romantics and, at worst, sinister reactionaries who were trying to maintain imperial control through Arab puppets. This argument could be supported by the fact that many of the Arabs are still at a pre-capitalist stage of development and governed by feudal traditions. So are many of the other peoples of the Third World, but they cannot be directly contrasted with the state of Israel, with its multi-party democratic system and trade unions. Progressive-minded Westerners therefore dubbed the Arabs as incurable reactionaries. In 1956 a British left-wing journalist who has since achieved considerable prominence as an editor and author replied to a letter from me in which I tentatively suggested that the British left showed an excessive bias in favour of Israel and a misunderstanding of Arab nationalism:

5. The subject is brilliantly analysed in a monograph by an Iraqi Arab, Khalid Kishtainy, entitled *The New Statesman and the Middle East* published by the Palestine Research Center, Beirut, 1972.

The Israelis are progressive, democratic and western-minded. The Arabs are obscurantist, totalitarian, lazy and violent. I am sorry that you appear to have fallen a victim to the charms of their way of life – which, I must admit, are considerable. I have always taken the Arab side against the French and still do: but I have never found working with them and for them agreeable. They are dirty, treacherous and untruthful, totally lacking in gratitude, intellectually dishonest and riddled with atavistic prejudices . . . I find it tragic that you should take the view you do. The Foreign Office has always been hopelessly handicapped in dealing with the Middle East because a great proportion of its officials are emotionally involved with the Arabs.

I have quoted this personal letter at length because it encapsulates with admirable frankness and clarity all the aspects of anti-Arab emotional prejudice in Western left-wing circles.

Since this letter was written, the question has been complicated by some new elements. First there was the Anglo-French–Israeli attack on Egypt of October 1956 which caused most of the European left to take, for a brief period, a more sympathetic view of Arab nationalism. Then there has been the slow dimming of Israel's progressive democratic image, especially after the 1967 war and the military occupation of Arab lands. This has been ignored by some Western liberals but others have felt the need to make some protest. One of these was the prominent pro-Zionist Richard Crossman who left the British cabinet to become editor of the *New Statesman*. On 31 July 1970 he published an open letter to the Israeli foreign minister deploring the loss of the early Zionist vision, and ending with the words: 'The Arabs can survive a decade of Jewish military domination. The Israel you and I believe in can't.' At the same time the cause of the Palestinian Arabs caught the imagination of many of the new generation of students in the West. A 'Palestine Week' became a regular annual feature of many university campuses. However, this new sympathy for the Arabs in the form of Palestinians was more than counterbalanced by the effect of a new phenomenon: the 'Arab oil shaikh' extorting his 'blackmail' payments from the West. It made no difference that the country which was taking the lead in putting up oil prices was not an Arab state but Iran, or that the peoples of the Arab world were still very much poorer than those of the West. 'The Arab shaikhs' were represented as a group of self-indulgent but ruthless men who were responsible for the West's economic difficulties. The word 'shaikh', with all its connotations of feudal power and sexual voracity, reinforced the impression. It was a gift for the cartoonists. One of them showed an obese Arab prince in his palace announcing that his contribution to World Hunger Year was to stop his wives from dining twice a week at the Savoy.

However much headway the Palestinian Arabs may have made in gaining support for their cause, a degree of bias against the Arabs is considered normal among Western liberals who would find it quite unacceptable if it was directed against other races.

That strong feeling in the liberal establishments of Western countries which has been called 'anti-anti-semitism' and is partly a reaction to the past persecution of the Jews and partly to guilt feelings about our own responsibility serves as an obstacle to understanding of the Arabs. At any time it is possible to secure hundreds of signatures of the most distinguished men and women in politics, the professions or the arts for an appeal for Soviet Jews to emigrate to Israel. A similar appeal to allow Palestinian Arabs to return to the homes they left under duress only a generation ago arouses little interest.

It is understandable that the great majority of Arabs are convinced that Zionist influence is the sole obstacle to their relations with the West. Some see the matter in simple nineteenth-century terms of Jewish financial and political power. Others, more sophisticated, speak of the crucial Jewish influence in all aspects of Western intellectual life – in teaching, the arts and the news media. But while it would be absurd to deny the strength of Zionism[6] in Western society, it is not by any means the only cause of misunderstanding between the Arabs and the West. (It is surely significant that a Palestinian Arab of the intellectual calibre of Walid Khalidi does not even mention Zionism in his 'Arabs and the West'.) The truth is that the struggle between Christendom and the World of Islam has never really ended, although it is being fought on different battlefields and with new weapons. In the nineteenth century it seemed as if the victory of Christendom was final, although its opponents never conceded defeat. Today we are not so sure. The overthrow of the régime in Iran, which was attempting to emulate the West, by a mass popular Islamic movement gave pause for thought. Today the phenomenon of Islamic revival is seen throughout the Muslim world but most strikingly among Iranians and Arabs. Its often violent manifestations have if anything increased the anti-Islamic and anti-Arab prejudices

6. I have equated Jews with Zionism in this context because despite the existence of an important minority of anti-Zionist Jews, the overwhelming majority of Western Jews are Zionist in the sense that they enthusiastically support the state of Israel.

of Westerners who have neither the time nor inclination to understand its origins.

We have discussed some of the reasons for the distortion of the Arab image in Western eyes. But it must be admitted, at the risk of incurring the anathema of the Race Relations Board, that generalizations about races or nations, however prejudiced, usually have *some* basis in fact. Some of the most tolerant and judicious Westerners still find aspects of the Arab world unattractive, mystifying and even repellent. The only remedy is to make the attempt to see the world through Arab eyes.

31. Through Arab Eyes

Renaissance and Revenge

It has been an underlying theme of this book that the prime motive force of Arab political life in the twentieth century has been the desire to recover status and dignity after a long period of humiliation at the hands of superior Western power. The three peoples of western Islam (or 'Inner Islam' as it is sometimes called to distinguish it from the 'Outer Islam' of central and eastern Asia) – Arabs, Turks and Iranians – are all imbued with a profound sense of their own glorious past. They are all inheritors of great empires which in earlier centuries were both more civilized and more powerful than Christian Europe and, following a long period of Christian ascendancy, these peoples have been seeking to bring their present up to the level of their past.

The Turks, who declined in power in relation to the West most recently and retained their national self-confidence as a 'governing race' until the first decades of this century, have been the least affected by this problem. It was the genius of Kemal Atatürk to see that if Turkey was to match the overbearing political, economic and military power of the West it must first abandon its pretensions to empire and concentrate on the development of the Turkish homeland in Anatolia. His secular reforms could not transform all aspects of Turkish society in a single generation (he died in 1938) but in the aftermath of the Second World War it was apparent that in many respects Turkey has become part of Europe.

The Iranians were less fortunate than the Turks in that their decline in power took place so much earlier that they were subjected to a long period of alien, predominantly Anglo-Russian, political and commercial domination. Iran's reforming dictator, Riza Shah, was a man of lesser ability than Atatürk and he was unable to preserve his country's independence and neutrality in the Second World War. Yet the Iranian empire, for all its variety of races and tongues, has a degree of unity which may be compared with that of Turkey. His son Mohammed Riza was a ruler of some ability who, once he had secured his authority with the help of the West, gave the country a degree of stability for more than two decades. His 'white revolution' of agrarian and other reforms and the industrialization and expansion of the economy sustained by increasing oil revenues appeared for a time to justify the Shah's increasingly ambitious claims for Iran's progress. He secured the confidence of the West which paid scant attention to the internal repression or the growing resentment of the mass of the Iranian people against the social disruption and loss of identity that were involved. The downfall of the Shah's régime and its replacement by the Ayatollah Khomeini's radical Islamic Republic was a challenge not only to the West but to all the Muslim Arab governments. But despite a degree of internal anarchy, serious unrest among Iranian minorities and a prolonged and bloody war with neighbouring Iraq, the break-up of the former Iranian empire was not seriously threatened.

The Arabs, the third people of Inner Islam, have faced far greater obstacles in their twentieth-century political renaissance. Unlike the Iranians and Turks, the Arabs had become accustomed to living under foreign rule following the dissolution of their own empire. In the western Arab world of North Africa the Ottoman imperial masters had already been replaced by Western Christian powers in the nineteenth century, and, when the eastern Arabs demanded their independence in the wake of the First World War they found themselves under a Western hegemony which in their eyes differed very little from direct colonial rule. Many of the new frontiers between the fledgeling states of the twentieth-century Arab world were arbitrarily drawn to suit the interests of the powers.

Arab Unity: Ideal or Fantasy?

Although the seeds of Arab nationalism were planted in the second half of the nineteenth century (see Chapter 7) it only began to flourish in the years between the two World Wars. All nationalists need a myth and an ideal, but the Arabs need one more than most. In their case it is the unification of the Arab-speaking peoples in a single nation.

The question is whether this has ever been, or can ever be a practical ideal. The fact that such a political unit would bear little relation to the first Arab/Islamic empire of the Golden Age is not a serious obstacle; other nations have been built on a dream-like view of the past. The political map of the Arab world shows that 180 million people live in a contiguous stretch of territory. The vast majority speak the same language; most belong to the same faith and all share the same cultural heritage. Why then, we may ask, have the Arabs not united like the Italians and the Germans in the nineteenth century?

Apart from the gain in world political influence, the economic advantages of unity are obvious. Some of the Arab states have vast natural resources and a labour shortage, while others are poor and over-populated. The fact that, despite their strong aspirations for unity, the Arabs have been unable to achieve it, has given rise to the belief that as a people they are innately quarrelsome and divisive.

The political map of the Arab world is deceptive. In the first place the continuing stretch of territory from Agadir on the Atlantic to Oman on the Indian Ocean is really an archipelago of inhabited islands on a desert sea. The mere physical obstacles to the political unity of the Arabs are immense.[1] Within these 'islands' a community of interest based on a common experience has grown up over the years. Thus although the boundaries between the present Arab states were often drawn quite arbitrarily by the powers, especially in the case of the partition of Greater Syria, a series of local patriotisms has developed. An Iraqi, Jordanian, Sudanese or Algerian does not necessarily see anything incompatible between his loyalty to his country and his belief that ultimately the whole Arab nation should be united under a single flag. In many ways a closer parallel can be seen with the Spanish-speaking states of Latin America than with Italy or Germany. The federations that were attempted between South American states in the last century were all abortive.

In his famous essay on *The Common Origin of the Arabs* the Syrian writer Edmond Rabbath quoted a remark of the French nineteenth-century philosopher–historian Ernest Renan: 'Language invites unity, but does not compel it.' Since the Arabic language is the prime element of Arab civilization, the invitation it offers is unusually strong for the Arabs. But it is a unity of the senses, not the limbs. It has been shrewdly observed that the Arabs are linked by a huge invisible nervous system. If you apply pressure at one point, the reaction may take place at some wholly different branch of the complex. But, to carry the metaphor further, the Arab world lacks a skeleton.

Nevertheless, the yearning to provide the common sensory system of the Arabs with a solid political structure has been so strong that it has already been attempted several times. The practical difficulties have always been underestimated. This was the case of the first and most famous experiment, the Syrian–Egyptian merger of 1958–61,

---

1. This was brought vividly home to me by driving from Tangiers to Cairo and, on another occasion, from Beirut to Kuwait via Baghdad. This meant crossing the two vast hiatuses of the Arab world – the Libyan and Syrian deserts.

and of the abortive Syrian–Iraqi–Egyptian merger of 1963. Some lessons had been learned through these experiments, especially by Egypt, which was anxious to apply them when the next proposal was made in 1969 for a federation of Libya, Sudan and Egypt. Yet on this occasion 'the moving spirit was the eager young Colonel Qaddafy, who had the same simplified vision of the unification of the Arab nation as his political mentor, the Gamal Abdul Nasser of the 1950s. One major problem in particular he tended to ignore or overlook – that of the presence of large non-Arab minorities in certain Arab countries, who might feel insecure and deprived in a Union of Arab States. In 1963 Abdul Nasser had come to realize that Iraq could not unite with any other Arab state until it had solved its Kurdish question. In 1969–70 it was the turn of Sudan to face this reality. To Colonel Qaddafy's disgust, President Nimeiry decided that nothing must obstruct his tackling of the problem of the Sudanese South and he backed out of the federation plans in 1971. Sudan's place was taken by Syria and the tripartite federation formally came into existence in September 1971. The federal institutions that were established never had real substance and disappeared when President Sadat refused Colonel Qaddafy's demands for an instant merger and Libya's relations with Egypt turned to bitter enmity. A further attempt in 1979 to form a Syrian–Libyan federation has failed to develop.

Other federations or mergers of individual Arab states have been proposed in recent years. In October 1972 the governments of the two Yemens agreed to unite and although nothing has happened, the blueprint for the union remains. Proposals for a federation of the three Maghreb states, which would have obvious economic advantages, have been put forward and discussed on numerous occasions and, in the most surprising move of all, Libya and Tunisia proclaimed their merger in a single Arab Islamic Republic. Within a month the plan had been dropped.

The great majority of politically conscious Arabs are aware that the political unity of the Arab nation, if it is ever to take place, must be achieved through a gradual evolutionary process. They look more to the European Economic Community as an example than the Kingdom of Italy or the German Empire of the nineteenth century. For this purpose, the Arab League as an association of sovereign states, would seem to be the most suitable instrument.

The main drawback of the League has been that it tends to be dominated by Egypt and other Arab states regard it as an instrument of Egyptian ambitions. Nuri Said of Iraq and Bourguiba of Tunisia made this charge most cogently but other Arab leaders have privately agreed. The headquarters of the League were in Cairo, a majority of the key posts in its civil service were held by the Egyptians and the three first secretary-generals of the League were all Egyptians. However, when in 1979 the Arab states agreed to boycott Egypt over its peace treaty with Israel and moved the League headquarters to Tunis, appointing a Tunisian secretary-general, the impotence of pan-Arab action without Egypt was merely underlined. There was only some advantage in the new location of the League headquarters as demonstrating the integration into the Arab world of its western wing – the Maghreb.

Much greater progress has been achieved towards the more modest and practical aim of strengthening links between neighbouring Arab states in different regions through forms of confederation. The precursor was the federation of United Arab Emirates which has defied the many pessimists to survive into its fifteenth year. The Gulf Cooporation Council founded in 1981 is of a confederal nature but already in three years had gone a long way towards establishing a common market of the six Arab Gulf states. The Egyptian–Sudanese Complementarity Agreement of 1982 is somewhat more ambitious in that it sets a target of fusing the two countries' domestic and foreign policies but aims to do this gradually over ten years.

It is difficult to see the League developing in the near future from a regional organization, similar to the European Council or the Organization of American States, which it is at present, into a federation or confederation of states. If, for example, the decisions of the Council of the League reached by a two-thirds majority were to be made binding on all its members, as has been suggested, the League would probably fall apart under the strain. Some Arabs criticize or deride the League for its failure to organize effective pan-Arab political action on an international scale, although this is not what it is constituted to do.

In a more unobtrusive way the Arab League has scored some achievements in carrying out the functions for which it *was* intended. In the social, cultural, educational and health fields it has acted on a regional scale as an Arab UNESCO or World Health Organization. Among other things, it has organized an Arab cultural treaty, an Arab union for wireless communication and telecommunications, a postal union, an air transport organization, a tourist union and a nationality agreement. The smaller branches of the League include a federation of Arab news agencies, an Arab film organization, an Arab regional literary organization, and an institute of Arab manuscripts. Most of these are severely handicapped by bureaucracy and the inadequacy and irregularity of their budgets, of a kind that is familiar to all international civil servants, but this makes their real achievements more remarkable.

It is in the economic field that the Arab League has the best hope of serving Arab unity in the near future. The objective of creating an Arab Common Market was agreed by the independent Arab states in 1957, the same year in which the first six European members of the EEC signed the treaty of Rome. A council of Arab economic unity was set up in that year to begin reducing internal tariffs and establishing common external tariffs. An Arab economic unity agreement was signed in 1962 by Jordan, Egypt, Morocco, Kuwait and Syria and later adhered to by Yemen, Iraq and Sudan. Another agreement establishing an Arab Common Market was signed in 1965 by Egypt, Jordan, Iraq, Syria and Kuwait. Yemen and Sudan adhered later but the Kuwait National Assembly voted against ratification. While some progress has been made towards reducing tariffs between the member states, complete freedom of movement of labour and capital must remain a distant goal.

The lack of real progress towards developing the economic complementarity of the Arab states and reducing their dependence on the advanced industrialized countries called for a new approach in the 1970s. The paradox appeared that while certain Arab states were becoming vastly wealthy this dependence was actually increasing as they imported new technology – mainly from the West – and invested their reserves in Western currencies.

In 1976 the Iraqi secretary-general for Economic Affairs of the Arab League, Dr Abdul-Hassan Zalzala, formed the Experts' Committee for the Strategy for Joint Arab Economic Action, known as the Committee of Twenty, which, together with the Federation of Arab Economists, proposed a New Framework for joint Arab economic planning, investment and development which was submitted to the Arab summit meeting in November 1980. The response of the Arab heads of state to the New Framework was neither as enthusiastic nor as comprehensive as its authors wished but in the opinion of one leading Arab economist: 'The pressure of reality will eventually move the Arab world towards complementarity in the service of development and security.'[2]

2. See Yusif A. Sayigh, 'A New Framework for Complementarity', in *Arab Resources, The Transformation of a Society*, London, 1983.

While the huge discrepancy between the Arab countries in the size of their capital resources and labour force makes the establishment of a genuine Arab Economic Community extremely difficult, the richer Arab states have done much to distribute their wealth among the less fortunate. Kuwait was the pioneer with the Kuwait Fund for Arab Economic Development, founded in 1961. Others followed, such as the Arab Fund for Economic and Social Development (1968), the Abu Dhabi Fund for Arab Economic Development (1971), the Arab Bank for Economic Development in Africa (1973), the Saudi Development Fund (1974), and the Jedda-based Islamic Development Bank. The great bulk of this aid goes first to Arab and secondly to non-Arab Muslim countries and as such has been criticized by other Third World states. Nevertheless, it represents a massive shift of resources from the rich to the poor and within the Arab context it represents a practical demonstration of unity.[3]

Another aspect of the underlying social and cultural unity of the Arab world, in contrast to the failure of political unification, has been the large-scale movement of population between the Arab states. This originated with the Palestinian Diaspora of the 1940s and 1950s which has constantly been replenished by a further exodus from Israel, the occupied territories and the refugee camps in the Arab states. While Palestinians are in many respects the most deprived and oppressed of the Arabs they are also the best educated, occupying key positions and forming a substantial part of the middle class in the eastern half of the Arab world, especially the Gulf states. Not surprisingly, the greatest movement in terms of numbers has been of citizens of the most populous Arab state – Egypt. Some 2 million Egyptians have found employment in other Arab states, a trend which was scarcely affected by Egypt's political isolation. Highly-trained Sudanese can be found in vital administrative posts in the Arabian Peninsula – to Sudan's detriment, it must be admitted – while most recently the tragedy of Lebanon has created a new diaspora in the Arab world of the most commercially talented of the Arabs.

The increasing movement of population within the Arab world – short-term, long-term and permanent – the growth of inter-Arab social, cultural and economic institutions and the great improvement

3. It is worth pointing out that Kuwait and Abu Dhabi are giving more than 10 per cent of their GNP in aid and Saudi Arabia more than 5 per cent. This compares with the 0·31 per cent of GNP provided by all the industrialized countries of the OECD since 1975, which has never approached even the 0·7 per cent recommended by the UN in World Development Year, or the 1 per cent called for by the Brandt Commission.

in communications and the exchange of information media have brought the Arabs closer to each other even as the political frontiers dividing them have in some cases become more firmly established. An Algerian film or television programme may appear in Iraq or vice versa and either may be shown on the screens of the Arab Gulf states. The Saudi-owned daily newspaper *Sharq Alawsat* (The Middle East), printed on green paper, is a familiar sight from Morocco to Arabia; it is the *International Herald Tribune* of the Arab world. Literary levels have risen to develop the common awareness of the problems facing the Arabs. Lebanese and Palestinians visiting the Maghreb are surprised to meet not only sympathy for, but considerable understanding of, their tragedy.

An important feature of this trend has been a degree of fusion of modern Arab culture. When I first went to the Middle East some thirty years ago it was considered possible or even probable by some that the regional Arab dialects would grow gradually further apart until they became separate languages, just as Latin fathered various European tongues. This was never likely because the vitality of the Holy Koran prevents classical Arabic from becoming a dead language like Latin or Greek. In fact the opposite has happened and today the 'modern classical' in which newspapers are written and current affairs are broadcast on radio and television is increasingly the common tongue of educated Arabs from the Atlantic to the Indian Ocean. It is less likely that a Syrian and a Moroccan will knit their brows as they endeavour to understand each other than a generation ago, still less that they would switch into French.

Idealistic Arabs who feel humiliated and depressed by the frequent failure of their rulers to reach a minimum of agreement and who despair, for example, of a reconciliation between the régimes in Iraq and Syria or Algeria and Morocco can take some comfort in the fact that the Arab world is not becoming more socially and culturally fragmented but the contrary. In the longer term this is more important. Thirty years ago Arab nationalism in the sense of a political pan-Arab movement was regarded as the driving force in the Middle East. Today it is often declared to have perished, to be replaced by the more fashionable movement of Islamic revival. This view is certainly an over-simplification. Since Islam is the principal ingredient of Arab civilization it could never be divorced from any Arab national movement. Neither Arab nationalism nor pan-Arabism are dead although they require new definitions.

The worldwide conviction that the Arabs are incapable of settling their internal differences and will always indulge in passionate mutual recrimination remains deeply rooted.[4] Certainly they have given good grounds for this belief in recent years. One of the reasons, as we have seen, is that the myth of the unity of the Arab nation is at once so powerful and so idealized that some degree of disillusion is inevitable. Yet if the Arabs have a capacity for quarrelling they also have a great talent for reconciliation. The spectacle of Arab leaders embracing only days after denouncing each other in the fiercest terms is familiar. This may be taken as a sign of their volatility or incorrigible sentimentality; it could also mean that the invisible ties which unite them are ultimately stronger than the physical barriers which divide them.

Palestine: the Open Wound

It is not my purpose to discuss at length the rights and wrongs of the burning Arab–Israeli conflict which has absorbed the attention and energies of the people of the Middle East for a generation and will continue to do so for many years. The question has been discussed and analysed, passionately and dispassionately, in countless books, articles and speeches. Many more have yet to be written. I have not concealed my view that an appalling injustice was done to the Arab people of Palestine, or that my own country bears a large share of the responsibility. No material compensation would be either possible or adequate. However, the realization of this bitter truth does not necessarily help to shape the views of the outsider – that is, someone who is not directly affected by the sufferings of the Palestinians or the Jewish people – as to the best, or rather, the least intolerable dénouement of the tragedy. In many ways it is impertinent for the outsider to express his opinion on this matter and tell those who are directly involved how they *ought* to feel if they were wise and objective. Yet we can never entirely avoid responsibility in this manner. The Palestine question is posed to the whole world if for no other reason than it could still provoke a global war.

My purpose here is no more than tentatively to describe the feelings of the Arabs towards Palestine. First consideration belongs naturally

4. 'Ghailan son of Kharasha said to Ahnaf, "What will preserve the Arabs from decline?" He replied, "All will go well if they keep their swords on their shoulders and their turbans on their heads and ride horseback and do not fall prey to the fools' sense of honour." "And what is the fools' sense of honour?" "That they regard forgiving one another as a wrong."' From the *Book of Proof* by al-Jahiz, a ninth-century Arab writer.

to the 4 million Arabs of Palestine, about half of whom live under Israeli rule, either as Israeli citizens or in the occupied territories, and about half in the diaspora. The Israeli Arabs, who now number about 600,000 or 15 per cent of the population of Israel, deserve their own special study. Here I must be content with the simple observation that since the creation of the state of Israel, the vast majority of those who have elected to remain under Israeli rule have remained physically loyal in the sense that they have not risen in any organized revolt or engaged in sabotage operations against the Israeli institutions. Their average living standards are higher than those of the majority of their fellow Arabs outside Israel although the gap has narrowed substantially in recent years through growing Arab prosperity and Israel's acute economic difficulties. At the same time, as long as Israel remains a Zionist state (in which, for example, a Law of Return gives citizenship only to Jewish immigrants) the Arabs will remain second-class citizens in certain important respects. This means that they can never become Israelis in the same sense as Jews, so long as the state is based on Zionism. The extent to which they resign themselves to this reality depends largely on the future status of the occupied territories. If Israel absorbs these into a Greater Israel, as appeared to be the policies of the Begin government, Palestinian Arabs will form nearly half the population of the enlarged state. It is difficult to imagine that the Israeli Arabs would not find themselves identifying with the much larger Arab minority in the West Bank and Gaza.

But what of the great majority of Palestinian Arabs who are not Israeli citizens? Close acquaintance with them over thirty years has led me to two conclusions: first that their attachment to the Land of Palestine is deep and genuine, but secondly that their sense of nationhood has only recently developed.

The first point has been widely disputed. It has been held that the Palestinian Arabs have not been resettled in other Arab lands because the Arab states have preferred to keep them as pawns in their struggle with Israel and the West which helped to create it. According to this view, the memory of Palestine is only kept alive among the younger generation which was born outside Palestine, as it indisputably *is* kept alive, in order to stoke the fires of hatred against Israel.

To deny that Palestinians remain in their refugee camps because the Arab governments prefer to keep them there is not to suggest that the Arabs have refrained from using their plight as a political argument for their cause. But there are some practical obstacles to resettlement. The great majority of the refugees are peasant farmers who know no other trade. Those who were educated in the professions or had technical skills soon left the camps and found work elsewhere. So also did the few who learned enough at the UNRWA schools to go on to some higher education. Life was never easy for them as stateless refugees but many of them prospered. Palestinians are found in key positions throughout the Arab world – doctors, bankers, industrialists, and administrators. But the peasant Palestinians remained. As we have seen, a glance at a political map of the Arab world may be deceptive. Much of the wide open space is desert, and although there are some areas (especially in Syria, Iraq and Sudan) which could be cultivated if they were reclaimed and developed the process requires a huge long-term investment of labour and money. The funds could be made available from those oil-producing countries which have surplus revenues – although these are not in any case the same as the Arab states which have unpopulated cultivable lands. But it has to be remembered that countries such as Syria or Iraq are already diverting a major part of their resources to the building of irrigation dams and the reclamation of land in order to raise the living standards of their own farming population. Apart from the ideological obstacle to resettling Palestinian farmers away from their homeland, there are formidable social and economic difficulties.

Nevertheless, when all these important considerations are taken into account, the crucial question remains: do the Palestinians really want to return? The very nature of the question means that the answer of an outsider must be largely subjective. He can only say whether he feels that the Palestinians' declaration of longing for their homeland is genuine or not. Certainly it is often expressed with moving eloquence by the Palestinian poets and writers who have grown up in exile or under Israeli rule. Thus Mahmoud Darwish, in his poem *The Reaction*, recalls his imprisonment.

> Dear homeland
> . . . They shut me in a dark cell,
> My heart glowed with sunny torches.
> They wrote my number on the walls,
> The walls transformed to green pastures,
> They drew the face of my executioner,
> The face was soon dispersed
> With luminous braids.
> I carved your map with my teeth upon the walls
> And wrote the song of fleeing night.
> I hurled defeat to obscurity

> And plunged my hands
> In rays of light.
> They conquered nothing.
> Nothing.
> They only kindled earthquakes.

Or Fadwa Touqan, the poet from the West Bank town of Nablus:

> . . . For out of your trodden hopes
> Out of your crucified growth,
> Out of your stolen smiles
> Your children's smiles,
> Out of the wreckage,
> And the torture,
> Out of the blood-clotted walls,
> Out of the quiverings
> Of life and death
> Life will emerge.
> O great land
> O deep wound,
> And sole love.

The passionate yearning survives translation. It is possible to maintain that this is a product of a bogus patriotism. The author can only say he does not believe it.

At the same time it is unquestionably true that for some years after the 1948 disaster many of the Palestinian Arabs, and especially the political and intellectual élite, submerged their Palestinian patriotism in a wider Arab nationalism. Some of the conservative ruling class gave their loyalty to Jordan, many more of the younger generation saw their hope in Nasserism, Baathism or other aspects of the modern Arab nationalist movement. But they all had the same dream: the recovery of Palestine by the Arabs. Gradually their hopes faded until they were given the *coup de grâce* by the Six Day War of June 1967. Harsh reality had shown that the Arab regular armies were incapable of recovering Palestine by force of arms. However much support and encouragement they had from their fellow Arabs, the Palestinians had to lead their own struggle and for this it was necessary to assert their own nationhood. This was the motive force behind the rise to prominence of the Palestinian guerrilla organizations in the late 1960s. At the same time, many of the younger Palestinian intellectuals moved sharply to the left politically as they identified themselves with all the oppressed peoples of the world. A powerful expression of this feeling is the climax of an angry autobiography of a young

Palestinian writer Fawaz Turki, who was driven from his home in Haifa at the age of eight and spent many years working and wandering in Asia and Australia:

Then it came about that we could not wait to be freed, and we broke out. With freedom from bondage came freedom of the spirit. Came humanity. A return to pride. A feeling of our place. A defiance. An exhilaration. A wonder. An awakening. A rebirth. Came a certainty that we were not the wretched natives of the earth. That we were not alone . . . I returned from my retreat in the East and went up on the rooftops to shout to the world that I was a Palestinian. I was no longer alone, hiding, shamefaced, embittered. I belonged to a people who shared their travails and their accomplishments with a commonwealth of men and women across the world who like them struggled to remove the leaf covering the nakedness of imperialist expression.[5]

Even if we grant that there is nothing bogus about the attachment of the former inhabitants of Palestine to its soil, what of the other Arabs? It is commonly said and believed that the habitually divided Arabs find in Palestine a convenient cause on which they can hope to unite, that the mass of the people are indifferent while the Arab governments shamelessly exploit the sufferings of the Arabs for their own purposes.

I once asked an intelligent and sensitive Palestinian, who worked for the Arab League and therefore was familiar with all the Arab states, whether it might be true that most other Arabs had no deep feelings about Palestine. His reply was categorical. Palestine was in the heart and mind of every Arab wherever he was living. It was the first thing he thought about in the morning and the last thing at night.

Was this the pardonable egocentricity of a sufferer? Undoubtedly, the young Palestinian had been stung into exaggeration in his reply. It could not be literally correct that an Iraqi, Sudanese or Moroccan farmer cares more about the recovery of Palestine than whether the rains will fail. Yet his answer was poetically true. No Arab has been unaffected by the loss of Palestine. As Walid Khalidi wrote in 1958:

It is sometimes suggested that the way to solve the Palestine problem is to approach it in a piecemeal fashion. You must nibble at the problem until you end up by swallowing it. Settle the refugees and the biggest obstacle to the solution will be removed. But the Palestine problem will remain as acute as ever with every Palestine refugee settled. The refugee may be outward

5. Fawaz Turki, *The Disinherited: Journal of a Palestinian Exile*, New York and London, 1972, p. 154.

evidence of the crime which must be tidied out of sight but nothing will remove the scar of Palestine from Arab hearts . . .[6]

The reason why this is so is that the loss of Palestine which was recovered from the crusaders, symbolizes the decline of the Arabs from power and greatness into impotence. It was the final humiliation of the Arabs at the hands of the West, and it should be no surprise that its recovery should be a spur to their renaissance.

Walid Khalidi is a Palestinian, although he was speaking for all the Arabs. It was an Egyptian, Abdul Rahman Azzam Pasha, the first secretary-general of the Arab League, who told the Anglo-American Committee of Inquiry on Palestine in 1945:

Our brother has gone to Europe and to the West and come back something else. He has come back a Russified Jew, a Polish Jew, a German Jew, an English Jew. He has come back with a totally different conception of things, Western and not Eastern. That does not mean we are necessarily quarrelling with anyone who comes from the West. But the Jew, our old cousin, coming back with imperialistic ideas, with materialistic ideas, with reactionary or revolutionary ideas and trying to implement them first by British pressure and then by American pressure, and then by terrorism on his own part – he is not the old cousin, and we do not extend to him a very good welcome. The Zionist, the new Jew, wants to dominate, and he pretends that he has got a particular civilizing mission with which he returns to a backward degenerate race in order to put the elements of progress into an area which has to progress. Well, that has been the pretension of every power that wanted to colonize and aimed at domination. The excuse has always been that the people are backward and that he has got a human mission to put them forward . . . the Arabs simply stand and say 'No.' We are not reactionary and we are not backward. Even if we are ignorant, the difference between ignorance and knowledge is ten years in school. We are a living, vitally strong nation, we are in our renaissance; we are producing as many children as any nation in the world. We still have our brains. We have a heritage of civilization and of spiritual life. We are not going to allow ourselves to be controlled either by great nations or small nations or dispersed nations.[7]

Although this was said forty years ago and three years before the creation of Israel, it is doubtful whether the Arab attitude towards the Zionist state has ever been more accurately expressed. In Arab eyes the seizure of Palestine was a crime committed against the Arabs which is neither forgotten nor forgiven. Since they always opposed it, they did not see why they should be responsible for compensating the

6. See *Middle East Forum*, xxxiii, 8 (Summer 1958), p. 22.
7. Quoted in Richard Crossman, *Palestine Mission*, London, 1950, p. 118.

victims – the Palestinian refugees. They understand still less that they should resettle them on their own territory. This is the rationale behind the failure of the few Arab oil states with surplus revenues – Saudi Arabia, Kuwait, Abu Dhabi and Qatar – to provide more financial aid for the refugees. On the other hand, the governments of the four Arab host states where the refugees are living – Lebanon, Syria, Jordan and Egypt – have contributed substantially from their very limited resources. Between 1949 and 1969 they provided a total of about $110 million (about $10 million contributed to UNRWA and some $100 million in services provided directly to the refugees). In each case the presence of so many Palestinians has greatly added to their own acute social and economic difficulties.

But even if the Arabs will never forgive the loss of Palestine in their hearts, the question which most concerns the world is whether they will ever accept Israel as a bitter reality. Here there is the greatest difficulty in finding out the truth. In 1972 the noted Israeli scholar and former military intelligence chief Dr Yehoshafat Harkabi published a book entitled *Arab Attitudes to Israel*. This remarkable and brilliantly documented compilation is an essential source for anyone concerned with the Arab–Israeli conflict. Yet it cannot provide an answer to our question about Arab acceptance of Israel, which is fortunate because anyone who read the book straight through would end with the conviction that there was no alternative to permanent war between Arabs and Jews. But the Arabs are not alone in expressing their feelings in colourful, rhetorical language, although it may be a specially strong characteristic of their race.

No one can doubt that any Arab would be happy to see the state of Israel disappear. But this does not mean that he sees this in terms of Arab armies advancing to occupy Tel Aviv and drive all its Jewish inhabitants into the Mediterranean. Some Arab leaders – usually those most distant from the scene of the conflict – may have believed this possible in the 1950s but the dream has faded for all except the most irrational. Today there are, with minor variations, two schools of thought among the Arabs. There are those who would accept an Israel within its pre-1967 borders and those who believe that if the Arabs keep up a combined diplomatic, economic and military pressure the Israeli state will disintegrate and wither away.

In the first camp are the leaders of the great majority of the Arab states, including Israel's Arab neighbours. Egypt has gone further to recognize Israel after it has withdrawn from Egyptian territory only. The fact that none of the rest has categorically and explicitly declared its readiness to recognize Israel on these terms[8] may be unfortunate in Western eyes but it is understandable in the light of the Arab feelings about Palestine we have discussed. The Arabs demand at least a simultaneous Israeli recognition of the Palestinian right to self-determination and this shows no signs of being forthcoming.

On the matter of practical attitudes towards Israel the Palestinians became divided into two similar camps in the years which followed the 1973 war. Yasir Arafat, and several of his closest colleagues, became ready to accept a Palestinian mini-state consisting of Jordan's West Bank and Gaza, provided just compensation is paid to those Palestinians who were displaced in 1948. Like other Arab leaders he has never stated explicitly his readiness to recognize Israel in return for Israel's recognition of an independent Palestinian state. The reason has been that Arafat's prime objective has been to hold the Palestinian liberation movement together and the principle adopted by its democratic institutions of which the Palestinians are justly proud – the quasi-parliament or Palestine National Council, the Central Committee and elected Executive – is that major decisions should be taken, as far as possible, unanimously. There is a powerful camp among the Palestinians which is rigidly opposed to acceptance of a West Bank state even as an interim goal. They declare their willingness to continue the struggle indefinitely because a reduced Arab Palestine would be weak and helpless at the hands of both Israel and Jordan. They also believe that while Israel is overwhelmingly powerful at present, the immense preponderance of the Arabs in human and material resources will eventually reverse the balance and that Israel will in any case destroy itself through its inner contradictions, although they have to admit that this will not happen in their own or their children's lifetime. It should be added that a minority of these hardliners has not hesitated to assassinate those courageous PLO representatives who declared their moderation publicly. Most of these murders are ascribed to the small Abu Nidal group which has been alternately sponsored by Iraq and Syria.

Nevertheless, there is no real doubt that Arafat has made the establishment of a small West Bank/Gaza state his real aim.

It is equally understandable that the Israelis remain sceptical. They can point to his speech at the UN General Assembly on 13 November

8. The proposals agreed at the Arab summit in Fez in September 1982, for example, refer to the right of all Middle East states to recognized and secure borders but do not mention Israel by name.

1974, in which he spoke only of the broader aim of replacing the state of Israel by a democratic secular state. Arafat's reply to that is that he is not going to abandon his dream. As he told *Le Monde* (7 January 1975): 'Is it a crime to dream? Is it forbidden to imagine the evolution that could occur during the coming years?'

To most of the world this is a totally impractical ideal, because Zionists would prefer to die than to see the destruction of the Israeli state.[9] It is assumed that if they found themselves with their backs to the wall they would make use of atomic weapons in desperation.

The fundamental inconsistency between the aims of Palestinian moderates and hardliners was long concealed because neither seemed likely to be realized. Israel, with powerful American support, rejected all hope of an independent Palestinian mini-state. After the PLO's expulsion from Jordan in 1970–71 it concentrated on building up a temporary Palestinian organization within Lebanon which included some impressive social services and even fledgeling industries. The PLO was not short of money – 'the richest revolutionaries in history' in the phrase of the Lebanese Druze leader, Walid Jumblatt – because of contributions from the Arab Gulf states and the Palestinian Diaspora. But the political cost was high in PLO involvement in the Lebanese civil war and the blame attached to the Palestinians for provoking the ruthless Israeli retaliation in which so many Lebanese civilians suffered. Sympathy for the Palestinian cause among many Lebanese turned to bitter hatred. The other Arab states, both unable and unwilling to offer the Palestinians any assistance, felt frustrated and humiliated. The Palestinians felt more isolated and neglected than ever. Moreover, it became apparent that Arafat and his moderate colleagues were neglecting their main constituency – the Palestinians in the occupied territories who overwhelmingly support his leadership and are quite prepared to accept and recognize the Zionist state if it means an end to the Israeli occupation.

Even after the Israeli invasion of Lebanon in 1982 caused the destruction of the Palestinian quasi-state the division over strategy among the Palestinians was still glossed over. The Palestinian National Council meeting in Algiers in February 1983 combined ringing

9. Many are also sceptical about statements by Palestinian spokesmen that all the Jews who are now in Israel would be allowed to remain if they accepted to live in a non-sectarian state. It is true that the Palestinian Covenant which refers to the expulsion of all Jews who have come since 1948 has never been formally amended yet I am personally convinced that the new policy is accepted by all the PLO leadership although I fully understand why Israelis refuse to believe that this is so.

affirmations of the continuation of the armed struggle *à l'outrance*, with the granting of a mandate to Yasir Arafat to pursue the path of political negotiation. It was only after the split within the PLO, caused by hardline rebels with Syrian support and Arafat's evacuation with his remaining loyalist fighters from his last Lebanese foothold in Tripoli, that reality had to be faced. The questions now at issue were whether the PLO could survive at all and whether Israel's moves to settle the West Bank with Jews and absorb it into Israel were on the point of becoming irreversible. There was even the fear that once Israel had done this it would find some means of persuading or forcing the majority of Arabs to leave so that what was left of Arab Palestine would finally disappear.

Yasir Arafat has to consider whether to disassociate himself finally from those who reject any political solution to the Palestinian problem. This inevitably involves some coordination with Jordan. It means retaining some faith that the world community, led by the United States, is prepared to accept that Palestinian self-determination is unavoidable if there is ever to be peace in the Middle East. This is the crux and it makes little difference whether the product of this self-determination is a small independent Palestinian state or an 'autonomous entity' linked with Jordan in the terms of President Reagan's Middle East plan.

The belief that no short- or even medium-term solution is possible will not die. In fact, there is underlying the feeling of all the Arabs, whether moderate or hardline in their political attitudes, the conviction that ultimately the Middle Eastern body will reject the Zionist transplant. It may take ten years, a century or, as with the Crusader states, 300 years, but it will happen. The only way, according to this view, that Israel could escape this fate would be by transforming itself into something different – a Middle Eastern state looking at the world through oriental eyes. This is the hope of the distinguished French Jewish orientalist Maxime Rodinson:

> As has been said, powerful factors have driven Israel into the role which she has assumed up till now. Other factors, however, could just as well drive her in an opposite direction. A different Israel is not an impossibility. Israel would, from that moment, be a Levantine state like any other, and no more a bridgehead of the West, forced by her situation to bear the brunt of the Arab world's hostility and to seek imperialist support.[10]

10. Maxime Rodinson, *Israel and the Arabs*, Harmondsworth, Penguin Books, 1968, p. 234.

It is an attractive dream, but the great doubt must remain whether Israel could transform itself in this way and retain the will to live. Zionism was Israel's *raison d'être*. Would an Israel without Zionism be no more than a self-contradiction?

Oil as Power

Oil executives, technicians and journalists from all over the world attending the Second Arab Petroleum Congress in Beirut in October 1960 were electrified by the paper presented by the fiery young Saudi director-general of petroleum and mineral resources, Abdullah Tariki. He was alleging that the oil companies by arbitrary and discriminatory pricing of Middle East oil had pocketed no less than $5,474,290,133, half of which under proper pricing would have gone to the Middle East producing countries.

Tariki was being deliberately provocative. Western oilmen had little difficulty in casting doubt on his statistical methods, and the argument became too technical for the non-specialist journalists to follow. But of one thing there could be no doubt. Tariki was expressing the innermost feelings of all his fellow Arabs. He was using his battery of figures to make the simple point that the price of oil in world trade was not determined by competitive forces of supply and demand but by a handful of all-powerful international oil companies. When oil executives dismissed Tariki's argument, saying that 'the price of oil is decided in the market place like everything else', they were being disingenuous. Middle Easterners felt in their bones this was not true, even if they did not have the means to prove it. What they did know was that the disposal of their only major but exhaustible natural resource was not in the hands of their own governments.

Basically, the argument was political and not economic. When oil was discovered and exploited in the Middle East by Western finance, technology and enterprise – first in Iran, then Iraq and later in Saudi Arabia and the Gulf states – the host states were all weak, impoverished and heavily dominated by Western economic and military power. Their governments were happy to receive the modest royalty payments from the oil companies for the oil that was exported.

From 1950 onwards royalty payments were abandoned for the new system of a fifty-fifty division of net profits between the oil companies and the ruler or government of the producing state. This coincided with a rapid expansion in exports and produced a speedy increase in revenues for the Middle East oil states. Those of Iraq, for example, rose from £13·9 million in 1951 to £32·6 million in 1952 and to £51·3 million in 1953. But although this in itself transformed the prospects of these countries and enabled them to launch ambitious social and economic development programmes, it did not alter the power structure of the international oil industry. The major oil companies remained in control and because they were able to provide an abundant supply of cheap oil for the rich industrialized nations, there was no clash of interest at this stage between them and the principal oil consumers.

Unfortunately, therefore, the fifty-fifty principle gave a bogus impression of fairness and of providing a basis for equal 'partnership' between the advanced industrialized non-communist countries and the technically backward Middle East oil states.[11] It did not answer the *political* need of the producing countries to acquire control over the resource which, in the case of the desert states of Arabia, was the very reason for their existence. Nor did it alleviate the bitter feeling that the foreign oil company was a 'state within a state', more powerful than the host government with whom it was sharing its profits. The only attempt to remedy this situation had been the hasty and ill-planned nationalization in 1951 of the Anglo-Iranian Oil Company by the populist Iranian leader Dr Muhammad Mossadegh. He was defeated partly through his own political incompetence but mainly because the AIOC, with the backing of the British government, was able to prevent Iran from selling its oil. Although the International Court of Justice ruled in Mossadegh's favour and the UN Security Council refused to take action, the West's political and economic strategy was enough to ensure Mossadegh's overthrow.

The lesson was not lost on the other oil-producing states, who temporarily abandoned any thoughts of nationalization. Abdul Nasser's takeover in 1956 of the Suez Canal Company, another 'state within a state', aroused the same kind of emotions among the Egyptians as Dr Mossadegh's oil nationalization had provoked among the Iranians. But the case was somewhat different. Nasser did not have to fight the international oil companies. However, he did have to go to war to keep the Suez Canal and he only won because the Western countries were divided on the issue.

11. This is how the principle was always warmly defended by the outstanding Lebanese millionaire contractor and politician, Emile Boustani, at the annual Arab Petroleum Congresses. His sparring matches with Abdullah Tariki became a popular feature of these meetings.

This did not mean that the Middle East oil-producing countries gave up thinking of other means of gaining more control over their only major source of wealth. They had good reason for discontent in the 1950s and 1960s. While the price of all the manufactured goods that they imported from the industrialized countries were rising the price of their oil was actually falling. Thus the posted price[12] of Saudi oil declined from \$2·18 a barrel in 1947 to \$1·80 in 1970 – a fall of 17 per cent. The fall in real terms of what Saudi oil revenues could buy was more like 50 per cent.[13] The terms of trade were moving inexorably against the Arab and Iranian oil producers.[14] Moreover, they were only receiving a small proportion of the price for which their oil was being sold to the main consuming nations. A much larger share was levied by the consumer governments in the form of taxes.

In 1959 the international oil companies suddenly cut the posted prices of crude oil in both Venezuela and the Middle East without consulting the governments concerned. When they followed this with a second round of cuts a year later the governments of the main producing countries were provoked into action. Representatives of Iraq, Iran, Kuwait, Saudi Arabia and Venezuela met in Baghdad and OPEC, the Organization for Petroleum Exporting Countries was born. OPEC pledged itself to restore oil prices and significantly demanded that in future the oil companies should consult with them whenever they believed cuts in prices were necessary.

The reaction in the main Western consuming countries to the formation of OPEC was both hostile and sceptical. It was hostile because there was very little sympathy with the plight of the oil states. Because of the foolish extravagance of some of their rulers it was easy to represent them as merely being greedy in wanting a better price for their oil. ('Why should the shaikhs get any more money? I think they should get less' was the typical reaction of one left-wing editor.) The reaction was sceptical because few believed that the OPEC members would be able to restore prices. The only method was to adopt

12. A posted price is that for which the producing company is prepared to sell oil to outsiders or to its own subsidiaries. It is used to value oil for tax purposes.

13. See Ibrahim Oweiss, 'Deciding a Price', *Middle East International*, February 1975, p. 12.

14. Moreover, they were deteriorating faster than for the Venezuelans. In order to ensure that Middle Eastern oil was made competitive with Venezuelan oil in the markets of Western Europe, the oil companies maintained and widened the gap between the two. In the 1960s the United States, which controlled Venezuelan oil, was concerned to conserve the oil resources of the western hemisphere.

prorationing – that is, the regulation and limitation of production on a planned basis – and this was something that was notoriously difficult to achieve. No one believed that the oil states would ever agree among themselves on their relative shares of the market or decide who should hold down production and by how much.

This scepticism was justified by events. OPEC's collective enthusiasm for prorationing soon waned, although Venezuela continued to be its advocate. But OPEC never abandoned its underlying aim which was to gain control over the exploitation of their main natural source of wealth. They might disagree on methods but this was their single purpose. It was clearly expressed in a 'Declaratory Statement of Petroleum Policy', issued at the sixteenth OPEC conference in Vienna in July 1968. This statement, which in spirit closely followed the UN General Assembly resolution of 25 November 1966 on a country's right of permanent sovereignty over the development of its natural resources, declared in its preamble that the best way for the OPEC member countries to ensure that their oil resources were used for their benefit was for them to be 'in a position to undertake themselves directly the exploitation of their hydrocarbon resources, so that they may exercise their freedom of choice in the utilization of hydrocarbon resources in the most favourable conditions'.

But were the oil-producing states capable of producing and marketing their oil and finding new sources of supply? This was the crucial question. Sudden expropriation of the foreign oil companies was ruled out as a result of the Iranian experience. A more gradual approach was required, and for this the vital need was for the oil states to develop their own body of men with experience and expertise who would be capable of running a national oil industry when the time came. Iran had an advantage over the Arab oil states because its oil industry was much older. Despite the disasters of the Mossadegh era it had established a National Iranian Oil Company, which in 1957 went into partnership with the Italian state oil company AGIP, headed by the brilliant and forceful Enrico Mattei, a dedicated opponent of the major oil companies, which he was apt to refer to as 'the cartel of the seven sisters'. This Italian–Iranian 'joint venture' set the pattern for similar deals in other Middle East countries, such as those between Egypt and the independent American oil companies to produce oil from the Red Sea and the Western Desert.

Iraq, Kuwait and Saudi Arabia all followed Iran's example and established their own national oil companies in the 1960s. But although this helped them to train more men with responsibility and experience in the oil industry it did not bring them much nearer to control over their main oil resources which were still part of the concessions of the major foreign oil companies – the American Aramco in Saudi Arabia, Anglo-American Kuwait Oil Company in Kuwait or the Anglo-American–French Iraq Petroleum Company in Iraq. From the moment that Iraq's revolutionary government had taken power in July 1958 it had asked for a 20 per cent participation in the ownership of the IPC on the strong ground that Article 34 of the original 1925 convention stipulated that when shares of the company were offered to the public, Iraqis should be given a preference for at least 20 per cent of the issue. When the company replied that the case had not arisen because IPC (although not the American, British and French parent companies) was private and not public and therefore none of its share capital was available for sale, the Iraqis understandably declared that their fathers had been hoodwinked in 1925. Similar demands by other oil states for a share in the foreign oil company which controlled most of their oil received the same reply. It was technically unfeasible. No one could ever assess the value of 20 per cent of IPC.

It was the Kassem government in Iraq which made the next important attempt of any Middle Eastern oil state to take control of its own oil resources. This was the issue of Law 80 on 19 December 1961 which expropriated all IPC's concession area except that in which they were operating. This left the company with only 0·5 per cent of its former concession. But Kassem's action must also be counted a failure. IPC refused to accept it and, as negotiations dragged on unsuccessfully, the company cut back production and exports so that Iraq, like Iran in 1952, fell back from its position among the major Middle East oil producers.

In 1965 there seemed to have been little change in the power structure of the international oil industry. OPEC was still in existence but its member countries had neither succeeded in restoring the cuts in oil prices nor in persuading the oil companies to accept their partnership in oil production. Joint ventures between national and foreign oil companies still only affected a tiny proportion of total Middle Eastern oil production.

Barely ten years later the situation had been totally transformed. The price of Middle East crude oil had quintupled; Algeria and Iraq had nationalized and the oil companies had come to terms: and even the more conservative oil states of Arabia had secured 60 per cent participation in the companies operating in their territory. On 5

March 1975 Kuwait chose the occasion of a summit meeting of OPEC countries at Algiers to announce that it was nationalizing the remaining 40 per cent share held by British Petroleum and Gulf Oil. No one doubted that the other Arabian oil states would soon follow.

How had this extraordinary revolution taken place? It was not a real *volte face* but the continuation of a trend which had been submerged for many years. It was helped to the surface by several factors such as the Middle East war of October 1973. Nevertheless, the shrewder independent oil experts had been predicting from the mid-1960s onwards that the managerial role of the oil companies in the Middle East was already in the process of being phased out. Soon they would be no more than agents drilling for oil, producing and marketing it on contract to the owner states. The oil states were in the vanguard of the Third World in fulfilling the 1966 UN General Assembly resolution about acquiring permanent sovereignty over natural resources.

In a very real sense, the use of the Arab 'oil weapon' in their struggle against Israel is only part of this trend. The Arabs have long regarded Israel as an instrument of Western imperialist domination. The use of oil power is a means of recovering their full sovereignty. Moreover it is not used directly against Israel but indirectly to induce the West to reduce its support for Israel.

Even if there had been no Arab–Israeli conflict the OPEC countries would sooner or later have taken over their oil industries. Although it is often forgotten, leading members of OPEC such as Iran, Venezuela and Nigeria are not Arab. The steep increase in oil prices began before the October 1973 war when the Arabs first made use of the 'oil weapon'. Nevertheless, the conflict with Israel has helped to radicalize the oil politics of the Arabs.

The use of the weapon had long been discussed by the Arabs before 1973. In 1956 during the Anglo-French–Israeli attack on Egypt the Syrians (without consulting the Iraqis) blew up the pipelines and pumping stations bringing Iraq oil across its territory. Britain had to bring in temporary petrol rationing, but it obtained supplies from the western hemisphere, and the Syrian action hardly affected the outcome of the war. In 1967 the Arabs made a more concerted action to cut off supplies in order to influence the disastrous course of the fighting between Israel and Egypt, Jordan and Syria. But for several reasons this was again a failure. The war ended in six days; the financial reserves of the oil states were too small to stand more than a short embargo, and the United States, the country they most wished to influence, was almost impervious to cuts since it imported very little Middle East oil. The oil states' main purpose in stopping exports was to prevent sabotage of the installations by an inflamed public. At the Khartoum Arab summit meeting in August–September 1967 it was agreed that exports should be resumed immediately.

In the aftermath of the Six Day War there was little talk of using the 'oil weapon' except in those states, such as Syria and Egypt, which were not major oil producers. Western countries were lulled into a feeling of security because the weapon had proved a failure. However, several important elements in the situation were changing in the 1970s. The Arab oil-exporting countries were becoming much stronger financially because of the increase in prices and oil revenues. Secondly, after the death of President Nasser, Egypt under President Sadat forged a new relationship with Saudi Arabia, the key Arab oil-producing country. Saudi Arabia had long been adamantly opposed to the political use of the oil weapon, which in the Saudi case would have to be used primarily against its Western friend, the United States. But King Feisal was becoming increasingly disillusioned by the United States' unremitting bias towards Israel. At the same time, it was a matter of crucial importance that the United States, with the depletion of its own oil reserves and with no prospect of any substantial increase in Venezuelan exports, was becoming increasingly dependent on Arab oil for a vital part of its energy supplies. The incentive and the opportunity for a concerted use of the Arab oil weapon existed. In the spring and summer of 1973, King Feisal and other leading Saudis made repeated warnings that it might be used, but the majority of US oil experts still dismissed these as empty threats.

The events of October 1973 showed how far both the Arab oil states' strength and strategy had improved since 1967. Experience had taught them that there was no use in imposing a selective embargo on 'hostile' (i.e. pro-Israeli) states without a general and concerted cutback in production because it was impossible to police. Having decided on an immediate cut in production of 5 per cent and then of 5 per cent each month until the Israelis withdrew from all occupied Arab territory they were able to declare their willingness to maintain supplies to those countries which were friendly or had shown their readiness to move to an even-handed position on the Arab–Israeli conflict. These included France, Britain, Spain, Belgium, India, Japan and most of the African and Islamic countries. A total boycott on the other hand was declared for the United States, the Netherlands and Denmark, which were dubbed as hostile to the Arabs.[15]

The oil weapon was crude and uneven in its effects. Iraq disassociated itself from its use at the outset on the ground that it damaged friendly countries, and demanded nationalization of Western interests as an alternative. But no one could doubt the power of the oil weapon and the immediate influence that it exerted on all the industrialized countries which were heavily dependent on Arab oil.

Nevertheless, the Arab oil-producers soon came to realize that the oil weapon could not be used to its fullest extent. Further cuts in production would bring the European countries and Japan to disaster and cause a collapse of the world economy. The threat of this could be enough to provoke a Western military invasion of the Arab oil fields. The Arabs were therefore obliged to abandon their declared aim of continuing the cuts until Israel withdrew from all the occupied territories. In March 1974 they lifted the embargo on the US, with Libya dissenting, and in July the Netherlands was also lifted from the blacklist.

The oil weapon was sheathed but its use had already caused a shift in the world balance of power in the Arabs' favour. It was more of a psychological than a material change. Certainly the October 1973 war accelerated the rise in oil prices. This increased their revenues and reserves and therefore the opportunities for Arab investors, both government and private, to buy their way into the Western economy. (The same happened incidentally to Iran, which was not involved in the 1973 war.) But this was only the intensification of a previous trend. The important change was in the *awareness* of Arab oil power. This created a new self-confidence among the Arabs and apprehension among the rest of the world. Arab oil ministers, such as the Saudi Shaikh Yamani, became figures of major international importance.

The image of the Arab oil shaikh gleefully planning to blackmail the rest of mankind from his luxurious desert palace was a gift for Western

15. A detailed blueprint for the whole Arab economic strategy in the October war was contained in a document entitled 'Economic Interests in the Service of Arab Causes' which was written in 1973 by three of the Arab world's leading economists for presentation to the economic committee of the Arab League. This remarkable paper not only suggested the methods for the use of the oil weapon which were actually used, but looked forward to the future use of Arab financial reserves and the coordination of industrialization policies in the Arab causes. It was discussed and analysed by Jim Muir in the *Sunday Times*, 17 March 1974.

cartoonists and journalists, which was duly exploited. From 1974 onwards, scarcely a day passed without a headline story in the European or American financial press of an Arab purchase of important real estate or stocks. 'The Arabs' were buying an island off the South Carolina coast, a leading women's magazine, or a majority shareholding in a major European company which was about to collapse. Readers of the Western press were additionally confused because many journalists found difficulty in remembering that Iranians were not Arabs. The picture of the Arabs as members of a financial Mafia on a global scale was fixed in the Western mind.[16]

While there were undeniably some elements of truth in this image, it was seriously distorted and exaggerated in several ways. In the first place, the future growth of Arab financial power was greatly overemphasized by the experts in 1974. It had been predicted, even before the 1973 Middle East war, that the Arabs would enjoy such large financial surpluses that a majority of the world's currency reserves would be in their hands by the early 1980s. Suddenly, in the early months of 1975, all these estimates were revised downwards. It was now predicted that the Middle East oil states would only build up surpluses for a few years. After that their expanding consumption of consumer goods and their ambitious industrialization plans would increase their imports to a point that they would again be in debt to the Western countries. Almost overnight the spectre which had been presented of the world's monetary system being drowned by an avalanche of petro-dollars, seemed to disappear.[17]

Secondly, the popular idea that 'the Arabs' would continue to raise oil prices indefinitely began to fade towards the end of 1974. Oil economists began to talk about a world surplus, and output was sharply cut back in some Arab countries, such as Kuwait, Libya and

16. Ironically, the image closely resembled the one that was popular in the earlier part of this century of International Jewry. A cartoon in the leading Israel newspaper *Haaretz* showed a sinister Arab shaikh holding the globe in his grasp. A very similar drawing formed the cover of the French edition of the notorious anti-semitic forgery *The Protocols of the Elders of the Zion* in the 1930s. The only difference was that it had an evil-looking Jew instead of the shaikh.

17. It is certainly arguable that the very high *per capita* incomes – among the highest in the world – which are usually ascribed to the Arab oil-producers of the Gulf are misleading. Since in exporting crude oil they are selling a wasting asset it should be regarded as the sale of capital rather than as income and at least a depletion factor taken into account when measuring their GDPs. This would place Kuwait, Qatar and the UAE much further down in the world league for *per capita* income and below the advanced industrialized states. See Dr Thomas R. Stanffer, *Oil Revenues: Income or Capital*, OPEC Fund Newsletter, September 1983.

Abu Dhabi. The possibility that OPEC might break up as its members fought for their shares of a reduced market was even discussed. But as this was happening a new point was raised. In a speech to the National Press Club in Washington on 3 February 1975, Dr Kissinger who was leading the move among the Western countries to try to force down oil prices, pointed out that they must remain high enough in the Western countries to encourage investment in the development of alternative sources of energy. Although Dr Kissinger appeared to believe that the two policies were perfectly compatible, the Western public was understandably confused. (The dilemma was greatest in Britain, whose economy suffered very severely from the oil price rises in 1973–4, but which was looking forward to becoming an oil exporter from the North Sea in the 1980s and therefore wanted prices to be maintained.)

Finally, it came to be dimly realized that neither OPEC nor even the Arab oil states (who have formed their own Organization of Arab Petroleum Exporting Countries, OAPEC, within OPEC) were anything like a monolithic bloc. They are not even a cartel in the normal sense because they have no agreement to share out the market between them. There is an immense disparity of interest between countries like Algeria or Iraq with their large and impoverished populations who need to be fed, housed and educated, and Kuwait and Abu Dhabi with their tiny populations which already have most of their material needs. About 76 per cent of OPEC oil revenues go to nine countries (including Algeria, Iraq and Iran) which have GNPs of only $450 per head, which is less than one tenth of the average for western European countries.[18] It is no surprise therefore that although Algeria and Saudi Arabia cooperated effectively over the use of the oil weapon during the 1973 war, they have since disagreed sharply over oil policy. Saudi Arabia occupies a unique position since it accounts for 30 per cent of OPEC's production and over 30 per cent of its reserves. By using its immense spare capacity to raise production or by a policy of conservation, Saudi Arabia can outplay all the rest. Moreover, increasing US dependence on imports of Saudi oil gives the Saudis a large measure of power over the American economy and hence over the entire non-communist industrialized world. But although the Saudis' approach to oil prices may be different for domestic reasons from Algeria, Iran or Iraq, their overall objective is the same: to secure a shift in resources to the Third World.

18. See the *Economist*, 15 February 1975, p. 72.

There was a strong element of comforting self-deception in the West's image of the greedy and selfish 'oil shaikh'. The question was often asked why he did not give away more of his wealth to help his fellow Asians or Africans. However, as we have seen, the great majority of oil revenues go to countries whose people are desperately poor by Western standards and need every cent for their own development. As for the rest, their record as givers of aid is considerably better than that of Western countries. Whereas the latter have never given as much as the 1 per cent of their GNP which was the target set for World Development Year, Kuwait gives between 6 and 8 per cent of its GNP. Saudi Arabia not only provides hundreds of millions of dollars to Arab, African and Islamic countries but is a massive contributor to World Bank funds.

It may also be worth mentioning that the governments of the main oil-consuming nations still take much more of the price for which a barrel of oil is sold than the oil-producing countries. OPEC figures for April 1973 showed that oil exports were being marketed in Western Europe for $16 a barrel. Of this 1·8 per cent was actual production costs and 9·6 per cent was revenue which went to producing countries. Just over 33 per cent was absorbed by companies' costs and profits and the remaining 55 per cent was accounted for by taxes levied by consuming governments.

In 1979–81 there was a further surge in OPEC prices which was largely caused by the near-panic among consumers provoked by the upheaval in Iran, the second largest Middle East producer. When this subsided a glut in the world market ensued; this was caused by reduced demand owing to the world recession, the fact that higher prices had caused the major industrialized countries to conserve their supplies of energy and switch to alternative sources of power and that new sources of oil outside OPEC, such as Mexico and the North Sea, had been discovered and developed. Prices fell from their high point of $34 a barrel to be held with difficulty at $29 a barrel. Throughout this period Saudi Arabia has used its position as the 'swing' producer within OPEC to stabilize prices – increasing or threatening to increase its output if it felt prices were rising too high or cutting production drastically to hold them at a lower level.

The twenty years of OPEC's existence have shown an astonishing swing in crude oil output. The production by the thirteen members rose from 11·5 million barrels per day in 1963 to nearly 40 million barrels per day in 1973, fell back to 27 million barrels per day in 1975, rose again to a peak of 31 million in 1977 before declining fairly steadily to as low as 15 million barrels per day in early 1983 before stabilizing at about 19 million by the end of the year.[19]

Arab oil-producers, together with the other members of OPEC, suffered a fall in oil revenues of 30 per cent in 1982 and a further cut of one third in 1983. But since there was no equivalent fall in the price of their imports from the developed countries they found themselves in deficit and had to dip into their reserves. On the other hand, by the end of 1983 OPEC appeared to be defying Western predictions, often made in gloating terms, of its imminent collapse. Inevitably, the trend in the oil market meant some reduction in the international power and influence of the major oil producers. But this could be exaggerated. The Arabs remained the owners of huge reserves of petro-dollars and collectively formed a major power bloc in the world economy. Moreover, since Arab oil has the lowest cost of production in the world it will be the last to be substituted by other forms of energy.

It is inevitable that the relationship between the main producers of oil and the consumers has taken on some of the aspects of an old-fashioned power struggle between nations. Because so many of the producers are Arab states and the main importers are European it even seems at times to be a continuation of the conflict between Islam and Christendom. The possibility of war over oil was clearly envisaged by President Ford and Dr Kissinger in January 1975, when they spoke of the use of military force in the case of the economic 'strangulation' of the West. Some powerful voices even advocated the immediate occupation of the Persian Gulf fields as a means of breaking the power of OPEC. Some of the leading oil producers discounted these statements as empty threats but in others it provoked an angry response. 'The US is living in the past,' President Boumedienne of Algeria told the French paper *l'Humanité*.

> They have ultra-advanced computers, but these cannot learn from history. To attempt to assume the leadership of the world in 1975 is an outdated concept . . . But how do they think they can attack any Arab country without provoking a response? You know, it only needs several determined groups to blow up all the oil installations.

However, in the 1980s the cold war between the West and the Arab oil-producers has subsided. This is partly because the West's dependence on Arab oil has been reduced but there has also been an

19. See *OPEC Annual Statistical Bulletin* for 1982 and 1983.

increased awareness on both sides of the common interest in bringing the world economy out of recession. The trading and financial links between the West and the Arab oil states are still of overwhelming importance to both. At the same time the fear has grown of external dangers to the security of Arab oil wells – from the Soviet occupiers of Afghanistan and more recently from the Iraq–Iran war which in 1983–4 even threatened to cause the closure of all tanker exports through the Gulf. The neo-imperialist view, which is still occasionally voiced by a few Western academics, that the West should have maintained its physical control over the Middle East in order to ensure continuing supplies of cheap energy, no longer seems relevant.

Some Arab Characteristics

In some ways it is absurd to talk about 'the Arab character'. If we are speaking of Arabs in the sense that the term has been used throughout this book, we are referring to 180 million people who have widely varying physical characteristics. Because of the admixtures of Turkish, Caucasian, Negro, Kurdish, Spanish or Berber blood an Arab today may be coal-black or blond-skinned and blue-eyed. These people live over a widely scattered area under very different political systems.

Yet I hope to have shown in these pages that there are certain common characteristics among the Arabic-speaking peoples. Even the variation in their physical appearance is a product of their racial colour-blindness. This is not absolute; Arabs are certainly aware of racial differences. But these affect their behaviour much less than that of peoples of most other nations and faiths.

It is to be hoped that this necessarily compressed account of the formation and present condition of the contemporary Arab world has provided some hint of how its character was created. One of the strongest influences has been a sense of past history. Writing in 1957, Professor Cantwell Smith said:

The Arabs are a proud and sensitive people. No adequate understanding of their situation today is possible unless due weight is given to both these factors. Further, some appreciation is needed of how much they have in their past of which to be proud, and how much in their present about which to be sensitive.[20]

20. Wilfred Cantwell Smith, *Islam in Modern History*, London, 1957, p. 93.

He went on to point out that the Arabs have a deep sense of betrayal at the hands of the rest of mankind, a feeling that history had been made to take the wrong turning. This causes them not only to glorify, but to idealize, their own past. As Professor Hamilton Gibb[21] has also shown, this had made the task of the Islamic modern reformers from Muhammad Abduh onwards difficult, if not impossible. Their aim was to strengthen the world of Islam in order to protect it against the dominating power of the West and for this purpose they sought to introduce the liberal humanitarian values of eighteenth-century Europe and America. But at the same time they could not admit that the values and practices of early Islam were anything less than perfect. In other words they were reformers who would not say they wanted a reformation.

In the Turkish Republic Kemal Atatürk chose the different path of outright secularism. He did not suppress Islam but he tried to eradicate its influence on Turkey's social and political life. In the Arab world the only open advocates of secularism are the Marxists, but they are a small minority who have to proceed with the greatest caution. Many of the leading communists in the Arab world are either non-Muslims or members of the non-Arab minorities. The reasons are understandable, but this fact serves to reduce their influence. This is not to say either that Arabs as a whole are passionately religious or that none of their modern leaders have shown interest in secular reforms of any kind. If a substantial number of Arab students are attracted to the Islamic revivalist ideas of the Muslim Brotherhood, the majority show little interest and are perfunctory in the performance of their Muslim duties. But they do not deny Islam because it is an integral part of their national heritage in a way that it is for no other people. In a real sense every Arab is a Muslim, even if he is a Christian – or a communist.

It can be seen that the twentieth-century Arab political reformer faces a uniquely difficult task. His problems are not made any easier by the atomism of the Arab mind, the 'intense feeling for the separateness and individuality of the concrete events' and 'aversion from the thought-processes of rationalism' which Professor Gibb detected (see p. 96). This essential characteristic of the Arabs is perfectly illustrated by their attitude to their language, which has a uniquely important role in their society and civilization.

There is one written or 'literary' Arabic language. This is the

21. H. A. R. Gibb, *Modern Trends in Islam*, London, 1947, pp. 63–84.

Arabic that is used in the modern Arab world in private letters, books, pamphlets, newspapers or public notices. It is also used in radio and television news bulletins and commentaries and for the most part by public speakers. But no Arab uses this Arabic for everyday conversation. To do so would be to invite ridicule, for it would be roughly equivalent to a contemporary Englishman addressing a friend in the language of Shakespeare ('Come on, you madcap, I'll to the alehouse with you presently.') For this he will use his own colloquial Arabic, which varies widely from one part of the Arab world to another. The colloquial Arabic of the former parts of Greater Syria (that is Lebanon, Syria, Jordon and Palestine) is fairly uniform and northern Sudanese speech is close to that of the Egyptians. Egyptian colloquial is widely understood because of familiarity with Egyptian films and radio programmes and the spread of Egyptian schoolteachers throughout the Arab world.

As might be expected, it is the common expressions of everyday use – the terms of greeting, for household articles or the most common verbs and adjectives – which vary most from one country to another. A highly educated Arab would obviously have less difficulty in communicating with another from a distant part of the Arab world than one who is illiterate because he can avoid colloquialisms and use a more classical form of the kind that is used in newspaper editorials.

The reasons for this are not far to seek. Classical Arabic, the language of the Holy Koran, is the living proof of the past glory of the Arabs and Islam. In contemporary Arabs it represents the 'ideal' of 'higher self' – something that we aspire to be but manifestly do not succeed in for most of our lives. But this is the language in which most political speeches, radio commentaries and newspaper editorials are spoken or written. At their best they are magnificent in sound and colour. They achieve their effect through the use of all the vast linguistic resources of the language: emphasis, exaggeration, elaborate metaphor and even a form of *saj*, a classical type of rhymed prose for which Arabic is ideally suited. The result is a semi-poetic rhetoric which can be highly intoxicating, sweeping the listeners or readers along on a current of words.

I have observed the Arab love of rhetoric on countless occasions. A Lebanese friend was once praising the oratory of a famous Arab politician: 'Yesterday I heard him speak for two hours without pausing or looking at any notes. He was magnificent.' 'What was he talking about?' I asked innocently. 'Oh, I don't remember,' he replied, apparently surprised that I should have asked. The acceptance of over-emphasis and exaggeration as normal is equally common. Three Arabs were discussing the Palestine guerrilla movement. Two of them were talking passionately but the third sat silent for a time, as he listened to what they were saying. All of a sudden one of the talkers rounded on him. 'And what have you got against Palestine liberation?' For an Arab real praise must be overstated; silence means disapproval.

This subject is brilliantly discussed in an article by a psychologist, E. Shouby.[22] He illustrated his central thesis with a story from his own experience of two friends: an English girl and an Arab youth.

> The girl complained that her Arab friend (a) was pestering her with his attentions and declarations of love; and (b) refused to take 'No' for an answer when she made it perfectly clear that she was not interested in him at all. The Arab confided (a) that the English girl was encouraging him to make love to her; and (b) that he had so far shown only a little interest and admiration. Both were strictly honest and truthful even to their conscious selves, but they did not know what a contrast could be created between Arab overassertion and exaggeration and British tact and understatement.

This Arab trait has been an incalculable drawback for the nation in the struggle for unity and independence in modern times. On countless occasions the Arabs have been led by their own rhetoric to believe that they were about to achieve their aspirations. They have woken to reality with a hangover which lasted until the next bout of self-intoxication. The supreme example of this behaviour occurred in the weeks before the Six Day War in 1967, when the Arabs whipped themselves into a state of collective euphoria in the belief they were about to triumph over Israel.

Yet if it is true that a people will show their national characteristics in time of stress, it is equally undeniable that these may be modified or even eradicated by a conscious act of national will. The Jews have not been regarded as a martial people since their last desperate revolt was crushed by the Emperor Hadrian in A.D. 135. Today they have in Israel one of the most formidable armies of the contemporary world. For the Arabs 1967 was a turning point, just as 1948 was for the Jews when they fought their war of independence. It is safe to say that the Arab character will never be the same after the Six Day War.

It would be absurd to suggest that no Arabs had diagnosed their national weaknesses before 1967. The difference was that after 1967

22. E. Shouby, 'The Influence of the Arabic Language on the Psychology of the Arabs', *Middle East Journal*, 5 (1951), pp. 284–302.

the Arabs as a whole were ready to listen to them and to take action. Ahmad Shukairy, chairman of the PLO, and Ahmad Said, director of Cairo's Voice of the Arabs – two of the greatest exponents of intoxicating rhetoric – were replaced. Six years later the results could clearly be seen during the October War. Arab military and civilian spokesmen were sober and restrained in their assessments of the way things were going. It was the Israelis who became wild and boastful, to the extent that amazed foreign correspondents were saying: 'But the Arabs are behaving like Israelis and the Israelis like Arabs.' In the last weeks of the war when the tide of the fighting had turned against the Arabs some of the old characteristics re-emerged in the Arab spokesmen. The interesting thing was that the Arab public remained sceptical. After 1967 they had taken the pledge.

It is doubtful whether the national psychology of the Arabs would have changed so swiftly if it had not been for the alteration in their world status. Just as the realistic estimates of their own and enemy losses were made possible by the Arab successes in the first week of the October War (there is no need to lie unless you are losing) so the growing political and economic self-confidence of the Arabs means it is less imperative to dwell on the glory of their Golden Age. Professors Gibb and Cantwell Smith and Mr E. Shouby were all writing about the Arabs in the 1950s. Although their different analyses of the Arab dilemma showed profound insight circumstances have radically changed in the past quarter of a century. Nothing that they said is irrelevant but it has to be modified in the 1980s.

The noted French arabist Jacques Berque remarked that the Arab '*a reçu le message et le coup de l'histoire moderne d'un seul bloc, et de l'exterieur, et non pas reparti, sur trois ou quatre siècles, comme chez nous*'. (He has received the message and the force of modern history at one blow; it has come from outside and has not been spread over three or four centuries as it has with us.)[23] The enforced pace of change for a society which remained dormant and impervious to the external world for several centuries has been so swift and ruthless that various signs of national neurosis were wholly to be expected.

Jacques Berque observed that the force of change for the Arabs came from outside. As we have seen, no Arab government had adopted a conscious and deliberate policy of impelling the secularization or europeanization of society in the manner of Kemal Atatürk in

23. Jacques Berque, *L'Anthologie de la littérature arabe contemporaine*, Paris, 1964, quoted in Salah Stétié, *Les Porteurs de feu et autres essais*, Paris, 1972, p. 12.

Turkey. It is not my intention to compare Arab with Turkish social life in the present day but it is my strong conviction that social change (I shall not beg the question by calling it 'social progress') is more likely to be pervasive and long-lasting if it takes place through the inner momentum of the whole of society rather than by government fiat. This view was strikingly advocated by a distinguished Lebanese writer and broadcaster Muhammad Naccache, whose wife was the first Muslim woman doctor in Lebanon. Pointing out that 'just as it is inhumane to force a young girl to wear the veil today so it is also to make an old woman, who has been accustomed to wear the veil all her life, unveil in the name of progress', he concluded:

> The path of progress is a one-way autostrade on which a driver may not stop, reverse or change his speed. It seems to me that Arab society has chosen the lane on the outside right where the speed is slow but the chances of safe arrival are greatest. From now on we should not, and can not, but go forward.[24]

Social change in Arab Muslim society is most commonly seen in terms of the emancipation of women. In the past nothing has done more to create barriers between Western and Arab society than the seclusion and subjection of Arab women. This has been condemned in countless ways which often showed the ignorance of the critic who ignores the fact that female emancipation is a relatively recent feature of our own society and which, in the view of many Western women, has still to be achieved.

The trend towards the social and political liberation of women is universal in the Arab world but it has advanced much further in some areas than in others. The strongest motive force behind it is education and every Arab government, without exception, accepts the principle that girls have the right to be taught at all levels. (The last converts to this principle were Yemen and Oman.) This view is not of course held by all the citizens of these countries. In the countryside especially the heads of many families still believe that primary education is sufficient for the needs of their daughters. This is as true of the Arab countries with 'progressive' régimes, such as Algeria or Egypt, as the more conservative such as Morocco or Saudi Arabia. Also every Arab state has the task of remedying past neglect of education. Whether the country was independent, or under Turkish or Western domina-

---

24. Muhammad Naccache, 'The Outside Lane', *Middle East Forum Special Issue on Social Change*, vol. xxxvi, no. 1, 1958, pp. 8–9.

tion, few schools were built before the middle of this century. Where there is a shortage of educational opportunities, preference, as might be expected, is given to boys.

Nevertheless, acceptance of the *principle* of female education by the state has in itself created a revolution. In those countries which had sufficient wealth to provide opportunities for secondary and higher education for all its youth, regardless of sex, a curious situation developed. Kuwait, for example, has been receiving substantial oil revenues for a generation and the great majority of Kuwaiti girls have been able to go to school. But the social mores of the country have hardly changed since the nineteenth century. The veil is customary in public. Women have no vote and the Kuwaiti parliament is all-male. Yet a substantial proportion of Kuwaiti girls are graduates either of Kuwait University or of other Arab or Western universities. I recall meeting in 1958 a leading Kuwaiti businessman, a multi-millionaire although illiterate, who was intensely proud of his five daughters who were all being educated abroad. The eldest was about to return to Kuwait after taking her MA in psychology at London University. The father saw nothing incongruous in the fact that she would have to put on her veil and re-enter a secluded life in Kuwait.

Such an anomaly could hardly endure. In the 1980s Kuwaiti girls are discarding the veil and a few of them are penetrating the professions and government ministries. The possibility of their being given the vote is discussed without embarrassment. Their sisters in Saudi Arabia are much less emancipated. Although the principle of female education has also been accepted there for some years, Saudi girls and women still make no appearance in public life. They may not work with men; they are banned from driving a car or even riding in one alone as a passenger. But even here it is difficult to see how change can be avoided.

Apart from Lebanon, which is a special case because of its non-Muslim majority, the Arab countries in which women play the biggest role in public life are Egypt and Tunisia. (If an Arab Palestine is re-created it would compete in this respect.) In Egypt the struggle for female emancipation began some fifty years ago. Hoda Sharawi, the wife of a nationalist leader, returned from an international women's rights conference and symbolically dropped her veil into the Mediterranean to the astonishment of the officials gathered on the Alexandria quayside to welcome her. The movement continued throughout the inter-war years and gathered momentum after the 1952 revolution. Although Gamal Abdul Nasser adopted a much more gradualist approach than Atatürk in Turkey, he clearly stated the principle in his National Charter of 1962:

Woman must be regarded as equal to man and she must therefore shed the remaining shackles that impede her freedom of movement, so that she may play a constructive and profoundly important part in shaping the life of the country.

But as in other social matters President Nasser recognized the strength of conservative feeling and was prepared to wait until the idea of women's equality had begun to be accepted by a much broader spectrum of the population than a highly educated minority before stating it as a principle of the Egyptian revolution. The still powerful conservative opinion was able to express itself during the debates of the National Congress of Popular Powers on the National Charter. The leading Cairo newspaper *al-Ahram* and its famous sceptical cartoonist Salah Jahin satirized these views and especially one al-Azhar Shaikh who had demanded that all Muslim women should be obliged to wear the veil. This led to a demonstration of al-Azhar students outside *al-Ahram*'s offices. The paper published an apology but on the principle it was unrepentant, and in general the whole Egyptian press has done much to promote the idea of female equality. Every year it is possible to observe a higher proportion of women employed as teachers, factory and office workers. There is a substantial number of women doctors, university teachers and lawyers and a proposal in 1964 to appoint some female judges aroused surprisingly little opposition. In some medical schools the girl students outnumber the boys. Egypt's first woman minister was appointed in 1962 and the public has now become quite accustomed to the idea of having a large handful of women members of parliament.

The spread of education has been the strongest single factor behind the emancipation of women in Egypt. But, as elsewhere in the Arab world, it has come up against strong resistance from conservative social custom, which is only gradually being eroded. For many years now the veil has not been the symbol of segregation in Egypt. But until very recently Egyptian girls were kept in a kind of moral purdah, which perhaps was even more irksome for the new generations. Any unmarried girl who was seen talking alone to a man, even within the walls of coeducational universities, destroyed her chances of getting married. Cases of parents or brothers assassinating one of the daughters of the family because of no more than a suspicion that she has been dishonoured still occur in every Arab Muslim society. (One peculiarly distressing case occurred in a Palestinian family in Lebanon only a few years ago. Two young men who were angry with a girl because she refused to have anything to do with them told her parents that they had seen her driving into the countryside with a married man. The parents waited until night when they took the girl from her bed and 'slit her throat like a sheep', according to the court report. It later appeared that the young men's accusation was false.) Dogmatic male chauvinism is by no means a monopoly of the older generation. As Muhammad Naccache shrewdly observed: 'There are still, of course, some young men who retain part of the old tradition. They expect to go out with the neighbour's daughter while forbidding their sister to go out with the neighbour's son.'

However, in urban society there has been a slow but steady change over the past ten or twenty years. In Cairo it is possible today to see a girl, who is neither a prostitute nor married, walking alone with a man or even sitting with him on a bench. It is still rare for a young Egyptian male to take a young girl out for the evening, but it is likely to become quite common in the next generation.

Social change is apparent in any of Egypt's big cities but it has still only just begun to affect the villages. Here male values are still supreme and it is virtually impossible for any girl to show independence. The new schools, rural centres, radio, television and the cinema, as well as the government's encouragement of political consciousness among women are certain to undermine the present system eventually but the evolution is gradual.

A change in the divorce and marriage laws will help to improve the status of Egyptian women as much as the spread of education. At present the minimum age for marriage is sixteen for girls and eighteen for boys. Divorce is easy for men although it was made rather more difficult by a new law introduced under President Sadat. The rate is 30 per cent in the country as a whole and higher than this in the cities. The highest rates of all are among very young married couples. A survey carried out in the 1960s by the Cairo magazine *al-Musawwar* showed that in one industrial area of Cairo 70 per cent of early marriages ended in failure and that the children rarely went to school.

For economic reasons polygamy is rare in all the Arab countries. In Egypt only about 4 per cent of all married males have more than one wife. But easy divorce increases the birth rate because one of the more common causes is the desire of the male to have more children.

In Egypt there is still a wide gap between the ideal of female equality declared by the Nasser revolution and the reality. The same

is true of all the other Arab states with régimes which have proclaimed themselves as progressive, revolutionary and socialist. This
includes Algeria, Iraq, Syria and even the semi-Marxist government
of Democratic Yemen. Like Egypt, they have renounced the drastic
secularizing policies of an Atatürk. To reject Islam in this way would
be virtually impossible. Since Islam is an integral part of Arab civilization it would amount to a denial of their own identity.

The patriarchal family system is still the basis of Arab society. The
family requires the support and loyalty of its members and in return
provides security and protection. Studies carried out in 1957 and 1958
on the group affiliation of Arab students at the American University
of Beirut showed that family had a clear preference over other
loyalties such as the nation, political party or religion. The order of
preference showed little difference between males, females, Christians and Muslims. When the study was repeated in 1972 there was
some decline in religious affiliations but the family still came first.[25]

This does not mean that the family system is not suffering severe
shocks in the Arab world. In the first place, as elsewhere in the world,
the effect of modernization and industrialization is to replace the
extended family of cousins and kinsmen, which once was wholly
typical of Arab life, by the nuclear family of parents and children.[26]
Also, the very fact that the family is so important and that the father's
authority is hallowed by tradition exacerbates the tensions of the
'generation gap', which is as much a phenomenon of Arab society as
of any other. As Levon Melikian showed in an essay, to which he gave
the inspired title 'The Dethronement of the Father', in an authoritarian culture such as that of the Middle East, where the father is
idealized, any discrepancy between the 'ideal' and the 'real' father
arouses the hostility of the children. Dr Melikian quoted some of the
typical complaints of students who came for counselling:

'My parents don't understand me . . . we seem to be living in two different
worlds.'
'We don't agree on many things but since they are my parents I have to obey
them.'
'I don't care whether he is my father or not . . . I am educated and I know
what is good for me . . . he is an ignorant man . . . if it comes to the worst I will
run away and live my own life.'

25. Levon H. Melikian and Lutfy N. Diab, 'Group Affiliations of University Students in
the Arab Middle East', *Journal of Social Psychology*, 49 (1959) pp. 145–59.
26. See E. Terry Prothro and Lutfy N. Diab, *Changing Family Patterns in the Arab East*,
Beirut, 1974.

'My father thinks that my views about religion and politics are dangerous; but what do you expect, it was his generation and its politics that brought us to the state in which we are . . . it was his generation and its religion that kept us backward . . . they lost Palestine.'[27]

An Arab psychiatrist with wide experience of mental health problems in various parts of the Arab world told the author of the devastating effects of this 'dethronement of the father'. Some of his patients suffered from what he called a 'father-denial complex'. A patient would say that he was an adopted child and that his 'so-called father' was not his real father, that he was illiterate, idle and unworthy. The psychiatrist pointed out that the loss of faith in the ideal father had provoked a search among Arab youth for 'father-substitutes'. Many thought they had found him in Gamal Abdul Nasser when he was at the height of his success. (The psychiatrist told of cases of adolescent Syrian girls who always carried Nasser's picture and referred to him as *Abuna*, i.e. 'our father'.)

We have no scope here for a proper discussion of the sexual *mores* of the Arabs of today. Little has yet been written on the subject above the level of gossipy newspaper articles or autobiographical observations which tend to be discreetly misleading. What is needed is a combination of an Arab Dr Kinsey and Richard Burton, whose acute and scholarly observations which he recorded in his 'Terminal Essay' for his translation of *The Thousand and One Nights* have never been surpassed, although they need updating.

A small beginning was made by Levon Melikian and E. Terry Prothro in their unique study 'Sexual Behaviour of University Students in the Arab Near East'[28] which Dr Melikian repeated and brought up to date in 1967 in his 'Social Change and Sexual Behaviour of Arab University Students.'[29]

One feature of these studies that would encourage any future investigator is that the male students seem to have had few taboos about answering the questions on the questionnaires frankly and honestly. For example, in Dr Melikian's survey 43 per cent were prepared to say that they had had their first sexual experience with another male, although the great majority said they had since abandoned homosexual practices. One interesting difference between the

27. Levon Melikian, 'The Dethronement of the Father', *Middle East Forum*, January 1960, pp. 24 ff.

28. *Journal of Social Psychology*, 49 (1954), pp. 59–64.

29. ibid., 73 (1967), pp. 169–75.

two surveys was the sharp decline in the number of students going to brothels. Between 1952 and 1967, prostitutes had been replaced by call-girls who go to the students' apartments. (This is borne out by the visible recession in the once thriving brothel quarter of Beirut.)

The chairman of the British Labour party once chose the occasion of a public dinner in 1970, at which the Prime Minister was present, to say in his speech that the Arabs are 'prone to homosexuality'. Apart from the curious aspect of this remark – that it would undoubtedly have been considered unacceptably racialistic if it had been said about a people other than the Arabs – it does represent a common Western belief. It is certainly true that the sexual taboos on women and the absolute insistence on virginity at marriage in Arab society cause young Arab males to seek their sexual outlets with their own sex. It is not regarded as any great shame although a certain amount of hypocrisy is involved because no Arab would admit to playing anything except the active role.[30]

In the chapter on pederasty in his 'Terminal Essay', Richard Burton described what he called a 'Sotadic Zone' which included the southern and eastern shores of the Mediterranean, Asia Minor, Persia, Afghanistan, the Punjab and then broadens out to cover China, Japan and Turkestan. He said: 'Within the Sotadic Zone the Vice is popular and endemic, held at the worst to be a mere peccadillo.' This was shrewd and observant of Burton, who, as he said, 'had made inquiries in many and distant countries'. But he went on to add that 'the races north and south of the limits here defined practise it only sporadically amid the opprobrium of their fellows who, as a rule, are physically incapable of performing the operation and look upon it with the liveliest disgust.'

Burton was less familiar with the areas outside his Sotadic Zone, and here he was confusing public attitudes with private practice. Homosexuality was no doubt as common in Europe in his time as we know it is today. Until an Arab Dr Kinsey has made his report our estimates have to be cautious, but it is quite probable that homosexuality as a way of life as opposed to adolescent sexual activity is more common in Western countries than in the Arab world. Several intelligent Arabs with wide human experience, both doctors and lawyers, have said to me with obvious sincerity that they have heard that

30. It is difficult to see how *all* could be active. The ribald suggestion of a friend of mine with long Middle East experience was that in every major city there must be one passive male who is had by all the rest.

homosexuality is widespread in Europe (especially, for some reason in France) whereas of course 'it is almost unknown among the Arabs'. It might interest the former chairman of the Labour party that in some major tourist centres of the Arab world young Arabs are convinced that all visiting Anglo-Saxons are homosexual, without exception.

The Way Ahead

In the 1980s the phenomenon of Islamic Revival or Reassertion has appeared to be so widespread that it has raised the question of whether the Arabs are not turning in an entirely new direction. The most striking manifestation of Islamic Reassertion has been outside the Arab World – in Iran – but none of the Arab states from the Gulf to the Maghreb has been immune. Mostly it has taken the form of a challenge to the established governments in which the younger generation – notably university students – have taken the lead. In Sudan in 1983 President Nimeiry has attempted to ride the storm by decreeing the Islamization of his own régime.

In Iran it could be debated whether girls have renounced Western dress for the Islamic *chador* and deliberately segregated themselves from men of their own free will or out of fear of the authorities. But in the Arab countries it has happened without any pressure from the rulers and even against their will. President Sadat of Egypt's comment on demands by fundamentalists for stricter Islamic laws was that 'women would not be forced to revert to dressing in "tents". They must live as equals.' Does this portend a mass movement which Arab rulers will be unable to withstand and will widen the gulf between the Arab peoples and the West? Certainly this must be regarded as a possibility but in my view it is an oversimplified judgement which fails to take into account a number of opposing factors. The most important is that while the Arabs will always feel the need to assert their identity in relation to the rest of the world – and especially the domineering West – they will equally strive for the knowledge and expertise which will enable them to catch up with the West in material terms to redeem their past humiliation. A good Muslim can maintain with perfect justice that there is nothing inherent in Islam which is contrary to economic progress, but only the most narrowminded and xenophobic will refuse to admit that there are values and experience in other civilizations and societies which are relevant to Muslims in the twentieth century. In their various ways all Arab rulers believe that the gate of *ijtihad* (the exercise of independent judgement) must be kept open. King Fahd of Saudi Arabia has urged this to a notable gathering of Saudi *ulama*. By their own nature, governments must reject the simple utopianism of the fundamentalist.

In many respects Europeans still find their south-eastern Arab neighbours alien and incomprehensible in spite of several decades of close association. Yet it can be asked whether the Arabs belong to the Western world. The question is neither irrelevant nor absurd. The answer would no doubt be an emphatic negative in the mountains of Yemen or in central Sudan, but many Arabs *feel* that they belong to the West. The vast majority of young Arabs who receive some of their higher education abroad will look for it in a European or American university if they have the opportunity, and tens of thousands of them are doing so today. They move in and out of Western cities with easy familiarity and have become part of the Western scene. (Thirty years ago it was widely said that middle-class Muslim Arabs would never bring themselves to work in restaurants. Today there are thousands of Arab students working in London coffee-bars, restaurants and hotels alongside the Spaniards and Portuguese who came in the 1960s.) Israel lies in the heart of the Arab world and it is generally assumed to be part of the West.

I would never suggest that this provides an adequate answer to the original question. It is true that tens of thousands of French-educated young Algerians feel that they belong to the culture of Voltaire and Balzac. It is equally true that French attempts to absorb the Algerian people and make them part of the French nation were doomed to failure. This provides the clue to the real answer which is that the past Western domination of the Arab nation has distorted and confused its search for identity in the modern world.

At the beginning of the Epilogue to his magisterial *Europe Leaves the Middle East 1936–1954* Professor Howard M. Sachar asks a different question: 'What, then, was left in the Middle East?' after the last Western soldiers had been evacuated. His conclusions are depressing. Of 'political liberalism and juridical egalitarianism . . . the traditions which sustained and distinguished French and British civilization', little remains. 'With the isolated exception of Lebanon and Israel, however, parliamentarianism has been a façade for political corruption at best, and, at worst, for plain and simple totalitarianism.' Professor Sachar's diagnosis of the cause is simple and familiar:

The fact cannot be skirted, therefore, that even the most enlightened of Western efforts to modernize and liberalize the Middle East foundered on the rock of Moslem *immobilism*. A socio-religious tradition that suffused all life and thought that once, long before, had known three glorious centuries of vitality and creativity during the Islamic Renaissance of the Middle Ages, had lapsed during the subsequent half-millenium into fatalism and intellectual paralysis . . .[31]

It is Professor Sachar's words '*Western efforts* to modernize and liberalize the Middle East' which are significant. It is because they were Western that they failed. The impact of the Western invasion and colonization of the Arab world was far-reaching. It stirred the Arabs profoundly after a long period of political and social stagnation and created many external changes. But the dynamic for progress or modernization had to come from within Arab society, and this is as true today as it ever was.

Parliamentary government of the kind that still exists in a handful of Western countries has failed in all the many Arab states which adopted it. In some of them, such as Morocco or Egypt, a form of elected assembly survives, but in no case is parliament sovereign. Real power lies with the president, king or ruler (and his family in the Arabian states) and either a small group of ministers or the executive of the single political party. In most of the Arab states the army plays a crucial political role – either because it is directly involved in government or because the head of state depends heavily on its support to remain in power. The only real exception is Lebanon, where the parliamentary system has been preserved as the only way of reflecting the pattern of interests which have to co-exist if the country is to survive. Power-sharing is compulsory for Lebanon; dictatorship is inconceivable because the dictator would be unable to impose his authority over all the sects to which he did not belong. One other possible exception is Kuwait, where the ruling family has allowed parliament to nibble away at its formerly absolute powers. But Kuwait can hardly be called a democracy in the Western sense as long as the majority of its inhabitants are non-citizens who have no vote.

In every Arab country public and private liberties are restricted to a greater or lesser extent. It may be that there is no society in the world where absolute freedom exists and that in any case the Arab masses as a whole have little interest in the principle or practice of democracy. But it is precisely because the educated élite among the Arabs has

31. Howard M. Sachar, *Europe Leaves the Middle East, 1936–1954*, London, 1974, pp. 608–9.

absorbed so many of the ideas of Western liberalism that they find the suppression of their liberties irksome.

The effect of restrictions on the personal freedom of the Arab middle class is partly mitigated by their increasing prosperity. A young Saudi or Libyan who finds the social laws at home oppressive can fly for the week-end to Cairo or Malta. An Iraqi intellectual who is afraid to publish his essays in Baghdad can have them appear in Beirut. The prohibition of foreign travel, which is such a common feature of dictatorial régimes, has never been rigorously applied in any Arab country (except for the former hermit states of Oman and Yemen), and today the Arabs are free to travel abroad and return if they have the means, as they do in hundreds of thousands every year.[32]

Arab society is not liberal in the Western sense, but neither is it totalitarian in the fascist or communist sense. Even the most authoritarian of modern Arab régimes, such as Abdul Nasser's Egypt, never attempted to mould the characters or interfere with the artistic expression of its people as fascist or communist governments have done in Europe. The doctrines of the Baath party, which holds power in Syria and Iraq, are too vague and mystical to hold the people in an ideological straitjacket. Arab society is everywhere in a state of transformation. The 'new middle class' is gaining steadily in power and influence as it replaces the old élite of landowners, merchants and semi-feudal political families. This new class bears little resemblance to the property-owning entrepreneurial middle class of the nineteenth century; it consists mainly of salaried administrators and 'technocrats' and because of the increase in the scope and function of the state in most Middle Eastern countries, the great majority are working directly or indirectly for the government.

However, there have been signs of a different trend in the 1980s. The 'open-door' policies in Egypt have led to some liberalization of the economy while even in Iraq, Syria and Algeria, which still profess socialism, there have been limited but significant moves to encourage the private sector. In the Arab Gulf states, on the other hand, where the government's control over the major national resource is unavoidable at the present stage, there are positive moves to encourage the growth of a class of private entrepreneurs. It is still too early to predict the growth of an independent Arab middle class which would be

---

32. The only exceptions now are the Palestinians who are stateless and therefore have no home to which to return.

sufficiently large and self-confident to challenge the overwhelming power of the state.

The transformation of a society which has been heavily traditional for many generations is bound to be open-ended. No one can tell what political and social institutions the Arab people will have developed by the end of this momentous century. All that can be said with certainty is that, however much they derive from foreign movements and ideas, they will have a specifically Arab and Islamic character. This does not mean that either President Muammar Qaddafy's 'Third Way' between capitalism and communism or the social order advocated by the Muslim Brothers will be adopted by the rest of the Arab world. But these are two examples of the search for an Arab ideology for the twentieth century. The same process will take place in the cultural arena. Arab writers, poets, musicians and painters have taken Western art forms which were virtually unknown in the Arab world before this century, such as the novel, sculpture, free verse or figurative paintings, and through vigorous experiment are producing something new which is neither oriental nor occidental but wholly Arab. As with the development of political institutions, the process is in some cases in its infancy, but it continues.

I have made clear my view that the most powerful political motivation in the present-day Arab world is the desire to redeem the century of humiliation at the hands of the West. To the thoughtful and sensitive Arab the present scene is profoundly depressing. It is not only – or even mainly – because the family of Arab states is so disunited and disputatious. The individual Arab régimes are mostly domineering and repressive with disastrous records in the field of human rights. Having been a byword for their instability in the early days of independence they have acquired a kind of permanence through the ruthless use of the powerful instruments in the hands of the modern state. Most Arab régimes have now been in power for fifteen years or more; change has only occurred through the death of the leader. Arguably they are now too stable and unresponsive to popular pressure.

Perhaps the most disastrous consequence of the oppressive nature of Arab régimes – especially when measured against the Arab desire to catch up with the West – is that so much Arab talent and brains prefer to emigrate. It has been pointed out that while 'in terms of high-level manpower resources, the number of universities, the size of the research and development pool, and the number of Ph.Ds, the Arab world is at a considerably greater advantage than modern

Japan was in its early years', there is another darker side to the picture.

Nearly half of all Arab science and engineering Ph.Ds have left the Arab world. Despite the fact that there are nigh on to sixty universities in the Arab world, the majority of Arab doctoral education continues to take place in Europe, the United States and the Soviet Union . . . Only two out of every five Arab researchers actually work in the Arab world. In terms of scientific activity and technical innovation the level of discovery in the Arab world of the 1980s does not even come close to the gains made in a number of Western countries half a century or more ago.[33]

Many reasons can be offered for the grim political outlook of the Arab world. There is a problem which is common to all nation-states carved out of former colonial empires – the task, which requires instant political maturity, of building a viable system of government. For the Arab states this difficulty has been compounded by the loss of Palestine to the Zionists. This is not meant to imply that without the gnawing Palestinian problem the Arab states would have developed humane and liberal systems of government. But who can doubt that the neuroses it has created – the anger, resentment and sense of humiliation – have made the task more difficult?

The catastrophe of 1967 provoked a wave of soul-searching among the Arabs. Some was productive and maturing. This was demonstrated in 1973 in the much improved performance of the Arab armies and the political use of the international oil crisis. But in some respects 1973 was a false dawn; Arab régimes seemed no less repressive and neurotic and the Palestinian problem was as far from solution as ever.[34] The terrible events in Lebanon in the 1980s and the faltering reaction to them of the Arab states were cause for deeper pessimism.

Inevitably, dissatisfaction with the existing systems has drawn attention to the alternatives. In general two utopian visions of the future are on offer to the Arabs which briefly, though misleadingly, may be described as coming from the right and left. The former, which in the 1980s appears to be predominant, is that of Islamic fundamentalism which says that all the Arabs need to prosper and triumph is to practise the principles of early Islam and, where

33. See Samir N. Anabtawi, 'Arab Institutions of Higher Learning', in *Arab Resources: The Transformation of a Society*, Ibrahim Ibrahim, ed., Washington and London, 1983, pp. 128–9.

34. For an important and provocative analysis see Fouad Ajami, *The Arab Predicament: Arab Political Thought and Practice since 1967*, Cambridge, 1981.

necessary, revive them. My own view, which I have already made clear, is that the fundamentalists are unlikely to achieve power in any Arab state or if they do, to be able to hold it, for the principal reason that their natural intolerance makes them incapable of compromise with the other forces seeking a change in the system.[35]

The other uncompromising criticism of the search for a specific Arab identity in the twentieth century comes from Marxists. In their view Arab socialism (or African socialism for that matter) is a myth. There is only one kind of socialism; this regards the class war as essential and inevitable and looks forward to a classless society and the withering of the state. Their attitude towards existing socialist revolutionary régimes in the Arab world, with the qualified exception of the People's Democratic Republic of Yemen, is that they are narrowly *petit-bourgeois* and military-dominated. In the view of the Marxist left, there is no alternative to the organization of the masses to overthrow these régimes and sweep away at the same time all the traditional social and religious customs and beliefs which still dominate Arab society. They are convinced that economic pressures alone will be enough to make this process inevitable.

My own view is that these assumptions are as unreal as those of the nostalgic right. I believe that revolution in the Arab world must be evolutionary if it is to succeed.

Moreover, in the mid-1980s the various reasons for Arabs' pessimism about their condition – the tragic turmoil in the Arab heartland of Greater Syria, the intolerable bloodshed of the Iraq–Iran war and signs of renewed rebellion in southern Sudan – diverted attention from some more favourable trends. In the North African Maghreb states there were distinctive moves towards liberalization of the régimes. Something similar was taking place in Egypt. The six Arab Gulf states were demonstrating that it is possible for Arab governments to move towards greater political and economic unity in a rational and practical manner. One might add the negative but important truth that all of them had survived huge cuts in their revenues without the political turmoil, financial disaster and break-

35. I am of course aware that Islamic fundamentalists have apparently won power in the Arabs' neighbour, Iran. There are many things to be said about this, such as that Ayatollah Khomeini and his followers are not fundamentalists so much as revolutionary innovators, that it is uncertain how long they will hold power, that reality has already forced them into numerous compromises with the infidel world and finally that circumstances in the Arab states are different in various ways. But obviously there is no room here for an adequate discussion of this fascinating subject.

down in their development plans that has affected other major oil-producing states in the Third World.

The Arabs, in common with most other peoples, are spending a deplorable proportion of their national income on arms but much of Arab wealth is also being properly used to improve educational and living standards. Above all, although with many setbacks and exceptions, there is a discernible trend towards greater liberty for the Arab individual.

None of this is likely to satisfy the impatient yearnings of the Arabs who have suffered so much disillusionment since the inspiring moments when they won independence from the old colonial powers. But I believe that it is enough to prevent them from turning *en masse* to utopian solutions which are despairing precisely because they are utopian and therefore bound to fail.

In spite of the fantastic, if exhaustible, wealth which the Arabs have found that they have inherited in the twentieth century and the power this has given them, they cannot aspire to the kind of dominant role they played in their golden era of the early Middle Ages. But it could be as historically important. I believe the Arabs have a unique opportunity to enhance the unity of mankind by acting as a link between Europe and the West and the peoples of Africa and Asia. In certain important respects they belong to all of them. To do this they will need, like the European nations, to transcend the darker aspects of their imperial past. The fact that some Arabs refuse to admit that they were ever imperialists in the same sense as the British, French or Americans is no help in this respect, but they do have the important advantage of their high degree of racial tolerance.

The growing sense of achievement of the Arabs in the modern age and the increase in their share of responsibility as some of the more fortunate of mankind will strengthen their self-confidence and reduce their sense of injured pride. Nostalgia for their own past greatness will no longer be a national handicap but a minor self-indulgence.

Index

Note: Proper names are indexed according to the common mode of reference where this differs from strict alphabetical order or from usual practice, e.g.,
Hajj Amin al-Husseini under Ha
Hussein ibn Ali under H
Abdul Raham al-Kawakibi under K
Ibn Saud under I.